For selected older vintages, re...

ITALY	0									
Barolo, Barbaresco	8									
Chianti Classico Ris.	8									
Brunello	8	8								
Amarone	6	8	5	9	8	5	7	9	7	7
SPAIN										
Ribera del Duero	5	6	8	8	8	5	8	7	8	7
Rioja (red)	6	6	8	8	7	6	8	8	7	6
PORTUGAL										
South	8	7	8	8	6	5	8	9	8	6
North	8	5	8	8	8	7	8	9	7	6
Port	8	7	8	8	9	6	7	9	7	6
USA										
California Cabernet	9	8	9	7	8	7	8	7	9	7
California Chardonnay	9	9	9	8	9	8	8	7	8	7
Oregon Pinot Noir	6	8	7	8	8	8	7	9	9	8
Wash. State Cabernet	7	8	9	8	8	7	8	9	9	8
AUSTRALIA										
Coonawarra Cabernet	6	9	10	8	8	9	9	6	8	10
Hunter Semillon	8	8	9	8	8	7	8	9	8	10
Barossa Shiraz	6	8	10	8	7	10	9	8	9	10
Marg. River Cabernet	9	6	9	9	8	8	10	8	10	7
NEW ZEALAND										
M'lborough Sauvignon	9	9	7	8	8	6	9	9	8	5
H'kes Bay Cab/Merlot	9	8	7	8	5	9	7	8	7	10
SOUTH AFRICA										
Stellenbosch Cabernet	9	9	8	8	9	5	9	8	7	8
S'bosch Chardonnay	9	8	8	9	8	6	7	7	8	6

Numerals (1–10) represent an overall rating for each year.
◑ Not ready ● Just ready ● At peak ◐ Past best ○ Not generally declared

OZ CLARKE

POCKET WINE BOOK 2009

PAVILION

This edition first published in 2008 by Pavilion Books

An imprint of
Anova Books Company Ltd
10 Southcombe Street
London W14 0RA

www.anovabooks.com
www.ozclarke.com

Editor Maggie Ramsay
Cartographer Andrew Thompson
Photography Michael Wicks
Desktop Publishing Jayne Clementson
Indexer Angie Hipkin

17th edition. First published in 1992.
Revised editions published annually.

A CIP catalogue for this book is available from the British
Library.

ISBN 978-1-862-05826-2

Printed and bound in China by SNP Leefung

Thanks are due to the following people for their invaluable help with the 2009
edition and the generous spirit in which they have shared their knowledge: Sarah
Ahmed, Nicolas Belfrage MW, Dan Berger, Stephen Brook, Bob Campbell MW,
Giles Fallowfield, Peter Forrestal, Roger Harris, James Lawther MW, John
Livingstone-Learmonth, Angela Lloyd, Dan McCarthy, Dave McIntyre, Charles
Metcalfe, Jasper Morris MW, Victor de la Serna, Stephen Skelton MW, Patricio
Tapia, Roger Voss, Stuart Walton.

CONTENTS

HOW TO USE THIS BOOK

The **World of Wine** section, starting on page 20, gives an overview of all the world's significant wine-producing countries. The most important countries are followed by a full list of the relevant entries in the A–Z section. Remember that regional A–Z entries guide you to further recommended producers in each region or appellation.

The A–Z section starts on page 56 and includes over 1600 entries on wines, producers, grapes and wine regions from all over the world. It is followed on page 308 by a **Glossary** of winemaking terms.

Detailed **Vintage Charts**, with information on which of the world's top wines are ready for drinking in 2009, can be found on the inside front and back covers; the front chart features vintages back to 1998; the back chart covers a selection of older vintages for premium wines.

Glass Symbols   These indicate the wines produced.

 ♥ Red wine   ♥ Rosé wine   ♀ White wine

The order of the glasses reflects the importance of the wines in terms of volume produced. For example:

 ♥ White followed by rosé wine

 ♥ Red followed by rosé, then white wine

Grape Symbols   These identify entries on grape varieties.

 ≡ Red grape   ≡ White grape

Star Symbols   These indicate wines and producers that are highly rated by the author.

★   A particularly good wine or producer in its category
★★   An excellent wine or producer in its category – one especially worth seeking out
★★★ An exceptional, world-class wine or producer

Best years   Recommended vintages are listed for many producer and appellation entries. Those listed in bold, e.g. **2006**, **00**, indicate wines that are ready for drinking now, although they may not necessarily be at their best; those appearing in brackets, e.g. (2007), (05), are preliminary assessments of wines that are not released at the time of going to press.

Cross References   Wine names, producers and regions that have their own entries elsewhere in the A–Z are indicated by SMALL CAPITALS. **Grape varieties** are not cross-referred in this way, but more than 70 varieties, from Albariño to Zinfandel, are included.

Special Features   The A–Z section includes special 2-page features on the world's most important wine styles, regions and grape varieties. These features include recommended vintages and producers, as well as lists of related entries elsewhere in the A–Z.

Index   The Index contains over 4000 recommended producers. Some of the world's most famous brand names are also included.

INTRODUCTION

The ice cap over the North Pole will have melted completely by the summer of 2013. Hey, don't get at me. This is the prediction of NASA in the USA, the space guys, the guys with all the global surveillance satellites, all the scientists. I could put a 'perhaps' or a 'maybe' or a 'might' in there. But why? We've been putting 'maybe's and 'might's into our talk about climate change for the best part of a generation and where has it got us? So I'm stopping. I'm going to make statements. If I'm wrong, get back to me in five years' time.

Evidence of change is all around us in our everyday lives. We shouldn't need boffins from NASA to kickstart us into doing something. Global warming is a fact. Climate change is here, and every sign is that it is becoming more rapid, more dramatic and more unpredictable – not just in the future, but in the present. Now for those of us in the north of Europe it's easy to smile a little smugly and start dreaming of tropical beach conditions, long summers punctuated by barbecues and picnics and never-ending cloudless skies. Bur climate change is not a predictable progression, it's a chaotic mess. Obviously in the short term areas like northern Europe, Canada, New Zealand, Tasmania and southern South America may benefit. In wine terms, areas that have vineyards can improve them and plant a far wider range of varieties in a far broader spread of places. Areas that don't have vineyards can get them. Scotland, Latvia, Alaska, Québec – why not?

Sure. So long as the Gulf Stream doesn't stop – and I suspect it will – the area of the world able to grow grapes will expand towards the poles. Scientists put the probable expansion at 500km (300 miles) during this century. The Baltic states, Sweden, northern England and the rest – go for it.

But what about the rest of the world? What about the places that supply us with all our wine today? How are they going to fare? Well, let's look back to February 2008. London had its hottest ever February days – up to 17°C. New York had its hottest ever February days, too. So I met up with an Australian friend of mine and we drank a refreshing pint outside my local. He told me that Sydney had endured relentless cyclones, storms and floods for two months – their summer. The few vineyards on the East coast were awash. Ah, I thought, but Australia is in the grip of a fierce drought. Wouldn't they welcome all that water? No. None of it got over the Dividing Range of mountains into the interior where farmers are gasping for life. It merely ruined the summer on the East coast. And I thought back a year, to 2007, in northern Europe. Lovely weather early on. April, the hottest ever. Vineyards burst into life weeks early. Then a totally miserable May, June, July and August. Crops wrecked – not just grapes, all kinds of crops – quality crushed, until nature relented for a lucky few with a fine autumn. That's global warming. 2007 was one of the warmest years ever in Europe. It's just that for most people the heat came at all the wrong times. The rains that should have quietly refreshed the land during winter came as deluges and floods during the summer months. That's global warming. It's happening.

A lot of good scientists have involved themselves in the effects of climate change on wine. Depending upon who you listen to, the increase in average growing season temperatures during the next 50 years will be between 2°C and 4°C. The average increase between 1950 and 2004 was 1.7°C. Until now, to be honest, this has led to a golden age for wine. Areas like Bordeaux, Rioja, the Rhine Valley, ripen their grapes every year. Thirty years ago they ripened them perhaps twice a decade. Places like New Zealand and Tasmania have stepped into the spotlight with cool-climate styles. All on the back of an increase in temperature of 1.7°C. Most winemakers would love to stop the warming right now. Many in Bordeaux think the present conditions are as good as they can get. If only it were that simple.

If we take the lower prediction – a 2°C rise by 2050 – Burgundy will become as warm as Châteauneuf-du-Pape near Avignon. If you want to produce Burgundy-like flavours, you'll need to plant Pinot Noir in Holland and Belgium, maybe even on the Baltic coast. Bordeaux's Cabernets will taste like those of southern France or Spain, and the Merlots of Pomerol and St-Émilion will disappear. Napa Valley will only be able to produce the baked jug wines that today spew out of California's Central Valley. And the Central Valley, California's largest wine region, would simply be too hot to produce a useable crop. Climate change will affect budbreak, flowering, fruiting and harvesting. Varieties that have been adapted to ancient sites since Roman times will no longer be suited to these regions and will have to migrate towards the poles to keep any kind of typicity of flavour.

Yet what *is* typicity? The flavour of a Bordeaux, of a Burgundy, of a Napa Cabernet or an Australian Chardonnay has already changed out of all recognition in 30 years. Typicity was a template created in times of uncertain ripening and rudimentary winemaking. We may actually prefer the 'new' typicity. But if the old typicity *did* exemplify the classic style, we are entering a post-classic era: 2°C change in the next 50 years will make the past irrelevant.

So what *will* I be drinking this year? Well, I may take this whole 'post-classic' thing quite seriously in **France**. I'll be drinking red **Bordeaux** from 2001, 2002 and 2004 – three recent vintages that are less lush, less hyped and less expensive than the big, ripe 2000, 2003 and 2005. More classic? Hmm. I'll be drinking the whites from 2006. I'll be looking for leafy, juicy **Loire** reds, as well as richer delights from the **Rhône** and **Languedoc-Roussillon**.

In **Italy** I'll be enjoying unoaked Veneto reds and whites. If I want oak, I'll get it sensitively applied in **Sicily** and **Puglia**. Oak and over-extraction are becoming a real problem for me in the new-wave **Spanish** reds, so I'll stick with the old wave – Garnachas from **Calatayud** and **Campo de Borja** and crianzas from **Rioja** and **Ribero del Duero**. There's lots of lightly oaked red in **Portugal** – thank goodness. The fruit's so good, why hide it with oak? Which brings me to **Austria**, **Hungary**, **Germany** and **Slovenia** – all full of crisp, tasty, unoaked whites.

I do drink oaked wines – I just get fed up when you can't taste the grape for the barrel. This isn't too much of a problem in **Chile** – I'm particularly taken with Pinot Noir, Sauvignon Blanc and aromatic whites just now. In **Argentina** the fruit is also tasty but sometimes the oak demon weaves one spell too many. It's difficult to get away from oak in **California**, but having spent a lot of last summer there I do have a new respect for some of their high-octane reds and whites and I'll be drinking them – cautiously.

New Zealand still hits the spot, although too many Sauvignons recently have had their tangy greenness dumbed down. But New Zealand still makes some of the world's best Chardonnay and Gewürztraminer – as well as increasingly brilliant reds. Let me at them. In **Australia** I'll be looking for real Aussie wines that remind me of the brave, brash beauty of the old days. And in **South Africa**, it's mostly whites I'm after.

And that just leaves **Belgium**, **Holland**, **Denmark** and **Britain**. Well, Britain's a given. English fizz is ever-present in my fridge. I've just tasted Belgian and Dutch Chardonnays and thought they might be from Chablis. Denmark is the EU's latest certified wine country. I'd better get over there and try out their grog.

SOME OF MY FAVOURITES

The following are some of the wines I've enjoyed most this year. They're not definitive lists of 'best wines', but all the wines, regions and producers mentioned here are on an exciting roll in terms of quality. Some are easy to find; others are very rare or expensive, but if you get the chance to try them, grab it! You can find out more about them in the A–Z on pages 56 to 307: the cross-references in small capitals will guide you to the relevant entries.

WORLD-CLASS WINES THAT DON'T COST THE EARTH
- Tim ADAMS Shiraz, Australia
- BOEKENHOUTSKLOOF Syrah, South Africa
- CARMEN Nativa Cabernet Sauvignon, Chile
- Viña Leyda, Cahuil Pinot Noir, SAN ANTONIO, Chile
- Ch. ROC DE CAMBES, Côtes de Bourg, France
- Ch. SOCIANDO-MALLET, Haut-Médoc, France
- STEENBERG Catharina, South Africa
- TRAPICHE Medalla Cabernet Sauvignon, Argentina
- VILLA MARIA Reserve Merlot, Hawkes Bay, New Zealand

BEST LOOKALIKES TO THE CLASSICS
Bordeaux-style red wines
- CULLEN Cabernet Sauvignon-Merlot, Australia
- OPUS ONE, California
- Miguel TORRES Manso de Velasco, Chile
- VERGELEGEN, South Africa

Burgundy-style white wines
- Ramey, Chardonnay, RUSSIAN RIVER VALLEY, California
- FROMM, Clayvin Vineyard Chardonnay, New Zealand
- HAMILTON RUSSELL Chardonnay, South Africa
- LEEUWIN ESTATE Art Series Chardonnay, Australia

Champagne-style wines
- Jansz (Vintage), YALUMBA, Australia
- NYETIMBER, England
- ROEDERER ESTATE L'Ermitage, California, USA

TOP-VALUE WINES
- CAVA fizz from Spain
- COTES DE GASCOGNE whites, France
- Hungarian whites
- Inycon FIANO, Sicily, Italy
- Old-vines Garnacha reds from Calatayud and Campo de Borja, ARAGON, Spain
- Peter LEHMANN whites, Australia

- Malbec (non-Reserva) from MENDOZA, Argentina
- Marqués de Casa Concha range, CONCHA Y TORO, Chile
- Trincadeira, ALENTEJO, Portugal
- Vin de Pays des Côtes Catalanes, ROUSSILLON, France
- Seigneurs d'Aiguilhe, COTES DE CASTILLON, France

REGIONS TO WATCH
- BIERZO, Spain
- CAMPANIA, Italy
- CENTRAL OTAGO, New Zealand
- La CLAPE and MINERVOIS, Languedoc, France
- COTES DE CASTILLON, France
- Leyda, SAN ANTONIO, Chile
- LIMARI, Chile
- PATAGONIA, Argentina
- Santa Lucia Highlands, MONTEREY COUNTY, California
- Sussex, England
- TASMANIA, Australia
- UCO VALLEY, Mendoza, Argentina

PRODUCERS TO WATCH
- Gérard Bertrand, Ch. l'HOSPITALET, Languedoc, France
- CASA MARIN, San Antonio, Chile
- Clos de los Siete, UCO VALLEY, Argentina
- The Crossings, Awatere, MARLBOROUGH, New Zealand
- Viña Falernia, Elquí, Chile
- O FOURNIER, Uco Valley, Argentina
- GIRARDIN, Burgundy, France
- Noemia, PATAGONIA, Argentina
- PALACIOS family, Spain (in PRIORAT, RIOJA, BIERZO and Valdeorras in GALICIA)
- S C Pannell, ADELAIDE HILLS and MCLAREN VALE, South Australia
- PONDALOWIE, Victoria, Australia
- Nicolas POTEL, Burgundy, France
- Philip Shaw, Orange, NEW SOUTH WALES, Australia

AUSTRALIA
- BROKENWOOD Semillon
- CAPE MENTELLE Cabernet Sauvignon
- GROSSET Watervale Riesling

- Henschke HILL OF GRACE Shiraz
- HOUGHTON Gladstones Shiraz
- LEEUWIN ESTATE Art Series Chardonnay
- MCWILLIAM'S Lovedale Semillon
- Charles MELTON Shiraz
- PRIMO ESTATE Moda Cabernet-Merlot
- ROCKFORD Basket Press Shiraz
- SKILLOGALEE Shiraz
- TYRRELL'S Vat 1 Semillon

RED BORDEAUX
- Ch. AUSONE
- Ch. CANON-LA-GAFFELIERE
- Ch. GRAND-PUY-LACOSTE
- Les Forts de LATOUR
- Ch. LEOVILLE-BARTON
- Ch. LEOVILLE-POYFERRE
- Ch. LYNCH-BAGES
- Ch. MARGAUX
- Ch. PICHON-LONGUEVILLE-LALANDE
- Ch. TERTRE-ROTEBOEUF

BURGUNDY
- CARILLON, Bienvenues-Bâtard-Montrachet (white)
- COCHE-DURY, Corton-Charlemagne (white)
- P Damoy, CHAMBERTIN (red)
- B Dugat-Py, Charmes-CHAMBERTIN (red)
- J-N GAGNARD, Bâtard-Montrachet (white)
- Anne GROS, Clos de Vougeot (red)
- LAFON, Volnay Santenots (red)
- Paul Pillot, CHASSAGNE-MONTRACHET (white)
- M Rollin, CORTON-CHARLEMAGNE (white)
- TOLLOT-BEAUT, Corton-Bressandes (red)

CALIFORNIA
- ALBAN
- Cline Cellars, Bridgehead ZINFANDEL, Contra Costa County
- DALLA VALLE
- LAUREL GLEN
- Long Meadow Ranch, NAPA VALLEY
- NEWTON Le Puzzle
- Ramey, Hyde Vineyard Chardonnay, CARNEROS
- RIDGE Geyserville
- St Supéry, Dollarhide Cabernet Sauvignon, NAPA VALLEY
- SHAFER Hillside Select Cabernet Sauvignon
- Sean Thackrey, Orion Rossi Vineyard Syrah, NAPA VALLEY
- Viader, NAPA VALLEY

ITALIAN REDS
- ALLEGRINI Amarone
- BOSCARELLI
- D'ALESSANDRO Cortona Syrah
- Giacomo CONTERNO, Barolo, Cascina Francia
- GAJA, Langhe, Sperss
- ISOLE E OLENA Cepparello
- PLANETA Santa Cecilia
- POLIZIANO Le Stanze
- SELVAPIANA Chianti Rufina, Riserva Bucerchiale
- TUA RITA Giusto di Notri

RHÔNE AND SOUTHERN FRANCE
- Ch. de BEAUCASTEL Roussanne Vieilles Vignes (white)
- CUILLERON, Condrieu les Chaillets
- Pierre Gaillard, CONDRIEU
- GRAILLOT, Crozes-Hermitage la Guiraude
- JAMET, Côte-Rôtie
- Dom. de la Janasse, CHATEAUNEUF-DU-PAPE Vieilles Vignes
- Raspail-Ay, GIGONDAS
- Le Vieux Donjon, CHATEAUNEUF-DU-PAPE

CABERNET SAUVIGNON
- SASSICAIA, Tuscany, Italy
- Long Meadow Ranch, NAPA VALLEY, California
- QUEBRADA DE MACUL, Domus Aurea, Chile
- SANTA RITA Floresta, Chile
- RIDGE Monte Bello, California
- STAG'S LEAP WINE CELLARS Fay, California
- TERRAZAS DE LOS ANDES Cheval des Andes, Argentina
- The Willows, BAROSSA, Australia

CHARDONNAY
- CARILLON, Bienvenues-Bâtard-Montrachet, France
- COCHE-DURY, Corton-Charlemagne, France
- CONCHA Y TORO Amelia, Chile
- Diamond Valley Vineyards, YARRA VALLEY, Australia
- J-N GAGNARD, Bâtard-Montrachet, France
- GIACONDA, Australia
- GROSSET Piccadilly, Australia
- HAMILTON RUSSELL, South Africa
- KUMEU RIVER, New Zealand
- NEWTON Unfiltered, California
- Ramey, Hudson Vineyard, CARNEROS, California

- RIDGE Monte Bello, California
- SAINTSBURY, Carneros, California
- SHAW & SMITH M3, Australia
- Tabalí/SAN PEDRO, Special Reserve, Limarí, Chile

MERLOT

- ANDREW WILL, Washington, USA
- Ch. ANGELUS, St-Émilion, France
- CASA LAPOSTOLLE Cuvée Alexandre, Chile
- CASABLANCA Nimbus Estate, Chile
- CONO SUR 20 Barrels, Chile
- LEONETTI CELLAR, Washington, USA
- ORNELLAIA Masseto, Tuscany, Italy
- Ch. PETRUS, Pomerol, France
- Ch. VALANDRAUD, St-Émilion, France
- WOODWARD CANYON, Washington, USA

PINOT NOIR

- ATA RANGI, New Zealand
- R Chevillon, NUITS-ST-GEORGES les St-Georges, France
- DRY RIVER, New Zealand
- FELTON ROAD, New Zealand
- FLOWERS Camp Meeting Ridge, California
- Freycinet, TASMANIA, Australia
- Anne GROS, Clos de Vougeot, France
- LAFON, Volnay Santenots, France
- Viña Leyda, Lot 21, SAN ANTONIO, Chile
- SAINTSBURY Carneros, California
- E Rouget, ECHEZEAUX, France
- VILLA MARIA Reserve, Marlborough, New Zealand

RIESLING

- Tim ADAMS, Clare Valley, Australia
- H DONNHOFF Oberhäuser Brücke, Nahe, Germany
- Gobelsburg, KAMPTAL, Austria
- GROSSET Watervale, Clare Valley, Australia
- Fritz HAAG Brauneberger Juffer Sonnenuhr, Mosel, Germany
- Dr LOOSEN Erdener Prälat, Mosel, Germany
- Mount Edward Drumlin, CENTRAL OTAGO, New Zealand
- MOUNT HORROCKS, Australia
- Horst SAUER Escherndorfer Lump, Franken, Germany

SAUVIGNON BLANC

- Cape Campbell, MARLBOROUGH, New Zealand

- CASAS DEL BOSQUE, Chile
- Didier DAGUENEAU, Pouilly-Fumé, France
- Neil ELLIS Groenekloof, South Africa
- Ch. SMITH-HAUT-LAFITTE, Pessac-Léognan, France
- SAINT CLAIR Wairau Reserve, New Zealand
- STEENBERG, South Africa
- VAVASOUR, New Zealand
- VERGELEGEN, South Africa
- VILLA MARIA Reserve Clifford Bay, New Zealand

SYRAH/SHIRAZ

- Tim ADAMS Aberfeldy, Clare Valley, Australia
- ALBAN, EdnaValley, California
- BROKENWOOD Graveyard Vineyard, Hunter Valley, Australia
- CAYUSE Cailloux Vineyard, Washington, USA
- EMILIANA Novas, Casablanca, Chile
- Esk Valley Reserve, HAWKES BAY, New Zealand
- JAMET, Côte-Rôtie, France
- MOUNT LANGI GHIRAN, Grampians, Victoria, Australia
- Penfolds GRANGE, South Australia
- Two Hands, BAROSSA, Australia
- TRINITY HILL Homage, Hawkes Bay, New Zealand
- The Willows, BAROSSA, Australia

FORTIFIED WINE

- Cossart Gordon Vintage Bual, MADEIRA WINE COMPANY
- CHAMBERS Rutherglen Muscat
- GONZALEZ BYASS Noé Pedro Ximénez
- GRAHAM Vintage Port
- HENRIQUES & HENRIQUES 15-year-old Madeira
- HIDALGO La Gitana Manzanilla
- NIEPOORT Vintage Port

SPARKLING WINE

- BILLECART-SALMON Cuvée N-F Billecart Champagne
- CAMEL VALLEY Pinot Noir, England
- CLOUDY BAY Pelorus, New Zealand
- DEUTZ Marlborough Cuvée, New Zealand
- Alfred GRATIEN Vintage Champagne
- Charles HEIDSIECK Mis en Caves Champagne
- Jansz, YALUMBA, Australia
- Charles MELTON Sparkling Red, Australia
- Le Mesnil Blanc de Blancs CHAMPAGNE

MODERN WINE STYLES

Not so long ago, if I were to have outlined the basic wine styles, the list would have been strongly biased towards the classics – Bordeaux, Burgundy, Sancerre, Mosel Riesling, Champagne. But the classics have, over time, become expensive and unreliable – giving other regions the chance to offer us wines that may or may not owe anything to the originals. *These* are the flavours to which ambitious winemakers the world over now aspire.

WHITE WINES

Ripe, up-front, spicy Chardonnay is the main grape and fruit is the key: apricot, peach, melon, pineapple and tropical fruits, spiced up with the vanilla and butterscotch richness of some new oak – often American oak – to make a delicious, approachable, fruit cocktail of taste. Australia and Chile are best at this style. Oak-aged Chenin and Sémillon can have similar characteristics.

Green and tangy New Zealand Sauvignon was the originator of this style – zingy lime zest, nettles and asparagus and passionfruit – and South Africa now has its own tangy, super-fresh examples. Chile's San Antonio and Casablanca regions have started to produce something similar, and there are hopeful signs in southern France and Hungary. Bordeaux and the Loire are the original sources of dry Sauvignon wines, and at last we are seeing an expanding band of modern producers matching clean fruit with zippy green tang. Riesling in Australia is usually lean and limy.

Bone-dry, neutral This doesn't sound very appetizing, but as long as it is well made it will be thirst-quenching and easy to drink. Many Italian whites fit this bill. Southern French wines, where no grape variety is specified, will be like this; so will many wines from Bordeaux, South-West France, Muscadet and Anjou. Modern young Spanish whites and dry Portuguese Vinho Verdes are good examples. I don't like seeing too much neutrality in New World wines, but cheap South African and California whites are 'superneutral'.

White Burgundy By this I mean the nutty, oatmealy-ripe but dry, subtly oaked styles of villages like Meursault at their best. Few people do it well, even in Burgundy itself, and it's a difficult style to emulate. California makes the most effort. Washington, Oregon, New York State and British Columbia each have occasional successes, as do top Australian, South African and New Zealand Chardonnays.

Perfumy, off-dry Gewurztraminer, Muscat and Pinot Gris from Alsace will give you this style and in southern Germany Gewürztraminer, Scheurebe, Kerner, Grauburgunder (Pinot Gris) and occasionally Riesling may also do it. In New Zealand Riesling, Pinot Gris and Gewürztraminer can be excellent. Irsai Olivér from Hungary and Torrontés from Argentina are both heady and perfumed. Albariño in Spain is leaner but heady with citrus scent. Viognier is apricotty and scented in southern Europe, Australia, Chile, California, South Africa and New Zealand.

Mouthfuls of luscious gold Good sweet wines are difficult to make. Sauternes is the most famous, but the Loire, and sometimes Alsace, can also come up with rich, intensely sweet wines that can live for decades. Germany's top sweeties are stunning; Austria's are similiar in style to Germany's, but weightier. Hungarian Tokaji has a wonderful sweet-sour smoky flavour. Australia, California and New Zealand also have some exciting examples and there are a few rare but excellent examples from South Africa and the USA.

RED WINES

Spicy, warm-hearted Australia is out in front at the moment through the ebullient resurgence of her Shiraz reds – ripe, almost sweet, sinfully easy to enjoy. France's southern Rhône Valley is also motoring, and the traditional appellations in the far south of France are looking good. In Italy Piedmont is producing delicious beefy Barbera and juicy exotic Dolcetto, Puglia has chocolaty Negroamaro and Sicily has Nero d'Avola. Spain's Ribera del Duero and Toro and Portugal's Alentejo also deliver the goods, as does Malbec in Argentina. California Zinfandel made in its most powerful style is spicy and rich; Lebanese reds have the succulent scent of the kasbah.

Juicy, fruity The excellent 2005 vintage brought Beaujolais' come-hither charms back into the spotlight. Even so, leafy, raspberryish Loire reds and Grenache and Syrah vins de pays are often better bets. Modern Spanish reds from Valdepeñas, Bierzo and La Mancha, and old-vine Garnachas from Campo de Borja and Calatayud, do the trick, as do unoaked Douros from Portugal and young Valpolicella and Teroldego in Italy. Argentina has some good examples from Bonarda, Tempranillo, Sangiovese and Barbera.

Deep and blackcurranty Chile has climbed back to the top of the Cabernet tree, though good producers in cooler parts of Australia produce Cabernets of thrilling blackcurranty intensity. New Zealand Merlot and Cabernet Franc are dense and rich yet dry. California too frequently overripens its Cabernet and Merlot, though restrained examples can be terrific. Top Bordeaux is on a rich blackcurranty roll since 2000: it's expensive but exciting – as is top Tuscan Cabernet.

Tough, tannic long-haul boys Bordeaux leads this field, and the best wines are really good after 10 years or so – but, except in years like 2005, minor properties won't age in the same way. It's the same in Tuscany and Piedmont – only the top wines last well – especially Brunello di Montalcino, Vino Nobile di Montepulciano, some IGT and DOCG wines from Chianti Classico, Barolo and Barbaresco. Portugal has some increasingly good Dão and Douro reds.

Soft, strawberryish charmers Good Burgundy definitely tops this group. Rioja in Spain can sometimes get there, as can Navarra and Valdepeñas. Pinot Noir in California, Oregon and New Zealand is frequently delicious, and Chile and Australia increasingly get it right too. Germany can hit the spot with Spätburgunder (Pinot Noir). Italy's Lago di Caldaro often smooches in; and over in Bordeaux, of all places, St-Émilion, Pomerol and Blaye can do the business.

SPARKLING AND FORTIFIED WINES

Fizz This can be white or pink or red, dry or sweet, and I sometimes think it doesn't matter what it tastes like as long as it's cold enough and there's enough of it. Champagne can be best, but frequently isn't – and there are lots of new-wave winemakers making good-value lookalikes. Australia is tops for tasty bargains, followed by California, New Zealand and England. Spain pumps out oceans of good basic stuff.

Fortified wines There's nothing to beat the top ports and sherries in the deep, rich, sticky stakes – though for the glimmerings of a new angle look to Australia, California and South Africa. The Portuguese island of Madeira produces fortifieds with rich, brown smoky flavours and a startling acid bite – and don't forget the luscious Muscats made all round the Mediterranean and in Rutherglen, Australia.

MATCHING FOOD AND WINE

Give me a rule, I'll break it – well, bend it anyway. So when I see the proliferation of publications laying down rules as to what wine to drink with what food, I get very uneasy and have to quell a burning desire to slosh back a Grand Cru Burgundy with my chilli con carne.

The pleasures of eating and drinking operate on so many levels that hard and fast rules make no sense. What about mood? If I'm in the mood for Champagne, Champagne it shall be, whatever I'm eating. What about company? An old friend, a lover, a bank manager – each of these companions would probably be best served by quite different wines. What about place? If I'm sitting gazing out across the shimmering Mediterranean, hand me anything, just as long as it's local – it'll be perfect.

Even so, there are some things that simply don't go well with wine: artichokes, asparagus, spinach, kippers and mackerel, chilli, salsas and vinegars, chocolate, all flatten the flavours of wines. The general rule here is avoid tannic red wines and go for juicy young reds, or whites with plenty of fruit and fresh acidity. And for chocolate, liqueur Muscats, raisiny Banyuls or Italy's grapy, frothy Asti all work, but some people like powerful Italian reds such as Barolo or Amarone. Don't be afraid to experiment. Who would guess that salty Roquefort cheese and rich, sweet Sauternes would go together? But they do, and it's a match made in heaven. So, with these factors in mind, the following pairings are not rules – just my recommendations.

FISH

Grilled or baked white fish White Burgundy or other fine Chardonnay, white Bordeaux, Viognier, Australian and New Zealand Riesling and Sauvignon.

Grilled or baked oily or 'meaty' fish (e.g. salmon, tuna, swordfish) Alsace or Austrian Riesling, Grüner Veltliner, fruity New World Chardonnay or Semillon; reds such as Chinon or Bourgueil, Grenache/Garnacha, or New World Pinot Noir.

Fried/battered fish Simple, fresh whites, e.g. Soave, Mâcon-Villages, Verdelho, Pinot Gris, white Bordeaux, or a Riesling Spätlese from the Pfalz.

Shellfish Chablis or unoaked Chardonnay, Sauvignon Blanc, Pinot Blanc; *clams and oysters* Albariño, Aligoté, Vinho Verde, Seyval Blanc; *crab* Riesling, Viognier; *lobster, scallops* fine Chardonnay, Champagne, Viognier; *mussels* Muscadet, Pinot Grigio.

Smoked fish Ice-cold basic fizz, manzanilla or fino sherry, Riesling, Sauvignon Blanc, Alsace Gewurztraminer or Pinot Gris.

MEAT

Beef and lamb are perfect with just about any red wine.

Beef/steak *Plain roasted or grilled* tannic reds, Bordeaux, New World Cabernet Sauvignon, Ribera del Duero, Chianti Classico, Pinotage.

Lamb *Plain roasted or grilled* red Burgundy, red Bordeaux, especially Pauillac or St-Julien, Rioja Reserva, New World Pinot Noir, Merlot or Malbec.

Pork *Plain roasted or grilled* full, spicy dry whites, e.g. Alsace Pinot Gris, lightly oaked Chardonnay; smooth reds, e.g. Rioja, Alentejo; *ham, bacon, sausages, salami* young, fruity reds, e.g. Beaujolais, Lambrusco, Teroldego, unoaked Tempranillo or Garnacha, New World Malbec, Merlot, Zinfandel/Primitivo, Pinotage.

Veal *Plain roasted or grilled* full-bodied whites, e.g. Pinot Gris, Grüner Veltliner, white Rioja; soft reds, e.g. mature Rioja or Pinot Noir; *with cream-based sauce* full, ripe whites, e.g. Alsace Pinot Blanc or Pinot Gris, Vouvray, oaked New World Chardonnay; *with rich red-wine sauce* (e.g. *osso buco*) young Italian reds, Zinfandel.

Venison *Plain roasted or grilled*
Barolo, St-Estèphe, Pomerol,
Côte de Nuits, Hermitage, big
Zinfandel, Alsace or German
Pinot Gris; *with red-wine sauce*
Piedmont and Portuguese reds,
Pomerol, St-Émilion, New
World Syrah/Shiraz or Pinotage,
Priorat.

Chicken and turkey Most red
and white wines go with these
meats – much depends on the
sauce or accompaniments. Try
red or white Burgundy, red
Rioja Reserva, New World
Chardonnay.

Duck Pomerol, St-Émilion, Côte
de Nuits or Rhône reds, New World
Syrah/Shiraz (including sparkling)
or Merlot; also full, soft whites from
Austria and southern Germany.

Game birds *Plain roasted or grilled*
top reds from Burgundy, Rhône,
Tuscany, Piedmont, Ribera del
Duero, New World Cabernet or
Merlot; also full whites such as
oaked New World Semillon.

Casseroles and stews Generally
uncomplicated, full-flavoured
reds. The thicker the sauce, the
fuller the wine. If wine is used in
the preparation, match the colour.
For strong tomato flavours
see Pasta.

HIGHLY SPICED FOOD

Chinese Riesling, Sauvignon,
Pinot Gris, Gewürztraminer,
unoaked New World Chardonnay;
fruity rosé; light Pinot Noir.

Indian Aromatic whites,
e.g. Riesling, Sauvignon Blanc,
Gewürztraminer, Viognier;
non-tannic reds, e.g. Valpolicella,
Rioja, Grenache.

Mexican Fruity reds, e.g. Merlot,
Cabernet Franc, Grenache,
Syrah/Shiraz, Zinfandel.

Thai/South-East Asian Spicy
or tangy whites, e.g. Riesling,
Gewürztraminer, New World
Sauvignon Blanc, dry Alsace
Muscat. Coconut is tricky: New
World Chardonnay may work.

EGG DISHES

Champagne and traditional-method
fizz; light, fresh reds such as
Beaujolais or Chinon; full, dry
unoaked whites; New World rosé.

PASTA, PIZZA

With tomato sauce Barbera,
Valpolicella, Soave, Verdicchio, New
World Sauvignon Blanc; *with meat-
based sauce* north or central Italian
reds, French or New World
Syrah/Shiraz, Zinfandel; *with cream-
or cheese-based sauce* gently oaked
Chardonnay, though the Italians
would drink unoaked whites from
northern Italy; Valpolicella or soft
Merlot; *with seafood/fish* dry, tangy
whites, e.g. Verdicchio, Vermentino,
Grüner Veltliner, Muscadet; *with
pesto* New World Sauvignon Blanc,
Dolcetto, Languedoc reds.
*Basic pizza, with tomato, mozzarella
and oregano* juicy young reds, e.g.
Grenache/Garnacha, Valpolicella,
Austrian reds, Languedoc reds.

SALADS

Sharp-edged whites, e.g. New
World Sauvignon Blanc, Chenin
Blanc, dry Riesling, Vinho Verde.

CHEESES

Hard Full reds from Italy, France
or Spain, New World Merlot or
Zinfandel, dry oloroso sherry,
tawny port.

Soft LBV port, Zinfandel, Alsace
Pinot Gris, Gewürztraminer.

Blue Botrytized sweet whites such as
Sauternes, vintage port, old oloroso
sherry, Malmsey Madeira.

Goats' Sancerre, Pouilly-Fumé,
New World Sauvignon Blanc,
Chinon, Saumur-Champigny.

DESSERTS

Chocolate Asti, Australian Liqueur
Muscat, Banyuls, Canadian
Cabernet Franc icewine.

Fruit-based Sauternes, Eiswein,
fortified European Muscats.

Christmas pudding Asti,
Australian Liqueur Muscat.

MATCHING WINE AND FOOD

With very special bottles, when you have found an irresistible bargain or when you are casting around for culinary inspiration, it can be a good idea to let the wine dictate the choice of food.

Although I said earlier that rules in this area are made to be bent if not broken, there are certain points to remember when matching wine and food. Before you make specific choices, think about some basic characteristics and see how thinking in terms of grape varieties and wine styles can point you in the right direction.

In many cases, the local food and wine combinations that have evolved over the years simply cannot be bettered (think of ripe Burgundy with *coq au vin* or *boeuf bourguignon*; Chianti Riserva with *bistecca alla Fiorentina;* Musadet and Breton oysters). Yet the world of food and wine is moving so fast that it would be madness to be restricted by the old tenets. Californian cuisine, fusion food, and the infiltration of innumerable ethnic influences coupled with the re-invigoration of traditional wines, continuous experiment with new methods and blends and the opening up of completely new wine areas mean that the search for perfect food and wine partners is, and will remain, very much an on-going process.

Here are some of the characteristics you need to consider, plus a summary of the main grape varieties and their best food matches.

Body/weight As well as considering the taste of the wine you need to match the weight or body of the wine to the intensity of the food's flavour. A heavy alcoholic wine will not suit a delicate dish; and *vice versa*.

Acidity The acidity of a dish should balance the acidity of a wine. High-acid flavours, such as tomato, lemon or vinegar, should need matching acidity in their accompanying wines, but, almost by mistake, I've tried a few reds with salad dressing and the wine's fruit was enhanced, not wrecked. Was I lucky? More research needed, I think. Use acidity in wine to cut through the richness of a dish but for this to work, make sure the wine is full in flavour.

Sweetness Sweet food makes dry wine taste unpleasantly lean and acidic. With desserts and puddings find a wine that is at least as sweet as the food (sweeter than the food is fine). However, many savoury foods, such as carrots, onions and parsnips, taste slightly sweet and dishes in which they feature prominently will go best with ripe, fruity wines that have a touch of sweetness.

Salt Salty foods, such as blue cheese, and sweet wines match, but salty foods and tannin are definitely best avoided.

Age/Maturity The bouquet of a wine is only acquired over time and should be savoured and appreciated: with age many red wines acquire complex flavours and perfumes and a relative simplicity in the flavour of the food is often a good idea.

Tannin Red meat, when cooked rare, can have the effect of softening tannic wine. Mature hard cheeses can make rough wine seem gentle. Avoid eggs and fish with tannic wines.

Oak Oak flavours in wine vary from the satisfyingly subtle to positively strident. This latter end of the scale can conflict with food, although it may be suitable for smoked fish (white wines only) or full-flavoured meat or game.

Wine in the food If you want to use wine in cooking it is best to use the same style of wine as the one you are going to drink with the meal (it can be an inferior version though).

14

RED GRAPES

Barbera Wines made to be drunk young have high acidity that can hold their own with sausages, salami, ham, and tomato sauces. Complex older or oak-aged wines from the top growers need to be matched with rich food such as beef casseroles and game dishes.

Cabernet Franc Best drunk with plain rather than sauced meat dishes, or, slightly chilled, with grilled or baked salmon or trout.

Cabernet Sauvignon All over the world the Cabernet Sauvignon makes full-flavoured reliable red wine: the ideal food wine. Cabernet Sauvignon seems to have a particular affinity with lamb, but it partners all plain roast or grilled meats and game well and would be an excellent choice for many sauced meat dishes such as beef casserole, steak and kidney pie or rabbit stew and substantial dishes made with mushrooms.

Dolcetto Dolcetto produces fruity purple wines that go beautifully with hearty meat dishes such as calves' liver and onions or casseroled game with polenta.

Gamay The grape of red Beaujolais, Gamay makes wine you can drink whenever, wherever, however and with whatever you want – although it's particularly good lightly chilled on hot summer days. It goes well with pâtés, bacon and sausages because its acidity provides a satisfying foil to their richness. It would be a good choice for many vegetarian dishes.

Grenache/Garnacha Frequently blended with other grapes, Grenache nonetheless dominates, with its high alcoholic strength and rich, spicy flavours. These are wines readily matched with food: barbecues and casseroles for heavier wines; almost anything for lighter reds and rosés – vegetarian dishes, charcuterie, picnics, grills, and even meaty fish such as tuna and salmon.

Merlot Merlot makes soft, rounded, fruity wines that are some of the easiest red wines to enjoy without food, yet are also a good choice with many kinds of food. Spicier game dishes, herby terrines and pâtés, pheasant, pigeon, duck or goose all team well with Merlot; substantial casseroles made with wine are excellent with Pomerols and St-Émilions; and the soft fruitiness of the wines is perfect for pork, liver, turkey, and savoury foods with a hint of sweetness such as Iberico, Parma or honey-roast ham.

Nebbiolo Lean but fragrant, early-drinking styles of Nebbiolo wine are best with Italian salami, pâtés, *bresaola* and lighter meat dishes. Top Barolos and Barbarescos need substantial food: *bollito misto*, rich hare or beef casseroles and *brasato al Barolo* (a large piece of beef marinated then braised slowly in Barolo) are just the job in Piedmont, or anywhere else for that matter.

Pinot Noir The great grape of Burgundy has taken its food-friendly complexity all over the wine world. However, nothing can beat the marriage of great wine with sublime local food that is Burgundy's heritage, and it is Burgundian dishes that spring to mind as perfect partners for the Pinot Noir: *coq au vin*, *boeuf bourguignon*, rabbit with mustard, braised ham, chicken with tarragon, *entrecôtes* from prized Charolais cattle with a rich red-wine sauce … the list is endless.

Pinot Noir's subtle flavours make it a natural choice for complex meat dishes, but it is also excellent with plain grills and roasts. New World Pinots are often richer and fruitier – excellent with grills and roasts and a good match for salmon or tuna.

In spite of the prevalence of superb cheese in Burgundy, the best Pinot Noir red wines are wasted on cheese.

Sangiovese Tuscany is where Sangiovese best expresses the qualities that can lead it, in the right circumstances, to be numbered among the great grapes of the world. And Tuscany is very much 'food with wine' territory. Sangiovese wines such as Chianti, Rosso di Montalcino, Vino Nobile di Montepulciano and the biggest of them all, Brunello, positively demand to be drunk with food. Drink them with *bistecca alla Fiorentina*, roast meats and game, calves' liver, casseroles, hearty pasta sauces, *porcini* mushrooms and Pecorino cheese.

Syrah/Shiraz Whether from France (the Rhône Valley and Languedoc), Australia, California, South America or South Africa, this grape always makes powerful, rich, full-bodied wines that are superb with full-flavoured food. The classic barbecue wine when drunk young, Shiraz/Syrah also goes with roasts, game, hearty casseroles and charcuterie. It can be good with tangy cheeses such as Manchego or Cheshire.

Tempranillo Spain's best native red grape makes juicy wines for drinking young, and matures well in a rich (usually) oaky style. Tempranillo is good with game, cured hams and sausages, casseroles and meat grilled with herbs; it is particularly good with roast lamb. It can partner some Indian and Mexican dishes.

Zinfandel California's much-planted, most versatile grape is used for a bewildering variety of wine styles from bland, slightly sweet pinks to rich, succulent, fruity reds. And the good red Zinfandels themselves may vary greatly in style,

from relatively soft and light to big and beefy, but they're always ripe and ready for spicy, smoky, unsubtle food: barbecued meat, haunches of lamb, venison or beef, game casseroles, sausages, Tex-Mex, the Beach Boys, The Eagles – anything rowdy – Zin copes with them all. The pale blush style of Zin goes well with tomato-based dishes, such as pizza and pasta, as well as with hamburgers.

WHITE GRAPES

Albariño Light, crisp, aromatic in a grapefruity way, this goes well with crab and prawn dishes as well as Chinese-style chicken dishes.

Aligoté This Burgundian grape can, at its best, make very versatile food wine. It goes well with many fish and seafood dishes, smoked fish, salads and snails in garlic and butter.

Chardonnay More than almost any other grape, Chardonnay responds to different climatic conditions and to the winemaker's art. This, plus the relative ease with which it can be grown, accounts for the marked gradation of flavours and styles: from steely, cool-climate austerity to almost tropical lusciousness. The relatively sharp end of the spectrum is one of the best choices for simple fish dishes; most Chardonnays are superb with roast chicken or other white meat; the really full, rich, New World blockbusters need rich fish and seafood dishes. Oaky Chardonnays are, surprisingly, a good choice for smoked fish.

Chenin Blanc One of the most versatile of grapes, Chenin Blanc makes wines ranging from averagely quaffable dry whites to the great sweet whites of the Loire. The lighter wines can be good as aperitifs or with light fish dishes or salads while the medium-sweet versions usually retain enough of their acidity to counteract the richness of creamy chicken and meat dishes. The sweet wines are good with fruit puddings and superb with those made with slightly tart fruit, or with foie gras or blue cheese.

Gewürztraminer Spicy and perfumed, Gewürztraminer has the weight and flavour to go with such hard-to-match dishes as *choucroute* and smoked fish. It is also a good choice for Chinese or any lightly spiced Oriental food, with its use of lemongrass, coriander and ginger, and pungent soft cheeses, such as Munster from Alsace.

Grüner Veltliner In its lightest form, this makes a peppery, refreshing aperitif. Riper, more structured versions keep the pepper but add peach and apple fruit, and are particularly good with grilled or baked fish.

Marsanne These rich, fat wines are a bit short of acidity, so match them with simply prepared chicken, pork, fish or vegetables.

Muscadet The dry, light Muscadet grape (best wines are *sur lie*) is perfect with seafood.

Muscat Fragrant, grapy wines coming in a multitude of styles, from delicate to downright syrupy. The drier ones are more difficult to pair with food, but can be delightful with Oriental cuisines; the sweeties really come into their own with most desserts. Sweet Moscato d'Asti, delicious by itself, goes well with rich Christmas pudding or mince pies.

Pinot Blanc Clean, bright and appley, Pinot Blanc is very food-friendly. Classic fish and chicken dishes, modern vegetarian food, pasta and pizza all match up well.

Pinot Gris In Alsace, this makes rich, fat wines that need rich, fat food: *choucroute*, *confit de canard*, rich pork and fish dishes. Italian Pinot Grigio wines are light quaffers. New World Pinot Gris is often delightfully fragrant and ideal with grilled fish.

Riesling Good dry Rieslings are excellent with spicy cuisine. Sweet Rieslings are best enjoyed for their own lusciousness but are suitable partners to fruit-based desserts. In between, those with a fresh acid bite and some residual sweetness can counteract the richness of, say, goose or duck, and the fuller examples can be good with Oriental food and otherwise hard-to-match salads.

Sauvignon Blanc Tangy green flavours and high acidity are the hallmarks of this grape. Led by New Zealand, New World Sauvignons are some of the snappiest, tastiest whites around and make good, thirst-quenching aperitifs. Brilliant with seafood and Oriental cuisine, they also go well with tomato dishes and goats' cheese.

Sémillon Dry Bordeaux Blancs are excellent with fish and shellfish; fuller, riper New World Semillons are equal to spicy food and rich sauces, often going even better with meat than with fish; sweet Sémillons can partner many puddings, especially rich, creamy ones. Sémillon also goes well with many cheeses, and Sauternes with Roquefort is a classic combination.

Viognier Fresh, young Viognier is at its best drunk as an aperitif. It can also go well with mildly spiced Indian dishes or chicken in a creamy sauce. The apricot aroma that typifies even inexpensive Viognier suggests another good pairing – pork or chicken dishes with apricot stuffing.

MAKING THE MOST OF WINE

Most wine is pretty hardy stuff and can put up with a fair amount of rough handling. Young red wines can knock about in the back of a car for a day or two and be lugged from garage to kitchen to dinner table without coming to too much harm. Serving young white wines when well chilled can cover up all kinds of ill-treatment – a couple of hours in the fridge should do the trick. Even so, there are some conditions that are better than others for storing your wines, especially if they are on the mature side. And there are certain ways of serving wines which will emphasize any flavours or perfumes they have.

STORING
Most wines are sold ready for drinking, and it will be hard to ruin them if you store them for a few months before you pull the cork. Don't stand them next to the central heating or the cooker, though, nor on a sunny windowsill, as too much warmth will flatten the flavour and give a 'baked' taste.

Light and extremes of temperature are also the things to worry about if you are storing wine long-term. Some wines, Chardonnay for instance, are particularly sensitive to exposure to light over several months, and the damage will be worse if the bottle is made of pale-coloured glass. The warmer the wine, the quicker it will age, and really high temperatures can spoil wine quite quickly. Beware in the winter of garages and outhouses, too: a very cold snap – say –4°C (25°F) or below – will freeze your wine, push out the corks and crack the bottles. An underground cellar is ideal, with a fairly constant temperature of 10°–12°C (50°–53°F). And bottles really do need to lie on their sides, so that the cork stays damp and swollen, and keeps out the air.

TEMPERATURE
The person who thought up the rule that red wine should be served at room temperature certainly didn't live in a modern, centrally heated flat. It's no great sin to serve a big, beefy red at the temperature of your central heating, but I prefer most reds just a touch cooler. Over-heated wine tastes flabby, and may lose some of its more volatile aromas. In general, the lighter the red, the cooler it can be. Really light, refreshing reds, such as Beaujolais, are nice lightly chilled. Ideally, I'd serve Burgundy and other Pinot Noir wines at larder temperature (about 15°C/59°F), Bordeaux and Rioja a bit warmer (18°C/64°F), Rhône wines and New World Cabernet at a comfortable room temperature, but no more than 20°C/68°F.

Chilling white wines makes them taste fresher, emphasizing their acidity. White wines with low acidity especially benefit from chilling, and it's vital for sparkling wines if you want to avoid exploding corks and a tableful of froth. Drastic chilling also subdues flavours, however – a useful ruse if you're serving basic wine, but a shame if the wine is very good. A good guide for whites is to give the cheapest and lightest a spell in the fridge, but serve bigger and better wines – Australian Chardonnays or top white Burgundies – perhaps half-way between fridge and central-heating temperature. If you're undecided, err on the cooler side, for whites or reds. To chill wine quickly, and to keep it cool, an ice bucket is more efficient if filled with a mixture of ice and water, rather than ice alone.

OPENING THE BOTTLE
There's no corkscrew to beat the Screwpull, and the Spinhandle Screwpull is especially easy to use. Don't worry if bits of cork crumble into the wine – just fish them out of your glass. Tight corks that refuse to budge might be

loosened if you run hot water over the bottle neck to expand the glass. If the cork is loose and falls in, push it right in and don't worry about it.

Opening sparkling wines is a serious business – point the cork away from people! Once you've started, never take your hand off the cork until it's safely out. Remove the foil, loosen the wire, hold the wire and cork firmly and twist the bottle. If the wine froths, hold the bottle at an angle of 45 degrees, and have a glass at hand.

AIRING AND DECANTING

Scientists have proved that opening young to middle-aged red wines an hour before serving makes no difference whatsoever. The surface area of wine in contact with air in the bottle neck is too tiny to be significant. Decanting is a different matter, because sloshing the wine from bottle to jug or decanter mixes it up quite thoroughly with the air. The only wines that really need to be decanted are those that have a sediment which would cloud the wine if they were poured directly – mature red Bordeaux, Burgundy and vintage port are the commonest examples. Ideally, if you are able to plan that far in advance, you need to stand the bottle upright for a day or two to let the sediment settle in the bottom. Draw the cork extremely gently. As you tip the bottle, shine a bright light through from underneath as you pour in a single steady movement. Stop pouring when you see the sediment approaching the bottle neck.

Contrary to many wine buffs' practice, I would decant a mature wine only just before serving; elderly wines often fade rapidly once they meet with air, and an hour in the decanter could kill off what little fruit they had left. By contrast, a good-quality young white wine can benefit from decanting.

GLASSES

If you want to taste wine at its best, to enjoy all its flavours and aromas, to admire its colours and texture, choose glasses designed for the purpose and show the wine a bit of respect. The ideal wine glass is a fairly large tulip shape, made of fine, clear glass, with a slender stem. When you pour the wine, fill the glass no more than halfway to allow space for aromas. For sparkling wines choose a tall, slender glass, as it helps the bubbles to last longer.

KEEPING LEFTOVERS

Leftover white wine keeps better than red, since the tannin and colouring matter in red wine is easily attacked by the air. Any wine, red or white, keeps better in the fridge than in a warm kitchen. And most wines, if well made in the first place, will be perfectly acceptable, if not pristine, after 2 or 3 days re-corked in the fridge. But for better results it's best to use one of the gadgets sold for this purpose. The ones that work by blanketing the wine with heavier-than-air inert gas are much better than those that create a vacuum in the air space in the bottle.

FRANCE

I've visited most of the wine-producing countries of the world, but the one I come back to again and again, with my enthusiasm undimmed by time, is France. The sheer range of its wine flavours, the number of wine styles produced, and indeed the quality differences, from very best to very nearly worst, continue to enthral me, and as each year's vintage nears, I find myself itching to leap into the car and head for the vineyards of Champagne, of Burgundy, of Bordeaux and the Loire. France is currently going through a difficult period – aware that the New World is making tremendous strides and is the master of innovation and technology, yet unwilling to admit to the quality and character of this new breed of wines. But the best French producers learn from the newcomers while proudly defining their Frenchness.

CLIMATE AND SOIL

France lies between the 40th and 50th parallels north, and the climate runs from the distinctly chilly and almost too cool to ripen grapes in the far north near the English Channel, right through to the swelteringly hot and almost too torrid to avoid grapes overripening in the far south on the Mediterranean shores. In the north, the most refined and delicate sparkling wine is made in Champagne. In the south, rich, luscious dessert Muscats and fortified wines dominate. In between is just about every sort of wine you could wish for.

The factors that influence a wine's flavour are the grape variety, the soil and climate, and the winemaker's techniques. Most of the great wine grapes, like the red Cabernet Sauvignon, Merlot, Pinot Noir and Syrah, and the white Chardonnay, Sauvignon Blanc, Sémillon and Viognier, find conditions in France where they can ripen slowly but reliably – and slow, even ripening always gives the best flavours to a wine. Since grapes have been grown for over 2000 years in France, the most suitable varieties for the different soils and mesoclimates have naturally evolved. And since winemaking was brought to France by the Romans, generation upon generation of winemakers have refined their techniques to produce the best possible results from their different grape types. The great wines of areas like Bordeaux and Burgundy are the results of centuries of experience and of trial and error, which winemakers from other countries of the world now use as role models in their attempts to create good wine.

WINE REGIONS

White grapes generally ripen more easily than red grapes and they dominate the northern regions. Even so, the chilly Champagne region barely manages to ripen its red or white grapes on its chalky soil. But the resultant acid wine is the ideal base for sparkling wine: with good winemaking and a few years' maturing, the young still wine can transform into a golden honeyed sparkling wine of incomparable finesse.

Alsace, on the German border, is warmer and drier than Champagne (the vineyards sit in a rain shadow created by the Vosges mountains that rise above the Rhine Valley) but still produces mainly dry white wines, from grapes such as Riesling, Pinot Gris and Gewurztraminer that are seldom encountered elsewhere in France. With its clear blue skies, Alsace can provide ripeness, and therefore the higher alcoholic strength of the warm south, but also the perfume and fragrance of the cool north.

South-east of Paris, heading into limestone country, Chablis marks the northernmost tip of the Burgundy region, and the Chardonnay grape here produces very dry wines, usually with a streak of green acidity and minerality, but nowadays with a fuller softer texture to subdue any harshness.

It's a good 2 hours' drive further south to the heart of Burgundy – the Côte d'Or, which runs between Dijon and Chagny. World-famous villages such as Gevrey-Chambertin and Vosne-Romanée (where the red Pinot Noir dominates) and Meursault and Puligny-Montrachet (where Chardonnay reigns) here produce the great Burgundies that have given the region renown over the centuries. Lesser Burgundies – but they're still good – are produced further south in the Côte Chalonnaise, while between Mâcon and Lyon are the Mâconnais white wine villages (Pouilly-Fuissé and St-Véran are particularly tasty) and the villages of Beaujolais, famous for bright, easy-going red wine from the Gamay grape. The 10 Beaujolais Crus or 'growths' are the most important communes and should produce wine with more character and structure.

South of Lyon, in the Rhône Valley, red wines begin to dominate. The Syrah grape makes great wine at Côte-Rôtie and Hermitage in the north, while in the south the Grenache and a host of supporting grapes (most southern Rhône reds will add at least Syrah, Cinsaut or Mourvèdre to their blends) make full, satisfying reds, of which Châteauneuf-du-Pape is the richest and most famous. The white Viognier makes lovely wine at Condrieu and Château-Grillet in the north.

The whole of the south of France has undergone considerable change over the last 20 years. Despite the financial woes of growers who over-extended themselves in the late 1990s, new ownership and a new generation are producing exciting wines from unpromising lands. The traditional Provence, Languedoc and Roussillon vineyards make increasingly impressive reds from

21

Grenache, Syrah, Mourvèdre and Carignan, as well as Cabernet Sauvignon. And, with the new Languedoc appellation (covering the whole of Languedoc and Roussillon), the possibilities and freedom to improve by blending will be extended. Many of the tastiest and most affordable wines are vins de pays. Roussillon also makes fine sweet Muscats and Grenache-based fortifieds.

The south-west of France is dominated by the wines of Bordeaux, but has many other gems benefiting from the cooling influence of the Atlantic. Dry whites from Gascony and Bergerac can be exciting. Jurançon down in the Basque country produces some remarkable dry and sweet wines, while Madiran, Cahors and Bergerac produce good to excellent reds.

But Bordeaux is the king here. The Cabernet Sauvignon and Merlot are the chief grapes, the Cabernet dominating the production of deep reds from the Médoc peninsula and its famous villages of Margaux, St-Julien, Pauillac and St-Estèphe on the left bank of the Gironde river. Round the city of Bordeaux are Pessac-Léognan and Graves, where Cabernet and Merlot blend to produce fragrant refined reds. On the right bank of the Gironde estuary, the Merlot is most important in the plump rich reds of St-Émilion and Pomerol. Sweet whites from Sémillon and Sauvignon Blanc are made in Sauternes, with increasingly good dry whites produced in the Entre-Deux-Mers, and especially in Graves and Pessac-Léognan.

The Loire Valley is the most northerly of France's Atlantic wine regions but, since the river rises in the heart of France not far from the Rhône, styles vary widely. Sancerre and Pouilly in the east produce tangy, *terroir*-influenced Sauvignon whites and some surprisingly good Pinot Noir reds. Along the river Cher, which joins the Loire at Tours, the best varieties are Sauvignon and Romorantin for whites, Gamay and Côt/Malbec for reds; watch out for ambitious vins de table. In central Touraine, Saumur and Anjou the focus is squarely on Chenin Blanc in styles which range from bone dry to lusciously sweet, even sparkling and, for the reds, Cabernet Franc with a little Cabernet Sauvignon. Down at the mouth of the river, as it slips past Nantes into the Atlantic swell, the vineyards of Muscadet produce one of the world's most famous and often least memorable dry white wines. Still, in common with the rest of the Loire, better vineyard practices have seen a general uplift in quality.

CLASSIFICATIONS

France has an intricate but eminently logical system for controlling the quality and authenticity of its wines. The system is divided into 4 broad classifications (in ascending order): **Vin de Table**, **Vin de Pays**, **VDQS** (Vin Délimité de Qualité Supérieure) and **AC** (Appellation Contrôlée). Within the laws there are numerous variations, with certain vineyards or producers singled out for special mention. The 1855 Classification in Bordeaux or the Grands Crus of Alsace or Burgundy are good examples. The intention is a system which rewards quality. Vin de Pays and VDQS wines can be promoted to AC, for example, after a few years' good behaviour. However, the AC system is now under increasing attack from critics, both inside and outside France, who feel that it is outmoded and ineffectual and that too many poor wines are passed as of Appellation Contrôlée standard.

2007 VINTAGE REPORT

What a year in Bordeaux! One of the warmest Aprils on record, then a miserable summer – sales of anoraks and umbrellas in the south-west rocketed in May, June, July and August – followed by vintage-saving sunny, dry weather in September and October. Producers really needed to be on top of their game in the vineyards to get through this. Mildew was a constant threat.

Woe betide those who missed their treatments (organic fundamentalists had to decide whether they wanted a crop or not). Then the Indian summer, a godsend for Bordeaux. Some growers picked really late, holding off until the end of October to get that last degree of ripeness. So what about the wines? Well, the dry whites are fresh and aromatic and there's some superb Sauternes. As to the reds, they're extremely varied – it's all down to the producer and *terroir*. Generally, colours are good, alcohol around the classic 12.5% and the wines aromatic. I'd say the best are good for relatively early drinking but don't go paying silly money.

The rest of the South-West suffered from the cool summer, with mildew reducing yields. Some growers claim that what was harvested is making better wine than in 2006.

In Burgundy the marvellous April weather led to an early harvest – if only it had not rained so much in between. Reds look pleasingly perfumed and fruity but will be light on depth and concentration; the secret to producing fine whites from a big crop was to have the courage to wait and pick late, the opposite decision to 2006. There will be some marvellous wines but others will seem lean and undernourished from a large crop.

Beaujolais wines are better than anticipated, with good colour, fruit and concentration.

In the Rhône Valley a sound late August and September led the 2007 vintage away from misfortune. The southern reds appear remarkably similar to 2006 in top appellations such as Châteauneuf-du-Pape – quite a rich layer of fruit and open appeal with sound tannins. The northern reds are relatively less full. The best sites have delivered mid-weight wines that have a little more depth than the somewhat similar 2004s. A good vintage for whites.

Cool nights and no big heat spikes meant that Languedoc and Provence had a slow harvest with plenty of time for grapes to ripen. Mildew was a problem for those growers who did not pay attention, and yields are down. One curiosity has been that the grapes, although healthy, have lacked juice. However, with a warm, dry September many growers are pronouncing a high-quality vintage.

In the Loire Valley, after a promising, unseasonably warm April, the 2007 vintage tested the steeliest of nerves. Mildew-inducing rainfall and cool, cloudy weather from May right through to August seriously hampered ripening and resulted in lower yields than normal. A sunny, warm September came to the rescue, producing tightly focused white wines, especially Muscadet and drier styles of Chenin Blanc. Purists will love 2007's lean and linear Sauvignons. As for sweet (*moelleux*) Chenin, the Layon was much more successful than Vouvray or Montlouis-sur-Loire thanks to good conditions for botrytis – expect some concentrated Coteaux du Layon and Bonnezeaux. Cabernet Franc reds, such as Bourgueil and Chinon, are reminiscent of 2002: leafy with an emphasis on red rather than black fruits and grippier tannins than the interceding vintages. The best reds – ripe yet elegant – came to those in no hurry to harvest and who extracted gently.

Alsace had something approaching a classic vintage, although the early part of the season was not without its hiccups. Most bizarre was a ferocious hailstorm in the second half of June, which led to some vineyards being denuded of up to 80% of their growth. Happily, the rest of the growing season saw normal meteorological service resumed, with July and August basking in hot sun. Harvests were unusually prolonged, thanks to fine late summer weather. All varieties look good, and there will be some great dessert wines (with Gewurztraminer and Pinot Gris the pick of the botrytized offerings).

23

In Champagne, the warmest April on record started the growing season three weeks early, but cooler temperatures, above-average rainfall and fewer sunshine hours in July and August slowed things down. In the end the harvest was only saved by a change in the weather just before picking was due to start in mid-August. Chardonnay looks to be best but some is underripe; Pinot Noir fared better than Pinot Meunier. Although production hit a record high, those restricting their yields got better levels of ripeness. In the best villages quality looks like being good enough for vintage wines.

French entries in the A–Z section (pages 56–307), by region.

ALSACE	PRODUCERS	Muré, Réné	Zind-Humbrecht
ACS	Adam, Jean-Baptiste	Schoffit, Dom.	
Alsace	Blanck, Paul	Trimbach	
Crémant d'Alsace	Deiss, Marcel	Turckheim, Cave	
	Hugel	Vinicole de	
	Mann, Albert	Weinbach	

BORDEAUX	St-Émilion	Coutet	Latour
ACS	St-Émilion Grand	Doisy-Daëne	Latour-Martillac
Barsac	Cru	Doisy-Védrines	Latour-à-Pomerol
Bordeaux	St-Estèphe	Ducru-Beaucaillou	Laville-Haut-Brion
Bordeaux-Côtes de	St-Georges-St-	l'Eglise-Clinet	Léoville-Barton
Francs	Émilion	l'Évangile	Léoville-Las-Cases
Bordeaux Supérieur	St-Julien	Falfas	Léoville-Poyferré
Cadillac	Ste-Croix-du-Mont	de Fargues	la Louvière
Canon-Fronsac	Sauternes	Ferrière	Lynch-Bages
Cérons		de Fieuzal	Magdelaine
Côtes de Bourg	CHATEAUX	Figeac	Malartic-Lagravière
Côtes de	Angélus	la Fleur-Pétrus	Malescot St-Exupéry
Castillon	d'Angludet	Gazin	Margaux
Entre-Deux-Mers	l'Arrosée	Gilette	Maucaillou
Fronsac	Ausone	Gloria	Meyney
Graves	Batailley	Grand-Puy-Ducasse	la Mission-Haut-
Haut-Médoc	Beau-Séjour	Grand-Puy-Lacoste	Brion
Lalande-de-Pomerol	Bécot	Gruaud-Larose	Monbousquet
Listrac-Médoc	Belair	Guiraud	Montrose
Loupiac	Beychevelle	Haut-Bages-Libéral	Moueix, J P
Lussac-St-Émilion	le Bon Pasteur	Haut-Bailly	Mouton-Cadet
Margaux	Bonnet	Haut-Bataillley	Mouton-
Médoc	Branaire-Ducru	Haut-Brion	Rothschild
Montagne-St-	Brane-Cantenac	Haut-Marbuzet	Nairac
Émilion	Calon-Ségur	d'Issan	Palmer
Moulis	Canon	Kirwan	Pape-Clément
Pauillac	Canon-la-Gaffeliere	Labégorce-Zédé	Pavie
Pessac-Léognan	Cantemerle	Lafaurie-Peyraguey	Pavie-Macquin
Pomerol	Chasse-Spleen	Lafite-Rothschild	Petit-Village
Premières Côtes de	Cheval Blanc	Lafleur	Pétrus
Blaye	Dom. de Chevalier	Lafon-Rochet	de Pez
Premières Côtes de	Clarke	Lagrange	Pichon-Longueville
Bordeaux	Climens	la Lagune	Pichon-Longueville-
Puisseguin-St-	La Conseillante	Langoa-Barton	Lalande
Émilion	Cos d'Estournel	Lascombes	le Pin

Pontet-Canet
Potensac
Poujeaux
Prieuré-Lichine
Rauzan-Ségla
Reynon
Rieussec
Roc de Cambes
St-Pierre
Siran
Smith-Haut-Lafitte

Sociando-Mallet
Suduiraut
Talbot
Tertre-Rôteboeuf
la Tour Blanche
Troplong-Mondot
Trotanoy
Valandraud
Vieux-Château-
    Certan
d'Yquem

SEE ALSO
Bordeaux Red
    Wines
Bordeaux White
    Wines
St-Émilion Premier
    Grand Cru Classé

**BURGUNDY AND
    BEAUJOLAIS**
ACS
Aloxe-Corton
Auxey-Duresses
Bâtard-Montrachet
Beaujolais
Beaujolais-Villages
Beaune
Blagny
Bonnes-Mares
Bourgogne
Bourgogne-Côte
    Chalonnaise
Bourgogne-Hautes-
    Côtes de Beaune
Bourgogne-Hautes-
    Côtes de Nuits
Brouilly
Chablis
Chablis Grand Cru
Chambertin
Chambolle-Musigny
Chassagne-
    Montrachet
Chénas
Chiroubles
Chorey-lès-Beaune
Clos des Lambrays
Clos de la Roche
Clos St-Denis
Clos de Tart
Clos de Vougeot
Corton
Corton-
    Charlemagne
Côte de Beaune
Côte de Beaune-
    Villages
Côte de Brouilly
Côte de Nuits-
    Villages
Coteaux du
    Lyonnais
Crémant de
    Bourgogne
Échézeaux

Fixin
Fleurie
Gevrey-Chambertin
Givry
Irancy
Juliénas
Ladoix
Mâcon
Mâcon-Villages
Maranges
Marsannay
Mercurey
Meursault
Montagny
Monthelie
Montrachet
Morey-St-Denis
Morgon
Moulin-à-Vent
Musigny
Nuits-St-Georges
Pernand-Vergelesses
Pommard
Pouilly-Fuissé
Pouilly-Vinzelles
Puligny-Montrachet
Régnié
Richebourg
la Romanée
la Romanée-Conti
Romanée-St-Vivant
Rully
St-Amour
St-Aubin
St-Bris
St-Romain
St-Véran
Santenay
Savigny-lès-Beaune
la Tâche
Viré-Clessé
Volnay
Vosne-Romanée
Vougeot

PRODUCERS
Angerville, Marquis
    d'
Boisset
Bouchard Père et
    Fils
Bouzereau
Brocard, Jean-Marc
Buxynoise, La
Carillon & Fils, Louis
Cathiard, Sylvain
Chablisienne, La
Chandon de Briailles
Clair, Bruno
Coche-Dury, J-F
Dauvissat, René &
    Vincent
Drouhin, Joseph
Dubeuf, Georges
Dujac
Durup, Jean
Faiveley, Joseph
Gagnard, Jean-Noël
Girardin, Vincent
Gouges, Henri
Grivot, Jean
Gros
Hospices de Beaune
Jadot, Louis
Lafarge, Michel
Lafon
Laroche, Michel
Latour, Louis
Leflaive, Dom.
Leflaive, Olivier
Leroy, Dom.
Liger-Belair
Méo-Camuzet
Montille, Dom. de
Mortet, Denis
Mugnier, J-F
Potel, Nicolas
Ramonet
Raveneau, Jean-
    Marie
Rion
Rodet, Antonin

Romanée-Conti,
    Dom. de la
Roumier, Georges
Rousseau, Armand
Sauzet
Tollot-Beaut
Verget
Vogüé, Comte
    Georges de
Vougeraie, Dom. de
    la

SEE ALSO
Aligoté
Beaujolais Nouveau
Burgundy Red
    Wines
Burgundy White
    Wines
Côte de Beaune
Côte de Nuits
Côte d'Or

CHAMPAGNE
Champagne AC
Champagne Rosé
Coteaux
  Champenois AC
Rosé des Riceys AC

PRODUCERS
Billecart-Salmon
Bollinger
Deutz
Gratien, Alfred
Heidsieck, Charles
Henriot
Jacquesson
Krug

Lanson
Laurent-Perrier
Moët & Chandon
Mumm, G H
Paillard, Bruno
Perrier, Joseph
Perrier-Jouët
Piper-Heidsieck
Pol Roger

Pommery
Roederer, Louis
Ruinart
Taittinger
Veuve Clicquot

**JURA AND
SAVOIE**
Arbois AC
Château-Chalon AC

Côtes du Jura AC
Crémant du Jura
  AC
l'Étoile AC

Savoie
Seyssel AC

**LOIRE VALLEY
ACS**
Anjou Blanc
Anjou Rouge
Anjou-Villages
Bonnezeaux
Bourgueil
Cabernet d'Anjou
Cheverny
Chinon
Côte Roannaise
Coteaux de
  l'Aubance
Coteaux du Layon
Crémant de Loire
Gros Plant du Pays
  Nantais VDQS
Jasnières
Menetou-Salon

Montlouis-sur-Loire
Muscadet
Pouilly-Fumé
Pouilly-sur-Loire
Quarts de Chaume
Quincy
Reuilly
Rosé de Loire
St-Nicolas-de-
  Bourgueil
Sancerre
Saumur
Saumur-Champigny
Saumur Mousseux
Savennières
Touraine
Val de Loire, Vin de
  Pays du
Vouvray

PRODUCERS
Baumard, Dom. des
Blot, Jacky
Bourgeois, Dom.
  Henri
Bouvet-Ladubay
Clos de la Coulée-
  de-Serrant
Clos Naudin, Dom.
  du
Couly-Dutheil
Dagueneau, Didier
Druet, Pierre-
  Jacques
l'Ecu, Dom. de
Huet
Hureau, Ch. du
Mellot, Alphonse
Pithon, Jo

Ragotière, Ch. de la
Richou, Dom.
Roches Neuves,
  Dom. des
Vacheron, Dom.
Villeneuve, Ch. de

SOUTHERN FRANCE

CORSICA
Vin de Corse AC
Arena, Dom.
  Antoine

**LANGUEDOC-
ROUSSILLON
ACS**
Banyuls
Blanquette de
  Limoux
Cabardès
Collioure
Corbières
Coteaux du
  Languedoc
Côtes du Roussillon
Côtes du
  Roussillon-Villages
Côtes de Thongue,
  Vin de Pays des

Crémant de Limoux
  AC
Faugères
Fitou
Gard, Vin de Pays
  du
Hérault, Vin de Pays
  de l'
Limoux
Maury
Minervois
Muscat de
  Frontignan
Muscat de
  Rivesaltes
Muscat de St-Jean-
  de-Minervois
Oc, Vin de Pays d'
Rivesaltes
St-Chinian

PRODUCERS
Alquier, Dom.
Antugnac, Dom. d'
Borie la Vitarèle
Canet-Valette,
  Dom.
Casenove, Ch. la
Cazes, Dom.
Clos de l'Anhel
Clos Bagatelle
Clos Centeilles
Clos Marie
Clot de l'Oum
Denois, J-L
Estanilles, Ch. des
Gauby, Dom.
Grange des Pères,
  Dom. de la
Hecht & Bannier
l'Hortus, Dom. de
l'Hospitalet, Ch.

Mas Blanc, Dom. du
Mas Bruguière
Mas la Chevalière
Mas de Daumas
  Gassac
Mont Tauch, les
  Producteurs du
Nizas, Dom. de
Peyre Rose, Dom.
Prieuré de St-Jean
  de Bébian
Primo Palatum
Sieur d'Arques, les
  Vignerons de
Skalli-Fortant de
  France
Tour Boisée, Ch.
Val d'Orbieu, les
  Vignerons du
Voulte-Gasparets,
  Ch. la

SOUTH-WEST

ACS

Béarn
Bergerac
Buzet
Cahors
Côtes de Duras
Côtes du Frontonnais
Côtes de Gascogne, Vin de Pays des
Côtes du Marmandais
Côtes de St-Mont VDQS
Crémant de Limoux
Gaillac
Irouléguy
Jurançon
Madiran
Marcillac
Monbazillac
Montravel
Pacherenc du Vic-Bilh
Pécharmant
Tursan VDQS

PRODUCERS

l'Ancienne Cure, Dom. de
Aydie, Ch. d'
Buzet, Vignerons
Cauhapé, Dom.
Cèdre, Ch. du
Chapelle Lenclos
Clos Triguedina
Clos Uroulat
Lagrezette, Ch.
Montus, Ch.
Plageoles, Robert
Plaimont, Producteurs
Primo Palatum
Rotier, Dom.
Tariquet, Dom. du
Tour des Gendres, Ch.

PROVENCE

ACS

Bandol
les Baux-de-Provence
Bellet
Bouches-du-Rhône, Vin de Pays des
Cassis
Coteaux d'Aix-en-Provence
Coteaux Varois
Côtes de Provence
Palette

PRODUCERS

d'Eole, Dom.
Esclans, Ch. d'
Pibarnon, Ch. de
Richeaume, Dom.
Romanin, Ch.
Sorin, Dom.
Trévallon, Dom. de
Vannières, Ch.

SEE ALSO

Clape, La
Languedoc-Roussillon
Pic St-Loup
Provence
Roussillon

RHÔNE VALLEY

ACS

Beaumes-de-Venise
Château-Grillet
Châteauneuf-du-Pape
Clairette de Die
Collines Rhodaniennes, Vin de Pays des
Condrieu
Cornas
Costières de Nîmes
Côte-Rôtie
Coteaux de l'Ardèche, Vin de Pays des
Coteaux du Tricastin
Côtes du Lubéron
Côtes du Rhône
Côtes du Rhône-Villages
Côtes du Ventoux
Côtes du Vivarais VDQS
Crémant de Die
Crozes-Hermitage
Gigondas
Hermitage
Lirac
Muscat de Beaumes-de-Venise
Rasteau
St-Joseph
St-Péray
Tavel
Vacqueyras
Vinsobres

PRODUCERS

Allemand, Thierry
Beaucastel, Ch. de
Chapoutier, M
Chave, Jean-Louis
Clape, A
Clos des Papes
Colombo, Jean-Luc
Coursodon, Pierre
Cuilleron, Yves
Delas Frères
Font de Michelle, Dom.
Graillot, Alain
Guigal
Jaboulet Aîné, Paul
Jamet
l'Oratoire St-Martin, Dom. de
Perret, André
Rayas, Ch.
Réméjeanne, Dom. la
Rostaing, Réné
St-Désirat, Cave de
St-Gayan, Dom.
Sang des Cailloux, Dom. le
Tain, Cave de

Vieux Télégraphe, Dom. du

SEE ALSO

Cairanne
Rhône Valley

27

ITALY

The cultivation of the vine was introduced to Italy 2500 to 3000 years ago, by the Greeks (to Sicily and the south) and by the Etruscans (to the north-east and central zones). Despite this great tradition, Italian wines as we know them today are relatively young. New attitudes have resulted, in the last 35 years or so, in a great change in Italian wine. The whole industry has been modernized, and areas like Tuscany, Piedmont, Veneto and Campania are now among the most dynamic of any in the world. With her unique characteristics, challenging wine styles and mass of grape varieties, Italy is now ready again to take on the role of leadership she has avoided for so long.

GRAPE VARIETIES AND WINE REGIONS

Vines are grown all over Italy, from the Austrian border in the north-east to the island of Pantelleria in the far south, nearer to North Africa than to Sicily. The north-west, especially Piedmont, is the home of many of the best Italian red grapes, like Nebbiolo (the grape of Barolo and Barbaresco), Dolcetto and Barbera, while the north-east (Friuli-Venezia Giulia, Alto Adige and the Veneto) is more noted for the success of native white varieties like Garganega and Prosecco, reds like Corvina and Corvinone, and imports like Pinot Grigio, Chardonnay and Sauvignon. The Po Valley is Lambrusco country west of Bologna, while Sangiovese rules in the hills to the east. Tuscany is best known for its Chianti, Brunello di Montalcino and other wines from the native Sangiovese grape as well as its famed Super-Tuscans. On the east coast, Verdicchio and Montepulciano make wines ranging from popular to serious. South of Rome, where the Mediterranean climate holds sway, modern winemakers are revelling in the chance to make exciting wines from varieties of long tradition, such as Negroamaro and Primitivo (in Puglia), Aglianico, Fiano and Greco (in Campania and Basilicata) and Gaglioppo (in Calabria). The islands have their own varieties: red Nero d'Avola and white Inzolia in Sicily, red Cannonau and Carignano and white Vermentino in Sardinia.

CLASSIFICATIONS

Vino da Tavola, 'table wine', is used for wine that is produced either outside the existing laws, or in an area where no delimited zone exists. Both cheap, basic wines and inspired innovative creations like Tignanello, Sassicaia and other so-called Super-Tuscans used to fall into this anonymous category. Now the fancy wines have become either DOC (particularly in Piedmont with its Langhe and Piemonte DOCs) or IGT. Remaining Vini da Tavola are labelled simply as bianco, rosso or rosato without vintages or varietal or geographical indications.

IGT (Indicazione Geografica Tipica) began taking effect with the 1995 vintage to identify wines from certain regions or areas as an equivalent of the French Vin de Pays. A great swathe of both ordinary and premium wines traded their Vino da Tavola status for a regional IGT, of which there are now some 120.

DOC (Denominazione di Origine Controllata) is the main classification for wines from designated zones made following traditions that were historically valid but often outdated. Recently the laws have become more flexible, encouraging producers to reduce yields and modernize techniques, while bringing quality wines under new appellations that allow for recognition of communes, estates and single vineyards. If anything, the problem today is a surfeit of DOCs: there are now over 350, a good number of which are unnecessary or repetitive.

DOCG (Denominazione di Origine Controllata e Garantita) was conceived as a 'super-league' for DOCs with a guarantee of authenticity that promised high class but didn't always provide it. Wines are made under stricter standards that have favoured improvements, but the best guarantee of quality remains the producer's name. Currently DOCGs number 35 and rising. Thus with IGTs, DOCs and DOCGs there are in excess of 500, far too many for clarity in marketing terms. What Italy's denominations need is a good pruning.

2007 VINTAGE REPORT

The shortest vintage in 50 years, partly owing to the continued reduction of Italy's vineyard area, in part due to the weather. Winter was mild with little rainfall, spring was positively summery and summer was seriously hot, so that many vines throughout the land suffered heat and/or water stress. The miracle is that good wines could be made in these global-warming conditions, but in fact some rainfall did occur in late summer/autumn, evenings and nights brought cooler temperatures and the result was a harvest featuring healthy grapes which, especially where late picked, often balanced physical ripeness (sugars) with polyphenolic maturity (tannins). Fans will be able to enjoy some big, concentrated Barolos and Barbarescos in future years, some excellent Chiantis and Brunellos and some full, fine Aglianicos from the south. Valpolicella was the only classic zone that took a knock, and that was from late-August hailstorms of great ferocity. White wines should be full-flavoured with, one hopes, reasonable acidity. Prices, however, after several years of stability, are set to rocket.

Italian entries in the A–Z section (pages 56–307).

REGIONS
Abruzzo
Alto Adige
Basilicata
Calabria
Campania
Emilia-Romagna
Friuli-Venezia Giulia
Lazio
Liguria
Lombardy
Marche
Piedmont
Puglia
Romagna
Sardinia
Sicily
Trentino
Tuscany
Umbria
Valle d'Aosta
Veneto

DOCS/DOCGS
Aglianico del
    Vulture
Amarone della
    Valpolicella
Asti
Barbaresco
Barbera d'Alba
Barbera d'Asti
Bardolino
Barolo
Bianco di Custoza
Bolgheri
Brunello di
    Montalcino
Carignano del Sulcis
Carmignano
Castel del Monte
Chianti
Chianti Classico
Chianti Rufina
Cirò
Colli Orientali del
    Friuli
Colli Piacentini
Collio
Erbaluce di Caluso
Est! Est!! Est!!! di
    Montefiascone
Falerno del Massico
Franciacorta
Frascati
Friuli Grave

Friuli Isonzo
Gattinara
Gavi
Ghemme
Lago di Caldaro
Langhe
Lugana
Marsala
Montecarlo
Montefalco
Montepulciano
    d'Abruzzo
Morellino di
    Scansano
Moscato d'Asti
Moscato Passito di
    Pantelleria
Nebbiolo d'Alba
Oltrepò Pavese
Orvieto
Primitivo di
    Manduria
Prosecco di
    Conegliano-
    Valdobbiadene
Recioto della
    Valpolicella
Recioto di Soave
Roero
Rosso Cònero
Rosso di Montalcino
Rosso di
    Montepulciano
Rosso Piceno
Salice Salentino
Sassicaia
Soave
Taurasi
Teroldego Rotaliano
Torgiano
Valpolicella
Valtellina Superiore
Verdicchio dei
    Castelli di Jesi
Vernaccia di San
    Gimignano
Vino Nobile di
    Montepulciano

PRODUCERS
Accademia dei
    Racemi
Allegrini
Altare
Ama, Castello di
Anselmi

Antinori
Argiolas
Ascheri
Avignonesi
Banfi
Bellavista
Biondi-Santi
Boscarelli
Bussola, Tommaso
Ca' del Bosco
Campo di Sasso
Case Basse
Castellare
Ceretto
Chiarlo, Michele
Clerico, Domenico
Conterno, Aldo
Conterno, Giacomo
Costanti
Dal Forno, Romano
D'Alessandro,
    Tenimenti Luigi
De Bartoli, Marco
Falesco
Felluga, Livio
Felsina, Fattoria di
Ferrari
Folonari, Tenute
    Ambrogio &
    Giovanni
Fontanafredda
Fonterutoli, Castello
    di
Fontodi
Foradori
Frescobaldi
Gaja
Giacosa, Bruno
Gravner
Isole e Olena
Jermann
Lageder, Alois
Lungarotti
le Macchiole
Maculan
Mascarello, Bartolo
Mascarello,
    Giuseppe
Masi
Mastroberardino
Monsanto
Montevertine
Ornellaia, Tenuta
    dell'
Pieropan
Planeta

Il Poggione, Tenuta
Poliziano
Prunotto
Querciabella
Quintarelli
Rampolla, Castello
    dei
Ratti, Renato
Ricasoli, Barone
Riecine
Rivera
Ruffino
Sala, Castello della
Salaparuta, Duca di
San Leonardo
Sandrone, Luciano
Schiopetto
Sella & Mosca
Selvapiana
Tasca d'Almerita
Terriccio, Castello
    del
Tiefenbrunner
Tua Rita
Viviani
Voerzio, Roberto
Volpaia, Castello di

SEE ALSO
Arneis
Barbera
Brachetto
Cannonau
Cortese
Dolcetto
Fiano
Goldmuskateller
Grechetto
Lagrein
Lambrusco
Malvasia
Maremma
Marzemino
Montepulciano
Nebbiolo
Nero d'Avola
Sangiovese
Solaia
Super-Tuscans
Tignanello
Tocai Friulana
Trebbiano
Vin Santo

GERMANY

Dull, semi-sweet wines with names like Liebfraumilch, Niersteiner Gutes Domtal and Piesporter Michelsberg used to dominate the export market, but they are rapidly vanishing off all but the most basic radar screens. Instead, and not before time, we are seeing a better range of single-estate wines, with a greatly improved quality. Throughout Germany, both red and white wines are year by year, region by region, grower by grower, becoming fuller, better balanced and drier.

GRAPE VARIETIES

Riesling makes the best wines, in styles ranging from dry to intensely sweet. Other white wines come from Grauburgunder/Ruländer (Pinot Gris), Weissburgunder (Pinot Blanc), Gewürztraminer, Silvaner, Scheurebe and Rieslaner, although Müller-Thurgau produces much of the simpler wine. In the past decade, plantings of red grape varieties have doubled to fully 30% of the nation's vineyard. Good reds are being made in the south of the country from Spätburgunder (Pinot Noir), Dornfelder and Lemberger.

WINE REGIONS

Many of the most delectable Rieslings come from villages such as Bernkastel, Brauneberg, Ürzig and Wehlen on the Mosel, and Kiedrich, Johannisberg and Rüdesheim in the Rheingau. Characterful dry Mosel Rieslings are the speciality of villages such as Winningen near Koblenz. The Nahe makes superb Rieslings in Schlossböckelheim and Traisen, and Niederhausen has the best vineyards in the entire region. Rheinhessen's top wines are the excellent racy Rieslings produced on steep riverside slopes in Nackenheim and Nierstein. Franken is the one place the Silvaner grape excels, often made in a powerful, dry, earthy style. The Pfalz is climatically similar to Alsace and has a similar potential for well-rounded, dry whites, plus rapidly improving reds. Baden also produces fully ripe wine styles, which should appeal to an international market accustomed to rich, dry wines. In Württemberg most of the red wines are thin and dull, but there are a few producers who understand the need for weight and flavour. The other smaller wine regions make little wine and little is exported, although the Ahr has a growing reputation for Pinot Noir.

CLASSIFICATIONS

Germany's classification system is based on the ripeness of the grapes and therefore their potential alcohol level.

Deutscher Tafelwein (table wine) is the most basic term, used for any blended wine; it accounts for only a tiny percentage of production.

Landwein (country wine) is a slightly more up-market version, linked to 19 regional areas. These must be Trocken (dry) or Halbtrocken (medium-dry).

QbA (Qualitätswein bestimmter Anbaugebiete) is 'quality' wine from one of 13 designated regions, but the grapes don't have to be very ripe, and sugar can be added to the juice to increase alcoholic content.

QmP (Qualitätswein mit Prädikat) or 'quality wine with distinction' is the top level; from August 2007 the term will be replaced by ' Prädikatswein'. There are 6 levels of QmP (in ascending order of ripeness): Kabinett, Spätlese, Auslese, Beerenauslese, Eiswein, Trockenbeerenauslese (TBA). The addition of sugar is strictly forbidden.

Since 2000, there have been 2 designations for varietal dry wines: **Classic** for 'good' wines and **Selection** for 'top-quality' wines, but they haven't really caught on. And an increasing number of good estates use single-vineyard names only on their top selections.

The Rheingau has introduced an official classification – Erstes Gewächs (First Growth) – for its best sites. Other regions have evolved similar classifications – called Grosses Gewächs (or Erste Lage in the Mosel) – to indicate top wines from top sites.

2007 VINTAGE REPORT

The early summer was dry and temperatures remained warm but moderate. Some heavy rain caused concern in August, and September started cool. But then it warmed up, allowing an October harvest in perfect conditions. Fine ripeness levels across Germany, after an unusually long growing season, and yields were generous. Some TBA and Eiswein made too. Has the potential to be a classic vintage.

German entries in the A–Z section (pages 56–307).

REGIONS	Johannisberg	Gunderloch	Schloss Lieser
Ahr	Kiedrich	Haag, Fritz	Schloss
Baden	Leiwen	Haart, Reinhold	Reinhartshausen
Franken	Nierstein	Heger, Dr	Schloss Saarstein
Hessische	Ockfen	Heyl zu Herrnsheim	Schloss Vollrads
Bergstrasse	Piesport	Heymann-	Selbach-Oster
Mittelrhein	Randersacker	Löwenstein	Van Volxem
Mosel-Saar-Ruwer	Rauenthal	Johner, Karl H	Wegeler
Nahe	Rüdesheim	Jost, Toni	Weil, Robert
Pfalz	Schlossböckelheim	Juliusspital	Wittmann
Rheingau	Trittenheim	Karthäuserhof	Wolf, J L
Rheinhessen	Ürzig	Keller	Zilliken
Saale-Unstrut	Wachenheim	Kesselstatt, von	
Sachsen	Wehlen	Koehler-Ruprecht	SEE ALSO
Württemberg	Winkel	Kühn, Peter Jakob	Gewürztraminer
	Winningen	Künstler, Franz	Kaiserstuhl
WINE TOWNS	Würzburg	Leitz, Josef	Liebfraumilch
AND VILLAGES		Loosen, Dr	Müller-Thurgau
Bad Dürkheim	PRODUCERS	Maximin Grünhaus	Ortenau
Bernkastel	Basserman-Jordan	Molitor, Markus	Rieslaner
Bingen	Becker, J B	Mosbacher, Georg	Riesling
Brauneberg	Bercher	Müller-Catoir	Scheurebe
Eltville	Biffar, Josef	Müller-Scharzhof,	
Erbach	Breuer, Georg	Egon	
Erden	Buhl, von	Prüm, J J	
Forst	Bürklin-Wolf	Prüm, S A	
Geisenheim	Diel, Schlossgut	Rebholz	
Graach	Dönnhoff	Richter, Max Ferd	
Hattenheim	Emrich-Schönleber	Sauer, Horst	
Hochheim	Fürst, Rudolf	Schaefer, Willi	
Iphofen	Grans-Fassian	Schäfer-Fröhlich	

AUSTRIA

I can't think of a European nation where the wine culture has changed so dramatically over a generation as it has in Austria. Austria still makes great sweet wines, but a new order based on world-class medium- and full-bodied dry whites and increasingly fine reds has emerged.

WINE REGIONS AND GRAPE VARIETIES

The Danube runs through Niederösterreich, scene of much of Austria's viticulture. The Wachau produces great Riesling and excellent pepper-dry Grüner Veltliner. The Riesling is powerful and ripe, closer in style to Alsace than Germany. Next along the Danube are Kremstal and Kamptal, rapidly improving as fine dry white regions with a few good reds. The Weinviertel, in the north-east, produces large quantities of decent reds and Grüner Veltliner whites. Burgenland, south of Vienna, produces the best reds from local varieties Zweigelt, Blaufränkisch and St-Laurent as well as from Merlot and Pinot Noir. Also, around the shores of the Neusiedler See, especially near the towns of Rust and Illmitz, Burgenland produces some superb dessert wines. Further south, in Steiermark, Chardonnay and Sauvignon are increasingly oak-aged, though many drinkers still prefer the racy unoaked 'classic' wines from these varieties.

Main vineyard areas

CLASSIFICATIONS

Wine categories are similar to those in Germany, beginning with **Tafelwein** (table wine) and **Landwein** (country wine). **Qualitätswein** must come from one of the 16 main wine-producing regions. Like German wines, quality wines may additionally have a special category: Kabinett, Spätlese, Auslese, Beerenauslese, Ausbruch, Trockenbeerenauslese. Since most Austrian wines are either dry or nobly sweet, these categories count for less than in Germany. The Wachau has a ripeness scale for dry whites: Steinfeder wines are made for early drinking, Federspiel wines can last three years or so and the most powerful wines are known as Smaragd. The first Austrian appellations, known as DAC, are starting to appear, but as yet they have had little impact.

2007 VINTAGE REPORT

The spring was mostly dry and warm with sporadic storm and hail damage. A mid-July heatwave caused some sunburn, but August was damp. Heavy rain marred early September, which was cool overall, delaying ripening. An Indian summer made for an easy harvest that was completed by mid-October. Outstanding Steiermark, while Niederösterreich whites had moderate sugars and good acidity. A good vintage for Burgenland reds, as thick skins protected grapes from rot, but the wines are not that concentrated. Some exceptional sweet wines were picked in early October and early November.

Austrian entries in the A–Z section (pages 56–307).

SPAIN

The late 1990s saw a dramatic turnaround in the quality of Spain's long-neglected wines. A drastic modernization of winemaking technology has now allowed regions like Priorat, Ribera del Duero, Rueda, Bierzo, Toro and La Mancha to muscle into the limelight, alongside Rioja and Jerez, with potent fruit-driven wines with the impact and style to convert the modern consumer.

WINE REGIONS
Galicia in the green, hilly north-west grows Spain's most aromatic whites. The heartland of the great Spanish reds, Rioja, Navarra and Ribera del Duero, is situated between the central plateau and the northern coast. Further west along the Duero, Rueda produces fresh whites and Toro good ripe reds. Cataluña is principally white wine country (much of it sparkling Cava), though there are some great reds in Priorat and increasingly in Terra Alta and Montsant. Aragón's reds and whites are looking good too, with an impressive relaunch of Aragón's great (but neglected for too long) native grape Garnacha. The central plateau of La Mancha makes mainly cheap reds and whites, though smaller private estates are improving spectacularly. Valencia, known for inexpensive and unmemorable wines, is now producing, with neighbouring Murcia, increasingly ambitious and rich reds. Andalucía's specialities are the fortified wines – sherry, Montilla and Málaga. There has been a notable rebirth of viticulture and winemaking in both the Balearics and the Canary Islands.

CLASSIFICATIONS
Vino de Mesa, the equivalent of France's Vin de Table, is the lowest level. For a while, it was used for some non-DO 'Super-Spanish'.

Vino de la Tierra is Spain's equivalent of France's Vin de Pays.

DO (Denominación de Origen) is the equivalent of France's AC, regulating grape varieties and region of origin. In Castilla-La Mancha, this category now encompasses single-estate DOs (Denominación de Origen – Vino de Pago).

DOCa (Denominación de Origen Calificada) is a super-category. Only two regions (Rioja and Priorat) have been promoted.

2007 VINTAGE REPORT

An uneven vintage, marked by humidity and uncommonly mild temperatures in most regions in early summer, which led to unusually high occurrences of mildew and oïdium (downy mildew) and cut the overall production levels. Some regions (for example, Jerez and Priorat) experienced torrential harvest rains and Ribera del Duero had a damaging frost in late September. Rueda had its largest harvest ever, up 24% on 2006, whereas Rías Baixas' harvest was down 39% and Rioja 30%, but with excellent grape quality. Penedès also enjoyed excellent results.

Spanish entries in the A–Z section (pages 56–307).

REGIONS	Ribera del Duero	Freixenet	Romeo, Benjamin
Andalucía	Rioja	González Byass	Sandeman
Aragón	Rueda	Guelbenzu	Torres
Balearic Islands	Somontano	Hidalgo	Valdespino
Canary Islands	Toro	López de Heredia	Vall-Llach
Castilla-La Mancha	Utiel-Requena	Lustau, Emilio	Vega Sicilia
Castilla y León	Valdepeñas	Marqués de	Vero, Viñas del
Cataluña		Cáceres	
Galicia	PRODUCERS	Marqués de Griñón	SEE ALSO
Valencia	Aalto	Marqués de	Airén
	Allende	Murrieta	Albariño
DO/DOCA	Artadi	Marqués de Riscal	Graciano
Bierzo	Barbadillo	Martínez Bujanda	Grenache Noir
Cariñena	Berberana	Mas Doix	Mourvèdre
Cava	Campillo	Mauro	Parellada
Costers del Segre	Campo Viejo	Muga	Tempranillo
Jerez y Manzanilla	Chivite	Osborne	
Jumilla	Clos Erasmus	Palacios, Alvaro	
Málaga	Clos Mogador	Pesquera	
La Mancha	Codorníu	Pingus, Dominio de	
Montilla-Moriles	Contino	Raïmat	
Navarra	CVNE	Remelluri	
Penedès	Domecq	Rioja Alta, La	
Priorat	Enate	Riojanas	
Rías Baixas	Faustino	Rodríguez, Telmo	

PORTUGAL

Investment and imagination are paying off in this attractive country, with climates that vary from the mild, damp Minho region in the north-west to the subtropical island of Madeira. Use of native grapes, occasionally blended with international varieties, means that Portugal is now a rich source of characterful wines of ever-increasing quality.

WINE REGIONS

The lush Vinho Verde country in the north-west gives very different wine from the parched valleys of the neighbouring Douro, with its drier, more continental climate. The Douro, home of port, is also the source of some of Portugal's best unfortified red wines. In Beiras, which includes Bairrada and Dão, soil types are crucial in determining the character of the wines.

Estremadura and Ribatejo use native and international varieties in regions influenced either by the maritime climate or by the river Tagus. South of Lisbon, the Terras do Sado and Alentejo produce some exciting table wines – and the Algarve is waking up. Madeira is unique, a volcanic island 850km (530 miles) out in the Atlantic Ocean.

CLASSIFICATIONS

Vinho de Mesa is the lowest level, but commercially important as so much off-dry to medium-dry rosé is exported in this category.

Vinho Regional (11 in number) is equivalent to French Vin de Pays, with laws and permitted varieties much freer than for IPR and DOC.

IPR (Indicação de Proveniência Regulamentada) is the intermediate step for wine regions hoping to move up to DOC status. Many have been promoted in the past few years, leaving just 4 IPRs, not all of which will definitely become DOCs.

DOC (Denominação de Origem Controlada) Equivalent to France's AC; there are now 25 DOC regions.

2007 VINTAGE REPORT

Cool, damp weather through most of the year meant losses of about one-fifth of the grape harvest to fungal diseases, but a warm, dry autumn allowed late-ripening red grapes to reach full maturity without the very high alcohol levels of recent years. White wines are some of the best that have been made for years. Wet weather in June also reduced yields, as flowers struggled to set into fruit. It was a year for the hard-working and conscientious in the vineyard, for growers who sprayed against oïdium and mildew. Other growers were hard hit, particularly in the Minho, Beiras and Alentejo. But Portuguese whites and fizz should be splendidly crisp and aromatic, and reds are elegant and balanced, especially those where the later-ripening Aragonez (Tempranillo), Touriga Franca, Touriga Nacional and Cabernet Sauvignon are the predominant grapes. Reds will not be blockbusters, but the best from the Douro, Dão, the Ribatejo, Terras do Sado and Alentejo will be aromatic and poised. There may well be 2007 vintage port declarations.

Portuguese entries in the A–Z section (pages 56–307).

USA

The United States has more varied growing conditions for grapes than any other country in the world, which isn't so surprising when you consider that the 50 states of the Union cover an area that is larger than Western Europe; and although Alaska doesn't grow grapes in the icy far north, Washington State does in the north-west, as does Texas in the south and New York State in the north-east, and even Hawaii, lost in the pounding surf of the Pacific Ocean, manages to grow grapes and make wine. Every state, including Alaska (thanks to salmonberry and fireweed), now produces wine of some sort or another; it ranges from some pretty dire offerings, which would have been far better distilled into brandy, to some of the greatest and most original wines to be found in the world today.

GRAPE VARIETIES AND WINE REGIONS

California is far and away the most important state for wine production. In its determination to match the best red Bordeaux and white Burgundy, California proved that it was possible to take the classic European role models and successfully re-interpret them in an area thousands of miles away from their home. However, there is more to California than this. The Central Valley produces the majority of the simple beverage wines that still dominate the American market. Napa and Sonoma Counties north of San Francisco Bay do produce great Cabernet and Chardonnay, but grapes like Zinfandel and Merlot also make their mark and the Carneros, Russian River Valley and

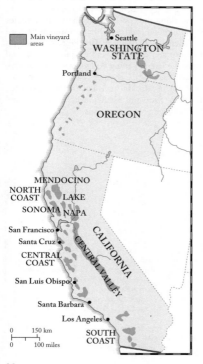

Sonoma Coast areas are highly successful for Pinot Noir, Chardonnay and sparkling wines. In the north, Mendocino and Lake Counties produce good grapes. South of San Francisco, in the cool, foggy valleys between Santa Cruz and Santa Barbara, Chardonnay, Pinot Noir and Syrah are producing exciting cool-climate but ripe-flavoured wines.

Oregon, with a cooler and more capricious climate than most of California, perseveres with Pinot Noir, Chardonnay, Pinot Gris, Pinot Blanc and Riesling with patchy success. Washington, so chilly and misty on the coast, becomes virtual desert east of the Cascade Mountains and it is here, in irrigated vineyards, that superb reds and whites can be made, with thrillingly focused fruit.

38

In New York, Long Island continues to impress with classically styled Merlot, Cabernet Sauvignon and Cabernet Franc, as well as Chardonnay to pair with the local lobster. Riesling shines in the Hudson Valley and especially the Finger Lakes; Chardonnay and fizz also do well here. Improved vineyard practices have enabled growers to cope with horrible weather through much of the first half of this decade, from vine-killing winter deep freeze to harvest-soaking rains.

Other states have seen dramatic growth in the wine industry this decade. Established industries in Virginia, Maryland, Pennsylvania, Texas and Missouri have led the way, but look also for new growth in North Carolina, Georgia and Michigan.

CLASSIFICATIONS

The AVA (American Viticultural Area) system was introduced in the 1980s. It does not guarantee a quality standard, but merely requires that at least 85% of grapes in a wine come from the specified AVA. There are over 170 AVAs, more than 100 of which are in California. AVAs come in all shapes and sizes, varying from the largest, Ohio River Valley, which spans an area of 26,000 square miles to the smallest, Cole Ranch, which covers a little less than a quarter of a square mile.

2007 VINTAGE REPORT

In California, lower rainfall than normal during the winter months and spring resulted in early bud-break, allowing for sufficient time on vine before a relatively early harvest, which began in mid-August. The summer was warm but not hot and the few heat spikes were of short duration. The start of harvest was rapid and furious, but then a slight cooling spell slowed things down in mid-September. Bunches and grapes were pretty small, concentrating fruit flavours and colour. Quality is rated very high as a result of a smaller crop than in 2005 and 2006 and early tasting promises some beautiful wines.

In Washington, a relatively mild winter was followed by a spring with cool but dry weather. Flowering took place under mild conditions, and it looked to be another early vintage by mid-summer. Many white grape varieties were harvested before the end of August. Very large day to night temperature swings led to high acidity levels in the resulting wines. In early September the weather turned unusually wet and cold. The red grapes were left to hang in an attempt to get higher sugars, but it remained cold and wet and many vineyards experienced bunch rot. As is predictable, the growers who cropped their vineyards at lower levels of fruit were able to harvest fruit earlier and in better condition. Overall the vintage will be variable for reds but very good for whites.

In Oregon, flowering was early and the set was a full crop. June was hot, leading to expectations of an early harvest, but in July the weather turned cold and humid. August continued the pattern of cold, wet weather. Problems with mildew, especially for biodynamic producers, resulted in lost fruit. September was more moderate, but with stormy weather late in the month. Many harvested fruit before the rains at lower than usual sugar levels. Botrytis was a problem for producers who attempted to wait through the storms. White and red wines will be lower in alcohol; their success will depend on the winemaker's skill.

A second consecutive outstanding vintage up and down the East Coast, with drought posing the only potential challenge to vintners unaccustomed to such dry conditions. Look for bigger, riper reds than usual.

USA entries in the A–Z section (pages 56–307) by state.

CALIFORNIA	Caymus Vineyards	Kendall-Jackson	Silver Oak Cellars
AVAS	Chateau Montelena	Kenwood	Silverado Vineyards
Alexander Valley	Chateau St Jean	Kistler	Simi
Anderson Valley	Chimney Rock	Kunde Estate	Sonoma-Cutrer
Cameros	Clos du Bois	Landmark	Spottswoode
Central Coast	Clos du Val	Laurel Glen	Stag's Leap Wine
Dry Creek Valley	Coppola, Francis	Marcassin	Cellars
Howell Mountain	Ford	Mariah	Steele
Mendocino Ridge	Cuvaison	Matanzas Creek	Sterling Vineyards
Mount Veeder	Dalla Valle	Merryvale	Swan, Joseph
Napa Valley	Dehlinger	Michael, Peter	Talbott
Oakville	Diamond Creek	Miner Family	Torres, Marimar
Paso Robles	Domaine Carneros	Vineyards	Turley
Russian River Valley	Domaine Chandon	Mondavi, Robert	Williams Selyem
Rutherford	Dominus	Moon Mountain	
Santa Cruz	Dry Creek Vineyard	Mumm Napa	**SEE ALSO**
Mountains	Duckhorn	Murray, Andrew	Central Valley
Santa Maria Valley	Dunn Vineyards	Navarro	Mendocino County
Santa Rita Hills	Ferrari-Carano	Newton	Monterey County
Sonoma Coast	Fetzer Vineyards	Opus One	Napa Valley
Sonoma Valley	Flora Springs	Phelps, Joseph	San Luis Obispo
Stags Leap	Flowers	Pine Ridge	County
District	Franciscan	Qupé	Santa Barbara
	Gallo	Rasmussen, Kent	County
PRODUCERS	Geyser Peak	Ravenswood	Sonoma County
Acacia	Grgich Hills Cellar	Ridge Vineyards	Zinfandel
Alban	Gundlach-Bundschu	J Rochioli Vineyards	
Araujo	Handley	Roederer Estate	
Arrowood	Harlan Estate	Saintsbury	
Atlas Peak	Hartford Family	Sanford	
Au Bon Climat	Hartwell	Scharffenberger	
Beaulieu Vineyard	Heitz Cellars	Cellars	
Beringer	Hess Collection	Schramsberg	
Bonny Doon	Iron Horse	Screaming Eagle	
Bronco Wine Co.	Vineyards	Seghesio	
Calera	Jordan	Shafer	

NEW YORK	**PRODUCERS**	Frank, Dr Konstantin	
STATE	Bedell Cellars	Lamoreaux Landing	
Finger Lakes AVA	Channing Daughters	Lenz Winery	
Long Island	Fox Run Vineyards		

OREGON	**PRODUCERS**	Cristom	Wright, Ken
Willamette Valley	Adelsheim Vineyard	Domaine Drouhin	
AVA	Argyle	Oregon	
	Beaux Frères	Domaine Serene	
	Bergström	Elk Cove	

WASHINGTON	**PRODUCERS**	Columbia Crest	Long Shadows
STATE	Andrew Will	DeLille Cellars	Vintners
AVAS	Betz Family Winery	Dunham Cellars	Quilceda Creek
Columbia Valley	Cadence	Hedges Cellars	Woodward Canyon
Walla Walla Valley	Cayuse Vineyards	Janiuk	
Yakima Valley AVA	Chateau Ste	L'Ecole No 41	
	Michelle	Leonetti Cellar	

SEE ALSO	Horton Vineyards	Texas	Virginia

AUSTRALIA

Australian wine today enjoys a reputation still well out of proportion to the quantity of wine produced (total output is about one-fifth that of France), though volumes are mushrooming. The New World wine revolution – emphasizing ripe, rich fruit, seductive use of oak, labelling by grape variety and consumer-friendly marketing – has been led by wine warriors from the southern seas. There's more than enough sunshine and not nearly enough rain to grow the grapes, so most growers are guaranteed ripeness but rely heavily on irrigation for their vines to survive. Dynamic and innovative winemakers ensure a steady supply of new wines, wineries and even regions, but consolidation and internationalization of larger operators seem to be causing an unwarranted and unwelcome dumbing down of flavour.

GRAPE VARIETIES

Varietal wines remain more prized than blends. Shiraz has long been a key varietal and is more fashionable than Cabernet Sauvignon. Renewed respect for old-vine Grenache and Mourvèdre has seen these former workhorse varieties transformed into premium wines. Merlot and – in cooler-climate regions – Pinot Noir lead the pack of alternative red varieties and Australia's endless appetite for experiment has found prospective new stars in Petit Verdot, Tempranillo, Nebbiolo and Sangiovese. Among white grapes the position of Chardonnay remains unchallenged, although Semillon and Riesling both have a longer track record. Sauvignon Blanc is enjoying a massive boost to its popularity both as a varietal and as part of a blend with Semillon, especially as an easy-drinking white. Rhône varieties Marsanne and Viognier (now fashionably included in blends with Shiraz) are both impressive and Verdelho and Pinot Gris are making a strong case for

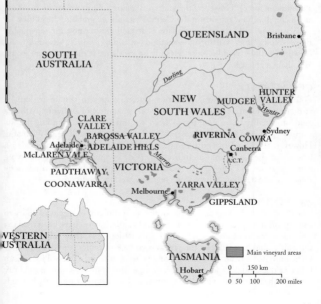

themselves as alternatives to Chardonnay. Sweet whites are produced from Semillon and Muscat – both the top-class Brown Muscat (a sub-variety of Muscat Blanc à Petits Grains) and the more workaday Muscat Gordo Blanco.

WINE REGIONS

Western Australia is a vast state, virtually desert except for its south-western coastal strip. The sun-baked region near Perth is best suited to throaty reds and fortified wines, yet winery and vineyard expertise has become more sophisticated and decent dry whites are now being made. The most exciting wines, both red and white, come from Margaret River and Great Southern down towards the coast.

South Australia dominates the wine scene – it grows the most grapes, makes the most wine and is home to most of the nation's biggest wine companies. There is more to it, however, than attractive, undemanding, gluggable wine. The Clare Valley produces outstanding cool-climate Riesling, as well as excellent Shiraz and Cabernet. The Barossa is home to some of the planet's oldest vines, particularly Shiraz and Grenache. Eden Valley, in the hills to the east of Barossa, excels at crisp, steely Rieslings and scented Shiraz. McLaren Vale, Coonawarra and the Limestone Coast also make many thrilling reds.

Victoria was Australia's major producer for most of the 19th century until her vineyards were devastated by the phylloxera louse. It's only recently that Victoria has regained her position as provider of some of the most startling wine styles in the country: stunning liqueur Muscats; the thrilling dark reds of Central Victoria; and the urbane Yarra Valley and Mornington Peninsula reds and whites.

New South Wales was home to the revolution that propelled Australia to the front of the world wine stage (in the Hunter Valley, an area that remains a dominant force). However, the state is a major bulk producer in Riverina, and a clutch of new regions in the Central Ranges are grabbing headlines.

Tasmania, with its cooler climate, is attracting attention for top-quality Pinot Noirs and Champagne-method sparkling wines. Riesling and Gewürztraminer would almost certainly be excellent, if the producers would give them a chance.

CLASSIFICATIONS

Formal appellation control, restricting certain grapes to certain regions, is virtually unknown; regulations are more of a guarantee of authenticity than a guide to quality. In a country so keen on inter-regional blending for its commercial brands, a system resembling France's AC could be problematic. However, the Label Integrity Program (LIP) guarantees all claims made on labels and the Geographical Indications (GI) committee is busy clarifying zones, regions and sub-regions – albeit with plenty of lively, at times acrimonious, debate about where some regional borders should go.

2008 VINTAGE REPORT

The 2008 Australian vintage is one of the most difficult in recent memory to sum up succinctly, except to say that some beautiful wines have been made as well as some dreadful ones. Initial speculation was that following the difficulties and low yields of the previous vintage the vines would not recover sufficiently to provide a more satisfying volume of fruit in 2008. However, a break in the drought and satisfactory winter rains combined with a mild dry run up to harvest: white yields are pretty much unchanged from 2007 but reds are up about 25%.

Heavy rains after most of the whites had been picked meant that the Hunter may well produce some excellent Semillon but the reds have suffered one of their worst vintages of recent times. The situation in Orange and Mudgee is likewise discouraging. Similarly, white varietals did exceptionally well in Canberra and those who picked reds before the rains are smiling.

In the Yarra Valley the Chardonnay is as good as the region has seen, thanks to lovely early season weather. Pinot Noir will be best in wineries with the best selection techniques and the capacity to allow the wines to evolve in the fermenters. The Cabernet and Shiraz will be delicious and show excellent detail if they were picked before the heat came.

McLaren Vale had the best-ever vintage for those who picked before the long heatwave shrivelled the remaining red grapes. Clare and Barossa experienced similar conditions.

Western Australia had an amazing harvest of sublime quality: so mild were the conditions that the Cabernet in Margaret River – which is normally picked in 3 days – was able to be taken off in small batches over 10 to 12 fine sunny days.

Australian entries in the A–Z section (pages 56–307).

STATES	PRODUCERS	Harewood	Seppelt
New South Wales	Adams, Tim	Henschke	Shaw & Smith
Queensland	Balnaves	Hollick	Skillogalee
South Australia	Bannockburn	Houghton	Stonier
Tasmania	Barossa Valley	Howard Park	Tahbilk
Victoria	Estate	Katnook Estate	Tapanappa
Western Australia	Barry, Jim	Knappstein	Tarrawarra
	Bay of Fires	Kooyong	Thomas
WINE REGIONS	Best's	Leasingham	Torbreck
Adelaide Hills	Binder, Rolf	Leeuwin Estate	Tower Estate
Barossa	Blass, Wolf	Lehmann, Peter	Turkey Flat
Beechworth	Boireann	Lindemans	Tyrrell's
Bendigo	Bowen Estate	Lubiana, Stefano	Vasse Felix
Canberra District	Brand's	Majella	Voyager Estate
Central Victoria	Brokenwood	McWilliam's	Weaver, Geoff
Clare Valley	Brown Brothers	Melton, Charles	Wendouree
Coonawarra	Burge, Grant	Merrill, Geoff	Westend
Geelong	Cape Mentelle	Mitchell	Wirra Wirra
Gippsland	Capel Vale	Morris	Wynns
Grampians and	Carlei	Moss Wood	Yalumba
Pyrenees	Chambers	Mount Horrocks	Yellowtail
Great Southern	Chapel Hill	Mount Langi Ghiran	
Heathcote	Clarendon Hills	Mount Mary	SEE ALSO
Hilltops	Clonakilla	Orlando	Grange
Hunter Valley	Coldstream Hills	Parker Coonawarra	Hill of Grace
Limestone Coast	Cullen	Estate	
McLaren Vale	D'Arenberg	Penfolds	
Margaret River	De Bortoli	Penley Estate	
Mornington	Domaine Chandon	Petaluma	
Peninsula	By Farr	Pierro	
Mudgee	Ferngrove	Plantagenet	
Padthaway	Fox Creek	Pondalowie	
Pemberton	Giaconda	Primo Estate	
Riverina	Glaetzer	Riposte	
Riverland	Grosset	Rockford	
Rutherglen	Hanging Rock	Rosemount Estate	
Swan District	Hardy Wine	St Hallett	
Yarra Valley	Company	Sandalford	

NEW ZEALAND

New Zealand's wines, though diverse in style, are characterized by intense fruit flavours, zesty acidity and pungent aromas – the product of cool growing conditions and high-tech winemaking.

GRAPE VARIETIES

Until recently, New Zealand's fame has rested on one grape variety: Sauvignon Blanc. The bracing, tangy style of New Zealand's first Sauvignons redefined the world's expectations of the grape. But this rapidly maturing wine industry has many more tricks up its sleeve. The other major white grapes are Chardonnay in a melony, peachy style, succulent Pinot Gris and fragrant Riesling, with Gewürztraminer on the rise and Viognier now making an appearance. Among reds, Cabernet Sauvignon and Merlot have been around for some time, either fruity and berryish or in a more serious Bordeaux style, sometimes blended with Cabernet Franc and/or Malbec; Syrah is fashionable, spicy and scented; and Pinot Noir, now the country's number one red, is bidding to be taken seriously in the Premier League of world wine.

WINE REGIONS

Nearly 1600km (1000 miles) separate New Zealand's northernmost wine region from the country's (and the world's) most southerly wine region, Central Otago. In terms of wine styles it is useful to divide the country into two parts. The warmer climate of Hawkes Bay and one or two pockets around Auckland produce the best Cabernet Sauvignon, Merlot and Cabernet Franc as well as increasingly good Syrah. Waiheke Island and Hawkes Bay's Gimblett Gravels have some of the most exciting red wine vineyards. Martinborough and Wairarapa are noted for Pinot Noir. In the South Island, Nelson is good for Pinot Noir and aromatic whites, while Marlborough is the hub of the industry, famous for Sauvignon Blanc, but also excellent for fizz, Chardonnay, Riesling and Pinot Noir. Waipara is small but produces very characteristic reds and whites, while Central Otago produces fabulous Pinot Noir, vibrant Riesling and an increasing amount of flavoursome Pinot Gris.

CLASSIFICATIONS

Labels guarantee geographic origin. The broadest designation is New Zealand, followed by North or South Island. Next come the 10 or so regions. Labels may also name specific localities and individual vineyards.

2008 VINTAGE REPORT

Predictions that La Niña would bring hot, dry conditions during late summer and early autumn were right on the nail: most New Zealanders enjoyed the best weather in memory. Winemakers were equally happy. Before picking began many claimed it would be an outstanding vintage. Rain in late February and March dampened the hopes of growers in the most northerly regions and caused varying levels of botrytis pressure as far south as Marlborough. Pre-vintage estimates put the likely harvest at 225,000–245,000 tonnes, considerably ahead of a record harvest of 205,000 tonnes in 2007. At the time of going to press, in the middle of the harvest, it now seems likely that the grape crop will exceed 245,000 tonnes. Growers, particularly in Marlborough, the country's largest region, have been surprised by the size of the harvest. A large crop has put pressure on processing capacity as well as dramatically reducing the price of Sauvignon Blanc grapes. Bulk wine that might have sold at $6.50–7 per litre last year is being traded at $4 per litre this year. Winemakers claim that Sauvignon Blanc quality is very good despite it being a large – and botrytis-affected – harvest. The quality of Pinot Noir looks promising, particularly in Central Otago.

New Zealand entries in the A–Z section (pages 56–307).

REGIONS	PRODUCERS	Isabel Estate	Pegasus Bay
Auckland	Ata Rangi	Jackson Estate	Saint Clair
Canterbury	Babich	Kumeu River	Seifried
Central Otago	Church Road	Le Brun	Seresin
Gisborne	Cloudy Bay	Martinborough	Sileni
Hawkes Bay	Coopers Creek	Vineyard	Stonyridge
Kumeu/Huapai	Craggy Range	Matua Valley	Te Mata
Marlborough	Delegat's	Millton	Trinity Hill
Martinborough	Dry River	Montana	Vavasour
Nelson	Felton Road	Neudorf	Villa Maria
Waiheke Island	Fromm	Ngatarawa	Wither Hills
	Giesen	Nobilo	
	Goldwater Estate	Palliser Estate	
	Hunter's	C J Pask	

SOUTH AMERICA

The only countries to have proved their ability to make fine wine are Chile and Argentina, though Uruguay is clearly trying to join them.

ARGENTINA

We have been talking about the Argentine renaissance for at least the last five years of this guide. Now it's a reality. After several economic crises and political instability, Argentina and its wines seem to be emerging from the ashes. The Upper Mendoza River region and the high Uco Valley, both located in Mendoza, are the main sources of great Malbec (Argentina's flagship red wine grape), but there are also interesting examples in cooler areas like Río Negro and Neuquén, down in Patagonia, and ripe and dense versions in Salta, to the north of the country. That region is also the best area for the perfumed and heady white Torrontés (the other Argentine speciality). Foreign investment is heavily focused on Mendoza, where more than 70% of the country's wine is made. New luxury hotels and spas in the wine country add glamour to this Argentine wine boom.

CHILE

We're seeing the name Carmenère more and more frequently on wine labels. Previously this grape's brilliance was hidden under the better-known title of 'Merlot' (Chilean Merlot is still some of the world's best due to its blending with Carmenère). Now the dark, rich, savoury flavours of Carmenère are proudly presented, especially from numerous established vineyard sites in the Central Valley and Rapel. Cabernet Sauvignon and Merlot, from Maipo and elsewhere, are still Chile's best-known wines, but superb, fragrant Pinot Noir is appearing from new coastal areas such as San Antonio, and excellent Syrah is being made in cool coastal areas like Limarí as well as the warmer Central Valley. Chile's fruity Chardonnay is some of the New World's best balanced, while exciting Sauvignon Blanc, Riesling and Gewürztraminer are becoming common from the coastal and southerly regions. Maule is experiencing a revival helped by old-vine Carignan and new investment from Spain and Italy.

URUGUAY

Most of the vines are on clay soils in the Canelones region around Montevideo, which has high rainfall in a relatively cool climate: the thick-skinned, rot-resistant black Tannat grape from South-West France is the leading variety. A clutch of modern wineries are working hard to soften the tannic Tannat; they are also producing snappy Sauvignon Blanc and fresh Cabernet Franc and Merlot. Best producers: Bouza, Carrau, Castillo Viejo, Los Cerros de San Juan, Filgueira, Juanicó, PISANO, Stagnari, Toscanini, Viñedo de los Vientos.

OTHER COUNTRIES

Look at Brazil, how vast it is. Yet in all this expanse, running from 33º South to 5º North, there's nowhere ideal to site a vineyard. The best attempts are made down towards the Uruguayan border, but half of Brazil's wine now comes from the Valle de San Francisco in the torrid north. Peru has seemingly good vineyard sites in the Ica Valley south of Lima, but nothing exciting winewise. Bolivia has few vineyards, but they're incredibly high. Venezuela's chief claim to fame is that some of her subtropical vines give three crops a year!

2008 VINTAGE REPORT

Hotter and very much drier than 2007, Chile's main wine regions have had practically no rain all season. A cold spring delayed flowering, December was unusually hot, then the temperature dropped in February and March – but still no rain – which delayed the harvest. This should result in good-quality Cabernet Sauvignon and Carmenère, though with slightly less fresh acidity than in 2007. Casablanca growers report good fruit concentration in Sauvignon and Chardonnay. In Argentina, 2008 was more challenging than the great 2006, and a good to very good vintage is expected. San Juan suffered heavy rain: very careful selection was necessary in the vineyards. Mendoza had a very hot January, followed by a much cooler, wetter February and March: good, fresh Malbec is predicted from careful growers.

South American entries in the A–Z section (pages 56–307).

SOUTH AFRICA

After a decline in 2006, 2007 saw a healthy increase in export sales. There are encouraging signs that 2008 will see even further growth. Markets too are spreading, with the US becoming an important destination for South African wine. Sales locally have also increased, though per capita consumption continues to decline. New wine producers are opening at the rate of one a week, mainly, but not exclusively, in the heart of the Western Cape winelands. If wine grapes are being harvested from further afield, they are also being sent further afield: South Africa is one country helping out the drought-stricken Australians with fruit!

Quality – especially that of white wines and blends – continues to improve and the new generation of winemakers are playing a major role in raising standards and broadening the range of styles.

GRAPE VARIETIES AND WINE REGIONS

The Cape's winelands run roughly 400km (250 miles) north and east of Cape Town, although small pockets of new vineyards are taking the winelands way outside their traditional territory. Wine, albeit in tiny quantities, is now being produced from grapes grown in the mountains above the Eastern Cape town of Plettenberg Bay, better known for its holidaymakers than its vines, and from vineyards in the Drakensberg region of KwaZulu-Natal. Plantings generally continue to decrease. New white grape vineyards – mainly Chenin Blanc, Chardonnay, Sauvignon Blanc and Colombard – outstrip reds by 5 to 1, and Chenin remains the most planted variety. Red varieties, led by Cabernet Sauvignon and Shiraz, cover just under 45% of the vineyards, with all major varieties either static or decreasing in area. The emphasis remains on classic, international varieties such as Cabernet Sauvignon, Merlot, Chardonnay and Sauvignon Blanc, with small quantities of Verdelho,

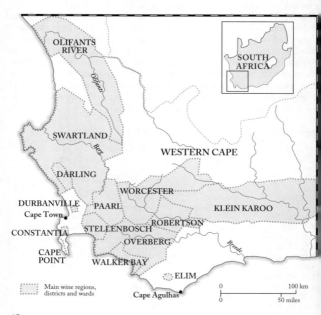

Malbec, Nebbiolo, Sangiovese, Tannat and Tempranillo in the mix. But it is without doubt Rhône varieties that still generate most excitement: as well as Syrah/Shiraz, there's Grenache, Cinsaut and Mourvèdre for reds, and Viognier, Grenache Blanc and Roussanne for whites.

With the major grape varieties being planted over the entire Western Cape winelands, there is little typicity of origin, although some areas are historically associated with specific varieties or styles. Stellenbosch lays claim to some of the best red wines; maritime-influenced Constantia, and Cape Point on the other side of the Peninsula mountain chain, produce exhilarating Sauvignon Blanc, a variety also showing great promise in other coastal areas, right from Cape Agulhas in the south to Durbanville and Darling on the west coast and even further north to Doring Bay near Vredendal in the Olifants River region, as well as upland Elgin in the Overberg district. Many of these areas are also producing distinctive blends of Semillon and Sauvignon Blanc. Other cool areas include Walker Bay, where the focus is Pinot Noir. Chardonnay, long associated with inland Robertson, is now making its mark with Cap Classique sparkling wines as well as citrous, nutty still wines. As a warmer area, Robertson is also recognized for fortifieds, both Muscadel (Muscat) and port styles. Inland areas such as Swartland along the west coast have good affinity with Shiraz and other Rhône varieties; white blends including Chenin, Chardonnay, Viognier are also starting to create waves.

CLASSIFICATIONS

The Wine of Origin (WO) system divides wine-producing areas into regions, districts, wards, estates and single vineyards. Varietal, vintaged wines for both export and the local market must be made from at least 85% of the named grape and vintage.

2008 VINTAGE REPORT

2008 has been dubbed 'a viticulturist's vintage', as vineyard work primarily determined success or otherwise. Winter 2007 was ideal in terms of low temperatures and plentiful rainfall; spring too was cool and wet, which resulted in vigorous growth. Similar conditions in early summer led to the harvest starting around two weeks late; more typical hot, dry conditions arrived in late February. The cool weather encouraged great flavour concentration, but showers and periods of humidity increased the likelihood of disease. There will be quality whites and reds (particularly Chardonnay, Sauvignon Blanc and Shiraz) showing accessibility and elegance, though stringent viticulture and grape selection will be determining factors. Quantities and alcohol levels are likely to be lower than usual.

South African entries in the A–Z section (pages 56–307).

WINE REGIONS	Boekenhoutskloof	Hartenberg Estate	Simonsig
Constantia WO	Bouchard Finlayson	Jordan	Spice Route
Durbanville WO	Buitenverwachting	Kanonkop	Springfield Estate
Elgin WO	Cape Point	Klein Constantia	Steenberg
Franschhoek WO	Cluver, Paul	KWV	Thelema
Paarl WO	De Trafford	L'Avenir	Veenwouden
Robertson WO	Distell	Meerlust	Vergelegen
Stellenbosch WO	Ellis, Neil	Morgenhof	Villiera
Walker Bay WO	Els, Ernie	Mulderbosch	Warwick
	Fairview	Rust en Vrede	
PRODUCERS	Glen Carlou	Rustenberg	SEE ALSO
Beck, Graham	Grangehurst	Sadie Family	Pinotage
Beyerskloof	Hamilton Russell	Saxenburg	

OTHER WINE COUNTRIES

ALGERIA With many vines over 40 years old, there should be great potential here, but political uncertainty hinders progress despite government support. The western coastal province of Oran produces three-quarters of Algeria's wine, including the soft but muscular Coteaux de Tlemcen wines and dark, beefy reds of the Coteaux de Mascara. Average production is around 75 million bottles a year.

BULGARIA After success in the 1980s and disarray in the 90s, some progress followed the introduction of new wine legislation in 2001, and investment in new vineyards is beginning to gather pace. Entry into the EU in 2007 has encouraged a more positive attitude in the vineyards, and there are signs of single-estate wines emerging, although in some regions there is a shortage of vineyard workers as they seek employment in wealthier EU states. New World influences are having some effect, although few wines shine. Cabernet Sauvignon and Merlot dominate, but local grapes – plummy Mavrud, meaty Gamza, deep Melnik, fruity white Dimiat and Misket – can be good. Established wineries such as BOYAR, Khan Krum and Suhindol have been joined by several new operations, Bessa Valley and Stork Nest estates being two of the largest; international wine consultant Michel Rolland is working with up-and-coming Telish Wine Cellars.

CANADA The strict VQA (Vintners Quality Alliance) maintains high standards in British Columbia and Ontario, and there has been enormous progress in the 2 most important regions – OKANAGAN VALLEY in British Columbia and the NIAGARA PENINSULA in Ontario – where the move from hybrid to vinifera varieties has been rapid. Sweet icewine is still Canada's trump card. Pinot Gris, Chardonnay, Riesling and Gewürztraminer lead the way in non-sweet whites; Merlot, Cabernet Franc, Cabernet Sauvignon, even Syrah, show potential in red wines.

CHINA Though China officially promotes wine, its potential remains unfulfilled as the majority of Chinese are reluctant to drink it. However, as the Chinese economy expands, demand for its wines is increasing, particularly in the cities. Home-grown premium wines are emerging and foreign investment proceeds apace with continual improvements in viticulture and winemaking. China now ranks as the sixth biggest wine producer in the world, with massive new plantings every year – mainly international grapes such as Chardonnay and Cabernet Sauvignon, with some traditional Chinese, German and Russian varieties. There are now over 400 wineries. Major producers include Changyu, Dynasty, Great Wall, HUADONG and newcomer Xintian. The south-west province of Yunnan has become popular with growers and several new wineries have been established here.

CROATIA Inland Croatia has an undercurrent of rising potential: bulk whites dominate but small private producers are emerging. Initiatives to sow vines in former minefields are helping to restore Croatia's viticultural heritage. What the country needs now is more investment, more technology in the vineyard and winery and a fair price for the grapes; planned membership of the EU will undoubtedly help. Tourism is flourishing and this should help popularize the wines – so long as foreigners can pronounce them. The best vineyards are on the Dalmatian coast, where international varieties are being planted alongside gutsy indigenous grapes: deep, tannic Plavac Mali – related to Zinfandel – has long produced the top red wines. GRGICH of California has a winery on the Peljesac peninsula. Frano Milos (also on the Peljesac peninsula) and Kozlovic and Matosevic in Istria are other names to look for.

CYPRUS COMMANDARIA has been famous since the Crusades, but otherwise Cypriot wine has no great reputation. However, Cyprus is modernizing, and regional press houses and wineries are being built in or near the vineyards. Investment by companies like Etko, Keo, Loel and Sodap is at last producing tasty modern reds and whites; Sodap uses Australian consultants. The first efforts with grapes like Cabernet Sauvignon and Sémillon are impressive.

THE CZECH REPUBLIC The vineyards of Bohemia in the north-west and Moravia in the south-east are mainly planted with white varieties – Grüner Veltliner, Müller-Thurgau, Riesling, Pinot Blanc, Pinot Gris – with pockets of red such as St-Laurent and Lemberger (Blaufränkisch).

ENGLAND The UK's winegrowing industry has celebrated more than 50 vintages since the 'revival' of commercial vineyards in the early 1950s. However, with around 1000ha (2470 acres) of vines, 350 vineyards (many very small), 120 wineries and an average annual output of around 2.2 million bottles, it is still minute. Nevertheless, producers have learnt which varieties are successful (Bacchus, Schönburger and Seyval Blanc for whites; Rondo, Regent, Dornfelder and Pinot Noir for reds; and, increasingly, Chardonnay, Pinot Noir and Pinot Meunier for quality sparklers), how to train and trellis them to cope with the (usually) cool summers and – most importantly – how to make sound, sometimes excellent, wines. In particular, sparkling wines have shown they can equal CHAMPAGNE in quality and the area planted to the classic Champagne varieties is now approaching 50% of the UK total. Growers from Champagne are taking notice and several famous houses have been looking for sites; a producer of very good Champagne from Avize has now planted 4ha (10 acres) in Hampshire and more are sure to follow. Regulations now require growers to submit their wines for testing before they can label them 'English'; wines labelled 'UK table wine' should be avoided. The most popular winemaking counties are: Kent (Balfour, Biddenden, CHAPEL DOWN, Sandhurst), East Sussex (BREAKY BOTTOM, Davenport), West Sussex (NYETIMBER, RIDGEVIEW), Surrey (DENBIES), Berkshire (STANLAKE PARK), Gloucestershire (THREE CHOIRS), Hampshire (Wickham), Devon (SHARPHAM) and Cornwall (CAMEL VALLEY).

GEORGIA Georgia faces many challenges – lack of regulation, resistance to change, counterfeiting and a recent ban on exports to Russia, its biggest market – but its diverse climates (from subtropical to moderate continental) and soils could produce every style imaginable. The tourist industry is vibrant and helping introduce Georgian wines to a wider audience. International and indigenous varieties abound; the peppery, powerful red Saperavi could be a world-beater. Most wine is still pretty rustic, but investment is beginning to have an effect, with GWS (Georgian Wines & Spirits Company, 75% owned by Pernod Ricard) leading the way.

GREECE Sadly, the Athens Olympics in 2004 didn't make quite the impact for the country's wines as had been hoped, although their reputation, their distribution and their sales continue to improve. The new generation of winemakers and grape growers, many of them trained in France, Australia or California, have a clear vision of the flavours they want to achieve and their wines are modern but marvellously original too. Polarization between cheap bulk and expensive boutique wines continues, but large companies such as Boutari, Kourtakis and Tsantalis are upping the quality stakes and flavours improve every vintage. More vineyard and marketing work – many labels are still difficult to understand – is needed. International plantings have led to surprising and successful blends with indigenous varieties such as the red Agiorgitiko, Limnio and Xynomavro, and white Assyrtiko (often blended with Sémillon), Moschofilero and Roditis. Quality areas: Naousa and Nemea for reds, SAMOS for sweet Muscats, Patras for dessert Mavrodaphne. Wineries to watch include: Aidarinis, Argyros, ANTONOPOULOS, Gentilini, GEROVASSILIOU, Hatzimichali, Kyr Yanni, Domaine Costa LAZARIDI, Mercouri, Papaïoannou, Strofilia and Tselepos.

HUNGARY Hungary makes remarkably good whites, improving reds and outstanding sweet wines, and has joined the EU, yet few of us have much idea about her as a wine country. Stringent regulations and investment/advice from Australian and western European companies and consultants – for example at the BALATONBOGLAR winery – have put Hungary back on the international wine map. There is renewed interest in native varieties such as Furmint and Irsai Olivér for whites, Kékfrankos (Blaufränkisch) and Kadarka (the traditional grape used in BULL'S BLOOD) for reds, and top Hungarian winemakers – Akos Kamocsay (at HILLTOP), Vilmos Thummerer and others – are now a solid force. But price and reputation remain low and many vineyards are being abandoned out of desperation. TOKAJI in particular has yet to develop the world-class reputation its wines deserve.

INDIA India's climate is generally unsuitable for wine production: only a small percentage of the 50,000ha (123,500 acres) of vines is used for wine; both international varieties and ancient Indian ones, such as Arkesham and Arkavati, are planted. Wine consumption is increasing rapidly. CHATEAU INDAGE, with vineyards in the Maharashtra hills east of Mumbai (Bombay), dominates the market and produces still and sparkling wines. Sula Vineyards is leading the way with screwcaps on all its wines and is planning to bring its area under vines up to 650ha (1600 acres). Advice from international wine guru Michel Rolland put Grover Vineyards in Bangalore on the map.

ISRAEL More small wineries continue to open and existing ones consolidate and enlarge. A lack of a decent labelling regime and regulatory authority means that quality is variable and labels not always 100% accurate. Most wine is locally consumed and only a few of the best are exported. Besides GOLAN HEIGHTS, some of Israel's most promising wines now come from Castel in the Judean Hills (particularly good Chardonnay), Galilee Heights in Galilee (good Cabernet) and Tishbi in Shomron. Non-Jews shouldn't be put off by a 'kosher' label: some of Israel's best reds and whites are kosher.

JAPAN As long as there is confusion between which wines are 100% locally grown and which are multi-country blends (which most are), Japanese wines, especially those made from indigenous varieties such as Koshu, will never really be appreciated by an international audience. One has to assume that the present situation suits most producers, who sell almost all their wines locally. However, the Japanese are increasingly interested in wine, and their national wine show now attracts entries from around the world. Despite humid conditions, wine is produced in almost every province. SUNTORY is in the best region, Yamanashi, and is expanding its vineyards. Other main players are Mercian, Sapporo, Manns and Domaine Sogga.

LEBANON CHATEAU MUSAR, Château Kefraya and Château Ksara survived the 25-year war. Peace has brought a new generation of producers and improved quality from the older companies – new releases from Musar, Kefraya, Ksara, Château Ka, Massaya and Clos St Thomas are vastly superior to those produced just a few years ago and are beginning to find their way into the high streets of the world. The 2007 outbreak of hostilities ended just in time for grapes to be harvested.

LUXEMBOURG With one of the world's highest levels of wine consumption per capita, very little wine is exported. Co-operatives dominate here and quality is about what you would expect. Plantings of Elbling and Rivaner (Müller-Thurgau) are in decline, and are being replaced with quality varietals such as Riesling, Pinot Noir, Chardonnay and Gewürztraminer. *Crémant* (sparkling) wines continue to increase in quality and popularity.

MEXICO In the far north-west of Mexico, in Baja California, some good reds are made by L A CETTO as well as by smaller companies such as Monte Xanic and Casa de Piedra. In the rest of the country, only high-altitude areas such as the Parras Valley and Zacatecas have the potential for quality wines. Casa Madero, in the Parras Valley, has some success with Cabernet Sauvignon. Other promising grape varieties include Nebbiolo, Petite Sirah, Tempranillo, Zinfandel and Barbera, with Viognier and Chardonnay also planted.

MOLDOVA Moldovan winegrowers suffered a major setback in 2006 when their main export market, Russia, banned imports of their wines, seemingly in retaliation for Moldova becoming too friendly with the West. Standards of winemaking and equipment leave much to be desired, but fruit quality is good, and international players, including PENFOLDS and winemakers Jacques Lurton, Hugh Ryman and Alain Thiénot, have worked with local wineries. However, chaotic social conditions have led to many attempts being abandoned.

MONTENEGRO This red-wine-dominated part of the former Yugoslavia shows some potential in the beefy Vranac grape with its bitter cherry flavours – but the worst wines are really poor.

MOROCCO Known for big, sweet-fruited reds that once found a ready blending market in France. Since the 1990s massive investment by Castel Frères is instigating a rebirth: the first results are tasty Syrah and Cabernet reds. The important Celliers de Meknès are also on the up, and Domaine el Baraka and Domaine Larroque are promising.

ROMANIA The huge vineyard area has declined somewhat in recent years as hybrid grape varieties are pulled up, to be replanted with *Vitis vinifera* grapes such as Pinot Noir, Cabernet Sauvignon, Merlot and the native Feteasca Negra for reds, Pinot Gris and Chardonnay for whites. International-backed ventures such as Cramele Recas, Halewood (Prahova Valley) and Carl Reh are a sign of the mini-revolution, but challenges remain. The appellation system is of limited value, although Dealul Mare, Murfatlar and Cotnari all have ancient reputations. Accession to the EU in 2007 has done little to help the fortunes of Romanian growers as there is now a shortage of labour to work the vineyards and there has been an increase in the amount of wine being imported into Romania from Spain and Italy.

SLOVAKIA The eastern part of the old Czechoslovakia, with its cool-climate vineyards, is dominated by white varieties – Pinot Blanc, Riesling, Grüner Veltliner, Irsai Olivér – with the occasional fruity Frankovka (Blaufränkisch) red. Western investment at the state winery at Nitra and smaller wineries such as Gbelce and Hurbanovo near the Hungarian border at Komárno, is rapidly improving the quality. With EU membership we may start to see some examples in the shops.

SLOVENIA Many of the old Yugoslav Federation's best vineyards are here. Potential is considerable, and some interesting wines are emerging, with whites generally better than reds. A simplified appellation system and the increasing popularity of Slovenia as a holiday and second-home region should increase availability. On the Italian border, Brda and Vipava have go-ahead co-operatives, and Kraski Teran is a red wine of repute. The Movia range, from the Kristancic family, looks promising.

SWITZERLAND Fendant (Chasselas) is the main grape for spritzy but neutral whites from the VAUD and VALAIS. Like the fruity DOLE reds, they are best drunk very young. German-speaking cantons produce whites from Müller-Thurgau and mostly light reds and rosés from Pinot Noir (Blauburgunder); top producers, such as Daniel GANTENBEIN, make more powerful versions. Italian-speaking TICINO concentrates on Merlots, which have been increasingly impressive since 2000. Serious wines, especially in Valais, use Syrah, Chardonnay, Marsanne and traditional varieties like Amigne and Petite Arvine. Pinot Noir from the Valais is greatly improved. See also NEUCHATEL.

THAILAND I first tasted Thai wine a few years ago: it was a light and fruity red and impressive for what I thought of as subtropical conditions. Since then, serious Shiraz and Chenin wines have shown that Thailand's high-altitude vineyards are capable of some tasty offerings. The Thai Wine Association is attempting to regulate the composition and quality of Thai wines and the once-common practice of blending local and imported wines (without declaring it on the label) is lessening.

TUNISIA Ancient wine traditions have had an injection of new life from international investment, and results so far are encouraging. Tourism soaks up most of the production and little is exported.

TURKEY The world's sixth-largest grape producer, but 97% ends up as table grapes or raisins. However, with EU membership a possibility in 2012 and with vast vineyards, good growing conditions and cheap labour on hand, Turkey could become a major player if the will-power and the investment are harnessed. Producers such as Diren, Kavaklidere, Turasan and Doluca are using modern technology to produce very drinkable wines. Local variety Buzbag can be good.

UKRAINE The Crimea's vineyards are the most important, producing hearty reds, sweet and sparkling wines; there's a surprisingly good sweet red sparkler, and sweet Muscatels are considered to be a cause for national pride, especially the Massandra brand. The Odessa region is successful with its sparkling wines, the three best-known facilities being the Inkerman winery, Novyi Svet and Zolota Balka. Future European investment is said to be in the pipeline, so let's see.

A–Z

OF WINES, PRODUCERS, GRAPES & WINE REGIONS

In the following pages there are over
1600 entries covering the world's top wines, as well as leading
producers, main wine regions and grape
varieties, followed on page 308 by a glossary of wine terms
and classifications.

On page 4 you will find a full explanation of
How to Use the A–Z. On page 317 there is an index
of all wine producers in the book, to help you find the
world's best wines.

AALTO *Ribera del Duero DO, Castilla y León, Spain* Former VEGA SICILIA winemaker Mariano García and former RIBERA DEL DUERO appellation boss Javier Zaccagnini teamed up to create this winery in 1999. From the outset, they have challenged top Spanish producers with their dense but elegant reds, Aalto★★ and old vines cuvée Aalto PS★★. Best years: (2005) 04 **03 01 00 99**.

ABRUZZO *Italy* This region stretches from the Adriatic coast to the mountainous Apennine interior. White Trebbiano d'Abruzzo DOC is usually dry and neutral; the MONTEPULCIANO D'ABRUZZO DOC is generally a strapping, peppery red of real character, but increasingly a rosé called Cerasuolo. Overproduction has been a problem, but quality is on the increase with new vineyard training techniques and the establishment of new DOCs.

ACACIA *Carneros AVA, California, USA* Leading producer of Chardonnay and Pinot Noir from CARNEROS. The regular Carneros Chardonnay★ is restrained but attractive. Pinot Noirs include the superb Beckstoffer Vineyard★★ and a Carneros★ – the wines have moved to a riper, meatier style of late. Best years: (Pinot Noir) 2006 05 **03 02 01 00 99 97 96 95**.

ACCADEMIA DEI RACEMI *Manduria, Puglia, Italy* Premium venture run by Gregory Perrucci, scion of a long-established family of bulk shippers of basic Puglian wines. Quality, modern-style reds mainly from Primitivo and Negroamaro under various producers' names: Felline (Vigna del Feudo★★), Pervini (PRIMITIVO DI MANDURIA Archidamo★★), Masseria Pepe (Dunico★★). Best years: (reds) (2007) 06 **05** 04 03 01.

ACHAVAL-FERRER *Uco Valley, Mendoza, Argentina* A former garage winery created in 1998, and now one of Argentina's most sought-after labels. 80-year-old vines in the La Consulta area of UCO VALLEY produce Finca Altamira★★★, a Malbec bursting with personality. Also superb single-vineyard Malbecs Bella Vista★★★ and Mirador★★★ and more approachable red blend Quimera★. Best years: (2006) 05 **04 03 02 01 99**.

JEAN-BAPTISTE ADAM *Alsace AC, Alsace, France* Long-established family vineyard in Ammerschwihr with a reputation for luscious, classically perfumed Gewurztraminer★★ from the newly created Kaefferkopf Grand Cru, as well as concentrated Riesling★★, herbaceous Pinot Gris★ and an exciting Pinot Noir★★ given 18 months in oak. Best years: (Kaefferkopf Gewurztraminer) (2007) 05 **04 02 01 00 99 98 97 95**.

TIM ADAMS *Clare Valley, South Australia* Important maker of fine, old-fashioned wine from his own and bought-in local grapes. Classic dry Riesling★★, oaky Semillon★★, and rich, opulent Shiraz★★ (sometimes ★★★) and Cabernet★★. The botrytis Semillon★ can be super, The Fergus★★ is a glorious Grenache-based blend, and minty, peppery Aberfeldy Shiraz★★★ is a remarkable, at times unnerving, mouthful of brilliance from 100-year-old vines. Best years: (Aberfeldy Shiraz) 2006 05 04 03 02 01 **00 99 98 96 94**.

ADELAIDE HILLS *South Australia* Small and exciting region 30 minutes' drive from Adelaide. High altitude affords a cool, moist climate ideal for fine table wines and superb sparkling wine. Consistently good Sauvignon Blanc and Chardonnay, plus promising Pinot Noir and exciting, fleshy Shiraz, and even Zinfandel. Best producers: Ashton Hills★, Bird in Hand★,

HENSCHKE★★, Longview, Nepenthe★★, S C Pannell★, PETALUMA★★, RIPOSTE★, SHAW & SMITH★★, Geoff WEAVER★★.

ADELSHEIM VINEYARD *Willamette Valley AVA, Oregon, USA* Over the past 3 decades, Adelsheim has established a reputation for excellent, generally unfiltered, Pinot Noir – especially cherry-scented Elizabeth's Reserve★ and Bryan Creek Vineyard★ – and for rich Chardonnay Caitlin's Reserve★. Also a bright, minerally Pinot Gris★. Best years: (Elizabeth's Reserve) 2006 05 **04 03 02**.

AGLIANICO DEL VULTURE DOC *Basilicata, Italy* Red wine from the Aglianico grape grown on the steep slopes of Mt Vulture. Despite the zone's location almost on the same latitude as Naples, the harvest here is sometimes later than in BAROLO, 750km (470 miles) to the north-west, because the Aglianico grape ripens very late at altitude. The best wines are structured, complex and long-lived. Best producers: Basilium★, D'Angelo★★, Cantine del Notaio★★, Paternoster★★, Tenuta del Portale, Le Querce★, Consorzio Viticoltori Associati del Vulture (Carpe Diem★). Best years: (2007) (06) 05 04 **03 01 00 98 97**.

AHR *Germany* The Ahr Valley is a small (545ha/1345-acre) mainly red wine region south of Bonn. Chief grape varieties are the Spätburgunder (Pinot Noir) and (Blauer) Portugieser. Adeneuer, Deutzerhof★, Meyer-Näkel★ and Stodden★ are the best of a growing band of serious producers.

AIRÉN Spain's – and indeed the world's – most planted white grape can make fresh, modern, but generally neutral-flavoured wines, with some eye-opening exceptions, such as Ercavio's stunning old-vines white from Toledo. Airén is grown all over the centre and south of Spain, especially in La MANCHA, VALDEPENAS and ANDALUCIA (where it's called Lairén).

ALBAN *San Luis Obispo County, California, USA* Based in the cool Arroyo Grande district of Edna Valley, RHONE specialist John Alban first produced Viognier in 1991. Today he offers 2 bottlings: Estate★★ and Central Coast★. Roussanne★★ is laden with honey notes. Syrah is represented by 3 bottlings: Reva★★★, Lorraine★★ and Seymour's Vineyard★★. Intense Grenache★★ and Pandora★★, a blend of about 60% Grenache, 40% Syrah, round out the line-up. These are some of America's purest expressions of Rhône varietals, despite some extremely high alcohol levels. Best years: (Syrah) (2006) **05 04 03 02 01 00 99 98 97**.

ALBARIÑO Possibly Spain's most characteristic white grape. It is a speciality of RIAS BAIXAS in Galicia in Spain's rainy north-west and, as Alvarinho, in Portugal's VINHO VERDE region. When well made, Albariño wines have fascinating flavours of apricot, peach, grapefruit and Muscat grapes, refreshingly high acidity, highish alcohol – and unrefreshingly high prices. The ever-present danger to quality is excessive yields.

ALENQUER DOC *Estremadura, Portugal* Maritime-influenced hills north of Lisbon, producing wines from (mostly) local grape varieties such as Castelão (Periquita) and Trincadeira, but also from Cabernet, Syrah and Chardonnay. Many wines are simply labelled ESTREMADURA. Best producers: Quinta do Carneiro, Quinta de Chocapalha★, D F J VINHOS, Quinta do Monte d'Oiro★★, Quinta de Pancas, Casa SANTOS LIMA★. Best years: (reds) 2005 **04 03 01 00**.

ALENTEJO *Portugal* A large chunk of southern Portugal south and east of Lisbon and, along with the DOURO, one of Portugal's fastest improving red wine regions. Potential is far from realized, but already some of Portugal's finest reds come from here. Vinho Regional wines are labelled Alentejano. **Best producers: (reds)** Azamor (Petit Verdot★), BACALHOA★ (Tinto da Ânfora Grande Escolha★★), Borba co-op★, CORTES DE CIMA★, Dona Maria, ESPORAO★★, José Maria da FONSECA★, Fundação Eugénio de Almeida (Cartuxa★, Pera-Manca★★), Paulo Laureano Vinus★, MALHADINHA NOVA★★, Monte da Penha, Mouchão★★, Quinta do Mouro★, João Portugal RAMOS★★, SOGRAPE★, Quinta da Terrugem★★/ALIANCA. **Best years: (reds)** 2005 **04 01 00**.

ALEXANDER VALLEY AVA *Sonoma County, California, USA* Important AVA, centred on the northern Russian River, which is fairly warm, with only patchy summer fog. Cabernet Sauvignon is highly successful here, with lovely, juicy fruit not marred by an excess of tannin. Chardonnay may also be good but is often overproduced and lacking in ripe, round flavours. Merlot and old-vine Zinfandel can be outstanding from hillside vineyards. **Best producers:** Alexander Valley Vineyards★, CLOS DU BOIS★, De Lorimier★, GEYSER PEAK★, JORDAN★, Murphy-Goode★★, SEGHESIO★★, SILVER OAK★★, SIMI★, Trentadue★★. See also RUSSIAN RIVER VALLEY AVA, SONOMA COUNTY. **Best years: (reds)** 2005 04 03 **02 01 00** 99 97 95 94 93 91 90.

ALGARVE *Portugal* Holiday region with mostly red wines in 4 DOCs: Lagoa, Lagos, Portimão and Tavira. There are some good wines. Look out for reds and rosés from Sir Cliff Richard's Vida Nova, Quinta do Barranco Longo and Morgado da Torre.

CAVES ALIANÇA *Beira Litoral, Portugal* Based in BAIRRADA, Aliança makes crisp, fresh whites and soft, approachable red Bairradas★. Also made, either from its own vineyards or bought-in grapes or wines, are reds from the DAO (Quinta da Garrida★) and ALENTEJO (Quinta da Terrugem★★). Quinta dos Quatro Ventos★★ from the DOURO is the top red, a blend of Tinta Roriz, Touriga Franca and Touriga Nacional.

ALIGOTÉ French grape, found mainly in Burgundy, whose basic characteristic is a lemony tartness. It can make extremely refreshing wine, especially from old vines, but is generally rather dull and lean. In ripe years it can resemble Chardonnay, especially if a little new oak is used. The best comes from the village of Bouzeron in the COTE CHALONNAISE, where Aligoté has its own appellation. Occasionally also found in Moldova and Bulgaria. Drink young. **Best producers: (Burgundy)** M BOUZEREAU, COCHE-DURY★, A Ente★, J-H Goisot★, Denis MORTET★, TOLLOT-BEAUT, Villaine★.

ALLEGRINI *Valpolicella DOC, Veneto, Italy* High-profile producer in VALPOLICELLA Classico, making single-vineyard La Grola★★ and Palazzo della Torre★★. These are now under the regional Veronese IGT – originally to distance them from the low regard in which much of Valpolicella was held until recently. These, and the barrique-aged La Poja★★★ (made solely with the Corvina grape), show the great potential that exists for Valpolicella as a table wine. Outstanding AMARONE★★★ and RECIOTO Giovanni Allegrini★★. **Best years: (Amarone)** (2007) (06) 04 03 01 00 97 95.

THIERRY ALLEMAND *Cornas AC, Rhône Valley, France* Thierry Allemand has a smallholding of some 5ha (12 acres) of vines. He is determined to keep yields low, uses little sulphur and seeks to make wines with clear fruit and precise tannins. He produces 2 unfiltered expressions of CORNAS at its intense and powerful best: Chaillot★★ is marginally the lighter; Reynard★★ is from a parcel of very old Syrah. Also makes St-Péray. Best years: (Reynard) (2007) 06 05 04 03 01 **00 99 98 96 95 94 91 90**.

ALLENDE *Rioja DOCa, Rioja, Spain* One of the most admired new names in RIOJA. Scented, uncompromisingly concentrated reds include Aurus★★★, Calvario★★ and the affordable Allende★. There is also a delicate white★. Best years: (reds) (2005) 04 **03 02 01 00 99 98**.

ALMAVIVA★★★ *Maipo, Chile* State-of-the-art joint venture between CONCHA Y TORO and the Baron Philippe de Rothschild company (see MOUTON-ROTHSCHILD), located in MAIPO Valley's Tocornal vineyard at the foot of the Andes. A memorably powerful red from old Cabernet Sauvignon vines planted in alluvial, stony soils; it can be drunk at 5 years but should age for 10. Best years: 2005 03 **02 01**.

ALOXE-CORTON AC *Côte de Beaune, Burgundy, France* An important village at the northern end of the COTE DE BEAUNE producing mostly red wines from Pinot Noir. Its reputation is based on the 2 Grands Crus, CORTON (mainly red) and CORTON-CHARLEMAGNE (white only). Other vineyards in Aloxe-Corton used to be a source of tasty, good-value Burgundy, but nowadays the reds rarely exhibit their former characteristic blend of ripe fruit and appetizing savoury dryness. Almost all the white wine is classified as Grand Cru. Best producers: d'Ardhuy, CHANDON DE BRIAILLES★★, M Chapuis★, Marius Delarche★, Dubreuil-Fontaine★, Follin-Arvelet★, Camille Giroud★, Antonin Guyon★, JADOT★, Rapet★, Comte Senard★, TOLLOT-BEAUT★★. Best years: (reds) (2007) 06 05 **03 02 99 97 96 95**.

DOM. ALQUIER *Faugères, Languedoc, France* This estate shows how good FAUGERES can be. Barrel aging of all wines, and low yields for the special cuvées, Les Bastides★★ and La Maison Jaune★. Also a good white blend of Roussanne and Marsanne. Best years: 2005 03 **01 00**.

ALSACE AC *Alsace, France* Tucked away on France's eastern border with Germany, Alsace produces some of the most individual white wines of all, rich in aroma and full of ripe, distinctive flavours. Alsace is almost as far north as CHAMPAGNE, but its climate is considerably warmer and drier. Wines from the 51 best vineyard sites can call themselves Alsace Grand Cru AC and account for 4% of production; quality regulations are now more stringent and many individual crus have further tightened the rules. Riesling, Muscat, Gewurztraminer and Pinot Gris are generally considered the finest varieties in Alsace and were originally the only ones permitted for Grand Cru wines, although Sylvaner is now legal in Zotzenberg and further changes will follow. Pinot Blanc can produce good wines too. Reds from Pinot Noir are improving fitfully. Alsace labels its wines by grape variety and, apart from the Edelzwicker blends and CREMANT D'ALSACE fizz, nearly all Alsace wines are made from a single variety, although blends from certain Grand Cru sites, such as Altenberg de Bergheim and Kaefferkopf, are now recognized. Medium-dry or sweeter wines are now, as of the 2004 vintage, labelled *moelleux*. Vendange Tardive means 'late-harvest'; the grapes (Riesling, Muscat, Pinot Gris or Gewurztraminer) are picked late and almost overripe, giving higher sugar levels and potentially more intense flavours. The resulting wines are usually rich and mouthfilling and often need 5 years or more to show their personality. Sélection de Grains Nobles – late-harvest wines made from superripe grapes of the same varieties – are invariably sweet and usually affected by noble rot; they are among Alsace's finest, but are very expensive to produce (and to buy). Best producers: J-B ADAM★★, Lucien Albrecht★, Barmès-Buecher★, J Becker, Léon Beyer★, P BLANCK★★, Bott-Geyl★★, A Boxler★, Ernest Burn★★, DEISS★★, Dirler-Cadé★★, Pierre Frick★, Rémy Gresser★, HUGEL★, Josmeyer★★, Kientzler★, Klur, Kreydenweiss★★, Seppi Landmann★, A MANN★★, Meyer-Fonné, Mittnacht Frères, MURE★★, Ostertag★★, Pfaffenheim co-op, Ribeauvillé co-op, Rieflé★, Rolly Gassmann★, Martin Schaetzel, Charles Schléret, Schlumberger★, SCHOFFIT★★, Louis Sipp, Bruno Sorg★, Marc Tempé, TRIMBACH★★, TURCKHEIM co-op★, WEINBACH★★, Paul Zinck★, ZIND-HUMBRECHT★★★. Best years: 2007 05 **04 02 01 00 98 97 96 95**.

ALTARE *Barolo DOCG, Piedmont, Italy* Elio Altare crafts some of the most
♀ stunning of Alba's wines: BARBERA D'ALBA★, Dolcetto d'Alba★★ and even finer BAROLO Vigneto Arborina★★ and Barolo Brunate★★★. Though he is a professed modernist, his wines are intense, full and structured while young, but with clearly discernible fruit flavours, thanks largely to tiny yields. He also makes 3 barrique-aged wines under the LANGHE DOC: Arborina★★★ (Nebbiolo), Larigi★★★ (Barbera) and La Villa★★ (Nebbiolo-Barbera). Altare is one of several producers that make L'Insieme★★ (a Nebbiolo-Cabernet-Barbera blend). Best years: (Barolo) (2007) (06) (04) **03** 01 **00 99 98 96 95**.

ALTO ADIGE *Trentino-Alto Adige, Italy* A largely German-speaking province, originally called Südtirol. The region-wide DOC covers 25 types of wine. Reds range from light and perfumed when made from the ubiquitous (but diminishing in importance) Schiava grape, to fruity and more structured from the Cabernets or Merlot, to dark and velvety if Lagrein is used. Excess oak can mar their delightful fruit. Whites include Chardonnay, Gewürztraminer, Pinot Bianco, Pinot Grigio, Riesling and Sauvignon, and are usually fresh and fragrant. There is also some good sparkling wine. Much of the wine comes from well-run co-ops, although there are some excellent individual producers. Sub-zones include the previously independent DOCs of Santa Maddalena and Terlano. Best producers: (individual) Abbazia di Novacella★, Casòn Hirschprunn★, Peter Dipoli★★, Egger-Ramer★, Franz Gojer★, Franz Haas★★, Haderburg★★, Hofstätter★★, Kränzl★, LAGEDER★★, Laimburg★, Loacker★, Josephus Mayr★, Muri-Gries★★, Josef Niedermayr★, Ignaz Niedrist★, Plattner Waldgries★, Peter Pliger-Kuenhof★★, Hans Rottensteiner★, Heinrich Rottensteiner★, TIEFENBRUNNER★★, Elena Walch★, Wilhelm Walch, Baron Widmann★; (co-ops) Caldaro★, Colterenzio★★, Girlan-Cornaiano★, Gries★★, Nals-Margreid★★, Prima & Nuova/Erste & Neue★, San Michele Appiano★★, Santa Maddalena★, Terlano★★, Termeno★★. See also TRENTINO.

ALTOS LAS HORMIGAS *Mendoza, Argentina* A rising star in Argentina,
♀ founded in 1995. Altos Las Hormigas Malbec is an opulent example of the grape, while Reserva Viña Hormigas★ is packed with pure, dense blackberry and cherry flavours. Colonia Las Liebres is a delightful, juicy Bonarda. Best years: (Viña Hormigas) (2006) 05 **04 03 02 01**.

ALVARINHO See ALBARINO.

CASTELLO DI AMA *Chianti Classico DOCG, Tuscany, Italy* Model estate of
♀ CHIANTI CLASSICO, with outstanding Chianti Classico★★, plus single-vineyard Riservas★★★ (Bellavista and La Casuccia). L'Apparita★★★ is

one of Italy's best Merlots. Also good Chardonnay Al Poggio★. Best years: (Chianti Classico) (2007) (06) **04 03 01 00 99 97 95**.

AMARONE DELLA VALPOLICELLA DOC *Veneto, Italy* A brilliantly individual, bitter-sweet style of VALPOLICELLA made from grapes shrivelled on mats for months after harvest. The wine, which can reach 16% of alcohol and more, differs from the sweet RECIOTO DELLA VALPOLICELLA in that it is fermented to near-dryness, the grapes having been left on the mats a month or two less. Wines from the Classico zone are generally the best, with exceptions from DAL FORNO, Corte Sant'Alda and Roccolo Grassi. Best producers: Accordini★★, ALLEGRINI★★★, Bertani★★, Brigaldara★, Brunelli★, BUSSOLA★★★, Michele Castellani★★, Corte Sant'Alda★★, Valentina Cubi★★, DAL FORNO★★★, Guerrieri-Rizzardi★★, MASI★, QUINTARELLI★★★, Le Ragose★★, Roccolo Grassi★, Le Salette★★, Serègo Alighieri★, Speri★★, Tedeschi★★, Tommasi★, Villa Monteleone★★, VIVIANI★★, Zenato★★. Best years: (2006) 04 **03 01 00 97**.

AMIGNE Ancient Swiss grape variety that is virtually limited to the region of Vétroz in the VALAIS. The wine has an earthy, nutty intensity and benefits from a few years' aging. Best producers: Bonvin, Fontannaz, Jean-René Germanier, Caves Imesch.

DOM. DE L'ANCIENNE CURE *Bergerac AC and Monbazillac AC, South-West France* Christian Roche exemplifies the best of BERGERAC, with textured elegant reds, crisp dry whites and balanced, luscious sweet MONBAZILLAC. Both reds and sweet whites have top cuvées called L'Abbaye★ and L'Extase★. Best years: (reds) 2005 03 **01 00**.

ANDALUCÍA *Spain* Fortified wines, or wines naturally so strong in alcohol that they don't need fortifying, are the speciality of this southern stretch of Spain. Apart from sherry (JEREZ Y MANZANILLA DO), there are the lesser, sherry-like wines of Condado de Huelva DO and MONTILLA-MORILES DO, and the rich, sweet wines of MALAGA DO. These regions also make some modern but bland dry whites; the best are from Condado de Huelva. Red wine is now appearing from producers in Málaga, Cádiz, Seville, Granada and Almería provinces.

ANDERSON VALLEY AVA *California, USA* Small appellation (less than 245ha/600 acres) in western MENDOCINO COUNTY that produces brilliant wines. Most vineyards are within 15 miles of the Pacific Ocean, making this one of the coldest AVAs in California. Delicate Pinot Noirs and Chardonnays, and one of the few places in the state for first-rate Gewürztraminer and Riesling. Superb sparkling wines with healthy acidity and creamy yeast are highlights as well. Best producers: Brutocao★, Greenwood Ridge★, HANDLEY★★, Lazy Creek★, NAVARRO★★★, ROEDERER ESTATE★★, SCHARFFENBERGER CELLARS★.

ANDREW WILL WINERY *Washington State, USA* Winemaker Chris Camarda makes delicious blends of BORDEAUX varietals from a range of older WASHINGTON vineyards. At the top are the complex Champoux Vineyard★★★ and the opulent Ciel du Cheval★★★. Wines from 2 newer vineyards, Sheridan Vineyard★ and Two Blondes Vineyard★, still show young vine character. Sorella★★, a blend of the best barrels each vintage, can be outstanding with age. Best years: (reds) (2006) 05 **04 03 01 00 99**.

CH. ANGÉLUS★★★ *St-Émilion Grand Cru AC, 1er Grand Cru Classé, Bordeaux, France* One of the best-known ST-EMILION Grands Crus (James Bond's choice in *Casino Royale*), with an energetic owner and talented winemaker. Rich, dark, spicy, modern St-Émilion. Promoted to Premier Grand Cru Classé in 1996 and on top form. Best years: 2006 05 04 **03 02 01** 00 **99 98 96 95 94 93 92 90 89 88 85**.

MARQUIS D'ANGERVILLE *Volnay, Côte de Beaune, Burgundy, France* The late Jacques d'Angerville for half a century produced an exemplary range of elegant Premiers Crus from VOLNAY, the subtlest of the COTE DE BEAUNE's red wine appellations. Quality is, if anything, improving further. Clos des Ducs and Taillepieds are ★★★. All should be kept for at least 5 years. Best years: (top reds) (2007) 06 05 03 02 99 **98 97 96 95 91 90**.

CH. D'ANGLUDET★ *Margaux AC, Haut-Médoc, Bordeaux, France* This English-owned château makes a gentle, unobtrusive but generally attractive red that is never overpriced. It ages well for at least a decade. Best years: 2006 05 04 **03 02 00 98 96 95 94 90 89 88 86**.

ANJOU BLANC AC *Loire Valley, France* Ill-defined AC; ranges from bone dry to sweet, from excellent to dreadful; the best are dry. Up to 20% Chardonnay or Sauvignon can be added, but many of the leading producers use 100% Chenin from top sites once dedicated to sweet COTEAUX DU LAYON. Best producers: M Angeli/Sansonnière★★, S Bernaudeau, des Chesnaies★, P Delesvaux★, Fesles★, L Herbel, Richard Leroy★, Montgilet/ V Lebreton, Mosse★, Ogereau★, Pierre-Bise★, Jo PITHON★★, RICHOU★, Roulerie★, Soucherie/P-Y Tijou★. Best years: (top wines) 2007 06 **05 04 03 02**.

ANJOU ROUGE AC *Loire Valley, France* Anjou reds (from Cabernets Sauvignon and Franc or Pineau d'Aunis) are increasingly successful. Usually fruity, easy-drinking wine, with less tannin than ANJOU-VILLAGES. Wines made from Gamay are sold as Anjou Gamay. Best producers: Brizé★, Germain-Saincrit, Putille, RICHOU★. Best years: (top wines) 2006 05 **04 03 02 01 96**.

ANJOU-VILLAGES AC *Loire Valley, France* Superior Anjou red from 46 villages, and made from Cabernet Franc and Cabernet Sauvignon. Anjou-Villages Brissac's schist soils produce particularly firmly structured wines which reward aging. Best producers: P Baudouin, Brizé★, P Delesvaux★, Deux Arcs, Germain-Saincrit★, Montgilet/V Lebreton★, de la Motte, Ogereau★, Pierre-Bise★, Putille★, RICHOU (Vieilles Vignes★★), Rochelles/J-Y Lebreton★★, Tigné★, la Varière/Beaujeau. Best years: 2006 05 04 **03 02 01 97 96**.

ANSELMI *Veneto, Italy* Roberto Anselmi (with PIEROPAN) has shown that the once much-maligned SOAVE can have personality when carefully made. Using ultra-modern methods he has honed the fruit flavours of his San Vincenzo★★ and Capitel Foscarino★★ and introduced small-barrel-aging for single-vineyard Capitel Croce★★ and luscious, SAUTERNES-like I Capitelli★★ (sometimes ★★★), as well as the Cabernet Sauvignon Realdà. All sold under the regional IGT rather than Soave DOC. Best years: (I Capitelli) 2006 05 04 **03 01 00**.

ANTINORI *Tuscany, Italy* World-famous Florentine family firm that has been involved in wine since 1385, but it is Piero Antinori, the current head, who has made the Antinori name synonymous with quality and innovation. The quality of its CHIANTI CLASSICO wines like Badia a Passignano★ (Riserva★★), Pèppoli★ and Tenute Marchese Antinori Riserva★★ is consistently good, but it was its development of the SUPER-TUSCAN concept of superior wines outside the DOC that launched a quality revolution during the 1970s. Introducing small-barrel-aging to Tuscany, TIGNANELLO★★ and, especially, SOLAIA★★★ can be great wines. Other Tuscan wines include VINO NOBILE La Braccesca★★, Bramasole Syrah from Cortona DOC, BRUNELLO DI MONTALCINO Pian delle Vigne★★ and BOLGHERI's Guado al Tasso★★ (Cabernet-Merlot). Interests further afield include PRUNOTTO in Piedmont, Tormaresca in PUGLIA, FRANCIACORTA's Monte Nisa and Bátaapáti in Hungary. A joint venture with CHATEAU STE MICHELLE in the USA acquired STAG'S LEAP WINE CELLARS in 2007. Best years: (reds) (2007) (06) **04 03 01 00 99 97.** See also Castello della SALA.

ANTONOPOULOS *Patras AO, Peloponnese, Greece* Boutique winery producing barrel-fermented Chardonnay★★, Cabernet Nea Dris (New Oak)★, a blend of Cabernets Sauvignon and Franc, and Private Collection★, a promising Agiorgitiko-Cabernet blend.

DOM. D'ANTUGNAC *Limoux AC, Languedoc, France* Two young Burgundians, Jean-Luc Terrier and Christian Collovray, are producing impressive Pinot Noir and Chardonnay in the cool LIMOUX region. Côte Pierre Lys is the Pinot Noir, with finesse and complexity. Chardonnay Les Gravas★ is barrel-fermented and aged, balancing richness with apples and cream freshness. Best years: (Les Gravas) 2005 04 **01**.

ARAGÓN *Spain* Aragón stretches south from the Pyrenees to Spain's central plateau. Winemaking has improved markedly, first of all in the cooler, hilly, northern SOMONTANO DO, and now also further south, in Campo de Borja DO, Calatayud DO and CARIÑENA DO; these 3 areas have the potential to be a major budget-price force in a world mad for beefy but fruity reds.

ARAUJO *Napa Valley AVA, California, USA* Boutique winery whose great coup was to buy the Eisele vineyard, traditionally a source of superb Cabernet under the Joseph PHELPS label. Araujo Cabernet Sauvignon★★★ is now one of California's most sought-after reds, combining great fruit intensity with powerful but digestible tannins. Altagracia is a red BORDEAUX blend; Syrah★★ is impressive. Also Viognier and an attractively zesty Sauvignon Blanc★★.

ARBOIS AC *Jura, France* The largest of the specific ACs in the Jura region. The majority of wines are red or rosé, but most widely seen outside the region are the whites, made from Chardonnay or the local Savagnin, which can give the wines a sherry-like flavour that is most concentrated in *vin jaune*. There is also a rare, sweet *vin de paille*. Good sparkling CREMANT DU JURA is made mainly from Chardonnay. Best producers: Ch. d'Arlay★, L Aviet★, Bourdy★, Désiré★, Dugois★, M Faudot★, F Lornet★, H Maire★, P Overnoy★, la Pinte★, J Puffeney★, Caves de la Reine Jeanne★, Renardière, Rijckaert★, Rolet★, A & M Tissot★, J Tissot★, Tournelle★. Best years: 2006 05 04 03 02 **01 00**.

DOM. ANTOINE ARENA *Patrimonio AC, Corsica, France* Family-owned vineyard in Patrimonio, which specializes in white wines based on Vermentino, white Bianco Gentile (a local grape which had fallen into disuse) and stunning reds under the Carco, Grotte di Sole★ and Morta Maio labels. Best years: (Grotte di Sole) (2005) 04 03 **01 00**.

ARGIOLAS *Sardinia, Italy* Sardinian star making DOC wines Cannonau (Costera★), Monica (Perdera) and Vermentino (Costamolino★) di Sardegna, but the best wines are the IGT Isola dei Nuraghi blends:

63

Turriga★★ and Korem★ are powerful, spicy reds; Angialis★★ is a golden, sweet white. All the wines are good value.

ARGYLE *Willamette Valley AVA, Oregon, USA* In 1987, Brian Croser and Rollin Soles planned a world-class New World sparkling wine firm; the cool WILLAMETTE VALLEY was ideal for late-ripened Pinot Noir and Chardonnay. Argyle sparkling wine★ was soon followed by barrel-fermented Chardonnay★ and Pinot Noir★. The Reserve★★, Nuthouse★★ and Spirithouse★★ bottlings show just how much potential this large winery possesses. Best years: (Pinot Noir) 2006 05 **04 03** 02.

ARNEIS Italian grape grown in the ROERO hills in PIEDMONT. Arneis is DOC in Roero, producing dry white wines which, at best, have an attractive (appley, herbal) perfume. Good ones can be expensive, but cheaper versions rarely work. COOPERS CREEK makes a good one in New Zealand. Best producers: Brovia★, Cascina Chicco★, Correggia★, Deltetto★, GIACOSA★, Malvirà★, Angelo Negro★, PRUNOTTO★, Sorilaria★, Vietti★, Gianni Voerzio★

CH. L'ARROSÉE★ *St-Émilion Grand Cru AC, Grand Cru Classé, Bordeaux, France* This small property, just south-west of the historic town of ST-EMILION, makes really exciting wine: rich, chewy and wonderfully luscious, with a comparatively high proportion (40%) of Cabernet. New investment from 2002. Drink after 5 years, but may be cellared for 10 or more. Best years: 2006 05 04 **03 02** 00 98 96 95 90.

ARROWOOD *Sonoma Valley AVA, California, USA* Richard Arrowood started his winery in 1986. The wines have mostly been tip-top – beautifully balanced Cabernet★★, superb Merlot★★, deeply fruity Syrah (Saralee's★, Kuljian★★, Le Beau Mélange★), lovely, velvety Chardonnay★ (Alary Vineyards★★) and fragrant Viognier★★. In 2006 the winery was acquired by Jackson Family Wines. Founder Arrowood now divides his time between this property and a new brand, Amapola Creek. Best years: (Cabernet Sauvignon) 2004 03 **02 01 00 99 97** 96 95 94 91 90.

ARTADI *Rioja DOCa, País Vasco, Spain* This former co-op is now producing some of RIOJA's deepest, most ambitious reds. These include Grandes Añadas★★★, Viña El Pisón★★★, Pagos Viejos★★ and Viñas de Gain★. Best years: (2005) 04 **03 01** 00 98 96 95 94.

ASCHERI *Piedmont, Italy* Winemakers in PIEDMONT for at least 5 centuries. The Ascheri style is forward and appealingly drinkable, whether it be BAROLO (Vigna dei Pola★, Sorano★), Dolcetto d'Alba (Vigna Nirane★) or NEBBIOLO D'ALBA. Montalupa Rosso and Bianco are made from Syrah and Viognier. The Cristina Ascheri MOSCATO D'ASTI is delightful.

ASTI DOCG *Piedmont, Italy* Asti Spumante, the world's best-selling sweet sparkling wine, was long derided as light and cheap, though promotion to DOCG signalled an upturn in quality. Made in the province of Asti, south-east of Turin, under a denomination which includes the rarer MOSCATO D'ASTI, the wine is now called simply Asti. Its light sweetness and refreshing sparkle make it ideal with fruit and a wide range of sweet dishes. Drink young. Best producers: Araldica, Bera★, Cinzano★, Contero, Giuseppe Contratto★, Cascina Fonda★, FONTANAFREDDA, Gancia★, Martini & Rossi★, Cascina Pian d'Or★.

ATA RANGI *Martinborough, North Island, New Zealand* Small, high-quality winery run by 2 families. Stylish, concentrated reds include seductively perfumed cherry/plum Pinot Noir★★★, a rare, herb-scented Syrah and an impressive Cabernet-Merlot-Syrah blend called Célèbre★★. Whites include big, rich Craighall Chardonnay★, delicately luscious Lismore Pinot Gris★★ and a concentrated, mouthwatering Sauvignon Blanc★. A succulent Kahu botrytis Riesling is made when vintage conditions allow. Best years: (Pinot Noir) (2007) 06 **03 01 00 99**.

ATLAS PEAK *Atlas Peak AVA, Napa, California, USA* Established in 1987 by ANTINORI of Italy, this mountaintop winery in the south-east corner of the NAPA VALLEY has been a leader in Californian Sangiovese without ever managing to achieve a consistent style. Good Chardonnay is also grown in these high, cool vineyards. Now owned by Constellation, the brand is being re-tooled with more of a focus on Cabernet Sauvignon. Best years: (reds) 2003 **01 99 97 95**.

AU BON CLIMAT *Santa Maria Valley AVA, California, USA* Pace-setting winery in this cool region, run by the talented Jim Clendenen, who spends much time in BURGUNDY. The result is a range of lush Chardonnays★★ and intense Pinot Noirs★★ (Isabelle Morgan and Knox Alexander bottlings can be ★★★). He also makes BORDEAUX-style reds and various Italian varietals, both red and white. Cold Heaven Viognier is made by Clendenen's wife, Morgan. QUPE operates from the same winery. Best years: (Pinot Noir) 2005 04 **03 02 01 00 99** 98 97 96 95; (Chardonnay) (2006) **05 04 03 02 01 00 99 98**.

AUCKLAND *North Island, New Zealand* Vineyards in this region are concentrated in the districts of Henderson, KUMEU/HUAPAI, Matakana and VAIHEKE ISLAND. Clevedon, south of Auckland, is a fledgling area that shows promise. Best years: (Cabernet Sauvignon) (2007) 05 **04 02 00 99 98**.

CH. AUSONE★★★ *St-Émilion Grand Cru AC, 1er Grand Cru Classé, Bordeaux, France* This beautiful property is situated on what are perhaps the best slopes in ST-EMILION. Owner Alain Vauthier has taken it to new heights since 1996 and the wines now display stunning texture and depth and the promise of memorable maturity. A high proportion (50%) of Cabernet Franc beefs up the Merlot. Production is 16–20,000 bottles a year (CHEVAL BLANC makes 80,000). Second wine: La Chapelle d'Ausone. Best years: 2006 05 04 03 02 01 00 99 98 **97 96 95 94 90 89 88 86 85 83 82**.

AUXEY-DURESSES AC *Côte de Beaune, Burgundy, France* Auxey-Duresses is a backwater village up a valley behind MEURSAULT. The reds should be light and fresh but can often lack ripeness. At its best, and at 3–5 years, the white is dry, soft, nutty and hinting at the creaminess of a good Meursault, but at much lower prices. Of the Premiers Crus, Les Duresses is the most consistent. Best producers: (reds) Comte Armand★★, J-P Diconne★, Maison Leroy, Duc de Magenta★, M Prunier★, P Prunier★; (whites) R Ampeau★, d'Auvenay (Dom. LEROY)★★, J-P Diconne★, DROUHIN★, J-P Fichet★, Gras, Olivier LEFLAIVE★, Maison Leroy★, M Prunier★. Best years: (reds) (2007) 06 05 **03 02 99**; (whites) (2007) 06 **05 04 02 00**.

AVIGNONESI *Vino Nobile di Montepulciano DOCG, Tuscany, Italy* The Falvo brothers led Montepulciano's revival as one of TUSCANY's best zones. Although international wines like Il Marzocco★ (Chardonnay) and Desiderio★★ (Merlot-Cabernet) at one time received more attention, today the focus is back on the top-quality classics, VINO NOBILE★ and its superior version, made only in top years, Grandi Annate★★. The VIN SANTO★★★ is the most sought-after in Tuscany; there's also a rare red version from Sangiovese, Occhio di Pernice★★★. Best years: (Vino Nobile) (2007) (06) 04 **03 01 00 99**.

CH. D'AYDIE *Madiran AC, South-West France* The Laplace family owns thi
top MADIRAN château, whose main wine is a full-blown Tannat-base
Madiran★; a softer Madiran cuvée called Autour du Fruit blends Tanna
with a little Cabernet. There is also a simple, fruity Aramis Vin de Pay
du Comté Tolosan. Best years: (Château d'Aydie) (2005) 04 **03 01**.

BABICH *Henderson, North Island, New Zealand* Family-run winery with som
prime vineyard land in MARLBOROUGH and HAWKES BAY. Irongat
Chardonnay★ is an intense, steely wine that needs plenty of cellaring
while full-flavoured varietal reds under the Winemakers' Reserve labe
show even greater potential for development. Flagship wine Th
Patriarch★★ is a red BORDEAUX blend from Hawkes Bay. Marlboroug
wines include stylish Sauvignon Blanc★, tangy Riesling and light
fruity Pinot Gris. Best years: (premium Hawkes Bay reds) (2007) 06 **04 0
00 98**.

BACALHÔA VINHOS DE PORTUGAL *Terras do Sado, Portugal* Forward
looking operation, using Portuguese and foreign grapes with equal ease
Quinta da Bacalhôa★ is an oaky, meaty Cabernet-Merlot blend, Pálácí
da Bacalhôa★★ even better; Tinto da Ânfora★ a rich and figgy ALENTEJ
red (Grande Escolha★★ version is powerful and cedary); and Cova d
Ursa★ a toasty, rich Chardonnay. Portugal's finest sparkling wine
vintage-dated Loridos Extra Bruto★, is a decent CHAMPAGNE lookalike. S
Syrah ('só' means 'only' in Portuguese, as in 'only Syrah') is characterful
atypical. Also excellent 20-year-old Moscatel de SETUBAL★★.

BAD DÜRKHEIM *Pfalz, Germany* This spa town has some good vineyard
and is the headquarters of the dependable Vier Jahreszeiten co-op. Bes
producers: Darting, Fitz-Ritter, Hensel, Karl Schaefer★, Egon Schmitt. Bes
years: (2007) 05 **04 03 02 01 99 98 97**.

BADEN *Germany* Very large, 16,000ha (39,520-acre) wine region stretchin
from FRANKEN to the Bodensee (Lake Constance). Its dry whites and reds sho
off the fuller, softer flavours Germany can produce in the warmer climate o
its southerly regions. Many of the best non-Riesling German wines com
from here, as well as many of the best barrel-fermented and barrel-age
wines. Good co-operative cellars at Achkarren, Bötzingen, Britzingen
Durbach, Königsschaffhausen, Pfaffenweiler and Sasbach. See als
KAISERSTUHL, ORTENAU.

BAGA Important red grape in BAIRRADA, which has been one of the fe
regions in Portugal to rely mainly on one variety. Also planted in smalle
quantities in DÃO and the RIBATEJO. It can give deep, comple
blackberryish wine, but aggressive tannin is a continuing problem.

BAIRRADA DOC *Beira Litoral, Portugal* Bairrada, along with the DOURO, DÃ
and ALENTEJO, can be the source of many of Portugal's best red wine
These can brim over with intense raspberry and blackberry fruit, thoug
the tannin levels are severe and may take quite a few years to softe
Traditionally made from a minimum of 50% of the tannic Baga grap
rules changed in 2003 to admit a load of 'international' grapes into th
Bairrada fold. The whites are coming on fast with modern vinificatio
methods. With an Atlantic climate, vintages can be very variable. Bes
producers: (reds) Caves ALIANCA★, Quinta das Bágeiras★, Quinta de Baixo★
Campolargo★, Cantanhede co-op, Quinta do Encontro, Caves do Freixo
Caves Messias (Quinta do Valdoeiro Reserva★), Casa de Saima★★, Caves SA

JOAO★★, SOGRAPE, Sidónio de Sousa★★; (whites) Caves SAO JOAO★★, SOGRAPE (Reserva★, Quinta de Pedralvites★). Best years: (reds) 2005 **04 03 01 00 97**.

ALATONBOGLÁR WINERY *Transdanubia, Hungary* Premium winery in the Lake Balaton region, which has benefited from heavy investment and the expertise of viticulturist Dr Richard Smart and wine consultant Kym Milne, but still needs to work to improve quality, particularly in the inexpensive but dumbed-down range sold under the Chapel Hill label.

ALEARIC ISLANDS *Spain* Medium-bodied reds and soft rosés were the mainstays of Mallorca's 2 DO areas, Binissalem and Plà i Llevant, until the Anima Negra winery began turning out its impressive, deep reds from the native Callet grape. Best producers: Anima Negra★★, José L Ferrer/ Franja Roja, Hereus de Ribas, Miquel Gelabert★, Miquel Oliver, Son Bordils★.

ALNAVES *Coonawarra, South Australia* Long-term residents of COONAWARRA, the grape-growing Balnaves family decided to become involved in making wine in the mid-1990s. With the talented Pete Bissell as winemaker, Balnaves is now among the best producers in the region. Reserve Cabernet The Tally★★★ is complex, wonderfully structured and deeply flavoured; the regular Cabernet★ is well priced and an excellent example of Coonawarra style.

ANDOL AC *Provence, France* A lovely fishing port with vineyards high above the Mediterranean, producing some of the best reds and rosés in Provence. The Mourvèdre grape gives Bandol its character – dense colour, warm, smoky black fruit and a herby fragrance. The reds happily age for 10 years, sometimes more, but can be very good at 3–4. The rosés, delicious and spicy but often too pricey, should be drunk young. There is a small amount of neutral, overpriced white. Best producers: (reds) la Bastide Blanche★, la Bégude★, Bunan★, Frégate★, le Galantin★, J P Gaussen★★, Gros' Noré★, l'Hermitage★, Lafran-Veyrolles★, la Laidière★, Mas Redorne★, la Noblesse★, PIBARNON★★, Pradeaux★★, Ray-Jane★, Roche Redonne★, Romassan, Ste-Anne★, Salettes★, SORIN, de Souviou★, la Suffrène, Tempier★, Terrebrune★, la Tour du Bon★, VANNIERES★★. Best years: 2004 03 01 **00 99 98 97 96 95**.

ANFI *Brunello di Montalcino DOCG, Tuscany, Italy* High-tech American-owned firm which is now a force in Italy. Chardonnay (Fontanelle★), Cabernet (Tavernelle★★) and Merlot (Mandrielle★) are successful, but even better are BRUNELLO Riserva Poggio all'Oro★★ and Brunello Poggio alle Mura★★, the latter made from Sangiovese clones developed by Banfi themselves. SUPER-TUSCANS Summus★★ (a blend of Sangiovese, Cabernet and Syrah) and Excelsus★★ (Cabernet-Merlot) are also very good. Also has cellars (Vigne Regali) in PIEDMONT for GAVI and fizz. Best years: (top reds) (2007) (06) (04) **03 01 99 98 97**.

ANNOCKBURN *Geelong, Victoria, Australia* Bannockburn emerged after more than 25 years under Gary Farr as one of Australia's most highly regarded medium-sized wineries. Now that he has moved on to the family By FARR label, the challenge is there for winemaker Michael Glover to maintain this position. The most famous wines have been the powerful, gamy and controversial Pinot Noir★ (Serre★★), MEURSAULT-like Chardonnay★★ and my favourite, the complex and classy Alain GRAILLOT-influenced Shiraz★★. Best years: (Shiraz) (2006) 05 04 03 **02 01 00** 99 98 97 96 94 92 91.

BANYULS AC *Roussillon, France* One of the best *vins doux naturels*, made mainly from Grenache, with a strong plum and raisin flavour. Rimage - vintaged early bottlings – and tawny (*tuilé*) styles are the best. Generally served as an apéritif in France and deserves a wider audience. Best producers: Cellier des Templiers★, CHAPOUTIER, Clos de Paulilles★, l'Étoile★, MAS BLANC★★, la Rectorie★★, la Tour Vieille★, Vial Magnères★.

BARBADILLO *Jerez y Manzanilla DO, Andalucía, Spain* The largest sherry company in the coastal town of Sanlúcar de Barrameda makes a wide range of good to excellent wines, in particular salty, dry manzanilla style (Solear★★, En Rama unfiltered★★★) and intense, nutty, but dry amontillados and olorosos (Amontillado Principe★★, Oloroso Cuco★★). Neutral dry white Castillo de San Diego is a bestseller in Spain.

BARBARESCO DOCG *Piedmont, Italy* This prestigious red wine, grown in the LANGHE hills south-east of Turin, is often twinned with its neighbour BAROLO to demonstrate the nobility of the Nebbiolo grape. Barbaresco can be a shade softer and less powerful, and is not required by law to age as long (2 years minimum compared with 3), but at the top level is often indistinguishable from Barolo. As in Barolo, traditionalists excel, led by Bruno GIACOSA. Even though the area is relatively compact (575ha/1420 acres), styles can differ significantly between vineyards and producers. Best vineyards: Asili, Bricco di Neive, Crichet Pajè, Gallina, Marcorino, Martinenga, Messoirano, Moccagatta, Montestefano, Ovello, Pora, Rabajà, Rio Sordo, Santo Stefano, Serraboella, Sorì Paitin. Best producers: Barbaresco co-op★★, Piero Busso★, CERETTO★★, Cigliuti★★, Stefano Farina★★, Fontanabianca★★, GAJA★★★, GIACOSA★★★, Lano★, Marchesi di Gresy★★, Moccagatta★★, Fiorenzo Nada★★, Castello di Neive★★, Oddero★, Paitin★★, Pelissero★★, Pio Cesare★★, PRUNOTTO★, Albino Rocca★★, Bruno Rocca★★, Sottimano★★, La Spinetta★★, Castello di Verduno★★, Vietti★★. Best years: (2007) (06) 04 **03** 01 **00 99 98 97 96 95**

BARBERA A native of north-west Italy, Barbera vies with Sangiovese as the most widely planted red grape in the country. When grown for high yields its natural acidity shows through, producing vibrant quaffers. Low yields from the top PIEDMONT estates create intensely rich and complex wines. Oaked versions can be stunning. Significant plantings in California, Argentina and Australia.

BARBERA D'ALBA DOC *Piedmont, Italy* Some outstanding Barbera come from this appellation. The most modern examples are supple and generous and can be drunk almost at once. More intense, dark-fruited versions require at least 3 years' age, but might improve for as much as 8. Best producers: G Alessandria★★, ALTARE★, Azelia★★, Boglietti★★, Brovia★, CERETTO★, Cascina Chicco★, Cigliuti★, CLERICO★, Elvio Cogno★, Aldo CONTERNO★, Giacomo CONTERNO★★, Conterno-Fantino★, Corino★★, Correggia★★, Elio Grasso★, Giuseppe MASCARELLO★, Moccagatta★, M Molino★★, Monfalletto-Cordero di Montezemolo★★, Oberto★★, Parusso★★, Pelissero★, F Principiano★★, PRUNOTTO★★, RATTI★, Albino Rocca★★, Bruno Rocca★, SANDRONE★★, P Scavino★★, La Spinetta★★, Vajra★★, Mauro Veglio★★, Vietti★★, Gianni Voerzio★★, Roberto VOERZIO★★★. Best years: (2007) 06 **04 03** 01.

BARBERA D'ASTI DOC *Piedmont, Italy* While Dolcetto d'Asti is usually light and simple, wines made from Barbera show a greater range of quality. Unoaked and barrique-aged examples can compete with the best

BARBERA D'ALBA and rival some of the better Nebbiolo-based reds. Best examples can be kept for 5–6 years, occasionally longer. **Best producers:** Araldica/Alasia★, La Barbatella★★, Pietro Barbero★★, Bava★, Bertelli★★, Braida★★, Cascina Castlèt★, Coppo★★, Hastae (Quorum★), Martinetti★★, Il Mongetto★★, PRUNOTTO★★, Cantine Sant'Agata★, La Spinetta★★, Vietti★★, Vinchio-Vaglio Serra co-op★. **Best years:** (2007) 06 **04 03 01**.

BARDOLINO DOC *Veneto, Italy* Zone centred on Lake Garda, giving, at best, light, scented red and rosé (*chiaretto*) wines to be drunk young, from the same grape mix as neighbouring VALPOLICELLA. Bardolino Superiore is now DOCG. **Best producers:** Cavalchina★, Corte Gardoni★, Guerrieri-Rizzardi★, Le Fraghe, MASI, Le Vigne di San Pietro★, Zeni.

BAROLO DOCG *Piedmont, Italy* Renowned red wine, named after a village south-west of Alba, from the Nebbiolo grape grown in around 1500ha (3700 acres) of vineyards in the steep LANGHE hills, the best coming from near the top (*bricco*) of those hills. Having in the post-WWII period gone to excesses of austerity, Barolo in the 1990s almost threatened to go too far in the other direction, its subtle floral/wild fruit aromas being drowned all too often under expensive but irrelevant oak smells of vanilla and toast. Thankfully 21st-century producers are finding their way back to the 'tar and roses' of the grape while managing to keep Nebbiolo's fierce tannins and biting acidity under control. Distinct styles of wine are said to be made in the zone's villages, though individual producers may make wines not conforming to the mould. Barolo and La Morra make the most perfumed wines; Monforte and Serralunga the most structured; Castiglione Falletto strikes a balance between the two. Barolo is nowadays frequently labelled by vineyard, though the producer's reputation often carries more weight. **Best vineyards:** Arione, Bricco delle Viole, Brunate, Bussia Soprana, Cannubi Boschis, Case Nere, Cerequio, Conca dell'Annunziata, Fiasco, Francia, Gavarini, Giachini, Ginestra, Monfalletto, Monprivato, Rocche dell'Annunziata, Rocche di Castiglione, Santo Stefano di Perno, La Serra, Vigna Rionda, Villero. **Best producers:** C Alario★★, G Alessandria★★, ALTARE★★, Azelia★★, Boglietti★★, Bongiovanni★★, Brovia★★, Burlotto★★, Cappellano★★, CERETTO★★, CHIARLO★, CLERICO★★★, Poderi Colla★, Aldo CONTERNO★★, Giacomo CONTERNO★★★, Conterno-Fantino★★, Corino★★, Luigi Einaudi★★, GIACOSA★★★, Elio Grasso★★, M Marengo★★, Bartolo MASCARELLO★★, Giuseppe MASCARELLO★★★, Monfalletto-Cordero di Montezemolo★★, Oberto★★, Oddero★★, Parusso★★, Pio Cesare★★, Pira★★, E Pira & Figli★★, F Principiano★, PRUNOTTO★★, Renato RATTI★, Revello★★, Giuseppe Rinaldi, Rocche dei Manzoni★★, SANDRONE★★★, P Scavino★★, M Sebaste★★, Vajra★★, Mauro Veglio★★, Vietti★★, Vigna Rionda★★, Gianni Voerzio★★, Roberto VOERZIO★★★. **Best years:** (2007) (06) 04 03 01 **00 99 98 97 96 95 90 89 88**.

BAROSSA VALLEY See pages 70–1.

BAROSSA VALLEY ESTATE *Barossa, South Australia* Half owned by local growers, with some of the best-sited vineyards in BAROSSA, and half by industry giant HARDY. Flagship reds are huge, gutsy Barossa beauties E&E Black Pepper Shiraz★★, Ebenezer Shiraz★★ and E&E Sparkling Shiraz★★, all of them bursting with ripe plum fruit, spice and plenty of vanilla oak. Other Ebenezer wines include intense, full-flavoured sparkling Pinot Noir. Excellent value in the E Bass Shiraz and budget-priced E Minor range. **Best years:** (E&E Black Pepper Shiraz) (2006) (05) (04) 02 **01 99 98 96 94**.

BAROSSA

South Australia

The Barossa Valley, an hour or so's drive north of Adelaide in South Australia, is the heart of the Australian wine industry. The giants of the industry have their major wineries here – Jacob's Creek, Wolf Blass, Penfolds and Yalumba – alongside around 50 or so smaller wineries, producing or processing up to 60% of the nation's wine. However, this percentage is based mostly on grapes trucked in from other regions, because the Barossa's vineyards themselves grow less than 10% of Australia's grapes. Yet Barossa-grown grapes, once rejected as uneconomical for their low yields, are now increasingly prized for those same low yields.

Why? Well, it's highly likely that the world's oldest vines are in the Barossa. The valley was settled in the 1840s by Lutheran immigrants from Silesia, who brought with them vines from Europe, most importantly, as it turned out, cuttings from the Syrah (or Shiraz) variety of France's Rhône Valley. And because Barossa has never been affected by the phylloxera louse, which destroyed many of the world's vineyards in the late 19th century, today you can still see gnarled, twisted old vines sporting just a few tiny bunches of priceless fruit that were planted by refugees from Europe all of a century and a half ago, and are still tended by their descendants. A new wave of winemakers has taken up the cause of the Barossa vines with much zeal and no small amount of national pride, and they now produce from them some of the deepest, most fascinating wines, not just in Australia, but in the world.

GRAPE VARIETIES

Shiraz is prized above all other Barossa grapes, able to conjure headswirling, palate-dousing flavours. Barossa is the main source of Shiraz grapes for Penfolds Grange, the wine that began the revolution in Australian red wine in the 1950s. Cabernet Sauvignon can be very good in the best years and similarly potent, as are the Rhône varieties of head Grenache and deliciously earthy Mourvèdre; some of the most exciting examples are from the original vines planted in the 19th century. All these varieties are largely grown on the hot, dry, valley floor, but just to the east lie the Barossa Ranges, and in these higher, cooler vineyards especially in those of the neighbouring Eden Valley, some of Australia's best and most fashionable Rieslings are grown, prized for their steely attack and lime fragrance. But even here you can't get away from Shiraz and some thrilling examples come from the hills, not least Henschke's Hill of Grace and Mount Edelstone.

CLASSIFICATIONS

The Barossa was among the first zones to be ratified within the Australian system of Geographical Indications and comprises the regions of Barossa Valley and Eden Valley. The Barossa lies within South Australia's collective 'super zone' of Adelaide.

See also GRANGE, SOUTH AUSTRALIA; and individual producers.

BEST YEARS

(Barossa Valley Shiraz) (2006) 05 04 **03 02 01 00 99 98 97 96 94 91 90 88**; (Eden Valley Riesling) 2007 06 05 04 03 02 **01 00 99 98 97 96 95 94 92 91 90 87**

BEST PRODUCERS

Shiraz-based reds
BAROSSA VALLEY ESTATE, Bethany, Rolf BINDER, Grant BURGE, Burge Family, Dutschke, Elderton (Command), GLAETZER, Greenock Creek (Block Shiraz, Seven Acres), HENSCHKE, Hewitson, JACOB'S CREEK (Centenary Hill), Jenke, Trevor Jones, Langmeil, Peter LEHMANN, Charles MELTON, PENFOLDS (RWT, GRANGE), Chris Ringland, ROCKFORD, ST HALLETT, Saltram, Schild Estate, Tim Smith, Spinifex, Thorn Clarke, TORBRECK, Torzi Matthews, TURKEY FLAT, Two Hands, The Willows, YALUMBA (Octavius).

Riesling
Bethany, Wolf BLASS (Gold Label), Grant BURGE, Leo Buring (Leonay), HENSCHKE, Hewitson, JACOB'S CREEK (Steingarten), Peter LEHMANN, Radford Dale, Ross Estate, ST HALLETT, Torzi Matthews, YALUMBA (Heggies, Mesh/with Jeffrey GROSSET, Pewsey Vale).

Cabernet Sauvignon-based reds
Rolf BINDER, Grant BURGE, Greenock Creek, HENSCHKE, Peter LEHMANN, ST HALLETT, The Willows.

Other reds (Grenache, Mourvèdre, Shiraz)
Rolf BINDER, Grant BURGE, Burge Family (Olive Hill), Charles Cimicky (Grenache), Elderton (CSM), HENSCHKE, Jenke (Mourvèdre), Langmeil, Peter LEHMANN, Charles MELTON, PENFOLDS (Bin 138 Old Vine), TORBRECK, TURKEY FLAT (Butcher's Block, Grenache Noir), Two Hands.

Semillon
Grant BURGE, HENSCHKE, Heritage, Jenke, Peter LEHMANN, ROCKFORD, TURKEY FLAT, The Willows.

71

JIM BARRY *Clare Valley, South Australia* After buying Australia's most famou
Riesling vineyard in 1986, they had to wait until 2005 for the trademark
to expire. Now Jim Barry has a flagship white, The Florita★, to head
quartet of classy, perfumed Rieslings. Medium-priced Lodge Hil
Shiraz★ is impressive, but the winery is best known for its rich, fruit
McRae Wood Shiraz★★ and heady, palate-busting Armagh Shiraz★★
Best years: (Armagh Shiraz) (2006) (05) 04 02 **01 99 98 96 95 92 89**.

BARSAC AC *Bordeaux, France* Barsac, lying close to the river Garonne and
with the little river Ciron running along its eastern boundary, is the
largest of the 5 communes in the SAUTERNES AC, and also has its own AC
which is used by most, but by no means all, of the top properties. In
general, the wines are a little less luscious than other Sauternes, but from
good estates they can be marvellous. **Best producers:** CLIMENS★★★
COUTET★★, DOISY-DAENE★★, Doisy-Dubroca★, DOISY-VEDRINES★★, Myrat★
NAIRAC★, Piada, Suau★. **Best years:** (2007) 05 **03 02 01 99 98 97 96 95 90 89**
88 86 83.

BASILICATA *Italy* Southern Italian region best known for one wine, the
potentially excellent, gutsy red called AGLIANICO DEL VULTURE.

BASSERMANN-JORDAN *Deidesheim, Pfalz, Germany* Since 1996, this
famous estate has been making rich yet elegant Rieslings of ★★ quality
from Deidesheim and FORST. **Best years:** (2007) 06 05 04 **03 02 01 99 98 97**
96 90.

CH. BATAILLEY★ *Pauillac AC, 5ème Cru Classé, Haut-Médoc, Bordeaux, France* A
byword for reliability and value for money among the PAUILLAC Classed
Growth estates. Marked by a full, obvious blackcurrant fruit, not too
much tannin and a luscious overlay of creamy vanilla. Lovely to drink a
only 5 years old, the wine continues to age well for at least 15 years. Bes
years: 2006 05 04 **03 02 00 98 96 95 94 90 89 88**.

BÂTARD-MONTRACHET AC *Grand Cru, Côte de Beaune, Burgundy, France*
This Grand Cru produces some of the world's greatest whites – full, rich
and balanced, with a powerful mineral intensity of fruit and fresh acidity
There are 2 associated Grands Crus: Bienvenues-Bâtard-Montrachet
and the minuscule Criots-Bâtard-Montrachet. All can age for a decade -
indeed, they ought to. **Best producers:** Blain-Gagnard★★, CARILLON★★★
DROUHIN★★★, Fontaine-Gagnard★★, J-N GAGNARD★★★, JADOT★★★, Louis
LATOUR★★, Dom. LEFLAIVE★★★, Olivier LEFLAIVE★★, Marc Morey★★★, Pierre
Morey★★★, Michel Niellon★★★, RAMONET★★★, SAUZET★★★, VERGET★★★
Best years: (2007) 06 05 04 03 02 01 **00 99 97 95 92 90 89**.

DOM. DES BAUMARD *Coteaux du Layon, Loire Valley, France* Well-sited
vineyards produce sensational QUARTS DE CHAUME★★★ that require
aging, as well as rich, honeyed, impeccably balanced COTEAUX DU LAYON
Clos de Ste-Cathérine★★. Also fine steely, mineral-scented SAVENNIERE
Clos du Papillon★★ and Clos St-Yves★★, with a late-harvest Tri
Spéciale★★ in top years. Idiosyncratic Vert de l'Or Verdelho varies in
sweetness according to vintage. CREMANT DE LOIRE and ANJOU reds are OK
but unexciting. Baumard made waves in 2006, switching all production
to Stelvin screwcap closures. **Best years:** (Quarts de Chaume) (2006) 05 0
02 **01 99 97 96 95 90 89**.

LES BAUX-DE-PROVENCE AC *Provence, France* This AC has proved that
organic and biodynamic farming can produce spectacular results, mainly
due to the warm dry climate. Good fruit and intelligent winemaking

produce some of the more easily enjoyable reds in Provence. Best producers: Hauvette★, Lauzières, Mas de la Dame★, Mas de Gourgonnier★, Mas Ste-Berthe★, ROMANIN★, Terres Blanches★. Best years: 2004 03 **02 01 00** 99 98 97.

BAY OF FIRES *Tasmania, Australia* The Tasmanian arm of Constellation has become more important in the past decade as HARDY's chief sparkling winemaker, Ed Carr, has increasingly focused on the region's ultra-cool climate. Hardy's best bubbly has been rebranded Bay of Fires Arras★★. There are also excellent sparkling wines under the Bay of Fires★ and Tigress★ labels as well as a brilliant range of cool-climate table wines which are the responsibility of talented Fran Austin.

BÉARN AC *South-West France* While the rest of South-West France has been producing some original flavours in recent years, Béarn's wines (90% red and rosé) are rarely special, despite some decent grape varieties. However, there seems to have been an improvement in quality since 2000. Best producers: Bellocq co-op, Cauhapé, Guilhemas, Lapeyre★, Nigri.

CH. DE BEAUCASTEL *Châteauneuf-du-Pape AC, Rhône Valley, France* The Perrin family makes some of the richest, most profound reds (often ★★★) in CHATEAUNEUF-DU-PAPE, with an unusually high percentage of Mourvèdre and Syrah, which can take at least a decade to show at their best. The white Roussanne Vieilles Vignes★★★ is exquisite and long-lived. They also produce COTES DU RHONE Coudoulet de Beaucastel red★★ and white★ and, under the Domaines Perrin label, a range of increasingly good southern reds, including RASTEAU★ and VINSOBRES★. Best years: (reds) (2007) 06 05 04 **03 01 00** 99 98 97 96 95 94 90 89 88 86 85; (whites) 2007 06 05 04 **03 01 00 99 98 97** 96 95 94 93 90.

BEAUJOLAIS AC *Beaujolais, Burgundy, France* Wine region in the beautiful hills that stretch down from Mâcon to Lyon, producing predominantly red wine from the Gamay grape in prolific quantities. Beaujolais is best known for BEAUJOLAIS NOUVEAU, which accounts for 40% of the production. The better-quality reds, each having their own appellation, come from the north of the region are BEAUJOLAIS-VILLAGES and the 10 single Cru villages; from north to south these are ST-AMOUR, JULIENAS, MOULIN-A-VENT, CHENAS, FLEURIE, CHIROUBLES, MORGON, REGNIE, BROUILLY and COTE DE BROUILLY. In good vintages simple Beaujolais is light, fresh, aromatic and delicious to drink, but in poorer vintages the wine can be drab and acidic. A little rosé is also made from Gamay, and a small quantity of Beaujolais Blanc is made from Chardonnay. Best producers: (reds) J-P Brun/Terres Dorées, L & J-M Charmet/La Ronze★, Chatelus, DUBOEUF, J-F Garlon★, JADOT.

BEAUJOLAIS NOUVEAU *Beaujolais AC, Burgundy, France* Also known as Beaujolais Primeur, this is the first release of bouncy, fruity Beaujolais on the third Thursday of November after the harvest. Once a simple celebration of the new vintage, then over-hyped, and now enjoyed by the true Beaujolais lover. Quality is generally reasonable and the wine is delicious until Christmas and the New Year, but thereafter, while drinkable, is likely to throw a slight sediment.

BEAUJOLAIS-VILLAGES AC *Beaujolais, Burgundy, France* Beaujolais-Villages can come from one of 38 villages in the north of the region. The best examples rival the BEAUJOLAIS Crus, having more body, character, complexity and elegance than simple Beaujolais and representing all the pleasure of the Gamay grape at its best. Best villages in addition to the 10 Crus are Lancié, Quincié and Perréon. Best producers: (reds) Ch. de Belleverne★, G Descombes★, DUBOEUF, Ch. du Pavé★.

BEAULIEU VINEYARD *Napa Valley AVA, California, USA* The late André Tchelistcheff, winemaker from the 1930s to the late 60s, had a major role in creating this icon for Napa Cabernet. After he left, Beaulieu lived on its reputation for too long. However, Private Reserve Cabernet Sauvignon★ seems to have returned to form. Tapestry★ (meritage red) is good, as are Chardonnay★ and Pinot Noir★ from CARNEROS, and Syrah★. Recent small-lot Cabernets Clone 4 and Clone 6 are fascinating. Best years: (Private Reserve) 2004 03 **01 00 99** 98 97 96 95 94 92 91 90 87 86 84.

BEAUMES-DE-VENISE AC *Rhône Valley, France* Area famous for its scented, honeyed sweet wine, MUSCAT DE BEAUMES-DE-VENISE. The local red wine is also very good, and received its own appellation from the 2004 vintage. It is full of dark fruit and crisp tannins and can age well for 8–10 years. Best producers: (reds) Balma Venitia (Beaumes-de-Venise) co-op, Beaumalric, Bernardins, Cassan★, Durban★, Fenouillet, les Goubert, Redortier.

BEAUNE AC *Côte de Beaune, Burgundy, France* Most of the wines are red, with delicious, soft red-fruits ripeness. There are no Grands Crus but some excellent Premiers Crus, especially Boucherottes, Bressandes, Clos des Mouches, Fèves, Grèves, Marconnets, Teurons, Vignes Franches. White-wine production is increasing – DROUHIN makes outstanding, creamy, nutty Clos des Mouches★★★. Best producers: (growers) Germain/Ch. de Chorey★★, LAFARGE★★, de MONTILLE★, Albert Morot★, Rateau, TOLLOT-BEAUT★★; (merchants) BOUCHARD PERE ET FILS★★, Champy★, Chanson★, DROUHIN★★, Camille Giroud★★, JADOT★★, Labouré-Roi★. Best years: (reds) (2007) 06 05 **03 02 99**; (whites) (2007) 06 **05 04** 02.

CH. BEAU-SÉJOUR BÉCOT★★ *St-Émilion Grand Cru AC, 1er Grand Cru Classé, Bordeaux, France* Demoted from Premier Grand Cru Classé in 1986 and promoted again in 1996, this estate is on top form. Brothers Gérard and Dominique Bécot produce firm, ripe, richly textured wines that need at least 8–10 years to develop. Best years: 2006 05 04 **03 02** 01 00 **99** 98 96 95 90 89 88 86 85.

BEAUX FRÈRES *Willamette Valley AVA, Oregon, USA* The goal here is to make ripe, unfiltered Pinot Noir★★ that expresses the essence of their 10ha (24-acre) vineyard atop Ribbon Ridge in the Chehalem Valley. A parcel known as the Upper Terrace★★★ yields exceptional fruit from Dijon clones. Best years: 2006 05 **04 03** 02.

Beaux Frères
2005 Pinot Noir
The Beaux Frères Vineyard

GRAHAM BECK WINES *Robertson WO, South Africa* A 2-cellar operation, overseen by Pieter Ferreira. ROBERTSON's potential for Cap Classique sparkling is realized in an elegant, rich NV Brut★, a toastily fragrant, creamy, barrel-fermented and ageworthy Blanc de Blancs★ and an occasional quirky sparkling Pinotage★. Single-vineyard duo The Ridge Syrah★ and flavoursome, succulent Lonehill Chardonnay★ lead the Robertson table wines. Viognier is good too. Top wines from FRANSCHHOEK include Old Road Pinotage★, The Joshua Shiraz-Viognier★★, DURBANVILLE-sourced Pheasants' Run Sauvignon Blanc★ and single-vineyard Coffestone Cabernet★. The William★, a Cabernet Sauvignon-Pinotage blend, shows much promise and aging potential.

J B BECKER *Walluf, Rheingau, Germany* Becker specializes in long-lived dry Rieslings – usually ★, some Spätlese trocken ★★. He also makes impressive dry Spätburgunder★ (Pinot Noir) reds. Best years: (Riesling Spätlese trocken) (2007) 06 05 04 **03 02** 01 99.

BEDELL CELLARS *Long Island, New York State, USA* Winemaker Kip Bedell helped establish LONG ISLAND's reputation with his Bordeaux-styled Merlot★ (Reserve★★) and red blends. The wines have continued to improve under new ownership, with Bedell still chief winemaker. Sister winery Corey Creek produces a noteworthy Gewürztraminer.

BEECHWORTH *Victoria, Australia* Beechworth was best known as Ned Kelly country before Rick Kinzbrunner planted the hilly slopes of sub-Alpine north-east Victoria and started making wines at GIACONDA. Now boutique wineries produce tiny volumes at high prices and are on a steep learning curve. BROKENWOOD has a major new vineyard here. Best producers: Amulet (Shiraz★★), Castanga★ (Shiraz★★), Cow Hill★, GIACONDA★★★, Savaterre (Chardonnay★★), Sorrenberg★.

BEIRAS *Portugal* This large, central Portuguese province includes the DOCs of DAO, BAIRRADA, Távora-Varosa and Beira Interior. Vinho Regional wines use Portuguese red and white varieties along with international grapes such as Cabernet Sauvignon and Chardonnay. Best producers: Caves ALIANCA, Quinta do Cardo, D F J VINHOS (Bela Fonte), Figueira de Castelo Rodrigo co-op, Quinta de Foz de Arouce★, Filipa PATO★, Luís PATO★★, Rogenda, Caves SAO JOAO (Quinta do Poço do Lobo), Quinta dos Termos. Best years: 2005 **04 03 01 00**.

CH. BELAIR★★ *St-Émilion Grand Cru AC, 1er Grand Cru Classé, Bordeaux, France* Belair is next to AUSONE on ST-EMILION's limestone plateau. Under owner-winemaker Pascal Delbeck the estate has been run biodynamically since 1994, and the soft, supremely stylish wines are currently on top form. Drinkable at 5–6 years, but also capable of long aging. Best years: 2006 05 04 **03 02 01 00** 99 98 95 90 89 88 86 85.

BELLAVISTA *Franciacorta DOCG, Lombardy, Italy* Specialist in FRANCIACORTA sparkling wines, with a very good Cuvée Brut★★ and 4 distinctive Gran Cuvées★★ (including an excellent rosé). Riserva Vittorio Moretti Extra Brut★★ is made in exceptional years. Also produces lovely still wines, including white blend Convento dell'Annunciata★★★, Chardonnay Uccellanda★★ and red Casotte★ (Pinot Nero) and Solesine★★ (Cabernet-Merlot).

BELLET AC *Provence, France* Tiny AC in the hills behind Nice; the wine, mostly white, is usually overpriced. Ch. de Bellet★, Ch. de Crémat★ and Dom. de Toasc are the most important producers. Best years: (2006) 05 **04**.

BENDIGO *Central Victoria, Australia* Warm, dry, former gold-mining region, which is now home to about 40 small-scale, high-quality wineries. The best wines are rich, ripe, distinctively minty Shiraz and Cabernet. Best producers: Balgownie, Blackjack★, Bress, Chateau Leamon, Passing Clouds, PONDALOWIE★, Turner's Crossing, Water Wheel. Best years: (Shiraz) (2006) 05 04 03 **02 01 00** 99 98 97 95 94 93 91 90.

BERBERANA *Rioja DOCa, Rioja, Spain* Now part of Spain's second largest wine company, Arco Bodegas Unidas, incorporating Lagunilla, Marqués de Monistrol and Dominio de Súsar, Berberana makes a pleasant, lightly oaked Crianza and respectable Reservas and Gran Reservas. Best years: (Reserva) 2004 **03 01** 98 96 95 94.

BERCHER *Burkheim, Baden, Germany* A top KAISERSTUHL estate. High points are the powerful oak-aged Spätburgunder★★ (Pinot Noir) reds, Grau-burgunder★★ (Pinot Gris) dry whites, which marry richness with perfect balance, and dry Muskateller★, which is firm, elegant and tangy. Best years: (whites) (2007) 06 05 **04** 03 02 01; (reds) (2007) 06 05 04 **03** 02 01.

BERGERAC AC *South-West France* Bergerac is the main town of the southern Dordogne and the overall AC for this underrated and improving area on the eastern edge of Bordeaux. The grape varieties are mostly the same as those used in the BORDEAUX ACs. The red is generally like a light, fresh claret, a bit grassy but with a good, raw blackcurrant fruit and hint of earth. Côtes de Bergerac AC wines have a higher minimum alcohol level. In general drink young, although a few estate reds can age for at least 3–5 years. Whites are generally fresh and dry for early drinking. **Best producers:** l'ANCIENNE CURE★, Bélingard, la Colline★, Court-les-Mûts, Eyssards, Les Miaudoux, Monestier, les Nicots, Panisseau, TOUR DES GENDRES★★, Tourmentine, les Verdots★. **Best years:** (reds) 2005 **04 03 02 01 00 98 96**.

BERGSTRÖM *Willamette Valley AVA, Oregon, USA* The Bergström family uses biodynamic farming to bring out the best character from the terroir of their 9ha (23-acre) estate vineyard. The primary focus is on Pinot Noir, with Bergström Vineyard Estate★★ and de Lancellotti Vineyard Estate★★ forming the greater part of the production. Pinot Noir Cumberland Reserve★★★ is a multi-vineyard blend that can rival many fine Burgundies in its complexity. Also small amounts of Chardonnay★, Sauvignon Blanc and Riesling★★. **Best years:** (reds) 2006 **05 04**.

BERINGER *Napa Valley AVA, California, USA* Beringer, part of the Foster's Wine Group, offers a serious range of top-class Cabernet Sauvignons. The Private Reserve Cabernet can be ★★★ and is one of NAPA VALLEY's finest yet most approachable; the Chabot Vineyard★★ can be equally impressive. The Knight's Valley Cabernet Sauvignon★ is made in a lighter style and is good value. Beringer also makes red★ and white★ Alluvium (meritage wines) from Knight's Valley. The powerful Private Reserve Chardonnay★★ is ripe and toasty. Bancroft Ranch Merlot★★ from HOWELL MOUNTAIN is also very good. **Best years:** (Cabernet Sauvignon) 2005 03 02 **01 00 99 98 97 96 95 94 93 91 90 87 86 84 81**.

BERNKASTEL *Mosel, Germany* Both a historic wine town in the Middle MOSEL and a large Bereich. Top wines, however, come only from vineyard sites within the town – the most famous of these is the overpriced Doctor vineyard. Many wines from the Graben and Lay sites are often as good and cost a fraction of the price. **Best producers:** Dr LOOSEN★★, Pauly-Bergweiler★, J J PRÜM★★, S A PRÜM★, SELBACH-OSTER★★, Studert-Prüm★, Dr H Thanisch★, WEGELER★★. **Best years:** (2007) **06 05 04 02 01 99 98 97 95**.

BEST'S *Grampians, Victoria, Australia* Viv and Chris Thomson run this historic winery, with vineyards dating back to 1868. There have been more recent plantings in the GRAMPIANS and at Lake Boga in the Murray Darling region. There are three ranges: As the Crow Flies quaffers from Lake Boga; medium-priced Kindred Spirits; and the premium Great Western wines. Of these the Bin No. 0 Shiraz★★ is superb, the Cabernet★ is good, and the Riesling★ shows flashes of brilliance. The Thomson Family Shiraz★★ is an outstanding cool-climate Shiraz. **Best years:** (Thomson Family Shiraz) (2006) 05 04 01 **99 98 97 95 94 93 91 90**.

BETZ FAMILY WINERY *Columbia Valley AVA, Washington State, USA* Bob Betz MW spent decades travelling the wine world promoting Washington wines before staking a claim in the goldrush of this young industry. Since 1997, he has crafted wines of uniquely stylish character. His BORDEAUX-style blends are the more sedate. Betz Family Clos de Betz★ is an easy-to-drink, early-maturing red. The Cabernet Sauvignon Père de Famille★★ is an ageworthy, powerful wine, spending time in a blend of new and used French oak. The Syrah La Côte Rousse★, named for its Red Mountain origin, is opulent; Syrah La Serenne★★ shows more polish and finesse. Best years: (2007) **05 06 05 04 01 99**.

CH. BEYCHEVELLE★ *St-Julien AC, 4ème Cru Classé, Haut-Médoc, Bordeaux, France* This beautiful château can make wine of Second Growth quality. It has a charming softness even when young, but takes at least a decade to mature into ST-JULIEN's famous cedarwood and blackcurrant flavour. In the best years it is worth its high price and, after a period of inconsistency, quality has become more regular since the late 1990s. Second wine: Amiral de Beychevelle. Best years: 2006 05 04 **03** 00 **99 98 96 95 90 89**.

BEYERSKLOOF *Stellenbosch WO, South Africa* Pinotage (Reserve★★) rules at maestro Beyers Truter's property: it contributes to every style from good fizz to a traditional vintage port style, including a flavoursome dry Pinotage rosé and two versions of a succulent Cabernet-Pinotage-Merlot blend called Synergy (Reserve★). There's also the striking Cabernet Sauvignon-based Field Blend★★ (previously named Beyerskloof). Best years: (Field Blend/Beyerskloof) **2003 02 01 00 99 98 97 96 95**.

BIANCO DI CUSTOZA DOC *Veneto, Italy* Dry white wine from the shores of Lake Garda, made from a blend of grapes including SOAVE's Garganega. Drink young. Best producers: Cavalchina★, Gorgo★, Montresor★, Le Vigne di San Pietro★, Zeni★.

BIENVENUES-BÂTARD-MONTRACHET AC See BATARD-MONTRACHET.

BIERZO DO *Castilla y León, Spain* Sandwiched between the rainy mountains of GALICIA and the arid plains of CASTILLA Y LEON. The arrival of Alvaro PALACIOS, of PRIORAT fame, and his nephew Ricardo Pérez Palacios, with their inspired Corullón★★ red, shed an entirely new and exciting light on the potential of the Mencía grape. Best producers: Bodega del Abad★, Casar de Burbia★, Pérez Caramés, Castro Ventosa★, Estefanía, Luna Beberide★, Paixar★★, Descendientes de José Palacios★★, Peique★, Pittacum★, Prada a Tope, Dominio de Tares★, Valtuille★★.

JOSEF BIFFAR *Deidesheim, Pfalz, Germany* Frequent changes in winemaker have led to somewhat inconsistent dry and sweet Rieslings (often ★, sometimes ★★) from Deidesheim, Ruppertsberg and WACHENHEIM. Best years: (2007) 06 05 04 **03 02 01 99** 98.

BILLECART-SALMON *Champagne AC, Champagne, France* High-quality family-controlled CHAMPAGNE house which makes extremely elegant wines that become irresistible with age. Greatly increased volumes have dumbed down the non-vintage Brut★, but non-

vintage Brut Rosé★★, Blanc de Blancs★★★, vintage Cuvée N-F Billecart★★★ and Cuvée Elisabeth Salmon Rosé★★ are all excellent. Clos Saint-Hilaire★★★ is a single-vineyard vintage Blanc de Noirs. Best years: (2000) 98 **97** 96 **95 90 89** 88 86 85 82.

ROLF BINDER *Barossa, South Australia* Rolf and Christa Binder's family winery was known as Veritas until 2004, when the name was changed to avoid confusion with a Veritas winery in the US. The motto *In vino veritas* – In wine there is truth – still holds true. There's certainly truth in the bottom of a bottle of Hanisch Shiraz★★★ or Heysen Shiraz★★★. The Shiraz-Mataro Pressings★★ (known locally as Bull's Blood) and

'Heinrich' Shiraz-Grenache-Mataro★★ blends are lovely big reds; Cabernet-Merlot★★ is also good. Under the Christa Rolf label, Shiraz-Grenache★ is good and spicy with attractive, forward black fruit.

BINGEN *Rheinhessen, Germany* A small town and also a Bereich, the vineyards of which fall in both the NAHE and RHEINHESSEN. The best vineyard is the Scharlachberg, which produces some exciting wines, stinging with racy acidity, and the whiff of minerals. **Best producers:** Kruger-Rumpf, Villa Sachsen. **Best years:** (2007) 06 05 04 **02 01 99**.

BIONDI-SANTI *Brunello di Montalcino DOCG, Tuscany, Italy* Franco Biondi-Santi's Il Greppo estate has created both a legend and an international standing for BRUNELLO DI MONTALCINO. The Biondi-Santi style has remained deeply traditional, while that of other producers has moved on. The very expensive Riserva★★, with formidable levels of tannin and acidity, deserves a minimum 10 years' further aging after release before serious judgement is passed on it. Franco's son, Jacopo, has created his own range of wines, including Sassoalloro★★, a barrique-aged Sangiovese, and Sangiovese-Cabernet-Merlot blend Schidione★★. **Best years:** (Riserva) (2007) (06) (04) (03) (01) (99) 97 95 90 88 **85 83 82 75 64 55 45**.

BLAGNY AC *Côte de Beaune, Burgundy, France* The red wine from this tiny hamlet above MEURSAULT and PULIGNY-MONTRACHET can be fair value, if you like a rustic Burgundy. Actually much more Chardonnay than Pinot Noir is grown here, but this is sold as Puligny-Montrachet, Meursault Premier Cru or Meursault-Blagny. **Best producers:** R Ampeau★, Lamy-Pillot★, Matrot★. **Best years:** (2007) 06 05 **04 03 02 99**.

DOM. PAUL BLANCK *Alsace AC, Alsace, France* One of ALSACE's most interesting and reliable domaines, although real character only shows in the Grand Cru wines. Riesling★★ and Vieilles Vignes Gewurztraminer★★ from the Furstentum Grand Cru (also the source of super-rich Pinot Gris SGN★★★) stand out. Riesling Schlossberg★★ and Pinot Gris Altenbourg★★ offer depth and finesse. **Best years:** (Grand Cru Riesling) (2007) 05 **04 02 01 00 98 97 96 95**.

BLANQUETTE DE LIMOUX AC *Languedoc-Roussillon, France* Sharp, refreshing fizz from the Mauzac grape, which makes up a minimum 90% of the wine and gives it its striking 'green apple skin' flavour – the balance is made up of Chardonnay and Chenin Blanc. The traditional (CHAMPAGNE) method is used. The more rustic *méthode rurale*, finishing off the original fermentation inside the bottle, is used under a separate appellation, Blanquette Méthode Ancestrale. **Best producers:** Collin, Fourn★, Guinot, Martinolles★, SIEUR D'ARQUES★, les Terres Blanches. See also CREMANT DE LIMOUX AC and pages 276–7.

WOLF BLASS *Barossa Valley, South Australia* Wolf Blass, with its huge range, remains a cornerstone (with PENFOLDS) of Australia's largest wine company, the Foster's Wine Group. The wines do still faintly reflect the founder's dictum that they must be easy to enjoy, though I long for them to do better. The reds show overt oak, sometimes clumsy, and occasionally capture the traditional Blass mint and blackcurrant charm. Whites are on the oaky side, except for the Rieslings, which are good, though sweeter and less vibrant than they used to be, including Gold Label Riesling★. Black Label★, a red blend released at 4 years old, is expensive but good. Ultra-expensive Platinum Label Shiraz★ is quite impressive. Regional varietals under the Blass label reflect the winemaking style rather than regional taste, whatever the label says. The Eaglehawk range is reliable quaffing wine. **Best years:** (Black Label) (2006)

(04) 03 02 **01 99 98** 97 96 95 91 90 88 86; (Platinum Shiraz) 2005 04 03 02 **01 99 98**.

BLAUBURGUNDER See PINOT NOIR.

BLAUER LEMBERGER See BLAUFRÄNKISCH.

BLAUFRÄNKISCH Good, ripe Blaufränkisch has a taste similar to raspberries and white pepper or even beetroot. Hungarian in origin, it does well in Austria, where it is the principal red grape of BURGENLAND. The Hungarian vineyards (where it is called Kékfrankos) are mostly just across the border on the other side of the Neusiedlersee. Called Lemberger in Germany, where almost all of it is grown in WURTTEMBERG. Also successful in NEW YORK STATE and (as Lemberger) in WASHINGTON STATE (getting better with global warming!).

BLAYE See PREMIERES COTES DE BLAYE AC.

JACKY BLOT Loire Valley, France   When he created Domaine de la Taille aux Loups in MONTLOUIS-SUR-LOIRE and VOUVRAY in 1988, Jacky Blot's use of barrel fermentation and new oak caused controversy. However, rigorous selection of pristine, ripe grapes produces sparkling, dry and sweet whites with tremendous fruit purity. Top Montlouis-sur-Loire cuvées Rémus (sec) ★★ and Romulus (Liquoreux)★★ are groundbreaking – with staggeringly good 'Plus' versions in exceptional vintages: Romulus Plus 2003★★, Remus Plus 2006★★. Since 2002 makes powerful, well-structured reds at Domaine de la Butte in BOURGUEIL AC from parcels of south-facing vineyards. Best years: (top whites) 2005 03 02 97 96 95 90.

BOEKENHOUTSKLOOF Franschhoek WO, South Africa   Perched high in the FRANSCHHOEK mountains, this small winery is named after the surrounding Cape beech trees. The flagship trio comprises punchy, savoury Syrah★★; deep, long-lived Cabernet Sauvignon★★; and sophisticated Semillon★★ from 100-year-old vines. Placed between these and the fruit-focused, good-value Porcupine Ridge★ range is the burly, expressive Chocolate Block★★, a Cabernet Sauvignon-Shiraz blend with Grenache and Cinsaut. Best years: (premium reds) **2005 04 03 02 01 00 99 98 97**.

BOIREANN Queensland, Australia   Fastidious attention to detail has turned this retirement project 1.5ha (3.5-acre) vineyard – planted to 11 varieties – into QUEENSLAND's most impressive winery. Hatfuls of stunning reds: Merlot★★, Cabernet Sauvignon★, Shiraz★ and Petit Verdot.

BOISSET Burgundy, France   Jean-Claude Boisset bought his first vineyards in 1964 and began a négociant company whose extraordinary success has enabled him to swallow up many other long-established names such as Jaffelin, Ponelle, Ropiteau and Héritier Guyot in the COTE D'OR, Moreau in CHABLIS, Cellier des Samsons and Mommessin in BEAUJOLAIS and others elsewhere in France. Most of these companies are designed to produce commercially successful rather than fine wine, excepting Domaine de la VOUGERAIE and, perhaps, Boisset itself. Also projects in LANGUEDOC, California, Canada, Chile and Uruguay.

BOLGHERI DOC Tuscany, Italy   Zone named after an arty village in the northern MAREMMA with, originally, simple white and rosé wines, later major reds based on Cabernet, Merlot and/or Syrah. There is a special sub-zone for SASSICAIA. The DOC Rosso Superiore now covers wines from the prestigious estates of Ca' Marcanda (GAJA), Grattamacco★★, Le MACCHIOLE★★, ORNELLAIA★★, Michele Satta★★ and ANTINORI's Guado al Tasso★★. Best years: (reds) (2007) (06) 05 **04 03 01 00 99 98 97**.

79

BORDEAUX RED WINES

Bordeaux, France

This large area of South-West France, centred on the historic city of Bordeaux, produces a larger volume of fine red wine than any other French region. Wonderful Bordeaux-style wines are produced in California, Australia, South Africa and South America, but the home team's top performers still just about keep the upstarts at bay. Around 800 million bottles of red wine a year are produced here. The best wines, known as the Classed Growths, account for a tiny percentage of this figure, but some of their lustre rubs off on the lesser names, making this one of the most popular wine styles.

GRAPE VARIETIES

Bordeaux's reds are commonly divided into 'right' and 'left' bank wines. On the left bank of the Gironde estuary, the red wines are dominated by the Cabernet Sauvignon grape, with varying proportions of Cabernet Franc, Merlot and Petit Verdot. At best they are austere but perfumed with blackcurrant and cedarwood. The most important left bank areas are the Haut-Médoc (especially the communes of Margaux, St-Julien, Pauillac and St-Estèphe) and, south of the city of Bordeaux, the ACs of Pessac-Léognan and Graves. On the right bank, Merlot is the predominant grape, which generally makes the resulting wines more supple and fleshy than those of the left bank. The key areas for Merlot-based wines are St-Émilion and Pomerol, Fronsac and Côtes de Castillon.

CLASSIFICATIONS

Red Bordeaux is made all over the region. At its most basic, the wine is simply labelled Bordeaux or Bordeaux Supérieur. Above this are the more specific ACs covering sub-areas (such as the Haut-Médoc) and individual communes (such as Pomerol, St-Émilion or Margaux). Single-estate Crus Bourgeois (although this classification has been officially declared null and void from 2007) are the next rung up on the quality ladder, followed by the Crus Classés (Classed Growths) of the Médoc, Graves and St-Émilion. The famous classification of 1855 ranked the top red wines of the Médoc (plus one from Graves) into 5 tiers, from First to Fifth Growths (Crus); there has been only one change, in 1973, promoting Mouton-Rothschild to First Growth status. Since the 1950s the Graves/Pessac-Léognan region has had its own classification, for red and white wines. St-Émilion's classification (for red wines only) has been revised several times, the last modification being in 2006; the possibility of re-grading can help to maintain quality. Curiously, Pomerol, home of Château Pétrus, arguably the most famous red wine in the world, has no official pecking order. Many top Bordeaux châteaux also make 'second wines', which are cheaper versions of their Grands Vins.

See also BORDEAUX, BORDEAUX-COTES DE FRANCS, BORDEAUX SUPERIEUR, CANON-FRONSAC, COTES DE BOURG, COTES DE CASTILLON, FRONSAC, GRAVES, HAUT-MEDOC, LALANDE-DE-POMEROL, LISTRAC-MEDOC, LUSSAC-ST-EMILION, MARGAUX, MEDOC, MONTAGNE-ST-EMILION, MOULIS, PAUILLAC, PESSAC-LEOGNAN, POMEROL, PREMIERES COTES DE BLAYE, PREMIERES COTES DE BORDEAUX, PUISSEGUIN-ST-EMILION, ST-EMILION, ST-ESTEPHE, ST-GEORGES-ST-EMILION, ST-JULIEN; and individual châteaux.

CHATEAU
LA CONSEILLANTE
POMEROL
APPELLATION POMEROL CONTROLÉE

2001

HÉRITIERS L. NICOLAS
PROPRIÉTAIRES A POMEROL (GIRONDE) - FRANCE
13,5% Vol.   750 ml
MISE EN BOUTEILLES AU CHATEAU
PRODUCE OF FRANCE

BEST PRODUCERS

Graves, Pessac-Léognan
Dom. de CHEVALIER, HAUT-BAILLY,
HAUT-BRION, la LOUVIERE,
MALARTIC-LAGRAVIERE, la MISSION-
HAUT-BRION, PAPE-CLEMENT,
SMITH-HAUT-LAFITTE.

Margaux BRANE-CANTENAC,
FERRIERE, MALESCOT ST-EXUPERY,
MARGAUX, PALMER, RAUZAN-SEGLA,
du Tertre.

Pauillac GRAND-PUY-LACOSTE,
HAUT-BAGES-LIBERAL, LAFITE-
ROTHSCHILD, LATOUR, LYNCH-
BAGES, MOUTON-ROTHSCHILD,
PICHON-LONGUEVILLE,
PICHON-LONGUEVILLE-LALANDE,
PONTET-CANET.

Pomerol le BON PASTEUR,
Certan-de-May, Clinet,
la CONSEILLANTE, l'EGLISE-CLINET,
l'EVANGILE, la FLEUR-PETRUS,
GAZIN, LAFLEUR, LATOUR-A-
POMEROL, PETIT-VILLAGE, PETRUS,
le PIN, TROTANOY, VIEUX-
CHATEAU-CERTAN.

St-Émilion ANGELUS, AUSONE,
BEAU-SEJOUR BECOT, BELAIR,
CANON, CANON-LA-GAFFELIERE,
CHEVAL BLANC, Clos Fourtet,
la Dominique, FIGEAC,
Grand Mayne, MAGDELAINE,
MONBOUSQUET, La Mondotte,
PAVIE, PAVIE-MACQUIN,
Rol Valentin, TERTRE-ROTEBOEUF,
TROPLONG-MONDOT,
VALANDRAUD.

St-Estèphe CALON-SEGUR, COS
D'ESTOURNEL, HAUT-MARBUZET,
LAFON-ROCHET, MONTROSE, les
Ormes de Pez.

St-Julien BRANAIRE-DUCRU,
DUCRU-BEAUCAILLOU, GRUAUD-
LAROSE, LAGRANGE, LANGOA-
BARTON, LEOVILLE-BARTON,
LEOVILLE-LAS-CASES, LEOVILLE-
POYFERRE, ST-PIERRE, TALBOT.

BORDEAUX WHITE WINES

Bordeaux, France

This is France's largest fine wine region but, except for the sweet wines of Sauternes and Barsac, Bordeaux's international reputation is based solely on its reds. From 52% of the vineyard area in 1970, white wines now represent only 12% of the present 120,000ha (296,500 acres) of vines. Given the size of the region, the diversity of Bordeaux's white wines should come as no surprise. There are dry, medium and sweet styles, ranging from dreary to some of the most sublime white wines of all. Bordeaux's temperate southern climate – moderated by the influence of the Atlantic and of 2 rivers, the Dordogne and the Garonne – is ideal for white wine production, particularly south of the city along the banks of the Garonne.

GRAPE VARIETIES

Sauvignon Blanc and Sémillon, the most important white grapes, are both varieties of considerable character and are usually blended together. They are backed up by smaller quantities of other grapes, the most notable of which is Muscadelle (unrelated to Muscat), which lends perfume to sweet wines and spiciness to dry.

DRY WINES

With the introduction of new technology and new ideas, many of them influenced by the New World, Bordeaux has become one of France's most exciting white wine areas. There are both oaked and unoaked styles. The unoaked are leafy, tangy and stony-dry. The barrel-fermented styles are delightfully rich yet dry, custard-cream softness mellowing leafy acidity and peach and nectarine fruit.

SWEET WINES

Bordeaux's most famous whites are its sweet wines made from grapes affected by noble rot, particularly those from Sauternes and Barsac. The noble rot concentrates the flavours, producing rich, honeyed wines replete with pineapple and peach flavours, and which develop a lanolin and beeswax depth and a barley sugar and honey richness with age. On the other side of the Garonne river, Cadillac, Loupiac and Ste-Croix-du-Mont also make sweet wines; these rarely attain the richness or complexity of a top Sauternes, but they are considerably less expensive.

CLASSIFICATIONS

The two largest dry white wine ACs in Bordeaux are Bordeaux Blanc and Entre-Deux-Mers. There are plenty of good dry wines in the Graves and Pessac-Léognan regions; the Pessac-Léognan AC, created in 1987, contains all the dry white Classed Growths. The great sweet wines of Sauternes and Barsac were classified as First or Second Growths in 1855.

See also BARSAC, BORDEAUX, BORDEAUX-COTES DE FRANCS, BORDEAUX SUPERIEUR, CADILLAC, CERONS, COTES DE BOURG, ENTRE-DEUX-MERS, GRAVES, LOUPIAC, PESSAC-LEOGNAN, PREMIERES COTES DE BLAYE, PREMIERES COTES DE BORDEAUX, STE-CROIX-DU-MONT, SAUTERNES; and individual châteaux.

Château RIEUSSEC
1er Grand Cru Classé 1855
SAUTERNES
2003
MIS EN BOUTEILLE AU CHÂTEAU

BEST YEARS

(dry) (2007) 06 **05 04 02 01 00
99 98 96 95**; (sweet) (2007) 05
**03 02 01 99 98 97 96 95 90
89 88 86 83**

BEST PRODUCERS

Dry wines
Pessac-Léognan Dom. de
CHEVALIER, Couhins-Lurton,
FIEUZAL, HAUT-BRION, LATOUR-
MARTILLAC, LAVILLE-HAUT-BRION,
la LOUVIERE, MALARTIC-LAGRAVIERE,
SMITH-HAUT-LAFITTE;
Graves Archambeau, Ardennes,
Brondelle, Chantegrive, Clos
Floridène, Magneau, Rahoul,
Respide-Médeville, St-Robert
(Cuvée Poncet-Deville), Vieux-
Ch.-Gaubert, Villa Bel Air.

Entre-Deux-Mers BONNET,
de Fontenille, Nardique-la-
Gravière, Ste-Marie, Toutigeac,
Turcaud.

Bordeaux AC l'Abbaye de Ste-
Ferme, Bauduc, DOISY-DAENE
(Sec), LYNCH-BAGES,
Ch. MARGAUX (Pavillon Blanc),
REYNON, Roquefort, TALBOT,
Thieuley, Tour de Mirambeau.

Premières Côtes de Blaye Charron
(Acacia), Haut-Bertinerie, Cave
des Hauts de Gironde co-op,
Tourtes (Prestige).

Sweet wines
Sauternes and Barsac CLIMENS,
Clos Haut-Peyraguey, COUTET,
DOISY-DAENE, DOISY-VEDRINES,
FARGUES, GILETTE, GUIRAUD,
LAFAURIE-PEYRAGUEY, NAIRAC,
Raymond-Lafon, RIEUSSEC,
Sigalas-Rabaud, SUDUIRAUT,
la TOUR BLANCHE, YQUEM.

Cadillac Fayau, Manos,
Mémoires.

Cérons Ch. de Cérons, Grand
Enclos du Ch. de Cérons.

Loupiac Clos Jean, Cros,
Mémoires, Noble.

Ste-Croix-du-Mont Loubens,
Pavillon, la Rame.

BOLLINGER *Champagne AC, Champagne, France* One of the great CHAMPAGNE houses, with good non-vintage (Special Cuvée★) and vintage wines (Grande Année★★★), made in a full, rich, rather old-fashioned style (Bollinger is one of the few houses to ferment its base wine in barrels.) It also produces a range of rarer vintages, including Vintage RD★★★, and a Vieilles Vignes Françaises Blanc de Noirs★★ from ancient, ungrafted Pinot Noir vines. Bollinger bought Champagne Ayala, a neighbour in Aÿ, in 2005. Best years: (Grande Année) 1999 **97** 96 **95** 92 90 89 88 85 82 79.

CH. LE BON PASTEUR★★ *Pomerol AC, Bordeaux, France* Owned by Michel Rolland, Bordeaux's most famous winemaker. The wines are expensive, but they are always deliciously soft and full of lush fruit. Best years: 2006 05 04 **03 01 00** 99 98 96 95 94 90 89 88 85.

BONNES-MARES AC *Grand Cru, Côte de Nuits, Burgundy, France* A large Grand Cru straddling the communes of CHAMBOLLE-MUSIGNY and MOREY-ST-DENIS, commendably consistent over the last few decades. Bonnes-Mares generally has a deep, ripe, smoky plum fruit, which starts rich and chewy and matures over 10–20 years. Best producers: d'Auvenay (Dom LEROY)★★★, BOUCHARD PERE ET FILS★★, DROUHIN★★, Drouhin-Laroze★★, DUJAC★★★, Robert Groffier★★★, JADOT★★★, D Laurent★★, J-F MUGNIER★★, ROUMIER★★★, de VOGUE★★★, VOUGERAIE★★★. Best years: (2007) 06 05 03 02 **01 00** 99 98 97 96 95 93 90 89.

CH. BONNET *Entre-Deux-Mers AC, Bordeaux, France* This region's pioneering estate for quality and consistency. Large volumes of good, fruity, affordable Entre-Deux-Mers★ and BORDEAUX AC rosé and red, particularly the barrel-aged Merlot-Cabernet Réserve★. Drink this at 3–4 years and the others young. A new special cuvée, Divinus★, was launched with the 2000 vintage. Owner André Lurton is also the proprietor of Ch. La LOUVIERE and other properties in PESSAC-LEOGNAN.

BONNEZEAUX AC *Loire Valley, France* One of France's great sweet wines, Bonnezeaux is a zone within the COTEAUX DU LAYON AC. Like SAUTERNES, the wine is influenced by noble rot, but the flavours are different and its structure finer, as only Chenin Blanc is used. Quality is variable, but top wines are world class. It can age very well in good vintages. Best producers: M Angeli/Sansonnière★★★, Fesles★★★, Godineau★★, des Grandes Vignes★★, Petit Val★★, Petits Quarts★★, Terrebrune★★, la Varière★★. Best years: (2007) 06 05 **04 03** 02 **01** 99 97 96 95 90 89.

BONNY DOON *Santa Cruz Mountains AVA, California, USA* Randall Grahm has a particular love for Rhône and Italian varietals: Le Cigare Volant★★ is a blend of Grenache and Syrah and is Grahm's homage to CHATEAUNEUF-DU-PAPE. His Ca' del Solo Italianate wines are delightful. Grahm's new Pacific Rim winery in WASHINGTON focuses entirely on Riesling.

BORDEAUX AC *Bordeaux, France* One of the most important ACs in France, covering reds, rosés and the dry, medium and sweet white wines of the entire Gironde region. Most of the best wines are allowed specific district or commune ACs (such as MARGAUX or SAUTERNES) but a vast amount of Bordeaux's wine – delicious, atrocious and everything in between – is sold as Bordeaux AC. At its best, straight red Bordeaux is marked by bone-dry leafy fruit and an attractive earthy edge, but far more frequently the wines are tannic and raw – and often overpriced. Good examples usually benefit from a year or so of aging. Bordeaux Blanc has joined the modern world with an increasing number of refreshing, pleasant wines. These may be labelled as Bordeaux Sauvignon. Drink as young as possible. Bordeaux Clairet is a pale red wine, virtually rosé but with a little more substance. Best producers: (reds) BONNET★, d:vin★, Dourthe (Numéro 1), Ducla, Fontenille★, Gadras, Sirius, Thieuley★, Tour de Mirambeau; (whites) l'Abbaye de Ste-Ferme★, Bauduc★, DOISY-DAENE★, Dourthe (Numéro 1★), LYNCH-BAGES★, MARGAUX (Pavillon Blanc★★), REYNON★, Roquefort★, TALBOT★, Thieuley★, Tour de Mirambeau★. See also pages 80–3.

BORDEAUX-CÔTES DE FRANCS AC *Bordeaux, France* Tiny area east of ST-EMILION; part of new Côtes de Bordeaux AC from 2007; the top wines are good value. The Thienpont family (Ch. Puygueraud) is the driving force. Best producers: les Charmes-Godard★, Franc-Cardinal, Francs (Les Cerisiers★★), Laclaverie★, Marsau★, Nardou, Pelan★, la Prade★, Puygueraud★★, Vieux Saule. Best years: 2005 **04 03 01 00 98**.

BORDEAUX SUPÉRIEUR AC *Bordeaux, France* Covers the same area as the BORDEAUX AC but the wines must have an extra 0.5% of alcohol, a lower yield and a longer period of maturation. Many of the best petits châteaux are labelled Bordeaux Supérieur. Best producers (reds): Barreyre★, Beaulieu Comtes des Tastes★, de Bouillerot★, de Courteillac★, Grand Village★, Parenchère★, Penin★, Pey la Tour★, le Pin Beausoleil★, Reignac★, Thieuley (Réserve Francis Courselle★), Tire-Pé★.

BORIE LA VITARÈLE *St-Chinian AC, Languedoc, France* The Izarn family produces two ST-CHINIANS, which express the different soils of their organic vineyard: Les Crès★, dominated by Syrah, is spicy and warm; Les Schistes is cooler, more elegant. Best years: 2005 04 03 **01** 00.

LUIGI BOSCA *Mendoza, Argentina* Founded by the Arizú family in 1901 and still family-owned, this winery has 400ha (1000 acres) in LUJAN DE CUYO and Maipú, planted mainly with Malbec, Cabernet Sauvignon, Syrah, Chardonnay and Sauvignon Blanc. Try the mineral Finca Los Nobles Chardonnay★, the dense, chocolaty Finca Los Nobles Malbec★ and the more complex and sophisticated Malbec-based blend Gala 1★★ and Cabernet-based Gala 2★. New Icono★ (from 2005 vintage) is a Malbec-Cabernet blend. Best years: (reds) (2006) 05 **04 03 02** 01 99.

BOSCARELLI *Vino Nobile di Montepulciano DOCG, Tuscany, Italy* Arguably Montepulciano's best producer, crafting rich and stylish reds with guidance from star enologist Maurizio Castelli. VINO NOBILE★★, Riserva del Nocio★★ and the barrique-aged SUPER-TUSCAN Boscarelli★★ are all brilliant. Best years: (2007) (06) 04 **03** 01 **00** 99 97.

BOUCHARD FINLAYSON *Walker Bay WO, South Africa* Pinotphile Peter Finlayson produces classy Pinot Noir (Galpin Peak★ and occasional barrel selection Tête de Cuvée★★). His love of Italian varieties is reflected in Hannibal★★, a multi-cultural mix led by Sangiovese with Pinot Noir, Nebbiolo, Barbera and Shiraz. Chardonnays (Kaimansgaat/Crocodile's Lair★ – now fresher, more citrusy and less obviously oaky – and full, nutty home-grown Missionvale★) are plausibly Burgundian. Sauvignon Blanc★ is tangy and fresh. Best years: (Pinot Noir) 2006 **05 04 03 02** 01 **00** 99 98.

BOUCHARD PÈRE ET FILS *Beaune, Burgundy, France* Important merchant and vineyard owner, with vines in some of Burgundy's most spectacular sites, including CORTON★★, CORTON-CHARLEMAGNE★★, Chevalier-Montrachet★★ and le MONTRACHET★★★. The firm is owned by Champenois Joseph HENRIOT, who is now realizing the full potential here. Wines from the company's own vineyards are sold under the Domaines du Château de Beaune label. Don't touch anything pre-1996. Best years: (top reds) (2007) 06 05 03 **02 00** 99 98.

BOUCHES-DU-RHÔNE, VIN DE PAYS DES *Provence, France* Wines fro
3 areas: the coast, a zone around Aix-en-Provence and the Camarg
Mainly full-bodied, spicy reds, but rosé can be good. Best producer
Ch. Bas, l'Île St-Pierre, Mas de Rey, la Michelle, TREVALLON★★, Valdition. Be
years: (reds) **2006 05 04 03 01 00**.

DOM. HENRI BOURGEOIS *Sancerre AC, Loire Valley, France* Large-scale outf
in SANCERRE with 67ha (166 acres) of domaine vineyards and a substanti
négociant business extending into other Loire appellations, plus Clc
Henri label in New Zealand. Reliably good wines from the vin de pay
Petit Bourgeois up. The Monts Damnés cuvées★ have bags of miner
character. Old-vine, soil-specific bottlings Jadis★★ (Kimmeridgian clay
d'Antan★★ (silex) and the rare barrel-fermented Étienne Henri★★ a
among the finest in Sancerre. Best years: (top wines) 2007 06 **05 04 02**.

BOURGOGNE AC *Burgundy, France* Bourgogne is the French nam
anglicized as 'Burgundy'. This generic AC mops up all the Burgundia
wine with no AC of its own, resulting in massive differences in style an
quality. The best wines will usually come from a single grower's vineyard
just outside the main village ACs of the COTE D'OR; such wines may be th
only way we can afford the joys of fine Burgundy. If the wine is from
grower, the flavours should follow a regional style. However, if the addres
on the label is that of a négociant, the wine could be from anywhere i
Burgundy. Pinot Noir is the main red grape, but Gamay from
declassified BEAUJOLAIS cru is, absurdly, allowed. Red Bourgogne is usuall
light, fruity in an upfront strawberry and cherry way, and should be drun
within 2–3 years. The rosé (Pinot Noir) can be pleasant, but little
produced. Bourgogne Blanc is a usually bone-dry Chardonnay wine an
most should be drunk within 2 years. Bourgogne Passe-tout-Grains
made from Gamay with a minimum 33% of Pinot Noir, while Bourgogn
Grand Ordinaire is rarely more than a quaffing wine, drunk in local bar
Best producers: (reds/growers) G Barthod★★, COCHE-DURY★, Dugat-Py★
Germain/Ch. de Chorey★, LAFARGE★, MEO-CAMUZET★★, P RION★★, ROUMIER★
VOUGERAIE; (reds/merchants) DROUHIN★, GIRARDIN★, JADOT★, Labouré-Ro
Maison Leroy★★, N POTEL★★; (reds/co-ops) BUXYNOISE★, Caves des Haute
Côtes★; (whites/growers) M BOUZEREAU★, Boyer-Martenot★, J-M BROCARD★
COCHE-DURY★★, J-P Fichet★, P Javillier★★, Ch. de Meursault★, Pierre Morey★
Guy Roulot★; (whites/merchants) DROUHIN★, FAIVELEY, JADOT★, Olivier LEFLAIV
RODET★; (whites/co-ops) BUXYNOISE, Caves des Hautes-Côtes. Best years: (reds
2007 06 **05 03 02**; (whites) **2007 06 05 04**. See also pages 88–91.

BOURGOGNE ALIGOTÉ AC See ALIGOTE.

BOURGOGNE-CÔTE CHALONNAISE AC *Côte Chalonnaise, Burgundy, Franc*
The AC covers vineyards to the west of Chalon-sur-Saône around th
villages of Bouzeron, RULLY, MERCUREY, GIVRY and MONTAGNY. Bes
producers: X Besson, BUXYNOISE co-op★, Villaine★. Best years: (reds) (2007) 0
04 03; (whites) **2007 06 05 04**.

BOURGOGNE-HAUTES-CÔTES DE BEAUNE AC *Burgundy, France* Th
hills behind the great COTE DE BEAUNE are a good source of affordabl
Burgundy. The red wines are lean but drinkable, as is the slightly shar
Chardonnay. Best producers: Caves des Hautes-Côtes★, J-Y Devevey★
L Jacob★, J-L Joillot★, Ch. de Mercey★/RODET, Naudin-Ferrand★
C Nouveau★. Best years: (reds) (2007) **06 05 03**; (whites) **2007 06 05 04**.

BOURGOGNE-HAUTES-CÔTES DE NUITS AC *Burgundy, Franc*
Attractive, lightweight wines from the hills behind the COTE DE NUITS
The reds are best, with an attractive cherry and plum flavour. The white

tend to be rather dry and flinty. Best producers: (reds) Bertagna★, D Duband★, FAIVELEY★, A-F GROS★, M GROS★, A Guyon★, Caves des Hautes-Côtes★, Jayer-Gilles★★, T LIGER-BELAIR★; (whites) Caves des Hautes-Côtes★, Champy★, Jayer-Gilles★★, Thévenot-le-Brun★, A Verdet★. Best years: (reds) (2007) **06 05 03**; (whites) **2007 06 05 04**.

BOURGUEIL AC *Loire Valley, France* Fine red wine from between Tours and Angers, made with Cabernet Franc, sometimes with a little Cabernet Sauvignon. A concerted quality drive, together with a good run of vintages, is shedding its reputation for rusticity; expect plump raspberry and plum fruit. Best producers: Y Amirault★★, Audebert (estate wines★), BLOT/la Butte★★, T Boucard★, P Breton★, la Chevalerie, Clos de l'Abbaye★, Max Cognard, DRUET★★, Forges, Lamé-Delisle-Boucard, la Lande/Delaunay, Nau Frères★, Ouches★, Les Pins, Raguenières★. Best years: 2006 05 **04 03 02 01 97 96 95**. See also ST-NICOLAS-DE-BOURGUEIL.

BOUVET-LADUBAY *Saumur AC, Loire Valley, France* Sparkling wine producer. Basic Bouvet Brut and Bouvet Rosé are good. Saphir, the top-selling wine, is over-sweet, but Trésor (Blanc★ and Rosé★), fermented in oak casks, is very good. Now also a good Brut Zéro. Weird and wonderful Rubis★ sparkling red is worth trying. The Nonpareils★ range of still wines are pricey for the quality.

BOUZEREAU *Meursault, Côte de Beaune, Burgundy, France* An extended family of vignerons – you'll find a good half dozen domaines with this name in the yellow pages – all making a range of whites from MEURSAULT and neighbouring villages, plus some less interesting COTE DE BEAUNE reds. Best at the moment are Dom. Michel Bouzereau & Fils★ and Vincent Bouzereau★. Best years: (whites) 2007 06 **05 04 02**.

BOWEN ESTATE *Coonawarra, South Australia* A COONAWARRA pioneer since the 1970s, Doug Bowen, now joined by his daughter, Emma, continues to make some of the region's best and most peppery Shiraz★★ as well as vibrant blackcurranty Cabernet★. Best years: (Shiraz) 2006 05 03 02 **01 00 98 97 96 94 93 92 91**.

BOYAR ESTATES *Bulgaria* The leading distributor of Bulgarian wines, selling more than 65 million bottles worldwide each year. Quality is erratic: many reds are raw and tannic, whites are merely decent.

BRACHETTO An unusual Italian grape native to Piedmont, Brachetto makes every style from dry and still to rich, sweet passito and sweet, frothy light red wines with a Muscat-like perfume, as exemplified by Brachetto d'Acqui DOCG. Best producers: (dry) Contero, Correggia★, Scarpa★; (Brachetto d'Acqui) BANFI★, Braida★, G Marenco★.

CH. BRANAIRE-DUCRU★★ *St-Julien AC, 4ème Cru Classé, Haut-Médoc, Bordeaux, France* After a long period of mediocrity, 1994 and subsequent vintages have confirmed a welcome return to full, soft, chocolaty form. Best years: 2006 05 04 03 **02 01** 00 **99 98 96 95 94**.

BRAND'S *Coonawarra, South Australia* COONAWARRA firm, owned by MCWILLIAM'S, with 100ha (250 acres) of new vineyards as well as some ancient vines planted in 1893. Ripe Laira Cabernet★ is increasingly attractive; Patron's Reserve★ (Cabernet with Shiraz and Merlot) is excellent. New life has been breathed into Shiraz★, and the opulent Stentiford's Reserve★★ (from 100-year-old vines) shows how good Coonawarra Shiraz can be. Merlot★★ is among Australia's best examples of the variety. Best years: (reds) (2006) 05 04 03 **02 01 00** 99 98 97 96 94 90.

BURGUNDY RED WINES

Burgundy, France

Rich in history and gastronomic tradition, the region of Burgundy (Bourgogne in French) covers a vast tract of eastern France, running from Auxerre, south-east of Paris, down to the city of Mâcon. As with its white wines, Burgundy's red wines are extremely diverse. The explanation for this lies partly in the fickle nature of Pinot Noir, the area's principal red grape, and partly in the historical imbalance of supply and demand between growers – who grow the grapes and make and bottle much of the best wine – and merchants, whose efforts originally established the reputation of the wines internationally.

WINE STYLES

Pinot Noir shows many different flavour profiles according to climate, soil and winemaking. The reds from around Auxerre (Épineuil, Irancy) in the north will be light, chalky and strawberry-flavoured. Also lighter though more rustic and earthy, are the reds of the Mâconnais in the south, while the Côte Chalonnaise offers solid reds from Givry and Mercurey.

The top reds come from the Côte d'Or, the heartland of Burgundy. Flavours sweep through strawberry, raspberry, damson and cherry – in young wines – to a wild, magnificent maturity of Oriental spices, chocolate, mushrooms and truffles. The greatest of all – the world famous Grand Cru vineyards such as Chambertin, Musigny, Richebourg and Clos de Vougeot – are in the Côte de Nuits, the northern part of the Côte d'Or from Nuits-St-Georges up towards Dijon. Other fine reds, especially Volnay, Pommard and Corton, come from the Côte de Beaune. Some villages tend towards a fine and elegant style (Chambolle-Musigny, Volnay), others towards a firmer, more tannic structure (Gevrey-Chambertin, Pommard).

The Beaujolais should really be considered as a separate region, growing Gamay on granitic soils rather than Pinot Noir on limestone, though a small amount of Gamay has also crept north to be included in the lesser wines of Burgundy.

CLASSIFICATIONS

Most of Burgundy has 5 increasingly specific levels of classification: regional ACs (e.g. Bourgogne), specified ACs covering groups of villages (e.g. Côte de Nuits-Villages), village wines taking the village name (Pommard, Vosne-Romanée), Premiers Crus (good village vineyard sites) and Grands Crus (the best individual vineyard sites).

See also ALOXE-CORTON, AUXEY-DURESSES, BEAUJOLAIS, BEAUNE, BLAGNY, BONNES-MARES, BOURGOGNE, BOURGOGNE-COTE CHALONNAISE, BOURGOGNE-HAUTES-COTES DE BEAUNE/NUITS, CHAMBERTIN, CHAMBOLLE-MUSIGNY, CHASSAGNE-MONTRACHET, CHOREY-LES-BEAUNE, CLOS DE LA ROCHE, CLOS ST-DENIS, CLOS DE VOUGEOT, CORTON, COTE DE BEAUNE, COTE DE NUITS, COTE D'OR, CREMANT DE BOURGOGNE, ECHEZEAUX, FIXIN, GEVREY-CHAMBERTIN, GIVRY, IRANCY, LADOIX, MACON, MARANGES, MARSANNAY, MERCUREY, MONTHELIE, MOREY-ST-DENIS, MUSIGNY, NUITS-ST-GEORGES, PERNAND-VERGELESSES, POMMARD, RICHEBOURG, la ROMANEE-CONTI, ROMANEE-ST-VIVANT, RULLY, ST-AUBIN, ST-ROMAIN, SANTENAY, SAVIGNY-LES-BEAUNE, la TACHE, VOLNAY, VOSNE-ROMANEE, VOUGEOT; and individual producers.

BURGUNDY WHITE WINES

Burgundy, France

White Burgundy has for generations been thought of as the world's leading dry white wine. The top wines have a remarkable succulent richness of honey and hazelnut, melted butter and sprinkled spice, yet are totally dry. Such wines are all from the Chardonnay grape and the finest are generally produced in the Côte de Beaune, the southern part of the Côte d'Or, in the communes of Aloxe-Corton, Meursault, Puligny-Montrachet and Chassagne-Montrachet, where limestone soils and the aspect of the vineyard provide perfect conditions for even ripening of grapes. However, Burgundy encompasses many more wine styles than this, even if no single one quite attains the peaks of quality of those 4 villages on the Côte de Beaune.

WINE STYLES

Chablis in the north traditionally produces very good steely wines, aggressive and lean when young, but nutty and rounded – though still very dry – after a few years. Modern Chablis is frequently a softer, milder wine, easy to drink young, and sometimes enriched (or denatured) by aging in new oak barrels.

There is no doubt that Meursault and the other Côte de Beaune villages can produce stupendous wine, but it is in such demand that unscrupulous producers are often tempted to maximize yields and cut corners on quality. Consequently white Burgundy from these famous villages must be approached with caution. Lesser-known villages such as Pernand-Vergelesses and St-Aubin often provide good wine at lower prices. There are also good wines from some villages in the Côte de Nuits, such as Morey-St-Denis, Nuits-St-Georges and Vougeot, though amounts are tiny compared with the Côte de Beaune.

South of the Côte d'Or the Côte Chalonnaise is becoming more interesting for quality white wine now that better equipment for temperature control is becoming more widespread and oak barrels are being used more often for aging. Rully and Montagny are the most important villages, though Givry and Mercurey can produce nice white, too. The minor Aligoté grape makes some attractive, if acidic, wine, especially in Bouzeron.

Further south, the Mâconnais is a large region, two-thirds planted with Chardonnay. There is some fair sparkling Crémant de Bourgogne, and some very good vineyard sites, in particular in St-Véran and in Pouilly-Fuissé. Increasingly stunning wines can now be found, though there's still a lot of dross.

See also ALOXE-CORTON, AUXEY-DURESSES, BATARD-MONTRACHET, BEAUJOLAIS, BEAUNE, BOURGOGNE, BOURGOGNE-COTE CHALONNAISE, BOURGOGNE-HAUTES-COTES DE BEAUNE/NUITS, CHABLIS, CHASSAGNE-MONTRACHET, CORTON, CORTON-CHARLEMAGNE, COTE DE BEAUNE, COTE DE NUITS, COTE D'OR, CREMANT DE BOURGOGNE, FIXIN, GIVRY, LADOIX, MACON, MACON-VILLAGES, MARANGES, MARSANNAY, MERCUREY, MEURSAULT, MONTAGNY, MONTHELIE, MONTRACHET, MOREY-ST-DENIS, MUSIGNY, NUITS-ST-GEORGES, PERNAND-VERGELESSES, POUILLY-FUISSE, POUILLY-VINZELLES, PULIGNY-MONTRACHET, RULLY, ST-AUBIN, ST-ROMAIN, ST-VERAN, SANTENAY, SAVIGNY-LES-BEAUNE, VIRE-CLESSE, VOUGEOT; and individual producers.

(2007) 06 05 **04 02 00** 99

BEST PRODUCERS

Chablis Barat, J-C Bessin, Billaud-Simon, P Bouchard, A & F Boudin, J-M BROCARD, D Dampt, R & V DAUVISSAT, D-E Defaix, Droin, DURUP, W Fèvre, J-H Goisot, J-P Grossot, LAROCHE, Long-Depaquit, Malandes, Louis Michel, C Moreau, Picq, Pinson, RAVENEAU, Vocoret.

Côte d'Or (Côte de Beaune) R Ampeau, d'Auvenay (LEROY), Blain-Gagnard, J-M Boillot, Bonneau du Martray, M BOUZEREAU, Boyer-Martenot, CARILLON, CHANDON DE BRIAILLES, Chassorney, Coche-Debord, COCHE-DURY, Marc Colin, Colin-Deléger, Arnaud Ente, J-P Fichet, Fontaine-Gagnard, J-N GAGNARD, A Gras, P Javillier, F Jobard, R Jobard, LAFON, H Lamy, Dom. LEFLAIVE, Matrot, Bernard Morey, Marc Morey, Pierre Morey, M Niellon, P Pernot, J & J-M Pillot, RAMONET, M Rollin, G Roulot, SAUZET, VERGET, VOUGERAIE.

Côte Chalonnaise S Aladame, H & P Jacqueson.

Mâconnais D & M Barraud, A Bonhomme, Bret Brothers, Cordier, Corsin, Deux Roches, J-A Ferret, Ch. Fuissé, Guffens-Heynen/VERGET, Guillot-Broux, O Merlin, Robert-Denogent, Ch. des Rontets, Saumaize-Michelin, la Soufrandière, J Thévenet.

Merchants BOUCHARD PERE ET FILS, Champy, DROUHIN, FAIVELEY, V GIRARDIN, JADOT, Labouré-Roi, Louis LATOUR, Olivier LEFLAIVE, Maison Leroy, Rijckaert, RODET, VERGET.

Co-ops BUXYNOISE, la CHABLISIENNE, Lugny, Viré.

CH. BRANE-CANTENAC★★ *Margaux AC, 2ème Cru Classé, Haut-Médoc,*
Bordeaux, France After a drab period, Brane-Cantenac returned to form
during the late 1990s. Henri Lurton has taken over the family property
and is making some superb wines, particularly the 2000, although don't
expect flavours to be mainstream – years like 2002 and 2003 are tasty but
wild. Best years: 2006 05 04 **03 02 01 00 99 98 96 95 89**.

BRAUNEBERG *Mosel, Germany* Small village with 2 famous vineyard sites,
Juffer and Juffer Sonnenuhr, whose wines have a honeyed richness and
creamy gentleness rare in the Mosel. Best producers: Bastgen★, Fritz
HAAG★★★, Willi Haag★, Paulinshof★, M F RICHTER★★, SCHLOSS LIESER★★.
Best years: (2007) 06 05 **04 03 02 01 99 98 97**.

BREAKY BOTTOM *Sussex, England* Small vineyard in the South Downs
near Lewes. Peter Hall is a quirky, passionate grower, making dry, nutty
Seyval Blanc★ that becomes creamy and BURGUNDY-like after 3–4 years.
Sparkling wines continue to improve: sparkling Seyval Blanc★ is
delicious, but there is a shift to more classic varieties, using early-ripening
clones of Chardonnay and Pinot Noir.

GEORG BREUER *Rüdesheim, Rheingau, Germany* Intense dry Riesling from
RUDESHEIM Berg Schlossberg★★, Berg Rottland★★ and RAUENTHAL
Nonnenberg★★. Also a remarkable Sekt★. Quality remains very high
despite Bernhard Breuer's untimely death in 2004. Best years: (Berg
Schlossberg) (2007) 06 05 **04 03 02 01 00 99 98 97 96**.

BRIGHT BROTHERS *Ribatejo, Portugal* The Fiúza-Bright operation is
located in the town of Almeirim; Fiúza-labelled wines are from local
vineyards planted to both Portuguese and French varieties. Australian
Peter Bright also makes Brightpink, Brightwhite and Brightred table
wines, in aluminium bottles, and red and white Fado ALENTEJO wines.

JEAN-MARC BROCARD *Chablis, Burgundy, France* Dynamic winemaker who
has built up this 80ha (200-acre) domaine almost from scratch, and is
now one of Chablis' most reliable and satisfying producers. The Premiers
Crus (including Montée de la Tonnerre★★, Montmains★★) and slow-
evolving Grands Crus (les Clos★★★ stands out) are tremendous, while
the basic Chablis, especially Vieilles Vignes★★, are some of the best on
the market. Brocard also produces a range of BOURGOGNE Blancs★ from
different soil types. Now adopting an increasingly organic – and in some
cases biodynamic – approach to his vineyards. Best years: (2007) 06 05 **04**
03 02 00.

BROKENWOOD *Hunter Valley, New South Wales, Australia* High-profile
winery with delicious traditional unoaked HUNTER Semillon★★
(sometimes ★★★). Best wine is classic Hunter Graveyard Vineyard
Shiraz★★★; MCLAREN VALE Rayner Vineyard Shiraz★★ has been stunning
but will disappear as the vineyard has been bought by WIRRA WIRRA.
Cricket Pitch reds and whites are cheerful, fruity ready-drinkers. New
Indigo vineyard at BEECHWORTH is making very promising Chardonnay,
Viognier and Pinot Noir. Best years: (Graveyard Vineyard Shiraz) (2006) 05
04 03 02 00 **99 98 96 95 94 93 91 90 89 88 86**.

BRONCO WINE CO. *California, USA* Maker of the Charles Shaw range of
wines – known as 'Two-Buck Chuck' because of their $2 price tag.
There's now a $5 Napa Cabernet Sauvignon. The company is run by
maverick Fred Franzia, who famously said 'wine's too damned
expensive'. He is grand-nephew of the late Ernest GALLO, and he owns
14,000ha (35,000 acres) of California vineyard land, marketing
10 million cases of wine under more than a dozen brands.

ROUILLY AC *Beaujolais, Burgundy, France* Largest of the 10 BEAUJOLAIS Crus; at its best, the wine is soft, fruity, rich and brightly coloured. Best producers: Ch. de la Chaize★, DUBOEUF (Ch. de Nervers★), A Michaud★, Ch. Thivin★★. Best years: **2007 06**.

ROWN BROTHERS *North-East Victoria, Australia* Highly successful family winery, producing a huge range of varietal wines, which have improved significantly in recent years. Good fizz and fine stickies★★. Top-of-the-range Patricia wines (Cabernet★★, sparkling Pinot-Chardonnay★★) are Brown's best yet. Premium grapes are from cool King Valley, mountain-top Whitlands and new vineyard at HEATHCOTE.

RÜNDLMAYER *Kamptal, Niederösterreich, Austria* Willi Bründlmayer makes wine in a variety of Austrian and international styles, but his outstanding dry Riesling (Alte Reben★★★) from the great Heiligenstein vineyard and Grüner Veltliner (Ried Lamm★★★) are the best; high alcohol is matched by superlative fruit and mineral flavours. Also excellent Chardonnay★★ and good Sekt★. Best years: (Zöbinger Heiligenstein Riesling) (2007) 06 05 **04 03** 02 01 00 99 98.

RUNELLO DI MONTALCINO DOCG *Tuscany, Italy* Powerful red wine produced from Sangiovese (known locally as Brunello). Traditionally needed over 10 years to soften, but modern practices result in more fruit-rich wines, yet still tannic enough to age very well, if not as spectacularly as sometimes claimed. Best producers: Agostina Pieri★★, Altesino★ (Montosoli★★), BANFI★ (Riserva★★), Barbi★, BIONDI-SANTI★★, Gianni Brunelli★★, Camigliano★★, La Campana★, Caparzo★ (La Casa★★), Casanova di Neri★★★, Casanuova delle Cerbaie★★★, CASE BASSE★★★, Castelgiocondo/ FRESCOBALDI (Riserva★), Centolani★ (Pietranera★★), Cerbaiona★★, Ciacci Piccolomini d'Aragona★★, Donatella Cinelli Colombini★★, Col d'Orcia★★, COSTANTI★★, Fuligni★★, La Gerla★★, Le Gode★★, Gorelli-Due Portine★, Greppone Mazzi★, Maurizio Lambardi★★, Lisini★★, Mastrojanni★★ (Schiena d'Asino★★★), Siro Pacenti★★★, Pian delle Vigne★★/ANTINORI, Piancornello★★, Pieve Santa Restituta★★, La Poderina★★, Poggio Antico★★, Poggio San Polo★★, IL POGGIONE★★ (Riserva★★★), Salvioni★, Livio Sassetti-Pertimali★★, Talenti★★, La Togata★★, Valdicava★★, Villa Le Prata★★. Best years: (2007) (06) (04) 03 01 **00** 99 98 97 95 90 88 85.

UCELAS DOC *Estremadura, Portugal* A tiny but historic DOC. The wines are whites based on the Arinto grape (noted for its high acidity). For attractive, modern examples try Quinta da Murta or Quinta da Romeira (Morgado de Santa Catherina★).

ON BUHL *Deidesheim, Pfalz, Germany* Large estate, sold in 2005 to Achim Niederberger, the new owner of BASSERMANN-JORDAN. Top Rieslings now invariably ★★. Best years: (Grosses Gewächs Rieslings) (2007) 06 05 04 **03** 02 01 99 98.

UITENVERWACHTING *Constantia WO, South Africa* Beautiful old property, part of the Cape's original CONSTANTIA wine farm. Sauvignon Blanc★ is penetrating and zesty; Husseys Vlei Sauvignon Blanc★ is bigger and more pungent. Ripe, fruit-laden Chardonnay★ and elegant, subtle Husseys Vlei★★ version. These and a light racy Riesling can improve with a little aging. The aristocratic Christine★★, with deep flavours and firm, dry structure, remains one of the Cape's most accurate BORDEAUX lookalikes. Best years: (Christine) (2004) 03 **02 01** 00 99 98 97 96 95.

BULL'S BLOOD *Hungary* Kékfrankos (Blaufränkisch) grapes sometimes replace robust Kadarka in the blend, thinning the blood; some producers blend with Cabernet Sauvignon, Kékoporto or Merlot. New regulations should improve the quality of Bikavér ('bull's blood') in the 2 permitte regions, Eger and Szekszárd. Winemakers such as Vilmos Thummere are working hard on this front, putting some balls back into the win

GRANT BURGE *Barossa Valley, South Australia* A leading producer in th BAROSSA, with extensive vineyard holdings and a wide range, includin chocolaty Filsell Shiraz★ and rich Meshach Shiraz★★, Cameron Val Cabernet★ and Shadrach Cabernet★ (now sourced entirely from Baross fruit), RHONE-style Grenache-Shiraz-Mourvèdre blend Holy Trinity★ fresh Thorn Riesling★, oaky Zerk Semillon, and the excellent-valu Barossa Vines range. Recent vintages have shown a welcome reduction i oak. Best years: (Meshach) (2006) (05) (04) 02 **99 98 96 95 94 91**.

BURGENLAND *Austria* 4 regions: Neusiedlersee, including Seewinkel fo sweet wines; Neusiedlersee-Hügelland, famous for sweet wines, now also bi reds and fruity dry whites; Mittelburgenland, for robust Blaufränkisch red and Südburgenland, for good reds. Best producers: FEILER-ARTINGER★★ Gesellmann★, Gernot Heinrich★★, Juris★, Kollwentz★★, KRACHER★★★ KRUTZLER★★, Helmut Lang★★, A & H Nittnaus★★, OPITZ★, Pöckl★★, Prieler★ Schröck★, Schwarz★, Ernst Triebaumer★★, UMATHUM★★, VELICH★★, Rober Wenzel★.

BURGUNDY See BOURGOGNE AC and pages 88–91.

BÜRKLIN-WOLF *Wachenheim, Pfalz, Germany* One of Germany's larges privately owned estates, with nearly 85ha (210 acres) of vineyards. Sinc the mid-1990s it has been in the first rank of the PFALZ's producers Biodynamic since 2005. The powerful, spicy dry Rieslings are now ★★ t ★★★. Best years: (Grosses Gewächs Rieslings) (2007) 06 05 **04 03 02 01 9**7

BURMESTER *Port DOC, Douro, Portugal* Shipper established in 1730, and no owned by the Galician firm Sogevinus, which also owns Cálem, Barro and Kopke. Vintage PORT has improved, as has the Vintage release under the Quinta Nova de Nossa Senhora do Carmo★ label. As well a refined 10- and 20-year-old tawnies★, there are some outstanding ol colheitas★★ which extend back over 100 years. Also decent Late Bottle Vintage and oak-aged DOURO red, Casa Burmester. Gilbert is a rang aimed at younger drinkers. Best years: (Vintage) **2003 00 97 95 94**.

TOMMASO BUSSOLA *Valpolicella DOC, Veneto, Italy* Tommaso Bussola AMARONE Vigneto Alto★★★ combines elegance with stunning power Amarone Classico TB★★ is similar with slightly less finesse, and eve the basic Amarone★ is a challenge to the palate. The Ripass VALPOLICELLA Classico Superiore TB★★ is one of the best of its genre, an the RECIOTO TB★★★ is consistently excellent. Best years: (2007) (06) 04 0 **01 00 99 97 95**.

LA BUXYNOISE *Côte Chalonnaise, Burgundy, France* One of Burgundy's to co-operatives, producing affordable, well-made Chardonnay and Pino Noir. The light, oak-aged BOURGOGNE Pinot Noir★ and the red and whit Clos de Chenôves★, as well as the nutty white MONTAGNY★, are all goo reasonably priced, and best with 2–3 years' age.

BUZET AC *South-West France* Good BORDEAUX-style red wines from th same mix of grapes, at a lower price. There is very little rosé and th whites are rarely exciting. Best producers: BUZET co-op, Dom. du Pech.

VIGNERONS DE BUZET *Buzet AC, South-West France* Controlling 90% o the production of BUZET, the local co-op has raised standards in this AC Some fine single-estate and branded reds, including Château de Padère

Château de Gueyze, Baron d'Ardeuil and the new wood-aged Grande Réserve. Best years: (Grande Réserve) (2005) 04 03 **01**.

A' DEL BOSCO *Franciacorta DOCG, Lombardy, Italy* Model estate, headed by Maurizio Zanella, making some of Italy's finest and most expensive international-style wines: outstanding sparklers in FRANCIACORTA Brut★★, Dosage Zero★, Satén★★ and the prestige Cuvée Annamaria Clementi★★★. Still wines include good Terre di Franciacorta Rosso★, remarkably good Chardonnay★★★, Pinero★★ (Pinot Noir) and BORDEAUX blend, Maurizio Zanella★★★. Also promising varietal Carmenère, Carmenero★.

ABARDÈS AC *Languedoc, France* Next door to MINERVOIS. Cabernet Sauvignon and Merlot are allowed, as well as the usual French Mediterranean grape varieties. At best, full-bodied, chewy and rustically attractive – and attractively priced. Best producers: Cabrol★, Jouclary, Pennautier★, Salitis, Ventenac. Best years: 2005 **04 03 02**.

ABERNET D'ANJOU AC *Loire Valley, France* Rosé made from both Cabernets; generally medium dry or semi-sweet. Drink young. Best producers: Hautes-Ouches, Ogereau, Petites Grouas, Terrebrune.

ABERNET FRANC Often unfairly dismissed as an inferior Cabernet Sauvignon, Cabernet Franc comes into its own in cool zones or areas where the soil is damp and heavy. It can have a leafy freshness linked to raw but tasty blackcurrant-raspberry fruit; lighter wines drink well lightly chilled. In France it thrives in the LOIRE VALLEY and BORDEAUX, especially ST-EMILION (AUSONE, CHEVAL BLANC) and POMEROL (LAFLEUR). Moderately successful where not overproduced in northern Italy, especially ALTO ADIGE and FRIULI, although some plantings here have turned out to be Carmenère, and increasingly preferred to Cabernet Sauvignon in Tuscany. It is the red of choice for many winemakers in the eastern United States, performing especially well in the FINGER LAKES and VIRGINIA. Experiments with Cabernet Franc on CALIFORNIA's North Coast and in WASHINGTON STATE show promise. There are also some good South African, Chilean and Australian examples.

ABERNET SAUVIGNON See pages 96–7.

ADENCE *Red Mountain AVA, Washington State, USA* A range of vineyard-specific reds. Tapteil Vineyard★★★, a powerful Cabernet Sauvignon-dominated blend, is the flagship; Ciel du Cheval Vineyard★★★ is more forward and juicy. Klipsun Vineyard★★ shows the characteristic firm tannins of the site. Best years: (2006) 05 **04 03 02 01 00 99**.

ADILLAC AC *Bordeaux, France* Sweet wine from the southern half of the PREMIERES COTES DE BORDEAUX. Styles vary from fresh, semi-sweet to richly botrytized. The wines have greatly improved in recent vintages. Drink young. Best producers: Fayau (Cuvée Grains Nobles★), Ch. du Juge, Manos★, Mémoires★, REYNON★. Best years: **2005 03 02 01 99 98**.

AHORS AC *South-West France* Important South-West red wine region. This dark, traditionally tannic wine is made from at least 70% Auxerrois (Malbec or Côt) and has an unforgettable, rich plummy flavour when ripe and well made – which is less often than I'd wish. Ages well. Best producers: la Caminade★, Cayrou, CEDRE★, Clos la Coutale★, Clos de Gamot★, CLOS TRIGUEDINA★, Gaudou, Gautoul★, Haut-Monplaisir, Haute-Serre, LAGREZETTE★, Lamartine★, les Laquets★, la Reyne, les Rigalets★. Best years: 2003 01 **00 98 96**.

95

CABERNET SAUVIGNON

 Wine made from Cabernet Sauvignon in places like Australi California, Chile, Bulgaria, even in parts of southern Franc has become so popular that many people may not realize whe it all started – and how Cabernet became the great, omnipreser red wine grape of the world.

WINE STYLES

Bordeaux Cabernet It all began in Bordeaux. With the exception of lively bunch of Merlot-based beauties in St-Émilion and Pomerol, th greatest red Bordeaux wines are based on Cabernet Sauvignon, wit varying amounts of Merlot, Cabernet Franc and possibly Petit Verd blended in. The blending is necessary because by itself Cabernet make such a strong, powerful, aggressive and assertive wine. Dark and tanni when young, the great Bordeaux wines need 10–20 years for th aggression to fade, the fruit becoming sweet and perfumed as fres blackcurrants, with a fragrance of cedarwood, of cigar boxes, minglin magically among the fruit. It is this character that has made red Bordeau famous for at least 2 centuries.

Cabernet worldwide When winemakers in other parts of the worl sought role models to try to improve their wines, most of ther automatically thought of Bordeaux and chose Cabernet Sauvignon. was lucky that they did, because not only is this variety easy to grow i almost all conditions – cool or warm, dry or damp – but that unstoppab personality always powers through. The cheaper wines are generall made to accentuate the blackcurrant fruit and the slightly earthy tannin They are drinkable young, but able to age surprisingly well. The mor ambitious wines are aged in oak barrels, often new ones, to enhance th tannin yet also to add spice and richness capable of developing over decade or more. Sometimes the Cabernet is blended – usually wit Merlot, sometimes with Cabernet Franc, and occasionally with othe grapes: Shiraz in Australia, Sangiovese in Italy, Tempranillo in Spain.

Europe Many vineyards in southern France now produce good affordable Cabernet Sauvignon. Spain has produced some goo Cabernet blends, as has Portugal. Italy's red wine quality revolution wa sparked off by the success of Cabernet in Tuscany, and all the leadin regions now grow it. Eastern Europe grows lots of Cabernet, but o widely varying quality, while the Eastern Mediterranean and Nort Africa are beginning to produce tasty examples. Germany has tried it bu is returning to Pinot Noir. Austria has had more success but is als returning to Blaufränkisch and Zweigelt.

New World There is a general move towards darker, denser, mor serious Cabernets, even in countries like Chile and Australia, whos Cabernet triumphs have until now been based on gorgeous blackcurran fruit, and New Zealand (previously light and green) and South Afric (previously pinched and unfriendly). I hope they don't ditch too much o the fruit, but I have to say that a lot of these new contenders are excellent Argentina is also pitching in with some powerful stuff. California' reputation was created by its strong, weighty Cabernets; she's at a bit o a crossroads right now, with some producers going to superhuma lengths to concentrate and overripen their wines, while others sho increasing restraint. I think I'm in the restraint camp for once.

BEST PRODUCERS

France
Bordeaux Dom. de CHEVALIER, COS D'ESTOURNEL, GRAND-PUY-LACOSTE, GRUAUD-LAROSE, LAFITE-ROTHSCHILD, LATOUR, LEOVILLE-BARTON, LEOVILLE-LAS-CASES, LYNCH-BAGES, Ch. MARGAUX, MOUTON-ROTHSCHILD, PICHON-LONGUEVILLE, RAUZAN-SEGLA; *Provence* TREVALLON.

Other European Cabernets
Italy BANFI, CA' DEL BOSCO, Col d'Orcia (Olmaia), GAJA, ISOLE E OLENA, LAGEDER, MACULAN, ORNELLAIA, Castello dei RAMPOLLA, SAN LEONARDO, SASSICAIA, SOLAIA, TASCA D'ALMERITA, Castello del TERRICCIO (Lupicaia), TUA RITA.

Spain BLECUA, MARQUES DE GRINON, TORRES.

New World Cabernets
Australia BALNAVES, CAPE MENTELLE, CULLEN, HOUGHTON (Jack Mann), HOWARD PARK, LEEUWIN (Art Series), MAJELLA, MOSS WOOD, PARKER ESTATE, PENFOLDS (Bin 707), PENLEY ESTATE, PETALUMA, SANDALFORD, WENDOUREE, The Willows, WIRRA WIRRA, Woodlands, WYNNS (John Riddoch), Zema.

New Zealand BABICH, CRAGGY RANGE, Esk Valley, GOLDWATER, Matariki, STONYRIDGE, TE MATA, Vidal, VILLA MARIA.

USA (California) ARAUJO, BERINGER, Bryant Family, CAYMUS, CHIMNEY ROCK, DALLA VALLE, DIAMOND CREEK, DOMINUS, DUNN, Grace Family, HARLAN, HARTWELL, LAUREL GLEN, Long Meadow Ranch, Peter MICHAEL, MINER, MONDAVI, NEWTON, PHELPS, RIDGE, St Supéry, SCREAMING EAGLE, SHAFER, SILVER OAK, SPOTTSWOODE, STAG'S LEAP, Viader; *(Washington)* ANDREW WILL, DELILLE, LEONETTI, QUILCEDA CREEK, WOODWARD CANYON.

Chile ALMAVIVA, CARMEN, CASABLANCA (Santa Isabel), CONCHA Y TORO, HARAS DE PIRQUE, QUEBRADA DE MACUL, SANTA RITA, TORRES.

Argentina CATENA, TERRAZAS DE LOS ANDES.

South Africa BEYERSKLOOF, BOEKENHOUTSKLOOF, BUITEN-VERWACHTING, Neil ELLIS, GRANGEHURST, KANONKOP, Le Riche, RUSTENBERG, SAXENBURG, THELEMA, VEENWOUDEN, VERGELEGEN.

CAIRANNE *Rhône Valley, France*   One of the top villages entitled to the COT▮ DU RHONE-VILLAGES appellation, offering full, herb-scented reds and soli▮ whites. Best producers: D & D Alary★★, Ameillaud★, Brusset★, Cave d▮ Cairanne★, les Hautes Cances★, ORATOIRE ST-MARTIN★★, Présidente★ Rabasse-Charavin★, M Richaud★★. Best years: (reds) (2007) 06 05 04 03 0▮ 00 99 98.

CALABRIA *Italy*   Italy's poorest, most backward and most corrupt region▮ CIRO, Donnici, Savuto and Scavigna DOC reds from the native Gaglioppo grape, and whites from Greco, are much improved thanks to greate▮ winemaking expertise. In a very restricted field the two leading producer▮ remain Librandi – who have recently added Magno Megonio★★, from th▮ obscure Magliocco variety, to an already fine range – and Odoardi, with thei▮ excellent Scavigna Vigna Garrone.

CALERA *San Benito, California, USA*   A pace-setter for California Pinot Noi▮ with 5 estate wines: Reed★★, Selleck★★, Jensen★★, Mills★★ an▮ newcomer Ryan★, which shows great potential. They are complex▮ fascinating wines with power and originality, and capable of aging▮ Mt Harlan Chardonnay★★ is excitingly original too. CENTRAL COAS▮ Chardonnay★ and Pinot Noir★ are good value. Small amounts o▮ Viognier★★ are succulent with sensuous fruit. Best years: (Pinot Noir▮ 2005 04 03 02 01 00 99 97 96 95; (Chardonnay) 2006 05 04 03 02 01 00 99

CALIFORNIA *USA*   California's importance is not simply in being th▮ fourth largest wine producer in the world (behind France, Italy and Spain)▮ Most of the revolutions in technology and style that have transformed th▮ expectations and achievements of winemakers in every country of the worl▮ – including France – were born in the ambitions of a band of Californian▮ winemakers during the 1960s and 70s. They challenged the old order, wit▮ its regulated, self-serving elitism, and democratized the world of fine win▮ to the benefit of every wine drinker. This revolutionary fervour is les▮ evident now. And there are times when Californians seem too intent o▮ establishing their own particular New World old order. A few figures▮ there are around 190,000ha (470,000 acres) of wine grape vineyards▮ producing around 20 million hectolitres (500 million gallons) of win▮ annually, about 90% of all wine made in the USA. A large proportio▮ comes from the hot, inland CENTRAL VALLEY. See also CENTRAL COAST▮ MENDOCINO COUNTY, MONTEREY COUNTY, NAPA VALLEY, SAN LUIS OBISPO COUNTY▮ SANTA BARBARA COUNTY, SONOMA COUNTY.

CH. CALON-SÉGUR★★ *St-Estèphe AC, 3ème Cru Classé, Haut-Médoc, Bordeaux▮ France*   Long considered one of ST-ESTEPHE's leading châteaux, but in th▮ mid-1980s the wines were not as good as they should have been▮ Vintages from the mid-1990s have been more impressive, with bette▮ fruit and a suppler texture. Second wine: Marquis de Calon. Best years▮ 2006 05 04 03 02 01 00 98 96 95 90 89 86.

CAMEL VALLEY *Cornwall, England*   The enterprising Lindos, Bob and Sam▮ are sparkling wine specialists who favour Seyval Blanc an▮ Reichensteiner over classic CHAMPAGNE varieties; the result is th▮ quintessentially English Camel Valley Brut★★. Sparkling Pinot Noir★★ (white and rosé) is also excellent, and still wines (dry white Bacchus★ Rosé★) are good, too.

‍CAMPANIA *Italy* Three regions – PUGLIA, SICILY and Campania – lead the evolution in Italy's south. Campania has made excellent progress in the white department, with varietals from Greco di Tufo, Fiano, Falanghina and several other native grapes. On the red side, other producers besides the venerable MASTROBERARDINO have begun to realize the potential of Campania's soil, climate and grapes, especially with the red Aglianico. DOC(G)s of note are SALERNO DEL MASSICO, Fiano di Avellino, Greco di Tufo, Ischia, TAURASI and Vesuvio. The leading red wines are Montevetrano★★★ (Cabernet-Merlot-Aglianico) and Galardi's Terra di Lavoro★★★ (Aglianico-Piedirosso), but also look for top Aglianicos from Antonio Caggiano★★, De Conciliis★, Feudi di San Gregorio★★, Luigi Maffini★, Michele Moio★, Salvatore Molettieri★, Orazio Rillo★, Cantina del Taburno★, San Paolo and others that fall outside the main DOCs.

‍CAMPILLO *Rioja DOCa, País Vasco, Spain* An upmarket subsidiary of Bodegas FAUSTINO, producing some exciting new red RIOJAS★. The wines are often Tempranillo-Cabernet Sauvignon blends, with masses of ripe, velvety fruit. Best years: (Reserva) 2004 03 01 99 98 96 95 94.

CAMPO DI SASSO *Tuscany, Italy* Brothers Piero and Lodovico ANTINORI's recently established venture in the commune of Bibbona, near BOLGHERI. Initial plantings include Cabernet Franc, Petit Verdot and Merlot. The first wine to emerge was the 2003 Insoglio del Cinghiale; Il Pino di Biserno came on stream in 2006; the top cru, Il Biserno, will follow.

CAMPO VIEJO *Rioja DOCa, Rioja, Spain* The largest producer of RIOJA is owned by Pernod Ricard. Reservas★ and Gran Reservas★ are reliably good, as are the elegant, all-Tempranillo Reserva Viña Alcorta and the barrel-fermented white Viña Alcorta. Albor Tempranillo is a good modern young Rioja, packed with fresh, pastilley fruit. Best years: (Reserva) 2004 03 01 98 96 95 94.

CANARY ISLANDS *Spain* The Canaries have a treasure trove of pre-phylloxera vines, and a total of 9 DOs. The sweet Malvasia from Lanzarote DO and La Palma DO is worth a try, and there are a couple of remarkable fresh dry whites, otherwise stick with the young reds. Best producers: El Grifo, Monje, Viña Norte, Tanajara★, Teneguía, Viñátigo★.

CANBERRA DISTRICT *New South Wales, Australia* Cool, high altitude (800m/2600ft) may sound good, but excessive cold and frost can be problematic. Lark Hill and Helm make exciting Riesling, Lark Hill and Brindabella Hills some smart Cabernet blends, and CLONAKILLA sublime Shiraz. Best producers: Brindabella Hills★, CLONAKILLA★★★, Doonkuna★, Helm★, Lake George★, Lark Hill★, Madew★, Mount Majura.

DOM. CANET-VALETTE *St-Chinian AC, Languedoc, France* Marc Valette is uncompromising in his quest to make great wine: organic cultivation, low yields and traditional *pigeage* (foot-stomping) are just some of his methods. The wines offer an enticingly rich expression of ST-CHINIAN's grape varieties and clay-limestone soils. Cuvées include Une et Mille Nuits (1001 Nights)★ and the powerful, complex Syrah-Grenache Le Vin Maghani★★. Best years: (Le Vin Maghani) (2004) 03 01 00 99.

CANNONAU Sardinian name of Spain's Garnacha and France's Grenache Noir. In SARDINIA it produces deep, tannic reds, but lighter, modern, dry red wines are gaining in popularity, although traditional sweet and

fortified styles can still be found. Best producers: (modern reds) ARGIOLA
SELLA & MOSCA; Dolianova, Dorgali, Jerzu, Alberto Loi, Ogliastra, Oliena, San
Maria La Palma and Trexenta co-ops.

CH. CANON★ *St-Émilion Grand Cru AC, 1er Grand Cru Classé, Bordeaux, Franc*
Canon can make some of the richest, most concentrated ST-ÉMILIONS, bu
it went into steep decline before being purchased in 1996 by Chane
Signs are that things have returned to form. In good vintages the wine
tannic and rich at first but is worth aging 10–15 years. Second wine: Clo
Canon. Best years: 2006 05 04 **03 02 01** 00 **98 89 88 85**.

CANON-FRONSAC AC *Bordeaux, France* This AC is the heart of th
FRONSAC region. The wines are quite sturdy when young but can age fo
10 years or more. Best producers: Barrabaque (Prestige★), Cassagne Hau
Canon (La Trufière★), la Fleur Cailleau, Gaby★, Grand-Renouil★, Hau
Mazeris, Moulin Pey-Labrie★★, Pavillon, Vrai Canon Bouché. Best years: 200
05 **03 01 00 98 96 95 90**.

CH. CANON-LA-GAFFELIÈRE★★ *St-Émilion Grand Cru AC, Grand Cru Class*
Bordeaux, France Owner Stephan von Neipperg has put this property a
the top of the list of ST-ÉMILION GRAND CRU CLASSES. The wines are firm, ric
and concentrated. He also owns Clos de l'Oratoire★, Ch. l'Aiguilhe★
in the COTES DE CASTILLON, and the remarkable micro-cuvée L
Mondotte★★. Best years: 2006 05 04 **03 02 01** 00 99 98 96 95.

CH. CANTEMERLE★ *Haut-Médoc AC, 5ème Cru Classé, Bordeaux, France* Wit
La LAGUNE, the most southerly of the Crus Classés. The wines are delica
in style and delightful in ripe vintages. Second wine: Les Allées d
Cantemerle. Best years: 2006 05 04 **03 01 00 98 96 95**.

CANTERBURY *South Island, New Zealand* The long, cool ripening season o
the arid central coast of South Island favours white varieties, particularl
Chardonnay, Pinot Gris, Sauvignon Blanc and Riesling, as well as Pino
Noir. The northerly Waipara district produces Canterbury's most excitin
wines, especially from Riesling and Pinot Noir. Best producers: Mountford★
PEGASUS BAY★★, Daniel Schuster★, Waipara West★. Best years: (Pinot Noir) (200
06 **03 02 01 00**; (Riesling) 2007 **06 04 02 01**.

CAPE MENTELLE *Margaret River, Western Australia* Leading MARGARET RIV
winery, owned by LVMH. Chief winemaker Rob Mann continues t
impress as Cape Mentelle produce superb, cedary Cabernet★★
impressive Shiraz★★ and Chardonnay★★, tangy Semillon-Sauvigno
Blanc★★ and wonderfully chewy Zinfandel★★. New Wallcliffe wine
are exceptional: densely concentrated Shiraz★★ and Sauvignon Blanc
Semillon★. All wines benefit from cellaring – whites up to 5 years, red
8–15. Best years: (Cabernet Sauvignon) (2005) 04 03 02 01 **94**.

CAPE POINT VINEYARDS *Cape Point WO, South Africa* Pioneering proper
influenced by bracing Atlantic breezes. Whites respond with vigour an
purity. Sauvignon Blanc★★ is astonishing, ocean-fresh, new and origina
Partially barrel-fermented Semillon★★ tantalizes with tangerine an
lemongrass intensity, while Isliedh★★, a barrel-fermented blend of bot
varieties, combines power with subtlety. Early reds, from a warmer sit
also show promise. Best years: (whites) **2007 06 05 04 03 02 01**.

CAPEL VALE *Geographe, Western Australia* The Pratten family's winer
sources fruit from its own vineyards in Geographe, Mount Barke
PEMBERTON and MARGARET RIVER. After an erratic history, this is now

winery very much on the up, using only the best varieties from each region, thoughtful winemaking, Larry Cherubino as consultant, and savvy marketing. Cheap and cheerful Debut range includes velvety Merlot★ and easy-drinking Pinot Noir. There's an impressive Regional Series, and two single-vineyard wines: intense yet fine Whispering Hill Riesling★★ and elegant, beautifully structured Whispering Hill Shiraz★★. Best years: (Whispering Hill Riesling) 2007 06 04 03 **02 01 00** 98 97.

ARIGNAN The dominant red grape in the south of France is responsible for much boring, cheap, harsh wine. But when made by carbonic maceration, the wine can have delicious spicy fruit. Old vines are capable of dense, rich, impressive reds, as shown by the odd success in France, California, Chile and South Africa. Although initially a Spanish grape (as Cariñena or Mazuelo), it is not that widespread there, but is useful for adding colour and acidity in RIOJA and CATALUÑA, and has gained unexpected respect in PRIORAT.

ARIGNANO DEL SULCIS DOC *Sardinia, Italy* Carignano is now producing wines of quite startling quality. Rocca Rubia★, a barrique-aged Riserva from the Santadi co-op, with rich, fleshy and chocolaty fruit, is one of SARDINIA's best reds. Baie Rosse★★ is a step up; even better is the more structured and concentrated Terre Brune★★. Best producer: Santadi co-op. Best years: (reds) (2007) (06) 05 **04 03 01 00** 99 98 97.

OUIS CARILLON & FILS *Puligny-Montrachet, Côte de Beaune, Burgundy, France* Excellent family-owned estate in PULIGNY-MONTRACHET. The emphasis is on traditional, finely balanced whites of great concentration, rather than new oak. Look out for Premiers Crus les Referts★★, Champs Canet★★ and les Perrières★★★, and the tiny but exquisite

production of Bienvenues-BATARD-MONTRACHET★★★. Reds from CHASSAGNE-MONTRACHET★, ST-AUBIN★ and MERCUREY★ are good, too. Best years: (whites) (2007) 06 05 **04 03 02 01 00** 99.

ARIÑENA DO *Aragón, Spain* The largest DO of ARAGON, baking under the mercilessly hot sun in inland eastern Spain, Cariñena has traditionally been a land of cheap, deep red, alcoholic wines from the Garnacha grape. (Confusingly the Carignan grape is called Cariñena in Spain, but is practically absent from the Cariñena region.) Since the late 1990s, however, temperature-controlled fermentation has been working wonders with this unfairly despised grape, and Tempranillo and international grape varieties like Cabernet Sauvignon are being planted widely. Best producers: Añadas★, San Valero (Monte Ducay, Don Mendo), Solar de Urbezo, Victoria★.

ARLEI *Victoria, Australia* Outstanding biodynamic producer, with Chardonnay★★ and Pinot Noir★ from YARRA VALLEY and Shiraz★★ from HEATHCOTE. Sergio Carlei's signature blends are Tre Rossi★ (Shiraz-Barbera-Nebbiolo), Tre Amici (Sangiovese-Cabernet-Merlot) and Tre Bianchi (Sauvignon with small amounts of Semillon and Chardonnay). The modestly priced Green Vineyards range offers very good regional varietals: Chardonnay and Pinot Noir from the Yarra, Heathcote Shiraz, Central Victorian Cabernet and Cardinia Ranges Pinot Gris.

101

CARMEN *Maipo, Chile* Some of the best reds in MAIPO, including Go
Reserve★★, a limited release made with Carmen's oldest Cabern
Sauvignon vines, Reserve Carmenère-Cabernet★★, balanced, compl
Wine Maker's Reserve★★ and organic Nativa Cabernet Sauvignon★
(sometimes ★★★). Best years: (reds) (2006) 05 **04 03 02 01 00 99**.

CARMENÈRE An important but forgotten constituent of BORDEAUX blends
the 19th century, historically known as Grande Vidure. Planted in Chil
it was generally labelled as Merlot until 1994 (and often still is). Whe
ripe and made with care, it has rich blackberry, plum and spice flavou
with an unexpected but delicious bunch of savoury characters – grill
meat, soy sauce, celery, coffee – thrown in. A true original. Also found
northern Italy, where it has been confused with Cabernet Fran
Argentina and China. Being replanted in Bordeaux.

CARMIGNANO DOCG *Tuscany, Italy* Red wine from the west of Florenc
renowned since the 16th century and revived in the 1970s by Capezzan
The blend (Sangiovese, plus 10–20% Cabernet) is one of Tuscany's mo
refined wines and can be quite long-lived. Although Carmignano
DOCG, DOC applies to a lighter red Barco Reale, rosé Vin Ruspo ar
fine VIN SANTO. Best producers: Ambra★ (Vigne Alte★★), Artimino
Capezzana★★, Le Farnete/E Pierazzuoli★ (Riserva★★), Piaggia★★, Pratesi
Villa di Trefiano★. Best years: (2007) (06) 04 **03 02 01 00 99 98 97 95**.

CARNEROS AVA *California, USA* Hugging the northern edge of Sa
Francisco Bay, Carneros includes parts of both NAPA and SONOM
Counties. Windswept and chilly with morning fog off the Bay, it is a to
cool-climate area, suitable for Chardonnay and Pinot Noir as both tab
wine and a base for sparkling wine. Merlot and even Syrah are al
coming on well. Best producers: ACACIA★★, Buena Vista★, Carneros Creek
DOMAINE CARNEROS★★, HdV★★, Ramey★★, RASMUSSEN★★, SAINTSBURY★
Truchard★★. Best years: (Pinot Noir) 2006 05 **04 03 02 01** 99 98.

CARNUNTUM *Niederösterreich, Austria* 890ha (2200-acre) wine region sou
of the Danube and east of Vienna, with a strong red wine tradition. Be
producers: Glatzer, G Markowitsch★, Muhr-van der Niepoort★, Pitnauer★.

CASA LAPOSTOLLE *Rapel, Chile* Owned by Marnier-Lapostolle of Franc
with consultancy from leading BORDEAUX winemaker Michel Rollan
Cuvée Alexandre Merlot★★, from the acclaimed Apalta area
COLCHAGUA, was its first big hit back in 1994, now eclipsed by red blend Cle
Apalta★★★. Also rich, creamy Cuvée Alexandre Chardonnay★ from th
CASABLANCA Valley and Borobo, a peculiar blend of Pinot Noi
Carmenère, Cabernet Sauvignon, Syrah and Merlot.

CASA MARÍN *San Antonio, Chile* Impressive whites, led by single-vineya
Sauvignon Blancs: Laurel★★ is powerful, full of mineral and intense chi
and fruit flavours, while Cipreses★★★ shows the influence of the Paci
Ocean in its citrus and stony aromas. Casona Vineyard Gewürztraminer
and Estero Sauvignon Gris★ are good, too – and there's juicy, coo
climate Pinot Noir★, with a single-vineyard Syrah to come.

CASABLANCA, VALLE DE *Aconcagua, Chile* Coastal valley with a coo
climate personality that is powerful proof of Chile's ability to do region
style. Whites dominate, with best results from Chardonnay, Sauvigno
Blanc and Gewürztraminer. Even so, the Pinot Noir is some of Chile
best, and Merlot and Carmenère – as well as a new community of Syra
(Casablanca, Casas del Bosque, Kingston, Loma Larga) – are very goo

Best producers: (whites) CASA LAPOSTOLLE★, CASABLANCA★, CASAS DEL BOSQUE★, CONCHA Y TORO★★, EMILIANA★, ERRAZURIZ★, MONTES, Morandé★, Veramonte★. Best years: (whites) **2007 06 04**.

ASABLANCA, VIÑA *Casablanca, Chile* The cool Santa Isabel Estate in CASABLANCA is the source of top wines such as quince-edged Chardonnay★, minty, exotic Merlot★★ and Cabernet Sauvignon★★. Under the Nimbus Estate label there is rose- and lychee-filled Gewürztraminer★, excellent, tangy, intense Sauvignon Blanc★, inky-black Cabernet Sauvignon★ and low-yield Merlot★★. Flagship red blend Neblus★ is made only in the best years.

ASAS DEL BOSQUE *Casablanca, Chile* This winery, located in the coolest area of CASABLANCA Valley, has a special focus on Sauvignon Blanc (Reserve★). The reds are good too, especially the red blend Estate Selection★ and Reserve Syrah★, all from Casablanca's cold slopes. Best years: (whites) **2007 06 04**.

ASE BASSE *Brunello di Montalcino DOCG, Tuscany, Italy* Gianfranco Soldera unblushingly proclaims his BRUNELLO DI MONTALCINO★★★ and Brunello di Montalcino Riserva★★★ wines (the latter usually under the Intistieti label) to be the best of their genre and, maddeningly, he's right. A fanatical biodynamist, Soldera believes perfect grapes are all you need to make great wine. He ages his wines for a minimum of 5 years in large old (and hence neutral) oak barrels; the result is a wine of brilliant colour and an amazing intensity and complexity of perfumes. Best years: (2007) (06) (04) (03) (01) 99 **98 97 95 93 90 88 85**.

H. LA CASENOVE *Côtes du Roussillon AC, Roussillon, France* Former photojournalist Étienne Montès, with consultant enologist Jean-Luc COLOMBO, has developed an impressive range, including a perfumed white Vin de Pays Catalan made from Macabeu and Torbat, MUSCAT DE RIVESALTES★, RIVESALTES★ and 2 predominantly Syrah reds: Dom. Saint-Luc Pla del Rei★★ and Commandant François Jaubert★★. Drink this with at least 5 years' bottle age. Best years: (François Jaubert) (2005) 04 **00**.

ASSIS AC *Provence, France* A picturesque fishing port near Marseille. The white wine, based on Ugni Blanc and Clairette, is overpriced but can be good if fresh. The red wine is dull, but the rosé can be pleasant (especially from a single estate). Best producers: Bagnol★, Caillol, Clos Ste-Magdelaine★, la Ferme Blanche★, Fontblanche, Ch. de Fontcreuse, Mas de Boudard. Best years: (white) 2006 **05 04 02 01**.

ASTEL DEL MONTE DOC *Puglia, Italy* An arid, hilly zone, and an ideal habitat for the Uva di Troia grape, producing long-lived red wine of astonishing character. There is also varietal Aglianico, some good rosé, and the whites produced from international varieties are improving. Best producers: RIVERA★, Santa Lucia, Tormaresca★/ANTINORI, Torrevento★. Best years: (2007) (06) **04 03 01 00 97**.

ASTELLARE *Chianti Classico DOCG, Tuscany, Italy* Fine estate with excellent CHIANTI CLASSICO★ and deeper, richer Riserva★★. Canonico di Castellare★ (Chardonnay), Coniale di Castellare★★ (Cabernet Sauvignon) and Spartito di Castellare★ (Sauvignon Blanc) are all ripe and fruity. Top wine I Sodi di San Niccolò★★ is an unusual Sangiovese-Malvasia blend, intense but finely perfumed.

ASTILLA-LA MANCHA *Spain* The biggest wine region in the world; hot, ry country with poor clay-chalk soil. The DOs of the central plateau, La ANCHA and VALDEPENAS, make white wines from the Airén grape, and some good reds from the Cencibel (Tempranillo). Méntrida DO, Manchuela DO Ribera del Júcar DO, Almansa DO and the new Uclés DO make fast improving reds. The most ambitious wines made here are those from MARQU DE GRIÑON's Dominio de Valdepusa★★ estate near the Tagus river and the Dehesa del Carrizal★ and Pago de Vallegarcía★ estates, both in the Toled mountains. Uribes Madero's Calzadilla★ in Cuenca province, Fine Sandoval★★ from Manchuela, Ercavio★ from Toledo and Manu Manzaneque's Cabernet-based reds★ and Chardonnay★ from Sierra Alcaraz in Albacete province are full of promise. Manzaneque now has his ow DO, Finca Élez, as do the Dominio de Valdepusa and Dehesa del Carriza

CASTILLA Y LEÓN *Spain* This is Spain's harsh, high plateau, with lor cold winters and hot summers (but always cool nights). A few rivers, notabl the Duero, temper this climate and afford fine conditions for viticulture. Aft many decades of winemaking ignorance, with a few exceptions like VEC SICILIA, the situation has changed radically for the better in all of the region DOs: RIBERA DEL DUERO, RUEDA, BIERZO, Cigales and TORO. Dynamic winemake such as Telmo RODRIGUEZ and Mariano García (AALTO and MAURO) have wo huge critical acclaim for the region.

CATALUÑA *Spain* Standards vary among the region's DOs. PENEDE between Barcelona and Tarragona, has the greatest number of technical equipped wineries in Spain, but doesn't make a commensurate number superior wines. In the south, mountainous, isolated PRIORAT has become a ne icon for its heady, raging reds, and the neighbouring DOs of Montsant an Terra Alta are following in its footsteps. Inland COSTERS DEL SEGRE and Cone de Barberá make potentially excellent reds and whites. Up the coast, Alel makes attractive whites and Ampurdán-Costa Brava (Empordá-Cos Brava), by the French border, is showing signs of life. Cataluña also make most of Spain's CAVA sparkling wines. The Catalunya DO allows (generall inexpensive blends from anywhere in the region.

CATENA ZAPATA *Mendoza, Argentina* Argentinian pioneer Nicol Catena's admiration for California is evident in the ripe, gentle, oaky Alamos range. However, Catena has vines in some of the best terroirs in MENDOZA and the wines in the Alta range – Chardonnay★, Cabernet Sauvignon★★ and Malbec★★ – are now developing a recognizable sense of place. Cabernet-based Nicolás Catena Zapata★★ and Malbec Argentino★★ are top-flight. Caro★, a joint venture with LAFITE-ROTHSCHILD, successfully combines French restraint with Argentinian panache.

SYLVAIN CATHIARD *Vosne-Romanée, Côte de Nuits, Burgundy, France* Sylvai Cathiard first achieved international recognition in the late 1990s and ha made brilliant wines even in difficult vintages since then. The stars ai VOSNE-ROMANEE Les Malconsorts★★★ and ROMANEE ST-VIVANT★★★ but he village Vosne-Romanée★★ and NUITS-ST-GEORGES Aux Murgers★★ a excellent too. Best years: (2007) 06 05 04 03 **02 01 00 99**.

DOM. CAUHAPÉ *Jurançon AC, South-West France* Henri Ramonteu has bee a major influence in JURANCON, proving that the area can make comple dry whites as well as more traditional sweet wines. Chant des Vignes★

a dry, unoaked Jurançon Sec; the oaked version is Sève d'Automne★. Top wines are dry La Canopée★★, sweet Noblesse du Temps★★ and barrel-fermented Quintessence★★★. Best years: (sweet wines) (2005) 04 01.

CAVA DO *Spain* Cava, the Catalan name for CHAMPAGNE-method fizz, is made throughout Spain, but most comes from CATALUNA. Grapes are the local trio of Parellada, Macabeo and Xarel-lo, although some good Cavas in Cataluña as well as VALENCIA are made with Chardonnay and Pinot Noir. The best-value, fruitiest Cavas are generally the youngest, with no more than the minimum 9 months' aging. A number of top-quality wines are now produced but are seldom seen abroad, since their prices are too close to those of Champagne to attract international customers. Best producers: Can Feixes, Can Ràfols dels Caus★, Castell de Vilarnau, Castellblanch, CODORNIU★, Colet★, FREIXENET, Juve y Camps, Marqués de Monistrol, Parxet★, RAIMAT, Raventós i Blanc, Rovellats, Signat★, Agustí Torelló★, Dominio de la Vega★, Jané Ventura.

CAYMUS VINEYARDS *Napa Valley AVA, California, USA* Caymus Cabernet Sauvignon★ is ripe, intense and generally tannic; it can be outstanding as a Special Selection★★★. Conundrum★ is an exotic, full-flavoured white blend. Also successful MONTEREY Chardonnay under the Mer Soleil★★ label. Best years: (Special Selection) 2005 04 03 **02 01 00 99 98 97 95 94 91 90 87 86 84**.

CAYUSE VINEYARDS *Walla Walla Valley AVA, Washington State, USA* Winemaker Christophe Baron has created a cult label here. His superb Viognier★★★ is crisp, floral and spicy, yet he is best known for his Syrahs. Using French clones, he farms a vineyard reminiscent of some in CHATEAUNEUF-DU-PAPE for its large stones. Vineyard-designated Syrahs include Cailloux★★, with a distinctive mineral flavour and chocolate depth, and En Cerise★★, with more cherry and raspberry flavour but equal richness. The Bionic Frog★★ sports a cartoon-ish label but is a serious Syrah, reminding me of a northern RHONE version. Cabernet-based Camaspelo★ is a fascinating redcurrant and jalapeño-scented wine. Best years: (Syrah) (2006) 05 **04 03** 02.

DOM. CAZES *Rivesaltes, Roussillon, France* The Cazes brothers make outstanding MUSCAT DE RIVESALTES★★, RIVESALTES Vieux★★ and the superb Aimé Cazes★★, but also produce a range of table wines. Soft red, white and rosé Le Canon du Maréchal★ are good, as are the Syrah-Grenache-Mourvèdre blend Alter★, the Cabernet-based Vin de Pays des Côtes Catalanes Le Credo★, COTES DU ROUSSILLON-VILLAGES Trilogy★ and the small production of barrel-fermented Chardonnay.

CH. DU CÈDRE *Cahors AC, South-West France* Pascal Verhaeghe leads the new generation of CAHORS winemakers. His wines are dark, richly textured, with a generous coating of chocolaty oak. There are 3 special cuvées: Le Prestige★; the 100% Auxerrois (Malbec) Le Cèdre★★, which is aged in new oak barrels for 20 months; and Cuvée GC★, which is fermented and aged in oak. All benefit from at least 5–6 years' bottle age. Best years: (Le Cèdre) 2003 01 00 **99 98**.

CENCIBEL See TEMPRANILLO.

CENTRAL COAST AVA *California, USA* Huge AVA covering virtually every vineyard between San Francisco and Los Angeles, with a number of sub-AVAs, such as SANTA CRUZ MOUNTAINS, Santa Ynez Valley, SANTA MARIA VALLEY and Monterey. There is superb potential for Pinot Noir and Syrah in Santa Lucia Highlands in the western Monterey area. See also MONTEREY COUNTY, SAN LUIS OBISPO COUNTY, SANTA BARBARA COUNTY.

CENTRAL OTAGO *South Island, New Zealand* The only wine region in New Zealand with a continental rather than maritime climate. Technically the ripening season is long and cool, suiting Pinot Noir, Gewürztraminer, Chardonnay and Pinot Gris, but there are usually periods of considerable heat during the summer to intensify flavour. Long autumns have produced some excellent Rieslings. There are already nearly 100 wineries and an explosion of plantings, both in good areas like Bannockburn and Lowburn, and in marginal zones. Latest expansion is to the Waitaki Valley in northern Otago. Best producers: Akarua★, Carrick★★, Chard Farm★, FELTON ROAD★★, Gibbston Valley★, Kawarau Estate★, Mt Difficulty★★, Mount Edward★, Mount Maude, Nevis Bluff★, Peregrine★★, Pisa Range★, Quartz Reef★★, Rippon★★, Two Paddocks★, Wild Earth★. Best years: (Pinot Noir) (2007) **06 05 03 02 01**.

CENTRAL VALLEY/VALLE CENTRAL *Chile* The heart of Chile's wine industry, encompassing the valleys of MAIPO, RAPEL, CURICO and MAULE. Most major producers are located here, and the key factor determining mesoclimate differences is the distance relative to the Coastal Ranges and the Andean Cordillera.

CENTRAL VALLEY *California, USA* This vast area grows 75% of California's wine grapes, used mostly for cheaper styles of wine, along with brandies and grape concentrate. It is a hot area, where irrigated vineyards tend to produce excess tonnages of grapes. It has often been said that it is virtually impossible to produce exciting wine in the Central Valley, but in fact the climatic conditions in the northern half are not unlike those in many parts of Spain and southern France and, viewed overall, quality has improved in recent years. Vineyards in the Lodi AVA have expanded to 40,500ha (nearly 100,000 acres), making Lodi the volume and quality leader for Chardonnay, Merlot, Zinfandel and Cabernet; Lodi Zinfandel shows most potential. Other sub-regions with claims to quality are the Sacramento Valley and the Delta area. Best producers: Ironstone★, McManis★, Michael-David★, RAVENSWOOD (Lodi★), Woodbridge/MONDAVI.

CENTRAL VICTORIA *Victoria, Australia* This zone comprises the regions of BENDIGO, HEATHCOTE, Goulburn Valley and the cooler Strathbogie Ranges and Upper Goulburn. Central Victoria, with its mostly warm conditions, produces powerful and individual wines. The few wineries on the banks of the Goulburn River feature fine Shiraz and Marsanne; reds from the high country are rich but scented and dry; whites are delicate and scented. Best producers: Jasper Hill★★, Mitchelton★, Paul Osicka★, PONDALOWIE★, TAHBILK★, Wild Duck Creek★.

CERETTO *Piedmont, Italy* This merchant house was one of the chief modern producers in BAROLO in the 1970s and 80s. Today, Barolo (Bricco Rocche★★, Brunate★ and Prapò★), BARBARESCO (Bricco Asili★), BARBERA D'ALBA Piana★ and white Arneis Blangè, while still good, are being overtaken by smaller, more specialist, growers. Ceretto also produces an oak-aged LANGHE red, Monsordo★, from Cabernet, Merlot, Pinot Nero and Nebbiolo. An unusual white counterpart, Arbarei, is 100% Riesling. A good fizz, La Bernardina, is made from Chardonnay and Pinot Noir.

CÉRONS AC *Bordeaux, France* An AC for sweet, soft, mildly honeyed wine in the GRAVES region of Bordeaux. The wine is not quite as sweet as SAUTERNES and not so well known, nor so highly priced. Most producers now make dry wine under the Graves AC. Best producers: Ch. de Cérons★, Chantegrive★, Grand Enclos du Château de Cérons★, Haura, Seuil. Best years: **2005 03 02 01 99 98 97 96 95 90 89**.

LA CETTO *Baja California, Mexico* Mexico's most successful winery relies on mists and cooling Pacific breezes to temper the heat of the Valle de Guadalupe in the northern part of Baja California. Italian Camillo Magoni makes ripe, fleshy Petite Sirah★, oak-aged Cabernet Sauvignon, Zinfandel and Nebbiolo. Whites, led by Chardonnay and Chenin, are greatly improved. Also good fizz.

CHABLAIS *Vaud, Switzerland* A sub-region of the VAUD, south-east of Lake Geneva along the right bank of the Rhône. Most of the vineyards lie on the alluvial plains but 2 villages, Yvorne and Aigle, benefit from much steeper slopes. Most of the thirst-quenchingly dry whites are made from Chasselas. The reds are from Pinot Noir, as is a rosé speciality, Oeil de Perdrix. Drink whites and rosés young. Best producers: Badoux, la Baudelière, Conne, J & P Testuz★.

CHABLIS AC *Burgundy, France* Chablis, lying closer to CHAMPAGNE than to the COTE D'OR, is Burgundy's northernmost outpost. When not destroyed by frost or hail, the Chardonnay grape makes a crisp, dry white wine with a steely mineral fruit which can be delicious. Several producers have taken to barrel-aging for their better wines, resulting in some full, toasty, positively rich dry whites. Others are intentionally producing a soft, creamy, early-drinking style, which is nice but not really typical Chablis. Outlying vineyards come under the Petit Chablis AC and these wines should be drunk young. The better straight Chablis AC should be drunk at 2–4 years, while a good vintage of a leading Chablis Premier Cru may take 5 years to show its full potential. About a quarter of Chablis is designated as Premier Cru, the best vineyards on the rolling limestone slopes being Fourchaume, Mont de Milieu, Montmains, Montée de Tonnerre and Vaillons. Best producers: Barat★, J-C Bessin (Fourchaume★★), Billaud-Simon★ (Mont de Milieu★★), Pascal Bouchard★, A & F Boudin★★, BROCARD★★, la CHABLISIENNE★, Collet★, D Dampt★, R & V DAUVISSAT★★, D-E Defaix★, Droin★, DROUHIN★, DURUP★ (Montée de Tonnerre★★), W Fèvre★★, J-P Grossot (Côte de Troesme★★), LAROCHE★★, Long-Depaquit, Malandes (Côte de Léchêt★★), Louis Michel★★, de Moor★, Christian Moreau★, Picq (Vaucoupin★★), Pinson★, RAVENEAU★★, Vocoret★★. Best years: (Chablis Premier Cru) (2007) 06 05 **04** 02 00 99.

CHABLIS GRAND CRU AC *Burgundy, France* The 7 Grands Crus (Bougros, les Preuses, Vaudésir, Grenouilles, Valmur, les Clos and les Blanchots) facing south-west across the town of Chablis are the heart of the Chablis vineyards. Oak barrel-aging takes the edge off taut flavours, adding a rich warmth to these fine wines. Droin and Fèvre are the most enthusiastic users of new oak, but use it less than they used to. Never drink young: 5–10 years are needed before you can see why you spent your money. Best producers: J-C Bessin★★, Billaud-Simon★★, Pascal Bouchard★, BROCARD★★, R & V DAUVISSAT★★★, D-E Defaix★★, Droin★★, W Fèvre★★★, LAROCHE★★, Long-Depaquit★★, L Michel★★★, Christian Moreau★★, Pinson★★, RAVENEAU★★★, Servin★, Vocoret★★. Best years: (2007) 06 05 02 **00** 99 98 97 96 95 92 90.

LA CHABLISIENNE *Chablis AC, Burgundy, France* Substantial co-op producing nearly a third of all CHABLIS. The wines are reliable and can aspire to something much better. The best are the oaky Grands Crus – especially les Preuses★★ and Grenouilles (sold as Ch. Grenouille★★) – but the basic unoaked Chablis★, the Vieilles Vignes★★ and the numerous Premiers Crus★ are good, as is the red BOURGOGNE Épineuil. Best years: (whites) (2007) 06 **05** 04 03 02.

CHAMPAGNE AC

Champagne, France

The Champagne region produces the most celebrated sparkling wines in the world. It is the most northerly AC in France – a place where grapes struggle to ripen fully, but provide the perfect base wine to make fizz. Champagne is divided into 5 distinct areas – the best are the Montagne de Reims, where the Pinot Noir grape performs brilliantly, and the Chardonnay-dominated Côte des Blancs south of Épernay. In addition to Chardonnay and Pinot Noir, the other main grape permitted for the production of Champagne is Pinot Meunier.

The wines undergo a second fermentation in the bottle, producing carbon dioxide which dissolves in the wine under pressure. Through this method Champagne acquires its crisp, long-lasting bubbles and a distinctive yeasty, toasty dimension to its flavour. If you buy a bottle of Coteaux Champenois, a still wine from the area, you can see why they decided to make bubbly instead; it usually tastes mean and tart, but is transformed by the Champagne method into one of the most delightfully exhilarating wines of all.

That's the theory anyway, and for 150 years or so the Champenois have persuaded us that their product is second to none. It can be, too, except when it is released too young or sweetened to make up for a lack of richness. When that periodically happens you know that, once again, the powers of marketing have triumphed over the wisdom and skills of the winemaker. But as Champagne expertise begins to turn out exciting sparklers in California, Australia and New Zealand, the Champagne producers must re-focus on quality or lose much of their market for good.

The Champagne trade is dominated by large companies or houses, called négociants-manipulants, recognized by the letters NM on the label. The récoltants-manipulants (RM) are growers who make their own wine, and they are becoming increasingly important for drinkers seeking characterful Champagne.

STYLES OF CHAMPAGNE

Non-vintage Most Champagne is a blend of 2 or more vintages. Quality varies enormously, depending on who has made the wine and how long it has been aged. Most Champagne is sold as Brut, which is a dry, but rarely bone-dry style, but more extremely dry styles – called Extra Brut, Ultra Brut, Brut Zero and the like – are appearing. Strangely, Extra Dry denotes a style less dry than Brut.

Vintage Denotes Champagne made with grapes from a single vintage. As a rule, it is made only in the best years, but far too many mediocre years were declared in the 1990s.

Blanc de Blancs A lighter, and at best highly elegant, style of Champagne made solely from the Chardonnay grape.

Blanc de Noirs White Champagne made entirely from black grapes, either Pinot Noir, Pinot Meunier, or a combination of the two.

Rosé Pink Champagne, made either from black grapes or (more usually) by mixing a little still red wine into white Champagne.

De luxe cuvée In theory the finest Champagne and certainly always the most expensive, residing in the fanciest bottles.

See also CHAMPAGNE ROSE; and individual producers.

BEST PRODUCERS

Houses BILLECART-SALMON, BOLLINGER, Cattier, Delamotte, DEUTZ, Drappier, Duval-Leroy, Gosset, Alfred GRATIEN, Charles HEIDSIECK, HENRIOT, JACQUESSON, KRUG, LANSON, LAURENT-PERRIER, Bruno PAILLARD, Joseph PERRIER, PERRIER-JOUET, Philipponnat, PIPER-HEIDSIECK, POL ROGER, POMMERY, Louis ROEDERER, RUINART, Salon, TAITTINGER, VEUVE CLICQUOT.

Growers Michel Arnould, Paul Bara, Barnaut, Beaufort, Beerens, Roger le Brun, Chartogne-Taillet, Paul Déthune, Diebolt Vallois, Daniel Dumont, Egly-Ouriet, René Geoffroy, Gimonnet, H Goutorbe, André Jacquart, Lamiable, Larmandier, Larmandier-Bernier, Launois, Margaine, Serge Mathieu, J Michel, Moncuit, Jérôme Prévost, Alain Robert, Secondé, Selosse, de Sousa, Tarlant, Vilmart.

Co-ops Beaumont des Crayères, H Blin, Nicolas Feuillatte, Jacquart, Mailly, Le Mesnil, Union Champagne.

De luxe cuvées Belle Époque (PERRIER-JOUET), N-F Billecart (BILLECART-SALMON), Blanc de Millénaires (Charles HEIDSIECK), Clos des Goisses (Philipponnat), Clos de Mesnil (KRUG), Comtes de Champagne (TAITTINGER), Cristal (Louis ROEDERER), Cuvée Josephine (Joseph PERRIER), Cuvée Sir Winston Churchill (POL ROGER), Cuvée William Deutz (DEUTZ), Dom Pérignon (MOET & CHANDON), Dom Ruinart (RUINART), Grand Siècle (LAURENT-PERRIER), Grande Dame (VEUVE CLICQUOT), Noble Cuvée (LANSON), Vintage RD (BOLLINGER).

CHAMBERS *Rutherglen, Victoria, Australia* Legendary family winery makin
sheer nectar in the form of Muscat and Tokay. The secret is Bi
Chambers' ability to draw on ancient stocks put down in wood by earlie
generations. His Grand★★ and Rare★★★ blends are national treasure
The Cabernet and Shiraz table wines are good, the whites pedestria

CHAMBERTIN AC *Grand Cru, Côte de Nuits, Burgundy, France* The village c
GEVREY-CHAMBERTIN, the largest COTE DE NUITS commune, has no fewer tha
9 Grands Crus (Chambertin, Chambertin-Clos-de-Bèze, Chapelle
Chambertin, Charmes-Chambertin, Griotte-Chambertin, Latricières
Chambertin, Mazis-Chambertin, Ruchottes-Chambertin and the rarel
seen Mazoyères-Chambertin), which can produce some of Burgundy
greatest and most intense red wine. Its rough-hewn fruit, seeming to wa
with fragrant perfumes for its first few years, creates remarkable flavour
as the wine ages. Chambertin and Chambertin-Clos-de-Bèze ar
neighbours on the slope above the village and the two greatest sites, bu
overproduction is a recurrent problem with some producers. Bes
producers: Denis Bachelet★★ (Charmes), BOUCHARD PERE ET FILS★★
Charlopin★, B CLAIR★★, P Damoy★★, DROUHIN★★, Drouhin-Laroze★★
C Dugat★★★, B Dugat-Py★★★, FAIVELEY★★, JADOT★★, D Laurent★★, Dom
LEROY★★★, Denis MORTET★★★, H Perrot-Minot★★, Ponsot★★, Rossigno
Trapet★★, J Roty★★ (Charmes), ROUMIER★★ (Ruchottes), ROUSSEAU★★★
J & J-L Trapet★★, VOUGERAIE★★. Best years: (2007) 06 05 03 02 **01 00** 99 9
97 96 95 93 90.

CHAMBOLLE-MUSIGNY AC *Côte de Nuits, Burgundy, France* AC with th
potential to produce the most fragrant, perfumed red Burgundy, whe
not over-cropped. Encouragingly, more young producers are nov
bottling their own wines. Best producers: Amiot-Servelle★, G Barthod★★,
J Confuron★, DROUHIN★★, DUJAC★★, R Groffier★★, Hudelot-Noëllat★★
JADOT★★, Dom. LEROY★★, F Magnien★, Marchand-Grillot★★, D MORTET★, J-
MUGNIER★★, RION★★, ROUMIER★★, VOGUE★★. Best years: (2007) 06 05 03 0
01 00 99 98 97 96 95 93 90.

CHAMPAGNE See pages 108–9.

CHAMPAGNE ROSÉ *Champagne, France* Good pink CHAMPAGNE – usually
little weightier than white – has a delicious fragrance of cherries an
raspberries. The top wines can age well, but most rosé Champagn
should be drunk on release, as young as possible. Best producers: (vintage
BILLECART-SALMON★★, BOLLINGER★★, Gosset★★, Charles HEIDSIECK★★
JACQUESSON★★, LAURENT-PERRIER (Grand Siècle Alexandra★★★), MOET &
CHANDON★★ (Dom Pérignon★★★), PERRIER-JOUET (Belle Époque★), PO
ROGER★★, POMMERY (Louise★★), Louis ROEDERER★★ (Cristal★★★), RUINAR
(Dom Ruinart★★★), TAITTINGER (Comtes de Champagne★★), VEUV
CLICQUOT★★ (Grande Dame★★); (non-vintage) Paul Bara★, E Barnaut★★
Beaumont des Crayères★, BILLECART-SALMON★★, Egly-Ouriet★★, Henr
Giraud★, Jacquart★, KRUG★★, LANSON★, LAURENT-PERRIER★, MOET &
CHANDON, RUINART★, TAITTINGER, Vilmart★. Best years: (2002) 00 99 98 96 9
90 89 88 85 82. See also pages 108–9.

CHANDON DE BRIAILLES *Savigny-lès-Beaune, Côte de Beaune, Burgundy, France*
The de Nicolays – François and his sister Claude – combine moderr
sophistication with traditional values to produce rich but refined reds
from SAVIGNY-LES-BEAUNE★, PERNAND-VERGELESSES★, ALOXE-CORTON★ anc
CORTON★, and an equally good range of whites from Pernand-
Vergelesses★★, Corton★★ and CORTON-CHARLEMAGNE★★★. Best years
(reds) (2007) 06 05 03 **02 99 98 96**.

CHANNING DAUGHTERS *Long Island, New York State, USA* A boutique winery in LONG ISLAND's Hamptons AVA that produces exciting but hard-to-find wines, including a racy Sauvignon Blanc★, a Muscat-based blend called Sylvanus★ and a juicy Blaufrankisch★.

CHAPEL DOWN *Kent, England* The UK's largest winery, producing around 500,000 bottles a year. Most grapes are grown under contract by growers in the south and east of England, although a recent purchase of land in Kent will see 32ha (80 acres) of CHAMPAGNE varieties planted in 2008. Wines of good to very good quality, especially non-vintage Chapel Down Brut, Pinot Reserve Sparkling and still Bacchus and Rosé.

CHAPEL HILL *McLaren Vale, South Australia* It would appear that the work of chief winemaker Michael Fragos and some exceptional vintages have added a further dimension to the powerful classy reds of Chapel Hill. The Cabernet Sauvignon★★ is a successful blend of mature MCLAREN VALE and COONAWARRA fruit, while the Shiraz★★ is all McLaren Vale. Good Unwooded Chardonnay★ and fascinating, bone-dry, honey-scented Verdelho★★. Best years: (Shiraz) 2006 05 04 02 **01 98 97 96 95 94 93 91**.

CHAPELLE-CHAMBERTIN AC See CHAMBERTIN AC.

CHAPELLE LENCLOS *Madiran AC, South-West France* A leading name in MADIRAN, Patrick Ducournau has tamed the savage Tannat grape with his invention of microoxygenation, or *microbullage* – bubbling tiny amounts of oxygen into the wine, either during fermentation or during barrel aging. Chapelle Lenclos★★ and Dom. Mouréou★ reds are ripe and concentrated, though they need at least 5 years to mature. Also sweet white PACHERENC DU VIC-BILH. Best years: (reds) (2005) 03 01 **00 99 98**.

M CHAPOUTIER *Rhône Valley, France* The biodynamic house of Chapoutier is in the vanguard of progress in viticulture and winemaking, and is producing serious, exciting wines. The HERMITAGE la Sizeranne★★ and special Ermitages (les Greffieux★★, l'Ermite★★, le Méal★★★ and le Pavillon★★★), white Hermitage de l'Orée★★ and l'Ermite★★★, CROZES-HERMITAGE les Varonniers★★, ST-JOSEPH les Granits★★ (red and white), and CHATEAUNEUF-DU-PAPE Barbe Rac★ and Croix de Bois★ are all good, but some reds show a surfeit of new oak. Large-volume Crozes-Hermitage les Meysonniers and COTES DU RHONE Belleruche are good value. Also BANYULS, COTEAUX DU TRICASTIN and Australian joint ventures. Best years: (la Sizeranne) (2007) 06 05 04 03 **01 00 99 98 95 94 91 90 89 88**.

CHARDONNAY See pages 112–13.

CHARMES-CHAMBERTIN AC See CHAMBERTIN AC.

CHASSAGNE-MONTRACHET AC *Côte de Beaune, Burgundy, France* Some of Burgundy's greatest white wine vineyards (part of le MONTRACHET and BATARD-MONTRACHET, all of Criots-Bâtard-Montrachet) are within the village boundary. The white Chassagne Premiers Crus are not as well known, but can offer nutty, toasty wines, especially if aged for 4–8 years; Blanchots Dessus, Chaumées, Ruchotte and Morgeots are among the best. Ordinary white Chassagne-Montrachet is usually enjoyable; the red is a little earthy, peppery and plummy and can be an acquired taste. Look out for reds from the following Premiers Crus: Clos de la Boudriotte, Clos St-Jean and Clos de la Chapelle. Best producers: (whites) Blain-Gagnard★★, B Colin★, B Colin, M Colin★★, P Colin★, Colin-Deléger★★, J-N GAGNARD★★, V GIRARDIN★★, V & F Jouard★, H Lamy★, B Morey★★, M Morey★★, M Niellon★★, J & J-M Pillot★, P Pillot★, RAMONET★★, VERGET★★; (reds) CARILLON★, R Clerget★, V GIRARDIN★★, B Morey★★, RAMONET★★. Best years: (whites) (2007) 06 05 **02 01 00 99**; (reds) (2007) 06 05 03 **02 99**.

CHARDONNAY

I never thought I'd see myself write this. Yes, we are gettin
bored with Chardonnay. Not all Chardonnay: there's probabl
more top Chardonnay being produced right now than eve
before. And for millions of wine drinkers the Chardonna
revolution (easy to pronounce, easy to swallow) has only ju
begun. But in the heart of the wine world – the middle market, wher
people care about flavour but also care about price – we're getting fed up
Far too much sugary, over-oaked, unrefreshing junk has been dumpe
into our laps recently, from countries and producers who should kno
better. Add to this the increasingly desperate dirt-cheap offerings at th
rump end of the market, and you'll see why I think the great golde
goose of Chardonnay has the carving knife of cynicism and greed firml
held against its neck. The next few years will show whether it wishes t
be the supremely versatile all-rounder or the sloppy jack of all trades an
master of none.

WINE STYLES

France Although a relatively neutral variety if left alone (this is wha
makes it so suitable as a base wine for top-quality Champagne-metho
sparkling wine), the grape can ripen in a surprising range of condition
developing a subtle gradation of flavours going from the sharp apple-co
greenness of Chardonnay grown in Champagne or the Loire Valle
through the exciting, bone-dry yet succulent flavours of white Burgund
to a round, tropical flavour in Languedoc-Roussillon.

Other regions Italy produces Chardonnay that can be bone dry and lea
or fat, spicy and lush. Spain does much the same. California an
Australia virtually created their reputations on great, viscous, almo
syrupy, tropical fruits and spice-flavoured Chardonnays; the be
producers are now moving away from this style. Some of the best Ne
World Chardonnays, dry but ripe and subtly oaked, are coming fro
South Africa. Unoaked versions from more mature vines off
increasingly characterful, food-friendly drinking. New Zealand
producing rich, deep, but beautifully balanced Chardonnays, while Chi
and Argentina are rapidly learning how to make fine wine from it to
Add Germany, Austria, Canada, New York State, Greece, Portuga
Slovenia, Moldova, Romania, even China, and you'll see it can perfor
almost anywhere.

Using oak The reason for all these different flavours lies in Chardonnay
wonderful susceptibility to the winemaker's aspirations and skills. Th
most important manipulation is the use of the oak barrel for fermentin
and aging the wine. Chardonnay is the grape of the great whi
Burgundies and these are fermented and matured in oak (not necessari
new oak); the effect is to give a marvellous round, nutty richness to
wine that is yet savoury and dry. This is enriched still further by aging th
wine on its lees.

The New World winemakers sought to emulate the gre
Burgundies, planting Chardonnay and employing thousands of oa
barrels (mostly new), and their success has caused winemake
everywhere else to see Chardonnay as the perfect variety – easy to gro
easy to turn into wine and easy to sell to an adoring public. But as in a
things, familiarity can breed contempt.

BEST PRODUCERS

France *Chablis* Billaud-Simon, A & F Boudin, DAUVISSAT, Fèvre, LAROCHE, RAVENEAU; *Côte d'Or* R Ampeau, J-M Boillot, Bonneau du Martray, BOUCHARD PERE ET FILS, CARILLON, COCHE-DURY, M Colin, DROUHIN, A Ente, J-P Fichet, J-N GAGNARD, V GIRARDIN, JADOT, F Jobard, LAFON, H Lamy, Dom. LEFLAIVE, B Morey, M Niellon, RAMONET, G Roulot, SAUZET, VERGET; *Mâconnais* D & M Barraud, Bret Brothers, Guffens-Heynen/VERGET, O Merlin, J Thévenet.

Other European Chardonnays
Austria BRUNDLMAYER, TEMENT, VELICH.

Germany JOHNER, REBHOLZ, WITTMANN.

Italy Castello di AMA, BELLAVISTA, CA' DEL BOSCO, GAJA, ISOLE E OLENA, LAGEDER, Lis Neris, Castello della SALA (Cervaro), TIEFENBRUNNER (Linticlarus), Vie di Romans.

Spain CHIVITE, ENATE, Manzaneque, Muñoz, Señorío de Otazu, TORRES.

New World Chardonnays
Australia BANNOCKBURN, Brookland Valley, CAPE MENTELLE, CULLEN, Evans & Tate, By FARR, GIACONDA, GROSSET, HOWARD PARK, LEEUWIN (Art Series), Oakridge (864), PENFOLDS (Yattarna), PETALUMA, PIERRO, Savaterre, SHAW & SMITH, TAPANAPPA (Tiers Vineyard), TARRAWARRA, TYRRELL'S, VOYAGER.

New Zealand BABICH, CLOUDY BAY, CRAGGY RANGE, DRY RIVER, FELTON ROAD, FROMM, GOLDWATER, ISABEL, KUMEU RIVER, MATUA VALLEY, MILLTON, MONTANA, Morton Estate, NEUDORF, PEGASUS BAY, SAINT CLAIR, SERESIN, VAVASOUR, Vidal, VILLA MARIA, WITHER HILLS.

USA ARROWOOD, AU BON CLIMAT, BERINGER, CALERA, CHATEAU ST JEAN, DOMAINE DROUHIN OREGON, FERRARI-CARANO, FLOWERS, HdV, IRON HORSE, KISTLER, MARCASSIN, MATANZAS CREEK, MERRYVALE, Peter MICHAEL, NEWTON, Ramey, RIDGE, ROCHIOLI, SAINTSBURY, SANFORD, SHAFER, STEELE, TALBOTT.

South Africa BUITENVERWACHTING, Chamonix, Neil ELLIS (Elgin), HAMILTON RUSSELL, JORDAN, MULDERBOSCH, THELEMA, VERGELEGEN, Waterford.

South America CATENA, CONCHA Y TORO (Amelia), CONO SUR (20 Barrels), DE MARTINO, Tabalí/SAN PEDRO.

CHASSELAS Chasselas is considered a table grape worldwide. Only in BADEN (where it is called Gutedel) and Switzerland (called FENDANT) is i thought to make decent light, dry wines with a slight prickle. A few Swiss examples, notably from CHABLAIS and DEZALEY, rise above this.

CH. CHASSE-SPLEEN★ *Moulis AC, Haut-Médoc, Bordeaux, France* Chasse-Spleen is not a Classed Growth – but during the 1980s it built a tremendous reputation for ripe, concentrated and powerful wines under the late proprietor, Bernadette Villars. The château is now run by Villars daughter Céline, and recent vintages are approaching the form of the old days. Second wine: l'Ermitage de Chasse-Spleen. Best years: 2006 05 04 03 02 01 00 99 96 95 90 89.

CHÂTEAU-CHALON AC *Jura, France* The most prized – and pricey – *vin jaune*, it is difficult to find, even in the Jura. But if you do find a bottle beware – the awesome flavour will shock your tastebuds like no other French wine. Aged like sherry under a yeast flor. Not released until 6 years after the vintage, it can be kept for much longer. Best producers Baud★, Berthet-Bondet★★, Bourdy★★, Chalandard★★, Crédoz★, Durand-Perron★★, J Macle★★, H Maire. Best years: (2000) 99 98 97 96 95 94 93 92 91 90 89 88 87.

CHÂTEAU-GRILLET AC★★ *Rhône Valley, France* This rare and very expensive RHONE white, made from Viognier and aged in used oak, has a magic reek of orchard fruit and harvest bloom when young but is best drunk after 5 years, and decanted. More reserved, more refined than CONDRIEU. Best years: 2006 05 **04** 03 01 00 98 95.

CHATEAU INDAGE *Maharashtra, India* India's first traditional-method sparkling wine appeared in the 1980s, with technical assistance from Champagne's PIPER-HEIDSIECK. Dry sparklers are firm, fresh and chunky – though quality is somewhat erratic. Omar Khayyám is produced from a blend of Chardonnay, Ugni Blanc, Pinot Noir and Pinot Meunier. A demi-sec and a good pink fizz are also produced. Red and white table wines use both international and indigenous Indian grape varieties such as Bangalore Purple and Arkavati.

CHATEAU MONTELENA *Napa Valley AVA, California, USA* NAPA winery producing classic California Chardonnay★★ and an estate Cabernet★★ which are impressive, if slow to develop. The Napa Valley Cabernet★ is an elegant wine for younger consumption. Best years: (Chardonnay) 2006 05 04 03 **02 01 00** 99 98; (Cabernet) 2005 03 02 **01 00 99 98 91** 90.

CHATEAU MUSAR *Ghazir, Lebanon* Founded by Gaston Hochar in the 1930s and now run by his Bordeaux-trained son Serge, Musar is famous for having made wine every year bar two (1976 and 84) throughout Lebanon's civil war. From an unlikely blend of primarily Cabernet Sauvignon and Cinsaut comes a wine of real, if wildly exotic, character with sweet, spicy fruit and good aging potential: Hochar says that red Musar★ 'should be drunk at 15 years'. Some recent vintages have not quite lived up to expectations, but latest harvests are encouraging. There is also a rosé, and a white from local Chardonnay and Sémillon lookalikes Obaideh and Merwah. Hochar Père et Fils is ready to drink upon release as is Musar Cuvée Reservée, which is not aged in oak. Best years: (red) 2000 **99 98 97 96 95 94 93** 91 89 88; (white) **1999 98 97**.

CHATEAU ST JEAN *Sonoma Valley AVA, California, USA* Once known almost entirely for its range of Chardonnays (Belle Terre★★, Robert Young★★), St Jean has emerged as a producer of delicious reds including a BORDEAUX-style blend called Cinq Cépages★★ and a Reserve Merlot★★. Now owned by the Foster's Group. Best years: (Chardonnay) (2006) **05 04 03 02 01 00 99**; (reds) (2005) 04 03 **02 01 00 99 97 95** 94.

CHATEAU STE MICHELLE *Washington State, USA* Pioneering winery with an enormous range of wines, including several attractive vineyard-designated Chardonnays★ (some ★★), Cabernet Sauvignons★ and Merlots★, especially Cold Creek Vineyard★★ and Indian Wells★ wines. Good Riesling, both dry and sweet, and increasingly interesting red Meritage★ and spicy Orphelin★★ Rhône-style blend. Partnership with Italy's ANTINORI and Germany's Ernst LOOSEN have produced dark, powerful Tuscan-style red Col Solare★★, attractive Riesling Eroica★ and a thrilling sweet version, Single Berry Select★★★, made in tiny quantities. Quality generally seems to be moving upwards. Best years: (premium reds) (2006) **05 04 03 02 01 00**.

CHÂTEAUNEUF-DU-PAPE AC *Rhône Valley, France* A large (3350ha/ 8275-acre) vineyard area between Orange and Avignon. The sweetly fruited red wine is based on Grenache, plus Syrah and Mourvèdre (10 other varieties are also allowed). Always choose Châteauneuf from a single estate, distinguished by the papal coat of arms or mitre embossed on the neck of the bottle. Only 5% of Châteauneuf is white; made mainly from Grenache Blanc, Bourboulenc and Clairette, these wines can be surprisingly good. Top reds, particularly old-vine cuvées, will age for 10 years or more; whites are best young. Best producers: (reds) P Autard★, L Barrot★, BEAUCASTEL★★★, Beaurenard★★, Bois de Boursan★★, H Bonneau★★, Bosquet des Papes★★, du Caillou★, les Cailloux★★, Chante-Perdrix★, CHAPOUTIER★, la Charbonnière★★, L Charvin★★, Clos du Mont Olivet★★, CLOS DES PAPES★★, Cristia★★, Font du Loup★, FONT DE MICHELLE★★, Fortia★★, la Gardine★★, Grand Tinel★★, Grand Veneur★, la Janasse★★, Marcoux★★, Mathieu★★, Millière★, Monpertuis★★, Mont-Redon★★, la Nerthe★★, Pégaü★★, RAYAS★★★, Roquette★, Roger Sabon★★, Solitude★★, Tardieu-Laurent★★, P Usseglio★★, la Vieille-Julienne★★, Le Vieux Donjon★, VIEUX TELEGRAPHE★★★, Villeneuve★; (whites) BEAUCASTEL★★★, CLOS DES PAPES★★, FONT DE MICHELLE★★, Grand Veneur★, Marcoux★★, RAYAS★★, St-Cosme★, VIEUX TELEGRAPHE★★. Best years: (reds) (2007) 06 **05 04 03 01 00 99 98 96 95 94 90 89 88**.

JEAN-LOUIS CHAVE *Rhône Valley, France* Jean-Louis Chave's red HERMITAGE★★★ is one of the world's great wines, surpassed only by the Cathelin★★★, produced in exceptional years. His wonderful, richly flavoured white Hermitage★★★ sometimes even outlasts the reds, as it quietly moves towards its honeyed, nutty zenith. Also produces a small amount of excellent red ST-JOSEPH★★ and an occasional stunning traditional sweet Vin de Paille★★. Expensive, but worth the money. Best years: (reds) (2007) 06 05 04 03 01 **00 99 98 97 96 95 94 92 91 90 89 88 86 85 83 82 79 78**; (whites) (2007) 06 05 04 03 **01 00 99 98 97 96 95 94 93 92 91 90 89 88 85 83**.

CHÉNAS AC *Beaujolais, Burgundy, France* The smallest of the BEAUJOLAIS Crus, Chénas offers a range of styles from light and elegant to austere and needing time to develop Burgundian tones. Best producers: Champagnon★, DUBOEUF, Nathalie Fauvin, H Lapierre★, B Santé★. Best years: **2007 06 05**.

CHENIN BLANC One of the most underrated and versatile white wine grapes in the world. In the LOIRE VALLEY, where it is also called Pineau de la Loire, it is responsible for sweet, dry and sparkling wines. The great sweet wines of COTEAUX DU LAYON, QUARTS DE CHAUME, BONNEZEAUX and VOUVRAY are some of the longest-lived of all wines. There is an increasing emphasis on barrel-fermented and aged dry wines, especially in ANJOU, the best of which are a revelation. In South Africa, Chenin Blanc remains both the most planted and most uprooted variety: vineyard area continues to decrease, but the best sites are being retained and the best wines are being compared favourably with their Loire counterparts. Styles range from sparkling through easy-drinking, dryish wines and modern barrel-fermented versions to botrytized dessert wines. New Zealand and Australia have produced good varietal examples, and it is also grown in California and Argentina.

CH. CHEVAL BLANC★★★ *St-Émilion Grand Cru AC, 1er Grand Cru Classé, Bordeaux, France* Along with AUSONE, the leading ST-EMILION estate. Right on the border with POMEROL, it seems to share some of its sturdy richness, but with an extra spice and purity of fruit that is impressively, recognizably unique. An unusually high percentage (60%) of

Cabernet Franc is often used in the blend. Appealing when young, yet with a remarkable ability to age for many decades. Best years: 2006 05 04 **03 02 01** 00 99 98 97 96 95 94 90 89 88 86 85 83.

CHEVALIER-MONTRACHET AC See MONTRACHET AC.

DOM. DE CHEVALIER *Pessac-Léognan AC, Cru Classé de Graves, Bordeaux, France* Some of Bordeaux's finest wines. The red★★ starts out firm and reserved but over 10–20 years gains heavenly cedar, tobacco and blackcurrant flavour. The brilliant white★★★ is both fermented and aged in oak barrels; in the best vintages it will still be improving at 15–20 years. Best years: (reds) 2006 05 04 **03 02 01** 00 **99 98 96 90 89 88**; (whites) 2006 **05 04 03 02 01** 00 99 98 96 95 94 90 89 88.

CHEVERNY AC *Loire Valley, France* A little-known area south of Blois. The local speciality is the white Romorantin grape, which makes a bone-dry wine under the AC Cour-Cheverny, but the best whites are from Chardonnay. Also pleasant Sauvignon, Pinot Noir, Gamay and bracing CHAMPAGNE-method fizz. Drink young. Best producers: Cazin, Cheverny co op, Courtioux, Gendrier/Huards★, Gueritte, H Marionnet, du Moulin, Salvard, Sauger, C Tessier/la Desoucherie, Tue-Boeuf★.

CHIANTI DOCG *Tuscany, Italy* The most famous of all Italian wines, but there are many styles, depending on what grapes are used, where they are grown, and by which producer. It can be a light, fresh, easy-drinking red wine with a characteristic hint of bitterness, or it can be an intense structured yet sleek wine in the same league as the best BORDEAUX. The vineyards are scattered over central Tuscany, either simply as 'Chianti' or Chianti plus the name of one of the 7 sub-zones: Colli Aretini, Colli Fiorentini, Colli Senesi, Colline Pisane, Montalbano, Montespertoli and Rufina. Sangiovese is the main grape; traditionally it was blended with the red Canaiolo and white Malvasia and Trebbiano. Modern wine-makers often make Chianti from Sangiovese alone or blended with 20% of Cabernet, Merlot, Syrah or, increasingly, with native grapes like Colorino. See also CHIANTI RUFINA, SUPER-TUSCANS. Best producers: (Chianti Colli Fiorentini) Baggiolino★, Le Calvane, Il Corno, Corzano e Paterno★,

Lanciola★, Malenchini★, Pasolini dall'Onda★, Poppiano★, La Querce, Sammontana, San Vito in Fior di Selva; (Chianti Colli Senesi) Campriano, Carpineta Fontalpino★, Casabianca, Casale-Falchini★, Farnetella★, Ficomontanino★, Pacina★, Paradiso★, Pietraserena.

CHIANTI CLASSICO DOCG *Tuscany, Italy* The original (if slightly enlarged) CHIANTI zone in the hills between Florence and Siena. Classico has led the trend in making richer, more structured and better-balanced wines. Nonetheless, until recently many producers used their best grapes for high-profile SUPER-TUSCANS. Since the '96 vintage, Classico can be made from 100% Sangiovese, though winemakers all too often accept the option of including 20% 'international' grapes (see CHIANTI). Riserva must be aged at least 27 months (usually in barrel) and must use only red grapes. The finest Riserva wines can improve for a decade or more. Many of the estates also offer regular bottlings of red wine, round and fruity, for drinking about 2–5 years after the harvest. **Best producers (Riserva or top cru):** Castello di AMA★★★, ANTINORI★ (Riserva★★), Badia a Coltibuono★, Brancaia★, Cacchiano★★, Capaccia★★, Carpineto★, Casaloste★★, CASTELLARE★, Castell'in Villa★, Collelungo★★, Colombaio di Cencio★★, Dievole★, Casa Emma★★, FELSINA★★, Le Filigare★, FONTERUTOLI★★, FONTODI★★, ISOLE E OLENA★★, Il Mandorlo★★, La Massa★★, Melini★, MONSANTO★★★, Il Palazzino★★, Paneretta★★, Panzanello★★, Poggerino★, Poggiopiano★★, Poggio al Sole (Casasilia★★★), Querceto★, QUERCIABELLA★★★, Castello dei RAMPOLLA★, RICASOLI (Castello di Brolio★★), RIECINE★★, Rignana★★, Rocca di Castagnoli★★, San Felice★★, San Giusto a Rentennano★★, San Polo in Rosso★, Casa Sola★★, Terrabianca★, Vecchie Terre di Montefili★★, Verrazzano★, Vignamaggio★, Villa Cafaggio★★, VOLPAIA★★. **Best years:** (2007) (06) **04 03 01 99 97 95 90.**

CHIANTI RUFINA DOCG *Tuscany, Italy* Smallest of the CHIANTI sub-zones, an enclave of the Apennine foothills to the east of Florence, where wines were noted for exceptional structure and longevity long before they joined the ranks of Chianti. Today the wines, particularly the long-lived Riserva Bucerchiale from SELVAPIANA and FRESCOBALDI's Montesodi, match the best of CHIANTI CLASSICO. Pomino DOC is a small (100ha/250-acre) high-altitude zone almost entirely surrounded by Chianti Rufina; dominated by Frescobaldi, it makes greater use of French varieties such as Merlot, Cabernet and Chardonnay. **Best producers (Rufina Riservas)** Basciano★★, Tenuta di Bossi★, Colognole★★, FRESCOBALDI★★, Grati/Villa di Vetrice★, Grignano★, Lavacchio★, SELVAPIANA★★★, Castello del Trebbio★. **Best years:** (2007) (06) **04 03 01 99 97 95.**

MICHELE CHIARLO *Piedmont, Italy* From his winery base south of Asti, Michele Chiarlo produces stylish wines from several PIEDMONT zones. Single-vineyard BAROLOS★★ and BARBARESCOS★★ top the list, but BARBERA D'ASTI★ and GAVI★ are reliable, too. The Monferrato DOC embraces Montemareto Countacc!★, a Barbera-Cabernet Sauvignon blend.

CHIMNEY ROCK *Stags Leap District AVA, California, USA* Powerful yet elegantly sculpted Cabernet Sauvignon★★ (Reserve★★) and a meritage blend called Elevage★★. There's also an ageworthy Elevage Blanc★ (a blend of Sauvignons Blanc and Gris), a tangy Fumé Blanc★ and a Cabernet Franc rosé. **Best years:** (Elevage) 2004 03 **02 01** 00 99 98 97 96 95.

CHINON AC *Loire Valley, France* Best red wine of the LOIRE VALLEY, made mainly from Cabernet Franc. Lovely light reds full of raspberry fruit and fresh summer earth to drink young, and heavyweights for keeping; always worth buying a single-estate wine. **Best producers:** P Alliet★★,

B Baudry★★, Baudry-Dutour★, Dom. de Beauséjour, Logis de la Bouchardière, P Breton★, Coulaine★, COULY-DUTHEIL★, DRUET★★, la Grille★, C Joguet★, la Noblaie, Rouet, Wilfrid Rousse, P Sourdais★. Best years: 2006 05 **04 03 02** 01 97 96 95.

CHIROUBLES AC *Beaujolais, Burgundy, France* The highest in altitude of the BEAUJOLAIS Crus, producing a light, fragrant, delicious Gamay wine exhibiting all the attractions of a youthful Cru. Best producers: Cheysson★, la Combe au Loup/Méziat★, la Grosse Pierre/A Passot★, Javernand, J Passot★. Best years: **2007** 06.

CHIVITE *Navarra DO, Navarra, Spain* Longtime leader in exports from NAVARRA. The Gran Feudo★ red and rosé are very good easy drinkers and unoaked Chardonnay★★ is excellent. The more upmarket reds have improved steadily in a restrained, claret-like style. The top range, called Colección 125, includes a red Reserva★, classy white Blanco★★ (barrel-fermented Chardonnay) and a characterful sweet Vendimia Tardía★★ from Moscatel de Grano Menudo (Muscat Blanc à Petits Grains).

CHOREY-LÈS-BEAUNE AC *Côte de Beaune, Burgundy, France* One of those tiny, forgotten villages that make good, if not great, Burgundy at prices most of us can afford, with some committed producers too. Can age for 5–8 years. Best producers: Arnoux★, DROUHIN★, Germain/Ch. de Chorey★, Maillard★, TOLLOT-BEAUT★★. Best years: (2007) 06 **05** 03 02 99.

CHURCH ROAD *Hawkes Bay, North Island, New Zealand* A premium-wine project owned by Pernod Ricard. The reds seem a bit Bordeaux-obsessed, although Reserve wines, made in the best years, can be very good. Reserve Chardonnay★★ leapt in quality in recent years to become one of the country's best. Best years: (reds) (2007) 06 **04 02 00** 98.

CHURCHILL *Port DOC, Douro, Portugal* Established in 1981, it was the first new PORT shipper for 50 years. The wines can be good, notably Vintage★, LBV★, Crusted★, single-quinta Gricha★ and a well-aged, nutty dry white port★, and are much more consistent since Quinta da Gricha was bought in 1999. Since 2003, Churchill Estates, an unfortified DOURO red, has also improved. Best years: (Vintage) **2003** 00 97 94 91 85; (Quinta da Gricha) **2003** 01 99.

CINSAUT Also spelt Cinsault. Found mainly in France's southern RHÔNE VALLEY, PROVENCE and LANGUEDOC-ROUSSILLON, giving a light wine with fresh, but rather fleeting, neutral fruit. Ideal for rosé wine. In blends, Cinsaut's low alcohol can help calm high-degree Grenache. Used in the blend for Lebanon's CHATEAU MUSAR. Popular as a bulk blender in South Africa, it is now being rediscovered by enthusiasts of the Rhône style.

CIRÒ DOC *Calabria, Italy* The legend that this was the wine offered to champions in the ancient Olympics has often seemed a more potent reason to buy it than for its quality. Yet Cirò Rosso, a full-bodied red from the Gaglioppo grape, has improved remarkably of late. Non-DOC Gaglioppo-based IGTs, like Librandi's Gravello★★ (an oak-aged blend with Cabernet), are genuinely exciting. The DOC also covers a dry white from Greco and a rare dry rosé. Best producers: Caparra & Siciliani★, Librandi★ (Riserva★★), San Francesco★. Best years: (reds) (2007) (06) 05 **04** 03 01 00.

BRUNO CLAIR *Marsannay, Côte de Nuits, Burgundy, France* Top producer from MARSANNAY with several single-vineyard cuvées there and an impressive range from other top vineyards including CHAMBERTIN Clos de Bèze★★, and Gevrey-Chambertin Clos St-Jacques★★. Also good-value SAVIGNY La Dominade★★ and a delicious Marsannay rosé★. Best years: (top reds) (2007) 06 05 03 02 **01 00** 99 **98** 96 90.

CLAIRETTE DE DIE AC *Rhône Valley, France* Sparkling wine made from a minimum of 75% Muscat, off-dry, with a creamy bubble and a honeyed, orchard-fresh fragrance. The *méthode Dioise* is used, which preserves the Muscat scent. An ideal light aperitif. Drink young. Best producers: Achard-Vincent★, Clairette de Die co-op, D Cornillon, Jacques Faure, J-C Raspail★. See also CREMANT DE DIE.

A CLAPE *Cornas, Rhône Valley, France* Leading estate in CORNAS – dense, tannic, consistently excellent wines, full of rich, roasted fruit and often ★★★. Second wine Renaissance is good lower-key Cornas. Clape also makes fine red and white COTES DU RHONE★ and decent ST-PERAY★. Best years: (Cornas) (2007) 06 05 04 03 **02** 01 **00 99** 98 97 96 95 94 91 90 89 88 86 85 83.

LA CLAPE *Coteaux du Languedoc AC, Languedoc, France* The mountain of La Clape rises above the flat coastal fields south-east of Narbonne; its vineyards produce some excellent whites from Bourboulenc and Clairette, plus fine, herb-scented reds and rosés, mainly from Grenache, Syrah and Mourvèdre. Whites and reds can age. Best producers: Bouisset, Camplazens★★, Capitoul, l'HOSPITALET★, Mire l'Étang, Négly, Pech-Céleyran★, Pech Redon★, Vires. Best years: (reds) 2005 04 **03 01** 00.

CLARE VALLEY *South Australia* Historic upland region north of Adelaide with a deceptively moderate climate, able to grow both hot-climate and cool-climate grapes successfully, including fine, aromatic Riesling, marvellously textured Semillon, scented Viognier, rich, robust Shiraz and Cabernet blends and peppery but voluptuous Grenache. Best producers: (whites) Tim ADAMS★★, Jim BARRY★, Wolf BLASS (Gold Label★), Leo Buring (Leonay★★), Crabtree, GROSSET★★★, KNAPPSTEIN★★ (Ackland Vineyard★★★), LEASINGHAM★, MITCHELL★, MOUNT HORROCKS★★, O'Leary Walker★★, PETALUMA★★★, Pikes★, SKILLOGALEE★, Taylors/Wakefield★; (reds) Tim ADAMS★★★, Jim BARRY★★, GROSSET★★, Kilikanoon★, KNAPPSTEIN★, LEASINGHAM★, MITCHELL★, O'Leary Walker★, Pikes★, SKILLOGALEE★, Taylors/Wakefield, WENDOUREE★★★. Best years: (Shiraz) 2006 05 04 03 02 **01** 99 98 97 96 94 93 92 91 90 88 86; (Riesling) **2006** 05 04 03 02 01 99 98 97 96 95.

CLARENDON HILLS *McLaren Vale, South Australia* Winery with a name for high-priced, highly extracted, unfined, unfiltered and unobtainable reds. Single-vineyard Astralis★★ is a hugely concentrated Syrah from old vines, aged in 100% French new oak. Other Syrah ★★ labels offer slightly better value, while Merlot★ and Cabernet Sauvignon★ aim to rub shoulders with great red BORDEAUX – although I'm not sure which ones. Several cuvées of Old Vines Grenache★★ are marked by saturated black cherry fruit and high alcohol. Best years: (Astralis) (2006) (05) 04 03 02 01 00 98 **96** 95 94.

CH. CLARKE★ *Listrac-Médoc AC, Bordeaux, France* This property had millions spent on it by the late Baron Edmond de Rothschild during the late 1970s, and from the 98 vintage leading Bordeaux winemaker Michel Rolland has been consultant enologist. The wines can have an attractive blackcurrant fruit and now a little more ripeness and polish. With a name like Clarke, how could they possibly fail to seduce? There is also a small production of dry white wine, le Merle Blanc. Best years: 2006 05 04 **03 01** 00 99 98 96.

DOMENICO CLERICO *Barolo DOCG, Piedmont, Italy* Domenico Clerico produces consistently superlative BAROLO (Ciabot Mentin Ginestra★★★ Pajana★★★, Per Cristina★★★) and excellent BARBERA D'ALBA★ (Trevigne★★), all wonderfully balanced. His range also includes LANGHE Arte★★, a barrique-aged blend of Nebbiolo and Barbera. Best years: (Barolo) (2007) (06) 04 **03** 01 **00 99 98 97 96 95 93 90 89 88**.

CH. CLIMENS★★★ *Barsac AC, 1er Cru Classé, Bordeaux, France* The leading estate in BARSAC, with a deserved reputation for fabulous, sensuous wines rich and succulent yet streaked with lively lemon acidity. Easy to drink at 5 years, but a good vintage will be richer and more satisfying after 10–15 years. Second wine: les Cyprès (also delicious). Best years: 2006 05 04 03 **02 01 00 99 98 97 96 95 90 89 88**.

CLONAKILLA *Canberra, Australia* Tim Kirk's small family winery, whose stellar Shiraz-Viognier★★★ is regarded as the benchmark for the style in Australia; it is elegant, lavender-scented, fleshily textured and complex, with the structure to age beautifully. Riesling and Viognier★ are good, too. A more modestly priced and increasingly interesting Shiraz is made from grapes purchased from nearby HILLTOPS.

CLOS DE L'ANHEL *Corbières AC, Languedoc, France* In just a few years, Sophie Guiraudon and Philippe Mathias have started to produce remarkable wines with a power unusual even for the CORBIERES. Top wine is smooth, rich Les Dimanches★★; also Les Terrassettes★ and Le Lolo de l'Anhel. Best years: (Les Dimanches) 2005 04 03 01 00.

CLOS BAGATELLE *St-Chinian AC, Languedoc-Roussillon, France* Siblings Luc and Christine Simon produce various ST-CHINIANS: top wine La Gloire de Mon Père★ is made from Syrah, Mourvèdre and Grenache, and aged in 100% new oak barrels; Sélection in only 25%. Unoaked Marie et Mathieu★ is fruit-driven; Cuvée Camille has spicy, herbal aromas. Also a MUSCAT DE ST-JEAN-DE-MINERVOIS.

CLOS DU BOIS *Alexander Valley AVA, Sonoma County, ornia, USA* I've always been partial to the house style here: gentle, fruit-dominated SONOMA Chardonnay, Merlot and Cabernet. Top vineyard selections can be exciting, especially the Calcaire★★ Chardonnay, as well as the rich, strong Briarcrest Cabernet Sauvignon★★ and Marlstone★★, a red BORDEAUX-style blend. Riesling is the latest project. Now owned by Constellation. Best years: (reds) 2003 02 **01 00 99 97 96 95 94 91 90 88 86**.

CLOS CENTEILLES *Minervois AC, Languedoc-Roussillon, France* Excellent MINERVOIS La Livinière and innovative vins de pays. Impressive Clos Centeilles★★ is the top wine; Capitelle de Centeilles★ and Carignanissime★ are 100% Cinsaut and 100% Carignan respectively. Best years: 2005 04 03 **01 00**.

CLOS DE LA COULÉE-DE-SERRANT *Savennières AC, Loire Valley, France* Nicolas Joly is biodynamics' most vocal proponent and now, with his winemaker daughter Virginie, produces the most powerfully concentrated, distinctive and ageworthy wines in SAVENNIERES. Eponymous top cuvée hails from monopole Clos de la Coulée de Serrant★★, a steep, walled 7ha (17-acre) vineyard with its own sub-appellation. Savennières Roche aux Moines★★ and Les Vieux Clos★ also impressive. Best years: 2006 05 04 03 02 **01 00 97 96 95 90 89**.

LOS ERASMUS★★★ *Priorat DOCa, Cataluña, Spain* Daphne Glorian's tiny estate turns out one of the most profound and personal reds in the fashionable region of PRIORAT. Her small winery (formerly that of Alvaro PALACIOS) also makes a convincing second wine, Laurel★. Best years: (2006) 05 04 03 02 01 **00 99 98 97 96 94**.

LOS DES LAMBRAYS AC★★★ *Grand Cru, Côte de Nuits, Burgundy, France* This 8.8ha (22-acre) Grand Cru vineyard in MOREY-ST-DENIS is almost entirely owned by the domaine of the same name, though Taupenot-Merme also has a few rows, not quite enough to make a barrel a year. Thierry Brouin, manager at the Dom. des Lambrays, has raised his game in recent years by a more severe selection of fruit for the Grand Cru, now using only old vines. Best years: (2007) 06 05 **04 03 02 00 99 96**.

LOS MARIE *Pic Saint-Loup, Coteaux du Languedoc AC, Languedoc, France* Since 1995, Christophe Peyrus has been making 4 powerful red wines, blends dominated by Syrah, that regularly wow tasters: Glorieuses★, L'Olivette★, Simon★ and Métairies du Clos★. Also white Cuvée Manon. Best years: (2005) 03 **01 00**.

LOS MOGADOR★★★ *Priorat DOCa, Cataluña, Spain* René Barbier Ferrer was one of the pioneers who relaunched the reputation of PRIORAT in the 1980s. The wine is a ripe, intense, brooding monster built to age. Best years: (2006) 05 04 03 01 **00 99 98 97 96 95 94**.

OM. DU CLOS NAUDIN *Vouvray AC, Loire Valley, France* Philippe Foreau runs this first-rate VOUVRAY domaine. Depending on the vintage, he produces a range of styles: dry★★, medium-dry★★ and sweet★★ (rare Réserve★★★), as well as Vouvray Mousseux★★ and Pétillant★★. The wines are supremely ageworthy. Best years: (Moelleux Réserve) 2006 05 03 97 96 95 90 89.

LOS DES PAPES *Châteauneuf-du-Pape AC, Rhône Valley, France* This top-grade red CHATEAUNEUF-DU-PAPE★★★ has a high 20% of Mourvèdre, which gives structure, complexity and potential longevity. Nevertheless, there is enough Grenache to ensure the wine's approachability in its youth and provide an initial blast of fruit. The white★★ takes on the nutty character of aged Burgundy after 5 or 6 years. Best years: (red) (2007) 06 05 04 03 **01 00 99 98 97 96 95 94 90 89 88 83 81**.

LOS DE LA ROCHE AC *Grand Cru, Côte de Nuits, Burgundy, France* The best and biggest of the 5 MOREY-ST-DENIS Grands Crus. The wine has a lovely, bright, red-fruits flavour when young, and should become richly chocolaty or gamy with age. Best producers: DROUHIN★★★, DUJAC★★★, Léchenaut★★, Dom. LEROY★★★, H Lignier★★, Perrot-Minot★★, Ponsot★★★, ROUSSEAU★★. Best years: (2007) 06 05 04 03 02 01 **00 99 98 97 96 95 93 90**.

LOS ST-DENIS AC *Grand Cru, Côte de Nuits, Burgundy, France* This small (6.5ha/16-acre) Grand Cru, which gave its name to the village of MOREY-ST-DENIS, produces wines which are sometimes light, but should be wonderfully silky, with the texture that only great Burgundy can regularly achieve. Best after 10 years or more. Best producers: Bertagna★★, Charlopin★★, DUJAC★★★, JADOT★★, Ponsot★★★. Best years: (2007) 06 05 04 03 02 01 **00 99 98 97 96 95 93 90**.

LOS DE TART AC★★★ *Grand Cru, Côte de Nuits, Burgundy, France* 7.5ha (18-acre) Grand Cru, a monopoly of the Mommessin family, run by Sylvain Pitiot. Intense, concentrated wines made by traditional methods with a modern result. Becoming exceptionally expensive. Best years: (2007) 06 05 04 03 02 **01 00** 99 96 **95 90**.

121

CLOS TRIGUEDINA★ *Cahors AC, South-West France* Jean-Luc Baldès mak
the CAHORS which is for many the reference to this appellation. In Prin
Probus★, he unites the strength of Cahors with elegance. H
experimental return to the 'black wine' of Cahors (a traditional style
which the must was 'cooked' to enhance colour) is revealed in a limite
release, The New Black Wine★. Best years: (2005) 03 01 **00 98**.

CLOS UROULAT *Jurançon AC, South-West France* Charles Hours makes tir
quantities of stunningly good JURANCON. Dry Cuvée Marie★★ has ri
fruit yet a deliciously refreshing finish. The rich sweet Jurançon★★ pu
together lemon, lime, honey and apricot: enjoyable young, but ag
magnificently. Best years: (sweet) 2005 03 **01 00 99 98**.

CLOS DU VAL *Napa Valley AVA, California, USA* Elegant Cabern
Sauvignon★ (STAGS LEAP DISTRICT★★), Chardonnay★, Merlot★, Pin
Noir★ and Zinfandel★. The Reserve Cabernet★ can age well. Best year
(Reserve Cabernet) 2003 **02 01 00** 99 97 96 95 94 91 90 87 86 84.

CLOS DE VOUGEOT AC *Grand Cru, Côte de Nuits, Burgundy, France* Enclose
by Cistercian monks in the 14th century, and today a considerable touri
attraction, this large (50ha/125-acre) vineyard is now divided among 8C
owners. As a result of this division, Clos de Vougeot has become one
the most unreliable Grand Cru Burgundies; the better wine tends
come from the upper and middle parts. When it is good it is wonderful
fleshy, turning deep and exotic after 10 years or more. Best produce
B Ambroise★★, Amiot-Servelle★★, Chopin★★, J-J Confuron★★
R Engel★★★ (to 2004), FAIVELEY★, GRIVOT★★★, Anne GROS★★★, JADOT★★
Dom. LEROY★★★, T LIGER-BELAIR★★, MEO-CAMUZET★★★, Denis MORTET★★
Mugneret-Gibourg★★★, Ch. de la Tour★★, VOUGERAIE★★. Best years: (200
06 05 03 02 01 **00 99 98 97 96 95 93 91 90**.

CLOT DE L'OUM *Cotes du Roussillon-Villages AC, Roussillon, France* Eric Monr
has been making powerful, dense wines since 2001, from 18ha (45 acre
of vines north of Perpignan, which he works organically. Wines includ
La Compagnie des Papillons★, Saint Bart Vieilles Vignes★ and top wir
Numéro Uno★★, a Syrah-Carignan blend.

CLOUDY BAY *Marlborough, South Island, New Zealand* New Zealand's mo
successful winery, Cloudy Bay achieved cult status with the first release
its zesty, herbaceous Sauvignon Blanc★★ in 1985. Sauvignon Blanc T
Koko★★ is very different: rich, creamy, oak-matured and bottle-age
Cloudy Bay also makes Chardonnay★★, a late-harvest Riesling★★
superb ALSACE-style Gewürztraminer★★ and Riesling★★, and goc
Pinot Noir★. Vintage Pelorus★★ is a high-quality old-style CHAMPAGN
method fizz and non-vintage Pelorus★★ is excellent too. Best year
(Sauvignon Blanc) **2007 06 04 03**.

PAUL CLUVER *Elgin WO, South Africa* Cool-loving varieties respond well
this high-lying area: Sauvignon Blanc shows mineral refinemen
Chardonnay★ is compact and layered. Also an often vibrant, dryis
Riesling★ and thrilling Noble Late Harvest botrytis dessert★★ versio
and a subtle Gewürztraminer★★. A silky Pinot Noir and flavoursom
savoury Cabernet Sauvignon show reds have promise too.

COBOS *Mendoza, Argentina* Small operation in LUJAN DE CUYO owned b
Andrea Marchiori, Luis Barraud and American Paul Hobbs. Cobc
offers voluptuous single-vineyard Malbec from Marchiori Vineyard★
in the Perdriel district of MENDOZA. Its Bramare Cabernet Sauvignon
and Malbec★★ are similarly ripe and succulent, while El Felin
Malbec★ offers simple, fresher flavours and great quality for its price.

COCHE-DURY *Meursault, Côte de Beaune, Burgundy, France* Jean-François Coche-Dury is a modest superstar, quietly turning out some of the finest wines on the COTE DE BEAUNE. His best wines are his CORTON-CHARLEMAGNE★★★ and MEURSAULT Perrières★★★, but even his BOURGOGNE Blanc★★ is excellent. His red wines, from VOLNAY★★ and MONTHELIE★, tend to be cheaper than the whites and are delicious to drink even when young. Best years: (whites) (2007) 06 05 04 03 02 **01 00 99 97 96 95**.

COCKBURN *Port DOC, Douro, Portugal* Best known for its Special Reserve ruby, Cockburn has more than that to offer. Vintage★ is stylish and Quinta dos Canais★ is a herby single quinta. Best years: (Vintage) **2003 00 97 94 91 70 63 60 55**; (dos Canais) **2003 01 00 95 92**.

CODORNÍU *Cava DO, Cataluña, Spain* The biggest CHAMPAGNE-method sparkling wine company in the world. Anna de Codorníu★ and Jaume Codorníu★ are especially good, but all the sparklers are better than the CAVA average. Drink young for freshness. Codorníu also owns RAIMAT in COSTERS DEL SEGRE, Masía Bach in the PENEDES and Bodegas Bilbaínas in RIOJA, and has a stake in Scala Dei in PRIORAT. They also own Artesa in NAPA, California.

COLCHAGUA, VALLE DE *Rapel, Chile* RAPEL sub-region and home to several exciting estates, such as the acclaimed Apalta hillside vineyard, where CASA LAPOSTOLLE, MONTES and others have plantings. Syrah and Carmenère do very well here. Chimbarongo and Los Lingues to the east are cooler due to the influence of the Andes, while the Nancagua and Santa Cruz are much warmer. New cool vineyards towards the coast in Lolol and Marchíhue are delivering exciting reds and whites, especially Syrah and Viognier. Best producers: Araucano/Lurton★, CASA LAPOSTOLLE★★, Casa Silva★, CONO SUR★★, EMILIANA (Coyam★★), MONTES★★, MontGras, Viu Manent★.

COLDSTREAM HILLS *Yarra Valley, Victoria, Australia* Founded by Australian wine guru James Halliday; owned by Foster's since 2005. Pinot Noir★ (Reserve★★) is usually good: sappy and smoky with cherry fruit and clever use of all-French oak. Chardonnay★ (Reserve★★) has subtlety and delicacy but real depth as well. Reserve Cabernet★ can be very good, though not always ripe; Merlot★★ ripens more successfully. Plans to dramatically increase production don't make a lot of sense in a cool region like the YARRA VALLEY. Best years: (Reserve Pinot Noir) 2006 05 04 **02 00 98 97 96**.

COLLI ORIENTALI DEL FRIULI DOC *Friuli-Venezia Giulia, Italy* This DOC covers 20 different types of wine. Best known are the sweet whites from Verduzzo in the Ramandolo sub-zone and the delicate Picolit, but it is the reds – from the indigenous Refosco and Schioppettino, as well as imports like Cabernet – and dry whites, from what used to be called Tocai Friulano (now just Friulano), Ribolla, Pinot Bianco, Pinot Grigio and Malvasia Istriana, that show how exciting the wines can be. Prices are high. Best producers: Ca' Ronesca★, Dario Coos★, Dorigo★, Dri★, Le Due Terre★★, Livio FELLUGA★★, Walter Filiputti★, Adriano Gigante★, Livon★, Meroi★, Miani★★, Davide Moschioni★★, Rocca Bernarda★, Rodaro★, Ronchi di Cialla★, Ronchi di Manzano★★, Ronco del Gnemiz★★, Scubla★, Sirch★, Specogna★, Le Vigne di Zamò★★, Zof★. Best years: (whites) (2007) 06 **04 02 01 00 99 98 97**.

COLLI PIACENTINI DOC *Emilia-Romagna, Italy* Home to some of EMILIA-ROMAGNA's best wines, this DOC covers 11 different types, the best of which are Cabernet Sauvignon and the red Gutturnio (a blend of Barbera and Bonarda) as well as the medium-sweet white and bubbly Malvasi Best producers: Luretta★, Lusenti, Castello di Luzzano/Fugazza Il Poggiarello★, La Stoppa★, Torre Fornello★, La Tosa (Cabernet Sauvignon★ Best years: (reds) (2007) 06 **04** 03 01 00.

COLLINES RHODANIENNES, VIN DE PAYS DES *Rhône Valley, Fran* Region between Vienne and Valence. The best wines are Gamay an notably, Syrah, although there are some good juicy Merlots, too. Be producers: P & C Bonnefond★, COLOMBO★, CUILLERON (Viognier★ P Gaillard★, J-M Gérin (Viognier), JAMET★★, R Jasmin, Monteillet, M Ogier ST-DESIRAT co-op, TAIN co-op, G Vernay★, Vins de Vienne (Sotanum★★ Best years: (reds) **2006** 05 04 03 01.

COLLIO DOC *Friuli-Venezia Giulia, Italy* Some of Italy's best and mo expensive dry white wines are from these hills on the Slovenian borde There are 19 types of wine, from local (Tocai) Friulano and Malvas Istriana to international varieties. The best are ageworthy. Best producer Borgo Conventi★, Borgo del Tiglio★★, La Castellada★, Damijan★, Liv FELLUGA★★, Marco Felluga★, Fiegl★, GRAVNER★★, JERMANN★★, Edi Keber Renato Keber★★, Livon★, Primosic★, Princic★, Puiatti★, Roncùs★★, Rus Superiore★★, SCHIOPETTO★★, Matijaz Tercic★★, Venica & Venica★★, Vi Russiz★★, Villanova★, Zuani★★. Best years: (whites) (2007) 06 **04** 02 01 0

COLLIOURE AC *Roussillon, France* This tiny fishing port tucked away in t Pyrenean foothills is also an AC, and makes a throat-warming red wi that is capable of aging for a decade but is marvellously rip-roaring whe young. Best producers: (reds) Abbé Rous, Baillaury★, Clos de Paulilles★, M BLANC★★, la Rectorie★★, la Tour Vieille★, Vial Magnères★. Best years: 200 **01** 00 99 98 96.

COLOMBARD In France, Colombard traditionally has been distilled make Armagnac and Cognac, but has now emerged as a table wine gra in its own right, notably as a Vin de Pays des COTES DE GASCOGNE. At best, it has a lovely, crisp acidity and fresh, aromatic fruit. The large plantings of the grape are in California, where it generally produc rather less distinguished wines. South Africa can produce attracti refreshing wines, though much is used in brandy production. Austral also has some bright-eyed examples.

JEAN-LUC COLOMBO *Cornas AC, Rhône Valley, France* Colombo has cause controversy with his criticism of traditional methods. His powerful, ri CORNAS is more opulent and has far less tannic grip than some. T cuvées are les Ruchets★★ and the lush old-vines la Louvée★★, made tiny quantities. Among négociant wines now produced, CONDRIEU★ CHATEAUNEUF-DU-PAPE les Bartavelles★ and red and white HERMITAGE Rouet★ stand out, although some labels don't always seem fully rip Also produces full, fragrant ST-PERAY la Belle de Mai★, good COTES t RHONE★ and vins de pays from the RHONE, the Marseille area an ROUSSILLON. Best years: (Cornas) (2007) 06 05 **04** 03 01 00 99 98 97 95.

COLUMBIA CREST *Washington State, USA* Begun as an offshoot of CHATE STE MICHELLE, it has grown into the largest winery in Washington Stat producing top-calibre wines at everyday prices. Two Vines budget label good. Grand Estates Shiraz★ and Grand Estates Chardonnay★ a strong suits, as is the new H3★ label for Horse Heaven Hills fruit. The are good young but will age for several years. Reserve Syrah★ can heavily oaked but has impressive style. Best years: (reds) (2006) **05** 04 03 0

OLUMBIA VALLEY AVA *Washington State, USA* The largest of WASHINGTON's viticultural regions, covering a third of the state's landmass and encompassing both the YAKIMA VALLEY and WALLA WALLA VALLEY. It produces 98% of the state's wine grapes: Merlot, Cabernet Sauvignon and Chardonnay are the most widely planted varieties. Best producers: ANDREW WILL★★, BETZ★, CADENCE★★, CHATEAU STE MICHELLE★, COLUMBIA CREST★, DELILLE CELLARS★★,

DUNHAM CELLARS★, Goose Ridge, HEDGES★, JANUIK★, L'ECOLE NO 41★★, LONG SHADOWS VINTNERS★★, Matthews Cellars★★, QUILCEDA CREEK★★★, WOODWARD CANYON★★. Best years: (reds) (2006) 05 **04 03 02 01 00**.

OMMANDARIA *Cyprus* Dark brown, treacly wine made from red Mavro and white Xynisteri grapes, sun-dried for 2 weeks before vinification and solera aging. Pretty decent stuff but only potentially one of the world's great rich wines. A lighter, drier style is also produced.

ONCHA Y TORO *Maipo, Chile* Chile's biggest winery, Concha y Toro has around 6000ha (15,000 acres) of vineyards and a talented group of winemakers. Casillero del Diablo★ is the excellent budget label and Marqués de Casa Concha is the next step up (reds ★★). Higher up, Trio★ and Terrunyo★★ are good labels for reds and whites. CASABLANCA-sourced Amelia★★ is the top Chardonnay and small amounts of various excellent reds come out under the Winemaker's Lot label (usually ★★). The classic Cabernet Sauvignon-based Don Melchor★★★ is impressively round and elegant in the current (2004) release. The recently launched Maycas range from LIMARI offers crisp Sauvignon Blanc, ripe and dense Syrah and mineral Chardonnay★. Trivento is an important Argentinian project. See also ALMAVIVA.

ONDRIEU AC *Rhône Valley, France* Wonderfully fragrant but expensive wine, made entirely from Viognier. Ranges from scented, full and opulent to sweet, late-harvested. Condrieu is a sensation everyone should try, but it is important to choose a good producer. Best drunk young. Best producers: G Barge★, P & C Bonnefond★★, CHAPOUTIER★, du Chêne★★, L Chèze★, COLOMBO★★, CUILLERON★★★, DELAS★★, P Dumazet★★, C Facchin★, P Faury★★, P Gaillard★★, Y Gangloff★★, J-M Gérin, GUIGAL★★ (Doriane★★★), F Merlin★★, Monteillet★★, Mouton★, R Niéro★, A Paret★★, A PERRET★★★, C Pichon★★, ROSTAING★★, St-Cosme★★, G Vernay★★★, F Villard★★.

ONO SUR *Rapel, Chile* Dynamic sister winery to CONCHA Y TORO, whose Pinot Noir put the grape on the Chilean map. The CASABLANCA-sourced 20 Barrels Pinot Noir★★ is rich and perfumed; top-of-the-range Ocio★★ is positively unctuous, yet refreshing, especially in the 2006 vintage. Minerally, crunchy 20 Barrels Sauvignon Blanc★★ is from one of Casablanca's coolest sites. Chardonnay★★, Merlot★★ and Cabernet Sauvignon★★, under 20 Barrels and Visión labels, are excellent, as is the Visión Riesling★★. Isla Negra offers drier, more 'European' flavours.

CH. LA CONSEILLANTE★★ *Pomerol AC, Bordeaux, France* Elegant, exotic, velvety wine that blossoms beautifully after 5–6 years but can age much longer. Second wine: Duo de Conseillante (from 2007). Best years: 2006 05 04 **03** 02 **01 00 99 98 96 95 94 90 89**.

CONSTANTIA WO *South Africa* The historic heart of South African wir
covering much of Simon van der Stel's original 1685 land grant. Tod
there are nine properties, stretching along the Constantiaberg fro
STEENBERG in the south to Constantia Glen in the north. Sauvignon Bla
thrust this cool-climate area into the limelight, but Chardonnays a
Semillons are also good. Constantia Uitsig's elegant, flavourson
Constantia White★ reflects an increasing trend for the Semillo
Sauvignon blend. Cap Classique sparkling wines are also gaining
popularity. Best producers: BUITENVERWACHTING★, Constantia Gle
Constantia Uitsig★, Eagles' Nest★, Groot Constantia (since 2004), H
Constantia, KLEIN CONSTANTIA★, STEENBERG★★. Best years: (whites) **2007
05 04 03 02 01**.

ALDO CONTERNO *Barolo DOCG, Piedmont, Italy* One of BAROLO's fine
traditionalist producers. He makes good Dolcetto d'Alba★, excelle
BARBERA D'ALBA Conca Tre Pile★★, a barrique-aged LANGHE Nebbiolo
Favot★★, red blend Quartetto★★ and 2 Langhe Chardonnays: unoak
Printaniè and Bussiador★, fermented and aged in new wood. Pride
the range, though, are his Barolos from the hill of Bussia. In top vintag
he produces Vigna Colonnello★★★, Vigna Cicala★★★ and excelle
Granbussia★★★, as well as a regular Barolo called Bussia Soprana★
All these Barolos, though accessible when young, need several years
show their true majesty, but retain a remarkable freshness. **Best yea**
(Barolo) (2007) (06) (04) **03** 01 **00 99 98 97 96 95 90 89 88**.

GIACOMO CONTERNO *Barolo DOCG, Piedmont, Italy* Aldo's late eld
brother Giovanni, now followed by his son Roberto, took an even mc
traditional approach to winemaking. The flagship wine is BARO
Monfortino★★★ (only released after some 5 or 6 years in large o
barrels) but Barolo Cascina Francia★★★ is also superb. Also excelle
traditional BARBERA D'ALBA★★. **Best years:** (Monfortino) (2007) (06) (04) (0
(01) 00 99 **98 97 96 95 90 89 88 85 82 71**.

CONTINO *Rioja DOCa, Rioja, Spain* An estate on some of the finest RIOJA lan
half-owned by CVNE. The wines include a Reserva★, a single-vineya
Viña del Olivo★★ and an innovative Graciano★ varietal. **Best yea**
(Reserva) (2005) (04) 03 02 **01 00 99 98 96 95 94 86 85**.

COONAWARRA *South Australia* On a flat limestone belt thinly veneer
with terra rossa soil, Coonawarra can produce sublime Cabernet wi
blackcurrant leafy flavours and spicy Shiraz that age for years. Merlot c
be good, too. An export-led boom fuelled significant new plantin
much of it outside the legendary terra rossa strip, and saw the productio
of disappointing light reds. An awareness of the risk to the regio
reputation has seen substantial changes to viticultural practice over t
past 5 years, accompanied by huge investment in revitalizing t
vineyards. **Best producers:** BALNAVES★★, BOWEN★, BRAND'S★★, HOLLICK
JACOB'S CREEK/Orlando★★, KATNOOK★★, Ladbroke Grove, Leconfield
LINDEMANS, MAJELLA★★★, Murdock, PARKER★★, PENFOLDS★★, PENLEY★
PETALUMA★★, WYNNS★★, Zema★★. **Best years:** (Cabernet Sauvignon) 2006
04 03 **02** 01 **00 99 98 97 96 94 91 90 86**.

COOPERS CREEK *Auckland, North Island, New Zealand* Successful HAWKES B
Chardonnay★ and tangy MARLBOROUGH Sauvignon Blanc★. GISBOR
Arneis★, Marlborough Riesling★ and Late Harvest Riesling★ are al
good. A smart range of Reserve reds from Hawkes Bay includes power
Syrah★ and complex Merlot★ and Cabernet Sauvignon blends★. Be
years: (Chardonnay) (2007) **06 04 02**.

FRANCIS FORD COPPOLA *Rutherford AVA, California, USA* Movie director Francis Ford Coppola, now a serious wine producer, with volume approaching 1 million cases, has split his winemaking activities between luxury and lifestyle brands. The historic Inglenook Niebaum winery, an elaborate NAPA tourist destination, has been renamed Rubicon Estate. Rubicon★★, a BORDEAUX blend, lacked grace in early vintages but has now taken on a more exciting personality. It still needs 5–6 years of aging. Coppola also offers Cask Cabernet★★, Edizione Pennino★ (Zinfandel), RC Reserve Syrah★ and tiny amounts of Merlot★★ and Cabernet Franc★★, as well as super-premium white blend Blancaneaux★. Coppola has also acquired the former Chateau Souverain winery in SONOMA COUNTY, which has been renamed Rosso & Bianco. Brands include Sofia bubblies and good-value Coppola Diamond Collection varietals. Best years: (Rubicon) 2003 **02 01 00 99 97 96 95 94 91 86**.

CORBIÈRES AC *Languedoc, France* This huge region now produces some of the best reds in the LANGUEDOC, with juicy fruit and more than a hint of wild hillside herbs. Excellent young, but wines from the best estates can age for years. White Corbières can be tasty – drink as young as possible. Best producers: (reds) Baillat★, Caraguilhes★, Cascadais★, CLOS DE L'ANHEL★★, Embres-et-Castelmaure★, Étang des Colombes★, Fontsainte★, Grand Crès★, Grand Moulin★, Haut-Gléon★, Hélène★, l'Ille★, Lastours★, Mansenoble★, Ollieux★, les Palais★, St-Auriol★, VOULTE-GASPARETS★★. Best years: (reds) (2005) 04 **03 01 00**.

CORNAS AC *Rhône Valley, France* Pure Syrah wines; attractive alternatives to pricey neighbours HERMITAGE and COTE-ROTIE. When young, the wines are a thick, impenetrable red, almost black in the ripest years. Many need 8 years' aging. Best producers: ALLEMAND★★, F Balthazar★★, CLAPE★★★, COLOMBO★★, Courbis★★, DELAS★, E & J Durand★★, Fauterie★, JABOULET★, J Lemenicier★, R Michel★★, V Paris★★, TAIN co-op★, Tardieu-Laurent★★, Tunnel★, A Voge★★. Best years: (2007) 06 05 04 **03 01 00 99 98 97 96 95 94 91 90 89 88 85 83**.

CORSE AC, VIN DE *Corsica, France* Overall AC for CORSICA with 5 superior sub-regions: Calvi, Cap Corse, Figari, Porto Vecchio and Sartène. Ajaccio and Patrimonio are entitled to their own ACs. The most distinctive wines, mainly red, come from local grapes (Nielluccio and Sciacarello for reds, Vermentino for whites). There are some rich sweet Muscats – especially from Muscat du Cap Corse. Best producers: ARENA★, Canarelli★, Clos d'Alzeto★, Clos Capitoro★, Clos Culombu★, Clos Landry★, Clos Nicrosi★, Gentile, Leccia, Maestracci★, Comte Peraldi★, Renucci★, Saparale, Signadore, Torraccia★.

CORSICA *France* This Mediterranean island has made some pretty dull and undistinguished wines in the past. The last decade has seen a welcome trend towards quality, with co-ops and local growers investing in better equipment and planting noble grape varieties – such as Syrah, Merlot, Cabernet Sauvignon and Mourvèdre for reds, and Chardonnay and Sauvignon Blanc for whites – to complement the local Nielluccio, Sciacarello and Vermentino. Whites and rosés are pleasant for drinking young; reds are more exciting and can age for 3–4 years. See also CORSE AC.

CORTES DE CIMA *Alentejo, Portugal* Excellent modern Portuguese reds. Blends of Aragonez (Tempranillo) and Syrah with local grapes such as Trincadeira and Touriga Nacional are used for spicy, fruity Chaminé★,

oaked red Cortes de Cima★ and a splendid dark, smoky Reserva★
Touriga★★ makes an aromatic varietal red and Incógnito★★ is a guts
black-fruited blockbuster Syrah. Best years: 2005 **04 03 01 00**.

CORTESE White grape variety planted primarily in south-eastern PIEDMON
in Italy; it can produce good, fairly acidic, dry whites. Sometimes labell
simply as Cortese Piemonte DOC, its main purpose in life is as th
principal grape in GAVI.

CORTON AC *Grand Cru, Côte de Beaune, Burgundy, France*   The only red Gran
Cru in the COTE DE BEAUNE; ideally the wines should have the burliness an
savoury power of the top COTE DE NUITS wines, combined with th
seductively perfumed fruit of Côte de Beaune. Red Corton should ta
10 years to mature, but many modern examples never get there. Ve
little white Corton is made. Best producers: B Ambroise★★, d'Ardhuy★
Bonneau du Martray★★, CHANDON DE BRIAILLES★★, Dubreuil-Fontaine★
FAIVELEY★★, Camille Giroud★★★, Guyon★★, JADOT★★★, Dom. LEROY★★
MEO-CAMUZET★★★, Prince de Merode★★, Senard★, TOLLOT-BEAUT★★★. Be
years: (reds) (2007) 06 05 03 02 **01 00** 99 98 96 95 90.

CORTON-CHARLEMAGNE AC *Grand Cru, Côte de Beaune, Burgundy, Franc*
Corton-Charlemagne, on the west and south-west flanks and at the to
of the famous Corton hill, is the largest of Burgundy's white Gran
Crus. It can produce some of the most impressive white Burgundies
rich, buttery and nutty with a fine mineral quality. The best show the
real worth only at 10 years or more. Best producers: B Ambroise★
Bonneau du Martray★★★, BOUCHARD PERE ET FILS★★, Champy★★, CHANDO
DE BRIAILLES★★★, COCHE-DURY★★★, DROUHIN★★, FAIVELEY★★
GIRARDIN★★★, JADOT★★★, P Javillier★★, Louis LATOUR★★, Rapet★★
Rollin★★, ROUMIER★★, TOLLOT-BEAUT★★★, VOUGERAIE★★. Best years: (200
06 05 04 03 02 **01 00** 99 97 95 92.

CH. COS D'ESTOURNEL★★★ *St-Estèphe AC,*
2ème Cru Classé, Haut-Médoc, Bordeaux, France
One of the leading châteaux of Bordeaux.
Despite a high proportion of Merlot (just
under 40%), the wine is classically made
for aging and usually needs 10 years to
show really well. Recent vintages have
been dark, brooding, powerful and, but for

a wobble in 1998 and 99, of the highest order. Small production of whi
from 2005. Second wine: les Pagodes de Cos. Best years: 2006 05 04 03
01 00 96 95 94 90 89 88 86 85.

COSTANTI *Brunello di Montalcino DOCG, Tuscany, Italy*   One of the origina
highly respected Montalcino estates making fine BRUNELLO★★ an
Rosso★★, as well as Vermiglio★, a tasty partially barrique-age
Sangiovese. Costanti's Brunello style went a bit oaky-modern in the 90
but is returning to its original elegant, restrained self. Calbello wine
from the hill of Montosoli, include excellent Rosso★★ and Merlo
Cabernet blend Ardingo★★. Best years: (Brunello) (2007) (06) (04) **03 01 9**
97 95 93 90 88 85 82.

COSTERS DEL SEGRE DO *Cataluña, Spain*   DO on the 'banks of the Segr
in western CATALUNA, with a great array of grape varieties, generally goo
quality and moderate prices. Best producers: Castell del Remei★, Celler
Cérvoles★, Tomás Cusiné★, RAIMAT★. Best years: (reds) 2005 04 **03 01 0**

COSTIÈRES DE NÎMES AC *Rhône Valley, France* Improving AC: reds are generally bright and perfumed, rosés are good young gluggers. Whites are usually tasty versions of Marsanne and Roussanne. Best producers: l'Amarine★, Grande Cassagne★, Lamargue, Mas des Bressades★, Mas Neuf, Mourgues du Grès★, Nages★, d'Or et de Gueules, la Patience, Tardieu-Laurent, la Tour de Beraud, la Tuilerie, Vieux-Relais★. Best years: 2007 **06 05 04 03**.

CÔTE DE BEAUNE *Côte d'Or, Burgundy, France* Southern part of the COTE D'OR; beginning at the hill of CORTON, north of the town of BEAUNE, the Côte de Beaune progresses south as far as les MARANGES, with white wines gradually taking over from red.

CÔTE DE BEAUNE AC *Côte de Beaune, Burgundy, France* Small AC, high on the hill above the town of Beaune, named to ensure maximum confusion with the title for the whole region. Best producers: Allexant, VOUGERAIE★. Best years: (2007) 06 **05** 03 02.

CÔTE DE BEAUNE-VILLAGES AC *Côte de Beaune, Burgundy, France* Red wine AC covering 16 villages, such as AUXEY-DURESSES, LADOIX, MARANGES. If the wine is a blend from several villages it is sold as Côte de Beaune-Villages. It can also cover the red wine production of mainly white wine villages such as MEURSAULT. Best producers: DROUHIN★, JADOT★. Best years: (2007) 06 **05** 03 02.

CÔTE DE BROUILLY AC *Beaujolais, Burgundy, France* Wine from the higher slopes of Mont Brouilly, a small but abrupt volcanic mountain in the south of the BEAUJOLAIS Crus area. The wine is deeper in colour and fruit and has more intensity than that of BROUILLY. Best producers: O Ravier★, Roches Bleues/Lacondemine★, Ch. Thivin (Zaccharie Geoffray★), Viornery★. Best years: **2007 06**.

CÔTE CHALONNAISE See BOURGOGNE-COTE CHALONNAISE.

CÔTE DE NUITS *Côte d'Or, Burgundy, France* This is the northern part of the great COTE D'OR and is *not* an AC. Almost entirely red wine country, the vineyards start in the southern suburbs of Dijon and continue south in a narrow swathe to below the town of NUITS-ST-GEORGES. The villages are some of the greatest wine names in the world – GEVREY-CHAMBERTIN, VOUGEOT and VOSNE-ROMANEE etc.

CÔTE DE NUITS-VILLAGES AC *Côte de Nuits, Burgundy, France* Although not much seen, the wines (mostly red) are often good, not very deep in colour but with a nice cherry fruit. Best producers: (reds) D Bachelet★, Chopin-Groffier★, J-J Confuron, JADOT★, Jayer-Gilles★, P Rossignol★. Best years: (reds) 2007 06 **05** 03 02.

CÔTE D'OR *Burgundy, France* Europe's most northern great red wine area and also the home of some of the world's best dry white wines. The name, meaning 'golden slope', refers to a 48km (30-mile) stretch between Dijon and Chagny which divides into the COTE DE NUITS in the north and the COTE DE BEAUNE in the south.

CÔTE ROANNAISE AC *Loire Valley, France* Small, improving AC in the upper LOIRE producing mostly light reds and rosés from Gamay. Non-appellation whites can be good. Best producers: Fontenay★, R Sérol★★.

CÔTE-RÔTIE AC *Rhône Valley, France* The Côte-Rôtie, or 'roasted slope', produces one of France's greatest red wines. On its vertiginous slopes, the Syrah manages to balance super ripeness with freshness, and the small amount of white Viognier sometimes included in the blend gives an unexpected exotic fragrance. Lovely young, it is better aged for 6–8 years. Best producers: G Barge★★, Bernard★, P & C Bonnefond★★, Bonserine★, B Burgaud★, Clusel-Roch★★, CUILLERON★★, DELAS★★,

Duclaux★★, Gallet★, Garon★, J-M Gérin★★, GUIGAL★★, JABOULET
JAMET★★★, Jasmin★★, S Ogier★★, Rosiers, ROSTAING★★, J-M Stéphan
Tardieu-Laurent★★, Vidal-Fleury★, F Villard★, Vins de Vienne★★. Best year
(2007) 06 05 04 **03** **01** **00** 99 98 97 95 94 91 90 89.

COTEAUX D'AIX-EN-PROVENCE AC *Provence, France* The first AC i
the south to acknowledge that Cabernet Sauvignon can enormous
enhance the traditional local grape varieties such as Grenache, Cinsau
Mourvèdre, Syrah and Carignan. The reds can age. Some quite goo
fresh rosé is made, while the whites, mostly still traditionally made, a
pleasant but hardly riveting. Best producers: Ch. Bas★, les Bastides★, l
Béates★, Beaupré★, Calissanne★, J-L COLOMBO (Côte Bleue★★), d'EOLE
Fonscolombe, Revelette★, Vignelaure★. Best years: (reds) 2005 04 **03** **01** **0**

COTEAUX DE L'ARDÈCHE, VIN DE PAYS DES *Rhône Valley, Fran*
Increasingly good, lively red wines made from Cabernet Sauvignon
Syrah, Merlot or Gamay and dry, fresh whites from Chardonna
Viognier or Sauvignon Blanc. Best producers: Vignerons Ardecho
Colombier, DUBOEUF, G Flacher, Louis LATOUR, Pradel, ST-DESIRAT, Vigier.

COTEAUX DE L'AUBANCE AC *Loire Valley, France* Smallish AC north
COTEAUX DU LAYON AC for sweet or semi-sweet white wines made from
Chenin Blanc. Top sweet wines are now labelled Sélection de Grain
Nobles, as in ALSACE. Best producers: Daviau/Bablut★★, Haute Perche
Montgilet/V Lebreton★★, Princé, RICHOU★★, Rochelles★. Best years: 2006 0
04 03 02 01 99 97 96 90.

COTEAUX CHAMPENOIS AC *Champagne, France* Still wines fro
Champagne. Fairly acid with a few exceptions, notably from Bouzy an
Ay. The best age for 5 years or more. Best producers: Paul Bara
BOLLINGER★, Egly-Ouriet★, Geoffroy, H Goutorbe, LAURENT-PERRIER, Josep
PERRIER, Ch. de Saran★/MOET & CHANDON. Best years: 2004 03 02 **00** 99 98 9

COTEAUX DU LANGUEDOC AC *Languedoc, France* Large and increasing
successful region situated between Montpellier and Narbonn
producing around 73 million bottles of beefy red and tasty rosé wine
Twelve 'crus', including Montpeyroux, Quatourze and Cabrières, hav
historically been allowed to append their names to the AC – these are i
the process of being delineated by climate and soil type. La CLAPE, Grès d
Montpellier and PIC ST-LOUP have already been officially recognized. Be
producers: l'Aiguelière★, Aupilhac★, Calage★, Clavel★, CLOS MARIE★,
Coste★, Grès St-Paul★, HECHT & BANNIER★, Lacroix-Vanel★, Mas C
Demoura, Mas des Chimères★, Mas Jullien★, Mas de Martin★, PEYRE ROSE★
Poujol★, PRIEURE DE ST-JEAN DE BEBIAN★★, Puech-Haut★, St-Martin de
Garrigue★, Terre Megère★. Best years: 2004 03 **01** **00** 99 98.

COTEAUX DU LAYON AC *Loire Valley, France* Sweet wine from the Layo
Valley, south of Angers. The wine is made from Chenin Blanc grape
that, ideally, are attacked by noble rot. In great years like 1996, and fro
a talented grower, this can be one of the world's exceptional sweet wine
Top wines are now labelled Sélection de Grains Nobles, as in ALSACE. S
villages are entitled to use the Coteaux du Layon-Villages AC and p
their own name on the label; these wines are definitely underpriced f
the quality. Three sub-areas, BONNEZEAUX, Chaume and QUARTS
CHAUME, have their own ACs. Best producers: P Aguilas★★, P Baudouin★
BAUMARD★★, Bergerie★★, Bidet★, Breuil★, Cady★★, P Delesvaux★★
Duloquet, Forges★★, Ogereau★★, Passavant★, Pierre-Bise★★, J PITHON★
Quarres★, J Renou★★, Roulerie★★, Sablonnettes★★, Sauveroy★, Soucheri
P-Y Tijou★★. Best years: (2007) 06 05 **04** **03** 02 01 99 97 96 95 90 89.

OTEAUX DU LOIR AC See JASNIERES AC.

OTEAUX DU LYONNAIS AC *Beaujolais, Burgundy, France* Good, light, BEAUJOLAIS-style reds and a few whites and rosés from scattered vineyards between Villefranche and Lyon. Drink young.

OTEAUX DU TRICASTIN AC *Rhône Valley, France* Bright, fresh, sometimes full, reds and rosés with attractive juicy fruit. Only a little of the nutty white is made but is worth looking out for. Drink it young. Best producers: Décelle, Grangeneuve★, Lônes, St-Luc★, la Tour d'Elyssas, Vieux Micocoulier. Best years: 2007 **06 05 04**.

OTEAUX VAROIS AC *Provence, France* North of Toulon and west of St-Tropez, this is an area to watch, with new plantings of classic grapes to improve quality. Best producers: Alysses★, Bremond, Calisse★, Chaberts, Deffends★, Garbelle, Routas★, St-Estève, St-Jean-le-Vieux, St-Jean-de-Villecroze★, Triennes★. Best years: 2005 **04 03**.

CÔTES DE BERGERAC AC See BERGERAC AC.

CÔTES DE BOURG AC *Bordeaux, France* The best red wines are earthy but blackcurranty and can age for 6–10 years. Very little white is made; most of it is dry and dull. Best producers: Brulesécaille★, Bujan★, FALFAS★, Fougas (Maldoror★), Garreau, Haut-Guiraud, Haut-Macô★, Haut-Mondésir★, Macay, Mercier, Nodoz★, ROC DE CAMBES★★, Tayac, Tour de Guiet★. Best years: 2005 **03 02 01 00 99 98 96 95**.

CÔTES DE CASTILLON AC *Bordeaux, France* Area east of ST-EMILION that has surged in quality recently. Can use new Côtes de Bordeaux AC label from 2007. There's still good value but prices are beginning to climb. The best wines are full and firm, yet well endowed with the lushness of St-Émilion. Best producers: Dom. de l'A★★, Aiguilhe★★, Belcier, Cap-de-Faugères★, la Clarière Laithwaite, Clos l'Eglise★, Clos Les Lunelles★ (from 2001), Clos Puy Arnaud★, Côte-Montpezat, Joanin Bécot★, Poupille★, Robin★, Veyry★, Vieux-Ch.-Champs-de-Mars★. Best years: 2005 **04 03 02 01 00 99 98**.

CÔTES DE DURAS AC *South-West France* AC between ENTRE-DEUX-MERS and BERGERAC, with good, fresh, leafy reds and whites from traditional BORDEAUX grapes. Drink young. Best producers: Clos du Cadaret, Duras co-op, Grand Mayne, Lafon, Landerrouat co-op, Laulan, Mouthes le Bihan★, Petit Malromé. Best years: (reds) 2005 04 03 **01 00**.

CÔTES DE FRANCS See BORDEAUX-COTES DE FRANCS.

CÔTES DU FRONTONNAIS AC *South-West France* From north of Toulouse, some of the most distinctive reds – often juicy and positively silky in texture – of South-West France. Négrette is the chief grape, but certain producers coarsen it with Cabernet, which rather defeats the object. Best producers: Baudare, Bellevue-la-Forêt★, Cahuzac★, la Colombière, Ferran, Flotis, Laurou, Montauriol, la Palme, Plaisance, le Roc★, St-Louis. Best years: 2005 04 03 **01 00**.

CÔTES DE GASCOGNE, VIN DE PAYS DES *South-West France* This is Armagnac country, but the tangy-fresh, fruity white table wines are tremendously good. Best producers: Aurin, Brumont/MONTUS, de Joy, Producteurs PLAIMONT★, St-Lannes, TARIQUET★.

CÔTES DU JURA AC *Jura, France* Jura's regional AC covers a variety of wines, including specialities *vin jaune* and *vin de paille*. Savagnin makes strong-tasting whites, and Chardonnay some good dry whites and CREMANT DU JURA. Distinctive reds and rosés from local Poulsard and Trousseau; wines can be better from Pinot Noir. Drink young. Best producers: Arlay★★, Berthet-Bondet★★, Bourdy★, Chalandard★, Clavelin★,

Delay★, Ch. de l'Étoile★, Joly★, A Labet★, J Maclé★★, Reverchon★
Rijckaert★★, Rolet★★, A & M Tissot★.

CÔTES DU LUBÉRON AC *Rhône Valley, France*   Production is dominated b
the co-ops east of Avignon; their light, easy wines drink young. Domain
wines have more body. Best producers: Bonnieux co-op, Ch. la Canorgue,
Citadelle★, Fontenille★, Ch. de l'Isolette★, la Tour-d'Aigues co-op, Ch. de
Tourettes, Val Joanis, la Verrerie★. Best years: 2007 **06 05 04**.

CÔTES DU MARMANDAIS AC *South-West France*   The red wines are fair
successful BORDEAUX lookalikes; Syrah is also permitted. Best producer
Beaulieu, Cave de Beaupuy, Cocumont co-op, Elian Da Ros★ (Chante Couco
Clos Baquey★).

CÔTES DE PROVENCE AC *Provence, France*   Large AC mainly for frui
reds and rosés to drink young. Whites have improved. Best producer
Barbanau★, la Bernarde★, Clos d'Alari★, Commanderie de Peyrassol★,
Courtade★★, Coussin Ste-Victoire★, Cressonnière★, Dupéré-Barrer
d'ESCLANS, Féraud★, Galoupet, Gavoty★, Jale, Mauvanne★, Minuty★, Ott★
Rabiega★, Réal Martin★, RICHEAUME★, Rimauresq★★, Roquefort★, Maîtr
Vignerons de St-Tropez, St-André de Figuière, SORIN★, Élie Sumeire★, L
Valentines.

CÔTES DU RHÔNE AC *Rhône Valley, France*   AC for the whole RHÔN
VALLEY. Over 90% is red and rosé, mainly from Grenache, with som
Cinsaut, Syrah, Carignan and Mourvèdre to add warm souther
personality. Modern winemaking has revolutionized the style; today
wines are generally juicy, spicy and easy to drink, ideally within 5 year
Most wine is made by co-ops. Best producers: (reds) Amouriers★
d'Andézon★, les Aphillanthes★, A Brunel★, L Charvin★★, CLAPE★, COLOMBO★
Coudoulet de BEAUCASTEL★★, Cros de la Mûre★, Estézargues co-op★
Fonsalette★★, FONT DE MICHELLE★, Gramenon★★, Grand Moulas★, Gran
Prébois★, GUIGAL★, Haut Musiel, Hugues★, JABOULET, la Janasse★
J-M Lombard★, Mas de Libian★, Mont-Redon, la Mordorée★, REMEJEANNE★
M Richaud★, Romarins, St-Estève, ST-GAYAN, Saint-Siffrein, Ste-Anne★, San
Duc★, Tardieu-Laurent★, Tours★, Vieille Julienne★, Vieux-Chêne★; (white
CLAPE★, Coudoulet de BEAUCASTEL★, P Gaillard★, REMEJEANNE★, Ste-Anne★
Best years: (reds) 2007 **06 05 04**.

CÔTES DU RHÔNE-VILLAGES AC *Rhône Valley, France*   AC covering 1
villages in the southern COTES DU RHONE that have traditionally mad
superior wine (especially CAIRANNE, RASTEAU, Laudun, Massif d'Uchau
Séguret, Valréas, Sablet, Visan). Best are spicy reds that can age well. Be
producers: Achiary★, Amouriers★, Beaurenard★, Bramadou, Bressy-Masson★
de Cabasse★, Cabotte★, Chapoton★, D Charvin★, la Charbonnière★
Chaume-Arnaud★, Combe★, Coriançon★, Cros de la Mûre★, Espigouette★
Estézargues co-op★, Les Goubert, Gourt de Mautens★★, Gramenon★, Gran
Moulas★, Grand Veneur★, Gravennes★, la Janasse★, Jérôme★, Mourchon★
Pélaquié★, Piaugier★, Rasteau co-op★, REMEJEANNE★, ST-GAYAN★, Ste-Anne★
Saladin, la Soumade★, Tours★, Trapadis★, Verquière★. Best years: (reds) 200
06 05 04 03 01 98.

CÔTES DU ROUSSILLON AC *Roussillon, France*   ROUSSILLON's catch-all A
dominated by co-ops. It's a hot area, and much of the wine is baked an
dull. But there's a lively bunch of estates making exciting reds and doin
surprisingly good things with whites. Best producers: (reds) la CASENOVE★★
Vignerons Catalans, CAZES★, Chênes★, J-L COLOMBO★, Ferrer-Ribière★, Forç
Réal, Joliette, Laporte★, Mas Crémat★, Mossé, Olivier Pithon★, Rivesaltes c
op, Sarda-Malet★. Best years: (reds) 2005 04 03 **01 00 99**.

CÔTES DU ROUSSILLON-VILLAGES AC *Roussillon, France* Wines from the best sites in the northern COTES DU ROUSSILLON. Villages Caramany,

Latour-de-France, Lesquerde and Tautavel may add their own name. Best producers: Vignerons Catalans, Calvet-Thunevin, CAZES★, Chênes★, Clos des Fées★, CLOT DE L'OUM★★, Fontanel★, Força Réal, Gardiés★, GAUBY★★, Jau, Mas Amiel★, Mas Crémat★, Roc des Anges, Schistes★. Best years: (reds) 2005 04 03 01 00 99.

DOMAINE DU
CLOS DES FÉES

★

2004

VIEILLES VIGNES
CÔTES DU ROUSSILLON VILLAGES

CÔTES DE ST-MONT VDQS *South-West France* A good VDQS for firm but fruity reds and some fair rosés and dry whites. Best producer: Producteurs PLAIMONT★.

CÔTES DE THONGUE, VIN DE PAYS DES *Languedoc, France* Zone north-east of Béziers. Many dull red quaffers, but dynamic estates can produce excellent results. Best producers: l'Arjolle★, Bellevue, les Chemins de Bassac, Condamine l'Évêque, Croix Belle.

CÔTES DU VENTOUX AC *Rhône Valley, France* AC with vineyards around the southern and western slopes of Mt Ventoux. When well made, the red wines can have a lovely juicy fruit, or in the case of JABOULET and Pesquié, some real stuffing. Best producers: Anges★, Bedoin co-op, Brusset, Cascavel★, La Croix des Pins★, Fenouillet, Font-Sane, Goult/Cave de Lumières★, JABOULET★, la Martinelle★, Pesquié★, St-Didier/Cave Courtoise★, Valcombe★, la Verrière, Vidal-Fleury, la Vieille Ferme. Best years: (reds) 2007 06 05.

CÔTES DU VIVARAIS AC *Rhône Valley, France* In the northern Gard and Ardèche, typical southern Rhône grapes (Grenache, Syrah, Cinsaut, Carignan) produce mainly light, fresh reds and rosés for drinking young. Best producers: Vignerons Ardechois, Gallety★, Vigier.

QUINTA DO CÔTTO *Douro DOC and Port DOC, Douro, Portugal* Unfortified DOURO wine expert. Quinta do Côtto red and creamy Paço de Teixeró VINHO VERDE are good, and Grande Escolha★★ can be excellent, oaky and powerful when young, rich and cedary when mature. Best years: (Grande Escolha) 2001 00 97 95 94 90 87 85.

COULY-DUTHEIL *Chinon AC, Loire Valley, France* Large merchant house vinifying 130ha (320 acres), of which 90 belong to the domaine. Best wines are Clos de l'Écho★, Clos de l'Écho Crescendo★ and Clos de l'Olive★. Top négociant blend is la Baronnie Madeleine★, which combines tasty raspberry fruit with a considerable capacity to age. Also sells a range of other Touraine wines. Best years: (reds) 2006 05 04 03 02 01 97 96 90 89.

PIERRE COURSODON *St-Joseph AC, Rhône Valley, France* Family-owned, 17-ha (42-acre) domaine producing rich, oaked ST-JOSEPH★ from very old vines. The red wines need up to 5 years before they show all their magnificent cassis and truffle and violet richness, especially the top wine, La Sensonne★★, aged in new oak. Whites, from the Marsanne grape, are good, too. Best years: (reds) 2007 06 05 04 03 01 00 99 98 95.

CH. COUTET★★ *Barsac AC, 1er Cru Classé, Bordeaux, France* BARSAC's largest Classed Growth property has been in great form in recent years, and with its finesse and balance is once again a classic Barsac. Extraordinarily intense Cuvée Madame★★★ is made in exceptional years. Best years: 2006 05 04 03 02 01 00 99 98 97 96 95 90 89 88.

133

CRAGGY RANGE *Hawkes Bay and Martinborough, North Island, New Zealan* Premium HAWKES BAY wines include stylish Les Beaux Caillou Chardonnay★★, a bold Cabernet blend called The Quarry★★, a ric Merlot blend known as Sophia★★ and the flagship Le Sol Syrah★★ Also elegant Seven Poplars Chardonnay★ and Gimblett Gravel Merlot★★ from Hawkes Bay; fine Te Muna Road Pinot Noir★★ an Riesling★ from MARTINBOROUGH; restrained yet intense Avery Sauvigno Blanc★ and tangy Rapaura Road Riesling★ from MARLBOROUGH. Bes years: (Syrah) (2007) **06 04 02 01**.

QUINTA DO CRASTO *Douro DOC and Port DOC, Douro, Portugal* Well situated property with very good traditional LBV★★ and Vintage★ port and massively enjoyable juicy red DOURO★★ and oaky but exceller Touriga Nacional★★. Flagship reds Vinha da Ponte★★ and Mari Teresa★★ can reach ★★★. Austere new Douro red Xisto★ is a join venture with Jean-Michel Cazes of Ch. LYNCH-BAGES of BORDEAUX. Bes years: (Vintage port) 2004 **03 00 99 97 95 94**; (Touriga Nacional) 2005 **04 0 01**; (Ponte) **2004 03 00**; (Maria Teresa) 2005 **03 01 98**.

CRÉMANT D'ALSACE AC *Alsace, France* Good CHAMPAGNE-method sparklin wine from ALSACE, usually made from Pinot Blanc and/or Pinot Gris Reasonable quality, if not great value for money. **Best producer** J-B ADAM★, BLANCK★, Cave de Cleebourg, Dopff & Irion, Dopff au Moulin★ J Gross★, Kuentz-Bas, MURE★, Ostertag★, Pfaffenheim co-op, P Sparr★ A Stoffel★, TURCKHEIM co-op★.

CRÉMANT DE BOURGOGNE AC *Burgundy, France* Most Burgundia Crémant is white and is made either from Chardonnay alone or blende with Pinot Noir. The result, especially in ripe years, can be full, sof almost honey-flavoured – if you give the wine 2–3 years' agin needed for mellowness to develop. **Best producers**: A Delorme, Simonne Febvre, A Sounit, Veuve Ambal; and the co-ops at Bailly★ (the best for rosé Lugny★, St-Gengoux-de-Scissé and Viré.

CRÉMANT DE DIE AC *Rhône Valley, France* AC for traditional-method fiz made entirely from the Clairette Blanche grape. Less aromatic tha CLAIRETTE DE DIE. **Best producers**: Jacques Faure, J-C Raspail.

CRÉMANT DU JURA AC *Jura, France* AC for fizz from Jura. Largel Chardonnay-based, with Poulsard, an interesting pale red grape, for th pinks. **Best producers**: Berthet-Bondet, Ch. de l'Étoile★, la Pinte, Pupillin co op★, A & M Tissot.

CRÉMANT DE LIMOUX AC *Languedoc, France* Sparkling wine made fron a blend of Chardonnay, Chenin Blanc, Mauzac and Pinot Noir; th wines generally have more complexity than BLANQUETTE DE LIMOUX. Drin young. **Best producers**: l'Aigle★, Antech, Fourn, Guinot, Laurens★ Martinolles★, SIEUR D'ARQUES★, Valent.

CRÉMANT DE LOIRE AC *Loire Valley, France* CHAMPAGNE-method sparklin wine in Anjou and Touraine, with more fruit and yeast character tha those of VOUVRAY and SAUMUR. Good to drink as soon as it is released. Ca be excellent value. **Best producers**: l'Aulée, BAUMARD, Berger Frères★, Brizé★ Fardeau★, Girault, Gratien & Meyer★, Lambert★, Langlois-Château★ Michaud★, Nerleux/Regis Neau, Passavant★.

CRIOTS-BÂTARD-MONTRACHET AC See BATARD-MONTRACHET AC.

CRISTOM *Willamette Valley AVA, Oregon, USA* Nestled in the Eola Hills, thi winery specializes in Pinot Noir (Marjorie Vineyard★, Sommer Reserve★). White wines include barrel-fermented Chardonnay, Pino Gris and Viognier. **Best years**: (Pinot Noir) 2006 **05 04 03 02**.

CROFT *Port DOC, Douro, Portugal* Owned by the Fladgate Partnership (along with TAYLOR and FONSECA) since 2001, these wines are showing distinct improvements, especially at basic level. Vintage ports★★ have traditionally been elegant, rather than thunderous. Single-quinta Quinta da Roêda★ is pretty good in recent vintages. Best years: (Vintage) **2003** 00 94 91 77 70 66 63 55 45; (Roêda) **1997 95**.

CROZES-HERMITAGE AC *Rhône Valley, France* The largest of the northern Rhône ACs. Ideally, the pure Syrah reds should have a full colour and a strong, clear, black fruit flavour. You can drink them young, but in ripe years from a hillside site the wine improves greatly for 2–5 years. The best whites are fresh and clean. In general drink white Crozes young, before the floral perfume disappears. Best producers: (reds) A Belle★★, Bruyères★★, CHAPOUTIER★ (Varonniers★★), Y Chave★ (Rouvre★★), Colombier★, Combier★ (Clos des Grives★★), E Darnaud★★, DELAS★ (Le Clos, Tour d'Albon★★), O Dumaine★, Entrefaux★, L Fayolle★★, Ferraton★, GRAILLOT★★, Hauts Chassis, JABOULET★, Murinais★, Pavillon-Mercurol★, Pochon★ (Ch. Curson★★), Remizières★★, G Robin★, Rousset (Picaudières★★), M Sorrel★, TAIN co-op (Les Hauts du Fief★), Tardieu-Laurent★★, Vins de Vienne★; (whites) Y Chave★, Colombier★, Combier★, Dard & Ribo★, DELAS★, O Dumaine★, Entrefaux★ (Cuvée des Pends★★), Fayolle Fils & Fille, Ferraton★, GRAILLOT★, Martinelles, Mucyn, Pochon (Ch. Curson★), Remizières★, M Sorrel★★. Best years: (reds) 2007 06 **05** 04 03 01 00 99 98 95.

YVES CUILLERON *Condrieu AC, Rhône Valley, France* With wines like Cuilleron's you can understand CONDRIEU's fame and high prices. Les Chaillets Vieilles Vignes★★★ is everything wine made from Viognier should be: opulent and rich, with perfumed honey and apricot aromas. La Petite Côte★★ is also exceptional, and the late-harvest les Ayguets★★★ is an extraordinary sweet whirl of dried apricots, honey and barley sugar. Cuilleron also makes ST-JOSEPH reds★★ and whites★★ and tiny quantities of ripe, dark, spicy COTE-ROTIE★★. A joint venture, les Vins de Vienne, with partners Pierre Gaillard, François Villard and Pierre-Jean Villa, produces Vin de Pays des COLLINES RHODANIENNES Sotanum★ (100% Syrah) and Taburnum★ (100% Viognier) from ancient terraces just north of Vienne. Best years: (Condrieu) **2007 06 05 04 03 01**.

CULLEN *Margaret River, Western Australia* One of the original and best MARGARET RIVER vineyards, established by Diana and Kevin Cullen and now run by their talented winemaker daughter Vanya. Superb Chardonnay★★★ is complex and satisfying; Sauvignon-Semillon★★ marries nectarines with melon and nuts. The Cabernet Sauvignon-Merlot★★★ is gloriously soft, deep and scented; this wine is now justifiably regarded as one of Australia's greats. Mangan Malbec-Petit Verdot-Merlot★★ is delicious. Best years: (Cabernet Sauvignon-Merlot) (2007) 05 04 03 02 01 **00 99** 98 97 96 95 94 92 91 90 86 84 82.

CURICÓ, VALLE DE *Valle Central, Chile* Most of the big producers here have planted Cabernet Sauvignon, Merlot, Carmenère, Chardonnay and Sauvignon Blanc. It's a bit warm for whites, but the long growing season provides good fruit concentration for reds. Best producers: Echeverría★★, SAN PEDRO★, Miguel TORRES★★, VALDIVIESO★.

CUVAISON *Napa Valley AVA, California, USA* Red wines include tasty, focused Merlot★, sound Cabernet Sauvignon★ and delicate Pinot Noir★. Decent Chardonnay; silky Reserve Chardonnay★ is worth seeking out. Best years: (Merlot) 2004 **03 02 01** 99 98 97 96 94.

CVNE *Rioja DOCa, Rioja, Spain* Compañía Vinícola del Norte de España is th full name of this firm, but it's usually known as 'coonay'. Viña Real★ one of RIOJA's few remaining well-oaked whites. Viña Real Reserva★ an Gran Reserva★ reds can be rich and meaty, and easily surpass the rathe commercial Crianzas; Imperial Gran Reserva★ is long-lived an impressive. Real de Asúa★ is a premium red. **Best years:** (reds) (2005) 0 03 02 01 98 96 95 94 91 90 89 87 86 85.

DIDIER DAGUENEAU *Pouilly-Fumé AC, Loire Valley, France* A much-neede innovator and quality fanatic in a complacent region. Wines benefit fro 4–5 years' aging and, although at times unpredictable, are generall intense and complex. The range starts with En Chailloux★★ and move up through flinty Buisson Renard★★ to barrel-fermented Silex★★ an Pur Sang★★. Since 2004, also making a sweet JURANCON. **Best years:** 200 06 05 **04** 03 02 01.

ROMANO DAL FORNO *Valpolicella DOC, Veneto, Italy* VALPOLICELL Superiore★★ from Monte Lodoletta vineyard, outside the Valpolicell Classico area, is a model of power and grace; AMARONE★★★ and RECIOT DELLA VALPOLICELLA★★★, from the same source, are even more voluptuou **Best years:** (Amarone) (2007) (06) (04) 03 01 **00** 97 96 95 90.

TENIMENTI LUIGI D'ALESSANDRO *Cortona DOC, Tuscany, Italy* Th vineyards have benefited from massive investment. Il Bosco★★ and th 'second' wine, Cortona Syrah★, are both 100% Syrah. The whit Fontarca★ blends Chardonnay with varying amounts of Viognier. Be years: (Il Bosco) (2007) (06) 04 **03** 01 **00** 99 97 95.

DALLA VALLE *Napa Valley AVA, California, USA* Stunning hillside winer producing some of NAPA's most esteemed Cabernets. Maya★★★ is magnificent blend of Cabernet Sauvignon and Cabernet Franc; th straight Cabernet Sauvignon★★★ is almost as rich. The wines drink we at 10 years, but will keep for 20 or more. **Best years:** (Maya) (2006) 05 03 0 01 00 **99 98** 97 96 95 94 91 90.

DÃO DOC *Beira Alta, Portugal* Dão has steep slopes ideal for vineyards, and great climate for growing local grape varieties, yet it's only just beginnin to realize its potential for characterful red and white wines. **Best producer** (reds) Caves ALIANCA (Quinta da Garrida★), Boas Quintas (Quinta Fonte d Ouro★), Quinta de Cabriz★, Quinta das Maias★, Quinta da Pellada★★, Quint da Ponte Pedrinha, Quinta dos ROQUES★★, Quinta de Sães★, Caves SAO JOAO SOGRAPE★ (Quinta dos Carvalhais★), Quinta da Vegia★★; (whites) Quinta c Cabriz, Quinta das Maias★, Quinta dos ROQUES★★, Quinta de Sães★, SOGRAPE **Best years:** (reds) 2005 **04** 03 01 00 **99** 97 96 95.

D'ARENBERG *McLaren Vale, South Australia* Chester Osborn makes block buster Dead Arm Shiraz★★, Custodian Grenache★, Coppermine Roa Cabernet Sauvignon★ and other blends from low-yielding old vine These are big, brash, character-filled wines, and are continually bein joined by more new ideas. **Best years:** (Dead Arm Shiraz) (2006) 05 04 03 0 01 00 97 96 95.

RENÉ & VINCENT DAUVISSAT *Chablis, Burgundy, France* CHABLIS at its mo complex – refreshing, seductive and beautifully structured, with the fru balancing the subtle influence of mostly older oak. Look for la Forest★★ the more aromatic Vaillons★★★ and the powerful les Clos★★★. Be years: (2007) 06 05 **04** 03 02 00 99 98 96 95.

MARCO DE BARTOLI *Sicily, Italy* Marco De Bartoli is most noted for a dr unfortified MARSALA-style wine called Vecchio Samperi – his idea of wh Marsala was before the English merchant, John Woodhouse, fir fortified it for export. Particularly fine is the 20-year-old Ventennale – dry, intense and redolent of candied citrus peel, dates and old, old raisins. Also excellent MOSCATO PASSITO DI PANTELLERIA Bukkuram★★.

DE BORTOLI *Riverina, New South Wales/Yarra, Victoria, Australia* Large, family-owned company currently producing some of Australia's most interesting wines. Some top stuff from the YARRA VALLEY: Sauvignon Blanc★, Chardonnay★★, Shiraz★★, Cabernet★ and Pinot Noir★★. The RIVERINA winery first gained prominence by producing a sublime, world-class botrytized Semillon (Noble One★★★) but in recent times has had consumers smiling because of the quality of its budget-priced labels – Sacred Hill, Deen and Montage. VICTORIA-based quaffers such as Sero, Windy Peak and Gulf Station have their admirers too. **Best years:** (Noble One) 2006 04 03 02 **00 98 96 95 94 93 90**.

DE MARTINO/SANTA INÉS *Maipo, Chile* Old-established winery and now one of MAIPO's rising stars, producing robust, concentrated red wines in the hands of talented Marcelo Retamal. Single Vineyard Carmenère★★ is one of Chile's best examples of this grape; De Martino Gran Familia Cabernet Sauvignon★★ is dense and complex. Single Vineyard Chardonnay★★ from LIMARI is perhaps Chile's best Chardonnay.

DE TRAFFORD *Stellenbosch WO, South Africa* David Trafford is a leading exponent of new-wave Chenin Blanc, in both dry and dessert styles. His rich, ageworthy dry Chenin Blanc★ from venerable Helderberg vines is barrel fermented on its own yeast; the Straw Wine★★ is honey-tinged and succulent. Among the reds, both Cabernet Sauvignon★ and Merlot★ are classically styled and built to age. Shiraz★★, brimming with spicy richness, remains remarkably elegant for its size. **Best years:** (reds) 2006 05 **04 03 02 01 00 99 98**.

DEHLINGER *Russian River Valley AVA, California, USA* Outstanding Pinot Noir★★★ from vineyards in the cool RUSSIAN RIVER region a few miles from the Pacific, best at 5–10 years old. Also mouthfilling Chardonnay★★ and bold, peppery Syrah★★. Recent vintages of Cabernet★★ and Bordeaux Blend★★ (Cabernet-Merlot) reflect a surge in quality. **Best years:** (Pinot Noir) (2005) 04 **03 02 01 00 99 98 97**.

MARCEL DEISS *Alsace AC, Alsace, France* Jean-Michel Deiss is fanatical about distinctions of *terroir* and, controversially for ALSACE, his top wines are now blends, named according to the vineyard – Grands Crus Altenberg, Mambourg and Schoenenbourg are all ★★★. These are outstanding wines of huge character, often with some residual sugar. Pinot Noir Burlenburg★★ is vibrant and delicious. Even basic Riesling St-Hippolyte★ and Pinot Blanc Bergheim are delightful. **Best years:** (Grand Cru blends) (2007) 05 **04 03 02 01 00 99**.

DELAS FRÈRES *Rhône Valley, France* Merchant (owned by ROEDERER) selling wines from the entire RHONE VALLEY, but with its own vineyards in the northern Rhône. Single-vineyard wines include dense, powerful red HERMITAGE★★ (les Bessards★★★), which needs a decade or more to reach its peak, perfumed COTE-ROTIE la Landonne★★ and ST-JOSEPH Ste-Épine★★. The CROZES-HERMITAGE Tour d'Albon★★ is good, as is the COTES DU RHONE St-Esprit. Look out for the aromatic CONDRIEU★★. **Best years:** (premium reds) (2007) 06 05 04 03 **01 00 99 98 97 96 95 94 91 90 89 88 78**.

DELEGAT'S *Henderson, Auckland, North Island, New Zealand* One of New Zealand's largest family-run wineries, specializing in Chardonnay (Reserve★), Cabernet and Merlot (Reserve★) from HAWKES BAY. The Oyster Bay label, based in MARLBOROUGH, is best known for Sauvignon Blanc★. Best years: (Oyster Bay Sauvignon Blanc) **2007 06 04 03**.

DELILLE CELLARS *Columbia Valley AVA, Washington State, USA* DeLille Cellars produces BORDEAUX-style wines from some of the better vineyards in YAKIMA VALLEY. The flagship is Chaleur Estate Red★★, a powerful ageworthy blend of Cabernet and Merlot. Chaleur Estate Blanc★★ (Semillon and Sauvignon Blanc) has a GRAVES-like character, albeit with a tad more alcohol. The second wine, D2★★, short for Deuxième, is an early-drinking red. Doyenne Syrah★★ shows outstanding potential. Best years: (Chaleur Estate Red) (2006) 05 **04 03 02 01 00 99**.

DENBIES *Surrey, England* UK's largest vineyard with 107ha (265 acres) of vines, planted on chalky slopes outside Dorking. Wines have been erratic over the years but have now reached a new plateau of quality with remarkably attractive whites, lively, refreshing rosé and decent fizz. Pinot Noir-based Redlands can be good too. Arrival of experienced winemaker John Worontschak can only be a good thing.

JEAN-LOUIS DENOIS *Vin de Pays d'Oc, Languedoc, France* Producer based in LIMOUX, who can't see a rule without breaking it. First he attempted to plant Riesling and was reprimanded by the French wine authorities (Riesling is permitted only in Alsace). Now he has made a red wine from Merlot and Cabernet, without any of the 'Mediterranean' varieties obligatory in Limoux. This wine is Chloé★, a wine that mixes the flavours of BORDEAUX with just an extra bit of Mediterranean warmth.

DEUTZ *Champagne AC, Champagne, France* This small company has been owned by ROEDERER since 1993 and considerable effort and investment have turned a good producer into an excellent one. The non-vintage Brut★★ is now regularly one of the best in CHAMPAGNE, often boasting a cedary scent, while the top wines are the classic Blanc de Blancs★★, the weightier Cuvée William Deutz★★ and the de luxe vintage blanc de blancs Amour de Deutz★★. Deutz has licensed Pernod Ricard in New Zealand to use its brand on their sparkling wine. Best years: (2004) (02) 00 **99** 98 96 **95 90 89 88**.

DÉZALEY *Lavaux, Vaud, Switzerland* The top wine commune in the VAUD, making surprisingly powerful, mineral wines from the Chasselas grape. Best producers: Louis Bovard★, Conne, Les Frères Dubois★, E & L Fonjallaz★, Pinget★, J & P Testuz★.

D F J VINHOS *Portugal* In the early 1990s, UK wine shippers D & F began working with one of Portugal's most innovative winemakers, José Neiva; in 1999 this relationship evolved into D F J Vinhos. Now Neiva has gone solo. The Bela Fonte brand includes varietal reds Baga, Jaen★ and Touriga Franca★, all from BEIRAS. Other labels include Segada from the RIBATEJO, Manta Preta★ from ESTREMADURA, Pedras do Monte from TERRAS DO SADO and Monte Alentejano from the ALENTEJO. At the top end are the Grand'Arte reds, including fruity, peppery Trincadeira★ and beefy Alicante Bouschet★, and prestige wines from the DOURO (Escada★), ALENQUER (Francos Reserva) and RIBATEJO (Consensus★).

DIAMOND CREEK *Napa Valley AVA, California, USA* Small Diamond Mountain estate specializing in Cabernet: Volcanic Hill★★★, Red Rock Terrace★★, Gravelly Meadow★★. Traditionally huge, tannic wines that, when tasted young, I swear won't ever come round. Yet there's usually a sweet inner core of fruit that envelops the tannin over 10–15 years; recent releases show wonderful perfume and balance even in their youth. Best years: 2005 04 03 02 01 00 **99 98** 97 96 95 94 92 91 90 87 86 84.

SCHLOSSGUT DIEL *Burg Layen, Nahe, Germany* Armin Diel has become one of the leading producers of classic-style Rieslings. Spätlese and Auslese from Dorsheim's top sites (Burgberg, Goldloch and Pittermännchen) are regularly ★★. Good Sekt too. Best years: (2007) 06 05 04 **03** 02 01 00 **99** 98.

DISTELL *Stellenbosch, South Africa* South Africa's largest wine company; some of the allied wineries – such as Neethlingshof★, Stellenzicht★ and Durbanville Hills★ – are performing well. The Fleur du Cap range is improving, whites especially. Two wineries in PAARL, Nederburg and Plaisir de Merle★, are run separately. Nederburg is starting to create a buzz with some unconventional blends as well as trademark botrytized dessert Edelkeur★, sold only through an annual auction.

CH. DOISY-DAËNE★★ *Sauternes AC, 2ème Cru Classé, Bordeaux, France* A consistently good property in BARSAC (although it uses the SAUTERNES AC for its wines) and unusual in that the sweet wine is made exclusively from Sémillon. It ages well for 10 years or more. The extra-rich Extravagant★★★ is produced in exceptional years. Doisy-Daëne Sec★ is a good, perfumed, dry white. Drink young. Best years: (sweet) 2006 05 04 03 **02 01 99 98 97 96 95** 90 89.

CH. DOISY-VÉDRINES★★ *Sauternes AC, 2ème Cru Classé, Bordeaux, France* Next door to DOISY-DAENE, Doisy-Védrines is a richly botrytized wine, fatter and more syrupy than most BARSAC wines. Like its neighbour, it also sells its wines under the SAUTERNES AC. Best years: (sweet) 2006 05 04 03 **02 01** 99 98 97 96 95 90 89 88 86.

DOLCETTO One of Italy's most charming grapes, producing, for the most part, purple wines bursting with fruit, though oak-aging is creeping into the equation a bit too much in the costlier versions. Virtually exclusive to PIEDMONT and LIGURIA, it boasts 11 DOCs and 1 DOCG (Dogliani) in Piemonte, with styles ranging from intense and rich in Alba, Ovada and Diano d'Alba, to lighter and more perfumed in Acqui and Asti. The most serious, longest-lasting wines are from Dogliani and Alba. Usually best drunk within 1–2 years, traditionally vinified wines can last 10 years or more. Best producers: (Alba) Alario★★, ALTARE★★, Boglietti★★, Bongiovanni★★, Bricco Maiolica★, Brovia★★, Elvio Cogno★★, Aldo CONTERNO★, Conterno-Fantino★★, B Marcarini★, Bartolo MASCARELLO★, Giuseppe MASCARELLO★★, Paitin★, Pelissero★★, PRUNOTTO★, RATTI★, Albino Rocca★★, SANDRONE★★, Vajra★★, Vietti★, Gianni Voerzio★, Roberto VOERZIO★; (Dogliani) M & E Abbona★, Chionetti★★, Luigi Einaudi★★, Pecchenino★★, San Fereolo★★, San Romano★.

DÔLE *Valais, Switzerland* Red wine from the VALAIS that must be made from at least 51% Pinot Noir, the rest being Gamay. Dôle is generally a light wine – the deeper, richer (100% Pinot Noir) styles may call themselves Pinot Noir. Most should be drunk young and lightly chilled. Best producers: M Clavien, Jean-René Germanier, A Mathier, Provins.

DOMAINE CARNEROS *Carneros AVA, California, USA* Very successful TAITTINGER-owned sparkling wine house. The vintage Brut now matches Taittinger's fizz from CHAMPAGNE, though I'd like it drier. Also vintage-dated Le Rêve★★★ and attractive Pinot Noirs★★.

139

DOMAINE CHANDON *Yarra Valley, Victoria, Australia* MOET & CHANDON
Aussie offshoot makes fine Pinot Noir-Chardonnay fizz. Non-vintage
Brut, Cuvée Riche and sparkling red Pinot-Shiraz★, and vintage
Brut★★, Rosé★★, Blanc de Blancs★, Blanc de Noirs★, YARRA VALLEY
Brut★★ and a Tasmanian Cuvée★★, plus new vintage ZD★★ (Zero
Dosage). Table wines, often of ★★ quality, under the Green Point label
with Reserve Shiraz★★ standing out. The Green Point name is also used
on fizz for export markets.

DOMAINE CHANDON *Napa Valley AVA, California, USA* California's first
French-owned (MOET & CHANDON) sparkling wine producer majors on
reasonable price and acceptable quality, but doesn't match the quality of
Moët's subsidiaries in Australia or Argentina. Reserve bottlings can be
rich and creamy. Blanc de Blancs is a CARNEROS Chardonnay; Étoile★ is
an aged de luxe wine, also made as a flavourful Rosé★.

DOMAINE DROUHIN OREGON *Willamette Valley AVA, Oregon, USA*
Burgundy wine merchant Robert DROUHIN bought 40ha (100 acres) in
OREGON in 1987, with plans to make fine Pinot Noir on New World land
with an Old World philosophy. The regular Pinot Noir★ is lean but
attractive, and the de luxe Pinot Noir Laurène★★ is supple and
voluptuous. Pinot Noir Louise★★ is a selection of the finest barrels in the
winery. Also very good Chardonnay Arthur★★. Best years: (Pinot Noir)
(2007) 06 05 **04 03 02 01 00 99 98 96 94 93**.

DOMAINE SERENE *Willamette Valley AVA, Oregon, USA* Ken and Grace
Evenstad purchased 17ha (42 acres) of land in the WILLAMETTE VALLEY in
1989, naming the property after their daughter, Serene. Devoted to
Pinot Noir and Chardonnay, they have established a fine reputation. The
full-bodied Pinot Noir Evenstad Reserve★★ is aged in French oak and
has striking black cherry and currant flavours. The Chardonnay Clos du
Soleil★★, made from Dijon clones, has a rich apple and hazelnut
character. Best years: (Pinot Noir) 2006 05 **04 03 02 01 00 99**.

DOMAINE VISTALBA *Argentina* French-owned company whose Fabre
Montmayou winery in LUJAN DE CUYO produces impressive Malbec★. The
almost black, chocolate-and-damsons Grand Vin★★ is a blend of
Malbec with Cabernet Sauvignon and Merlot. Phebus Malbec is
seductively mineral and floral. Latest releases from the Infinitus winery,
down in PATAGONIA, are exciting.

DOMECQ *Jerez y Manzanilla DO and Rioja DOCa, Spain* The largest of the sherry
companies, best known for its refreshing fino, La Ina★, is now in a state
of flux after the acquisition by Pernod Ricard of Allied Domecq. At the
top of the range, dry Amontillado 51-1A★★★, Sibarita Palo
Cortado★★★ and Venerable Pedro Ximénez★★ are spectacular.
Domecq also makes light, elegant RIOJA, Marqués de Arienzo★.

DOMINUS★★ *Napa Valley AVA, California, USA* Owned by Christian MOUEIX,
director of Bordeaux superstar PETRUS. Wines are based on Cabernet with
leavenings of Merlot and Cabernet Franc. Its reputation was marred by
excessively tannic early releases, but recent wines are mellow and
delicious. Best years: (2006) 05 04 03 02 **01 00 99 97 96 95 94 91 90**.

DONAULAND See WAGRAM.

DÖNNHOFF *Oberhausen, Nahe, Germany* Helmut Dönnhoff is the quiet
winemaking genius of the NAHE, conjuring from a string of top sites some
of the most mineral dry and naturally sweet Rieslings in the world. The
very best are the subtle, long-lived wines from the Niederhäuser
Hermannshöhle★★★ and Oberhäuser Brücke vineyards. Eiswein★★★

equally exciting. **Best years:** (Hermannshöhle Riesling Spätlese) (2007) 06 05 04 **03** 02 01 00 99 98 97 96.

OURO DOC *Douro, Portugal* As prices soar for the best wines, deciding whether to use top grapes for unfortified DOURO wine or PORT has become much harder for Douro producers. Quality can be superb when the lush, scented fruit is not smothered by new oak. Reds may improve for 10 years or more. Whites from higher-altitude vineyards have improved, but best drunk young. **Best producers:** (reds) ALIANÇA (Quinta dos Quatro Ventos★★), Maria Doroteia Seródio Borges (Fojo★★), Casal de Loivos★★, Chryseia★★★, Quinta do COTTO (Grande Escolha★★), Quinta do CRASTO★★, FERREIRA★ (Barca Velha★★★, Quinta da Leda★), Quinta da Gaivosa★, Quinta de Macedos★, Quinta de Maritávora★, Muxagat, NIEPOORT★★★, Quinta do NOVAL★★, Quinta do Passadouro (Reserva★★), Pintas★★, Poeira★★, Quinta do Portal★, RAMOS PINTO★ (Duas Quintas Reserva Especial★★), Quinta de Roriz★, Quinta de la ROSA★, SOGRAPE, Quinta do Vale Dona Maria★★, Quinta do Vale Meao★★, Quinta do Vale da Raposa★, Quinta do Vallado★ (Sousão★★, Tinta Roriz★★), Xisto★. **Best years:** (reds) 2005 **04** 03 01 00 97 95.

OW *Port DOC, Douro, Portugal* The grapes for Dow's Vintage PORT★★★ come mostly from the Quinta do Bomfim, also the name of the excellent single quinta★★★. Dow ports are relatively dry compared with those of GRAHAM and WARRE (the 2 other major brands belonging to the Symington family). There are also good Crusted★ and some excellent aged tawnies★★. Quinta Senhora da Ribeira★, opposite VESUVIO, has made impressive ports since 1998. **Best years:** (Vintage) **2003** 00 97 94 91 85 83 80 77 70 66 63 60 55 45; (Bomfim) **1999** 98 95 92 87 86 84.

OSEPH DROUHIN *Beaune, Burgundy, France* Burgundian merchant with substantial vineyard holdings in CHABLIS and the COTE D'OR, and DOMAINE DROUHIN OREGON. Consistently good, if expensive, wines from all over Burgundy. Look for BONNES-MARES★★, ROMANEE-ST-VIVANT★★★, BEAUNE Clos des Mouches (red★★ and white★★★), le MUSIGNY★★★ and le MONTRACHET★★★ from the Marquis de Laguiche. Drouhin offers fine value in Chablis★ and less glamorous Burgundian ACs, such as RULLY★ and

ST-AUBIN★. The whites are impressively consistent; the reds are less powerful than some as the policy is to pursue elegance and style. Top reds and whites should be aged for at least 5 years; often better nearer 10. **Best years:** (top reds) (2007) 06 05 03 02 **00** 99 96 95.

IERRE-JACQUES DRUET *Bourgueil AC, Loire Valley, France* A passionate producer of BOURGUEIL and small quantities of CHINON★★. Druet makes various Bourgueils – les Cent Boisselées★, Grand Mont★ and Vaumoreau★★ – each a complex expression of the Cabernet Franc grape. Best aged for at least 3–5 years. **Best years:** (top cuvées) 2006 05 **04** 03 02 01 00 99 97 96 90 89.

DRY CREEK VALLEY AVA *Sonoma, California, USA* Best known for Sauvignon Blanc, Zinfandel and Cabernet Sauvignon, this valley runs west of ALEXANDER VALLEY AVA, and similarly becomes hotter moving northwards. **Best producers:** DRY CREEK VINEYARD★, Duxoup★, FERRARI-CARANO★★, GALLO (Zinfandel★, Cabernet Sauvignon★), Lambert Bridge★, Michel-Schlumberger★, Nalle★★, Pezzi King★, Preston★, Quivira★, Rafanelli (Zinfandel★★). **Best years:** (reds) 2005 03 **02** 01 00 99 98 97 96 95.

DRY CREEK VINEYARD *Dry Creek Valley AVA, California, USA* An earl
advocate of Fumé Blanc★, Dry Creek remains faithful to the brisk rac
style and also makes a serious Reserve★ which improves with aging
DCV3★ (sometimes ★★) is from original plantings and displays subt
notes of fig and herb. A drink-young Chardonnay (Reserve★) i
attractive, but the stars are red Meritage★, Merlot★, Old Vin
Zinfandel★★ and a superb Dry Chenin Blanc★★. Best years: (Old Vin
Zin) 2005 **03 02 01 00 99 97 96 95 94**.

DRY RIVER *Martinborough, North Island, New Zealand* Low yields and a
uncompromising attitude to quality at this tiny winery have created som
of the country's top Gewürztraminer★★★ and Pinot Gris★★★, a
intense, succulent yet minerally Pinot Noir★★★, sleek Chardonnay★
and powerful, long-lived Craighall Riesling★★★. Excellent Syrah★★ i
made in tiny quantities. Owned since 2002 by 2 Americans but founde
Neil McCallum continues as chief winemaker. Best years: (Craigha
Riesling) 2006 **03 01 00 99 98**; (Pinot Noir) (2007) **06 03 01 00 99**.

GEORGES DUBOEUF *Beaujolais, Burgundy, France* Known as the King o
Beaujolais, Duboeuf is responsible for more than 10% of the win
produced in the region. Given the size of his operation, the quality of th
wines is good. Duboeuf also makes and blends wine from the Mâconnai
(ST-VERAN★), the southern RHONE VALLEY and the LANGUEDOC. His BEAUJOLA
NOUVEAU is usually reliable, but his top wines are those he bottles fo
independent growers, particularly Jean Descombes★★ in MORGON, Dom
des Quatre Vents★ and la Madone★ in FLEURIE and Dom. de la Tour d
Bief★ in MOULIN-A-VENT.

DUCKHORN *Napa Valley AVA, California, USA* Best known for its very chunky
tannic Merlot★ – now, thankfully, softer and riper. The Cabernet
Sauvignon★ and Sauvignon Blanc provide easier drinking. Paraduxx is
Zinfandel-Cabernet blend; Decoy is the budget line. The company'
Pinot Noir★ project is Goldeneye in MENDOCINO. Best years: (Merlot) 200
03 02 01 99 98 97 96 95 94 91 90 86.

CH. DUCRU-BEAUCAILLOU★★★ *St-Julien AC, 2ème Cru Classé, Haut-Médoc
Bordeaux, France* Traditionally the epitome of ST-JULIEN, mixing charm and
austerity, fruit and firm tannins. Vintages from the mid-1980s to 199
were flawed; back on form since 94. Second wine: la Croix d
Beaucaillou. Best years: 2006 **05 04 03 02 01 00 99 98 96 95 94**.

DUJAC *Morey-St-Denis, Côte de Nuits, Burgundy, France* Owner Jacques Seysses
estate is based in MOREY-ST-DENIS, with some choice vineyards elsewhere i
the COTE DE NUITS. The wines are all perfumed and elegant, including
small quantity of Morey-St-Denis★ white wine, but the outstanding
bottlings are the Grands Crus – Échézeaux★★★, CLOS DE LA ROCHE★★★
BONNES-MARES★★★ and CLOS ST-DENIS★★★, to which CHAMBERTIN and
ROMANEE-ST-VIVANT have been added since 2005. All need to age for
decade or more. Son Jeremy makes négociant cuvées under the labe
Dujac Fils et Père. Best years: (Grands Crus) (2007) **06 05 04 03 02 01 00 9
98 96 95 93 91 90 89**.

DUNHAM CELLARS *Columbia Valley AVA, Washington State, USA* Family
owned winery in a rustic, remodelled airplane hangar near the Wall
Walla airport. The wines here are powerful and extracted, includin
Cabernet Sauvignon★★, Syrah★, a limited-release Lewis Vineyar
Syrah Reserve★★, Trutina★ (a BORDEAUX-style blend), Three Legge
Red (named after one of the winery dogs) and 'Shirley May
Chardonnay. Best years: (reds) (2006) 05 **04 03 02 01 00 99**.

DUNN VINEYARDS *Howell Mountain AVA, California, USA* Massive, concentrated, hauntingly perfumed, long-lived Cabernet Sauvignon★★★ from HOWELL MOUNTAIN; NAPA VALLEY Cabernets★★ are less powerful but still scented. Thankfully Randy Dunn has resisted the move towards high alcohol, and his wines' ability to age beautifully is evidence of this. Best years: 2005 03 01 **00 99 97 96 95 94 93 92 91 90 88 87 86 85 84 82**.

DURBANVILLE WO *South Africa* Tucked into the folds of the Tygerberg Hills, Durbanville borders Cape Town's northern suburbs. Cool breezes from both the Atlantic Ocean and False Bay suit Sauvignon Blanc: wines are vivid, often with an invigorating minerality. Semillon also does well. Merlot shows promise both as a varietal wine and blended with Cabernet Sauvignon, though the latter sometimes struggles to ripen. Best producers: Bloemendal, Diemersdal, Durbanville Hills★, Meerendal, Nitida★.

DURIF See PETITE SIRAH.

JEAN DURUP *Chablis, Burgundy, France* The largest vineyard owner in CHABLIS, Jean Durup is a great believer in unoaked Chablis, which tends to be clean without any great complexity. Best are the Premiers Crus Fourchaume★ and Montée de Tonnerre★★. Wines appear under a variety of labels, including l'Eglantière, Ch. de Maligny and Valéry. Best years: (2007) **06 05 02**.

ÉCHEZEAUX AC *Grand Cru, Côte de Nuits, Burgundy, France* The Grands Crus of Échezeaux and the smaller and more prestigious Grands-Échezeaux are sandwiched between the world-famous CLOS DE VOUGEOT and VOSNE-ROMANEE. Look for subtlety, intricacy, delicacy from Échezeaux and a little more weight, deepening over the years to a gamy, chocolaty richness from the 'Grands' version. Best producers: R Arnoux★★, BOUCHARD PERE ET FILS★★, Cacheux-Sirugue★★★, DROUHIN★★, DUJAC★★★, R Engel★★★ (to 2004), GRIVOT★★★, A-F GROS★★★, Jayer-Gilles★★★, Mugneret-Gibourg★★★, Perdrix★, Dom. de la ROMANEE-CONTI★★★, E Rouget★★★. Best years: (2007) 06 05 04 03 02 **01 00 99 98 97 96 95 93 90**.

DOM. DE L'ECU *Muscadet Sèvre-et-Maine, Loire Valley, France* One of the finest producers in MUSCADET, Guy Bossard's biodynamically run estate also produces GROS PLANT DU PAYS NANTAIS white, a velvety red vin de pays Cabernet blend and a refreshing sparkler, Ludwig Hahn. It is his Muscadet, though, that stands out, especially the top cuvées from different soil types: Gneiss, Orthogneiss★ and fuller-bodied, minerally Granite★★. Best years: (Granite) 2006 **05 04 03 02 01 00**.

EDEN VALLEY See BAROSSA, pages 70–1.

CH. L'ÉGLISE-CLINET★★★ *Pomerol AC, Bordeaux, France* A tiny 5.5ha (13-acre) domaine in the heart of POMEROL, with a very old vineyard – one of the reasons for the depth and elegance of the wines. The other is the winemaking ability of owner Denis Durantou. The wine is expensive and in limited supply. It can be enjoyed young, though the best vintages should be cellared for 10 years or more. Second wine: La Petite Église. Best years: 2006 05 04 **03 02 01 00 99 98 96 95 94 93 92 90 89**.

ELGIN WO *South Africa* This high-lying ward within the Overberg district is being targeted by some of the Cape's leading winemakers. Summer cloud helps to keep temperatures reasonable, creating good conditions for pure-fruited Sauvignon Blanc, Chardonnay, Riesling and Pinot Noir. Best producers: Paul CLUVER★, Neil ELLIS★★, Iona, Oak Valley★, THELEMA★.

ELK COVE *Willamette Valley AVA, Oregon, USA* Back in 1974, Elk Cove was one of the pioneers of the WILLAMETTE VALLEY. Today the Campbell family produces Pinot Gris★, Riesling and a Riesling-based dessert wine called

Ultima. Basic Pinot Noir★★ frequently matches the more expensiv single-vineyard Pinot Noirs – Roosevelt, Windhill★ and La Bohème★ Best years: (Pinot Noir) (2006) 05 **04 03 02 01**.

NEIL ELLIS *Stellenbosch WO, South Africa* Winemaker and négocian renowned for powerful, invigorating Groenekloof Sauvignon Blanc★ and striking STELLENBOSCH reds (blackcurranty Cabernet Sauvignon★ supple Cabernet-Merlot★). An ageworthy single-vineyard Syrah★ an Cabernet★ (both from Jonkershoek Valley fruit), and a subtly deliciou Chardonnay★★ from cool ELGIN, confirm his versatility. Best year (Cabernet) **2005 04 03 01 00 99 98**; (whites) **2007 06 05 04 03 02 01**.

ERNIE ELS *Stellenbosch WO, South Africa* Jean Engelbrecht's joint venture wit his golfing friend Ernie Els has resulted in a dark, serious BORDEAUX blen under the Ernie Els★★ label. Engelbrecht Els★ forges Shiraz wit Bordeaux varieties (Cabernets Sauvignon and Franc, Merlot, Malbe and Petit Verdot), in a dense, rich, international style. The Guardia Peak range offers quality blends and good-value varietal wine Engelbrecht also makes outstanding Cirrus Syrah★★ in partnership wit SILVER OAK of California. Best years: (Ernie Els) **2005 04 03 02 01 00**.

ELTVILLE *Rheingau, Germany* Large wine town, making some of th RHEINGAU's most racy Rieslings. Best producers: Langwerth von Simmern★ Staatsweingut. Best years: (2007) 06 05 04 **03 02 01 99**.

EMILIA-ROMAGNA *Italy* This region is divided into the western zone c Emilia, best known for LAMBRUSCO, and the eastern zone of ROMAGNA, wher Sangiovese is dominant. See also COLLI PIACENTINI.

EMILIANA *Colchagua, Chile* Venture from the Guilisasti family, mai shareholders at CONCHA Y TORO, with leading winemaker Alvaro Espinoz contributing his biodynamic and organic approach to viticulture. Adob is good entry-level range, Novas★★ range is significantly better, and re five-variety blend Coyam★★ (sometimes ★★★) is one of Chile's mos fascinating wines. 'Super Coyam', called 'Ge'★★, is a dense, powerfu long-distance runner. Best years: (2006) 05 04 03 **02 01**.

EMRICH-SCHÖNLEBER *Monzingen, Nahe, Germany* Although Monzinge is not the most prestigious of NAHE villages, Werner Schönleber ha steadily brought his 14ha (35-acre) property into the front ranks. H vigorous, spicy Rieslings are consistently ★ to ★★ and his Eisweins ar ★★★. Best years: (2007) 06 05 04 **03 02 01 00 99**.

ENATE *Somontano DO, Aragón, Spain* Barrel-fermented Chardonnay★ is ric buttery and toasty, Gewürztraminer★ is exotic and convincing International grape varieties also feature in the red Crianza, Reserva (100% Cabernet Sauvignon), Reserva Especial★★ (Cabernet-Merlot and blockbuster Merlot-Merlot★ and Syrah-Shiraz. Best years: (red **2005 04 03 01 00 99 98**.

ENTRE-DEUX-MERS AC *Bordeaux, France* This large AC between the river Garonne and Dordogne increasingly represents some of the freshes snappiest dry white wine in France. In general, drink the latest vintag though better wines will last a year or two. Most of Bordeaux's basic re wine under the Bordeaux AC comes from here too. Sweet wines are sol as PREMIERES COTES DE BORDEAUX, St-Macaire, LOUPIAC and STE-CROIX-DL MONT. Best producers: BONNET★, Castenet Greffier, de Fontenille★ Landereau★, Marjosse★, Nardique la Gravière★, Ste-Marie★, Tour d Mirambeau★, Toutigeac★, Turcaud★.

OM. D'EOLE *Coteaux d'Aix-en-Provence AC, Provence, France* Top wines from this organic estate are rosé Cuvée Caprice★ and Cuvée Léa★★, a 50:50 blend of Syrah and Grenache. Best years: 2005 03 **01** 00.

RBACH *Rheingau, Germany* Erbach's famous Marcobrunn vineyard is one of the top spots for Riesling along the Rhine. The village wines are elegant while those from Marcobrunn more powerful and imposing. Best producers: Jakob Jung★, Knyphausen★, Langwerth von Simmern★★, SCHLOSS REINHARTSHAUSEN★★, Schloss Schönborn★. Best years: (2007) 06 05 **04** 03 02 **01** 99 98.

RBALUCE DI CALUSO DOC *Piedmont, Italy* Usually a dry or sparkling white from the Erbaluce grape, but Caluso Passito, where the grapes are semi-dried before fermenting, can be a fine sweet wine. Best producers: (Caluso Passito) Cieck★, Ferrando★, Orsolani★.

RDEN *Mosel, Germany* Middle MOSEL village with the superb Prälat and Treppchen vineyards. Wines are rich and succulent with a strong mineral character. Best producers: Christoffel★★, Dr LOOSEN★★★, Mönchhof★★, Peter Nicolay★, Dr Weins-Prüm★. Best years: (2007) 06 05 **04** 03 02 01 99 97.

RRÁZURIZ *Aconcagua, Chile* Traditional winery run by dynamic Eduardo Chadwick. Its portfolio includes SENA and Arboleda – originally joint ventures with MONDAVI, now 100% Errázuriz, and much improved as a result. The classic label is Don Maximiano Founder's Reserve★ (sometimes ★★), a Cabernet Sauvignon-based red from Aconcagua, also the source of La Cumbre Shiraz★ and dense red The Blend★. Single-vineyard Cabernet Sauvignon Viñedo Chadwick★★ comes from Tocornal, a classic area of MAIPO. Also very good 'Wild Ferment' Chardonnay★★ and Pinot Noir★ from CASABLANCA. Best years: (reds) (2006) 05 04 **03** 02 01.

CH. D'ESCLANS *Côtes de Provence AC, Provence, France* Sacha Lichine has created what is claimed to be the 'most expensive rosé in the world', Garrus, an explosive, wood-aged blend of old-vine Grenache and Rolle. For lesser mortals, there are Les Clans, the château wine and the sweeter Whispering Angel. First vintage was 2006.

SPORÃO *Reguengos DOC, Alentejo, Portugal* Huge estate in the heart of the ALENTEJO, where Australian David Baverstock makes a broad range of wines. Principal labels are Esporão (red★★ and white★ Reservas), Vinha da Defesa★, Monte Velho and Alandra. Also some delightful varietals: Trincadeira★, Aragonês★, Touriga Nacional★, Syrah★, Alicante Bouschet★ and Verdelho★. Best years: (reds) 2005 **04 01** 00.

EST! EST!! EST!!! DI MONTEFIASCONE DOC *Lazio, Italy* Trebbiano-based white whose quality is distinctly inferior to the renown it has earned in myth. Best producers: Bigi (Graffiti), FALESCO (Poggio dei Gelsi★), Mazziotti (Canuleio★).

CH. DES ESTANILLES *Faugères AC, Languedoc, France* The Louisons know that quality begins in the vineyard. Their best site is the Clos de Fou, with its very steep schistous slope planted with Syrah; the grape 'dominates' the Prestige cuvée★★ (i.e. 100% – but AC regulations do not allow them to say so). Also a wood-fermented and aged rosé, plus fine COTEAUX DU LANGUEDOC white★. Best years: (reds) 2005 **04** 02 01.

ESTREMADURA *Portugal* Portugal's most productive region, occupying t
western coastal strip and with an increasing number of clean, character
wines. The leading area is ALENQUER DOC and there are eight other DO
regions; however, much of the wine, including some of the region's best,
simply labelled as Vinho Regional Estremadura. Spicy, perfumed reds a
often based on Castelão, but Aragonez (Tempranillo), Cabernet Sauvigno
Syrah and Touriga Nacional contribute to top examples, which can bene
from 4 or 5 years' aging. Top producers also make fresh, aromatic whites. B
producers: Agrovitis (Fonte das Moças★), Quinta de Chocapalha★, Quinta
Cortezia★, D F J VINHOS (Francos Reserva★), Grand'Arte Touriga Nacional★), Quir
dos Loridos (Merlot★), Quinta do Monte d'Oiro★★, Quinta de Pancas, Compan
Agricola do Sanguinhal, Casa SANTOS LIMA★. See also BUCELAS. Best years: (red
2005 **04 03 01 00**.

L'ÉTOILE AC *Jura, France* A tiny area within the COTES DU JURA which has
own AC for whites, mainly Chardonnay and Savagnin, and for *vin jau*
Fizz now comes under the CREMANT DU JURA AC. Best producers: C
l'Étoile★, Geneletti★, Joly★, Montbourgeau★★.

CH. L'ÉVANGILE★★ *Pomerol AC, Bordeaux, France* A neighbour to PETR
and CHEVAL BLANC, this estate has been wholly owned and managed by t
Rothschilds of LAFITE-ROTHSCHILD since 1999. The wine is quintessent
POMEROL – rich, fat and exotic. Recent vintages have been very go
(sometimes ★★★), but expect further improvement as the Rothschi
effect intensifies. Second wine: Blason de l'Evangile. Best years: 2006
04 **03 02 01 00 99 98 96 95 94 93 90 89 88 85**.

FAIRVIEW *Paarl WO, South Africa* Owner Charles Back believes Sou
Africa's strength, especially in warmer areas, lies with Rhône varieti
These are expressed in the Goats range: the spicy Goat-Roti★ partne
Shiraz with Viognier; Goats do Roam and Goats do Roam in Villag
reds and rosé feature Pinotage with Shiraz, Grenache, Cinsa
Mourvèdre and Viognier, while the whites★ include Grenache Bla
Clairette and Viognier as part of the mix. Complementing these is Bor
Doe, a Merlot-led, classic BORDEAUX-style blend. The French authoriti
are not amused but fans on both sides of the Atlantic can't get enoug
Fine Shiraz★★ (Solitude★★, The Beacon★★, Jakkalsfontein★★
Carignan★, Merlot★, Cabernet Sauvignon★ and Pinotage
(Primo★★). Good whites include Oom Pagel Semillon★★, Viognie
and outstanding sweet wine La Beryl★★★. Back also owns SPICE ROU
Best years: (Shiraz) **2006 05 04 03 02 01 00 99**.

JOSEPH FAIVELEY *Nuits-St-Georges, Côte de Nuits, Burgundy, France* Th
Burgundian merchant makes impressive but severely tannic red win
that demand aging (CORTON★★, CHAMBERTIN-Clos-de-Bèze★★, Maz
Chambertin★★), principally from its own substantial vineyard holdin
In lesser wines, the fruit may not hold out against the tannin, and ev
aging may not help. The much cheaper MERCUREY reds★ from the Cô
Chalonnaise can be attractive, if on the lean side. But watch
developments now that Erwan Faiveley has taken over from his fath
François. Whites from Mercurey★ and RULLY★, and the oak-ag
BOURGOGNE Blanc represent reasonably good value. Best years: (top re
(2007) 06 05 03 99 **98 97 96 95 93 90**; (whites) (2007) 06 05 **04 02 00 9**

FALERNO DEL MASSICO DOC *Campania, Italy* Falernian was one of t
ancient Romans' star wines. Today's DOC, with a white Falanghina a
reds from either Aglianico and Piedirosso or from Primitivo, has so

promised more than it has delivered. Best producers: Michele Moio★, Villa Matilde★ (Vigna Camarato★★). Best years: (reds) (2007) (06) **05 04 03 01 00**.

ALESCO *Lazio, Italy* Property of the phenomenal Cotarella brothers: Renzo is ANTINORI's technical director (so responsible for SOLAIA, TIGNANELLO, etc.); Riccardo is a high-profile consultant enologist, working all over Italy from Piedmont to Sicily. Located at Montefiascone, the town of EST! EST!! EST!!!, their Poggio dei Gelsi★ is considered best of the genre, but they are better known for their Merlot Montiano★★, the essence of smooth if somewhat soulless modernity. Best years: (Montiano) (2007) (06) 04 **03 01 00 99 98 97**.

H. FALFAS★ *Côtes de Bourg AC, Bordeaux, France* Biodynamic estate making concentrated, structured wine that needs 4–5 years to soften. Le Chevalier★ is an old-vines cuvée. Best years: **2005 04 03 02 01 00**.

H. DE FARGUES★★ *Sauternes AC, Bordeaux, France* Property run by the Lur-Saluces family, who until 1999 also owned Ch. d'YQUEM. The quality of this fine, rich wine is more a tribute to their commitment than to the inherent quality of the vineyard. Best years: 2006 05 04 03 **02 01 99 98 97 96 95 90 89 88 86 83**.

Y FARR *Geelong, Victoria, Australia* Having established BANNOCKBURN as one of Australia's best boutique wineries, Gary Farr is now making wine with his son, Nick, from his 4.8ha (12-acre) family vineyard. Farr, one of the great individuals of Australian wine, is a traditionalist at heart who is relishing his new beginning and making wines of rare quality. The Viognier★ is heady, complex and alluring; the Chardonnay★ austere yet tangy and elegant; the Pinot Noir★★ ethereal, fine and deliciously varietal; the Shiraz★★ meaty, savoury and minerally, dry and firm. Nick Farr makes more moderately priced wines under the Farr Rising label.

AUGÈRES AC *Languedoc, France* The schistous hills north of Béziers in the Hérault produce red wines whose ripe, soft, rather plummy flavour marks them out from other LANGUEDOC reds. Best producers: Abbaye Sylva Plana★, ALQUIER★, Léon Barral★, Chenaie★, ESTANILLES★, Faugères co-op, Grézan, Haut-Fabrègues, Haut Lignières, HECHT & BANNIER★, la Liquière★, Moulin de Ciffre, Ollier-Taillefer (Castel Fossibus★), Saint-Antonin. Best years: 2005 04 **03 01 00 99**.

AUSTINO *Rioja DOCa, País Vasco and Rioja, and Cava DO, Spain* Family-owned and technically very well equipped, this RIOJA company makes fair Reserva V and Gran Reserva I red Riojas, as well as a more modern, oak-aged red, Faustino de Autor, and fruit-driven Faustino de Crianza. But they could try harder – and they should. Best years: (reds) (2005) **04 03 01 99 98 96 95 94 92 91 90**.

EILER-ARTINGER *Rust, Neusiedlersee, Burgenland, Austria* Hans Feiler and now his son Kurt make supreme Ausbruch dessert wines★★★. Their dry whites are ★. Solitaire★★ is a suave red blend of Merlot with Blaufränkisch and Zweigelt. Best years: (sweet whites) (2007) 06 05 04 **02 01 00 99 98 95**; (Solitaire) (2007) 06 05 **04 03 02 01 00**.

LIVIO FELLUGA *Colli Orientali del Friuli DOC, Friuli-Venezia Giulia, Italy* A younger generation has continued the great work of Livio Felluga at this large Friuli estate. Merlot-Cabernet blend Vertigo★★, raspberryish straight Merlot Riserva Sossò★★, white Pinot Grigio★, Picolit Riserva★★ and Tocai Friulano★ are all class acts. Shàrjs★ combines Chardonnay with Ribolla and oak, but there's more to stimulate the palate in Terre Alte★★, an aromatic blend of Tocai, Pinot Bianco and Sauvignon. Best years: (whites) (2007) 06 **04 02 01 00**.

147

FATTORIA DI FELSINA *Chianti Classico DOCG, Tuscany, Italy* Full, chunk
CHIANTI CLASSICO★★ wines which improve with several years' bottle ag
Quality is good to outstanding; most notable are the single-vineyar
Riserva Rancia★★★ and (under the regional IGT Toscana) Sangiove
Fontalloro★★★. Also good are Chardonnay I Sistri★★ and Cabern
Maestro Raro★★★. Best years: (Fontalloro) (2007) (06) 04 03 01 00 99 98 9
95 93 90 88 85.

FELTON ROAD *Central Otago, South Island, New Zealand* Runaway succe
with vineyards in the old goldfields of Bannockburn. Intensely fruit
seductive Pinot Noir★★ is surpassed by very limited quantities
concentrated, complex Block 3 Pinot Noir★★★ and the equally limite
edition Block 5★★★. Cornish Point Pinot Noir★★, from a separa
vineyard, is fleshy and scented. Three classy Rieslings (all ★★) cover th
range from dry to sweet. Mineral, citrus unoaked Chardonnay★ can b
one of New Zealand's best; barrel-fermented Chardonnay★★ is funk
and delicious. Best years: (Pinot Noir) (2007) 06 05 03 02 01.

FENDANT *Valais, Switzerland* Chasselas wine from the steep slopes of th
VALAIS. Good Fendant should be slightly *spritzig*, with a nutty characte
However, the average Fendant is overcropped, thin and virtual
characterless. Best drunk very young. Best producers: Chappaz, Jean-Ren
Germanier, Gilliard, Caves Imesch, Fils Maye, Taillefer.

FERNGROVE *Great Southern, Western Australia*
Ambitious new winery based in Frankland River,
where it has 285ha (700 acres) of vines (along with
140ha/345 acres at Mount Barker). The quality
potential in Frankland River is unquestioned, being
sunny yet cool. Lack of water is a limiting factor,
but that also means yields are naturally limited and
flavours intensified. So far Majestic Cabernet
Sauvignon★ is pretty serious, Dragon Shiraz★ and
King Malbec★ improve with each vintage, while
Cossack Riesling★★ and Diamond Chardonnay★
are very good. The flagship Stirlings Shiraz-
Cabernet blend★★ has at last shown its potential.

FERRARI *Trento DOC, Trentino, Italy* Founded in 1902, the firm is a leader f
sparkling wine. Consistent, classy wines include Ferrari Brut★
Maximum Brut★, Perlé★, Rosé★ and vintage Giulio Ferrari Riserva d
Fondatore★★, aged 8 years on its lees and an Italian classic. Ar
relation? No, apparently Ferrari is one of the commonest names in Ital

FERRARI-CARANO *Dry Creek Valley AVA, California, USA* Balanced, elegar
Chardonnay; the regular bottling★★ has delicious apple-spice frui
while the Reserve★★ is deeply flavoured with more than a touch of oal
Fumé Blanc★ is also good. A new line of premium whites is calle
PreVail. Red wines are equally impressive, including Trésor★★ (
BORDEAUX blend), Siena★★ (Sangiovese-Cabernet Sauvignon), Syrah★
Merlot★ and Zinfandel★. Reds can age for 5–10 years. Best years: (red
2006 05 03 02 01 00 99 97 96 95.

FERREIRA *Port DOC and Douro DOC, Douro, Portugal* Old PORT house owned b
SOGRAPE. Ferreira is best known for excellent tawny ports: creamy, nutt
Quinta do Porto 10-year-old★ and Duque de Braganza 20-year-old★★
The Vintage★★ is increasingly good. Ferreira's unfortified win
operation, known as Casa Ferreirinha, produces Portugal's most sough
after red, Barca Velha★★★; made from DOURO grape varieties (mainl

Tinta Roriz), it is produced only in the finest years – just 15 vintages since 1953. Marginally less good years are now sold as Casa Ferreirinha Reserva★ (previously Reserva Especial). Quinta da Leda reds★★ are also fine. Best years: (Vintage) **2003 00 97 95 94 91 85 83 82 78 77 70 66 63**; (Barca Velha) **1999 95 91 85 83 82 81 78**.

H. FERRIÈRE★★ *Margaux AC, 3ème Cru Classé, Haut-Médoc, Bordeaux, France* Ferrière was bought by the Merlaut family, owners of Ch. CHASSE-SPLEEN, in 1992. It is now managed by Claire Villars, and the ripe, rich and perfumed wines are among the best in MARGAUX AC. Best years: 2006 05 04 **03 02 01 00 99 98 96**.

ETZER VINEYARDS *Mendocino County, California, USA* Important winery that I feel could push the quality level a bit higher. Locals swear by the quality of the special cellar door releases, but we never see these in the outside world. Basic wines are good, with tasty Gewürztraminer, Riesling and Syrah★; Barrel Select bottles can be ★. Bargain-priced Valley Oaks line is decent value. Also a leader in organic viticulture with the slowly improving Bonterra range: Chardonnay, Viognier★, Merlot, Roussanne★, Zinfandel★, Cabernet Sauvignon and Sangiovese. Best years: (Barrel Select reds) 2005 **03 02 01 99 98 97 96**.

IANO Exciting, distinctive, low-yielding southern Italian white grape variety. Best producers: (Molise) Di Majo Norante; (Fiano di Avellino DOC in CAMPANIA) Colli di Lapio★, Feudi di San Gregorio★★, MASTROBERARDINO★, Terredora di Paolo★, Vadiaperti★; (others) L Maffini (Kràtos★★), PLANETA (Cometa★★), Settesoli (Inycon★).

CH. DE FIEUZAL *Pessac-Léognan AC, Cru Classé de Graves, Bordeaux, France* Under new ownership since 2001; efforts are being made to recapture the form of the 1980s, with help from the owner of ANGELUS. The red★ is drinkable almost immediately, but can age. The white★, a gorgeous, perfumed (and ageworthy) wine, is the star performer. Second wine (red and white): l'Abeille de Fieuzal. Best years: (reds) 2006 05 **01 00 98 96 95 90 89 88**; (whites) 2006 05 **03 02 01 00 99 98 96**.

CH. FIGEAC★★ *St-Émilion Grand Cru AC, 1er Grand Cru Classé, Bordeaux, France* Leading property whose wine traditionally has a delightful fragrance and gentleness of texture. It has an unusually high percentage (70%) of Cabernets Franc and Sauvignon, making it more structured than other ST-EMILIONS. After an unconvincing run of vintages from the mid-1980s, recent vintages have been far more like the lovely Figeac of old. Second wine: la Grange Neuve de Figeac. Best years: 2006 05 04 **03 02 01** 00 **99 98 96 95 90 89**.

FINGER LAKES AVA *New York State, USA* Cool region in central NEW YORK STATE, where some winemakers are establishing a regional style for dry Riesling. Chardonnay and sparkling wines also star, with Pinot Noir and Cabernet Franc the best reds. Best producers: Anthony Road, Chateau Lafayette Reneau★, FOX RUN★, Dr Konstantin FRANK★, Heron Hill, LAMOREAUX LANDING★, Red Newt, Swedish Hill, Wagner, Hermann J Wiemer★.

FITOU AC *Languedoc, France* One of the success stories of the 1980s. Quality subsequently slumped, but with the innovative MONT TAUCH co-op taking the lead, Fitou is once again an excellent place to seek out dark, herb-scented reds. Best producers: Abelanet, Bertrand-Bergé★★, Lerys★, Milles Vignes, MONT TAUCH co-op★, Nouvelles★, Rochelierre, Rolland, Roudène★. Best years: 2004 03 **01 00 99 98**.

FIXIN AC *Côte de Nuits, Burgundy, France* Although it's next door to GEVREY
CHAMBERTIN, Fixin rarely produces anything really magical. The wines a
often sold as CÔTE DE NUITS-VILLAGES. Increased quality from Joliet's Clos (
la Perrière estate. Best producers: Charlopin★, Coillot, Galeyrand★, Pier
Gelin★, Alain Guyard★, Joliet/Clos de la Perrière★★. Best years: (reds) (200
06 05 **03 02 99**.

FLEURIE AC *Beaujolais, Burgundy, France* The best-known BEAUJOLAIS Cr
Fleurie reveals the happy, carefree flavours of the Gamay grape at its bes
plus heady perfumes and a delightful juicy fruit. But demand has mea
that too many wines are overpriced and dull. Best producers: J-M Aujoux
Berrod★, P-M Chermette★/Vissoux, M Chignard★, Clos de la Roilette
Depardon★, DUBOEUF (la Madone★, Quatre Vents★), Fleurie co-op★,
Madone/Despres★, Métrat★, A & M Morel★, Verpoix★. Best years: **2007 06 0**

CH. LA FLEUR-PÉTRUS★★ *Pomerol AC, Bordeaux, France* Like the bette
known PETRUS and TROTANOY, this is owned by the dynamic MOUEIX famil
Unlike its stablemates, it is situated entirely on gravel soil and tends t
produce tighter wines with less immediate fruit but considerable elegan
and cellar potential. Among POMEROL's top dozen properties. Best year
2006 05 04 **03 02 01 00 99 98 96 95 94 90 89**.

FLORA SPRINGS *Napa Valley AVA, California, USA* Best known for red win
such as Merlot★★, Cabernet Sauvignon★★ and a BORDEAUX blend calle
Trilogy★★. Barrel-fermented Chardonnay★★ tops the whites, an
Soliloquy★, a barrel-fermented Sauvignon Blanc, has attractive melo
fruit. The winery also works with Italian varietals; a weighty Pino
Grigio★ and a lightly spiced Sangiovese★ are consistent successes. Be
years: (Trilogy) 2005 04 03 **02 01 00 99 97 96 95 94 91**.

FLOWERS *Sonoma Coast AVA, California, USA* Small producer whose esta
vineyard, Camp Meeting Ridge, a few miles from the Pacific, yiel
wines of great intensity. Camp Meeting Ridge Pinot Noir★★★ an
Chardonnay★★★ are usually made with native yeasts and offe
wonderful exotic aromas and flavours. Wines from purchased fruit with
SONOMA COAST designation are ★★. Best years: (Chardonnay) (2006) **05 0**
03 01 00 99; (Pinot Noir) (2006) **05 04 03 01 00 99 98 97 96**.

TENUTE AMBROGIO & GIOVANNI FOLONARI *Tuscany, Italy* A fe
years ago the Folonari family, owners of the giant RUFFINO, split asunde
and these two brothers went their own way. Their properties/bran
include Cabreo (Sangiovese-Cabernet Il Borgo★, Chardonnay I
Pietra★) and Nozzole (powerful, long-lived Cabernet Il Pareto★★) i
CHIANTI CLASSICO, plus VINO NOBILE estate Gracciano-Svetoni, Campo d
Mare in BOLGHERI and BRUNELLO producer La Fuga.

FONSECA *Port DOC, Douro, Portugal* Owned by the same group as TAYLO
(Fladgate Partnership), Fonseca makes ports in a rich, densely plumm
style. Vintage★★★ is magnificent, the aged tawnies★★ uniform
superb. Guimaraens★★ is the 'off-vintage' wine, Crusted★ and La
Bottled Vintage★ are among the best examples of their styles, as is Bi
No. 27★ of a premium ruby port. Quinta do Panascal is the single-quint
vintage. Best years: (Vintage) 2003 00 97 **94 92 85 83 77 75 70 66 63 5**

JOSÉ MARIA DA FONSECA *Terras do Sado, Portugal* Go-ahead compar
making a huge range of wines, from fizzy Lancers Rosé to serious red
Best include Vinya★ (Syrah-Aragonez), Domingos Soares Franc
Private Collection★, and Garrafeiras with codenames like CO★★
RA★★ and TE★★. Optimum★★ is top of the range. Periquita is th
mainstay, with Clássico★ made only in the best years. Also SETUBAL mad

mainly from the Moscatel grape: 5-year-old★ and 20-year-old★★. Older vintage-dated Setúbals are rare but superb.

OM. FONT DE MICHELLE *Châteauneuf-du-Pape AC, Rhône Valley, France* CHATEAUNEUF-DU-PAPE reds★★, in particular Cuvée Étienne Gonnet★★, and whites★★ that are stylish but still heady, with richness and southern herb fragrance – and good value for money. **Best years:** (Étienne Gonnet red) (2007) 06 05 04 **03 01 00 99 98 97 95 94 90 89.**

ONTANAFREDDA *Barolo DOCG, Piedmont, Italy* This large Piedmontese property used to be the hunting lodge of the King of Italy. As well as BAROLO Serralunga d'Alba★, it also produces several single-vineyard Barolos★ (La Delizia★★), a range of PIEDMONT varietals, 4 million bottles of ASTI and a good dry sparkler, Contessa Rosa. **Best years:** (Barolo) (2007) (06) 04 **03** 01 00 99 97.

ASTELLO DI FONTERUTOLI *Chianti Classico DOCG, Tuscany, Italy* This estate has belonged to the Mazzei family since the 15th century. The focus is on CHIANTI CLASSICO Riserva★★, along with excellent SUPER-TUSCAN Siepi★★★ (Sangiovese-Merlot). Belguardo★ is a more recent venture in the MAREMMA, with IGT and MORELLINO DI SCANSANO wines.

ONTODI *Chianti Classico DOCG, Tuscany, Italy* The Manetti family has built this superbly sited estate into one of the most admired in CHIANTI CLASSICO, with excellent *normale*★★ and fine Riserva Vigna del Sorbo★★. SUPER-TUSCAN Flaccianello della Pieve★★★, from a single vineyard of old vines, has served as a shining example to other producers of how excellent Sangiovese can be without the addition of other varieties. Two varietals, Pinot Nero and Syrah★, are made under the Case Via label. **Best years:** (Flaccianello) (2007) (06) **04 03** 01 00 99 97 95 93 90 88 85.

ORADORI *Teroldego Rotaliano DOC, Trentino, Italy* Producer of dark, spicy, berry-fruited wines, including a regular TEROLDEGO ROTALIANO★ and barrique-aged Granato★★. Foradori's interest in Syrah is producing excellent results, both in the varietal Ailanpa★★ and the smoky, black-cherry lushness of Cabernet-Syrah blend Karanar★. **Best years:** (Granato) (2007) (06) **04 03** 01 00 99 97.

ORST *Pfalz, Germany* Village with outstanding vineyard sites, including the Ungeheuer or 'Monster'; wines from the Monster can indeed be quite savage, with a marvellous mineral intensity and richness. Equally good are the Kirchenstück, Jesuitengarten, Freundstück and Pechstein. **Best producers:** BASSERMANN-JORDAN★★, von BUHL★★, BÜRKLIN-WOLF★★, MOSBACHER★, E Müller, WEGELER★, Werlé★, WOLF★★. **Best years:** (2007) 06 05 **04 03** 02 01 99 98.

O FOURNIER *Uco Valley, Mendoza, Argentina* A rising star in the UCO VALLEY, producing exciting Tempranillo and Malbec from old vines in the La Consulta area. Alfa Crux★★, a blend of Tempranillo, Malbec and Merlot, is the current top of the line, while Alfa Crux Malbec★★ is an excellent, juicy expression of Argentina's flagship red grape. Also top Syrah★★. B Crux★ is the lighter, but delicious, second label. O Fournier also has a venture in RIBERA DEL DUERO, Spain, with top Fournier★★ and Alfa Spiga★ cuvées. A new venture in Chile is based in MAULE and SAN ANTONIO; the first release is Centauri, a San Antonio Sauvignon Blanc. **Best years:** (reds) 2005 04 03 **02.**

OX CREEK *McLaren Vale, South Australia* Impressive, opulent, superripe MCLAREN VALE reds. Reserve Shiraz★★ and Reserve Cabernet Sauvignon★★ have wowed the critics; JSM (Shiraz-Cabernets)★★ is rich and succulent; Merlot★★ is a little lighter but still concentrated and

powerful. Vixen sparkling Shiraz★ is also lip-smacking stuff. Whites a
comparatively ordinary, albeit fair value for money.

FOX RUN VINEYARDS *Finger Lakes AVA, New York State, USA* A leader i
crafting a regional style from Dry Riesling★, as well as a reliable produc
of complex, ALSACE-style Gewürztraminer★ and an elegant Reser
Chardonnay★. There are also spicy, attractive reds from Pinot Noir ar
Cabernet Franc, and a complex, fruit-forward red Meritage.

FRANCIACORTA DOCG *Lombardy, Italy* CHAMPAGNE-method fizz mad
from Pinot and Chardonnay grapes. Still whites from Pinot Bianco ar
Chardonnay and reds from Cabernet, Barbera, Nebbiolo and Merlot a
all DOC with the appellation Terre di Franciacorta. Best produce
BELLAVISTA★★, Fratelli Berlucchi★, Guido Berlucchi★, CA' DEL BOSCO★
Castellino★, Cavalleri★, La Ferghettina★, Enrico Gatti★, Monte Rossa★,
Mosnel★, Ricci Curbastro★, San Cristoforo★, Uberti★, Villa★.

FRANCISCAN *Napa Valley AVA, California, USA* Consistently good wines at fa
prices: the Cuvée Sauvage Chardonnay★★ is a blockbusting, savou
mouthful, and the Cabernet Sauvignon-based meritage Magnificat★
very attractive. Part of huge Constellation, which also owns Mou
Veeder Winery (and numerous other premium brands), where lean b
intense Cabernet Sauvignon★★ of great mineral depth and complexity
made, and Estancia, with remarkably good-value Chardonnay★ ar
Pinot Noir★ from CENTRAL COAST and Cabernet Sauvignon★ fro
ALEXANDER VALLEY, as well as its own Meritage★.

DR KONSTANTIN FRANK *Finger Lakes AVA, New York State, USA* The goo
doctor was a pioneer of *vinifera* grapes in the FINGER LAKES region in th
1960s. Now under the direction of his grandson Fred, the wine
continues to spotlight the area's talent with Riesling★ and Rkatsiteli, a
obscure Georgian grape. There's also some nice Chateau Frank fizz.

FRANKEN *Germany* 6000ha (14,820-acre) wine region specializing in d
wines – recognizable by their squat Bocksbeutel bottles (familiar because
the Portuguese wine Mateus Rosé). Silvaner is the traditional variet
although Müller-Thurgau now predominates. The most famous vineyards a
on slopes around WURZBURG, RANDERSACKER, IPHOFEN and Escherndorf.

FRANSCHHOEK WO *South Africa* Huguenot refugees settled in th
picturesque valley, encircled by breathtaking mountain peaks, in the 17t
century. Many wineries and other landmarks still bear French name
The valley is recognized for its whites – Semillon is a local speciality
few vines are 100 years old) – though reds are establishing a reputatio
La Motte Pierneef Shiraz-Viognier★, Stony Brook Cabernet Sauvigno
Reserve★ and Chamonix Pinot Noir★ are among the most promisin
Best producers: Graham BECK★, BOEKENHOUTSKLOOF★★, Cabrière Estat
Chamonix★ (Reserve Chardonnay★★), La Motte★, La Petite Ferm
L'Ormarins, Solms-Delta★, Stony Brook. Best years: (reds) **2005 04 03 02 01 0**

FRASCATI DOC *Lazio, Italy* One of Italy's most famous whites, frequent
referred to as Rome's quaffing wine. The wine may be made fro
Trebbiano or Malvasia or any blend thereof; the better examples have
higher proportion of Malvasia. Good Frascati is worth seeking out, mo
notably Vigna Adriana★★ (though it's now an IGT) from Castel
Paolis. Other light, dry Frascati-like wines come from neighbourin
DOCs in the hills of the Castelli Romani and Colli Albani, includir
Marino, Montecompatri, Velletri and Zagarolo. Best producers: Casa

Marchese★, Castel de Paolis★★, Colli di Catone★, Piero Costantini/Villa Simone★, Fontana Candida★, Zandotti★.

FREIXENET *Cava DO, Cataluña, Spain* The second-biggest Spanish sparkling wine company (after CODORNIU) makes the famous Cordon Negro Brut CAVA in a vast network of cellars in Sant Sadurní d'Anoia. Freixenet also owns the Castellblanch, Segura Viudas, Conde de Caralt and Canals & Nubiola Cava brands as well as PENEDES winery René Barbier and a stake in PRIORAT's Viticultors del Priorat (Morlanda). Its international expansion has gathered pace in recent years with interests in Champagne, California, Australia and Bordeaux.

FRESCOBALDI *Tuscany, Italy* Ancient Florentine company selling large quantities of inexpensive blended CHIANTI, but from its own vineyards (some 800ha/1980 acres in total) it produces good to very good wines at Nipozzano (CHIANTI RUFINA Nipozzano Riserva★★ and Montesodi★★), Tenuta di Pomino★, and Castelgiocondo★ in BRUNELLO DI MONTALCINO, where the Sangiovese and Merlot grapes for the SUPER-TUSCAN (and super-expensive) Luce della Vita are grown. Frescobaldi is now sole

owner of the famous Bolgheri estate, ORNELLAIA. Best years: (premium reds) (2007) (06) **04 03 01 00 99 98 97 95 90**.

FRIULI GRAVE DOC *Friuli-Venezia Giulia, Italy* DOC in western Friuli covering 19 wine types. Good affordable Merlot, Refosco, Chardonnay, Pinot Grigio, Traminer and Tocai. Best producers: Borgo Magredo★, Di Lenardo★, Le Fredis★, Organni★, Pighin★, Pittaro★, Plozner★, Pradio★, Russolo★, Vigneti Le Monde★, Villa Chiopris★, Vistorta★. Best years: (2007) 06 **04 02 01 00 98**.

FRIULI ISONZO DOC *Friuli-Venezia Giulia, Italy* Classy southern neighbour of COLLIO with wines of outstanding value. The DOC covers 20 styles, including Merlot, Chardonnay, Pinot Grigio and Sauvignon. The best from neighbouring Carso DOC are also good. Best producers: (Isonzo) Borgo San Daniele★, Colmello di Grotta★, Sergio & Mauro Drius★★, Masùt da Rive★, Lis Neris★★, Pierpaolo Pecorari★★, Giovanni Puiatti★, Ronco del Gelso★★, Vie di Romans★★, Tenuta Villanova★; (Carso) Castelvecchio, Edi Kante★★. Best years: (whites) (2007) 06 **04 03 02 01 00 99 98 97**.

FRIULI-VENEZIA GIULIA *Italy* North-east Italian region bordering Austria and Slovenia. The hilly DOC zones of COLLIO and COLLIO ORIENTALI produce some of Italy's finest whites from Chardonnay, Pinot Bianco, Pinot Grigio, Sauvignon and Tocai, and excellent reds mainly from Cabernet, Merlot and Refosco. Good-value wines from the DOCs of Friuli Aquileia, FRIULI ISONZO, Friuli Latisana and FRIULI GRAVE, in the rolling hills and plains.

FROMM *Marlborough, South Island, New Zealand* Small winery where low-yielding vines and intensively managed vineyards are the secret behind a string of winning white wines, including fine Burgundian-style Clayvin Vineyard Chardonnay★★, German-style Riesling★★ and Riesling Auslese★. Despite its success with whites, Fromm is perhaps best known for intense, long-lived reds, including Clayvin Vineyard Pinot Noir★★★, Fromm Vineyard Pinot Noir★★ and a powerful, peppery Syrah★★. Best years: (Pinot Noir) 2006 **05 04 03 02 01 00 99**.

FRONSAC AC *Bordeaux, France* Small area west of POMEROL making good-value Merlot-based wines. The top producers have taken note of the feeding frenzy in neighbouring Pomerol and sharpened up their act accordingly, with finely structured wines, occasionally perfumed, and better with at least 5 years' age. Best producers: Dalem★, la Dauphine★ Fontenil★, la Grave, Haut-Carles (Carles★), Magondeau Beau-Site, Mayne-Vieil (Cuvée Aliénor★), Moulin Haut-Laroque★, Richelieu★, la Rivière★ (Aria★), la Rousselle★, Tour du Moulin, les Trois Croix★, la Vieille Cure★, Villars★. Best years: 2006 05 **03 01 00 98 96 95 90**.

FUMÉ BLANC See SAUVIGNON BLANC, pages 268–9.

RUDOLF FÜRST *Bürgstadt, Franken, Germany* Paul Fürst's dry Rieslings★★ are unusually elegant for a region renowned for its earthy white wines, while his Burgundian-style Spätburgunder (Pinot Noir) reds★★ and barrel-fermented Weissburgunder (Pinot Blanc) whites★★ are some of the best in Germany. Sensual, intellectual wines with excellent aging potential. Best years: (dry Riesling) (2007) 06 05 **04 03 02 01 99**; (reds) (2007) 06 05 04 **03 02 01 00**.

JEAN-NOËL GAGNARD *Chassagne-Montrachet, Côte de Beaune, Burgundy, France* Now run by Gagnard's daughter Caroline Lestimé, who consistently makes some of the best wines of CHASSAGNE-MONTRACHET, particularly Premiers Crus Caillerets★★★ and Morgeot★. Top wine is rich, toasty BATARD-MONTRACHET★★★. All whites are capable of extended cellaring. Reds★ are good, but not in the same class. Best years: (whites) (2007) 06 05 **04 03 02 01 00 99**.

GAILLAC AC *South-West France* The whites, mainly from Mauzac and Ondenc, with their sharp but attractive green apple bite, are rather stern but, from a decent producer, can be extremely refreshing. Sweet whites are getting better. Some more serious reds are made, which require some aging. The reds and fizz are the current stars of Gaillac; the fizz is ideally not quite dry and packed with fruit. Drink as young as possible. Best producers: Albert, Bosc-Long, Causses-Marines★, Clément-Termes, Escausses, de Gineste, Labarthe★, Labastide-de-Lévis co-op, PLAGEOLES★★, ROTIER★, Técou co-op★, des Terrisses★.

GAJA *Barbaresco DOCG, Piedmont, Italy* Angelo Gaja brought about the transformation of PIEDMONT from an old-fashioned region that Italians swore made the finest red wine in the world yet the rest of the world disdained, to an area buzzing with excitement. He introduced international standards and charged staggeringly high prices, thus giving other Piedmont growers the chance to get a decent return for their labours. Into this fiercely conservative area, full of fascinating grape varieties and proudest of the native Nebbiolo, he introduced French grapes like Cabernet Sauvignon (Darmagi★★), Sauvignon Blanc (Alteni di Brassica★) and Chardonnay (Gaia & Rey★★). He has also renounced the Barbaresco and Barolo DOCGs for his best wines! Gaja's traditional strength has been in single-vineyard wines from the BARBARESCO region: his Sorì San Lorenzo★★★, Sorì Tildìn★★★ and Costa Russi★★★, now sold under the LANGHE DOC, are often cited as Barbaresco's best of the modern style, although, excellent as these blends are, they tend to be more 'Gaja' than 'Barbaresco'. Only one 100% Nebbiolo bottling of Barbaresco DOCG★★★ is now made. Sperss★★★ and Conteisa★★★ – from BAROLO, but sold as Langhe DOC wines – are also outstanding. Barbera Sitorey★ and Nebbiolo-based Langhe Sito Moresco★ are less exciting. Gaja has also invested in

BRUNELLO DI MONTALCINO (Pieve Santa Restituta) and BOLGHERI (Ca' Marcanda). Best years: (Barbaresco) (2007) (06) 04 **03** 01 **00 99 98 97 96 95 93 90 89 88 85 82 79 78 71 64 61**.

GALICIA *Spain* Up in Spain's hilly, verdant north-west, Galicia is renowned for its Albariño whites. There are 5 DOs: RIAS BAIXAS can make excellent, fragrant Albariño, with modern equipment and serious winemaking; Ribeiro DO has also invested heavily in new equipment, and better local white grapes such as Treixadura are now being used; it's a similar story with Godello in the mountainous Valdeorras DO, where new producers such as the young Rafael Palacios, from the ubiquitous Rioja-based family, are reaching new heights for ageworthy, individual whites. Some young reds from the Mencía grape are also made there and in the Ribeira Sacra DO. Monterrei DO is technically backward but shows some potential with its native white grape, Doña Blanca. Most wines are best drunk young.

GALLO *Central Valley, California, USA* Gallo, the world's second-largest wine company – and for generations a byword for cheap, drab wines – has made a massive effort to change its reputation since the mid-1990s. This began with the release of Sonoma Estate Chardonnay and Cabernet Sauvignon. The Gallo of Sonoma label has been discontinued and replaced by the umbrella Gallo Family label, with emphasis on Sonoma Chardonnay and Cabernet Sauvignon, Zinfandel and Cabernet Sauvignon from DRY CREEK VALLEY and ALEXANDER VALLEY and other Chardonnay from several vineyards. New vineyards in RUSSIAN RIVER VALLEY and the SONOMA COAST have been planted to Pinot Noir and Pinot Gris (some of it to make the premium MacMurray wines). Even so, Gallo continues to produce oceans of ordinary wine. Turning Leaf and Sierra Valley aren't going to turn many heads, but the company has taken Rancho Zabaco upscale and added a parallel brand, Dancing Bull, in which Sauvignon Blanc★ and Zinfandel★★ are budding stars. In 2002, Gallo acquired historic Louis M Martini in NAPA VALLEY, adding the famed Monte Rosso vineyard to its holdings, and then bought Mirassou, Barefoot Cellars, William Hill and CENTRAL COAST's Bridlewood.

GAMAY The only grape allowed for red BEAUJOLAIS. In general Gamay wine is rather rough-edged and quite high in raspy acidity, but in Beaujolais, so long as the yield is not too high, it can achieve a wonderful, juicy-fruit gluggability, almost unmatched in the world of wine. Elsewhere in France, it is successful in the Ardèche and the Loire and less so in the Mâconnais. In Switzerland it is blended with Pinot Noir to create DOLE and Goron. There are occasional plantings in Canada, New Zealand, Australia, South Africa, Italy (MONTECARLO DOC) and even England, which could become interesting.

GANTENBEIN *Fläsch, Graubunden, Switzerland* Since 1982 Daniel Gantenbein has focused on producing intense and powerful versions of the Burgundian varieties, and has won a fine reputation above all for his Pinot Noir★★, as well as Chardonnay and Riesling. Best years: (Pinot Noir) (2006) 05 04 **03 02 00 99**.

GARD, VIN DE PAYS DU *Languedoc, France* Mainly reds and rosés from the western side of the RHONE delta. Most red is light, spicy and attractive. Rosés can be fresh when young, and with modern winemaking whites can be good. Best producers: des Aveylans★, Baruel★, Cantarelles, Coste Plane, Grande Cassagne★, Guiot★, Mas des Bressades★.

GARNACHA BLANCA See GRENACHE BLANC.

GARNACHA TINTA See GRENACHE NOIR.

GATTINARA DOCG *Piedmont, Italy* One of the most capricious of Italy's top red wine areas. The Nebbiolo wines should be softer and lighter than BAROLO, with a delicious, black plums, tar and roses flavour if you're lucky. Drink within 10 years. Vintages follow those for Barolo. Best producers: Antoniolo★, S Gattinara, Nervi★, Travaglini★.

DOM. GAUBY *Côtes du Roussillon-Villages AC, Roussillon, France* Gérard Gauby used to make burly but very tannic wines; now his wines are softer but marvellously concentrated and balanced. Highlights include powerful COTES DU ROUSSILLON-VILLAGES Vieilles Vignes★★ and Syrah-dominated La Muntada★★ as well as a gorgeously seductive white vin de pays la Coume Ginestre★. Best years: (reds) 2005 04 03 **02 01 00** 99.

GAVI DOCG *Piedmont, Italy* This fashionable and rapidly improving Cortese-based, steely, lemony white can age up to 5 years, providing it starts life with sufficient fruit. La Scolca's Spumante Brut Soldati★ is an admirable sparkling wine. Best producers: Battistina★, Bergaglio★,

Broglia★, La Chiara★, CHIARLO★, FONTANAFREDDA★, La Giustiniana★★, Pio Cesare, San Pietro★, La Scolca★, Tassarolo★, Villa Sparina★.

CH. GAZIN★★ *Pomerol AC, Bordeaux, France* One of the largest châteaux in POMEROL, situated next to the legendary PETRUS. The wine, traditionally a succulent, sweet-textured Pomerol, seemed to lose its way in the 1980s but has now got much of its richness and character back under the management of owner Nicolas de Bailliencourt. Best years: 2006 05 04 **03 02 01 00** 99 98 96 95 94 90 89 88.

GEELONG *Victoria, Australia* Cool-climate, maritime-influenced region revived in the 1960s after destruction by phylloxera in the 19th century. Can be brilliant; potentially a match for the YARRA VALLEY. Impressive Pinot Noir, Chardonnay, Riesling, Sauvignon and Shiraz. Best producers: Austin's, BANNOCKBURN★, By FARR★, Scotchmans Hill★.

GEISENHEIM *Rheingau, Germany* Village famous for its wine school, where the Müller-Thurgau grape was bred in 1882. Geisenheim's most famous vineyard is the Rothenberg, which produces strong, earthy wines. Best producers: Johannishof★, WEGELER★. Best years: (2007) 06 05 **04 03** 02 01 99 98.

GEROVASSILIOU *Macedonia AO, Greece* Bordeaux-trained Evángelos Gerovassiliou has 40ha (100 acres) of vineyards and a modern winery in Epanomi in northern Greece. High-quality fruit results in Syrah-dominated Domaine Gerovassiliou red★ and some fresh, modern whites, including a fine Viognier★ that lacks a little perfume but has fantastic fruit, barrel-fermented Chardonnay and Fumé, and the Domaine Gerovassiliou white, a most original Assyrtiko-Malagousia blend.

GEVREY-CHAMBERTIN AC *Côte de Nuits, Burgundy, France* A new generation of growers has restored the reputation of Gevrey as a source of well-coloured, firmly structured, powerful, perfumed wines that become rich and gamy with age. Village wines should be kept for at least 5 years, Premiers Crus and the 9 Grands Crus for 10 years or more, especially

CHAMBERTIN and Clos-de-Bèze. The Premier Cru Clos St-Jacques is worthy of promotion to Grand Cru. Best producers: D Bachelet★★, Louis Boillot★, A Burguet★★, B CLAIR★★, P Damoy★★, DROUHIN★, C Dugat★★★, B Dugat-Py★★, DUJAC★★, S Esmonin★★, FAIVELEY★★, Fourrier★★, Geantet-Pansiot★★, JADOT★★, Denis MORTET★★★, Rossignol-Trapet★★, J Roty★★, ROUSSEAU★★★, Sérafin★★, J & J-L Trapet★★. Best years: (2007) 06 05 03 02 **01 00 99 98 96 95 93 90**.

GEWÜRZTRAMINER *Gewürz* means spice, and the wine certainly can be spicy and exotically perfumed, as well as being typically low in acidity. It is thought to have originated in the village of Tramin, in Italy's ALTO ADIGE, and the name Traminer is used by many producers. In parts of Germany and Austria it is known as Clevner. It makes an appearance in many wine-producing countries; quality is mixed and styles vary enormously, from the fresh, light, florally perfumed wines produced in Alto Adige to the rich, luscious, late-harvest ALSACE Vendange Tardive. Best in France's Alsace and also good in Austria's Styria (STEIERMARK), Chile and New Zealand.

GEYSER PEAK *Alexander Valley AVA, Sonoma County, California, USA* Australian winemaker Daryl Groom set the tone for wines that tend to be accessible and fruit-driven. Typical are the fruity SONOMA COUNTY Cabernet★ and Merlot★ – ripe, juicy and delicious upon release. The Reserve Alexandre Meritage★★, a BORDEAUX-style blend, is made for aging, and the Reserve Shiraz★★ has a cult following. Block Collection features limited production, single-vineyard wines. There's also a highly popular Sauvignon Blanc★ (Block Collection★★). The winery was sold in December 2007 to Constellation and Groom left to pursue other wine ventures. Best years: (Alexandre) 2005 **02 01 00 99 98 97 94 91**.

GHEMME DOCG *Piedmont, Italy* Near neighbour and similar to GATTINARA. Best producers: Antichi Vigneti di Cantalupo★, Ioppa★.

GIACONDA *Beechworth, Victoria, Australia* In spite of (or perhaps because of) Giaconda's tiny production, Rick Kinzbrunner is one of Australia's most influential winemakers. Following on from his success, BEECHWORTH has become one of the country's most exciting viticultural regions. His tightly structured, minerally, savoury Chardonnay★★★ is one of Australia's best – as are both the serious and beautiful Pinot Noir★★★ and the deep, gamy HERMITAGE-style Warner Vineyard Shiraz★★★. The Cabernet★ is ripe, deep and complex. Best years: (Chardonnay) 2007 06 05 04 02 **01 00 99 98 96 93 92**.

BRUNO GIACOSA *Barbaresco DOCG, Piedmont, Italy* One of the great winemakers of the LANGHE hills, indeed of Italy, still basically a traditionalist, though he has reduced maturation time for his BARBARESCOS and BAROLOS to a maximum of 4 years. Superb Barbarescos Asili★★★, Santo Stefano★★★ and Rabaja★★★, and Barolos including Rocche di Falletto★★★ and Falletto★★. Also excellent Dolcetto d'Alba★, ROERO Arneis★, MOSCATO D'ASTI★★ and sparkling Extra Brut★★.

GIESEN *Canterbury and Marlborough, South Island, New Zealand* A large winery that played a significant part in putting CANTERBURY on the map with a string of fine sweet and dry Rieslings. Has now bought 400ha (1000 acres) of vineyard in MARLBOROUGH and seems intent upon producing vast quantities of budget-priced Sauvignon Blanc rather than stellar Riesling. Best years: (Sauvignon Blanc) **2007 06 04**.

GIGONDAS AC *Rhône Valley, France*   Gigondas wines, mostly red and mad
mainly from Grenache, have fistfuls of chunky personality. Most drin
well with 5 years' age; some need a little more. Best producers
P Amadieu★, la Bouïssière★★, Brusset★★, Cassan★★, Cayron★★, Clos de
Cazaux★★, Clos du Joncuas★, Cros de la Mûre★★, DELAS★, des Espiers★★
Font-Sane★, la Fourmone★, les Goubert★, Gour de Chaulé★, Grapillo
d'Or★★, GUIGAL★, JABOULET★, Longue-Toque★, Montvac★, Moulin de l
Gardette★★, les Pallières★★, Piaugier★, Raspail-Ay★★, Redortier★, St
Cosme★★, ST-GAYAN★★, Santa Duc★★, Tardieu-Laurent★★, la Tourade★★
Tourelles★, Trignon★. Best years: 2007 06 05 **04 03 01 00 99 98 97 95 9**

CH. GILETTE★★ *Sauternes AC, Bordeaux, France*   These astonishing wines ar
stored in concrete vats as opposed to the more normal wooden barrels
This virtually precludes any oxygen contact, and it is oxygen that ages th
wine. Consequently, when released at up to 30 years old, they ar
bursting with life and lusciousness. Best years: **1986 85 83 82 81 79 78 7**
75 70 67 61 59 55 53 49.

GIPPSLAND *Victoria, Australia*   Diverse wineries along the southern
VICTORIA coast, all tiny but with massive potential. Results are erratic
occasionally brilliant. Nicholson River's BURGUNDY-style Chardonnay ca
sometimes hit ★★. Bass Phillip Reserve★★ and Premium★★ Pino
Noirs are among the best in Australia, with a cult following. McAlister★
a red BORDEAUX blend, has also produced some tasty flavours. Bes
producers: Bass Phillip★★, McAlister★, Nicholson River★.

VINCENT GIRARDIN *Santenay, Côte de Beaune, Burgundy, France*   The bes
grower in SANTENAY and now a thriving négociant, with an establishmen
in MEURSAULT★★. Bright, glossy reds from Santenay★★, MARANGES★ and
CHASSAGNE-MONTRACHET★★ are surpassed by excellent VOLNAY★★ and
POMMARD Grands Épenots★★★. Chassagne-Montrachet white
(Morgeot★★, Caillerets★★★) are perfectly balanced with good frui
depth. CORTON-CHARLEMAGNE★★★ is exceptional. He has also revived th
moribund Henri Clerc estate in PULIGNY-MONTRACHET. Best years: (reds
(2007) 06 05 **04 03 02 99**; (whites) (2007) **06 05 04 02**.

GISBORNE *North Island, New Zealand*   Gisborne, with its hot, humid climate
and fertile soils, delivers both quality and quantity. Christened (by loca
growers) 'The Chardonnay Capital of New Zealand'; Gewürztraminer and
Chenin Blanc are also a success. Good reds, however, are hard to find. Bes
producers: MILLTON★★, MONTANA. Best years: (Chardonnay) (2007) **05 04 02**.

GIVRY AC *Côte Chalonnaise, Burgundy, France*   Important COTE CHALONNAIS
village. The reds have an intensity of fruit and ability to age that ar
unusual in the region. There are some attractive, fairly full, nutty white
too. Best producers: Bourgeon★, Chofflet-Valdenaire★, B CLAIR★, Clos
Salomon★, Joblot★★, F Lumpp★★, Ragot★, Sarrazin★. Best years: (reds
(2007) **05 03 02 99**; (whites) (2007) **06 05 04 02**.

GLAETZER *Barossa Valley, South Australia*   Colin Glaetzer has been one of the
BAROSSA VALLEY's most enthusiastic and successful winemakers for decades
He made his reputation working for other people, and now he and hi
son Ben make 4 tip-top Barossa wines for the family label. There is fleshy
Wallace Shiraz-Grenache★, rich, superripe Bishop Shiraz★★ (from
30–60-year-old vines), the amazingly opulent, succulent and velvet
Amon-Ra Shiraz★★ and Anaperenna★★ (formerly Godolphin), a deep
dense Shiraz-Cabernet blend. Ben also makes reds and whites for the

Heartland label using fruit from their vineyards in Langhorne Creek and LIMESTONE COAST, but recent releases have lost their initial zip. Best years: (Bishop Shiraz) 2006 **05 04 02 01 99 98 96**.

GLEN CARLOU *Paarl WO, South Africa* Started by the Finlaysons in the 1980s and now owned by Donald Hess. David Finlayson remains as winemaker. Elegant standard Chardonnay★ and restrained single-vineyard Quartz Stone Chardonnay★★ lead the whites. Reds feature sweet-textured Pinot Noir★; deep, dry Syrah★; Grand Classique★, a red BORDEAUX blend with excellent aging potential; and concentrated Gravel Quarry Cabernet★. Best years: (Chardonnay) **2007 06 05 04 03 02 01**.

CH. GLORIA★ *St-Julien AC, Haut-Médoc, Bordeaux, France* An interesting property, created out of tiny plots of Classed Growth land scattered all round ST-JULIEN. Generally very soft and sweet-centred, the wine nonetheless ages well. Second wine: Peymartin. Best years: 2006 05 04 **03 02 01 00 99 98 96 95 90 89**.

GOLAN HEIGHTS WINERY *Golan Heights, Israel* Israel's leading quality wine producer. Cool summers, high-altitude vineyards and modern winemaking with kosher standards have resulted in good Sauvignon Blanc and Cabernet Sauvignon★, balanced, oaky Chardonnay★ and good bottle-fermented fizz★. Yarden is the top label.

GOLDMUSKATELLER Moscato Giallo (Orange Muscat) is known as Goldmuskateller in the ALTO ADIGE. Here and elsewhere in Italy's north-east, sometimes under the name Fior d'Arancio, it makes scented wines in dry, off-dry and sweet (*passito*) styles. Best producers: Bolognani★, Viticoltori Caldaro★, LAGEDER★, Thurnhof★, Vignalta.

GOLDWATER ESTATE *Waiheke Island, Auckland, New Zealand* The first vineyard on WAIHEKE ISLAND. Top wines are intense, long-lived 'Goldie' Cabernet-Merlot★★ and elegant, cedary Esslin Merlot★★, with considerable depth and structure. Chardonnay★★ from Waiheke looks exciting. Attractive New Dog Sauvignon Blanc★ and Roseland Chardonnay★ from MARLBOROUGH fruit. In 2006 Goldwater merged with Marlborough's VAVASOUR. Best years: (Waiheke reds) (2006) (05) **04 02 00 99**.

GONZÁLEZ BYASS *Jerez y Manzanilla DO, Andalucía, Spain* Tio Pepe★ fino is the world's biggest-selling sherry. The old sherries are superb: intense, dry Amontillado del Duque★★★; 2 rich, complex olorosos, sweet Matusalem★★ and medium Apóstoles★★; treacly Noé Pedro Ximénez★★★. One step down is the Alfonso Dry Oloroso★. The firm pioneered the rediscovery of single-vintage (non-solera) dry olorosos★★ and palos cortados★★.

HENRI GOUGES *Nuits-St-Georges, Côte de Nuits, Burgundy, France* The original Henri Gouges was mayor of NUITS-ST-GEORGES in the 1930s and was instrumental in classifying the large number of Premiers Crus in his appellation. Today, the domaine is back on form, producing impressive, meaty, long-lived reds (Les St Georges★★★, Clos des Porrets★★, Les Vaucrains★★) as well as excellent white Nuits-St-Georges Premier Cru La Perrière★★. Best years: (2007) 06 05 02 01 **00 99 98 96 90**.

GRAACH *Mosel, Germany* Important Middle MOSEL wine village with 4 vineyard sites, the most famous being Domprobst (also the best) and Himmelreich. A third, the Josephshöfer, is wholly owned by the von KESSELSTATT estate. The wines have an attractive fullness to balance their steely acidity, and great aging potential. Best producers: von KESSELSTATT★,

Dr LOOSEN★★, Markus MOLITOR★★, JJ PRUM★★, S A PRUM★, Max Fer
RICHTER★, Willi SCHAEFER★★★, SELBACH-OSTER★★, Dr Weins-Prüm★. Bes
years: (2007) 06 05 **04 03 02 01 00 99 98 97 94**.

GRACIANO Rare, low-yielding but excellent Spanish grape, traditional i
RIOJA, NAVARRA and Extremadura. It makes dense, highly structured
fragrant reds, and its high acidity adds life when blended with low-aci
Tempranillo. In Portugal it is called Tinta Miúda. Also grown by BROW
BROTHERS in Australia.

GRAHAM Port DOC, Douro, Portugal Part of the Symington empire, makin
rich, florally scented Vintage Port★★★, sweeter than DOW's and WARRE's
but with the backbone to age. In non-declared years makes a fine vintag
wine called Malvedos★★. Six Grapes★ is one of the best premiun
rubies, and Crusted★★ and 10-year-old★ and 20-year-old★★ tawnie
are consistently good. Best years: (Vintage) **2003 00 97 94 91 85 83 80 7
75 70 66 63 60**; (Malvedos) **2001 99 95 92 90**.

ALAIN GRAILLOT Crozes-Hermitage AC, Rhône Valley, France Excellent famil
estate producing powerfully concentrated, rich, fruity reds. The top win
is CROZES-HERMITAGE la Guiraude★★, but the regular Crozes
Hermitage★★ is wonderful too, and great for early drinking, as are the
ST-JOSEPH★★ and a lovely fragrant white Crozes-Hermitage★. Keep to
reds for at least 5 years. Son Max has Dom. des Lises estate. Best years: (
Guiraude) 2007 06 05 **04 03 01 00 99 95 89**.

GRAMPIANS AND PYRENEES Victoria, Australia Two adjacent cool-climat
regions in central western VICTORIA, producing some of Australia's mos
characterful Shiraz, distinguished Riesling, subtle Pinot Gris and savour
Chardonnay. Best producers: BEST'S★, Blue Pyrenees, Dalwhinnie★★, MOUN
LANGI GHIRAN★★, Redbank★, SEPPELT★★, Summerfield★, Taltarni. Best years
(Shiraz) 2006 05 04 03 **02 01 99 98 97 96 94 91 90**.

CH. GRAND-PUY-DUCASSE★ Pauillac AC, 5ème Cru Classé, Haut-Médoc
Bordeaux, France After great improvement in the 1980s, form dipped i
the early 90s but recovered again in 95. Approachable after 5 years, bu
the best vintages can improve for considerably longer. Second win
Artigues-Arnaud. Best years: 2006 05 04 **03 02 00 96 95 90 89**.

CH. GRAND-PUY-LACOSTE★★ Pauillac AC, 5ème
Cru Classé, Haut-Médoc, Bordeaux, France Classic
PAUILLAC, with lots of blackcurrant and cigar-box
perfume. It begins fairly dense, but as the wine
develops, the flavours mingle with the sweetness
of new oak to become one of Pauillac's most
memorable taste sensations. Second wine:
Lacoste-Borie. Best years: 2006 05 04 03 02 00 **99
98 96 95 94 90 89 88 86 85 83**.

GRANDS-ÉCHÉZEAUX AC See ECHÉZEAUX AC.

GRANGE★★★ Barossa Valley, South Australia In 1950, Max Schubert, chie
winemaker at PENFOLDS, visited Europe and came back determined t
make a wine that could match the great BORDEAUX reds. Undeterred by
lack of Cabernet Sauvignon grapes and French oak barrels, he set to worl
with BAROSSA Shiraz and barrels made from the more pungent American
oak. Initially ignored and misunderstood, Schubert eventually achieved
global recognition for his wine, a stupendously complex, thrillingly ric
red that only begins to reveal its magnificence after 10 years in bottle –

but is better after 20. Best years: (2005) (04) (02) 01 99 98 96 94 92 91 90 **88 86 84 83 76 71 66 62 53**.

OM. DE LA GRANGE DES PÈRES★★ *Vin de Pays de l'Hérault, Languedoc, France* With only 500 cases produced each year, demand is high for the meticulously crafted unfiltered Cabernet Sauvignon-based red★★. The white★★ is produced in even smaller quantities. Best years: (red) 2003 02 01 00 **99 98**.

GRANGEHURST *Stellenbosch WO, South Africa* Boutique winery known for modern Pinotage★, Cabernet-Merlot★★ with Bordeaux-ish appeal and Nikela★, a blend of all three varieties and owner/winemaker Jeremy Walker's answer to the Cape blend. Recent additions to the range include two Cabernets (Reserve★) and Shiraz-Cabernet Reserve★. Best years: (Cabernet-Merlot) **2003 02 01 00 09 98 97 95**.

GRANS-FASSIAN *Leiwen, Mosel, Germany* LEIWEN owes its reputation largely to Gerhard Grans. Both sweet and dry Rieslings have gained in sophistication over the years: Spätlese★★ and Auslese★★ from TRITTENHEIMER Apotheke are particularly impressive. Eiswein is ★★★ in good vintages. Best years: (2007) 06 05 **04 03 02 01 99 98 97**.

ALFRED GRATIEN *Champagne AC, Champagne, France* This small company makes some of my favourite CHAMPAGNE. Its wines are made in wooden casks, which is very rare nowadays. The non-vintage★★ blend is usually 4 years old when sold, rather than the normal 3 years. The vintage★★★ is deliciously ripe and toasty when released but can age for another 10 years. The prestige cuvée, Cuvée Paradis★★, is non-vintage. Best years: (1998) **97 96 95 91 90 89 88 85 83**.

GRAVES AC *Bordeaux, France* The Graves region covers the area south of Bordeaux to Langon, but the generally superior villages in the northern half broke away in 1987 to form the PESSAC-LEOGNAN AC. In the southern Graves, a new wave of winemaking has produced plenty of clean, bone-dry white wines with lots of snappy freshness, as well as more complex soft, nutty barrel-aged whites, and some juicy, quick-drinking reds. Sweet white wines take the Graves Supérieures AC; the best make a decent substitute for the more expensive SAUTERNES. Best producers: Archambeau★, Ardennes★, Brondelle★, Chantegrive★, Clos Floridène★★, Crabitey★, l'Hospital, Léhoul★, Magence, Magneau★, Rahoul, Respide-Médeville★, St-Robert (cuvée Poncet Deville★), Seuil, Venus, Vieux-Ch.-Gaubert★, Villa Bel-Air★; (sweet) Brondelle, Léhoul. Best years: (reds) **2005 04 01 00 98 96 95 90**; (dry whites) **2006 05 04 02 01 00 98 96 95**.

GRAVNER *Friuli-Venezia Giulia, Italy* Josko Gravner, FRIULI's most zealous winemaker, sets styles with his wood-aged, oxidative whites. Along with high-priced Chardonnay★★, Sauvignon★★ and Ribolla Gialla★, he combines 6 white varieties in Breg★★. Reds are Rosso Gravner★ (predominantly Merlot) and Rujno★★ (Merlot-Cabernet Sauvignon).

GREAT SOUTHERN *Western Australia* A vast, cool-climate region encompassing the sub-regions of Mount Barker, Frankland River, Denmark, Albany and Porongurup. Mount Barker is particularly successful with Riesling and Shiraz; Frankland River with Riesling, Shiraz and Cabernet; Denmark with Chardonnay and Pinot Noir; Albany with Pinot Noir; Porongurup with Riesling. Plantings have boomed in recent years, especially in Frankland River. Best producers: Alkoomi★, Castle Rock, FERNGROVE★, Forest Hill★, Frankland Estate★, Gilberts★, Goundrey★, HAREWOOD★★, HOUGHTON★★, HOWARD PARK★★, PLANTAGENET★★, West Cape Howe★★.

GRECHETTO Italian grape centred on UMBRIA, the main component
 orvieto DOC, also making tasty, anise-tinged dry white varietal
Occasionally used in VIN SANTO in TUSCANY. **Best producers:** Antone
Barberani-Vallesanta★, Caprai, FALESCO★, Palazzone, Castello della SALA.

GRENACHE BLANC A common white grape in the south of France, b
without many admirers. Except me, that is, because I love the pea
scented wine flecked with anise that a good producer can achieve. Low
yield examples take surprisingly well to oak. Generally best within a ye
of the vintage, although the odd old-vine example can age attractivel
Grown as Garnacha Blanca in Spain, where it's now producing som
stunning examples in PRIORAT. A few old vines are contributing to som
interesting wines in South Africa.

GRENACHE NOIR Among the world's most widely planted red grapes
the bulk of it in Spain, where it is called Garnacha Tinta. It is a ho
climate grape and in France it reaches its peak in the southern RHON
especially in CHATEAUNEUF-DU-PAPE, where it combines great alcohol
strength with rich, refined raspberry fruit and a perfume hot from th
herb-strewn hills. It is generally given more tannin, acid and structure b
blending with Syrah, Mourvèdre, Cinsaut or other southern Frenc
grapes. It can make wonderful rosé in TAVEL, LIRAC and COTES DE PROVENC
as well as in NAVARRA in Spain. It takes centre stage in ARAGON
Calatayud, Campo de Borja and CARINENA, and forms the backbone of th
impressive reds of PRIORAT; in RIOJA it adds weight to the Tempranillo.
is also the basis for the *vins doux naturels* of BANYULS and MAURY
southern France. Also grown in CALIFORNIA and SOUTH AUSTRALIA, where
has only recently been accorded much respect as imaginative winemake
realized there was a great resource of century-old vines capable of makir
wild and massively enjoyable reds. More is being planted in South Afric
where it is a popular component in Rhône-style blends. See als
CANNONAU.

GRGICH HILLS CELLAR *Rutherford AVA, California, USA* Mike Grgich w
winemaker at CHATEAU MONTELENA when its 1973 Chardonnay shocke
Paris judges by finishing ahead of French versions in the famous 197
tasting. At his own winery he makes classic California Chardonnay★★
which ages for at least a decade, ripe, tannic Cabernet★, plumm
Merlot★ and a huge, old-style Zinfandel★. **Best years:** (Chardonna
(2006) 05 **04 03 02 01 00 99 98 97 95**.

GRIOTTE-CHAMBERTIN AC See CHAMBERTIN AC.

JEAN GRIVOT *Vosne-Romanée, Côte de Nuits, Burgundy, France* After changin
directions a few times, Étienne Grivot settled into a successful stric
from 1995 and has raised his game from 2004 with increasingly ripe ye
always fine and complex wines from a host of VOSNE-ROMANÉE Premie
Crus (Beaumonts★★★) as well as brilliant CLOS DE VOUGEOT★★★ an
RICHEBOURG★★★. Expensive, but try VOSNE-ROMANEE★★ for value. Be
years: (2007) **06** 05 04 03 02 **01 00 99 98 97 96 95**.

GROS *Côte de Nuits, Burgundy, France* Brilliant COTE DE NUITS wines from vario
members of the family, especially Anne Gros, Michel Gros, Gros Frère
Soeur and Anne-Françoise Gros. Look out for CLOS DE VOUGEOT★★★
ECHEZEAUX★★★ and RICHEBOURG★★★ as well as good-value HAUTES-COTES D
NUITS★. **Best years:** (2007) 06 05 04 03 02 **01 00 99 98 96 95 93 90**.

ROS PLANT DU PAYS NANTAIS VDQS *Loire Valley, France* Gros Plant can be searing stuff, but this acidic wine is well suited to the seafood guzzled in the region. Look for a *sur lie* bottling and drink the youngest available. **Best producers:** Brochet, les Coins, l'ecu, la Grange, Saupin.

ROSSET *Clare Valley, South Australia* Jeffrey Grosset is a perfectionist, crafting tiny quantities of hand-made wines. A Riesling specialist, he sources single-vineyard Watervale★★★ and Polish Hill★★★ from his own properties; both are supremely good and age well. Cabernet blend Gaia★★ is smooth and seamless. Also outstanding Piccadilly (ADELAIDE HILLS) Chardonnay★★★ and very fine Pinot Noir★★ and Semillon-Sauvignon★★. **Best years:** (Riesling) 2007 06 05 **04 03 02 01 00 99 98 97 96 94 93 92 90**.

H. GRUAUD-LAROSE★★ *St-Julien AC, 2ème Cru Classé, Haut-Médoc, Bordeaux, France* One of the largest ST-JULIEN estates. Until the 1970s these wines were classic, cedary St-Juliens; since the early 80s, the wines have been darker, richer and coated with new oak, yet inclined to exhibit an unnerving feral quality. Recent vintages have mostly combined considerable power with finesse, despite disappointments in 02 and 03. Second wine: Sarget de Gruaud-Larose. **Best years:** 2006 05 04 **01** 00 **99 98 96 95** 90 89 88.

RÜNER VELTLINER Austrian grape, also grown in the Czech Republic, Slovakia and Hungary. It is at its best in Austria's KAMPTAL, KREMSTAL and the WACHAU, where the soil and cool climate bring out all the lentilly, white-peppery aromas. Styles vary from light and tart to savoury, mouthfilling yet appetizing wines equalling the best in Europe.

UELBENZU *Spain* Family-owned bodega making good Azul★, from Tempranillo, Cabernet and Merlot, and rich, concentrated Cabernet Sauvignon-based Evo★. Lautus★★, from old vines, incorporates Garnacha in the blend. Guelbenzu has estates in both NAVARRA and ARAGON; the wines are non-DO and are labelled as Vinos de la Tierra Ribera del Queiles. **Best years:** (Evo) (2005) 04 **03** 01 00 99 98.

UIGAL *Côte-Rôtie AC, Rhône Valley, France* Marcel Guigal is the most internationally famous name in the RHONE, producing wines from his own vineyards in COTE-ROTIE under the Ch. d'Ampuis★★★ label as well as Dom. de Bonserine★ and the Guigal range from purchased grapes (Côte-Rôtie Brune et Blonde is ★★ since 1998). La Mouline, la Turque and la Landonne all rate ★★★ in most critics' opinions. Well, I have definitely had profound wines from La Landonne and La Mouline, and to my surprise and delight the considerable new oak aging had not dimmed the Côte-Rôtie beauty and fragrance. However, Guigal is uniquely talented; lesser producers using this amount of new oak rarely manage to save the balance of the wine. CONDRIEU★★ (la Doriane★★★) is wonderfully fragrant. HERMITAGE★★ is also good, ST-JOSEPH★★ improving, as are the red and white COTES DU RHONE★ and chunky GIGONDAS★. **Best years:** (top reds) 2007 06 05 04 03 01 00 **99 98 97 95 94 91 90 89 88 85 83 82 78**.

CH. GUIRAUD★★ *Sauternes AC, 1er Cru Classé, Bordeaux, France* Since the 1980s this SAUTERNES estate has returned to the top-quality fold. High price reflects the fact that only the best grapes are selected and 50% new oak used each year. New ownership from 2006. Keep best vintages for 10 years or more. Second wine (dry): G de Guiraud. **Best years:** 2006 05 04 03 **02 01 99 98 97 96 95** 90 89 88.

GUNDERLOCH *Nackenheim, Rheinhessen, Germany* Fritz and Agnes Hasselbach's estate has become one of Germany's best. Sensationally concentrated and luscious Beerenauslese★★★ and Trockenbeeren-auslese★★★ dessert Rieslings are expensive but worth it. Dry and off-dry Rieslings, at least ★, however, are good value. Late-harvest Spätlese and Auslese are ★★ year in, year out. Best years: (2007) 06 05 **04 03 02 01 00 99 98 97 96 95 93**.

GUNDERLOCH

2004

Nackenheim
ROTHENBERG
Riesling Auslese

GUNDLACH-BUNDSCHU *Sonoma Valley AVA, California, USA* Family-owned winery, founded in 1858. From the Rhinefarm Vineyards come outstanding juicy, fruity Cabernet Sauvignon★★, rich and tightly structured Merlot★★, Zinfandel★ and Pinot Noir★. Whites include Chardonnay★, attractive Riesling and dramatic dry Gewürztraminer★★. The Bundschu family also operates the boutique winery Bartholomew Park, which specializes in Cabernet blends. Winemaker Linda Trotta one of the state's best.

FRITZ HAAG *Brauneberg, Mosel, Germany* MOSEL grower with vineyards in the BRAUNEBERGER Juffer and Juffer Sonnenuhr. Pure, elegant Rieslings at least ★★ quality, Auslese reaching ★★ or ★★★. Best years: (2007) 06 05 04 0 **02 01 99 98 97 96 95**.

REINHOLD HAART *Piesport, Mosel, Germany* Theo Haart produce sensational Rieslings – with blackcurrant, peach and citrus aromas – from the great Piesporter Goldtröpfchen vineyard. Ausleses are often ★★★. Wines from his vineyards in Wintrich can be bargains. Best years: (2007) 06 05 04 **02 01 99 98 97 96 95**.

HAMILTON RUSSELL VINEYARDS *Hemel en Aarde Valley WO, South Africa* Well-established WALKER BAY property focusing on Pinot Noir and Chardonnay. Pinot Noir★★ is broad-shouldered and delicately scented while Chardonnay★★ is minerally and exciting – and is pushing toward ★★★ since recent winemaking changes. Two separate operations Southern Right and Ashbourne, focus on Pinotage (Ashbourne★), while Southern Right Sauvignon Blanc★ is zingy and easy-drinking. Best year. (Pinot Noir) (2007) 06 05 04 03 02 01 00 99 98; (Chardonnay) 2007 06 0 04 03 02 01 00 99 98.

HANDLEY *Mendocino County, California, USA* Outstanding producer o sparkling wines, including one of California's best Brut Rosés★ Aromatic Gewürztraminer★★ and Riesling★★ are among the state' finest. Two bottlings of Chardonnay, from the DRY CREEK VALLEY★ and ANDERSON VALLEY★, are worth seeking out. The Anderson Valley estat Pinot Noirs (regular★, Reserve★★) are in a lighter, more subtle style. A new Syrah★ is excellent and Brightlighter White is a terrific white blend. Best years: (Pinot Noir Reserve) (2005) 04 **03 01** 00 99 98.

HANGING ROCK *Macedon Ranges, Victoria, Australia* Highly individual, guts sparkling wine Macedon Cuvée★★ (stunning late-disgorged Cuvée★★★) stands out at John and Ann (née TYRRELL) Ellis's ultra-cool climate vineyard high in the Macedon Ranges. Tangy estate-grown 'The Jim Jim' Sauvignon Blanc★★ is mouthwatering stuff, while HEATHCOTE Shiraz★★ is the best red.

HARAS DE PIRQUE *Maipo, Chile* Located in Pirque, a sub-region of MAIPO in the foothills of the Andes, this winery started production in 2002 and soon became an important player in Maipo. Elegance★★, a dense and spicy Cabernet Sauvignon, leads Haras de Pirque's portfolio. Character★★, another Cabernet, is equally charming, yet fruitier and more approachable. A great discovery for Chilean Cabernet lovers.

ARDY WINE COMPANY *McLaren Vale, South Australia* Despite the takeover of BRL Hardy by American giant Constellation, wines under the Hardys flagship label so far still taste reassuringly Australian. Varietals (especially Shiraz and Grenache) under Nottage Hill and Tintara labels are among Australia's most reliably good gluggers. Top of the tree are the Eileen Hardy Shiraz★★★ and Thomas Hardy Cabernet★★★, both dense reds for hedonists. Eileen Hardy Chardonnay★★ is more elegant, tightly structured and focused than it used to be. Also 'ecologically aware' Banrock Station, inexpensive Oomoo wines, good-value Omni sparkling wine and top-quality BAY OF FIRES range. Best years: (Eileen Hardy Shiraz) (2006) (05) (04) 03 02 01 00 **98 97 96 95 93 88 87**.

AREWOOD *Great Southern, Western Australia* James Kellie made a name for himself as white winemaker for HOWARD PARK before his family purchased one of Denmark's finest vineyards, Harewood Estate. His portfolio now shows evidence of Kellie's knowledge of the GREAT SOUTHERN and his winemaking skill, especially with opulent Cabernet★★ from Mount Barker and Porongurup, gutsy yet silky smooth Frankland River Shiraz★★ and elegant single-vineyard estate Chardonnay★.

ARLAN ESTATE *Oakville AVA, California, USA* Estate in the western hills of OAKVILLE, whose BORDEAUX blend has become one of California's most sought-after reds. Full-bodied and rather tannic, Harlan Estate★★★ offers layers of ripe black fruits and heaps of new French oak. Dense but thrilling upon release, the wine is built to develop for 10 years.

ARTENBERG ESTATE *Stellenbosch WO, South Africa* Shiraz is the prime performer at this Bottelary Hills winery. Regular Shiraz★ is fleshy and accessible, while two flagships, The Stork★ and single-vineyard Gravel Hill★★, reflect the soils they grow in. Merlot★ and Cabernet also perform well, but The Mackenzie Cabernet-Merlot blend★ tops both. Whites include a pair of Chardonnays (standard, and refined, complex The Eleanor★) and an off-dry, limy Riesling★. Best years: (premium reds) **2005 04 03 02 01 00 98**.

ARTFORD FAMILY *Russian River Valley AVA, California, USA* Owned by Jess Jackson (of KENDALL-JACKSON). Very limited production wines from RUSSIAN RIVER, Green Valley and SONOMA COAST fruit bear the Hartford Court label. Pinot Noirs include the massive Arrendell Vineyard★★★. Seascape Vineyard Chardonnay★★ has textbook cool-climate intensity and acidity. Hartford label wines are blended from various sources. Sonoma Coast bottlings of Chardonnay★ and Pinot Noir★ are deeply flavoured and good value. Old-vine Zinfandels include Fanucchi-Wood Road★★, Highwire★, Dina's★ and Russian River Valley★.

ARTWELL *Stags Leap District AVA, Napa Valley, California, USA* Wine collector Bob Hartwell has been producing a gloriously fruity and elegant Cabernet Sauvignon★★ from his small vineyard in the STAGS LEAP DISTRICT since 1993. Recently, an equally supple Merlot★★ and lower-priced Misté Hill★ Cabernet have been added. Best years: (Cabernet Sauvignon) (2005) 02 **01 00 99 98 97 96 94**.

HATTENHEIM *Rheingau, Germany* RHEINGAU village with 13 vineyard sites, including a share of the famous Marcobrunn vineyard. Best producers: Barth★, Lang, Langwerth von Simmern★, SCHLOSS REINHARTSHAUSEN★★, Schloss Schönborn★. Best years: (2007) 06 05 04 **03 02 01 99 98 95**.

CH. HAUT-BAGES-LIBÉRAL★ *Pauillac AC, 5ème Cru Classé, Haut-Médo*
Bordeaux, France Little-known PAUILLAC property that has quietly bee
gathering plaudits for some years now: loads of unbridled delicious fru
a positively hedonistic style – and its lack of renown keeps the price ju
about reasonable. The wines will age well, especially the latest vintage
Best years: 2006 05 04 03 **02 01** 00 **99 98 96 95 94 90 89.**

CH. HAUT-BAILLY★ *Pessac-Léognan AC, Cru Classé de Graves, Bordeaux, Fran*
Traditionally one of the softest and most charming of the PESSAC-LEOGNA
Classed Growths, and on good form during the 1990s. New ownershi
from 1998 has produced erratic returns so far, some wines being to
tough, some being almost milky soft, some being delicious (200
onwards). Drinkable early, but ages well. Second wine: la Parde-de
Haut-Bailly. Best years: 2006 05 04 **01** 00 **99 98 96 95 90 89 88 86.**

CH. HAUT-BATAILLEY★ *Pauillac AC, 5ème Cru Classé, Haut-Médoc, Bordeau*
France This estate has produced too many wines that are ligh
attractively spicy, but rarely memorable. Owner François-Xavier Borie
GRAND-PUY-LACOSTE is changing this and from 2004 the wines have show
improvement, becoming distinctly more substantial. Best years: 2006 05
03 02 01 00 98 96 95 90 89.

CH. HAUT-BRION *Pessac-Léognan AC, 1er Cru Classé, Graves, Fran*
This property's excellent gravel-based vineyard is now part of Bordeaux
suburbs. The red wine★★★ almost always deserves its status. There
also a small amount of white★★★ which, at its best, is magically rich y
marvellously dry, blossoming out over 5–10 years. Second wine: (re
Bahans-Haut-Brion. Best years: (red) 2006 05 04 03 02 01 00 **99 98 97 9
95 94 93 90 89 88**; (white) 2006 05 **04 03 02 01** 00 98 96 95.

CH. HAUT-MARBUZET★★ *St-Estèphe AC, Haut-Médoc, Bordeaux, Fran*
Impressive ST-ESTEPHE wine worthy of classification with great, ric
mouthfilling blasts of flavour and lots of new oak. Best years: 2006 05
03 02 **01** 00 **99 98 96 95 94 90 89 88 86 85.**

HAUT-MÉDOC AC *Bordeaux, France* The finest gravelly soil is here in th
southern half of the MEDOC peninsula; this AC covers all the decen
vineyard land not included in the 6 village ACs (MARGAUX, MOULIS, LISTRA
ST-JULIEN, PAUILLAC and ST-ESTEPHE). Wines vary in quality and style. Be
producers: d'Agassac★, Belgrave★, Belle-Vue★, Bernadotte★, Cambon
Pelouse★, Camensac, CANTEMERLE★, Charmail★, Cissac★, Citran★, Coufran
LAGUNE★, Lanessan★, Malescasse★, Maucamps★, Peyrabon★, Sénéjac
SOCIANDO-MALLET★★, la Tour-Carnet★, Tour-du-Haut-Moulin★, Villegeorg
Best years: 2006 05 04 **03 02 01** 00 **96 95 94 90 89 88 86 85.**

HAUTES-CÔTES DE BEAUNE AC See BOURGOGNE-HAUTES-COTES DE BEAUNE A
HAUTES-CÔTES DE NUITS AC See BOURGOGNE-HAUTES-COTES DE NUITS A

HAWKES BAY *North Island, New Zealand* One of New Zealand's mo
prestigious wine regions. Plenty of sunshine, moderately predictable weath
during ripening and a complex array of soils make it ideal for a range of wir
styles. Traditionally known for Cabernet Sauvignon and, particularly, Merlo
it has recently produced some superb Syrahs. Free-draining Gimblett Grave
is the outstanding area, followed by the Ngatarawa Triangle. Best producer
Alpha Domus★, Bilancia★, CHURCH ROAD★, Clearview★, COOPERS CREEK★, CRAGC
RANGE★★, Esk Valley★★, Matariki★, MATUA VALLEY★, Newton Forrest
(Cornerstone★★), NGATARAWA★, Paritua★, C J PASK★, Sacred Hill★, SILENI★
Southbank★, Stonecroft★, Te Awa★, TE MATA★★, TRINITY HILL★★, Unison★
Vidal★★, VILLA MARIA★★. Best years: (premium reds) (2007) (06) **04 02 00 98.**

HEATHCOTE *Central Victoria, Australia*   This wine region's unique feature is the deep russet Cambrian soil, formed more than 600 million years ago, which is found on the best sites and is proving ideal for Shiraz. Jasper Hill★★★, Heathcote Winery★, Red Edge★ and Wild Duck Creek★ are the best of the long-established vineyards, while BROWN BROTHERS and TYRRELL's (Rufus Stone★★ is outstanding and good value) have extensive new plantings. Heathcote Estate★★ is a brilliant newcomer. **Best years:** (Shiraz) 2006 05 04 03 **02 01 00** 97 96 95 94 91 90.

HECHT & BANNIER *Languedoc, France*   An exciting new partnership of two young Dijon wine marketing graduates, Gregory Hecht and François Bannier. They are selecting and aging some rich, finely crafted wines from MINERVOIS★, COTEAUX DU LANGUEDOC★, FAUGERES★ and ST-CHINIAN★. Coteaux du Languedoc Jonquières★★ is their best wine.

HEDGES *Columbia Valley AVA, Washington State, USA*   Top wines here are Cabernet-Merlot blends using fruit from prime Red Mountain AVA vineyards: Three Vineyards★ is powerful and ageworthy, with bold tannins but plenty of cassis fruit; Red Mountain Reserve★ shows more polish and elegance. Red CMS★ (Cabernet-Merlot-Syrah) and crisp white CMS (Chardonnay-Marsanne-Sauvignon) form the bulk of the production. **Best years:** (top reds) (2006) 05 **04 03 02 01 00** 99.

DR HEGER *Ihringen, Baden, Germany*   Joachim Heger specializes in powerful, dry Grauburgunder (Pinot Gris)★★, Weissburgunder (Pinot Blanc)★ and red Spätburgunder (Pinot Noir)★, with Riesling a sideline in this warm climate. Winklerberg Grauburgunder★★ is serious stuff, while his ancient Yellow Muscat vines deliver powerful dry wines★ and rare but fabulous TBAs★★. Wines from rented vineyards are sold under the Weinhaus Joachim Heger label. **Best years:** (white) (2007) 06 05 **04 03 02 01 00** 98.

CHARLES HEIDSIECK *Champagne AC, Champagne, France*   Charles Heidsieck, owned by Rémy Cointreau, is the most consistently fine of all the major houses, with vintage★★★ Champagne only declared in the very best years. The non-vintage★★, marked with a bottling date (for example, Mis en Cave en 2004), is regularly of vintage quality; these age well for 5 years. **Best years:** 2000 96 **95** 90 89 88 85 82.

HEITZ CELLARS *Napa Valley AVA, California, USA*   Star attraction here is the Martha's Vineyard Cabernet Sauvignon★★. Many believe that early bottlings of Martha's Vineyard are among the best wines ever produced in CALIFORNIA. After 1992, phylloxera forced the replanting of Martha's Vineyard and although bottling only resumed in 1996, the 1997 vintage was exceptional and set the tone for the modern era. Heitz also produces a Bella Oaks Vineyard Cabernet Sauvignon★, a Trailside Vineyard Cabernet★ and a straight Cabernet★ that takes time to understand but can be good. Grignolino Rosé is an attractive picnic wine. **Best years:** (Martha's Vineyard) 2002 **97 96** 92 91 86 85 75.

HENRIOT *Champagne AC, Champagne, France*   In 1994 Joseph Henriot bought back the name of his old-established family company. Henriot CHAMPAGNES have an austere clarity – no Pinot Meunier is used. The range includes non-vintage Brut Souverain★, Blanc Souverain and Rosé Brut★, vintage Brut★★ and Rosé, and de luxe Cuvée des Enchanteleurs★★. **Best years:** 1998 96 **95** 90 89 88 85.

HENRIQUES & HENRIQUES *Madeira DOC, Madeira, Portugal*   The wines to look for are the 10-year-old★★ and 15-year-old★★ versions of the classic varieties. Vibrant Sercial and Verdelho, and rich Malmsey and

167

Bual are all fine examples of their styles. Henriques & Henriques also h
vintage Madeiras★★★ of extraordinary quality.

HENRY OF PELHAM *Niagara Peninsula VQA, Ontario, Canada* A pioneer
vinifera wines in this region. Best are Reserve Chardonnay★, Proprietor
Reserve Riesling★, Riesling Icewine★ and a Cabernet-Merlot blend.

HENSCHKE *Eden Valley, South Australia* Fifth-generation winemak
Stephen Henschke and his viticulturist wife Prue make some
Australia's grandest reds from old vines: HILL OF GRACE★★★ is stunning
Mount Edelstone Shiraz★★★, Tappa Pass★★, Cyril Henschk
Cabernet★★, Johann's Garden Grenache★, Henry's Seven★ Shira
blend and Keyneton Estate★ are also top wines. The whites have lifted
recent years, led by the seductive, perfumed Julius Riesling★★, toasty y
fruity Louis Semillon★★ and Croft Chardonnay★. Best years: (Mou
Edelstone) (2007) (06) 05 04 02 01 99 **96 94 92 91 90 88 86 84 82**.

HÉRAULT, VIN DE PAYS DE L' *Languedoc, France* A huge region, coverin
the entire Hérault *département*. Red wines predominate, based c
Carignan, Grenache and Cinsaut, and most of the wine is sold in bul
But things are changing. There are lots of hilly vineyards with gre
potential, and MAS DE DAUMAS GASSAC followed by GRANGE DES PERES an
Gérard Depardieu's Référence are making waves internationally. White
are improving, too. Best producers: Bosc, Capion★, la Fadèze, GRANGE D
PERES★★, Jany, Limbardié★, Marfée, MAS DE DAUMAS GASSAC★.

HERMITAGE AC *Rhône Valley, France* Great Hermitage, from a stee
vineyard above the town of Tain l'Hermitage in the northern RHONE,
revered throughout the world as a rare, rich red wine – expensive
memorable and classic. Not all Hermitage achieves such an excitin
blend of flavours, but the best growers, with mature red Syrah vines, ca
create superbly original wine, needing 5–10 years' aging even in a ligh
year and a minimum of 15 years in a ripe vintage. White Hermitag
from Marsanne and Roussanne, is less famous but the best wines, mad
by traditionalists, can outlive the reds, sometimes lasting as long as 4
years. Best producers: A Belle★, CHAPOUTIER★★, J-L CHAVE★★★, Y Chave
Colombier★, COLOMBO★, DELAS★★, B Faurie★★, L Fayolle★, Ferraton★
GUIGAL★★, JABOULET (la Chapelle)★, Remizières★, J-M Sorrel★, M Sorrel★★
TAIN co-op★★, Tardieu-Laurent★★, les Vins de Vienne★★. Best years: (red
2007 06 05 04 03 **01 00 99 98 97 96 95 94 91 90 89 88 85 83 78**.

THE HESS COLLECTION *Mount Veeder AVA, California, USA* Known fo
powerful MOUNT VEEDER Cabernet Sauvignon★ – but after a change i
winemaking direction, recent vintages lack polish and balance; Moun
Veeder Mountain Cuvée★ is better. Hess Estate Cabernet★ is good value
Chardonnay★ is ripe with tropical fruit and balanced oak. Vineyard
designated Napa Chardonnay★ and Cabernet★ can be good. Budget labe
Hess Select. Best years: (Cabernet) 2003 **01 00 99 98 97 96 95 94 91 90**.

HESSISCHE BERGSTRASSE *Germany* A small (436ha/1070-acre), war
region near Darmstadt. Lovely Eiswein★★ is made by the Staatsweingu
Simon-Bürkle★ is reliable too. Riesling is still the most prized grape.

HEYL ZU HERRNSHEIM *Nierstein, Rheinhessen, Germany* Organic esta
whose main strength is substantial dry whites from Riesling
Weissburgunder (Pinot Blanc) and Silvaner. However, Auslese an
higher Prädikat wines of recent vintages have been of ★★ – an
sometimes ★★★ – quality. Only wines from the top sites (Brudersber

Pettental, Rothenberg) carry the vineyard designation. Quality slipped recently, but new owner Detlev Meyer seems keen to restore its reputation. Best years: (2007) 06 05 04 **03 02 01** 99 98 97.

HEYMANN-LÖWENSTEIN Winningen, Mosel, Germany A leading estate of the Lower MOSEL. Its dry Rieslings are unusually full-bodied for the region; those from the Röttgen and Uhlen sites often reach ★★. Also powerful Auslese★★. Best years: (2007) 06 05 **04 03 02 01 00** 99 98.

HIDALGO Jerez y Manzanilla DO, Andalucía, Spain Hidalgo's Manzanilla La Gitana★★ is deservedly one of the best-selling manzanillas in Spain. Hidalgo is family-owned, and only uses grapes from its own vineyards. Brands include Mariscal★, Fino Especial and Miraflores, Amontillado Napoleon★★, Oloroso Viejo★★ and Jerez Cortado★★.

HILL OF GRACE★★★ Eden Valley, South Australia A stunning wine with dark, exotic flavours made by HENSCHKE from a single plot of Shiraz. The Hill of Grace vineyard was first planted in the 1860s, and the old vines produce a powerful, structured wine with superb ripe fruit, chocolate, coffee, earth, leather and the rest. Can be cellared for 20 years or more. Best years: (2007) (06) (05) (04) 02 01 99 98 97 96 95 **94 93 92 91** 90 88 86 85 82.

HILLTOP Neszmély, Hungary Under chief winemaker Akos Kamocsay, this winery provides fresh, bright wines, especially white, at friendly prices. Indigenous varieties such as Irsai Olivér and Cserszegi Füszeres line up with Gewürztraminer, Sauvignon Blanc★, Pinot Gris and Chardonnay. Hilltop also produces a good but controversial TOKAJI.

HILLTOPS New South Wales, Australia Promising high-altitude cherry-growing region with a small but fast-growing area of vineyards around the town of Young. Good potential for reds from Cabernet Sauvignon and Shiraz. Best producers: Chalkers Crossing, Grove Estate, MCWILLIAM's/Barwang★, Woodonga Hill.

FRANZ HIRTZBERGER Wachau, Niederösterreich, Austria The respected grower died in 2007, but his son, also Franz, has taken over. The finest wines are the concentrated, elegant Smaragd Rieslings from Singerriedel★★★ and Hochrain★★. The best Grüner Veltliner comes from Honivogl★★★. Best years: (Riesling Smaragd) (2007) 06 05 **04 03 02 01** 00 99 98 97 95.

HOCHHEIM Rheingau, Germany Village best known for having given the English the word 'Hock' for Rhine wine, but with good individual vineyard sites, especially Domdechaney, Hölle (hell!) and Kirchenstück. Best producers: Joachim Flick, Franz KUNSTLER★★, Werner★. Best years: (2007) 06 05 **04 03 02 01** 99 98 97 96.

HOLLICK Coonawarra, South Australia Ian Hollick makes a broader range of good wines than is usually found in COONAWARRA: irresistible sparkling Merlot★ (yes, Merlot), subtle Chardonnay★, tobaccoey Cabernet-Merlot★ and richer Ravenswood Cabernet Sauvignon★★. Also attractive Sauvignon-Semillon and good limy Riesling★. Best years: (Ravenswood) (2006) 05 02 **01 99 98** 96 94 93 91 90 88.

HORTON VINEYARDS Virginia, USA Horton's Viognier★ established Virginia's potential as a wine region and ignited a rush of wineries wanting to make the next CONDRIEU. Innovations include a sparkling Viognier and varietals such as Tannat and Petit Manseng. The Cabernet Franc★ is consistently among the best wines of the eastern US.

DOM. DE L'HORTUS Pic St-Loup, Coteaux du Languedoc AC, Languedoc, France One of PIC ST-LOUP's leading estates. Bergerie de l'Hortus★, a ready-to-drink unoaked Mourvèdre-Syrah-Grenache blend, has delightful flavours of herbs, plums and cherries. Big brother Grande Cuvée★★ needs time for the fruit and oak to come into harmony. The white Grande Cuvée★ is a Chardonnay-Viognier blend. Best years: (Grande Cuvée red) (2005) 04 03 **01 00 99 98**.

HOSPICES DE BEAUNE *Côte de Beaune, Burgundy, France* Scene of a theatrical auction on the third Sunday in November each year, now under the auspices of Christie's, the Hospices is an historic foundation which sells the wine of the new vintage from its holdings in the CÔTE D'OR to finance its charitable works. Pricing reflects charitable status rather than common sense, but the auction trend is regarded as an indicator of which way the market is heading. Much depends on the Hospices winemaking, which has been variable, as well as on the maturation and bottling which are in the hands of the purchaser of each lot.

CH. L'HOSPITALET *La Clape, Coteaux du Languedoc AC, Languedoc, France* With his purchase of this domaine in La CLAPE, Gérard Bertrand has entered the big time in the Languedoc. Best wines are l'Expérience de l'Émotion, a range of *terroir*-based wines including Vin de Pays d'Oc, Cigalus★★, with 50% Cabernet Sauvignon, as well as CORBIÈRES Autrement, a blend of Syrah and Carignan. Best years: (2005) 04 **03 01 00**.

HOUGHTON *Swan District, Western Australia* WESTERN AUSTRALIA's biggest winery, owned by Constellation, sources fruit from its own outstanding vineyards and from growers in premium regions. The budget-priced Line range includes the flavoursome White Classic★ (formerly White Burgundy, or HWB in the EU), good Semillon-Sauvignon Blanc★ and Chenin Blanc; also recently improved Chardonnay and Cabernet. Moondah Brook Cabernet★★ and Shiraz★★ are a leap up in quality and even better value. Houghton has had enormous success with its regional range: a Riesling★★ and Shiraz★★ from Frankland River; a MARGARET RIVER Cabernet★★; and some of the best wines yet seen from the emerging PEMBERTON region. Dense, oaky Gladstones Shiraz★★★ and powerful, lush Jack Mann Cabernet Sauvignon★★★ have also contributed to Houghton's burgeoning profile. Best years: (Jack Mann) (2007) (05) (04) (02) 01 99 98 **96 95 94**.

HOWARD PARK *Margaret River, Western Australia*

Howard Park now has wineries at Denmark in GREAT SOUTHERN (for whites) and at MARGARET RIVER (for reds). The classic Cabernet Sauvignon-Merlot★★★ and occasional Best Barrels Merlot★★ are matched by intense, floral Riesling★★ and supremely classy Chardonnay★★. The exciting Scotsdale Shiraz★★ and Leston Cabernet★ are part of a range of regional reds. The MadFish label is good for Riesling★, Shiraz★, Sauvignon-Semillon★ and unwooded Chardonnay★. Best years: (Cabernet) (2007) 05 04 03 02 **01 99 96 94 92 91 90 88 86**; (Riesling) 2006 05 04 **03 02 01 97 95 92 91 89 86**.

HOWELL MOUNTAIN AVA *Napa Valley, California, USA* NAPA's north-eastern corner is noted for powerhouse Cabernet Sauvignon and Zinfandel as well as exotic, full-flavoured Merlot. Best producers: BERINGER (Merlot★★), DUNN★★★, La Jota★★, Ladera★★, Liparita★, PINE RIDGE (Cabernet Sauvignon★), Viader★★, White Cottage★★. Best years: (reds) 2005 03 **02 01 00** 99 98 97 96 95 94 91 90.

HUADONG WINERY *Shandong Province, China* The first producer of varietal and vintage wines in China, Huadong has received massive foreign investment as well as state support. Money, however, can't change the climate, and excessive moisture from the summer rainy season causes problems. Even so, Riesling and Chardonnay (under the Tsingtao label) are not at all bad and Cabernet Sauvignon and Chardonnay in special 'feng shui' bottles are pretty tasty.

HUET *Vouvray AC, Loire Valley, France* Complex, traditional VOUVRAY that can age for decades. Biodynamic methods are bringing the individual traits of its three excellent sites – le Haut-Lieu, Clos du Bourg and le Mont – into even sharper focus. These yield dry★★, medium-dry★★★ or sweet★★★ wines, depending on the vintage – in 2006 and 2007 the emphasis is on drier wines, including base wines for its very good Vouvray Mousseux★★. Best years: 2007 06 05 04 03 02 **01 00 99 98 97 96 95 90 89**.

HUGEL *Alsace AC, Alsace, France* Best wines are sweet ALSACE Vendange Tardive★★ and Sélection de Grains Nobles★★★. Big-volume Tradition wines are rather dull, but Jubilee wines can be ★★. Best years: (Vendange Tardive Riesling) (2007) 05 **03 01 00 98 97 96 95 90 89 88**.

HUNTER VALLEY *New South Wales, Australia* NEW SOUTH WALES' oldest wine zone overcomes a tricky climate to make fascinating, ageworthy Semillon and rich, buttery Chardonnay. Shiraz is the mainstay for reds, aging well but often developing a leathery overtone; Cabernet is occasionally successful. Premium region is the Lower Hunter Valley; the Upper Hunter has few wineries but extensive vineyards. Best producers: Allandale★, BROKENWOOD★★, Capercaillie, De Iuliis★, Hope★, Lake's Folly★, Margan Family, Mount Pleasant★★/MCWILLIAM'S, Meerea Park★, ROSEMOUNT, THOMAS★★, TOWER★, Keith Tulloch★, TYRRELL'S★★. Best years: (Shiraz) 2007 06 04 03 02 00 99 **98 97 96 94 91**.

HUNTER'S *Marlborough, South Island, New Zealand* One of MARLBOROUGH's stars, with fine, if austere, Sauvignon★, savoury Burgundian Chardonnay★, vibrant Riesling★ and sophisticated Pinot Noir★. Also attractive Miru Miru fizz★. Best years: (Chardonnay) (2007) **06 05 03 01 00**.

CH. DU HUREAU *Saumur-Champigny AC, Loire Valley, France* The Vatan family produces exemplary silky SAUMUR-CHAMPIGNY reds. The basic red★ is deliciously bright and fruity. Special cuvées Lisagathe★★ and Fevettes★★ need a bit of time. Jasmine-scented white SAUMUR★ is exceptional in top years. Decent fizz and occasional sweet Coteaux de Saumur, too. Best years: (top reds) (2007) 06 05 **04 03 02 01 99 97 96**.

INNISKILLIN *Niagara Peninsula, Ontario, Canada* One of Canada's leading wineries, with good Pinot Noir★ and Cabernet Franc, well-rounded Chardonnay★ and rich Vidal Icewine★★, Cabernet Franc Icewine★ and Riesling Icewine★. Another Inniskillin winery is in the OKANAGAN VALLEY in British Columbia. Best years: (Vidal Icewine) 2005 **04 03 02 00 99 98**.

IPHOFEN *Franken, Germany* Important wine town in FRANKEN for dry Riesling and Silvaner. Both are powerful, with a pronounced earthiness. Best producers: JULIUSSPITAL★, Johann Ruck★, Hans Wirsching★, Zehntkeller★. Best years: (2007) 06 05 **04 03 02 01 00 99 98**.

IRANCY AC *Burgundy, France* This northern outpost of vineyards, just south-west of CHABLIS, is an unlikely champion of the clear, pure flavours of the Pinot Noir grape. But red Irancy can be delicate and lightly touched by the ripeness of plums and strawberries, and can age well. Best producers: Bienvenu, J-M BROCARD, Cantin, A & J-P Colinot★, Delaloge, Patrice Fort★. Best years: (2007) **06 05 03 02**.

IRON HORSE VINEYARDS *Sonoma County, California, USA* Outstanding sparkling wines with vintage Brut★★ and Blanc de Blancs★★ delicious on release but highly suitable for aging. The Brut LD★★★ (Late Disgorged) is a heavenly mouthful – yeasty and complex. Wedding Cuvée★ blanc de noirs and Brut Rosé★ complete the line-up. Still wines include a lovely Pinot Noir★★, a stunningly fresh, crisp Chardonnay★★, a seductive Viognier★★ and a sensational Pinot Noir Rosé★.

IROULÉGUY AC *South-West France* A small AC in the Basque Pyrenees. Cabernet Sauvignon, Cabernet Franc and Tannat give fascinating, robust reds that are softer than MADIRAN. Whites are from Petit Courbu and Manseng. **Best producers:** Arretxea★, Brana★, Etxegaraya, Ilarria★, Irouléguy co-op (Mignaberry★). **Best years:** (reds) 2005 04 **03 01 00**.

ISABEL ESTATE *Marlborough, South Island, New Zealand* Aromatic, plum-and-cherry Pinot Noir★★, stylish, concentrated Chardonnay★★, aromatic Riesling★ and Pinot Gris★, plus a solid Sauvignon Blanc★. **Best years:** (Pinot Noir) **2006 04 03 01 00**.

ISOLE E OLENA *Chianti Classico DOCG, Tuscany, Italy* Paolo De Marchi has long been one of the pacesetters in CHIANTI CLASSICO. His Chianti Classico★★, characterized by clean, elegant and spicily perfumed fruit, excels in every vintage. The powerful SUPER-TUSCAN Cepparello★★★, made from 100% Sangiovese, is the top wine. Excellent Syrah★★, Cabernet Sauvignon★★★, Chardonnay★★ and VIN SANTO★★★. **Best years:** (Cepparello) (2007) (06) 04 **03 01** 99 98 97 95 90 88.

CH. D'ISSAN★ *Margaux AC, 3ème Cru Classé, Haut-Médoc, Bordeaux, France* This lovely moated property disappointed me far too often in the distant past but pulled its socks up in the 1990s. When successful, the wine can be one of the most delicate and scented in the MARGAUX AC. **Best years:** 2006 05 04 **03 02 01 00** 99 98 96 95 90 89.

PAUL JABOULET AÎNÉ *Rhône Valley, France* During the 1970s, Jaboulet led the way in raising the world's awareness of the great quality of RHONE wines. Although many of the wines are still good, they are no longer the star in any appellation. Best wines are top red HERMITAGE La Chapelle★ (this was a ★★★ wine in its heyday) and whites La Chapelle and Chevalier de Stérimberg★★. CROZES-HERMITAGE Thalabert is of regular quality, as are whites Mule Blanche★ and Raymond Roure★. Attractive CORNAS Dom. St-Pierre★, reliable COTES DU RHONE Parallèle 45, good-value COTES DU VENTOUX★ and sweet, perfumed MUSCAT DE BEAUMES-DE-VENISE★★. In January 2006, Jaboulet was bought by Swiss financier Jean-Jacques Frey, owner of Ch. la LAGUNE. **Best years:** (La Chapelle) 2006 05 04 **03 01** 99 98 97 96 95 94 91 90 89 88 78.

JACKSON ESTATE *Marlborough, South Island, New Zealand* An established grapegrower with vineyards in MARLBOROUGH's most prestigious district. Tangy, appley Sauvignon Blanc★★ and barrel-fermented Grey Ghost Sauvignon Blanc★★ both improve with a little age; restrained Chardonnay and Pinot Noir. **Best years:** (Sauvignon Blanc) **2007 06 04 03**.

JACOB'S CREEK *Barossa Valley, South Australia* Australia's leading export brand, selling more than 7 million cases a year, is owned by Pernod Ricard. The company is taking advantage of the strength of the Jacob's Creek name to rebrand wines formerly sold under the Orlando label, hence Jacob's Creek Steingarten Riesling★★ from Eden Valley, Jacob's Creek St Hugo Cabernet Sauvignon★ from COONAWARRA and rich Jacob's Creek Centenary Hill Shiraz★★ from the BAROSSA: I'm not sure I agree with this marketing ploy. Flagship reds remain Orlando Jacaranda

Ridge Cabernet★ from Coonawarra and Orlando Lawson's Shiraz★★ from PADTHAWAY. Watch for new super-premium Jacob's Creek Johann Shiraz-Cabernet and new mid-price Barossa Range wines. Jacob's Creek Reserve and Limited Release★★ wines are very good. Basic Jacob's Creek Cabernet and Semillon-Chardonnay seem stretched, but Riesling★ and Grenache-Shiraz are fine. Best years: (St Hugo) (2006) 05 04 03 02 **01 00 99 98 96 94 91 90 88 86**.

ACQUESSON *Champagne AC, Champagne, France* Top-class small producer of classic vintage Brut★★. Its non-vintage is an austerely-styled one-off that changes each year to produce the best possible blend. Cuvée No 732★★ (the fifth version made), based on the 2004 harvest, was released in October 2007. Superb single-cru Champagnes from Avize★★, Aÿ★★ and Dizy★★ plus a Dizy saignée Rosé★. Best years: (2002) (00) **97 96 95 93 90 89 88 85**.

LOUIS JADOT *Beaune, Burgundy, France* Leading merchant with a broad range of fine wines under head winemaker Jacques Lardière. The whites have power and structure, the reds look good across the price levels. The greatest here are Chevalier-Montrachet les Demoiselles★★★ and CHAMBERTIN Clos de Bèze★★★. SANTENAY★, PERNAND-VERGELESSES★ and ST-AUBIN★ offer the best value. In recent years Jadot has purchased some top BEAUJOLAIS vineyards, such as Ch. des Jacques★ in MOULIN-A-VENT. Best years: (top reds) (2007) 06 05 03 02 **00 99 98 97 96 90**; (top whites) (2007) 06 05 **04 02 00 99**.

JAMET★★★ *Côte-Rôtie AC, Rhône Valley, France* Jean-Paul and Jean-Luc Jamet are 2 of the most talented growers of COTE-ROTIE, one of France's most famous red wine appellations. The full-bodied wines, from excellent vineyards on vertiginous slopes above the Rhône, led by the marvellous Côte Brune, age well for a decade or more. Good Syrah Vin de Pays★★ too. Best years: 2007 06 05 **04 03 01 00 99 98 97 96 95 91 90 89 88**.

JANUIK *Columbia Valley AVA, Washington State, USA* Before starting his own operation, Mike Januik oversaw all the operations at CHATEAU STE MICHELLE. His experience and knowledge of Washington's vineyards allow him to source fruit from only exceptional sites. His Chardonnays (Elerding★ and Cold Creek★★) are among the top in the state. Lewis Vineyard Syrah★★ is rich, earthy and bold, and Cabernet Sauvignons (Champoux Vineyard★★ and Ciel du Cheval★★) are chocolaty, complex and ageworthy. Best years: (reds) (2006) 05 **04** 03 02.

JARDIN See JORDAN, South Africa.

JASNIÈRES AC *Loire Valley, France* Tiny AC north of Tours. Reputation for long-lived, bone-dry whites from Chenin Blanc, though new movers and shakers here and in neighbouring appellation Coteaux du Loir (which additionally makes delicate Pineau d'Aunis and Gamay reds) are picking Chenin riper. Sweet wine may be made in good years. Best producers: Bellivière★★, Le Briseau★, J Gigou★★, Les Maisons Rouges. Best years: 2007 05 **04** 03 02 01 99 97 96.

JEREZ Y MANZANILLA DO/SHERRY See pages 174–5.

JERMANN *Friuli-Venezia Giulia, Italy* Silvio Jermann produces non-DOC Chardonnay★, Sauvignon Blanc★, Pinot Bianco★ and Pinot Grigio★. Deep, long-lived Vintage Tunina★★ is based on Sauvignon-Chardonnay with Ribolla, Malvasia and Picolit. Barrel-fermented Chardonnay★★ is labelled, rather ungrammatically, 'Were dreams, now it is just wine'. Vinnae★ is based on Ribolla; Capo Martino★ is also a blend of local varieties. The wines are plump but pricey.

JEREZ Y MANZANILLA DO/SHERRY

Andalucía, Spain

The Spanish now own the name outright. At least in the EU, the only wines that can be sold as sherry come from the triangle of vineyard land between the Andalucian towns of Jerez de la Frontera (inland), and Sanlúcar de Barrameda and Puerto de Santa María (by the sea). New agreements signed by the EU have phased out such other appellations as South African Sherry.

The best sherries can be spectacular. Three main factors contribute to the high-quality potential of wines from this region: the chalky-spongy albariza soil where the best vines grow, the Palomino Fino grape - unexciting for table wines but potentially great once transformed by the sherry-making processes – and a natural yeast called flor. All sherry must be a minimum of 3 years old, but fine sherries age in barrel for much longer. Sherries must be blended through a solera system. About a third of the wine from the oldest barrels is bottled, and the barrels topped up with slightly younger wine from another set of barrels and so on, for a minimum of 3 sets of barrels. The idea is that the younger wine takes on the character of older wine, as well as keeping the blend refreshed.

MAIN SHERRY STYLES

Fino and manzanilla Fino sherries derive their extraordinary, tangy, pungent flavours from flor. Young, newly fermented wines destined for these styles of sherry are deliberately fortified very sparingly to just 15–15.5% alcohol before being put in barrels for their minimum of 3 years' maturation. The thin, soft, oatmeal-coloured mush of flor grows on the surface of the wines, protecting them from the air (and thereby keeping them pale) and giving them a characteristic sharp, pungent tang. The addition of younger wine each year feeds the flor, maintaining an even layer. Manzanillas are fino-style wines that have matured in the cooler seaside conditions of Sanlúcar de Barrameda, where the flor grows thickest and the fine, salty tang is most accentuated.

Amontillado True amontillados are fino sherries that have continued to age after the flor has died (after about 5 years) and so finish their aging period in contact with air. These should all be bone dry. Medium-sweet amontillados are concoctions in which the dry sherry is sweetened with mistela, a blend of grape juice and alcohol.

Oloroso This type of sherry is strongly fortified after fermentation to deter the growth of flor. Olorosos therefore mature in barrel in contact with the air, which gradually darkens them while they remain dry, but develop rich, intense, nutty and raisiny flavours.

Other styles Manzanilla pasada is aged manzanilla, with greater depth and nuttiness. Palo cortado is an unusual, deliciously nutty, dry style somewhere in between amontillado and oloroso. Sweet oloroso creams and pale creams are almost without exception enriched solely for the export market. Sweet varietal wines are made from sun-dried Pedro Ximénez or Moscatel.

See also individual producers.

Argüeso (Manzanilla San León, Manzanilla Fina Las Medallas).

BARBADILLO (Manzanilla Eva, Manzanilla En Rama, Manzanilla Solear, Amontillado Príncipe, Amontillado de Sanlúcar, Oloroso Seco Cuco, Palo Cortado Obispo Gascón).

Delgado Zuleta (Manzanilla Pasada La Goya).

Díez Mérito (Imperial Fino, Don Zoilo Imperial Amontillado, Victoria Regina Oloroso).

DOMECQ (Fino La Ina, Amontillado 51-1A, Sibarita Palo Cortado, Venerable Pedro Ximénez).

El Maestro Sierra.

Equipo Navazos (La Bota de…)

Garvey (Palo Cortado, Amontillado Tio Guillermo, Pedro Ximénez Gran Orden).

GONZALEZ BYASS (Tio Pepe Fino, Amontillado del Duque, Matusalem Oloroso Muy Viejo, Apóstoles Oloroso Viejo, Noé Pedro Ximénez, Oloroso Viejo de Añado).

HIDALGO (Manzanilla La Gitana, Manzanilla Pasada, Jerez Cortado, Amontillado Napoleon, Oloroso Viejo).

LUSTAU (Almacenista single-producer wines, East India Solera, Puerto Fino).

OSBORNE (Amontillado Coquinero, Fino Quinta, Oloroso Bailén, Oloroso Solera India, Pedro Ximénez).

Rey Fernando de Castilla.

Sánchez Romate (Pedro Ximénez Cardenal Cisneros).

Tradición.

VALDESPINO (Amontillado Coliseo, Amontillado Tio Diego, Amontillado Don Tomás, Palo Cortado Cardenal, Fino Inocente, Oloroso Don Gonzalo, Pedro Ximénez Niños).

Williams & Humbert (Pando Fino, Alegría Manzanilla).

175

JOHANNISBERG *Rheingau, Germany* Probably the best known of all th
Rhine wine villages, with 10 vineyard sites, including the famous Schlos
Johannisberg. Best producers: Prinz von Hessen★, Johannishof★★, Schlos
Johannisberg★. Best years: (2007) 06 05 **04 03 02 01** 99 98.

KARL H JOHNER *Bischoffingen, Baden, Germany* Johner specializes in nev
oak-aged wines from his native BADEN. The vividly fruity Pinot Noir
and Pinot Blanc★ are excellent, the Chardonnay SJ★★ is one o
Germany's best examples of this varietal, and the rich, silky Pinot Noi
SJ★★ can be one of Germany's finest reds. Best years: (Pinot Noir SJ) (2007)
06 05 **04 03 02 01** 00.

JORDAN *Alexander Valley AVA, Sonoma County, California, USA* Ripe, fruit
Cabernet Sauvignon★ with a cedar character rare in California. Th
winery has recently moved towards greater use of mountain-grow
Cabernet. Chardonnay★ is nicely balanced. J★ fizz is an attractiv
mouthful, now made independently by Judy Jordan's J Wine Co.; J als
makes top-notch RUSSIAN RIVER Pinot Noir★. Best years: (Cabernet) 2003 0
01 00 99 97 96 95 94 91 86.

JORDAN *Stellenbosch WO, South Africa* Meticulously groomed hillside vine
yards, with a variety of aspects and soils. Chardonnays (regular★★ wit
creamy complexity; Nine Yards★★, dense, nutty, but balanced) an
delicious peppery Chenin★★ head a strong white range. Syrah★★
Cabernet Sauvignon★, Merlot★ and BORDEAUX-blend Cobblers Hill★
are understated but beautifully balanced for aging. Sophia★ is a ric
Bordeaux-blend red. Sold under the Jardin label in the USA. Best year
(Chardonnay) 2007 **06 05 04 03 02 01**; (Cobblers Hill) **2005 04 03 02 0**
00 99.

TONI JOST *Bacharach, Mittelrhein, Germany* Peter Jost has put the MITTELRHEI
on the map. From the Bacharacher Hahn site come some delicious, rac
Rieslings★; Auslese★★ adds creaminess without losing that pine-need
scent. Best years: (2007) 06 05 **04 03 02 01** 99 98 97.

J P VINHOS See BACALHOA VINHOS DE PORTUGAL.

JULIÉNAS AC *Beaujolais, Burgundy, France* One of the more norther
BEAUJOLAIS Crus, Juliénas is attractive, 'serious' Beaujolais which can be bi
and tannic enough to develop in bottle. Best producers: G Descombes★
DUBOEUF★, P Granger★, Ch. de Juliénas★, J-P Margerand★, Pelletier★
B Santé★, M Tête★. Best years: **2007 06 05**.

JULIUSSPITAL *Würzburg, Franken, Germany* A 16th-century charitabl
foundation, with 170ha (420 acres) of vineyards, known for its dry wine
– especially from IPHOFEN and WURZBURG. Look out for the Würzburge
Stein wines, sappy Müller-Thurgau, grapefruity Silvaners★★ an
petrolly Rieslings★★. Best years: (2007) 06 05 **04 03 02 01** 00.

JUMILLA DO *Murcia and Castilla-La Mancha, Spain* Jumilla's reputation is fo
big alcoholic reds, but dense, serious reds from Monastrell (Mourvèdre
show the region's potential. Whites are almost non-existent today. Bes
producers: Casa Castillo★★, Casa de la Ermita, Hijos de Juan Gil★, Luzón★,
Nido★, Agapito Rico★. Best years: 2006 **05 04 03 01** 00 99 98 96.

JURA See ARBOIS, CHATEAU-CHALON, COTES DU JURA, CREMANT DU JURA, l'ETOIL

JURANÇON AC *South-West France* The sweet white wine made from late
harvested and occasionally botrytized grapes can be heavenly, with flora
spicy, apricot-quince flavours. The dry lemony wine, Jurançon Sec, ca
be ageworthy. Best producers: Bru-Baché★★, Castera★, CAUHAPE★★, Clo
Guirouilh★, Clos Lapeyre★, Clos Thou★, CLOS UROULAT★★, Larrédya★, PRIM
PALATUM★, Souch★★. Best years: (sweet) (2005) 03 **02 01** 00 99 98.

KAISERSTUHL *Baden, Germany* A 4000ha (10,000-acre) volcanic stump rising to 600m (2000ft) and overlooking the Rhine plain. Pinot varieties excel. Best producers: BERCHER★★, Dr HEGER★★, Karl H JOHNER★★, Franz Keller★, Königsschaffhausen co-op, Salwey★, Schneider★★. Best years: (dry whites) (2007) 06 05 **04 02 01 99 98**.

KAMPTAL *Niederösterreich, Austria* 3870ha (9560-acre) wine region centred on the town of Langenlois, making some impressive dry Riesling and Grüner Veltliner. Best producers: BRUNDLMAYER★★★, Ehn★★, Hiedler★, Hirsch★, Jurtschitsch★, Fred Loimer★★, Schloss Gobelsburg★★, Topf. Best years: (2007) 06 05 **04 03 02 01 00 99**.

KANONKOP *Stellenbosch WO, South Africa* Winemaker Abrie Beeslaar is confidently creating traditional, long-lived red wines – now, thanks to virus-free vine material, often with brighter fruit. Muscular, savoury BORDEAUX-blend Paul Sauer★★ really does mature for 10 years or more. A straight Cabernet Sauvignon★ adds to this enviable red wine reputation: Pinotage★★, from 50-year-old vines, is indelibly associated with the estate. Best years: (Paul Sauer) 2004 **03 02 01 00 99 98 97 96 95 94 91**.

KARTHÄUSERHOF *Trier, Mosel-Saar-Ruwer, Germany* Top Ruwer estate which has gone from strength to strength under Christoph Tyrell and winemaker Ludwig Breiling. Rieslings combine aromatic extravagance with racy brilliance. Most wines are now ★★, some Auslese and Eiswein ★★★. Best years: (2007) 06 05 **04 03 02 01 99 97 95 94**.

KATNOOK ESTATE *Coonawarra, South Australia* Chardonnay★★ has consistently been the best of the fairly expensive whites, though Riesling★ and Sauvignon★★ are pretty tasty, too. Well-structured Cabernet Sauvignon★ and treacly Shiraz★ lead the reds, with Odyssey Cabernet Sauvignon★★ and Prodigy Shiraz★★ reaching a higher level. Best years: (Odyssey) (2006) (05) (04) 03 02 **01 00 99 98 97 96 94 92 91**.

KÉKFRANKOS See BLAUFRANKISCH.

KELLER *Flörsheim-Dalsheim, Rheinhessen, Germany* Klaus Keller and son Klaus-Peter are the leading winemakers in the hill country of RHEINHESSEN, away from the Rhine riverbank. They produce a range of varietal dry wines and naturally sweet Rieslings, as well as extra-special dry Rieslings★★ from the Dalsheimer Hubacker site. Astonishing TBA★★★ from Riesling and Rieslaner. Best years: (2007) 06 05 **04 03 02 01 00 99**.

KENDALL-JACKSON *Sonoma County, California, USA* Jess Jackson founded KJ in bucolic Lake County in 1982 after buying a vineyard there; now based in SONOMA COUNTY, with operations throughout the state, and producing about 4 million cases. Since the 2004 vintage, KJ's volume leader, the Vintner's Reserve Chardonnay (2 million cases) is made entirely from estate-grown fruit. Higher levels of quality are found in the Grand Reserve reds and whites, the vineyard-based Highland Estates★ series and the top of the range Stature (red Meritage★★).

KENWOOD *Sonoma Valley AVA, California, USA* This winery has always represented very good quality at reasonable prices. The Sauvignon Blanc★ highlights floral and melon flavours with a slightly earthy finish. Jack London Zinfandel★★ is impressive, while long-lived Artist Series Cabernet Sauvignon★★ is the flagship. RUSSIAN RIVER VALLEY Pinot Noir★ is superb value. Best years: (Zinfandel) 2005 04 **03 02 01 00 99 98 97 96 95 94**.

VON KESSELSTATT *Trier, Mosel, Germany* Good traditional Rieslings (★ to ★★) from some top sites at GRAACH (Josephshöfer) and PIESPORT in the MOSEL, Scharzhofberg in the Saar and Kasel in the Ruwer. Best years: (2007) 06 05 **04 03 02 01 99**.

KIEDRICH *Rheingau, Germany* Top vineyard here is the Gräfenberg, givin long-lived, mineral Rieslings. Wines from Sandgrub and Wasseros ar also often good. Best producers: Prinz von Hessen, Knyphausen★, WEIL★★ Best years: (2007) 06 05 04 **03 02 01** 99 98 97 96.

CH. KIRWAN★ *Margaux AC, 3ème Cru Classé, Haut-Médoc, Bordeaux, France* Thi MARGAUX estate has shown considerable improvement since the mid 1990s. Investment in the cellars, more attention to the vineyards and th advice of consultant Michel Rolland (until 2007) have produced wines o greater depth and power but less perfume. Second wine: Les Charmes d Kirwan. Best years: 2006 05 04 **03 01 00** 99 98 96 95.

KISTLER *Sonoma Valley AVA, California, USA* One of California's hottes Chardonnay producers. Wines are made from many different vineyard (Kistler Vineyard, Durell Vineyard and Dutton Ranch can be ★★★ McCrea Vineyard and the ultra-cool-climate Camp Meeting Ridg Vineyard ★★). All possess great complexity with good aging potentia Kistler also makes a number of single-vineyard Pinot Noirs★★ that g from good to very good. Best years: (Kistler Vineyard Chardonnay) 2005 0 **03 02 01 00** 99 98 97.

KLEIN CONSTANTIA *Constantia WO, South Africa* Showpiece estate fas regaining deserved stature. The area's aptitude for white wines i reflected in crisp, nicely weighted Sauvignon Blanc★ (expressive, vibrar Perdeblokke★★ from a higher vineyard), good Chardonnay, excellen barrel-fermented white blend Madame Marlbrook★★, attractive off-dr Riesling and Vin de Constance★★ (recent vintages ★★★), a thrillin Muscat dessert wine based on the 18th-century Constantia. In reds, Nev World-style Shiraz★ looks promising. Best years: (Vin de Constance) 200 **02 01 00** 99 98 97 96 95 94 93 92 91 90.

KNAPPSTEIN *Clare Valley, South Australia* The owners, Lion Nathan, have given young winemaker Paul Smith enough scope to revitalize Knappstein, with some outstanding single-vineyard wines from mature vines: Ackland Riesling★★★, Enterprise Cabernet★★ and Yertabulti Shiraz★★. The Hand Picked Riesling★★ is reliably good and Three★ intriguingly combines Gewürztraminer with Riesling and Pinot Gris. The Enterprise Brewery★ (established 1878) has been re-opened with refreshing results. Best years: (Enterprise Cabernet Sauvignon) (2006) (05) 04 03 02 **01 00** 99 98; (Enterprise Ale) 2009 08.

KNAPPSTEIN LENSWOOD VINEYARDS See RIPOSTE.

EMMERICH KNOLL *Unterloiben, Wachau, Niederösterreich, Austria* Since th late 1970s, some of the greatest Austrian dry white wines. His rich complex Riesling and Grüner Veltliner are packed with fruit an invariably ★★ quality, with versions from both the Loibenberg an Schütt sites ★★★. They repay keeping for 5 years or more. Best year (Riesling Smaragd) (2007) 06 05 **04** 03 02 01 00 99 98 97 96 95 94.

KOEHLER-RUPRECHT *Kallstadt, Pfalz, Germany* Bernd Philippi make powerful, very concentrated dry Rieslings★★★ from the Kallstadte Saumagen site, the oak-aged botrytized Elysium★ and Burgundian-styl Spätburgunder (Pinot Noir)★. Best years: (Saumagen Riesling) (2007) 06 0 04 **03 02 01 00** 99 98 97.

KOOYONG *Mornington Peninsula, Australia*   Owned by the Gjergja family, who also have nearby Port Phillip Estate, and driven by the winemaking talents of Sandro Mosele. From 1995, 30ha (74 acres) at Kooyong were planted to Pinot Noir (the Haven★★★, Ferrous★★ and Meres★ Vineyards) and Chardonnay (the Faultline★★ and Farrago★ Vineyards). Entry-level Clonale Chardonnay★ and Massale Pinot Noir★ show varietal character at bargain prices, while the Kooyong Estate Chardonnay★★ is structured, complex and restrained and the Estate Pinot Noir★★ needs time to show its seductive best.

ALOIS KRACHER *Illmitz, Burgenland, Austria*   Unquestionably Austria's greatest sweet winemaker until his untimely death in 2007. Nouvelle Vague wines are aged in new barriques while Zwischen den Seen wines are aged in large casks. The Scheurebe Beerenauslesen and TBAs, and the Welschrieslings, Chardonnay-Welschrieslings and Grande Cuvée are all ★★★. Best years: (whites) (2007) 06 05 04 **02 01 00 99 98 96 95**.

KREMSTAL *Niederösterreich, Austria*   2170ha (5365-acre) wine region around Krems, producing some of Austria's best whites. From 2007 the DAC appellation can be used for dry Riesling and Grüner Veltliner. Best producers: Malat★★, Mantlerhof★, Sepp Moser★, NIGL★★, NIKOLAIHOF★★, Franz Proidl★, Salomon★★, Stadt Krems★. Best years: (2007) 06 **05 04 03 02 01 00 99**.

KRUG *Champagne AC, Champagne, France*   Serious CHAMPAGNE house, making seriously expensive wines. The non-vintage Grande Cuvée★★ used to knock spots off most other de luxe brands in its rich, rather over-the-top traditional style. Under new owners LVMH, the style seems to have changed dramatically: it's fresher, leaner, more modern – good, but that's not why I buy Krug. Also an impressive vintage★★, a rosé★★ and ethereal, outrageously expensive, single-vineyard Clos du Mesnil★★★ Blanc de Blancs. Brand-new Clos d'Ambonnay is next up. Best years: 1996 95 **90 89 88 85 82 81 79**.

KRUTZLER *Deutsch-Schützen, Südburgenland, Austria*   One of Austria's finest red wines, Perwolff★★, is a generously oaked blend of Blaufränkisch and Cabernet Sauvignon. The Blaufränkisch Reserve★ is almost as fine. Best years: (2007) 06 05 04 **03 02 01** 00 99 98.

PETER JAKOB KÜHN *Oestrich, Rheingau, Germany*   A brilliant grower and winemaker, Kühn frequently makes headlines with his substantial dry Rieslings and full, juicy Auslese. These wines are usually ★★. Best years: (2007) 06 05 **04 03 02 01 99** 98.

KUMEU/HUAPAI *Auckland, North Island, New Zealand*   A small but significant viticultural area north-west of Auckland. The 11 wineries profit from their proximity to New Zealand's largest city, but most make little or no wine from grapes grown in their home region. Best producers: COOPERS CREEK★, KUMEU RIVER★★, MATUA VALLEY★, West Brook. Best years: (reds) (2007) **05 04 02 00**.

KUMEU RIVER *Kumeu, Auckland, North Island, New Zealand*   This family winery has been transformed by New Zealand's first Master of Wine, Michael Brajkovich, with adventurous, high-quality wines: a big, complex Chardonnay★★★ (Maté's Vineyard★★★), complex oak-aged Pinot Gris★ and a MARLBOROUGH Sauvignon Blanc. Only Pinot Noir disappoints so far. Best years: (Chardonnay) 2007 **06 05 02 00**.

KUNDE ESTATE *Sonoma Valley, California, USA*   The Kunde family have grown wine grapes in SONOMA COUNTY for more than 100 years; in 1990 they started producing wines, with spectacular results. The Chardonnays are all impressive – Kinneybrook★★, Wildwood★★ and the powerful buttery Reserve★★. The Century Vines Zinfandel★★ gets rave reviews, as does the peppery Syrah★★, the zesty Sauvignon Blanc★★ and the explosively fruity Viognier★★. Best years: (Zinfandel) 2005 **02 01 00 99 9** **96 94**.

FRANZ KÜNSTLER *Hochheim, Rheingau, Germany* Gunter Künstler makes some of the best dry Rieslings in the RHEINGAU – powerful, mineral wines★★, with the Hölle wines often ★★★. Sweet wine quality has been erratic lately, but the best are fantastic. Powerful, earthy and pricey Pinot Noir. Best years: (2007) 06 05 04 **03 02 01 98 97**.

KWV *Paarl WO, South Africa* This industry giant aims to get back on course with help from Neil ELLIS, Charles Back (FAIRVIEW) and Ian McKenzie (ex Southcorp), who are mentoring the winemaking team. The flagship Cathedral Cellar range features bright-fruited, well-oaked Triptych★ (Cabernet-Merlot-Shiraz), rich bold Cabernet Sauvignon★ and modern-style Pinotage. Among whites, barrel-fermented Chardonnay shows pleasing fruit/oak balance, and Sauvignon★ is tangy. Produced in best years only, and in very limited quantities, single-vineyard Perold is an ultra-ripe international-style Shiraz lavishly adorned with new American oak. PORT-style and Muscadel fortifieds remain superb value.

LA ROSA *Cachapoal, Rapel, Chile* Recently rejuvenated old family operation. The La Palma unoaked Chardonnay and La Palma Merlot are good easy drinkers. The La Capitana★ and Don Reca★ labels are a step up in quality and always terrific value. New icon Ossa Sixth Generation proves La Rosa can also produce world-class reds.

CH. LABÉGORCE-ZÉDÉ★ *Margaux AC, Haut-Médoc, Bordeaux, France* Cherished and improved by Luc Thienpont of POMEROL until 2005, this property is now owned by neighbouring Ch. Labégorce. The wine isn't that perfumed, but is well poised between concentration and finesse. Ages for 5 years or more. Second wine: Domaine Zédé. Best years: 2006 05 0 **03 01 00 99 98 96 95 90 89**.

LADOIX AC *Côte de Beaune, Burgundy, France* Most northerly village in the CÔTE DE BEAUNE. The village includes some of the Grand Cru CORTON, and the lesser vineyards may be sold as Ladoix-Côte de Beaune or CÔTE DE BEAUNE-VILLAGES. Reasonably priced reds, quite light in colour and a little lean in style, from several good growers. Best producers: (reds) Cachat Ocquidant★, Chevalier, E Cornu★, M Mallard★, Prince de Merode★; (whites) R & R Jacob★, S Loichet★. Best years: (reds) (2007) 06 05 **03 02 99**.

MICHEL LAFARGE *Volnay, Côte de Beaune, Burgundy, France* The doyen of VOLNAY; son Frédéric is now in charge. Some outstanding red wines, notably Volnay Clos des Chênes★★★, Volnay Clos du Château des Ducs★★★ (a monopole) and less fashionable BEAUNE Grèves★★. BOURGOGNE Rouge★ is good value. Top wines may seem a little lean at first, but will blossom after 10 years' or more aging. Best years: (top reds) (2007) 06 05 04 03 02 99 **98 97 96 95 93 91 90**.

CH. LAFAURIE-PEYRAGUEY★★ *Sauternes AC, 1er Cru Classé, Bordeaux, France* One of the most improved SAUTERNES properties of the 1980s and now frequently one of the best Sauternes of all, sumptuous and rich when young, and marvellously deep and satisfying with age. Best years: 2005 04 **03 02 01 99 98 97 96 95 90 89 88 86 85 83**.

CH. LAFITE-ROTHSCHILD★★★ *Pauillac AC, 1er Cru Classé, Haut-Médoc, Bordeaux, France* This PAUILLAC First Growth is frequently cited as the epitome of elegance, indulgence and expense. Since the late 1990s vintages have been superb, with added depth and body to match the wine's traditional finesse. Second wine: les Carruades de Lafite-Rothschild. Best years: 2006 05 04 03 02 01 00 **99 98 97 96 95 94 90 89 88 86 85 82**.

CH. LAFLEUR★★★ *Pomerol AC, Bordeaux, France* Using some of POMEROL's most traditional winemaking, this tiny estate can seriously rival the great PETRUS for texture, flavour and aroma. But a high percentage of Cabernet Franc (50%) makes this a more elegant style of wine. Second wine: Pensées de Lafleur. Best years: 2006 05 04 03 02 01 00 **99 98 96 95 90 89 88**.

LAFON *Meursault, Côte de Beaune, Burgundy, France* One of Burgundy's current superstars, with prices to match. Early exponent of biodynamics for brilliant MEURSAULT including Clos de la Barre★★, Charmes★★★, Perrières★★★, le MONTRACHET★★★ and exciting long-lived reds from VOLNAY (Santenots-du-Milieu★★★). Since 1999, also MACON★ (Clos du Four★, Clos de la Crochette★). Best years: (whites) (2007) 06 05 04 03 02 00; (reds) (2007) 06 05 03 02 99 **98 97 96 95 91 90**.

CH. LAFON-ROCHET★ *St-Estèphe AC, 4ème Cru Classé, Haut-Médoc, Bordeaux, France* Good-value, affordable Classed Growth claret. Recent vintages have seen an increase of Merlot in the blend, making the wine less austere. Delicious and blackcurranty after 10 years. Best years: 2006 05 04 03 02 01 00 **99 98 96 95 94 90 89 88**.

ALOIS LAGEDER *Alto Adige DOC, Trentino-Alto Adige, Italy* Leading producer in ALTO ADIGE, making good, medium-priced varietals and pricey estate and single-vineyard wines such as Löwengang Cabernet★ and Chardonnay★★, Sauvignon Lehenhof★★, Cabernet Cor Römigberg★★, Pinot Noir Krafuss★, Pinot Bianco Haberlehof★ and Pinot Grigio Benefizium Porer★. Also owns the historic Casòn Hirschprunn estate, source of excellent Alto Adige blends. White Contest★★ is based on Pinot Grigio and Chardonnay, with small amounts of Marsanne and Roussanne. The red equivalent, Casòn★★, is Merlot-Cabernet based; a second red, Corolle★, and white Etele★ show similar style.

LAGO DI CALDARO DOC *Trentino-Alto Adige, Italy* At its best a lovely, barely red, youthful glugger from the Schiava grape, tasting of strawberries and cream and bacon smoke. However, far too much Caldaro is overproduced. Known in German as Kalterersee. Kalterersee Auslese (Lago di Caldaro Scelto) is not sweet, but has 0.5% more alcohol. Best producers: Caldaro co-op★, LAGEDER★, Prima & Nuova/Erste & Neue★, San Michele Appiano co-op, Schloss Sallegg★.

CH. LAGRANGE★★ *St-Julien AC, 3ème Cru Classé, Haut-Médoc, Bordeaux, France* Since the Japanese company SUNTORY purchased this large estate in 1983 it has become a single-minded wine of good fruit, meticulous winemaking and fine quality, an occasional surfeit of tannin being the only cautionary note. Second wine: les Fiefs de Lagrange. Best years: 2006 05 04 03 02 **01 00 99** 98 96 95 90 89 88.

LAGREIN Black grape in Italy's TRENTINO-Alto Adige, producing – when not over-oaked – deep-coloured, brambly, chocolaty reds called Lagrein Dunkel or Scuro, and full-bodied, attractively scented rosé (known as Kretzer). Best producers: Colterenzio co-op (Cornell★), Graziano Fontana★, Franz Gojer★, Gries co-op★, Hofstätter★, LAGEDER★, Laimburg★, Muri-Gries★, J Niedermayr★, I Niedriest★, Plattner-Waldgries★, Hans Rottensteiner★, Santa Maddalena co-op★, Simoncelli★, Terlano co-op★★, Thurnhof★★, TIEFENBRUNNER★★, Zemmer★.

CH. LAGREZETTE *Cahors AC, South-West France* Splendid CAHORS estate
owned by Alain-Dominique Perrin, boss of luxury jewellers Cartier. The
cellars are overseen by enologist Michel Rolland. There's a merchant
range of Caves de Grezette (red Expression de Grezette★), oak-aged
Chevaliers and Ch. Lagrezette★. Cuvée Dame Honneur★ and le
Pigeonnier★★ are special cuvées, mainly from Malbec. Best years: (2004)
03 02 **01 00 99**.

CH. LA LAGUNE★ *Haut-Médoc AC, 3ème Cru Classé,
Haut-Médoc, Bordeaux, France* The closest MEDOC
Classed Growth to Bordeaux city. The soils are
sandy-gravel and the wines round and elegant in
style. Took a dip in the late 1990s but new
investment from 2000, and quality has
improved. Second wine: Moulin de la Lagune.
Best years: 2005 04 **03 02 00 98 96 95 90 89**.

GRAND CRU CLASSE

CHATEAU LA LAGUNE
2003
HAUT-MÉDOC

LALANDE-DE-POMEROL AC *Bordeaux, France* To the north of its more
famous neighbour POMEROL, this AC produces ripe, plummy wines with
an unmistakable mineral edge that are very attractive to drink at 3–5
years old, but age reasonably well too. Even though they lack the
concentration of top Pomerols, the wines are not particularly cheap. Best
producers: Annereaux★, Bertineau St-Vincent★, La Croix des Moines★, la
Croix-St-André★, les Cruzelles★, la Fleur de Boüard★★, Garraud★, Grand
Ormeau★, Haut-Chaigneau, les Hauts Conseillants, Jean de Gué★, Laborderie
Mondésir★, Perron (La Fleur★), Sergant, la Sergue★, Siaurac★, Tournefeuille★,
Viaud. Best years: 2006 05 04 **03 02 00 98 96 95 90 89**.

LAMBRUSCO *Emilia-Romagna, Italy* 'Lambrusco' refers to a family of black
grape varieties, grown in 3 DOC zones on the plains of Emilia and
around Mantova in LOMBARDY, but it is the screwcap bottles of non-DOC
Lambrusco that made the name famous, even though some contain no
wine from Lambrusco grapes at all. Proper Lambrusco is a dry or semi-
sweet fizzy red with high acidity to partner the rich local foods, such as
rich, buttery cheese sauces and salami, and is worth trying (especially
Lambrusco di Sorbara and Grasparossa di Castelvetro). Best producers:
Barbieri, Barbolini, F Bellei★, Casali, Cavicchioli★, Chiarli, Vittorio Graziano★,
Oreste Lini, Stefano Spezia, Venturini Baldini.

LAMOREAUX LANDING *Finger Lakes AVA, New York State, USA* One of the
most important wineries in FINGER LAKES. Its Chardonnay Reserve★ is a
consistent medal winner, and the Pinot Noir★ is arguably the region's
best. Merlot★ and Cabernet Franc★ are also attractive, as are Riesling★
and good, quaffable fizz.

LANDMARK *Sonoma County, California, USA* This producer concentrates on
Chardonnay and Pinot Noir. Chardonnays include Overlook★★ and the
oakier Damaris Reserve★★ and Lorenzo★★. Tropical-fruited Courtyard
Chardonnay★ is lower-priced. Pinot Noir from Kastania Vineyard★★
(SONOMA COAST) is beautifully focused.

LANGHE DOC *Piedmont, Italy* Important DOC covering blends (Rosso or
Bianco) and varietals from the Langhe hills around Alba, the 'varietals'
crucially allowing 15% grapes other than that announced on the label.
The range of varietals such as Chardonnay, Barbera and Nebbiolo
embrace many former vino da tavola blends of the highest order, as well
as most of what Angelo Gaja used to sell as Barbaresco and Bando. Best
producers: (reds) ALTARE★★, Boglietti (Buio★★), Bongiovanni (Falletto★★),
CERETTO★★, CHIARLO★, Cigliuti★★, CLERICO★★, Aldo CONTERNO★★,

Conterno-Fantino (Monprà★★), Luigi Einaudi★, GAJA★★★, A Ghisolfi★★, Marchesi di Gresy (Virtus★★), F Nada (Seifile★★), Parusso (Bricco Rovella★★), Rocche dei Manzoni (Quatr Nas★), Vajra★, Gianni Voerzio (Serrapiu★★), Roberto VOERZIO★★. Best years: (reds) (2007) (06) 04 **03 01 00 99 98 97 96 95**.

CH. LANGOA-BARTON★★ *St-Julien AC, 3ème Cru Classé, Haut-Médoc, Bordeaux, France* Owned by the Barton family since 1821, Langoa-Barton is usually less scented and elegant, though often richer than its ST-JULIEN stablemate LEOVILLE-BARTON, but it is still extremely impressive and excellent value. Drink after 7 or 8 years, although it may keep for 15. Second wine: Réserve de Léoville-Barton (a blend from the young vines of both Barton properties). Best years: 2006 05 04 **03** 02 **01** 00 99 98 96 95 90 89 88 86 85.

LANGUEDOC-ROUSSILLON *France* This vast area of southern France, running from Nîmes to the Spanish border and covering the *départements* of the GARD, HERAULT, Aude and Pyrénées-Orientales, is still a source of undistinguished cheap wine, but is also one of France's most exciting wine regions. The transformation is the result of better grape varieties, modern winemaking and ambitious producers, from the heights of GRANGE DES PERES to very good local co-ops. The best wines are the reds, particularly those from CORBIERES, COTEAUX DU LANGUEDOC, MINERVOIS and PIC ST-LOUP, and some new-wave Cabernets, Merlots and Syrahs, as well as the more traditional *vins doux naturels*, such as BANYULS, MAURY and MUSCAT DE RIVESALTES; but we are now seeing exciting whites as well, particularly as new plantings of Chardonnay, Marsanne, Roussanne, Viognier and Sauvignon Blanc mature. A super-appellation for the whole of Languedoc and Roussillon, called simply Languedoc AC, was agreed in 2007 and includes all of Coteaux du Languedoc, Corbières, Minervois and the ROUSSILLON appellations. Producers can opt into this new appellation or stick to the old areas. See also BOUCHES-DU-RHONE, CABARDES, COLLIOURE, COSTIERES DE NIMES, COTES DU ROUSSILLON, COTES DE THONGUE, FAUGERES, FITOU, LIMOUX, MUSCAT DE FRONTIGNAN, MUSCAT DE ST-JEAN-DE-MINERVOIS, OC, RIVESALTES, ST-CHINIAN.

LANSON *Champagne AC, Champagne, France* Non-vintage Lanson Black Label★ is reliably tasty and, like the rosé★ and vintage★★ wines, especially de luxe Noble Cuvée★★, improves greatly with aging. In 2006, Lanson (and associated brands Besserat de Bellefon, Gauthier, Massé and Alfred Rothschild) was bought by Boizel Chanoine Champagne, where Bruno PAILLARD is the majority shareholder. Best years: (1999) 98 **97 96 95 93 90 89 88 85 83 82**.

DOM. LAROCHE *Chablis, Burgundy, France* Dynamic CHABLIS producer, with good St Martin★ and impressive Grand Cru Les Clos★★★. One of the first Burgundians to use screwtop closures. Also owns MAS LA CHEVALIERE in the Languedoc and L'AVENIR in Stellenbosch, South Africa. Best years: (Chablis) (2007) **06 05 03 02 00 99**.

CH. LASCOMBES *Margaux AC, 2ème Cru Classé, Haut-Médoc, Bordeaux, France* One of the great underachievers in the MARGAUX AC and little worth drinking in the 1980s and 90s, but new American ownership and invest-ment and the advice of consultant enologist Michel Rolland have begun to make a difference – and the 2004 is the best effort for a generation. Best years: 2006 05 04 03 **01** 00 **96 95**.

CH. LATOUR★★★ *Pauillac AC, 1er Cru Classé, Haut-Médoc, Bordeaux, France*
Latour's reputation is based on powerful, long-lasting classic wines. Strangely, in the early 1980s there was an attempt to make lighter, more fashionable wines, with mixed results. The late 80s saw a return to classic Latour, much to my relief. Its reputation for making fine wine in less successful vintages is well deserved. After 30 years in British hands it returned to French ownership in 1993. Spanking new cellars from 2004. Second wine: les Forts de Latour. Best years: 2006 05 04 03 02 01 00 **99 98 97 96 95 94 93 90 89 88 86**.

LOUIS LATOUR *Beaune, Burgundy, France* Merchant almost as well known for his COTEAUX DE L'ARDECHE Chardonnays as for his Burgundies. Latour's white Burgundies are much better than the reds, although the red CORTON-Grancey★★ can be very good. Latour's oaky CORTON-CHARLEMAGNE★★, from his own vineyard, is his top wine, but there is also good CHEVALIER-MONTRACHET★★, BATARD-MONTRACHET★★ and le MONTRACHET★★. Even so, as these are the greatest white vineyards in Burgundy, there really should be more top performances. Best years: (top whites) (2007) 06 05 **04 02 00 99**.

CH. LATOUR-MARTILLAC *Pessac-Léognan AC, Cru Classé de Graves, Bordeaux, France* The vineyard here is strictly organic, and has many ancient vines. The deep, dark, well-structured reds★ improved considerably in the 1990s. Whites★ are thoroughly modern and of good quality. Good value as well. Best years: (reds) 2006 05 04 **03** 02 **01** 00 **98** 96 95 90; (whites) 2006 **05 04 02 01 00 99 98 96**.

CH. LATOUR-À-POMEROL★ *Pomerol AC, Bordeaux, France* Directed by Christian MOUEIX of PETRUS fame, this property makes luscious wines with loads of gorgeous fruit and enough tannin to age well. Best years: 2006 05 04 03 02 **01 00 99 98 95 90 89 88 85**.

LATRICIÈRES-CHAMBERTIN AC See CHAMBERTIN AC.

LAUREL GLEN *Sonoma Mountain AVA, California, USA* Owner/winemaker Patrick Campbell makes only Cabernet★★ at his mountaintop winery. This is rich wine with deep fruit flavours, aging after 6–10 years to a perfumed, complex BORDEAUX style. Counterpoint is a label for wine that does not make it into the top-level Cabernet. Terra Rosa is made from bought-in Argentinian wine. A wine called Reds, from Lodi-grown fruit, is great value. Best years: (2005) **02 01 99 98 97 96 95 94 91 90**.

LAURENT-PERRIER *Champagne AC, Champagne, France* Large, family-owned CHAMPAGNE house, offering flavour and quality at reasonable prices. Non-vintage★ is light and savoury; the vintage★★ is delicious, and the top wine, Grand Siècle★★★, is among the finest Champagnes of all. Non-vintage rosé★ is good and vintage Alexandra Rosé★★★ is excellent. Best years: 1999 **97 96 95 90 88 85 82**.

L'AVENIR *Stellenbosch WO, South Africa* Chenin Blanc and Pinotage remain the focus under new owner Chablis merchant Michel LAROCHE. Three Pinotages, from cheerfully fruity, via well-oaked★ to flagship, ageworthy Grand Vin Pinotage★★ are echoed by a stylish pair of Chenin Blancs (L'Avenir★). Promising Chardonnay★, Cabernet★ and BORDEAUX-blend Stellenbosch Classic★. Best years: (Pinotage) **2006 05 04 03 02 01 00 99 98**.

CH. LAVILLE-HAUT-BRION★★★ *Pessac-Léognan AC, Cru Classé de Graves, Bordeaux, France* One of the finest white PESSAC-LEOGNANs, with a price tag to match. Fermented in barrel, it needs 10 years or more to reach its savoury but luscious peak. Best years: 2006 05 **04 03 02 01 00 98 96 95 94 93 90 89**.

DOMAINE COSTA LAZARIDI *Drama, Greece* State-of-the-art, Bordeaux-inspired winery making good use of indigenous and international varieties. Fresh gooseberry Amethystos white★ (Sauvignon Blanc, Sémillon and Assyrtiko); a fascinatingly intense Viognier★ with a stunning, oily, peach kernel finish; tasty Château Julia Chardonnay★; and fine Amethystos Cava★, an oak-aged Cabernet from very low yields.

LAZIO *Italy* Region best known for FRASCATI, Rome's white glugger. There are also various bland whites from Trebbiano and Malvasia, such as EST! EST!! EST!!! DI MONTEFIASCONE. The region's most interesting wines are reds based on Cabernet, Merlot and Sangiovese; the local Cesanese can also do well. Some of the best come from Castel de Paolis (Quattro Mori★★), Paolo di Mauro (Vigna del Vassallo★★), Cerveteri co-op (Tertium★) and FALESCO (Montiano★★), with other good wines from Casale del Giglio★, Pietra Pinta★ and Trappolini★.

LE BRUN *Marlborough, South Island, New Zealand* CHAMPAGNE-method specialist, with vintage Blanc de Blancs★, and tasty blended vintage and non-vintage bubblies. Quality has languished in recent years but may get a boost from new brand owner Lion Nathan. New release 1998 Blanc de Blancs is delicious. Best years: (Blanc de Blancs) **1998 97 96 95**.

LEASINGHAM *Clare Valley, South Australia* A wing of HARDY, Leasingham is one of CLARE VALLEY's largest wineries, and is well respected. Riesling★★ can be among Clare's best, and Sparkling Shiraz★★ is excellent. Bin 56 Cabernet-Malbec★ and Bin 61 Shiraz★ are powerful, mid-price reds, while Classic Clare Shiraz★★ and Cabernet★ are high-alcohol, heavily oaked, heavily-priced blockbusters. Budget-priced ranges Magnus and Circa 1893 are good value.

L'ECOLE NO 41 *Walla Walla Valley AVA, Washington State, USA* Velvety and deeply flavoured Seven Hills Vineyard Merlot★, good Cabernet Sauvignon★ and lush Syrah★★; a BORDEAUX blend called Apogee★★ from the Pepper Bridge vineyard in WALLA WALLA is dark and challenging. The best wines are the barrel-fermented Semillons: a nutty COLUMBIA VALLEY★★ version and exciting single-vineyard Fries Vineyard★★ and Seven Hills Vineyard★★. The Chardonnay★ is pleasant and minerally. Best years: (top reds) (2006) 05 **04 03 02 01**.

LEEUWIN ESTATE *Margaret River, Western Australia* MARGARET RIVER's high flier, with pricey Chardonnay (Art Series★★★) that gets Burgundy lovers drooling. Art Series Cabernet Sauvignon★★ (sometimes ★★★) has improved dramatically since 1998 and exhibits superb blackcurrant and cedar balance. Art Series Riesling★★ is complex and fine, and look out for exceptional Shiraz★★ to come. New labels Prelude and Siblings give Leeuwin pleasure at lower prices. Best years: (Art Series Chardonnay) (2007) 06 05 04 **02 01 00 99 98 97 96 95**.

DOM. LEFLAIVE *Puligny-Montrachet, Côte de Beaune, Burgundy, France* Famous white Burgundy producer with extensive holdings in some of the greatest vineyards of PULIGNY-MONTRACHET, including les Pucelles★★★, Chevalier-MONTRACHET★★★, BATARD-MONTRACHET★★★ and a tiny slice of le MONTRACHET★★★. After a disappointing patch, Anne-Claude Leflaive has taken the family domaine right back to the top using biodynamic methods. These extraordinarily fine wines can age for 20 years and are understandably expensive. More reasonably priced Mâcon-Verzé was launched in 2004. Best years: (2007) 06 05 **03** 02 **01 00 99**.

OLIVIER LEFLAIVE *Puligny-Montrachet, Côte de Beaune, Burgundy, France* Négociant Olivier Leflaive specializes in crisp, modern white wines from the COTE D'OR and the COTE CHALONNAISE, but standards are far from consistent. Lesser ACs – ST-ROMAIN★, MONTAGNY★, ST-AUBIN★, RULLY★ – offer good value, but the rich, oaky BATARD-MONTRACHET★★★ is the star turn. Best years: (top whites) (2007) **06 05 04 02**.

PETER LEHMANN *Barossa Valley, South Australia* BAROSSA doyen Lehmann buys grapes from many local growers and owns the superb Stonewell vineyard, which contributes its fruit and name to his best Shiraz★★★. Juicy, old-fashioned, fruit-packed reds include Grenache-Shiraz★, Mentor★★ and Eight Songs Shiraz★★. Also lemony Semillon★★ and Chenin★, and dry, long-lived Eden Valley Riesling★★ (Reserve★★★). Bought by California-based Donald HESS in 2003. Befuddling array of new budget lines like 'Weighbridge' and 'My Word is my Bond' – but the quality is holding up so far. Best years: (Stonewell Shiraz) (2006) (04) 03 0
01 **99 98 96 94 93 92 91 90 89**.

JOSEF LEITZ *Rüdesheim, Rheingau, Germany* Some of the RHEINGAU's best dr and off-dry Rieslings come from this RUDESHEIM grower, especially from the Berg Rottland★★ and Berg Schlossberg★★ sites, whose recent vintages have been the best yet. Best years: (2007) 06 05 **04 03 02 01 00 99**.

LEIWEN *Mosel, Germany* This unspectacular village has become a hotbed of the MOSEL Riesling revolution. Nowhere else in the region is there such a concentration of dynamic estates and new ideas. Best producers: GRANS-FASSIAN★★, Carl Loewen★★, Josef Rosch★★, St Urbans-Hof★★, Heinz Schmitt. Best years: (2007) 06 05 **04 03 02 01 99 98**.

LEMBERGER See BLAUFRÄNKISCH.

LENZ WINERY *Long Island AVA, New York State, USA* A leading LONG ISLAND winery going from strength to strength. The Estate Merlot★★ is elegant and powerful with soft, balanced tannins; dry Gewürztraminer★ is spicy and tasty. In good vintages the Pinot Noir★ has deep, ripe fruit Chardonnay★ is mostly good.

LEONETTI CELLAR *Walla Walla Valley AVA, Washington State, USA* Rich and velvety Cabernet Sauvignon★★ and Merlot★★ aged in a combination of French and American oak. A dense and powerful Reserve★★★ uses the best barrels. Sangiovese★★ has very fine texture and lots of new wood The focus is on vineyard management and most of the fruit is now estate grown. Best years: (2006) 05 **04 03 02 01 00**.

CH. LÉOVILLE-BARTON★★★ *St-Julien AC, 2ème Cru Classé, Haut-Médoc, Bordeaux, France* Made by Anthony Barton, whose family has run this ST-JULIEN property since 1826, this fine claret is a traditionalist's delight. Dark, dry and tannic, and not overly oaked, the wines are often underestimated, but over 10–15 years they achieve a lean yet sensitively proportioned beauty rarely equalled in Bordeaux. Moreover, they are never overpriced. Second wine: Réserve de Léoville-Barton. Best years: 2006 05 04 03 02
01 00 **99 98 96 95 94 93 90 89 88 86 85**.

CH. LÉOVILLE-LAS-CASES★★★ *St-Julien AC, 2ème Cru Classé, Haut-Médoc Bordeaux, France* The largest of the 3 Léoville properties, making wines of startlingly deep, dark concentration. I now find them so dense and thick in texture that it is difficult to identify them as ST-JULIEN. Second wine: Clos du Marquis. Best years: 2006 05 04 03 02 01 00 **99 98 96 95 94 93 90 89 88 86 85**.

CH. LÉOVILLE-POYFERRÉ★★ *St-Julien AC, 2ème Cru Classé, Haut-Médoc, Bordeaux, France* Since the 1986 vintage Didier Cuvelier has gradually increased the richness of the wine without wavering from its austere style. A string of excellent wines in the 90s frequently show more classic ST-JULIEN style than those of neighbour LEOVILLE-LAS-CASES. Second wine: Moulin-Riche. Best years: 2006 05 04 03 02 **01** 00 **99 98 96 95 94 90** 89 86.

DOM. LEROY *Vosne-Romanée, Côte de Nuits, Burgundy, France* In 1988 Lalou Bize-Leroy bought the former Dom. Noëllat in VOSNE-ROMANEE, renaming it Domaine Leroy, which should not be confused with her négociant house, Maison Leroy, which contains stocks of great mature vintages, or her personal estate, Dom. d'Auvenay. Here she produces fiendishly expensive, though fabulously concentrated, wines with biodynamic methods and almost ludicrously low yields from top vineyards such as CHAMBERTIN★★★, CLOS DE VOUGEOT★★★, MUSIGNY★★★, RICHEBOURG★★★ and ROMANEE-ST-VIVANT★★★. Best years: (top reds) (2007) 06 05 03 02 **01 00 99 98 97 96 95 90** 89.

LIEBFRAUMILCH *Pfalz, Rheinhessen, Nahe and Rheingau, Germany* Sweetish and low in acidity, Liebfraumilch rightly has a downmarket image. It can come from any of these four regions and 70% of the blend must be Müller-Thurgau, Kerner, Riesling and Silvaner.

LIGER-BELAIR *Côte de Nuits, Burgundy, France* Vicomte Louis-Michel Liger-Belair makes stylish, perfumed wines at the family estate in VOSNE-ROMANEE, including the monopoly of la ROMANEE★★★ itself, while his cousin Thibault Liger-Belair makes rich, plump wines from his NUITS-ST-GEORGES base, including Premier Cru les St Georges★★ and Grands Crus RICHEBOURG★★ and CLOS DE VOUGEOT★★. Best years: (Vicomte) (2007) 06 05 03 02 **01 00** 99; (Thibault) (2007) 06 05 **04 03 02**.

LIGURIA *Italy* Thin coastal strip of north-west Italy, running from the French border at Ventimiglia to the Tuscan border. Best-known wines, though mostly drunk by natives or tourists, are the Cinqueterre, Colli di Luna, Riviera Ligure di Ponente and Rossese di Dolceacqua DOCs.

LIMARÍ VALLEY *Chile* Best known in Chile for pisco (the local brandy), during the past decade this valley – 400km (250 miles) north of Santiago – has shown that its cold ocean influence and its clay and chalky soil can produce world-class wines. Chardonnay and Syrah are the top performers, both expressing fresh, vibrant flavours and subtle yet clear minerality. Tabalí are the best producers so far (Syrah★★) but expect more in the near future. Best producers: DE MARTINO, Maycas/CONCHA Y TORO, Tabalí/SAN PEDRO, Tamaya.

LIMESTONE COAST *South Australia* Zone for south-east of South Australia, including COONAWARRA, PADTHAWAY, Mount Benson and Wrattonbully. Plantings near Mount Gambier, Bordertown and Robe may seek official recognition in the future. New vineyards in this far-flung area have Coonawarra-like terra rossa soil with great potential. The Foster's Wine Group, YALUMBA, HARDY and Pernod Ricard are all involved.

LIMOUX AC *Languedoc, France* The first AC in the LANGUEDOC to allow Chardonnay and Chenin Blanc, which must be vinified in oak. Production is dominated by the SIEUR D'ARQUES co-op. From 2004 a red

187

Limoux AC has been made from Merlot and Cabernet with loca
varieties. **Best producers: d'ANTUGNAC★, Begude★, SIEUR D'ARQUES★.**

LINDEMANS *Murray Darling, Victoria, Australia* Large, historic company that i
a key part of the Foster's Wine Group even though it suffered from th
corporate chaos of the Southcorp days. Traditionally strong i
COONAWARRA, where the best wines are the mineral St Georg
Cabernet★★, spicy Limestone Ridge Shiraz-Cabernet★★ and the re
BORDEAUX-blend Pyrus★★. Reserve-label reds from the LIMESTONE COAS
are good value. Decent mass-market wines in the Bin range. Using th
Lindemans name for non-Australian blends is a worrying developmen
Best years: (Coonawarra reds) 2006 05 04 01 99 98 96 94 91 90 88 86.

LIRAC AC *Rhône Valley, France* Underrated AC between TAVEL an
CHATEAUNEUF-DU-PAPE. Reds have the dusty, spicy red fruit of Châteauneu
without quite the intensity. They age well but are delicious young
Refreshing rosé has lovely strawberry fruit, and whites can be good
drink them young before the perfume goes. **Best producers: Amido★
Aquéria★, Bouchassy★, Devoy Martine, Duseigneur, la Genestière, Joncier★
Lafond-Roc-Épine★★, Lorentine★, Maby★, Mont-Redon★, la Mordorée★★
Pélaquié★, Roger Sabon★★, St-Roch★, Ségriès★, Tavel co-op★, Zobel. Bes
years: 2007 06 05 04 03 01.**

LISTRAC-MÉDOC AC *Haut-Médoc, Bordeaux, France* Set back from th
Gironde and away from the best HAUT-MEDOC gravel ridges, Listrac wine
can be good but never thrilling, and are marked by solid fruit, a slightl
coarse tannin and an earthy flavour. More Merlot is now being used t
soften the style. **Best producers: Cap Léon Veyrin, CLARKE★, Ducluzea
Fonréaud, Fourcas-Dupré★, Fourcas-Hosten, Fourcas-Loubaney, Grand Listra
co-op, Mayne-Lalande★, Saransot-Dupré. Best years: 2005 03 01 00 96 95 9**

LOIRE VALLEY *France* The Loire river cuts right through the heart o
France. The middle reaches are the home of world-famous SANCERRE an
POUILLY-FUME. The region of TOURAINE makes good Sauvignon Blanc an
Gamay, while at VOUVRAY and MONTLOUIS the Chenin Blanc makes some prett
good fizz and still whites, ranging from sweet to very dry. The Loire's bes
reds are made in SAUMUR-CHAMPIGNY, CHINON and BOURGUEIL, mainly fron
Cabernet Franc, with ANJOU-VILLAGES improving fast. Anjou is famous for ros
but the best wines are white, either sweet from the Layon Valley or dry fron
SAVENNIERES and ANJOU where a new generation of producers are making riche
barrel-fermented and aged wines. Near the mouth of the river around Nante
is MUSCADET. *See also* ANJOU BLANC, ANJOU ROUGE, BONNEZEAUX, CABERNET D'ANJOU
CHEVERNY, COTE ROANNAISE, COTEAUX DE L'AUBANCE, COTEAUX DU LAYON, CREMAN
DE LOIRE, GROS PLANT DU PAYS NANTAIS, JASNIERES, MENETOU-SALON, POUILLY-SUR-LOIR
QUARTS DE CHAUME, QUINCY, REUILLY, ROSE DE LOIRE, ST-NICOLAS-DE-BOURGUEI
SAUMUR, SAUMUR MOUSSEUX, VAL DE LOIRE.

LOMBARDY *Italy* Lombardy, whose capital is Milan, is a larger consume
than producer. Many of the best grapes, especially from OLTREPO PAVESE, go t
provide base wine for Italy's *spumante* industry. However, there are som
interesting wines in Oltrepò Pavese, VALTELLINA, LUGANA and high-qualit
sparkling and still wines in FRANCIACORTA.

LONG ISLAND *New York State, USA* Long Island encompasses 3 AVAs: th
Hamptons; North Fork; and the broader Long Island AVA. People hav
likened growing conditions to BORDEAUX, and the long growing seaso

combined with a maritime influence, does produce similarities. Certainly Merlot and Cabernet Franc are the best reds, with Chardonnay the best white. Best producers: BEDELL★★, CHANNING DAUGHTERS★, LENZ★★, Macari, Martha Clara, Palmer★, Paumanok★, Pellegrini★, Pindar, Raphael, Shinn Estate, Wölffer★. Best years: (reds) (2007) 06 **02 01 00 98 97**.

ONG SHADOWS VINTNERS *Columbia Valley AVA, Washington State, USA* Long Shadows Vintners is a series of small partnerships led by Allen Shoup, encompassing a coterie of wineries located in the heart of the COLUMBIA VALLEY appellation. It includes Pedestal★★ with Michel Rolland, Feather★ with Randy DUNN, Poet's Leap★ with Armin Diel of Schlossgut DIEL, Saggi★ with Ambrogio and Giovanni FOLONARI, Sequel★★ with John Duval and Chester-Kidder★ with Allen Shoup and Gilles Nicault, the head winemaker for the group. The arrangement is unique in that each winery is individually owned and managed as a separate partnership. Best years: (reds) (2006) **05 04**.

DR LOOSEN *Bernkastel, Mosel, Germany* Loosen's estate has portions of some of the MOSEL's most famous vineyards: Treppchen and Prälat in ERDEN, Würzgarten in URZIG, Sonnenuhr in WEHLEN, Himmelreich in GRAACH and Lay in BERNKASTEL. Most of the wines achieve ★★, and Spätlese and Auslese from Wehlen, Ürzig and Erden frequently ★★★. His basic Riesling is excellent, year in year out. A joint venture with CHATEAU STE MICHELLE in Washington is proving exciting. Best years: (2007) 06 05 **04 03 02 01 00 99 98 97 96 95**. See also J L WOLF.

ÓPEZ DE HEREDIA *Rioja DOCa, Rioja, Spain* Family-owned RIOJA company, still aging wines in old oak casks. Younger red wines are called Viña Cubillo★, and mature wines Viña Tondonia★ and Viña Bosconia★. Good, oaky whites, especially Viña Gravonia★. Best years: (Viña Tondonia) **1998 96 95 94 93 91 87 86 85**.

OUPIAC AC *Bordeaux, France* A sweet wine area across the Garonne river from BARSAC. The wines are attractively sweet without being gooey. Drink young in general, though the best can age. Best producers: Clos Jean★, Cros★, Loupiac-Gaudiet, Mémoires★, Noble★, Ricaud, les Roques★. Best years: 2005 **03 02 01 99 98 97 96 95 90**.

CH. LA LOUVIÈRE *Pessac-Léognan AC, Bordeaux, France* The star of PESSAC-LEOGNAN's non-classified estates, its reputation almost entirely due to André Lurton. Well-structured reds★ and fresh, Sauvignon-based whites★★ are excellent value. Best years: (reds) 2006 05 04 **02 01 00 99 98 96 95 90 89**; (whites) 2006 **05 04 03 02 01 00 99 98 96 95**.

STEFANO LUBIANA *Tasmania, Australia* One of the new stars of the Tasmanian wine scene. Vintage★ and non-vintage★ sparkling wines rank with the best in Australia. Chardonnay★ is restrained and elegant, Sauvignon Blanc shows greengage and passionfruit characters, while the Pinot Noir★ has weight, concentration and a velvety texture.

LUGANA DOC *Lombardy, Italy* Dry white (occasionally sparkling) from the Trebbiano di Lugana grape. Well-structured wines from the better producers can develop excitingly over a few years. Best producers: Ca' dei Frati★★, Ottella★, Provenza★, Visconti★, Zenato★, Zeni.

LUJÁN DE CUYO *Mendoza, Argentina* The first DOC in Argentina, declared in 1989, with an average altitude of 1000m (3200ft), Luján de Cuyo's reputation lies in its magnificent old Malbec vines. Best producers: Luigi BOSCA★, CATENA★★, COBOS★, Dominio del Plata★, Finca la Anita, Fabre Montmayou/DOMAINE VISTALBA★, TERRAZAS DE LOS ANDES★★, WEINERT★. Best years: (Malbec) 2006 05 **04 02**.

LUNGAROTTI *Torgiano DOC, Umbria, Italy* Leading, nearly sole, producer of TORGIANO. The Torgiano Riserva (Vigna Monticchio★★) is DOCG. Also makes red San Giorgio★ (Cabernet-Sangiovese) and Chardonnay Palazzi★.

LUSSAC-ST-ÉMILION AC *Bordeaux, France* Much of the wine from this AC, which tastes like a lighter ST-EMILION, is made by the first-rate local co-op and should be drunk within 4 years of the vintage; certain properties are worth seeking out. Best producers: Barbe-Blanche★, Bel-Air, Bellevue, Courlat★, la Grenière, Lussac★, Lyonnat★, Mayne Blanc, des Rochers★. Best years: **2005 03 01 00 98 96 95 90**.

EMILIO LUSTAU *Jerez y Manzanilla DO, Andalucía, Spain* Specializes in supplying 'own-label' wines to supermarkets. Quality is generally good and there are some real stars at the top, especially the Almacenista range★★: very individual sherries from small, private producers.

CH. LYNCH-BAGES *Pauillac AC, 5ème Cru Classé, Haut-Médoc, Bordeaux, France* I am a great fan of Lynch-Bages red★★★ – with its almost succulent richness, its gentle texture and its starburst of flavours, all buttered blackcurrants and mint – and it is now one of PAUILLAC's most popular wines. Sadly, it's no longer underpriced but it's still worth the money. Impressive at 5 years, beautiful at 10 and irresistible at 20. Second wine Haut-Bages-Averous. Since 1990 there has been a small amount of white wine, Blanc de Lynch-Bages★. Best years: (reds) 2006 05 04 03 02 01 00 **99 98 96 95 94 90 89 88 86 85**.

LE MACCHIOLE *Bolgheri, Tuscany, Italy* Eugenio Campolmi died prematurely in 2002, having established Le Macchiole as one of the leading quality estates of the new Tuscany. Mainstay is Paleo Rosso★★, a pure Cabernet (from 2001 100% Cabernet Franc). Best known is the Merlot Messorio★★, while Scrio★★ is one of the best Syrahs in Italy. Best years: (2007) (06) 04 **03 01 00 99 98 97 96 95**.

MÂCON AC *Mâconnais, Burgundy, France* The basic Mâconnais AC, but most whites in the region are labelled under the superior MACON-VILLAGES AC. The wines are rarely exciting. Chardonnay-based Mâcon Blanc especially, is a rather expensive basic quaffer. Drink young. Mâcon Supérieur has sensibly been discontinued. Best producers: Bertillonnes, Bruyère, DUBOEUF, LAFON★.

MÂCON-VILLAGES AC *Mâconnais, Burgundy, France* There is a sea of modestly priced and often modest wines under this appellation, which covers 26 villages. Co-ops still dominate production, but these days a handful of growers make more exciting wines from individually named villages such as Mâcon-Lugny and Mâcon la Roche Vineuse. Co-ops dominate production. Best villages: Bussières, Chaintré, Chardonnay, Charnay, Clessé, Cruzille, Davayé, Igé, Lugny, Prissé, la Roche Vineuse, Uchizy, Verzy. Best producers: D & M Barraud★★, A Bonhomme★★, Bret Brothers★★, Deux Roches★, E Gillet★, la Greffière★★, Guillot-Broux★★, LAFON★, J-J Litaud★, Jean Manciat★, O Merlin★★, R Michel★, Rijckaert★, Robert-Denogent★★, Saumaize-Michelin★, J Thévenet★★, Valette★★, VERGET★, J-J Vincent★. Best years: (2007) **06 05 04**. See also VIRE-CLESSE.

MACULAN *Breganze DOC, Veneto, Italy* Fausto Maculan makes an impressive range under the Breganze DOC, led by Cabernet-Merlot blend Fratta★★ and Cabernet Palazzotto★, along with excellent reds★★ and whites★★ from the Ferrata vineyards. Even more impressive are sweet Torcolato★★ and outstanding Acininobili★★★, made mainly from botrytized Vespaiolo grapes.

ADEIRA DOC *Madeira, Portugal* The subtropical holiday island of Madeira seems an unlikely place to find a serious wine. However, Madeiras are very serious wines indeed and the best can survive to a great age. Modern Madeira was shaped by the oïdium epidemic of the 1850s, which wiped out the vineyards, and phylloxera, which struck in the 1870s. Replantation was with hybrid, non-vinifera vines greatly inferior to the 'noble' and traditional Malvasia (or Malmsey), Boal (or Bual), Verdelho and Sercial varieties. There are incentives to replant the hybrids with European varieties, but progress is slow, and most of the replantations are of the red Tinta Negra. The typically burnt, tangy taste of inexpensive Madeira comes from *estufagem*, heating in huge vats, but modern controls give better flavours than used to be possible. The best wines are aged naturally in the subtropical warmth. All except dry wines are fortified early on and may be sweetened with fortified grape juice before bottling. Basic 3-year-old Madeira is made mainly from Tinta Negra, whereas higher-quality 10-year-old, 15-year-old and vintage wines (from a single year, aged in cask for at least 20 years) tend to be made from 1 of the 4 'noble' grapes. Colheita is an early-bottled vintage Madeira, which can be released after 5 years in wood (7 years for Sercial). **Best producers:** Barbeito, Barros e Souza, H M Borges, HENRIQUES & HENRIQUES, Vinhos Justino Henriques, MADEIRA WINE COMPANY, Pereira d'Oliveira.

MADEIRA WINE COMPANY *Madeira DOC, Madeira, Portugal* This company ships more than half of all Madeira exported in bottle. Among the brand names are Blandy's, Cossart Gordon, Leacock and Miles. Now controlled by the Symington family from the mainland. Big improvements are taking place in 5-, 10- and 15-year-old wines, including a tasty 5-year-old (a blend of Malvasia and Bual) called Alvada★. The vintage wines★★★ are superb. Specially blended 'early release' colheita wines are surprisingly tasty and complete.

MADIRAN AC *South-West France* The gentle hills of Vic-Bilh, north of Pau, have seen a steady revival of the Madiran AC. Several of the best producers use new oak and micro-oxygenation, which helps to soften the rather aggressive wine, based on the tannic Tannat grape – if you're lucky, you'll taste damsons and bitter chocolate. **Best producers:** AYDIE★★, Barréjat★, Berthoumieu★, Bouscassé★★, Capmartin★, CHAPELLE LENCLOS★★, du Crampilh★, Cave de Crouseilles, Laffitte-Teston★, MONTUS★★,

Producteurs PLAIMONT, PRIMO PALATUM★, Viella★. **Best years:** (2005) 04 03 02 01 00 98 97 96.

CH. MAGDELAINE★ *St-Émilion Grand Cru AC, 1er Grand Cru Classé, Bordeaux, France* Dark, rich, aggressive wines, yet with a load of luscious fruit and oaky spice. In lighter years the wine has a gushing, easy, tender fruit and can be enjoyed at 5–10 years. Owned by the quality-conscious company of MOUEIX. **Best years:** 2006 05 04 **03 01 00 99** 98 96 95 90 89 88.

MAIPO, VALLE DEL *Valle Central, Chile* Birthplace of the Chilean wine industry and increasingly encroached upon by Chile's capital, Santiago. Cabernet is king and many premium-priced reds come from here. Good Chardonnay from vineyards close to the Andes. **Best producers:** ALMAVIVA★★★, Antiyal★★, CARMEN★★, CONCHA Y TORO★★, Cousiño Macul, DE MARTINO★, El Principal★★, ERRAZURIZ (Viñedo Chadwick★★), HARAS DE PIRQUE★★, QUEBRADA DE MACUL★★, SANTA RITA★, Tarapacá.

MAJELLA *Coonawarra, South Australia* The Lynn family are long-ter
grapegrowers turned successful winemakers. A trademark lush, swe
vanillin oakiness to the reds is always balanced by dense, opulent frui
The profound Malleea★★★ (Cabernet-Shiraz) is the flagship, while th
Cabernet Sauvignon★★★ (a succulent, fleshy cassis bomb) an
Shiraz★★ are almost as good and very reasonably priced; th
Musician★★ (Cabernet-Shiraz) is an early-drinking bargain.

MÁLAGA DO *Andalucia, Spain* Málaga is a curious blend of sweet win
alcohol and juices; production is dwindling. The best are intensely nutt
raisiny and caramelly. A 'sister' appellation, Sierras de Málaga (created i
2001) includes non-fortified wines. **Best producers:** Gomara★, Lópe
Hermanos★★, Jorge Ordóñez★★, Telmo RODRIGUEZ★, Friedrich Schatz★.

CH. MALARTIC-LAGRAVIÈRE★ *Pessac-Léognan AC, Cru Classé de Grave*
Bordeaux, France A change of ownership in 1997 and massive investmen
in the vineyard and cellars have seen a steady improvement here since th
98 vintage. The tiny amount of white★★ is made from a majority o
Sauvignon Blanc and usually softens after 3–4 years into a lovely nutt
wine. **Best years:** (reds) 2006 05 04 **03** 02 **01** 00 **99** 98 96 90 89; (whites) 200
05 04 03 02 01 **99**.

MALBEC A red grape, rich in tannin and flavour, from South-Wes
France. A major ingredient in CAHORS wines, where it is known a
Auxerrois, it is also planted in the LOIRE, where it is called Côt. Howeve
it is at its best in Chile and especially in Argentina, where it produce
lush-textured, ripe, perfumed, damsony reds. In California, Australi
and New Zealand it sometimes appears in BORDEAUX-style blends. I
South Africa it is used both in blends and for varietal wines.

CH. MALESCOT ST-EXUPÉRY★ *Margaux AC, 3ème Cru Classé, Haut-Médo*
Bordeaux, France Once one of the most scented, exotic reds in Bordeaux
a model of perfumed MARGAUX. In the 1980s Malescot lost its reputatio
as the wine became pale, dilute and uninspired, but since 1995 it ha
begun to rediscover that cassis and violet perfume and return to it
former glory. Can reach ★★, for example in 2004. **Best years: 2006 05 0**
03 02 01 00 99 98 96 95 90.

HERDADE DA MALHADINHA NOVA *Alentejo DOC, Portugal* 2003 arriva
on the ALENTEJO wine scene, owned by the Soares family (who also have a
Algarve wine-shop chain). Ultra-modern winery and wines, makin
Monte da Peceguinha red, white and rosé, and top wines, Malhadinh
Tinto★★ and Malhadinha Branco★.

MALVASIA This grape, probably of Greek origin, is widely planted in Ital
and is found in many guises, both white and red. In Friuli, it is known a
the Malvasia Istriana and produces light, fragrant wines of great charm
while in TUSCANY, UMBRIA and the rest of central Italy it is used to improv
the blend for wines like ORVIETO and FRASCATI. On the islands, Malvasia i
used in the production of rich, dry or sweet wines in Bosa and Cagliar
(in SARDINIA) and in Lipari off the coast of SICILY to make really tast
apricotty sweet wines. As a black grape, Malvasia Nera is blended wit
Negroamaro in southern PUGLIA and with Sangiovese in CHIANTI. Variant
of Malvasia also grow in Spain and mainland Portugal. On the island o
MADEIRA it produces sweet, varietal fortified wine, usually known by it
English name: Malmsey.

A MANCHA DO *Castilla-La Mancha, Spain* Spain's vast central plateau is Europe's biggest delimited wine area. Since 1995, DO regulations have allowed for irrigation and the planting of new, higher-quality grape varieties, including Macabeo (Viura), Verdejo, Chardonnay, Cabernet Sauvignon, Petit Verdot, Merlot and Syrah – and also banned new plantings of the simple white Airén grape. Whites are rarely (see AIREN) exciting but nowadays are often fresh and attractive. Reds can be light and fruity, or richer. Best producers: Ayuso, Campos Reales★, Vinícola de Castilla (Castillo de Alhambra, Señorío de Guadianeja), Finca Antigua★, Fontana★, Muñoz (Blas Muñoz★), Rodriguez & Berger (Santa Elena), Torres Filoso (Arboles de Castillejo), Casa de la Viña.

DOM. ALBERT MANN *Alsace AC, Alsace, France* Powerful, flavoursome and ageworthy wines from a range of Grand Cru vineyards, including intense, mineral Rieslings from Furstentum★★ and Schlossberg★★ and rich Furstentum Gewurztraminer★★. Impressive range of Pinot Gris culminates in some astonishingly concentrated Sélections de Grains Nobles★★★. Basic wines are increasingly stylish. Best years: (Sélection de Grains Nobles Gewurztraminer) (2007) 05 **01 00 98 97 94 89**.

MARANGES AC *Côte de Beaune, Burgundy, France* AC right at the southern tip of the COTE DE BEAUNE. Slightly tough red wines of medium depth which are mainly sold as COTE DE BEAUNE-VILLAGES. Less than 5% of production is white. Best producers: B Bachelet★, M Charleux★, Contat-Grangé★, DROUHIN, GIRARDIN★. Best years: (reds) (2007) **06 05 03 02 99**.

MARCASSIN *Sonoma County, California, USA* Helen Turley focuses on cool-climate Chardonnay and Pinot Noir. Incredible depth and restrained power are the hallmarks here. Tiny quantities of single-vineyard Chardonnays (Alexander Mountain Upper Barn, Three Sisters Vineyard, Marcassin Vineyard) and Pinot Noirs (Marcassin Vineyard, Blue Slide Vineyard) often rank ★★★. Best years: (2005) (04) 03 02 01 **00 99 98 97 96 95**.

MARCHE *Italy* Adriatic region producing increasingly good reds from Montepulciano and Sangiovese, led by ROSSO CONERO and ROSSO PICENO, also from the curiously aromatic, indigenous Lacrima di Morro d'Alba. Good international varietals such as Cabernet, Chardonnay and Merlot under the Marche IGT or Esino DOC are becoming more common, as well as blends with the native grapes. Best of the reds are Boccadigabbia's Akronte★★ (Cabernet), Oasi degli Angeli's Kurni★★ (Montepulciano), Monte Schiavo's Adeodato★★ (Montepulciano), Umani Ronchi's Pelago★★ (Montepulciano-Cabernet-Merlot), La Monacesca's Camerte★★ (Sangiovese-Merlot) and Le Terrazze's Chaos★★ (Montepulciano-Merlot-Syrah). However, the truly original wines here are whites based on VERDICCHIO, from Bucci★★, Colonnara★, Coroncino★★, Garofoli★★, Mancinelli★, La Monacesca★★, Monte Schiavo★★, Sartarelli★, Umani Ronchi★.

MARCILLAC AC *South-West France* Strong, dry red wines (and a little rosé), largely made from a local grape, Fer. The reds are rustic but full of fruit and should be drunk at 2–5 years old. Best producers: Cros/Philippe Teulier, Laurens, Marcillac-Vallon co-op, Jean-Luc Matha.

MAREMMA *Tuscany, Italy* The name given to the Tuscan Tyrrhenian coast, notably the southern part, which was only discovered wine-wise in the early 1970s, thanks to SASSICAIA. DOCs include (south to north): Capalbio, Parrina, Bianco di Pitigliano, MORELLINO DI SCANSANO,

193

Montecucco, Monteregio di Massa Marittima, Val de Cornia, BOLGHER
And of course there's IGT Maremma Toscana. In these clime
compared with inland, Sangiovese comes softer and jammier, th
BORDEAUX grapes thrive and vintages count for much less.

MARGARET RIVER *Western Australia* Planted on the advice of agronomi
John Gladstones from the late 1960s, this coastal region quick
established its name as a leading area for Cabernet, with marvellous
deep, BORDEAUX-like structured reds. Now Chardonnay, concentrate
and opulent, vies with Cabernet for top spot, but there is also fine grass
Semillon, often blended with citrus-zest Sauvignon. Increasingly popul
Shiraz provides the occasional gem, but there's too much dull stuff. Be
producers: Brookland Valley★★, CAPE MENTELLE★★, CULLEN★★★, Devil
Lair★★, Edwards, Gralyn★, HOWARD PARK★★, Juniper Estate, LEEUW
ESTATE★★★, MOSS WOOD★★★, PIERRO★★, SANDALFORD★★, Stella Bella★
VASSE FELIX★★, VOYAGER ESTATE★★, Windance, Woodlands★★, Xanadu. Be
years: (Cabernet-based reds) 2007 05 04 03 **01 00 99 98 96 95 94 91 90**.

MARGAUX AC *Haut-Médoc, Bordeaux, France* AC centred on the village
Margaux. Gravel banks dotted through the vineyards mean the wines ar
rarely heavy and should have a divine perfume after 7–12 years. Be
producers: (Classed Growths) Boyd-Cantenac★, BRANE-CANTENAC★
Dauzac★, FERRIERE★★, Giscours★, ISSAN★, KIRWAN★, LASCOMBES, MALESCOT S
EXUPERY★, MARGAUX★★★, PALMER★★, PRIEURE-LICHINE★, RAUZAN-SEGLA★
Tertre★; (others) ANGLUDET★, Bel-Air Marquis d'Aligre★, Eyrins★,
Gurgue★, LABEGORCE-ZEDE★, Monbrison★, SIRAN★. Best years: 2006 05 04 0
02 01 00 99 96 95.

CH. MARGAUX★★★ *Margaux AC, 1er Cru Classé, Haut-Médoc, Bordeaux, Fran*
Frequently the greatest wine in the MEDOC. Has produced almost flawle
wines since 1978, and inspired winemaker Paul Pontallier continues
produce the best from this great terroir. Also some delicious whit
Pavillon Blanc★★, from Sauvignon Blanc, but it must be the mo
expensive BORDEAUX AC wine by a mile. Second wine: Pavillon Rouge★
Best years: (reds) 2006 05 04 03 02 **01 00 99 98 96 95 94 93 90 89 88 86 8**
(whites) 2006 05 04 02 01 00 **99 98 96 95**.

MARIAH *Mendocino Ridge AVA, Mendocino County, California, USA* Boutiqu
winery producing Zinfandel from a vineyard at 600m (2000f
overlooking the Pacific Ocean. The wines have cherry fruit and natural
high acidity. Mariah Vineyard Zinfandel★★ is the flagship; Poc
Ranch★ is lighter but elegant. A tiny amount of fruit-forward Syrah★
also made. Best years: (Zinfandel) 2005 **02 01 00 99**.

MARLBOROUGH *South Island, New Zealand* Marlborough, a wide, fla
pebbly plain around the town of Blenheim, has enjoyed such spectacul
success as a quality wine region that it is difficult to imagine that the fir
commercial vines were planted as recently as 1973. Marlborough is now hon
to more than half the country's vines. Its long, cool and relatively dry ripenir
season, cool nights and free-draining stony soils are the major assets. I
snappy, aromatic Sauvignon Blanc first brought the region fame worldwid
Fine-flavoured Chardonnay, steely Riesling, elegant CHAMPAGNE-method fiz
and luscious botrytized wines are other successes. Pinot Noir is no
establishing a strong regional identity. Best producers: Cape Campbell★, Cliffo
Bay★, CLOUDY BAY★★, The Crossings★, Dog Point★, Forrest Estate★★, Fox
Island★, Framingham★, FROMM★★, HUNTER'S★, ISABEL★, JACKSON ESTATE★, Lawsor
Dry Hills★, LE BRUN, MONTANA, Mount Riley★, Nautilus★, SAINT CLAIR★★, SERESIN

toneleigh★, VAVASOUR★★, VILLA MARIA★★, WITHER HILLS★★. Best years: Chardonnay) 2007 **06 05 03 01**; (Pinot Noir) (2007) **06 05 04 03 01 00**; (Sauvignon lanc) **2007 06 04**.

1ARQUÉS DE CÁCERES *Rioja DOCa, Rioja, Spain* Go-ahead RIOJA winery making crisp, aromatic, modern whites★ and rosés★, and fleshy, fruity reds (Reservas★) with the emphasis on aging in bottle, not barrel. There is also a luxury red, Gaudium★. Best years: (reds) (2005) **04 03 01 99 98 96 95 94 92 91 90 89**.

1ARQUÉS DE GRIÑÓN *Castilla-La Mancha, Spain* From his estate at Malpica, near Toledo, now with its own Dominio de Valdepusa DO, Carlos Falcó (the eponymous Marqués) produces some impressive wines: Dominio de Valdepusa Cabernet Sauvignon★, Petit Verdot★★, Syrah★ and the top wine, Eméritus★★, a blend of the 3 varieties. A new Graciano★★ vineyard went into production in 2005, with stunning results. The joint venture with the Arco/BERBERANA group, which developed the Marqués de Griñón wines from RIOJA, is now being phased out. Best years: (Eméritus) 2003 **02 01 00 99 98**.

1ARQUÉS DE MURRIETA *Rioja DOCa, Rioja, Spain* This RIOJA bodega faithfully preserves the traditional style of long aging. The splendidly ornate Castillo de Ygay★★ label now includes wines other than Gran Reserva. There's a more modern-styled, upmarket cuvée, Dalmau★★. Whites are dauntingly oaky, reds packed with savoury mulberry fruit. Best years: (reds) (2005) 04 **03 01 00 99 96 95 94 92 91 89 87 85**.

1ARQUÉS DE RISCAL *Rioja DOCa, País Vasco and Rueda DO, Castilla y León, Spain* A producer which has restored its reputation for classic pungent RIOJA reds (Reserva★). Expensive, Cabernet-based Barón de Chirel★★ is made only in selected years. Increasingly aromatic RUEDA whites★. Best years: (Barón de Chirel) **2001 96 95 94**.

1ARSALA DOC *Sicily, Italy* Fortified wines, once as esteemed as sherry or Madeira. A taste of an old Vergine (unsweetened) Marsala, fine and complex, will show why. Today most is sweetened. Purists say this mars its delicate nuances, but DOC regulations allow for sweetening Fine and Superior versions. Best producers: DE BARTOLI★★, Florio (Baglio Florio★, Terre Arse★), Pellegrino (Soleras★, Riserva 1962★).

1ARSANNAY AC *Côte de Nuits, Burgundy, France* Village almost in Dijon, best known for its pleasant but quite austere rosé. Reds are much better: light, but frequently one of Burgundy's most fragrant wines. Whites mostly dull. Best producers: Audoin★, P Charlopin★★, B CLAIR★★, Geantet-Pansiot★★, JADOT★, MEO-CAMUZET★, D MORTET★★, Pataille★★, J & J-L Trapet★. Best years: (reds) (2007) **06 05 03 02**.

1ARSANNE Undervalued white grape yielding rich, nutty, long-lived wines in the northern Rhône (HERMITAGE, CROZES-HERMITAGE, ST-JOSEPH and ST-PERAY), often with the more lively Roussanne. Also used in southern Rhône, PIC ST-LOUP and other LANGUEDOC wines, and performs well in Australia at Mitchelton and TAHBILK. As Ermitage, it produces some good wines in Swiss VALAIS.

1ARTINBOROUGH *North Island, New Zealand* A cool, dry climate, free-draining soil and a passion for quality are this region's greatest assets. Mild autumn weather promotes intense flavours balanced by good acidity: top Pinot Noir and complex Chardonnay, intense Cabernet, full Sauvignon

Blanc and honeyed Riesling. **Best producers:** ATA RANGI★★, CRAGGY RANGE★
DRY RIVER★★★, Escarpment★, MARTINBOROUGH VINEYARD★★, Murdoch James★
Nga Waka★, PALLISER ESTATE★★. **Best years:** (Pinot Noir) (2007) 06 **03 01 00**.

MARTINBOROUGH VINEYARD *Martinborough, North Island, New Zealand*
Famous for Pinot Noir★★ but also makes impressive Chardonnay★
spicy Riesling★, creamy Pinot Gris★ and luscious botrytized styles★
when vintage conditions allow. Good vineyard sites and sensitive
winemaking have produced a string of very elegant wines. **Best years:**
(Pinot Noir) (2007) 06 **03 01 00**.

MARTÍNEZ BUJANDA *Rioja DOCa, País Vasco, Spain* This family-owned firm
known for producing some of the best modern RIOJA, was split in two in
2007: Carlos and Pilar Martínez-Bujanda retain the Finca Valpiedra and
Finca Antigua estates and the Cosecheros y Criadores wine company,
while Jesús Martínez-Bujanda keeps the Valdemar winery in Rioja.
Whites and rosés are young and crisp, reds★ are full of fruit and age well.

MARZEMINO This red grape of northern Italy's TRENTINO province makes
deep-coloured, plummy and zesty reds that are best drunk within 3–
years. **Best producers:** Battistotti★, La Cadalora★, Cavit★, Concilio Vini★
Isera co-op★, Letrari★, Mezzacorona, Eugenio Rosi★, Simoncelli★, Spagnolli★
De Tarczal★, Vallarom★, Vallis Agri★.

DOM. DU MAS BLANC *Banyuls AC, Roussillon, France* Run by the Parcé
family, this estate makes great traditional BANYULS, specializing in the
rimage (early-bottled vintage) style. La Coume★★ is the top name in this
range. Also Banyuls Hors d'Age from a solera laid down in 1955. Jean-
Michel Parcé also makes traditional-style red COLLIOURE Cosprons★★.
Best years: 2003 01 **00 98 96**.

MAS BRUGUIÈRE *Pic St-Loup, Coteaux du Languedoc AC, Languedoc, France* The
basic PIC ST-LOUP red★ has rich, spicy Syrah character, while La
Grenadière★★ develops buckets of black fruit and spice after 3 years.
Super-cuvée Le Septième★★ (seventh generation) is a blend of
Mourvèdre with some Grenache. Calcadiz is an easy-drinking red from
young vines. Aromatic, fruity and refreshingly crisp Roussanne white Les
Mûriers★. **Best years:** (reds) 2004 03 **01 00 99**.

MAS LA CHEVALIÈRE *Vin de Pays d'Oc, Languedoc, France* State-of-the-art
winery created by Chablis producer Michel LAROCHE in the early 1990s.
Innovative wines include La Croix Chevalière★, a blend of Syrah,
Grenache and Mourvèdre, and Mas la Chevalière Rouge★, from the
estate vineyard. Also new range of inexpensive varietals. **Best years:** 2006
01 00 99 98.

MAS DE DAUMAS GASSAC *Vin de Pays de l'Hérault, Languedoc, France* Aimé
Guibert proves that the HERAULT, normally associated with cheap table
wine, can produce fine, ageworthy reds.
The tannic yet rich Cabernet
Sauvignon-based red★ and Réserve de
Gassac★★ and the lush, scented white★
(Viognier, Chardonnay, Petit Manseng
and Chenin) are impressive, if
expensive. Sweet Vin de Laurance★★ is
a triumph. **Best years:** (reds) 2005 **04** 03 02
01 00 99 98 97 96 95 94.

1AS DOIX *Priorat DOCa, Cataluña, Spain* The Doix and Llagostera families own some extraordinary old Garnacha and Cariñena vineyards, which provide the grapes for some equally impressive wines. Doix Vinyes Velles★★★ is probably the first of the new generation PRIORATS to reach the heights of the pioneers such as CLOS ERASMUS, CLOS MOGADOR and Alvaro PALACIOS' L'Ermita. Best years: (2006) 05 04 03 **02 01**.

ARTOLO MASCARELLO *Barolo DOCG, Piedmont, Italy* Bartolo Mascarello died in 2005 following a long period of incapacitation; his daughter Maria Teresa has run the winery since the early 1990s. Proudly traditional, the BAROLO★★★ wines have an exquisite perfume and balance. The Dolcetto★ and Barbera★ can need a little time to soften. Best years: (Barolo) (2007) (06) (04) 03 01 **00 99 98 97 96 95 90 89 88 86 85**.

GIUSEPPE MASCARELLO *Barolo DOCG, Piedmont, Italy* The old house of Giuseppe Mascarello (now run by grandson Mauro) is renowned for dense, vibrant Dolcetto d'Alba (Bricco★★) and intense Barbera (Codana★★), but the pride of the house is BAROLO from the superb south-west-facing Monprivato★★★ vineyard in Castiglione Falletto. A little is now produced as a Riserva, Cà d'Morissio★★★, in top years. Small amounts are also made from the Bricco, Santo Stefano di Perno and Villero vineyards. Best years: (Monprivato) (2007) (06) (04) 03 01 **00 99 98 97 96 95 93 91 90 89 88 85 82 78**.

MASI *Veneto, Italy* Family firm, one of the driving forces in VALPOLICELLA. Brolo di Campofiorin★ (effectively if not legally a *ripasso* Valpolicella) is worth looking out for, as is AMARONE (Mazzano★★ and Campolongo di Torbe★★). Valpolicella's Corvina grape is also used in red blend Toar★; Osar★ is made from a local grape, Oseleta, rediscovered by Masi. The wines of Serègo Alighieri★★ are also produced by Masi. Best years: (Amarone) (2007) (06) 04 **03 01 00 97 95 93 90**.

MASTROBERARDINO *Campania, Italy* This family firm has long flown the flag for CAMPANIA in southern Italy, though it has now been joined by others. Best known for red TAURASI★★ and white Greco di Tufo★ and Fiano di Avellino★. Best years: (Taurasi Radici) (2007) (06) (05) 04 **03 01 99 97 96 95 90 89 88 85 68**.

MATANZAS CREEK *Bennett Valley AVA, Sonoma County, California, USA* Sauvignon Blanc★★ is taken seriously here, and it shows in a complex, zesty wine; Chardonnay★★ is rich and toasty but not overblown. Merlot★★ has silky, mouthfilling richness. Limited-edition Journey Chardonnay★★ and Merlot★★ are opulent but pricey. Owned by Jess Jackson (of KENDALL-JACKSON). Best years: (Chardonnay) 2005 04 **03 02 01 00 99 98 97**; (Merlot) 2004 03 02 01 **00 99 97 96 95**.

MATETIC VINEYARDS *San Antonio, Chile* Matetic has been making high-quality wines from the SAN ANTONIO Valley – especially under the EQ label – since it burst on to the scene in 2001. Exceptional, concentrated and scented Syrah★★ is the star, but there's also a fleshy Pinot Noir★, juicy Sauvignon Blanc★ and refreshing new Coastal★ Sauvignon.

MATUA VALLEY *Auckland, North Island, New Zealand* In 2001 Matua became part of Beringer-Blass (now Foster's Group), with the consequent introduction of an uninspired budget range. Top wines are still good, with whites more consistent than reds: sensuous, scented Ararimu Chardonnay★★; lush, strongly varietal Gewürztraminer★; tangy MARLBOROUGH Sauvignon Blanc★; fine Merlot★; and Ararimu★, a blend of Cabernet Sauvignon, Merlot and occasionally Syrah. Second label: Shingle Peak. Best years: (Ararimu red) **2003 02 00 98**.

CH. MAUCAILLOU★ *Moulis AC, Haut-Médoc, Bordeaux, France* Maucaillou shows that you don't have to be a Classed Growth to make high-quality claret. Expertly made by the Dourthe family, it is soft but classically flavoured. It is accessible early on but ages well for 10–12 years. **Best years:** 2006 05 **04 03 02 00 98 96 95 90**.

MAULE, VALLE DEL *Valle Central, Chile* The most southerly sub-region of Chile's CENTRAL VALLEY, with wet winters and a large day/night temperature difference. Nearly 30% of Chile's vines are planted here, with nearly 10,000ha (25,000 acres) of Cabernet Sauvignon. Merlot does well on the cool clay soils, and there is some tasty Carmenère and Syrah. Whites are mostly Chardonnay and Sauvignon Blanc. A new and exciting community of producers has recently been redefining Maule's identity, and there's a feeling that Maule's old 'bulk' mentality must give way to a quality focus if the area's great potential is to be realized. **Best producers:** J Bouchon, Calina★ (KENDALL-JACKSON), Casa Donoso, Gillmore, La Reserva de Caliboro, Terra Noble.

MAURO *Castilla y León, Spain* After making a name for himself as VEGA SICILIA's winemaker for 30 years, Mariano García propelled his family's estate to the forefront in Spain and abroad. Wines include Crianza★★, Vendimia Seleccionada★★ and Terreus★★★. **Best years:** (2006) 05 **04 03 02 01 00 9**... 98 97 96 95 94.

MAURY AC *Roussillon, France* A *vin doux naturel*, mainly from Grenach... Noir. This strong, sweetish wine can be made in either a young, fresh style (vintage) or the locally revered old *rancio* style. **Best producers:** I Coume du Roy★, Mas Amiel★★, Maury co-op★, Maurydoré★, la Pleiade★.

MAXIMIN GRÜNHAUS *Grünhaus, Mosel-Saar-Ruwer, Germany* One of Germany's great wine estates. Dr Carl von Schubert vinifies separately the wines of his 2 top vineyards, Abtsberg and Herrenberg, both of monastic origin. He makes chiefly dry and medium-dry wines of great subtlety. In good vintages the top wines are certainly ★★★ and are among the most long-lived white wines in the world. **Best years:** (2007) 0... 05 04 **03 01 00 99 97 95 94 93 92 90 89 88 85**.

MAZIS-CHAMBERTIN AC See CHAMBERTIN AC.

MAZOYÈRES-CHAMBERTIN AC See CHAMBERTIN AC.

McLAREN VALE *South Australia* Sunny maritime region south of Adelaide producing superb full-bodied wines from Shiraz, Grenache and Cabernet. Its warmth means that the whites rarely impress, though Coriole's Fiano has raised eyebrows. More than 60 small wineries, plus big boys Hardy and the Foster's Wine Group. **Best producers:** Cascabel, CHAPEL HILL★★, CLARENDON HILLS★★, Coriole★, D'ARENBERG★, FOX CREEK★★, HARDY★★, Kangarilla Road★, Maxwell★, Geoff MERRILL★, Mitolo★★, Oliver's Taranga, SC Pannell★, Penny's Hill, Pirramimma, RockBare, ROSEMOUNT, Tatachilla★, WIRRA WIRRA★★, Woodstock.

McWILLIAM'S *Riverina, New South Wales, Australia* Large family winery whose Hanwood Estate and J J McWilliam brands are joint ventures with California's GALLO, delivering good flavours at a fair price. Best are the Mount Pleasant wines from the HUNTER VALLEY: classic bottle-aged Semillons (Elizabeth★★★, Lovedale★★★), buttery Chardonnays★ and special-vineyard Shirazes – Old Paddock & Old Hill, Maurice O'Shea (★★ in the best years) and Rosehill★. Classy liqueur Muscat★★ from RIVERINA, and good table wines from HILLTOPS Barwang★ vineyard. McWilliam's own Lillydale in the YARRA which is making sublime Chardonnay, BRAND'S in COONAWARRA and have just purchased the

Evans & Tate label following the collapse of the MARGARET RIVER-based company. Best years: (Elizabeth Semillon) (2007) (06) (05) (04) 03 02 01 **00 99 98 97 96 95 94 87 86 84 83 79**.

MÉDOC AC *Bordeaux, France* The Médoc peninsula north of Bordeaux on the left bank of the Gironde river produces a good fistful of the world's most famous reds. These are all situated in the HAUT-MÉDOC, the southern, more gravelly half of the area. The Médoc AC, for reds only, covers the northern part. Merlot dominates in these flat clay vineyards and the wines can be attractive in warm years: dry but juicy. Best at 3–5 years old. Best producers: Bournac★, Escurac★, les Grands Chênes★, Greysac★, Goulée★, L'Inclassable★, Loudenne, Lousteauneuf★, les Ormes-Sorbet★, Patache d'Aux, POTENSAC★★, Preuillac, Ramafort★, Rollan de By★ (Haut Condissas★), la Tour de By★, la Tour Haut-Caussan★, Tour St-Bonnet★, Vieux-Robin. Best years: 2006 05 **04 03 01 00 96 95**.

MEERLUST *Stellenbosch WO, South Africa* Elegant, fresh Chardonnay★ was the earliest beneficiary of new cellarmaster Chris Williams's thoughtful, informed approach; a maiden Cabernet★★ shows he's as adroit with reds. It bodes well for his first vintages of complex Rubicon★, one of the Cape's first BORDEAUX blends, refined, distinctive Merlot and a ripe Pinot Noir from this venerable estate. Best years: (Rubicon) (2004) **03 01 00 99 98 97 96 95 94**; (Chardonnay) (2007) **06 05 04 03 01 00**.

ALPHONSE MELLOT *Sancerre AC, Loire Valley, France* Ambitious biodynamic producer of white and red SANCERRE, made with obsessive attention to detail by Alphonse 'Junior', the 19th generation of the family. The white cuvée La Moussière★ is unoaked, with fresh, intense citrus flavours; the oaked cuvée Edmond★★ needs a few years to mature to a fascinating rich flavour. Red and white Génération XIX★★ are outstanding, with a fine balance of fruit and oak. Since 2005, also makes aromatic, fruity Chardonnay and Pinot Noir, Les Pénitents, in neighbouring Vin de Pays des Coteaux Charitois. Best years: (Edmond) 2007 06 **05 04 03 02 01 00**.

CHARLES MELTON *Barossa Valley, South Australia* One of the leading lights in the renaissance of hand-crafted Shiraz, Grenache and Mourvèdre in the BAROSSA. Fruity Grenache rosé Rose of Virginia★, RHÔNE blend Nine Popes★★, heady, sumptuous Grenache★★, smoky Shiraz★★ and Sparkling Red★★ have all attained cult status. Cabernet Sauvignon is variable, but ★★ at best. Best years: (Nine Popes) (2006) (05) 04 **03 02 01 99 98 96 95 94 91 90**.

MENDOCINO COUNTY *California, USA* The northernmost county of the North Coast AVA. It includes cool-climate ANDERSON VALLEY, excellent for sparkling wines and a little Pinot Noir; and the warmer Redwood Valley AVA, with good Zinfandel and Cabernet. Coro is a stylish Zinfandel-based blend made by numerous Mendocino wineries. Best producers: Brutocao★, FETZER, Fife★, Goldeneye★, HANDLEY★★, Husch, Lazy Creek★, McDowell Valley★, NAVARRO★★★, ROEDERER ESTATE★★, Saracina★, SCHARFFENBERGER CELLARS★. Best years: (reds) (2005) 04 **03 01 00 99 97 96 95 94 93 91 90**.

MENDOCINO RIDGE AVA *California, USA* One of the most unusual AVAs in California. Mendocino Ridge starts at an altitude of 365m (1200ft) on the timber-covered mountaintops of western MENDOCINO COUNTY. Because of the topography, the AVA is non-contiguous: rising above the fog, the vineyards are commonly referred to as 'islands in the sky'. Currently only 30ha (75 acres) are planted, primarily with Zinfandel. Best producers: Edmeades★, Greenwood Ridge★, MARIAH★, STEELE★★.

MERLOT

Red wine without tears. That's the reason Merlot has vaulted from being merely Bordeaux's red wine support act, well behind Cabernet Sauvignon in terms of class, to being the red wine drinker's darling, planted like fury all over the world. It is able to claim some seriousness and pedigree, but – crucially – can make wine of a fat, juicy character mercifully low in tannic bitterness, which can be glugged with gay abandon almost as soon as the juice has squirted from the press. Yet this doesn't mean that Merlot is the jelly baby of red wine grapes. Far from it.

WINE STYLES

Bordeaux Merlot The great wines of Pomerol and St-Émilion, on the right bank of the Dordogne, are largely based on Merlot and the best of these – for example, Château Pétrus, which is almost 100% Merlot – can mature for 20–30 years. In fact there is more Merlot than Cabernet Sauvignon planted throughout Bordeaux, and I doubt if there is a single red wine property that does not have some growing, because the variety ripens early, can cope with cool conditions and is able to bear a heavy crop of fruit. In a cool, damp area like Bordeaux, Cabernet Sauvignon cannot always ripen, so the soft, mellow character of Merlot is fundamental component of the blend even in the best, Cabernet dominated, Médoc estates, imparting a supple richness and approachability to the wines. Up-and-coming areas like Blaye and Côte de Castillon depend on it.

Other European regions The south of France has briskly adopted the variety, producing easy-drinking, fruit-driven wines, but in the hot Languedoc the grape often ripens too fast to express its full personality and can seem a little simple, even raw-edged, unless handled well. Italy has long used very high-crop Merlot to produce a simple, light quaffer in the north, particularly in the Veneto, though Friuli and Alto Adige make fuller styles and there are some very impressive examples from Tuscany and as far south as Sicily. The Swiss canton of Ticino is often unjustly overlooked for its intensely fruity, oak-aged versions. Eastern Europe has the potential to provide fertile pastures for Merlot and so far the most convincing, albeit simple, styles have come from Hungary and Bulgaria; the younger examples are almost invariably better than the old. Spain has developed decent Merlot credentials since the mid-1990s, but has few sites cool enough for the variety.

New World Youth is also important in the New World, nowhere more so than in Chile. Chilean Merlot, mostly blended with Carmenère, has leapt to the front of the pack of New World examples with gorgeous garnet-red wines of unbelievable crunchy fruit richness that cry out to be drunk virtually in their infancy. California Merlots often have more serious pretensions, but the nature of the grape is such that its soft, juicy quality still shines through. The cooler conditions in Washington State have produced some impressive wines, and the east coast of the US has good examples from places such as Long Island. With some French input, South Africa is starting to get Merlot right, and in New Zealand the warm, dry conditions of Hawkes Bay and Waiheke Island are producing classic styles. Only Australia seems to find Merlot problematic, but there are some fine exceptions from cooler areas, including some surprisingly good fizzes – red fizzes, that is!

WOODWARD CANYON

2005

Columbia Valley
Merlot

BEST PRODUCERS

France

Bordeaux (St-Émilion) ANGELUS, AUSONE, BEAU-SEJOUR BECOT, Clos Fourtet, la Mondotte, TERTRE-ROTEBOEUF, TROPLONG-MONDOT, VALANDRAUD; *(Pomerol)* le BON PASTEUR, Certan-de-May, Clinet, la CONSEILLANTE, l'EGLISE-CLINET, l'EVANGILE, la FLEUR-PETRUS, GAZIN, LATOUR-A-POMEROL, PETIT-VILLAGE, PETRUS, le PIN, TROTANOY.

Other European Merlots

Italy (Friuli) Livio FELLUGA; *(Tuscany)* Castello di AMA, AVIGNONESI, Castelgiocondo (Lamaione), Ghizzano, Le MACCHIOLE, ORNELLAIA, Petrolo, San Giusto a Rentennano, TUA RITA; *(Lazio)* FALESCO; *(Sicily)* PLANETA.

Spain (Navarra) Nekeas; *(Penedès)* Can Ràfols dels Caus; *(Somontano)* ENATE; *(Vino de la Tierra de Castilla)* Pago del Ama.

Switzerland Gialdi (Sassi Grossi), Daniel Huber, La Capellaccia, Terreni alla Maggia, Christian Zündel.

New World Merlots

USA (California) ARROWOOD, BERINGER, CHATEAU ST JEAN, MATANZAS CREEK, MERRYVALE, NEWTON, Pahlmeyer, SHAFER, STERLING; *(Washington)* ANDREW WILL, LEONETTI, QUILCEDA CREEK, WOODWARD CANYON; *(New York)* BEDELL, LENZ.

Australia BRAND'S, CLARENDON HILLS, COLDSTREAM HILLS, Elderton, James Irvine, PARKER COONAWARRA ESTATE, PETALUMA, Tatachilla, YALUMBA (Heggies).

New Zealand CRAGGY RANGE, Esk Valley, GOLDWATER, C J PASK, Sacred Hill (Broken Stone), TRINITY HILL, VILLA MARIA.

South Africa STEENBERG, THELEMA, VEENWOUDEN, VERGELEGEN.

Chile CARMEN, CASA LAPOSTOLLE (Cuvée Alexandre), CASABLANCA (Santa Isabel), CONCHA Y TORO, CONO SUR (20 Barrels).

MENDOZA *Argentina* The most important wine province in Argentina accounting for around 80% of the country's wine. Situated in the eastern foothills of the Andes, Mendoza's bone-dry climate produces powerful high-alcohol reds. Just south of Mendoza city, Maipú and LUJAN DE CUYO are ideal for Malbec, Syrah and Cabernet Sauvignon. High-altitude regions nearer the Andes, such as UCO VALLEY, produce better whites, particularly Chardonnay, but also thrilling reds. Best producers: ACHAVAL-FERRER★★, ALTOS LAS HORMIGAS★, Luigi BOSCA, CATENA★★, COBOS★, Finca El Retiro★, O FOURNIER★★, Nieto Senetiner (Cadus★★), NORTON★, Salentein★ TERRAZAS DE LOS ANDES★★, Familia ZUCCARDI★.

MENETOU-SALON AC *Loire Valley, France* Attractive, chalky-clean Sauvignon whites and cherry-fresh Pinot Noir reds and rosés from west of SANCERRE. Best producers: R Champault, Chatenoy★, Chavet★, J-P Gilbert★, P Jacolin, J Mellot, H Pellé★, J-M Roger★, J Teiller★, Tour St-Martin★.

MÉO-CAMUZET *Vosne-Romanée, Côte de Nuits, Burgundy, France* Super-quality estate, run by Jean-Nicolas Méo. New oak barrels and luscious, rich fruit combine in superb wines, which also age well. CLOS DE VOUGEOT★★★, RICHEBOURG★★★ and CORTON★★ are the grandest wines, along with the VOSNE-ROMANEE Premiers Crus, aux Brulées★★, Cros Parantoux★★★ and les Chaumes★★. Fine NUITS-ST-GEORGES aux Boudots★★ and aux Murgers★★, and now also some less expensive négociant wines. Best years: (2007) 06 05 04 03 02 **01 00 99 97 96 95 93 90**.

MERCUREY AC *Côte Chalonnaise, Burgundy, France* Most important of the 4 main COTE CHALONNAISE villages. The red is usually pleasant and strawberry-flavoured, sometimes rustic, and can take some aging. There is not much white, but I like its buttery, even spicy, taste. Best at 3–4 years old. Best producers: (reds) FAIVELEY★, Hasard★, E Juillot★, M Juillot★, Lorenzon★★, F Raquillet★★, RODET★, de Suremain★★, de Villaine★★; (whites) FAIVELEY (Clos Rochette★), M Juillot★, O LEFLAIVE★, Ch. de Chamirey★/RODET. Best years: (reds) (2007) 05 **03 02 01** 99.

MERLOT See pages 200–1.

GEOFF MERRILL *McLaren Vale, South Australia* High-profile winemaker with an instinctive feel for wine. There's a nicely bottle-aged Reserve Cabernet★ in a light, early-picked, slightly eccentric style, Reserve Shiraz★ (Henley Shiraz★★) and Chardonnay★ (Reserve★★). Also a moreish unoaked and ageworthy Bush Vine Grenache★★.

MERRYVALE *Napa Valley AVA, California, USA* A Chardonnay powerhouse (Reserve★★, Silhouette★★, Starmont★★), but reds are not far behind, with BORDEAUX-blend Profile★★ and juicy Reserve Merlot★★. Best years: (Chardonnay) 2006 **05 04 03 02 01 00** 99.

MEURSAULT AC *Côte de Beaune, Burgundy, France* The biggest and most popular white wine village in the COTE D'OR. There are no Grands Crus, but a whole cluster of Premiers Crus, of which Perrières, Charmes and Genevrières stand out. The general standard is better than in neighbouring Puligny. The golden wine is lovely to drink young but better aged for 5–8 years. Virtually no Meursault red is now made. Best producers: R Ampeau★★, M BOUZEREAU★★, V Bouzereau★, Boyer-Martenot★, Coche-Bizouard★★, COCHE-DURY★★★, Deux MONTILLE★, DROUHIN★, A Ente★★★, J-P Fichet★, Henri Germain★, V GIRARDIN★, Grux★, JADOT★★, P Javillier★★, François Jobard★★, Rémi Jobard★★, LAFON★★★, Christophe Mary★★, Matrot★★, Mikulski★, Pierre Morey★★, G Roulot★★★. Best years: (2007) 06 05 **04 02 01 00** 99.

CH. MEYNEY★ *St-Estèphe AC, Haut-Médoc, Bordeaux, France*   One of the most reliable ST-ESTEPHES, producing broad-flavoured wine with dark, plummy fruit. Second wine: Prieur de Meyney. Best years: 2006 05 04 03 **02 01 00** 99 98 96 95 94 90 89.

PETER MICHAEL WINERY *Sonoma County, California, USA*   British-born Sir Peter Michael has turned a country retreat into an impressive winery known for its small-batch wines. Les Pavots★★ is the estate red BORDEAUX blend, and Mon Plaisir★★ and Cuvée Indigène★ are his top Chardonnays, both noted for their deep, layered flavours. Best years: (Les Pavots) (2005) 04 03 02 **01 00** 99 97 96 95 94 91 90.

MILLTON *Gisborne, North Island, New Zealand*   Organic vineyard using biodynamic methods, whose top wines include the sophisticated Clos de Ste Anne Chardonnay★★, Opou Vineyard Riesling★ and complex barrel-fermented Chenin Blanc★. Chardonnays and Rieslings both age well. Best years: (whites) **2007 05 04 02 00**.

MINER FAMILY VINEYARDS *Oakville AVA, California, USA*   Dave Miner has 32ha (80 acres) planted on a ranch 300m (1000 ft) above the OAKVILLE valley floor. Highlights include yeasty, full-bodied Chardonnay★ (Oakville Ranch★★, Wild Yeast★★) as well as intense Merlot★★ and Cabernet Sauvignon★★ that demand a decade of aging. Also a stylish Viognier★★ and a striking Rosé★ from purchased fruit.

MINERVOIS AC *Languedoc, France*   Attractive, mostly red wines from north-east of Carcassonne, made mainly from Syrah, Carignan and Grenache. The local co-ops produce good, juicy, quaffing wine at reasonable prices, but the best wines are made by the estates: full of ripe, red fruit and pine-dust perfume, for drinking young. It can age, especially if a little new oak has been used. A village denomination, La Livinière, covering 6 superior communes whose wines can be particularly scented and fine, can be appended to the Minervois label. Best producers: (reds) Aires Hautes★, Ch. Bonhomme★, Borie de Maurel★, CLOS CENTEILLES★★, Pierre Cros★, Fabas★, la Grave, HECHT & BANNIER★, Maris★, Oustal Blanc★, PRIMO PALATUM★, Pujol, Rieux, Senat★★, Ste-Eulalie★, TOUR BOISEE★, Villerambert-Julien★. Best years: (2005) 04 03 01 00 99.

CH. LA MISSION-HAUT-BRION★★★ *Pessac-Léognan AC, Cru Classé de Graves, Bordeaux, France*   Traditionally I have found la Mission long on power but short on grace, but in the difficult years of the 1990s it showed impressive consistency allied to challenging intensity and fragrance. Occasionally better (as in 2000) than stablemate HAUT-BRION. Best years: 2006 05 04 03 02 **01 00** 98 96 95 94 90 89 88 85.

MISSION HILL *Okanagan Valley VQA, British Columbia, Canada*   The winery has expanded its facilities and its operations and hired consultant Michel Rolland to help Kiwi winemaker John Simes craft some of the most noteworthy wines from OKANAGAN VALLEY. Excellent Chardonnay★★, Pinot Blanc★ and Pinot Grigio★ are joined by Merlot★, Cabernet Sauvignon, Pinot Noir and Shiraz★, and a red BORDEAUX-style blend, Oculus★★.

MITCHELL *Clare Valley, South Australia*   Jane and Andrew Mitchell turn out some of CLARE VALLEY's most ageworthy Watervale Riesling★★ and a classy barrel-fermented Growers Semillon★. Growers Grenache★ is a huge unwooded and heady fruit bomb, if you're in the mood... Peppertree Shiraz★★ and Sevenhill Cabernet Sauvignon★ are plump, chocolaty and typical of the region.

203

MITTELRHEIN *Germany* Small (465ha/1150-acre), northerly wine region Almost 70% of the wine here is Riesling, but the Mittelrhein is in decline as the vineyard sites are steep and difficult to work. The best growers (like Ton, JOST★, Müller★, Perll★ and Weingart★★), clustered around Bacharach and Boppard, make wines of a striking mineral tang and dry, fruity intensity. Best years: (2007) 06 05 **04 02 01** 99.

MOËT & CHANDON *Champagne AC, Champagne, France* Moët & Chandon dominates the CHAMPAGNE market (more than 25 million bottles a year), and has become a major producer of sparkling wine in California, Argentina, Brazil and Australia too. Non-vintage has started to exhibit distressing unreliability, and some recent releases have really not been acceptable. There has been a change of winemaker and hopefully this will put the vintage release at least back on track. Interestingly, the vintage rosé★★ can show a rare Pinot Noir floral fragrance. Dom Pérignon★★★ is the de luxe cuvée. It can be one of the greatest Champagnes of all, but you've got to age it for a number of years after release or you're wasting your money. Best years: 2003 (02) 00 99 **98** 96 **95 90 88 86 85 82**.

MARKUS MOLITOR *Bernkastel-Wehlen, Mosel, Germany* Dynamic estate with fine vineyards throughout Middle MOSEL and Saar. Brilliant Riesling Auslesen, often ★★★, and probably the best Spätburgunder (Pinot Noir)★ from the Mosel. Best years: (2007) 06 05 **04 03 02 01 00** 99.

MONBAZILLAC AC *South-West France* BERGERAC's leading sweet wine. Most is light, pleasant, but forgettable, from the co-op. However, an increasing number of estates are making wines of a richness to approach SAUTERNES, and the ability to age 10 years. Best producers: l'ANCIENNE CURE★, Bélingard (Blanche de Bosredon★), la Borderie★, Grande Maison★, Haut-Bernasse, Haut-Montlong (Grande Cuvée), Theulet★, Tirecul-la-Gravière★★, Les Verdots★, Treuil-de-Nailhac★. Best years: 2005 03 02 **01 99 98** 97 96.

CH. MONBOUSQUET★ *St-Émilion Grand Cru AC, Grand Cru Classé, Bordeaux, France* Gérard Perse, owner of Ch. PAVIE, has transformed this struggling estate into one of ST-EMILION's 'super-crus'. The reward was promotion to Grand Cru Classé in 2006. Rich, voluptuous and very expensive, the wine is drinkable from 3–4 years but will age longer. Also a plush white Monbousquet★ (BORDEAUX AC). Best years: 2006 05 **04 03 02 01 00 99 98** 96 95 94.

ROBERT MONDAVI *Napa Valley, California, USA* A Californian institution, best known for open and fruity regular Cabernet Sauvignon★ and the Reserve Cabernet★★, possessing enormous depth and power. A regular★ and a Reserve★★ Pinot Noir are velvety smooth and supple wines with style, perfume and balance. For many years the Mondavi signature white was Fumé Blanc (Sauvignon Blanc), but in recent years Chardonnay★ (Reserve★★) has overtaken it. The Robert Mondavi Winery is now part of Constellation's Icon Estates portfolio; Mondavi's lower-priced 'lifestyle' lines, Private Selection and Woodbridge (from Lodi in the CENTRAL VALLEY), are promoted separately. Best years: (Cabernet Sauvignon Reserve) (2005) 04 03 **02 01 00 99 98** 97 96 95 94 92 91 87.

MONSANTO *Chianti Classico DOCG, Tuscany, Italy* Fabrizio Bianchi, with his daughter Laura, makes a range of Sangiovese-based wines topped by the CHIANTI CLASSICO Riserva Il Poggio★★★, a complex and attentiondemanding single-vineyard cru which until recently would have been considered too 'traditional' for its discreet austerity and need of bottle age. 100% Sangiovese IGT 'Fabrizio Bianchi'★★ is almost as fine. Best years: (2007) (06) (04) 01 **99 97 88 82 77**.

MONT TAUCH, LES PRODUCTEURS DU *Fitou, Languedoc-Roussillon, France* A big, quality-conscious co-op producing a large range of wines, from good gutsy FITOU★ and CORBIERES to rich MUSCAT DE RIVESALTES★ and light but gluggable Vin de Pays du Torgan. Top wines: Les Quatre★, Les Douze★. Best years: (Les Douze) (2005) 03 **01 00**.

MONTAGNE-ST-ÉMILION AC *Bordeaux, France* A ST-EMILION satellite which can produce rather good red wines. The wines are normally ready to drink in 4 years but age quite well in their slightly earthy way. Best producers: Calon★, Croix Beauséjour★, Faizeau★, Gachon★, Laurets, Maison Blanche, Montaiguillon★, Négrit, Roc-de-Calon, Rocher Corbin★, Roudier, Teyssier, Vieux-Ch.-St-André★. Best years: 2005 03 **01 00** 98 96 95.

MONTAGNY AC *Côte Chalonnaise, Burgundy, France* Wines from this Côte Chalonnaise village can be rather lean, but are greatly improved now that some producers are aging their wines for a few months in new oak. Generally best with 2–5 years' bottle age. Best producers: S Aladame★★, BOUCHARD PERE ET FILS★, la BUXYNOISE★, Davenay★, FAIVELEY, Louis LATOUR★, O LEFLAIVE★, A Roy★, J Vachet★. Best years: (2007) **05 04 02**.

MONTALCINO See BRUNELLO DI MONTALCINO DOCG.

MONTANA *Auckland, Gisborne, Hawkes Bay and Marlborough, New Zealand* Owned since 2005 by French giant Pernod Ricard, which produces an estimated 40% of New Zealand's wine. Montana's MARLBOROUGH Sauvignon Blanc★ and GISBORNE Chardonnay are in a considerable way to thank for putting New Zealand on the international wine map. Estate bottlings of whites, especially in the Terroir series, are also generally good. Montana is now one of the world's biggest producers of Pinot Noir★, and each vintage the quality improves and the price stays fair. Consistent Lindauer fizz and, with the help of the Champagne house DEUTZ, austere yet full-bodied Deutz Marlborough Cuvée NV Brut★★. CHURCH ROAD, in HAWKES BAY, aims to produce premium reds, but Chardonnay★★ is better. As well as Corbans, Pernod Ricard also acquired Stoneleigh, with top-selling Marlborough Sauvignon Blanc★ and Riesling★ and tasty new Rapaura Series★. Extensive plantings in Waipara are now bearing exciting results under the Camshorn label.

MONTECARLO DOC *Tuscany, Italy* Distinctive reds (Sangiovese with Syrah) and whites (Trebbiano with Sémillon and Pinot Grigio). Also non-DOC Cabernet, Merlot, Pinot Bianco, Roussanne and Vermentino. Best producers: Buonamico★, Carmignani★, Montechiari★, La Torre★, Wandanna★. Best years: (reds) (2007) 04 03 01 00 99 97.

MONTEFALCO DOC *Umbria, Italy* Good Sangiovese-based Montefalco Rosso is outclassed by dense, massive Sagrantino di Montefalco DOCG (dry) and glorious sweet red Sagrantino Passito from dried grapes. Best producers: (Sagrantino) Adanti★, Antonelli★, Caprai★★ (25 Anni★★★), Colpetrone★★. Best years: (Sagrantino) (2007) (06) 04 **03 01 00** 99 98 97.

MONTEPULCIANO Grape grown mostly in eastern Italy (unconnected with TUSCANY's Sangiovese-based wine VINO NOBILE DI MONTEPULCIANO). Can produce deep-coloured, fleshy, spicy wines with moderate tannin and acidity. Besides MONTEPULCIANO D'ABRUZZO, it is used in ROSSO CONERO and ROSSO PICENO in the MARCHE and also in UMBRIA, Molise and PUGLIA.

MONTEPULCIANO D'ABRUZZO DOC *Abruzzo, Italy* The Montepulciano grape's most important manifestation, dark and deeply brambly when red, bright pink and intensely fruity when rosé (Cerasuolo). Quality varies from insipid or rustic to concentrated and characterful. Best producers: Barba, Cataldi Madonna★, Contesa★★, Cornacchia★, Filomusi Guelfi★, Illuminati★, Marramiero★★, Masciarelli★★, A & E Monti★, Montori★ Nicodemi★, Roxan★, Cantina Tollo★, Umani Ronchi★, La Valentina★ Valentini★★, L Valori★, Ciccio Zaccagnini★. Best years: (2007) (06) 04 **03 0** 00 98 97 95.

MONTEREY COUNTY *California, USA* Large CENTRAL COAST county south of San Francisco in the Salinas Valley. The most important AVAs are Monterey, Arroyo Seco, Chalone, Carmel Valley and Santa Lucia Highlands. Best grapes are Chardonnay, Riesling and Pinot Blanc, with some good Cabernet Sauvignon and Merlot in Carmel Valley and superl Pinot Noir in the Santa Lucia Highlands in the cool middle of the county. Best producers: Bernardus★★, Estancia★, Jekel★, Joullian★ Mer Soleil★★, Morgan★★, TALBOTT★★, Testarossa★★. Best years: (reds) 2005 04 03 **01 00 99 97 96 95 94 91 90**.

MONTES *Colchagua, Chile* One of Chile's pioneering wineries in the modern era, notable for innovative development of top-quality vineyard land on the steep Apalta slopes of COLCHAGUA and the virgin country of Marchíhüe out towards the Pacific. Sauvignon Blanc★ (Leyda★★) and Chardonnay★ (Alpha★★) are good and fruit-led; all the reds are more austere and need bottle age. Since the 2001 vintage, top-of-the-line Montes Alpha M★★ has begun to shine. The most impressive reds however, are Montes Alpha★★ and Montes Folly★★, two massive Syrahs, and Purple Angel★★, a vibrant, scented Carmenère. New Montes Alpha Pinot Noir shows ripe flavours and extensive use of oak

MONTEVERTINE *Tuscany, Italy* Based in the heart of CHIANTI CLASSICO Montevertine is famous for its non-DOC wines, particularly Le Pergole Torte★★★. This was the first of the SUPER-TUSCANS made solely with Sangiovese, and it remains one of the best. A little Canaiolo is included in the excellent Montevertine Riserva★★. Best years: (Le Pergole Torte (2007) (06) **04 03 01 00 99 97 95 93 90 88 85**.

MONTHELIE AC *Côte de Beaune, Burgundy, France* Attractive, mainly red wine village lying halfway along the COTE DE BEAUNE behind MEURSAULT and VOLNAY. The wines generally have a lovely cherry fruit and make pleasant drinking at a good price. Best producers: BOUCHARD PERE ET FILS, COCHE-DURY★, Darviot-Perrin★, P Garaudet★, R Jobard★, LAFON★★, O LEFLAIVE★ G Roulot★★, de Suremain★. Best years: (reds) (2007) **06 05 04 03 02 99**.

MONTILLA-MORILES DO *Andalucía, Spain* Sherry-style wines that used to be sold almost entirely as lower-priced sherry substitutes. However, the wines *can* be superb, particularly the top dry amontillado, oloroso and rich Pedro Ximénez styles. Best producers: Alvear (top labels★★), Aragón Gracia Hermanos, Pérez Barquero★★, Toro Albalá★★.

DOM. DE MONTILLE *Côte de Beaune, Burgundy, France* Brought to fame by *Mondovino* star Hubert de Montille, and now run by son Étienne Consistent producer of stylish reds that demand aging, from VOLNAY (especially Mitans★★, Champans★★, Taillepieds★★★) and POMMARD (Pezerolles★★, Rugiens★★). Also top PULIGNY Les Caillerets★★★. Very expensive. From 2005 outstanding VOSNE-ROMANEE Malconsorts★★★ Étienne and his sister have also started a négociant business, Deux Montille★. Best years: (2007) 06 05 04 03 02 99 96 **93 88 85 83**.

MONTLOUIS-SUR-LOIRE AC *Loire Valley, France* On the opposite bank of the Loire to VOUVRAY, Montlouis makes similar styles (dry, medium, sweet and CHAMPAGNE-style fizz), if a touch less fine. Mousseux, the green, appley fizz, is best drunk young. Still wines need 5–10 years, particularly the sweet Moelleux. Best producers: L Chatenay★, F Chidaine★, S Cossais★, Delétang★, Levasseur-Alex Mathur★, des Liards/Berger★, Taille aux Loups★★/BLOT. Best years: (2007) 06 05 04 03 02 01 99 97 96 95.

MONTRACHET AC *Côte de Beaune, Burgundy, France* This world-famous Grand Cru straddles the boundary between the villages of CHASSAGNE-MONTRACHET and PULIGNY-MONTRACHET. Wines have a unique combination of concentration, finesse and perfume; white Burgundy at its most sublime. Chevalier-Montrachet, immediately above it on the slope, yields slightly leaner wine that is less explosive in its youth, but good examples become ever more fascinating with age. Best producers: BOUCHARD★★★, M Colin★★★, DROUHIN (Laguiche)★★★, LAFON★★★, Louis LATOUR★★, Dom. LEFLAIVE★★★, LEROY★★★, RAMONET★★★, Dom. de la ROMANEE-CONTI★★★, SAUZET★★, Thénard★★. Best years: (2007) 06 05 04 03 02 01 00 99 97 95 92 90 89 85.

MONTRAVEL AC *South-West France* Dry white, medium-dry and sweet white wines from the western end of the BERGERAC region. Sweet whites from Côtes de Montravel AC and Haut-Montravel AC. Red Montravel is made from a minimum 50% Merlot. Best producers: le Bondieu, Masburel★, Moulin Caresse★, Perreau, Pique-Sègue, Puy-Servain★, le Raz. Best years: (sweet) 2005 02 01 98 96; (red) 2005 03 01.

CH. MONTROSE★★ *St-Estèphe AC, 2ème Cru Classé, Haut-Médoc, Bordeaux, France* A leading ST-ESTEPHE property, once famous for its dark, brooding wine that would take around 30 years to reach its prime. In the late 1970s and early 80s the wines became lighter, but Montrose has now returned to a powerful style, though softer than before. Recent vintages have been extremely good. Sold in 2006, so let's see what happens to the style. Second wine: la Dame de Montrose. Best years: 2006 05 04 03 01 00 99 98 96 95.

CH. MONTUS *Madiran AC, South-West France* Alain Brumont has led MADIRAN's revival, using 100% Tannat and deft public relations. The top wine is aged in new oak. He has 3 properties: Montus (Prestige★★), Bouscassé (Vieilles Vignes★★) and Meinjarre. Montus and Bouscassé also make enjoyable dry PACHERENC DU VIC-BILH★ and COTES DE GASCOGNE. Also fine Moelleux Vendémiaire★★. Best years: (Prestige) 2005 03 01 00 99 98 97 96.

MOON MOUNTAIN *Sonoma Valley AVA, California, USA* Formerly known as Carmenet (which is now a brand of the Foster's Group – the wines are not related), Moon Mountain specializes in intensely flavoured reds from mountain vineyards. Full-throttle Cabernet Franc★★ and Reserve Cabernet Sauvignon★★ can age for a decade. Reserve Sauvignon Blanc★★ from Edna Valley grapes features plenty of creamy oak. Best years: (reds) 2005 04 03 02 01 00 99 98 97 96 95 94.

MORELLINO DI SCANSANO DOC *Tuscany, Italy* Morellino is the local name for the Sangiovese grape in the south-west of TUSCANY. The wines can be robust and robust, but the best are delightfully perfumed. Best producers: E Banti★, Belguardo★/FONTERUTOLI, Carletti/POLIZIANO (Lohsa★), Cecchi★, Il Macereto★, Mantellassi★, Morellino di Scansano co-op★, Moris Farms★★, Podere 414★, Poggio Argentaria★★, Le Pupille★★. Best years: (2007) 06 04 03 01 00 99 98 97.

MOREY-ST-DENIS AC *Côte de Nuits, Burgundy, France* Morey has 5 Grand
Crus (CLOS DES LAMBRAYS, CLOS DE LA ROCHE, CLOS ST-DENIS, CLOS DE TART and
a share of BONNES-MARES) as well as some very good Premiers Crus. Basic
village wine is sometimes unexciting, but from a quality grower the wine
has good fruit and acquires an attractive depth as it ages. A tiny amount
of startling nutty white wine is also made. Best producers: Pierre Amiot★,
Arlaud★★, Dom. des Beaumonts★, CLAIR★★, DUJAC★★★, Dom. de
Lambrays★★, H Lignier★★★, Lignier-Michelot★, H Perrot-Minot★★,
Ponsot★★, ROUMIER★★, ROUSSEAU★★, Sérafin★★, Taupenot-Merme★★. Best
years: (2007) 06 05 03 02 **01 00 99 98 97 96 95 93 90**.

MORGENHOF *Stellenbosch WO, South Africa* A 300-year-old Cape farm
grandly restored and run with French flair by owner Anne Cointreau-
Huchon. The range spans Cap Classique sparkling to PORT styles. Best
are a well-oaked, muscular Chenin Blanc, structured Merlot★ and the
dark-berried, supple Première Sélection★, a BORDEAUX-style blend.

MORGON AC *Beaujolais, Burgundy, France* The longest-lasting of BEAUJOLAIS
Cru, wines that should have the structure to age and delightful cherry
fruit. There are, however, many more Morgons, made in a commercial
style for early drinking, which are nothing more than a pleasant, fruity
and pricey – drink. Best producers: N Aucoeur★, DUBOEUF (Jean
Descombes★), J Foillard, M Jonchet★, M Lapierre★. Best years: **2007 06 05**.

MORNINGTON PENINSULA *Victoria, Australia* Exciting cool-climate
maritime region dotted with small vineyards. Chardonnay runs the
gamut from honeyed to harsh; Pinot Noir can be very stylish in warm
years, especially as more vineyards in the mild Moorooduc area mature.
Best producers: Dexter, Hurley, KOOYONG★★, Main Ridge★, Moorooduc★,
Paringa Estate★★, Port Phillip Estate★, Scorpo, STONIER★★, Ten Minutes by
Tractor★, T'Gallant★, Tuck's Ridge, Willow Creek, Yabby Lake★★. Best years:
(Pinot Noir) 2006 05 04 **03 02 01 00 99 98 97 95 94**.

MORRIS *Rutherglen, Victoria, Australia* Historic winery, in the process of being
sold by Pernod Ricard. David Morris has been making old favourites like
Liqueur Muscat★★ and Tokay★★ (Old Premium★★★), 'ports',
'sherries' and robust table wines to very high quality levels. Let's hope the
new owners appreciate it.

DENIS MORTET *Gevrey-Chambertin, Côte de Nuits, Burgundy, France* Before his
untimely death in January 2006, Denis Mortet had built a brilliant
reputation for his GEVREY-CHAMBERTIN (various cuvées, all ★★★) and tiny
amounts of CHAMBERTIN★★★. Early vintages are deep coloured and
powerful; recent years show increased finesse, a trend being continued by
son Arnaud. Best years: (2007) 06 05 **04 03 02 01 00 96 95 93**.

GEORG MOSBACHER *Forst, Pfalz, Germany* This small estate makes dry
white and dessert wines in the village of FORST. Best of all are the dry
Rieslings★★ from the Forster Ungeheuer site, which are among the
lushest in Germany. Delicious young, but worth cellaring for more than
3 years. Best years: (2007) 06 05 04 **02 01 99 98 97**.

MOSCATO D'ASTI DOCG *Piedmont, Italy*
Utterly beguiling, delicately scented,
gently bubbling wine, made from
Moscato Bianco grapes grown in the
hills between Acqui Terme, Asti and
Alba in north-west Italy. The DOCG is
the same as for ASTI, but only select
grapes go into this wine, which is

frizzante (semi-sparkling) rather than fully sparkling. Drink while they're bubbling with youthful fragrance. Best producers: Araldica/Alasia★, ASCHERI★, Bava★, Bera★★, Braida★, Cascina Castlèt★, La Caudrina★★, Michele CHIARLO, Giuseppe Contratto★, Coppo★, Cascina Fonda★, Forteto della Luja★, Icardi★, Marenco★, Beppe Marino★, La Morandina★, Marco Negri★, Perrone★, Cascina Pian d'Or★, Saracco★★, Scagliola★, La Spinetta★★, I Vignaioli di Santo Stefano★, Gianni Voerzio★.

MOSCATO PASSITO DI PANTELLERIA DOC *Sicily, Italy* Powerful dessert wine made from the Muscat of Alexandria, or Zibibbo, grape. Pantelleria is a small island south-west of SICILY, closer to Africa than it is to Italy. The grapes are picked in mid-August and laid out in the hot sun to shrivel for a couple of weeks. They are then crushed and fermented to give an amber-coloured, intensely flavoured sweet Muscat. The wines are best drunk within 5–7 years of the vintage. Best producers: Benanti★, D'Ancona★, DE BARTOLI★★, Donnafugata (Ben Ryé★), Murana★, Nuova Agricoltura co-op★, Pellegrino.

MOSEL-SAAR-RUWER *Germany* A collection of vineyard areas on the Mosel and its tributaries, the Saar and the Ruwer, amounting to 9080ha (22,435 acres). The Mosel river rises in the French Vosges before forming the border between Germany and Luxembourg. In its first German incarnation in the Upper Mosel the light, tart Elbling grape holds sway, but with the Middle Mosel begins a series of villages responsible for some of the world's very best Riesling wines: LEIWEN, TRITTENHEIM, PIESPORT, BRAUNEBERG, BERNKASTEL, GRAACH, WEHLEN, URZIG and ERDEN. The wines have tremendous slatiness and an ability to blend the greenness of citrus leaves and fruits with the golden warmth of honey. Great wines are rarer in the lower part of the valley as the Mosel approaches Koblenz, although WINNINGEN is an island of excellence. The Saar can produce wonderful, piercing wines in villages such as Serrig, Ayl, OCKFEN and Wiltingen. Ruwer wines are slightly softer; the estates of MAXIMIN GRUNHAUS and KARTHAUSERHOF are on every list of the best in Germany. From late 2007 only the name 'Mosel' will appear on labels.

MOSS WOOD *Margaret River, Western Australia* Seminal MARGARET RIVER winery at the top of its form. Supremely good, scented Cabernet★★★ needing 5 years to blossom, classy Chardonnay★★, pale, fragrant Pinot Noir★ and crisp, fruity but ageworthy Semillon★★. Range is expanding with excellent Ribbon Vale★★ wines and very good entry-level Amy's Cabernet. Best years: (Cabernet) (2007) 05 04 03 **02 01 00 99 98 96 95 94 91 90 85**.

J P MOUEIX *Bordeaux, France* As well as owning PETRUS, la FLEUR-PETRUS, MAGDELAINE, TROTANOY, Hosanna and other properties, the Moueix family runs a thriving merchant business specializing in the wines of the Right Bank, particularly POMEROL and ST-EMILION. Quality is generally high.

MOULIN-À-VENT AC *Beaujolais, Burgundy, France* Potentially the greatest of the BEAUJOLAIS Crus, taking its name from an ancient (now renovated) windmill that stands above Romanèche-Thorins. The granitic soil yields a majestic wine that with time transforms into a rich Burgundian style more characteristic of the Pinot Noir than the Gamay. Best producers: Champagnon★, DUBOEUF (Tour du Bief★), Ch. des Jacques★/JADOT, Ch. du Moulin-à-Vent★, Dom. Romanesca★, P Sapin (Le Vieux Domaine). Best years: **2007 06 05**.

MOULIS AC *Haut-Médoc, Bordeaux, France* Small AC within the HAUT-MEDOC
Much of the wine is excellent – delicious at 5–6 years old, though good
examples can age 10–20 years – and not overpriced. **Best producers:**
Anthonic, Biston-Brillette★, Branas-Grand-Poujeaux, Brillette, CHASSE-SPLEEN★,
Duplessis, Gressier-Grand-Poujeaux★, MAUCAILLOU★, Moulin-à-Vent,
POUJEAUX★. **Best years:** 2006 05 **03 02 01 00 96 95 90 89**.

MOUNT HORROCKS *Clare Valley, South Australia* Stephanie Toole has
transformed this label into one of the CLARE VALLEY's best, with taut,
minerally, limy Riesling★★★ from a single vineyard in Watervale; classy
cedary Semillon★; and complex, savoury Shiraz★; and a delicious sticky (dessert
wine), the Cordon Cut Riesling★★★, which shows varietal character with
a satisfying lush texture.

MOUNT LANGI GHIRAN *Grampians, Victoria, Australia* This winery made its
reputation with remarkable dark plum, chocolate and pepper Shiraz★★.
Delightful Riesling★, honeyed Pinot Gris★ and melony unwooded
Chardonnay★. Joanna★★ Cabernet is dark and intriguing. **Best years**
(Shiraz) 2005 04 **03 99 98 97 96 95 94 93**.

MOUNT MARY *Yarra Valley, Victoria, Australia* Founder and YARRA VALLEY
pioneer, Dr John Middleton, died in 2006 but this classic property
continues to produce controversial cult wines. It uses only estate-grown
BORDEAUX grapes, with dry white Triolet★★ blended from Sauvignon,
Semillon and Muscadelle, and Quintet (★★★ for keen Francophiles)
from Cabernet Sauvignon and Franc, Merlot, Malbec and Petit Verdot
that ages beautifully. The Pinot Noir★★ is almost as good. **Best years**
(Quintet) (2006) 05 03 02 01 **00 99 98 97 96 95 94 93 92 91 90 88 86 84**.

MOUNT VEEDER AVA *Napa Valley, California, USA* Small AVA in south-
west NAPA, with Cabernet Sauvignon and Zinfandel in an impressive,
rough-hewn style. **Best producers:** Chateau Potelle★, Robert Craig★★, HESS
COLLECTION, Lokoya★★, Mayacamas★, Mount Veeder Winery★.

MOURVÈDRE The variety originated in Spain, where it is called Monastrell.
It dominates the JUMILLA DO and also Alicante, Bullas and Yecla. It needs
lots of sunshine to ripen, which is why it performs well on the
Mediterranean coast at BANDOL. It is increasingly important as a source of
body and tarry, pine-needle flavour in the wines of CHATEAUNEUF-DU-PAPE
and parts of Languedoc-Roussillon. It is beginning to make a reputation
in Australia and California, where it is sometimes known as Mataro, and
is also starting to make its presence felt in South Africa.

MOUTON-CADET *Bordeaux AC, Bordeaux, France* The most widely sold red
BORDEAUX in the world was created by Baron Philippe de Rothschild in
the 1930s. Blended from the entire Bordeaux region, the wine is
undistinguished – and never cheap. A new label and somewhat fruitier
style were introduced in 2004. Also a white, rosé, MEDOC and GRAVES.

CH. MOUTON-ROTHSCHILD★★★ *Pauillac AC, 1er Cru Classé, Haut-Médoc,
Bordeaux, France* Baron Philippe de Rothschild died in 1988, having
raised Mouton from a run-down Second Growth to its promotion to
First Growth in 1973, and a reputation as one of the greatest wines in the
world. It can still be the most magnificently opulent of the great MEDOC
reds, but inexcusable inconsistency frequently makes me want to
downgrade it. Recent vintages seem back on top form. When young, it is
rich and indulgent on the palate, aging after 15–20 years to a complex
bouquet of blackcurrant and cigar box. There is also a white wine, Ail

d'Argent. Second wine: Le Petit-Mouton. Best years: (red) 2006 05 04 03 02 01 00 **99 98 97 96 95 90 89 88 86 85**.

MUDGEE *New South Wales, Australia* Small, long-overlooked region neigh-bouring HUNTER VALLEY, with a higher altitude and marginally cooler temperatures. Major new plantings are giving it a fresh lease of life and producers are beginning to make the best use of very good fruit. Best producers: Abercorn, Farmer's Daughter, Huntington Estate★, Miramar★, Oatley, ROSEMOUNT.

MUGA *Rioja DOCa, Rioja, Spain* A traditional family winery making high-quality, rich red RIOJA★, especially the Gran Reserva, Prado Enea★★. It is the only bodega in Rioja where every step of red winemaking is still carried out in oak containers. The modern Torre Muga Reserva★ marks a major stylistic change. The new top cuvée is Aro★★. Whites and rosés are good too. Best years: (Torre Muga Reserva) (2004) **03 01 99 98 96 95**.

J-F MUGNIER *Chambolle-Musigny, Côte de Nuits, Burgundy, France* Since giving up his other career as an airline pilot in 1998, Frédéric Mugnier has produced a series of beautifully crafted, lightly extracted wines at the Château de Chambolle-Musigny, especially from les Amoureuses★★ and Grand Cru le MUSIGNY★★★. In 2004 the 9ha (23-acre) NUITS-ST-GEORGES Clos de la Maréchale★★ vineyard came back under his control; first vintages are very stylish and a small section has been grafted over to white wine production. Best years: (2007) 06 05 04 02 **01 00 99 98 96 93 90 89**.

MULDERBOSCH *Stellenbosch WO, South Africa* Consistency is one of the hallmarks of this white-dominated range. Sleek, gooseberry-infused Sauvignon Blanc★★ is deservedly a cult wine; drink young and fresh. Purity and intensity mark out the Chardonnays (regular★ and barrel-fermented★★) and oak-brushed Chenin Blanc★ (previously labelled Steen op Hout)★. The handful of reds includes Faithful Hound, a Cabernet-Merlot blend, BORDEAUX-like but easy-drinking. Best years: (barrel-fermented Chardonnay) **2006 05 04 03 02 01 00**.

MÜLLER-CATOIR *Neustadt-Haardt, Pfalz, Germany* This PFALZ producer makes wine of a piercing fruit flavour and powerful structure unsurpassed in Germany, including Riesling, Scheurebe, Rieslaner, Gewürztraminer, Muskateller and Pinot Noir – all ★★. BA and TBA are invariably ★★★. Best years: (2007) 06 05 **04 03 02 01 99 98 97 94**.

EGON MÜLLER-SCHARZHOF *Scharzhofberg, Mosel-Saar-Ruwer, Germany* Some of the world's greatest – and most expensive – sweet Rieslings are this estate's Auslese, Beerenauslese, Trockenbeerenauslese and Eiswein: all usually rating ★★★. Regular Kabinett and Spätlese wines are pricey but classic. Best years: (2007) 06 05 04 03 02 **01 99 97 95 93 90 89 88 83**.

MÜLLER-THURGAU The workhorse grape of Germany, largely responsible for LIEBFRAUMILCH, with 14% of the country's vineyards, but diminishing. When yields are low it produces pleasant floral wines, but this is rare since modern clones are all super-productive. It is occasionally better in England – and a few good examples, with a slightly green edge to the grapy flavour, come from Switzerland (here known as Riesling-Sylvaner), Luxembourg (as Rivaner) and Italy's TRENTINO and ALTO ADIGE, which latter boasts one of Europe's highest vineyards in TIEFENBRUNNER's Feldmarschall at 1000m (3280 ft). In New Zealand, Müller-Thurgau acreage is in terminal decline.

MUSCAT

It's strange, but there's hardly a wine grape in the world which makes wine that actually tastes of the grape itself. Yet there's one variety which is so joyously, exultantly grapy that it more than makes up for all the others – the Muscat, generally thought to be the original wine vine. In fact there seem to be about 200 different branches of the Muscat family worldwide, but the noblest of these and the one that always makes the most exciting wine is called Muscat Blanc à Petits Grains (the Muscat with the small berries). These berries can be crunchily green, golden yellow, pink or even brown – as a result Muscat has a large number of synonyms. The wines they make may be pale and dry, rich and golden, subtly aromatic or as dark and sweet as treacle.

WINE STYLES

France Muscat is grown from the far north-east right down to the Spanish border, yet is rarely accorded great respect in France. This is a pity, because the dry, light, hauntingly grapy Muscats of Alsace are some of France's most delicately beautiful wines. It pops up sporadically in the Rhône Valley, especially in the sparkling wine enclave of Die. Mixed with Clairette, the Clairette de Die Tradition is a fragrant grapy fizz that deserves to be better known. Muscat de Beaumes-de-Venise is a delicious manifestation of the grape, this time fortified, fragrant and sweet. Its success has encouraged the traditional fortified winemakers of Languedoc-Roussillon, especially in Frontignan and Rivesaltes, to make fresher, more perfumed wines than the flat and syrupy ones they've produced for generations.

Italy Various types of Muscat are grown in Italy. In the north-west, especially Piedmont, Moscato Bianco/Moscato di Canelli makes the fragrantly sweet sparklers called Asti or (less bubbly) Moscato d'Asti. Orange Muscat (Moscato Giallo/Goldmuskateller) is used in the north-east for making passito-style dessert (or occasionally dry) wines, while Muscat of Alexandria prevails in the south, especially in relation to the great passitos of Pantelleria. Italy also has red varieties: Moscato Nero for rare sweet wines in Lazio, Lombardy and Piedmont; Moscato Rosa/Rosenmuskateller for delicately sweet wines in Trentino-Alto Adige and Friuli-Venezia Giulia.

Other regions Elsewhere in Europe, Muscat is a component of some Tokajis in Hungary, Crimea has shown how good it can be in the Massandra fortified wines, and the rich golden Muscats of Samos and Patras are among Greece's finest wines. As Muskateller in Austria and Germany it makes primarily dry, subtly aromatic wines. In Spain, Moscatel de Valencia is sweet, light and sensational value, Moscatel de Grano Menudo is on the resurgence in Navarra and Castilla-La Mancha and it has also been introduced in Mallorca. Portugal's Moscatel de Setúbal is also wonderfully rich and complex. California grows Muscat, often calling it Muscat Canelli, but South Africa and Australia make better use of it. With darker berries, and called Brown Muscat in Australia and Muscadel in South Africa, it makes some of the world's sweetest and most luscious fortified wines, especially in the north-east Victoria regions of Rutherglen and Glenrowan in Australia.

BEST PRODUCERS

Sparkling Muscat
France (Clairette de Die) Achard-Vincent, Clairette de Die co-op, Jean-Claude Raspail.

Italy (Asti) G Contratto, Gancia; *(Moscato d'Asti)* Bera, Braida, Caudrina, Saracco, La Spinetta, Gianni Voerzio.

Dry Muscat
Austria (Muskateller) Gross, Lackner-Tinnacher, POLZ, TEMENT.

France (Alsace) Dirler-Cadé, Kientzler, Kuentz-Bas, Ostertag, Rolly Gassmann, SCHOFFIT, Bruno Sorg, TRIMBACH, WEINBACH, ZIND-HUMBRECHT.

Germany (Muskateller) BERCHER, Dr HEGER, MULLER-CATOIR, REBHOLZ.

Spain (Alicante) Bocopa co-op; *(Málaga)* Jorge Ordóñez; *(Penedès)* TORRES (Viña Esmeralda).

Italy (Goldmuskateller) LAGEDER.

Sweet Muscat
Australia (Liqueur Muscat) All Saints, Baileys of Glenrowan, BROWN BROTHERS, Buller, Campbells, CHAMBERS, MCWILLIAM'S, MORRIS, SEPPELT, Stanton & Killeen, YALUMBA.

France (Alsace) Ernest Burn, Rolly Gassmann, René MURE, SCHOFFIT; *(Beaumes-de-Venise)* Bernardins, Durban, Paul JABOULET, Pigeade; *(Frontignan)* la Peyrade; *(Lunel)* Lacoste; *(Rivesaltes)* CAZES, Jau.

Greece SAMOS co-op.

Italy (Goldmuskateller) Viticoltori Caldaro, Thurnhof; *(Pantelleria)* DE BARTOLI, Murana.

Portugal (Moscatel de Setúbal) BACALHOA, J M da FONSECA.

South Africa KLEIN CONSTANTIA.

Spain (Navarra) Camilo Castilla, CHIVITE; *(Terra Alta)* Vinos Piñol; *(Valencia)* Gandía; *(Alicante)* Gutiérrez de la Vega, Enrique Mendoza, Primitivo Quiles; *(Jumilla)* Silvano García; *(Sierras de Málaga)* Jorge Ordóñez, Telmo RODRIGUEZ.

G H MUMM *Champagne AC, Champagne, France* Mumm's top-selling non vintage brand, Cordon Rouge, disappointing in the 1990s, improved when Dominique Demarville took over as winemaker in 1998, but he left in 2006 to join VEUVE CLICQUOT. His efforts at improving quality were confirmed by the 2005 release of Mumm Grand Cru★ and elegant new de luxe Cuvée R Lalou★★, launched in 2007 with the 1998 vintage, but it remains to be seen whether standards continue to improve under Pernod Ricard's ownership. Best years: 1998 96 **95 90 89 88 85 82**.

MUMM NAPA *Napa Valley AVA, California, USA* The California offshoot of Champagne house MUMM has always made good bubbly, and after a slight dip is now back on form. Cuvée Napa Brut Prestige★ is a fair drink. Blanc de Noirs★ is better than most pink Champagnes. Elegant vintage-dated Blanc de Blancs★★ and flagship DVX★★. Part of Pernod Ricard.

RENÉ MURÉ *Alsace AC, Alsace, France* The pride and joy of this domaine's fine vineyards is the Clos St-Landelin, a parcel within the Grand Cru Vorbourg and the label for all the top wines. The Clos is the source of lush, concentrated wines, with particularly fine Riesling★★ and Pinot Gris★★. The Muscat Vendange Tardive★★ is rare and remarkable, as is the opulent old-vine Sylvaner Cuvée Oscar★. The Vendange Tardive★★ and Sélection de Grains Nobles★★★ wines are among the best in Alsace. Best years: (Clos St-Landelin Riesling) (2007) 05 **04 02 01 00 97 96 95**.

ANDREW MURRAY VINEYARDS *Santa Barbara County, California, USA* Working with RHONE varieties, winemaker Andrew Murray has created an impressive array of wines. Rich, aromatic Viognier★ and Roussanne★★ as well as several Syrahs, including Roasted Slope★★ and Hillside Reserve★★. Espérance★ is a spicy blend patterned after serious COTES DU RHONE. Best years: (Syrah) 2005 **04 03 02 01 00 99 98 97**

MUSCADET AC *Loire Valley, France* AC for the region around Nantes in north-west France, best drunk young and fresh as an apéritif or with the local seafood. Wines from 3 better quality zones (Muscadet Coteaux de la Loire, Muscadet Côtes de Grand-Lieu and Muscadet Sèvre-et-Maine) are typically labelled *sur lie*. They must be matured on the lees for a maximum of 12 months and show greater depth of flavour and more fruit. Ironically, ageworthy top cuvées from specific vineyards or soils (granite, gneiss, schist) are usually aged *sur lie* for well over 12 months so cannot use this term on the label. Best producers: Bidière, Bonhomme, Bonnet-Huteau, Chéreau-Carré★, Choblet/Herbauges★, Bruno Cormerais, Michel David★, Dorices★, Douillard, l'ECU★, Gadais★, Jacques Guindon★, les Hautes Noëlles★/Serge Bâtard, l'Hyvernière, Landrons★, Luneau-Papin★, Metaireau★, RAGOTIERE★, Sauvion★, la Touché★. Best years: (sur lie) **2007 05 03 02**.

MUSCAT See pages 212–13.

MUSCAT OF ALEXANDRIA This grape rarely shines in its own right but performs a useful job worldwide, adding perfume and fruit to what would otherwise be dull, neutral white wines. It is common for sweet and fortified wines throughout the Mediterranean basin (in Sicily it is called Zibibbo) and in South Africa (where it is also known as Hanepoot), as well as being a fruity, perfumed bulk producer there and in Australia, where it is known as Gordo Blanco or Lexia.

MUSCAT DE BEAUMES-DE-VENISE AC *Rhône Valley, France* Delicious Muscat *vin doux naturel* from the southern Rhône. It has a fruity acidity and a bright fresh feel, and is best drunk young to get all that lovely grapey perfume and bright fruit at its peak. Best producers: Beaumalric★, Beaumes-de-Venise co-op, Bernardins★★, DELAS★, Durban★★, Fenouillet★, JABOULET★★, Pigeade★★, Vidal-Fleury★.

MUSCAT BLANC À PETITS GRAINS See MUSCAT, pages 212–13.

MUSCAT DE FRONTIGNAN AC *Languedoc, France* Muscat *vin doux naturel* on the Mediterranean coast. Quite impressive but can be a bit cloying. Muscat de Mireval AC, a little further inland, can have a touch more acid freshness and quite an alcoholic kick. Best producers: (Frontignan) Cave de Frontignan, la Peyrade★, Robiscau; (Lunel) Lacoste★; (Mireval) la Capelle★, Mas des Pigeonniers, Moulinas.

MUSCAT DE LUNEL, MUSCAT DE MIREVAL See MUSCAT DE FRONTIGNAN.

MUSCAT DE RIVESALTES AC *Roussillon, France* Made from Muscat Blanc à Petits Grains and Muscat of Alexandria, the wine can be very good from go-ahead producers who keep the aromatic skins in the juice for longer periods to gain extra perfume and fruit. Most delicious when young. Best producers: Baixas co-op (Dom. Brial★, Ch. les Pins★), la CASENOVE★, CAZES★★, Chênes★, Corneilla, Fontanel★, Força Réal★, l'Heritier, Jau★, Laporte★, MONT TAUCH★, de Nouvelles★, Piquemal★.

MUSCAT DE ST-JEAN-DE-MINERVOIS AC *Languedoc, France* Up in the remote Minervois hills, a small AC for fortified Muscat made from Muscat Blanc à Petits Grains. Less cloying than some Muscats from the plains of LANGUEDOC-ROUSSILLON, more tangerine and floral. Best producers: CLOS BAGATELLE, Combebelle, Vignerons de Septimanie.

MUSIGNY AC *Grand Cru, Côte de Nuits, Burgundy, France* One of a handful of truly great Grands Crus, combining power with an exceptional depth of fruit and lacy elegance – an iron fist in a velvet glove. Understandably expensive. A tiny amount of BOURGOGNE Blanc is currently made from the Musigny vineyard by de VOGUE★★. Best producers: DROUHIN★★★, JADOT★★★, D Laurent★★★, Dom. LEROY★★★, J-F MUGNIER★★★, J Prieur★★, ROUMIER★★★, VOGUE★★★, VOUGERAIE★★★. Best years: (2007) 06 05 04 03 02 01 00 99 **98 97 96 95 93 90 89 88**.

NAHE *Germany* 4120ha (10,180-acre) wine region named after the River Nahe, which rises below Birkenfeld and joins the Rhine by BINGEN, opposite RUDESHEIM in the RHEINGAU. The Rieslings from this geologically complex region are often among Germany's best. The finest vineyards are those of Niederhausen and SCHLOSSBOCKELHEIM, situated in the dramatic, rocky Upper Nahe Valley, and at Dorsheim and Münster in the lower Nahe.

CH. NAIRAC★ *Barsac AC, 2ème Cru Classé, Bordeaux, France* An established name in BARSAC which, by dint of enormous effort, produces a sweet wine sometimes on a par with the First Growths. The influence of aging in new oak casks, adding spice and even a little tannin, means this can age for 10–15 years. Best years: 2005 04 03 **02 01 99 98 97 96 95**.

NAPA VALLEY See pages 216–17.

NAPA VALLEY AVA *California, USA* An AVA so inclusive that it is almost completely irrelevant. It includes vineyards that are outside the Napa River drainage system – such as Pope Valley and Chiles Valley. A number of sub-AVAs have been and are in the process of being created; a few such as CARNEROS and STAGS LEAP DISTRICT are discernibly different from their neighbours, but the majority are similar in nature, and many fear that these sub-AVAs will simply dilute the magic of Napa's name. See also HOWELL MOUNTAIN, MOUNT VEEDER, NAPA VALLEY, OAKVILLE, RUTHERFORD.

NAPA VALLEY

California, USA

From the earliest days of California wine, and through all its ups and downs, the Napa Valley has been the standard-bearer for the whole industry and the driving force behind quality and progress. The magical Napa name – derived from an Indian word for plenty – applies to the fertile valley itself, the county in which it is found and the AVA for the overall area, but the region is so viticulturally diverse that the appellation is virtually meaningless.

The valley was first settled by immigrants in the 1830s, and by the late 19th century Napa, and in particular the area around the communities of Rutherford and Oakville, had gained a reputation for exciting Cabernet Sauvignon. Despite the long, dark years of Prohibition, this reputation survived and when the US interest in wine revived during the 1970s, Napa was ready to lead the charge.

GRAPE VARIETIES

Most of the classic French grapes are grown and recent replantings have done much to match varieties to the most suitable locations. Cabernet Sauvignon is planted in profusion and Napa's strongest reputation is for varietal Cabernet and Bordeaux-style (or meritage) blends, mostly Cabernet-Merlot. Pinot Noir and Chardonnay, for both still and sparkling wines, do best in the south, from Yountville down to Carneros. Zinfandel is grown mostly at the north end of the valley. Syrah and Sangiovese are relatively new here.

SUB-REGIONS

The most significant vine-growing area is the valley floor running from Calistoga in the north down to Carneros, below which the Napa River flows out into San Pablo Bay. It has been said that there are more soil types in Napa than in the whole of France, but much of the soil in the valley is heavy, clayish, over-fertile, difficult to drain and really not fit to make great wine. Some of the best vineyards are tucked into the mountain slopes at the valley sides or in selected spots at higher altitudes.

There is as much as a 10°C temperature difference between torrid Calistoga and Carneros at the mouth of the valley, cooled by Pacific fog and a benchmark for US Pinot Noir and cool-climate Chardonnay. About 20 major sub-areas have been identified along the valley floor and in the mountains, although there is much debate over how many have a real claim to individuality. Rutherford, Oakville and Yountville in the mid-valley produce Cabernet redolent of dust, dried sage and ultra-ripe blackcurrants. Softer flavours come from Stags Leap to the east. The higher-altitude vineyards of Diamond Mountain, Spring Mountain and Mount Veeder along the Mayacamas mountain range to the west produce deep Cabernets, while Howell Mountain in the north-east has stunning Zinfandel and Merlot.

See also CARNEROS AVA, HOWELL MOUNTAIN AVA, MOUNT VEEDER AVA, NAPA VALLEY AVA, OAKVILLE AVA, RUTHERFORD AVA, STAGS LEAP DISTRICT AVA; and individual producers.

BEST PRODUCERS

**Cabernet Sauvignon and
meritage blends**
Abreu, Altamura, Anderson's
Conn Valley, ARAUJO, Barnett
(Rattlesnake Hill), BEAULIEU,
BERINGER, Bryant Family,
Burgess Cellars, Cafaro,
Cakebread, CAYMUS, CHATEAU
MONTELENA, Chateau Potelle
(VGS), CHIMNEY ROCK, Cliff
Lede, Clos Pegase, CLOS DU
VAL, Colgin, Conn Creek
(Anthology), Corison,
Cosentino, Robert Craig,
DALLA VALLE, Darioush,
Del Dotto, DIAMOND CREEK,
DOMINUS, DUNN, Elyse, Far
Niente, FLORA SPRINGS, Forman,
Freemark Abbey, Frog's Leap,
Grace Family, Groth, HARLAN
ESTATE, HARTWELL, HEITZ, Jarvis,
Ladera, La Jota, Lewis Cellars,
Livingston Moffett, Lokoya,
Long Meadow Ranch, Long
Vineyards, Markham,
Mayacamas, MERRYVALE,
Peter MICHAEL, MINER, MONDAVI,
Monticello, Mount Veeder
Winery/FRANCISCAN, NEWTON,
OPUS ONE, Pahlmeyer,
Paradigm, Robert Pecota,
Peju Province (HB Vineyard),
PHELPS, PINE RIDGE, Plumpjack,
Pride Mountain, Quintessa,
Raymond, Rubicon/COPPOLA,
Rudd Estate, Saddleback,
St Clement, SCREAMING EAGLE,
Seavey, SHAFER, SILVER OAK,
SILVERADO, SPOTTSWOODE,
Staglin Family, STAG'S LEAP WINE
CELLARS, STERLING, Swanson,
The Terraces, Philip Togni,
Turnbull, Viader, Villa Mt Eden
(Signature Series), Vine Cliff,
Vineyard 29, Von Strasser,
Whitehall Lane, ZD.

NAVARRA DO *Navarra, Spain* This buzzing region has increasing number of vineyards planted to Cabernet Sauvignon, Merlot and Chardonnay in addition to Tempranillo, Garnacha and Moscatel (Muscat). This translates into a wealth of juicy reds, barrel-fermented whites and modern sweet Muscats, but quality is still more haphazard than it should be. Best producers: Artazuri, Camino del Villar★, Camilo Castilla (Capricho de Goya Muscat★★), CHIVITE★ (Señorío de Arínzano estate★★), Iñaki Núñez★ Inurrieta★, Lezaun★, Magaña★, Castillo de Monjardin★, Nekeas co-op★ Ochoa, Palacio de la Vega, Parraldea, Príncipe de Viana, Quaderna Via, Señorío de Otazu, Señorío de Sarria. Best years: (reds) **2005 04 03 01 99 98**.

NAVARRO VINEYARDS *Anderson Valley AVA, California, USA* Small but extremely high-calibre family-owned producer of sensational Gewürztraminer★★★, Pinot Gris★★, Riesling★★, Dry Muscat★★ and late-harvest Riesling★★★, perfectly balanced Pinot Noir★★ and a dozen other stellar wines.

NEBBIOLO The grape variety responsible for the majestic wines of BAROLO and BARBARESCO, found almost nowhere outside north-west Italy. Its name may derive from the Italian for fog, *nebbia*, because it ripens late when the hills are shrouded in autumn mists. It needs a thick skin to withstand this fog, so often gives very tannic wines that need years to soften. When grown in the limestone soils of the Langhe hills around Alba, Nebbiolo produces wines that are only moderately deep in colour but have a wonderful array of perfumes and an ability to develop great complexity with age. Barolo is usually considered the best and longest-lived of the Nebbiolo wines; the myth that it needs a decade or more to be drinkable has been dispelled by new-style Barolo, and the best Barolos now reach a plateau within 10 years and then subtly mature for decades. Barbaresco also varies widely in style between the traditional and the new. NEBBIOLO D'ALBA and ROERO produce lighter styles. The variety is also used for barrique-aged blends, often with Barbera and/or Cabernet and sold under the LANGHE DOC. Nebbiolo is also the principal grape for reds of northern PIEDMONT – Carema, GATTINARA and GHEMME. In LOMBARDY it is known as Chiavennasca and is the main variety of the Valtellina DOC and VALTELLINA SUPERIORE DOCG wines. Outside Italy, rare good examples have been made in Australia, California and South Africa.

NEBBIOLO D'ALBA DOC *Piedmont, Italy* Red wine from Nebbiolo grown around Alba, but excluding the BAROLO and BARBARESCO zones. Vineyards in the LANGHE and ROERO hills are noted for sandy soils that produce a fragrant, fruity style for early drinking, though some growers make wines that improve for 5 years or more. Best producers: Alario★, ASCHERI, Bricco Maiolica★★, CERETTO, Cascina Chicco★, Correggia★★, GIACOSA★, Giuseppe MASCARELLO★, Pio Cesare★, PRUNOTTO★, RATTI★, SANDRONE★, Vietti★. Best years: (2007) (06) **04 03 01 00 99 98**.

NELSON *South Island, New Zealand* A range of mountains separates Nelson from MARLBOROUGH at the northern end of South Island. Nelson is made up of a series of small hills and valleys with a wide range of mesoclimates. Pinot Noir, Chardonnay, Riesling and Sauvignon Blanc do well. Best producers: Greenhough★, Himmelsfeld, Kina Beach, NEUDORF★★, Rimu Grove★, SEIFRIED★, Spencer Hill. Best years: (whites) **2007 06 05 04 03 02**.

NERO D'AVOLA The name of SICILY's great red grape derives from the town of Avola near Siracusa, although it is now planted all over the island. Its deep colour, high sugars and acidity make it useful for blending, especially with the lower-acid Nerello Mascalese, but also with Cabernet, Merlot and Syrah. On its own, and from the right soils, it can be brilliant, with a soft, ripe, spicy black fruit character. Examples range from simple quaffers to many of Sicily's top reds.

NEUCHÂTEL *Switzerland* Swiss canton with high-altitude vineyards, mainly Chasselas whites and Pinot Noir reds and rosé. **Best producers:** Ch. d'Auvernier, Châtenay-Bouvier, Montmollin, Porret.

NEUDORF *Nelson, South Island, New Zealand* Owners Tim and Judy Finn produce some of New Zealand's most stylish and sought-after wines, including gorgeous, honeyed Chardonnay★★★, rich but scented Pinot Noir★★, Sauvignon Blanc★★, Riesling★★ and Pinot Gris★. **Best years:** (Chardonnay) 2007 **06 05 04 03 02 01**; (Pinot Noir) 2006 **05 03 02 01 00**.

NEW SOUTH WALES *Australia* Australia's most populous state is responsible for about 25% of the country's grape production. The largest centres of production are the irrigated areas of RIVERINA, and Murray Darling, Swan Hill and Perricoota on the Murray River, where better viticultural and winemaking practices and lower yields have led to significant quality improvements. Smaller premium-quality regions include the old-established HUNTER VALLEY, Cowra and higher-altitude MUDGEE, Orange and HILLTOPS. CANBERRA is an area of tiny vineyards at chilly altitudes, as is Tumbarumba at the base of the Snowy Mountains.

NEW YORK STATE *USA* Wine grapes were first planted on Manhattan Island in the mid-17th century, but it wasn't until the early 1950s that a serious wine industry began to develop in the state as *vinifera* grapes were planted to replace natives such as *Vitis labrusca*. Weather conditions, particularly in the north, can be challenging, but improved vineyard practices have made a good vintage possible in most recent years. The most important region is the FINGER LAKES in the north of the state, but LONG ISLAND is the most exciting; the Hudson River Region has a couple of good producers and a few upstarts are producing noteworthy wines amid the ocean of plonk along the shores of Lake Erie. **Best producers:** (Hudson River) Clinton, Millbrook★. See also FINGER LAKES and LONG ISLAND.

NEWTON *Napa Valley AVA, California, USA* Spectacular winery and steep vineyards high above St Helena, owned by French luxury giant LVMH. Cabernet Sauvignon★★, Merlot★★ and Claret★ are some of California's most pleasurable examples. Even better is the single-vineyard Cabernet Sauvignon-based Le Puzzle★★★. Newton pioneered the unfiltered Chardonnay★★★ style and this lush mouthful is one of California's best. Age Chardonnays for up to 5 years, reds for 10–15. **Best years:** (Cabernet Sauvignon) 2005 03 02 01 **00 99 97 96 95 94 91 90**.

NGATARAWA *Hawkes Bay, North Island, New Zealand* Viticulture here is organic, with Chardonnay★, botrytized Riesling and Cabernet-Merlot under the premium Alwyn Reserve label. The Glazebrook range includes attractive Chardonnay★ and Cabernet-Merlot★, both of which are best drunk within 5 years. **Best years:** (reds) (2007) **06 04 02 00 98**.

NIAGARA PENINSULA *Ontario, Canada* Sandwiched between lakes Er▮ and Ontario, the Niagara Peninsula benefits from regular through▮ breezes created by the Niagara escarpment, the cool climate bringing o▮ distinctive characteristics in the wine. Icewine, from Riesling and Vida▮ is the showstopper, with growing international acclaim. Chardonna▮ leads the dry whites, with Pinot Noir, Merlot and Cabernet Fran▮ showing most promise among the reds. Best producers: Cave Spring★ Chateau des Charmes★, HENRY OF PELHAM★, INNISKILLIN★★, Konzelmann▮ Reif Estate★, Southbrook★, Stoney Ridge, THIRTY BENCH★. Best year▮ (icewines) 2005 04 **03 02 00 99 98.**

NIEPOORT *Port DOC, Douro, Portugal* Remarkable small PORT shipper ▮ Dutch origin. Outstanding Vintage ports★★★, old tawnies★★★ an▮ colheitas★★★. Unfiltered LBVs★★ are among the best in their class▮ intense and complex. The Vintage port second label is calle▮ Secundum★★. Niepoort also produces fine red, white and rosé DOUR▮ Redoma★★; red Vertente★★, Batuta★★★ and Charme★★ are alread▮ established as three of Portugal's leading reds. Best years: (Vintage) 2005 0▮ **00 97 94 92 91 87 85 82 80 77 70 66 63.**

NIERSTEIN *Rheinhessen, Germany* Confusingly, both a small town and ▮ large Bereich which includes the infamous Grosslage Gutes Domta▮ The town boasts 23 vineyard sites and the top ones (Pettenthal, Bruders▮ berg, Hipping, Oelberg and Orbel) are some of the best in the Rhi▮ Valley. Best producers: GUNDERLOCH★★, HEYL ZU HERRNSHEIM★★, Kühlin▮ Gillot★, St Antony★, Schneider★. Best years: (2007) 06 05 **04 03 02 01 9▮**

NIGL *Senftenberg, Kremstal, Austria* Consistently fine and crystalline Rieslin▮ and Grüner Veltliner from this organic estate. Top vineyard is calle▮ Piri★ but each year Martin Nigl releases his best wines under th▮ Privat★★ label. Best years: (2007) 06 05 **04 03 02 01 00 99.**

NIKOLAIHOF *Wachau, Niederösterreich, Austria* The Saahs family make▮ some of the best wines in the WACHAU as well as in nearby Krems-Stein i▮ KREMSTAL, including steely, intense Rieslings from the famous Steine▮ Hund vineyard, always ★★. A biodynamic estate. Best years: (2007) 06 0▮ 04 02 **01 99 98.**

DOM. DE NIZAS *Languedoc, France* Owned by NAPA-based CLOS DU VA▮ Nizas makes an intense, New World-style limited-production re▮ Réserve★, which needs aging, and an old-vine Carignan. Other notab▮ wines include a sweet Muscat and less expensive, ready-to-drink, red an▮ white Le Mas, the red a blend of Cabernet Sauvignon, Merlot and Syra▮ Best years: (Réserve) (2005) **03 01.**

NOBILO *Kumeu/Huapai, Auckland, North Island, New Zealand* Wines range fro▮ medium-dry White Cloud to premium varietals. Tangy thoug▮ restrained Sauvignon Blanc and a vibrant Chardonnay★ are the to▮ wines from MARLBOROUGH. In 1998 Nobilo bought Selaks, with winerie▮ in AUCKLAND and Marlborough (Drylands); since then they have adde▮ the intense Drylands Marlborough Sauvignon Blanc★, Chardonnay▮ and Riesling★ to their list. The Selaks label has the most characte▮ Nobilo is now part of Constellation Brands.

NORTON *Luján de Cuyo, Mendoza, Argentina* Austrian-owned winery wher▮ reds impress more than whites (though Torrontés★ is good), wit▮ chocolaty Sangiovese, soft, rich Merlot★ and good Barbera. Higher u▮ the scale, quality has enormously improved in the past few vintage▮ especially in Reserva★ releases, while top-of-the-line Privada★★ i▮ enjoyable young but ages beautifully.

QUINTA DO NOVAL *Port DOC, Douro, Portugal*
Owned by AXA-Millésimes, this property is the source of extraordinary Quinta do Noval Nacional★★★, made from ungrafted vines – virtually unobtainable except at auction. Other Noval ports (including Quinta do Noval Vintage★★★ and Silval★★) are excellent too. Also fine colheitas★★ and some

stunning 40-year-old tawnies★★★. First DOURO red, Quinta do Noval Tinto★★, from 2004. Best years: (Nacional) 2003 00 97 94 87 85 70 66 63 62 60 31; (Vintage) 2004 03 00 97 95 94 91 87 85 70 66 63 60 31.

NUITS-ST-GEORGES AC *Côte de Nuits, Burgundy, France* This large AC is one of the few relatively reliable 'village' names in Burgundy. Although it has no Grands Crus, many of its Premiers Crus (it has 38!) are extremely good. The red can be rather slow to open out, often needing at least 5 years, but it ages to a delicious, chocolaty, deep figs-and-prune fruit. Minuscule amounts of white are made by GOUGES★, l'Arlot, Chevillon and RION★. Best producers: l'Arlot★★, R Arnoux★★, S CATHIARD, J Chauvenet★★, R Chevillon★★, J-J Confuron★★, FAIVELEY★★, H GOUGES★★, GRIVOT★★, Jayer-Gilles★★, Lechenaut★★, T LIGER-BELAIR★★, MEO-CAMUZET★★, A Michelot★, Mugneret★★, J-F MUGNIER★★, POTEL★★, RION★★. Best years: (reds) (2007) 06 05 03 02 **01 00 99 98 96 95 93 90**.

NYETIMBER *West Sussex, England* England's flagship sparkling wine producer, using classic CHAMPAGNE varieties. Two wines are made – Classic Cuvée★★ (Chardonnay, Pinot Noir and Pinot Meunier) and Chardonnay-based Blanc de Blancs★★ – though they have also released a 2003 Pinot Meunier Blanc de Noirs. A new winemaking team took over in 2007, although Nyetimber still retains the services of the Champagne-based enologist who has been there from the start. Although some recent bottlings showed quality inconsistencies, the wines continue to exhibit exceptional depth, with delicious toasty flavours and great length. New plantings have taken the area under vine from 16ha (40 acres) to 104ha (257 acres) and a new winery is planned. Since their reputation has been based on well-aged sparklers, let's hope they don't try to expand too fast. Best years: 2003 **00 99**.

OAKVILLE AVA *Napa Valley, California, USA* This region is cooler than RUTHERFORD, which lies immediately to the north. Planted primarily to Cabernet Sauvignon, the area contains some of NAPA's best vineyards, both on the valley floor (MONDAVI, OPUS ONE, SCREAMING EAGLE) and hillsides (HARLAN ESTATE, DALLA VALLE), producing wines that display lush, ripe black fruits and firm tannins. Best years: (Cabernet Sauvignon) (2005) (04) 03 **02 01 00 99 97 96 95 94 91 90**.

OC, VIN DE PAYS D' *Languedoc-Roussillon, France* Important Vin de Pays covering LANGUEDOC-ROUSSILLON. Overproduction and consequent underripeness have not helped its reputation, but an increasing number of fine reds and whites show what can be done. Best producers: l'Aigle★, Condamine Bertrand, Croix de St-Jean, J-L DENOIS★, l'HOSPITALET, J & F Lurton★, MAS LA CHEVALIERE, Ormesson★, Pech-Céleyran (Viognier★), Quatre Sous★, St-Saturnin★, SKALLI-FORTANT, VAL D'ORBIEU (top reds★), Virginie.

OCKFEN *Mosel-Saar-Ruwer, Germany* Village with one famous individual vineyard site, the Bockstein. The wines can be superb in a sunny year, never losing their cold steely streak but packing in delightful full-

flavoured fruit as well. Best producers: St Urbans-Hof★★, Dr Heir
Wagner★, ZILLIKEN★★. Best years: (2007) 06 05 04 **03 02 01 99 97 95**.

OKANAGAN VALLEY *British Columbia, Canada* The oldest and mos
important wine-producing region of British Columbia and first home c
Canada's rich, honeyed icewine. The Okanagan Lake helps temper th
bitterly cold nights but October frosts can be a problem. Chardonnay
Pinot Blanc, Pinot Gris and Pinot Noir are the top performers. South c
the lake, Cabernet, Merlot and even Shiraz are now being grow
successfully. Best producers: Blue Mountain★, Burrowing Owl★, Gehringer★
INNISKILLIN, MISSION HILL★★, Quails' Gate, SUMAC RIDGE★, Tinhorn Creek. Bes
years: (reds) 2006 05 04 03 **02 01 00**.

OLTREPÒ PAVESE DOC *Lombardy, Italy* Italy's main source of Pinot Nerc
used mainly for sparkling wines that may be called Classese when mad
here by the CHAMPAGNE method, though base wines supply *spuman*
industries elsewhere. Still reds from Barbera, Bonarda and Pinot Ner
and whites from the Pinots, Riesling and Chardonnay can be impressiv
Major producer of mediocre Pinot Grigio. Best producers: Cà di Frara★
Le Fracce★, Frecciarossa★, Fugazza, Castello di Luzzano, Mazzolino★
Monsupello★, Montelio★, Vercesi del Castellazzo★, Bruno Verdi★. Best years
(reds) (2007) 06 **04 03 01**.

WILLI OPITZ *Neusiedlersee, Burgenland, Austria* The eccentric and publicity
conscious Willi Opitz produces a remarkable, unusual range of desse
wines from his 12ha (30-acre) vineyard, including red Eiswein. The bes
are ★★, but dry wines are average.

OPUS ONE★★ *Oakville AVA, California, USA* BORDEAUX-blend wine, a join
venture initially between Robert MONDAVI and the late Baron Philipp
de Rothschild of MOUTON-ROTHSCHILD, now between Constellatio
and Baroness Philippine de Rothschild. Various Opus bottlings hav
been in the ★★ range, one or two nudging ★★★, in a beautifull
cedary, minty manner. Best years: 2004 03 02 **01 99 98 97 96 95 94 93 9**
91 90 86 85 84.

DOM. DE L'ORATOIRE ST-MARTIN *Côtes du Rhône AC, Rhône Valley, Franc*
Careful fruit selection in a mature vineyard is the secret of Frédéric an
François Alary's concentrated Côtes du Rhône-Villages CAIRANNE red
and whites. Haut-Coustias white★ is ripe with peach and exotic frui
aromas, while the red★★ is a luscious mouthful of raspberries, herbs an
spice. Top red Cuvée Prestige★★ is deep and intense with darkly spic
fruit. Best years: (Cuvée Prestige) 2007 06 05 04 03 01 00 99 98.

OREGON *USA* Oregon shot to international stardom in the early 1980
following some perhaps overly generous praise of its Pinot Noir, but it is onl
with the release of a succession of fine recent vintages and some soul
searching by the winemakers about what style they should be pursuing that w
can now begin to accept that some of the hype was deserved. Consistency i
still a problem, however, with surprisingly warm weather now offerin
challenges along with the traditional ones of overcast skies and unwelcom
rain. Chardonnay can be quite good in an austere, understated style. Th
rising star is Pinot Gris which can be delicious, with surprising complexity
Pinot Blanc is also gaining momentum. The WILLAMETTE VALLEY is considere
the best growing region, although the more BORDEAUX-like climate of th
Umpqua and Rogue Valleys can produce good Cabernet Sauvignon an
Merlot. Best producers: (Rogue, Umpqua) Abacela★, Bridgeview★, Foris★, Henr
Estate, Valley View. Best years: (reds) (2006) **04 03 02**.

ENUTA DELL'ORNELLAIA *Bolgheri, Tuscany, Italy* This beautiful property was developed by Lodovico ANTINORI, brother of Piero. Now owned by FRESCOBALDI. Ornellaia★★, a Cabernet-Merlot blend, doesn't quite have the style of neighbouring SASSICAIA. Also outstanding Merlot, Masseto★★. Best years: (Ornellaia) (2007) (06) (05) 04 03 **01 00 99 98 97 96 95**.

ORTENAU *Baden, Germany* A chain of steep granitic hills between Baden-Baden and Offenburg, which produce the most elegant (generally dry) Rieslings in BADEN, along with fragrant, medium-bodied Spätburgunder (Pinot Noir) reds. Best producers: Laible★★, Männle, Nägelsförst★, Schloss Neuweier★, Wolff Metternich★.

ORVIETO DOC *Umbria, Italy* Traditionally a lightly sweet (*abboccato*) white wine made from a blend of grapes including TREBBIANO and Umbria's native Grechetto, Orvieto at the basic level is today usually dry and ordinary. In the superior Classico zone, however, the potential for richer, more complex wines exists, especially in the Superiore category. Not generally a wine for aging. There are also some very good botrytis-affected examples. Best producers: (dry) Barberani-Vallesanta★ (Superiore Castagnolo★★), La Carraia★, Decugnano dei Barbi★, Palazzone★ (Superiore Campo del Guardiano★★), Castello della SALA★, Salviano★, Conte Vaselli★, Le Velette★; (sweet) Barberani-Vallesanta (Calcaia★★), Decugnano dei Barbi★, Palazzone (Muffa Nobilis★★), Castello della SALA★.

OSBORNE *Jerez y Manzanilla DO, Andalucía, Spain* The biggest drinks company in Spain, Osborne does most of its business in brandy and other spirits. Its sherry arm in Puerto de Santa María specializes in the light Fino Quinta★. Amontillado Coquinero★, rich, intense Bailén Oloroso★★ and Solera India Oloroso★★ are very good indeed. It has also created a large red wine estate at Malpica de Tajo in CASTILLA-LA MANCHA.

PAARL WO *South Africa* South Africa's second most densely planted district after Worcester, accounting for just under 18% of all vineyards. A great diversity of soil and climate favour everything from Cap Classique sparkling wines to sherry styles, but reds are setting the quality pace, especially Shiraz. Its white RHONE counterpart, Viognier, solo and in some expressive white blends, is also performing well. FRANSCHHOEK, Simonsberg-Paarl, Voor Paardeberg and Wellington are wards within the Paarl district. Best producers: (Paarl) Boschendal, DISTELL (Nederburg, Plaisir de Merle★), FAIRVIEW★★, GLEN CARLOU★, Rupert & Rothschild★, Scali★, VEENWOUDEN★★, Vilafonté★, Welgemeend★; (Wellington) Diemersfontein★, Mont du Toit★. Best years: (premium reds) 2006 **05 04 03 02 01 00**.

PACHERENC DU VIC-BILH AC *South-West France* Individual whites from an area overlapping the MADIRAN AC. The wines are mainly dry, but there are some medium-sweet/sweet late-harvest wines. Most Pacherenc is best drunk young. Best producers: AYDIE★, Berthoumieu★, Brumont (Bouscassé★, MONTUS★), du Crampilh★, Damiens, Laffitte-Teston★, PLAIMONT★, Sergent★, Viella. Best years: (sweet) (2006) 05 **04 02 01 00**.

PADTHAWAY *South Australia* This wine region has always been the alter ego of nearby COONAWARRA, growing whites to complement Coonawarra's reds; Chardonnay has been particularly successful. Nowadays there are some excellent reds, especially from Henry's Drive; even GRANGE has included Padthaway grapes. Orlando's premium Lawson's Shiraz★★ is 100% Padthaway, HARDY'S Eileen Hardy Shiraz★★★ usually includes Padthaway fruit. Best producers: Browns of Padthaway, Henry's Drive★★, LINDEMANS★, Orlando/JACOB'S CREEK★, Padthaway Estate, SEPPELT, Stonehaven★.

BRUNO PAILLARD *Champagne AC, Champagne, France* Bruno Paillard is on
of the very few individuals to have created a new CHAMPAGNE house ove
the past century. Paillard still does the blending himself. Non-vintag
Première Cuvée★ is lemony and crisp; Réserve Privée★ is a blanc d
blancs; vintage Brut★★ is a serious wine. De luxe cuvée Nec Plu
Ultra★★ is a barrel-fermented blend of Grands Crus made in to
vintages. Also owns Philipponnat and the great single-vineyard site, Clo
des Goisses★★★. Best years: 1999 96 **95 90 89 88**.

ALVARO PALACIOS *Priorat DOCa, Cataluña, Spain* The young Alvar
Palacios was already a veteran with Bordeaux and Napa experience whe
he launched his boutique winery in the rough hills of southern CATALUN
in the late 1980s. He is now one of the driving forces of the area's rebirth
His expensive, highly concentrated reds (L'Ermita★★★, Finca Dofi★★
Les Terrasses★) from old Garnacha vines and a dollop of Caberne
Sauvignon, Merlot, Cariñeña and Syrah have won a cult following. Bes
years: (2006) (05) 04 03 **01 00 99 98 97 96 95 94**.

PALETTE AC *Provence, France* Tiny AC just east of Aix-en-Provence. Eve
though the local market pays high prices, I find the reds and rosés rathe
tough and charmless. However, Ch. Simone manages to achieve a whit
wine of some flavour from basic southern French grapes. Best producer
Crémade, Ch. Simone★.

PALLISER ESTATE *Martinborough, North Island, New Zealand* State-of-the-ar
winery producing some of New Zealand's best Sauvignon Blanc★★
(certainly the best outside MARLBOROUGH) and Riesling★, delightful
Chardonnay★★ and Pinot Gris★, and impressive, rich-textured Pino
Noir★★. Exciting botrytized dessert wines in favourable vintages
Méthode★ fizz is good, too. Best years: (Pinot Noir) (2007) **06 03 01 00**

CH. PALMER★★ *Margaux AC, 3ème Cru Classé, Haut-Médoc, Bordeaux, Franc*
This estate was named after a British major-general who fought in th
Napoleonic Wars, and is one of the leading properties in MARGAUX AC
The wine is wonderfully perfumed, with irresistible plump fruit. Th
very best vintages can age for 30 years or more. Second wine: Alter Eg
(frequently an excellent, scented red). Best years: 2006 05 04 03 02 **01** 00 9
98 96 95 90 89 88 86 85.

CH. PAPE-CLÉMENT *Pessac-Léognan AC, Cru Classé de Graves, Bordeaux, Franc*
The expensive red wine★★ from this GRAVES Classed Growth has no
always been as consistent as it should be – but things settled down into
high-quality groove during the 1990s. In style it is mid-way between th
refinement of HAUT-BRION and the firmness of la MISSION-HAUT-BRION. Mor
elegance and seduction since 2001. Also produces a small amount of fine
aromatic white wine★★. Second wine: (red) Clémentin. Best years: (reds
2006 05 04 03 02 **01** 00 **99 98 96 95 90** 89 88; (white) 2006 **05 04 03 02 0
00 99 98**.

PARELLADA This Catalan exclusivity is the lightest of the trio of white
grapes that go to make CAVA wines in north-eastern Spain. It also make
still wines, light, fresh and gently floral, with good acidity. Drink it a
young as possible, while it still has the benefit of freshness.

PARKER COONAWARRA ESTATE *Coonawarra, South Australia* Following
the death of founder John Parker the estate has been bought by th
Rathbone family who own Yering Station in the YARRA VALLEY and MOUN
LANGI GHIRAN. The top label, cheekily named First Growth★★ in

imitation of illustrious BORDEAUX reds, has enjoyed much critical acclaim. It is released only in better years. Second-label Terra Rossa Cabernet Sauvignon★ is lighter and leafier. The Merlot★★ is among the best in Australia. Best years: (First Growth) (2006) 05 04 01 99 **98 96 93 91 90**.

C J PASK *Hawkes Bay, North Island, New Zealand* Chris Pask made the first wine in the now-famous Gimblett Gravels area of HAWKES BAY. Flagship Declaration label includes an intense Syrah★, rich Merlot★ and a powerful Cabernet-Merlot-Malbec★ blend. Mid-range wines under the Gimblett Road label. Best years: (reds) (2007) **06** 04 02 00 98.

PASO ROBLES AVA *California, USA* A large AVA at the northern end of SAN LUIS OBISPO COUNTY. Cabernet Sauvignon and Zinfandel perform well in this warm region, and Syrah is gaining an important foothold, but too many producers are chasing OTT alcohol levels. The Perrin family from Ch. de BEAUCASTEL selected this AVA to plant RHONE varieties for their California project, Tablas Creek, whose whites so far outshine their mid-weight reds. Best producers: Adelaida★, Eberle★, Justin★, J Lohr★, Peachy Canyon★, Tablas Creek★, Wild Horse★.

PATAGONIA *Argentina* Located 750 km (465 miles) south of MENDOZA, Patagonia used to be called 'the vineyards of the winds'. Those constant winds, along with relentless sunshine and cool nights, allow a super-healthy viticulture where Malbec flavours are fresh and scented and plump, Cabernet and Merlot are juicy and perhaps, Pinot Noir may flourish. There are two main areas: Río Negro, to the east, is where the first vines were planted in the 19th century. The Neuquén area to the north-west has seen dramatic development during the past 5 years. Best producers: (Río Negro) Humberto Canale, Chacra★★, Infinitus★★/DOMAINE VISTALBA, Noemía★★; (Neuquén) Fin del Mundo, NQN, Familia Schroeder★.

LUÍS PATO *Bairrada, Beira Litoral, Portugal* Leading 'modernist' in BAIRRADA, passionately convinced of the Baga grape's ability to make great reds on clay soil. He labels his wines as BEIRAS after arguing with Bairrada's bosses. Wines such as the Vinhas Velhas★, Vinha Barrosa★★, Vinha Pan★★ and the flagship Quinta do Ribeirinho Pé Franco★★ (from ungrafted vines) rank among Portugal's finest modern reds: some can reach ★★★ with age. Good white, Vinha Formal★, is 100% Bical. Also some good fizz. Daughter Filipa makes delightful reds and whites under Lokal★★ and Ensaios FP★★ labels. Best years: (reds) 2005 **04 03 01 00 97 96 95 92**.

PAUILLAC AC *Haut-Médoc, Bordeaux, France* The deep gravel banks around the town of Pauillac in the HAUT-MEDOC are the heartland of Cabernet Sauvignon. For many wine lovers, the king of red wine grapes finds its ultimate expression in the 3 Pauillac First Growths (LATOUR, LAFITE-ROTHSCHILD and MOUTON-ROTHSCHILD). The large AC also contains 15 other Classed Growths. The uniting characteristic of Pauillac wines is their intense blackcurrant fruit flavour and heady cedar and pencil-shavings perfume. These are the longest-lived of BORDEAUX's great red wines. Best producers: Armailhac★, BATAILLEY★, Clerc-Milon★, Duhart-Milon★, Fonbadet, GRAND-PUY-DUCASSE★, GRAND-PUY-LACOSTE★★, HAUT-BAGES-LIBERAL★, HAUT-BATAILLEY★, LAFITE-ROTHSCHILD★★★, LATOUR★★★, LYNCH-BAGES★★★, MOUTON-ROTHSCHILD★★★, Pibran★, PICHON-LONGUE-VILLE★★★, PICHON-LONGUEVILLE-LALANDE★★, PONTET-CANET★★. Best years: 2006 05 04 03 02 **01 00 96 95 90 89 88 86**.

CH. PAVIE★★ *St-Émilion Grand Cru AC, 1er Grand Cru Classé, Bordeaux, France* The style of the wine may be controversial – dense, rich, succulent – and it has as many enemies as friends, but there's no doubting the progress

225

made at Pavie since Gérard Perse acquired the property in 1998. The price has also soared. Pavie-Decesse★ and MONBOUSQUET★ are part of the same stable. Best years: 2006 05 04 **03 02 01 00 99 98 90 89 88 86.**

CH. PAVIE-MACQUIN★★ *St-Émilion Grand Cru AC, 1er Grand Cru Classé Bordeaux, France* This has become one of the stars of the ST-EMILION grand cru since the 1990s, with promotion to Premier Grand Cru Classé in 2006. Rich, firm and reserved, the wines need 7–8 years and will age longer. Best years: 2006 05 04 03 02 **01** 00 **99 98 96 95 94 90.**

PÉCHARMANT AC *South-West France* Improving red wines from small AC north-east of BERGERAC. The wines are full-bodied and have a delicious, full, piercing flavour of blackcurrants and attractive grassy acidity. Good vintages easily last 10 years and match a good HAUT-MEDOC. Best producers: Beauportail, Bertranoux, Costes★, Grand Jaure, Haut-Pécharmant★, Métairie-Haute★, Tiregand★. Best years: 2005 04 03 01 **00 98 96.**

PEGASUS BAY *Canterbury, South Island, New Zealand*
Matthew Donaldson and Lynette Hudson make lush, mouthfilling Chardonnay★★, an almost chewy Pinot Noir★★ and its even richer big sister Prima Donna Pinot Noir★★, powerful Sauvignon Blanc-Semillon★★ and very stylish Riesling★★. These are some of the most original wines in New Zealand, and all will age well. Best years: (Pinot Noir) (2007) 06 **04 03 02 01 00 99.**

PEMBERTON *Western Australia* Exciting emergent cool-climate region, deep in the Karri forests of the south-west, which has long divided opinion about which varieties will most suit the region. At this stage, the whites have done best, especially taut, tangy Sauvignon Blanc and thrilling, minerally Chardonnay. There have also been the occasional superb examples of Riesling, Viognier, Semillon and Marsanne as well as Western Australia's only distinguished sparkling wine. Best of the reds has been Pinot Noir, with Shiraz rewarding the patient in its best vintages. HOUGHTON leads the way – thanks to the outstanding fruit coming from the vineyard they purchased more than a decade ago – with its Pemberton range: sparkling Chardonnay-Pinot Noir★, Sauvignon Blanc★★, Chardonnay★★, but dull Merlot. Best producers: Angelus, Bellarmine★, HOUGHTON★★, Lillian, Merum, Picardy★, Salitage, Smithbrook.

PENEDÈS DO *Cataluña, Spain* The booming CAVA industry is based in Penedès, and the majority of the still wines are white, made from the Cava trio of Parellada, Macabeo and Xarel-lo, clean and fresh when young, but never exciting. Better whites are made from Chardonnay. The reds are variable, the best made from Cabernet Sauvignon and/or Tempranillo and Merlot. Best producers: Albet i Noya★, Can Feixes★, Can Ràfols dels Caus★★, Cavas Hill, Jean León★, Marques de Monistrol, Masía Bach★, Albert Milá i Mallofré, Puig y Roca★, Sot Lefriec★, TORRES★, Vallformosa, Jané Ventura★.

PENFOLDS *Barossa Valley, South Australia* While it was part of the giant Southcorp group, Penfolds proved that quality can go hand in hand with quantity, but so far its performance as part of the Foster's Wine Group has been uneven, particularly at the lower end. It still makes the country's most famous red wine, GRANGE★★★, and other superb reds such as RWT Shiraz★★★, Magill Estate★★, St Henri★, Bin 707 Cabernet★★, Bin 389 Cabernet-Shiraz★, Bin 28 Kalimna★ and Bin 128 Coonawarra

Shiraz. Its Cellar Reserve wines are difficult to find but outstanding, and occasional releases of Special Bin reds are among Australia's best. However, further down the range a dispiriting blandness has entered into previously reliable wines like Koonunga Hill and Rawson's Retreat. Whites are led by expensive but excellent Yattarna Chardonnay★★; there's also citrus Eden Valley Riesling★ and decent Rawson's Retreat Riesling. Thomas Hyland Cabernet, Shiraz and Chardonnay are pretty good. Best years: (top reds) 2006 05 04 **02 98 96 94 91 90**.

PENLEY ESTATE *Coonawarra, South Australia* Kym Tolley, a member of the PENFOLD family, combined the names when he left Southcorp and launched Penley Estate in 1991. From 1997 Cabernet Sauvignon★★★ has been outstanding. Chardonnay and Hyland Shiraz can reach ★★; Gryphon Merlot★ and fizz★ are also worth a try. Best years: (Cabernet Reserve) (2007) (06) 05 04 **02 00 99 98 96 94 93 92 91**.

PERNAND-VERGELESSES AC *Côte de Beaune, Burgundy, France* The little-known village of Pernand-Vergelesses contains a decent chunk of the great Corton hill, including much of the best white CORTON-CHARLEMAGNE Grand Cru vineyard. The red wines sold under the village name are very attractive when young, with a nice raspberry pastille fruit and a slight earthiness, and will age for 6–10 years. Best vineyard: Île de Vergelesses. As no one ever links poor old Pernand with the heady heights of Corton-Charlemagne, the whites sold under the village name can be a bargain. The wines can be a bit lean and dry to start with but fatten up beautifully after 2–4 years in bottle. Best producers: (reds) CHANDON DE BRIAILLES★★, C Cornu★, Denis Père et Fils★, Dubreuil-Fontaine★, Laleure-Piot★; (whites) CHANDON DE BRIAILLES★★, Dubreuil-Fontaine★, Germain/Ch. de Chorey, A Guyon, JADOT, J-M Pavelot★, Rapet★, Rollin★. Best years: (reds) (2007) 06 05 **03 02 99**; (whites) (2007) **06 05 04 02**.

ANDRÉ PERRET *Condrieu AC, Rhône Valley, France* A top CONDRIEU grower, with 2 standout cuvées: Clos Chanson★★ is direct and full, Chéry★★★, made with some later-picked grapes, is gloriously musky, floral and rich. Impressive white and red ST-JOSEPH, notably Les Grisières★★ from old Syrah vines. Best years: (Condrieu) **2007 06 05 04 03**.

JOSEPH PERRIER *Champagne AC, Champagne, France* The NV Cuvée Royale★ is biscuity and creamy. Prestige Cuvée Josephine★★ has length and complexity, but the much cheaper Cuvée Royale Vintage★★ is the best deal. Best years: (1999) 98 96 **95 90 89 88 85 82**.

PERRIER-JOUËT *Champagne AC, Champagne, France* Perrier-Jouët has had three owners in the past 9 years (it's now owned by Pernod Ricard). This doesn't help consistency, but Perrier-Jouët had fallen so low during the 1990s that any change would be beneficial. Certainly the NV is now a decent drink once more, the Blason Rosé★ is charming and the de luxe vintage cuvée Belle Époque★ (known as Fleur de Champagne in the US) reasonably classy. So keep up the improvement for this great label. Best years: (2002) 99 98 96 **95 90 89 85 82**.

PESQUERA *Ribera del Duero DO, Castilla y León, Spain* Tinto Pesquera reds, richly coloured, firm, fragrant and plummy-tobaccoey, have long been among Spain's best. Made by the small firm of Alejandro Fernández, they are 100% Tempranillo and sold as Crianza and Reserva★. Gran Reserva★★ and Janus★★★ are made in the best years. Condado de Haza (Alenza★) is a separate estate. New ventures in Zamora (Dehesa La Granja★) and La MANCHA (Vínculo). Best years: (Pesquera Crianza) 2005 04 **01 99 96 95 94 93 92 91 90 89**.

PESSAC-LÉOGNAN AC *Bordeaux, France* AC created in 1987 for the northern (and best) part of the GRAVES region and including all the Graves Classed Growths. The supremely gravelly soil tends to favour red wines over the rest of the Graves. Now, thanks to cool fermentation and the use of new oak barrels, this is also one of the most exciting areas of France for top-class white wines. Best producers: (reds) Carbonnieux★, les Carmes Haut-Brion★, Dom. de CHEVALIER★★, FIEUZAL★, HAUT-BAILLY★, HAUT-BRION★★★, Larrivet-Haut-Brion★, LATOUR-MARTILLAC★, la LOUVIERE★, MALARTIC-LAGRAVIERE★, la MISSION-HAUT-BRION★★★, PAPE-CLEMENT★★, SMITH-HAUT-LAFITTE★★; (whites) Brown★, Carbonnieux★, Dom. de CHEVALIER★★★, Couhins-Lurton★★, FIEUZAL★, HAUT-BRION★★★, LATOUR-MARTILLAC★, LAVILLE-HAUT-BRION★★★, la LOUVIERE★★, MALARTIC-LAGRAVIERE★★, PAPE-CLEMENT★★, Rochemorin★, SMITH-HAUT-LAFITTE★★. Best years: (reds) 2006 05 04 02 **01 00 99 98 96 95**; (whites) 2006 **05 04 02 01 00 99 98 96**.

PETALUMA *Adelaide Hills, South Australia* This public company, which includes KNAPPSTEIN, STONIER, Mitchelton in Victoria and Smithbrook in Western Australia, was founded by Brian Croser, probably Australia's most influential winemaker. It was taken over by brewer Lion Nathan in 2001 and Croser is no longer involved. CHAMPAGNE-style Croser★ is stylish but lean. Chardonnay★★ and COONAWARRA (Cabernet-Merlot)★★ are consistently fine and Hanlin Hill Riesling★★★ from the CLARE VALLEY is at the fuller end of the spectrum and matures superbly. Best years: (Coonawarra) (2007) (06) 05 04 (03) **02 01 00** 99 97 94 **91** 90 88.

PETIT VERDOT A rich, tannic variety, grown mainly in Bordeaux's HAUT-MEDOC to add depth, colour and violet fragrance to top wines. Late ripening and erratic yield limit its popularity, but warmer-climate plantings in Australia, California, South Africa, Chile, Argentina, Spain and Italy are giving exciting results.

CH. PETIT-VILLAGE★ *Pomerol AC, Bordeaux, France* This top POMEROL used to be rather dry and dense, but has considerably softened up in recent vintages. New cellar and even better from 2006. Generally worth aging for 8–10 years. Best years: 2006 05 04 **03 01 00** 99 98 96 95 90 89 88.

PETITE ARVINE A Swiss grape variety from the VALAIS, Petite Arvine has a bouquet of peach and apricot, and develops a spicy, honeyed character. Dry, medium or sweet, the wines have good aging potential – thank goodness: I've still got one from 1969. Best producers: Chanton★, Chappaz★, Caves Imesch★, Maye, Dom. du Mont d'Or★, Varone.

PETITE SIRAH Once used primarily as a blending grape in California, this variety is identical to the Rhône blender Durif. Some 275 California wineries now make a varietal Petite Sirah. At its best, it is deep, tannic and long-lived, but can be monstrously huge and unfriendly. Australian and Mexican examples are softer though still hefty, and can occasionally develop a floral scent and blackberry fruit. Best producers: L A CETTO★ (Mexico), De Loach★, FETZER, Fife, Foppiano, RAVENSWOOD★, Stags' Leap Winery★★, TURLEY★★.

CH. PÉTRUS★★★ *Pomerol AC, Bordeaux, France* One of the most expensive red wines in the world (alongside other superstars from POMEROL, such as le PIN). The powerful, concentrated wine produced here is the result of the caring genius of Pétrus' owners, the MOUEIX family, who have maximized the potential of the vineyard of almost solid clay, although the impressive average age of the vines has been much reduced by recent replantings. Drinkable for its astonishingly rich, dizzying blend of fruit and spice flavours after a decade, but top years will age for much longer, developing exotic scents of tobacco and chocolate and truffles as they mature. Best years: 2006 05 04 03 02 01 00 **99 98 96 95 90 89 88 86 85.**

OM. PEYRE ROSE *Coteaux du Languedoc AC, Languedoc, France* Organic viticulture, ultra-low yields and total absence of oak are all marks of the individuality of Marlène Soria's wines. Syrah is the dominant grape in both the raisin- and plum-scented Clos des Cistes★ and the dense, velvety Clos Syrah Léone★★. Best years: (reds) 2004 03 01 **00 99 98 97 96.**

CH. DE PEZ★ *St-Estèphe AC, Haut-Médoc, Bordeaux, France* One of ST-ESTÈPHE's leading non-Classed Growths, de Pez makes mouthfilling, satisfying claret with sturdy fruit. Slow to evolve, good vintages often need 10 years or more. Owned by Champagne house ROEDERER. Best years: 2006 05 04 03 02 **01 00 99 98 96 95 90 89.**

PFALZ *Germany* This immense wine region, with 23,360ha (57,720 acres), makes a lot of mediocre wine, but the quality estates can match the best that Germany has to offer. The Mittelhaardt has a reputation for Riesling, especially round the villages of BAD DÜRKHEIM, WACHENHEIM, FORST and Deidesheim, though Freinsheim, Kallstadt, Ungstein, Gimmeldingen and Haardt also produce fine Riesling as well as Scheurebe, Rieslaner and Pinot Gris. In the Südliche Weinstrasse the warm climate makes the area an ideal testing ground for Spät-, Weiss- and Grauburgunder (aka Pinots Noir, Blanc and Gris), as well as Gewürztraminer, Scheurebe, Muscat and red Dornfelder, the last often dark and tannic, sometimes with oak influence.

JOSEPH PHELPS *Napa Valley AVA, California, USA* Joseph Phelps' BORDEAUX-blend Insignia★★ is usually one of California's top reds, strongly fruit-driven with a lively spicy character. Phelps' pure Cabernets include Napa Valley★ and huge Backus Vineyard★★, beautifully balanced with solid ripe fruit. The Napa Merlot★ is ripe and elegant, with layers of fruit. Phelps was the first California winery to successfully major on Rhône varietals, and makes an intense Viognier★ and complex Syrah★. Le Mistral★ is a splendid Rhône red blend from Phelps' vineyards in MONTEREY COUNTY. Soon to release Chardonnay and Pinot Noir from a

project at cold Freestone near the Sonoma coast. Best years: (Insignia) (2005) 04 03 02 **01 00 99 96 95 94 93 91 85.**

CH. DE PIBARNON *Bandol AC, Provence, France* Blessed with excellently located vineyards, Pibarnon is one of BANDOL's leading properties. The reds★★, extremely attractive when young, develop a truffly, wild herb character with age. Average white and a ripe, strawberryish rosé. Best years: (reds) 2005 03 01 **00 99 98 96.**

PIC ST-LOUP *Coteaux du Languedoc AC, Languedoc, France* This COTEAUX DU LANGUEDOC Cru, north of Montpellier, is one of the coolest growing zones in the Midi and, along with la CLAPE, produces some of the best reds in the Languedoc. Syrah is the dominant variety, along with Grenache and Mourvèdre. Whites from Marsanne, Roussanne, Rolle and Viognier are showing promise. **Best producers:** Cazeneuve★, CLOS MARIE★, Ermitage du Pic St-Loup, l'Euzière★, l'HORTUS★, Lancyre★, Lascaux★, Lavabre★, MAS BRUGUIERE★, Mas de Mortiès★. **Best years:** (reds) 2005 04 **03 01 00 99 98**.

FRANZ X PICHLER *Wachau, Niederösterreich, Austria* One of Austria's most famous producers of dry wines. Top wines Grüner Veltliner and Riesling 'M'★★★ (for monumental) and Riesling Unendlich★★★ (endless) – alcoholically potent but balanced – are amazing. Red Arachon★★ is a joint venture with TEMENT and Szemes in BURGENLAND. **Best years** (Riesling/Grüner Veltliner Smaragd) (2007) 06 05 04 **03 02 01 00** 99 98 97.

CH. PICHON-LONGUEVILLE★★★ *Pauillac AC, 2ème Cru Classé, Haut-Médoc, Bordeaux, France* Despite its superb vineyards, Pichon-Longueville (called Pichon-Baron until 1988) wines were 'also-rans' for a long time. In 1987 the property was bought by AXA and Jean-Michel Cazes of LYNCH-BAGES took over the management. The improvement was immediate and thrilling. Cazes has now left, but most recent vintages have been of First Growth standard, with firm tannic structure and rich dark fruit. Cellar for at least 10 years, although it is likely to keep for 30. Second wine: les Tourelles de Pichon. **Best years:** 2006 05 04 03 02 01 **00** 99 98 96 95 90 89 88 86.

CH. PICHON-LONGUEVILLE-LALANDE★★★ *Pauillac AC, 2ème Cru Classé, Haut-Médoc, Bordeaux, France* The inspirational figure of May de Lencquesaing forged the modern reputation of this property. It's now (2007) controlled by Champagne house ROEDERER but with the same winemaking and management team. Divinely scented and lush at 6–7 years, the wines usually last for 20 at least. Recent years have been excellent. Second wine: Réserve de la Comtesse. **Best years:** 2006 05 04 03 02 **01** 00 **99 98 96 95 90 89 88 86 85 83 82**.

PIEDMONT *Italy* The most important Italian region for the tradition of quality wines. In the north, there is Carema, GHEMME and GATTINARA. To the south, in the LANGHE hills, there's BAROLO and BARBARESCO, both masterful examples of the Nebbiolo grape, and other wines from Dolcetto and Barbera grapes. In the Monferrato hills, in the provinces of Asti and Alessandria, the Barbera, Moscato and Cortese grapes hold sway. Recent changes in the system have created the broad DOCs of Langhe and Monferrato and the regionwide Piemonte appellation, designed to classify all wines of quality from a great range of grape varieties. See also ASTI, ERBALUCE DI CALUSO, GAVI, MOSCATO D'ASTI, NEBBIOLO D'ALBA, ROERO.

PIEROPAN *Veneto, Italy* Exceptionally good SOAVE Classico★ and, from 2 single vineyards, Soave Classico crus Calvarino★★ and La Rocca★★. Excellent RECIOTO DI SOAVE Le Colombare★★ and opulent Passito della Rocca★★, a barrique-aged blend of Sauvignon, Riesling Italico (Welschriesling) and Trebbiano di Soave. Single-vineyard Soaves can improve for 5 years or more, as can the Recioto and other sweet styles.

PIERRO *Margaret River, Western Australia* Mike Peterkin doesn't make that much Pierro Chardonnay★★★, yet it is a masterpiece of elegance and complexity. The Semillon-Sauvignon LTC★ is full with just a hint of leafiness, while the Pinot Noir★ approaches ★★ as the vines age. Dark, dense Cabernet Sauvignon-Merlot★ is the serious, BORDEAUX-like member of the family. The Fire Gully range is from a vineyard next door to MOSS WOOD. Best years: (Chardonnay) (2007) 06 05 04 **03 02 01 00** 99.

PIESPORT *Mosel, Germany* Generic Piesporter Michelsberg wines, soft, sweet and forgettable, have nothing to do with the excellent Rieslings from the top Goldtröpfchen site. With their intense peach and blackcurrant aromas they are unique among MOSEL wines. Best producers: GRANS-FASSIAN★★, Reinhold HAART★★, Kurt Hain★, von KESSELSTATT★, Lehnert-Veit, St Urbans-Hof★★. Best years: (2007) 06 05 04 **02 01 00 99** 98 97 96.

CH. LE PIN★★★ *Pomerol AC, Bordeaux, France* Now one of the most expensive wines in the world. The first vintage was 1979 and the wines, which are concentrated but elegant, are produced from 100% Merlot. The tiny 2ha (5-acre) vineyard lies close to those of TROTANOY and VIEUX-CH.-CERTAN. Best years: 2006 05 04 02 **01 00 99** 98 96 95 94 90 89 88 86 85.

PINE RIDGE *Stags Leap District AVA, California, USA* Wines come from several NAPA AVAs, but its flagship Cabernet remains the supple, plummy STAGS LEAP DISTRICT★★. Andrus Reserve★★, a BORDEAUX blend, has more richness and power, while the HOWELL MOUNTAIN Cabernet★ offers intense fruit and structure for long aging. CARNEROS Merlot★ is spicy and cherry fruited, and Carneros Chardonnay★ looks good. Best years: (Stags Leap Cabernet) 2005 03 **02 01 00 99** 97 96 95 94 91.

PINGUS, DOMINIO DE *Ribera del Duero DO, Castilla y León, Spain* Peter Sisseck's tiny vineyards and winery have attracted worldwide attention since 1995 due to the extraordinary depth and character of the cult wine they produce, Pingus★★★. Second wine Flor de Pingus★★ is also super. Best years: (Pingus) (2005) 04 **03 01 00** 99 96 95.

PINOT BIANCO See PINOT BLANC.

PINOT BLANC Wines have a clear, yeasty, appley taste, and good examples can age to a delicious honeyed fullness. In ALSACE it is taking over the 'workhorse' role from Sylvaner and Chasselas and is the mainstay of most CREMANT D'ALSACE. Important in northern Italy as Pinot Bianco and especially in ALTO ADIGE where it reaches elevated levels of purity, complexity and longevity. Taken seriously too in southern Germany and Austria (as Weissburgunder), producing imposing wines with ripe pear and peach fruit and a distinct nutty character. Also successful in Hungary, Slovakia, Slovenia and the Czech Republic and promising in California (notably from Robert Sinskey), Oregon and Canada.

PINOT GRIGIO See PINOT GRIS.

PINOT GRIS At its finest in ALSACE; with lowish acidity and a deep colour the grape produces fat, rich wines that somehow mature wonderfully. It is very occasionally used in BURGUNDY (as Pinot Beurot) to add fatness to a wine. Italian Pinot Grigio, often boring, occasionally delicious, is currently so popular worldwide that New World producers are tending to use the Italian name in preference to the French version. Also successful in Austria and Germany as Ruländer or Grauburgunder, and as Malvoisie in the Swiss VALAIS. There are good Romanian and Czech examples, as well as spirited ones in Hungary (as Szürkebarát). In a crisp style, it can be successful in Oregon and is showing promise in California, Virginia and OKANAGAN VALLEY in Canada. Now very fashionable in New Zealand and cooler regions of Australia.

231

PINOT NOIR

There's this myth about Pinot Noir that I think I'd better lay to rest. It goes something like this. Pinot Noir is an incredibly tricky grape to grow and an even more difficult grape to vinify; in fact Pinot Noir is such a difficult customer that the only place that regularly achieves magical results is the thin stretch of land known as the Côte d'Or, between Dijon and Chagny in France, where mesoclimate, soil conditions and 2000 years of experience weave an inimitable web of pleasure.

This just isn't so. The thin-skinned, early-ripening Pinot Noir is undoubtedly more difficult to grow than other great varieties like Cabernet or Chardonnay, but that doesn't mean that it's impossible to grow elsewhere – you just have to work at it with more sensitivity and seek out the right growing conditions. And although great red Burgundy is a hauntingly beautiful wine, many Burgundians completely fail to deliver the magic, and the glorious thing about places like New Zealand, California, Oregon, Chile, Australia and Germany is that we are seeing an ever-increasing number of wines that are thrillingly different from anything produced in Burgundy, yet with flavours that are unique to Pinot Noir.

WINE STYLES

France All France's great Pinot Noir wines come from Burgundy's Côte d'Or. Rarely deep in colour, they should nonetheless possess a wonderful fruit quality when young – raspberry, strawberry, cherry or plum – that becomes more scented and exotic with age, the plums turning to figs and pine, and the richness of chocolate mingling perilously with truffles and well-hung game. Strange, challenging, hedonistic. France's other Pinots – in north and south Burgundy, the Loire Valley, Jura, Savoie, Alsace and now occasionally in the south of France – are lighter and milder, and in Champagne its pale, thin wine is used to make sparkling wine.

Other European regions Since the 1990s, helped by good vintages, German winemakers have made considerable efforts to produce serious Pinot Noir (generally called Spätburgunder). Italy, where it is called Pinot Nero or Blauburgunder, and Switzerland (as Blauburgunder) both have fair success with the variety, especially in Alto Adige. Austria and Spain have produced a couple of good examples, and Romania, the Czech Republic and Hungary produce significant amounts of Pinot Noir, though of generally low quality.

New World Light, fragrant wines have bestowed upon Oregon the reputation for being 'another Burgundy'; but I get more excited about the sensual wines of the cool, fog-affected areas of California: the ripe, stylish Russian River Valley examples; the exotically scented wines of Carneros, Anderson Valley and Sonoma Coast; the startlingly original offerings from Santa Barbara County (notably Santa Rita Hills) and Santa Lucia Highlands on east-facing slopes of western Monterey County.

New Zealand produces wines of thrilling fruit and individuality, most notably from Martinborough, Canterbury's Waipara district and Central Otago, with its wild thyme-flavoured wines. In the cooler regions of Australia – including Yarra Valley, Adelaide Hills, north-east Victoria and Tasmania – producers are beginning to find their way with the variety. New Burgundian clones bode well for South African Pinot Noir. Chile's Leyda and Bio-Bio areas are beginning to shine.

BEST PRODUCERS

France (*Burgundy*) d'ANGERVILLE,
l'Arlot, Comte Armand, D Bachelet,
G Barthod, J-M Boillot, BOUCHARD
PERE ET FILS, CATHIARD, CHANDON DE
BRIAILLES, R Chevillon, CLAIR,
J-J Confuron, DROUHIN, C Dugat,
B Dugat-Py, DUJAC, FAIVELEY, GIRARDIN,
GOUGES, GRIVOT, Anne Gros, JADOT,
LAFARGE, LAFON, Dom. LEROY, H
Lignier, MEO-CAMUZET, de MONTILLE,
MORTET, J-F MUGNIER, Ponsot, POTEL,
RION, Dom. de la ROMANEE-CONTI,
E Rouget, ROUMIER, ROUSSEAU, Sérafin,
TOLLOT-BEAUT, de VOGUE;
(*Alsace*) J-B ADAM.

Germany BECKER, BERCHER, FURST,
Huber, JOHNER, Meyer-Näkel,
REBHOLZ, Stodden.

Switzerland GANTENBEIN, Adrian Mathier.

Italy CA' DEL BOSCO, Franz Haas,
Haderburg, Hofstätter, Nals-Margreid.

New World Pinot Noirs
USA (*California*) ACACIA, AU BON
CLIMAT, Byron, CALERA, Clos Pepe,
Davis Bynum, DEHLINGER, Dutton-
Goldfield, Merry Edwards, Gary
Farrell, FLOWERS, HARTFORD FAMILY,
KISTLER, Kosta-Browne, La Crema,
LANDMARK, Littorai, MARCASSIN,
Morgan, Papapietro Perry, Patz &
Hall, RASMUSSEN, ROCHIOLI, SAINTSBURY,
SANFORD, Sea Smoke, Siduri, SWAN,
Talley, WILLIAMS SELYEM; (*Oregon*)
ARGYLE, BEAUX FRERES, DOMAINE
DROUHIN, DOMAINE SERENE, Ken WRIGHT.

Australia Ashton Hills, BANNOCKBURN,
Bass Phillip, Bindi, Castle Rock,
COLDSTREAM HILLS (Reserve), Curly
Flat, Diamond Valley, By FARR,
Freycinet, GIACONDA, KOOYONG,
Paringa, STONIER, TARRAWARRA,
Yabby Lake.

New Zealand ATA RANGI, Carrick,
CRAGGY RANGE (Te Muna Road), DRY
RIVER, Escarpment, FELTON ROAD,
Foxes Island, FROMM, Greenhough
(Hope Vineyard), ISABEL,
MARTINBOROUGH VINEYARD, NEUDORF,
PALLISER ESTATE, PEGASUS BAY, Peregrine,
Quartz Reef, SERESIN, VAVASOUR,
WITHER HILLS.

South Africa BOUCHARD FINLAYSON,
HAMILTON RUSSELL.

Chile CONO SUR (20 Barrels, Ocio),
Viña Leyda, Porta, Villard.

233

PINOT MEUNIER An important ingredient in CHAMPAGNE, along with Pinot Noir and Chardonnay – though it is the least well known of the three. Occasionally found in the LOIRE, and also grown in Germany under the names Müllerrebe, Müller-Traube or Schwarzriesling.

PINOT NERO See PINOT NOIR.
PINOT NOIR See pages 232–3.

PINOTAGE A Pinot Noir x Cinsaut cross, conceived in South Africa in 1925 and covering 6% of the country's vineyards. Highly versatile; classic versions are full-bodied and well-oaked with ripe plum, spice and maybe some mineral, banana or marshmallow flavours. New Zealand and California have interesting examples. **Best producers:** (South Africa) Ashbourne★, Graham BECK★, BEYERSKLOOF★★, Clos Malverne★, DeWaal★ (Top of the Hill★★), Diemersfontein★, FAIRVIEW★, GRANGEHURST★, Kaapzicht★, KANONKOP★★, Laibach★, L'AVENIR★★, Newton Johnson★, SIMONSIG★ (Redhill★★), Stony Brook★, Tukulu; (New Zealand) Te Awa★.

PIPER-HEIDSIECK *Champagne AC, Champagne, France* They've put a big effort into restoring Piper's reputation and the work has paid off. Non-vintage★ is now gentle and biscuity, and the vintage★★ is showing real class. They've also launched a plethora of new cuvées: Sublime (demisec), Divin (blanc de blancs), Rosé Sauvage and Rare★★, a de luxe non-vintage blend. **Best years:** 2000 96 **95** 90 89 **85** 82.

PISANO *Canelones, Uruguay* Family-owned winery with some of Uruguay's truest expressions of the Tannat grape: RPF is a good example and pure, dense Axis Mundi is from old vines. The more sophisticated Arretxea★ blends Tannat with Cabernet and Merlot. **Best years:** (reds) 2005 04 **02** 00.

DOM. JO PITHON *Coteaux du Layon AC, Loire Valley, France* Fine sweet COTEAUX DU LAYON★★ and QUARTS DE CHAUME★★, made entirely from botrytized fruit, see plenty of oak and drink fairly young. Les Blanches Bergères★★ is the most striking of 3 trailblazing dry, barrel-fermented and aged ANJOU BLANCS, and a young-vines SAVENNIERES shows promise, as does new red ANJOU Cabernets. **Best years:** (dry whites) (2007) 06 05 **04** 03 02.

DOM. ROBERT PLAGEOLES *Gaillac AC, South-West France* Both traditionalists and modernizers, Robert and Bernard Plageoles have revived 14 ancient Gaillac grape varieties, including the almost extinct Ondence, which they blend in their sweet Vin d'Autan★★. Dry wines include Mauzac, Ondenc and a bone-dry Mauzac Nature★ fizz.

PRODUCTEURS PLAIMONT *Madiran AC, Côtes de St-Mont VDQS and Vin de Pays des Côtes de Gascogne, South-West France* This grouping of Gascon co-ops is the largest, most reliable and most go-ahead producer of COTES DE GASCOGNE and COTES DE ST-MONT. The whites, full of crisp fruit, are reasonably priced and are best drunk young. The reds, especially Ch. de la Roque★ and Ch. de Sabazan★, are very good too. Also good MADIRAN (Arte Benedicte) and PACHERENC DU VIC-BILH.

PLANETA *Sicily, Italy* Rapidly expanding, dynamic estate. Chardonnay★★ is already one of the best in southern Italy; Cabernet Sauvignon Burdese★★ and Merlot★★ are becoming some of Italy's most impressive; and rich, peppery Santa Cecilia★★ (Nero d'Avola) has star quality. The white Cometa★★ is a fascinating Sicilian version of FIANO. Gluggable Cerasuolo di Vittoria★ and La Segreta red★ and white★ blends are marvellously fruity.

PLANTAGENET *Great Southern, Western Australia* Influential winery in the GREAT SOUTHERN region. The spicy Shiraz★★ is among the best produced in the West; limy Riesling★★ and classy Cabernet Sauvignon★ also impress. Omrah is the second label, made from bought-in grapes – Sauvignon Blanc★, Chardonnay★ and Pinot Noir★ stand out. Best years: (Shiraz) 2007 05 04 03 **02 01 99 98 97 95 93 90 86 85**.

TENUTA IL POGGIONE *Brunello di Montalcino DOCG, Tuscany, Italy* Extensive property (more than 100ha/250 acres of vineyard) which set the standard for traditional-style BRUNELLO DI MONTALCINO★★ (Riserva★★★) at a reasonable price. Also fine ROSSO DI MONTALCINO★ and SUPER-TUSCAN Cabernet-Sangiovese blend San Leopoldo★. Best years: (2007) (06) (04) **03 01 99 98 97 95 90 88 85**.

POL ROGER *Champagne AC, Champagne, France* Non-vintage Brut Réserve★ (formerly known as White Foil) is biscuity and dependable rather than thrilling. The new ultra-dry wine is called Pure. Pol Roger also produces a vintage★★, a vintage rosé★★ and a vintage Chardonnay★★. Its top Champagne, the Pinot-dominated Cuvée Sir Winston Churchill★★, is a deliciously refined drink. All vintage wines will improve with at least 5 years' keeping. Best years: 1999 **98 96 95 90 89 88 85 82**.

POLIZIANO *Vino Nobile di Montepulciano DOCG, Tuscany, Italy* A leading light in Montepulciano. VINO NOBILE★★ is smoother if more international than average, especially the Riserva Vigna Asinone★★. SUPER-TUSCAN Le Stanze★★★ (Cabernet Sauvignon-Merlot) has been outstanding in recent vintages – the fruit in part coming from owner Federico Carletti's other estate, Lohsa, in MORELLINO DI SCANSANO. Best years: (Vino Nobile) (2007) (06) 04 **03 01 99 98 97 95**.

POLZ *Steiermark, Austria* Consistent producer of aromatic dry white wines: few wines fail to reach ★, and with Weissburgunder (Pinot Blanc), Morillon (Chardonnay), Muskateller and Sauvignon Blanc the combination of intensity and elegance frequently deserves ★★. Steierische Klassik indicates wines vinified without any new oak. Best years: (2007) 06 05 **04 03 02 01**.

POMEROL AC *Bordeaux, France* This AC includes some of the world's most sought-after red wines. Pomerol's unique quality lies in its deep clay (though gravel also plays a part in some vineyards) in which the Merlot grape flourishes. The result is seductively rich, almost creamy wine with wonderful mouthfilling fruit flavours: often plummy, but with blackcurrants, raisins and chocolate, too, and mint to freshen it up. Best producers: Beauregard★, Bonalgue, le BON PASTEUR★★, Certan-de-May★, Clinet★★, Clos l'Église★★, Clos René, la CONSEILLANTE★★, l'EGLISE-CLINET★★★, l'EVANGILE★★, Feytit-Clinet★, la FLEUR-PETRUS★★, GAZIN★★, Hosanna★★ (previously Certan-Guiraud), LAFLEUR★★★, LATOUR-A-POMEROL★, Montviel, Nénin★, PETIT-VILLAGE★, PETRUS★★★, Le PIN★★★, TROTANOY★★, VIEUX-CHATEAU-CERTAN★★. Best years: 2006 05 04 **01 00 98 96 95 94 90 89 88 86 85**.

POMINO DOC See CHIANTI RUFINA.

POMMARD AC *Côte de Beaune, Burgundy, France* The first village south of Beaune. At their best, the wines should have full, round, beefy flavours. Can age well, often for 10 years or more. There are no Grands Crus but les Rugiens Bas and les Épenots (both Premiers Crus) occupy the best sites. Best producers: Aleth-Girardin★, Comte Armand★★★, J-M Boillot★★, Courcel★★, Dancer★, M Gaunoux★, V GIRARDIN★★, LAFARGE★★, Lejeune★, de MONTILLE★★, J & A Parent★, Ch. de Pommard★, Pothier-Rieusset★. Best years: (2007) 06 05 03 02 99 **98 97 96 95 90**.

PORT DOC

Douro, Portugal

The Douro region in northern Portugal, where the grapes for port are grown, is wild and beautiful, and now classified as a World Heritage Site. Steep hills covered in vineyard terraces plunge dramatically down to the Douro river. Grapes are one of the few crops that will grow in the inhospitable climate, which gets progressively drier the further inland you travel. But not all the Douro's grapes qualify to be made into port. A quota is established every year, and the rest are made into increasingly good unfortified Douro wines.

Red port grapes include Touriga Franca, Tinta Roriz, Touriga Nacional, Tinta Barroca, Tinta Cão and Tinta Amarela. Grapes for white port include Côdega, Gouveio, Malvasia Fina, Rabigato and Viosinho. Grapes for both are partially fermented, and then *aguardente* (grape spirit) is added – fortifying the wine, stopping the fermentation and leaving sweet, unfermented grape sugar in the finished port.

PORT STYLES

Vintage Finest of the ports matured in bottle, made from grapes from the best vineyards. Vintage port is not 'declared' every year (usually there are 3 or 4 declarations per decade), and only during the second calendar year in cask if the shipper thinks the standard is high enough. It is bottled after 2 years, and may be consumed soon afterwards, as is not uncommon in the USA; at this stage it packs quite a punch. The British custom of aging for 20 years or more can yield exceptional mellowness. Vintage port throws a thick sediment, so requires decanting.

Single quinta (Vintage) A true single-quinta wine comes from an individual estate; however, many shippers sell their vintage port under a quinta name in years which are not declared as a vintage, even though it may be sourced from 2 or 3 different vineyards. It is quite possible for these 'off vintage' ports to equal or even surpass the vintage wines from the same house.

Aged tawny Matured in cask for 10, 20, 30 or even 40 years before bottling, older tawnies have delicious nut and fig flavours.

Colheita Tawny from a single vintage, matured in cask for at least 7 years – potentially the finest of the aged tawnies.

Late Bottled (Vintage) (LBV) Port matured for 4–6 years in vat, then usually filtered to avoid sediment forming in the bottle. Traditional unfiltered LBV has much more flavour and requires decanting; it can generally be aged for another 5 years or more.

Crusted Making a comeback, this is a blend of good ports from 2–3 vintages, bottled without filtration after 3–4 years in cask. A deposit (crust) forms in the bottle and the wine should be decanted.

Reserve (most can be categorized as Premium Ruby) has an average of 3–5 years' age. A handful represent good value.

Ruby The youngest red port with only 1–3 years' age. Ruby port should be bursting with young, almost peppery, fruit, and there has been an improvement in quality of late, except at the cheapest level.

Tawny Cheap tawny is either an emaciated ruby, or a blend of ruby and white port, and is both dilute and raw.

White Only the best taste dry and nutty from wood-aging; most are coarse and alcoholic, best with tonic water and a slice of lemon.

BEST PRODUCERS

Vintage BURMESTER, CHURCHILL, COCKBURN, CROFT, Delaforce, DOW, FERREIRA, FONSECA, GRAHAM, NIEPOORT, Quinta do NOVAL, Portal, RAMOS PINTO, SMITH WOODHOUSE, TAYLOR, WARRE.

Single quinta (Vintage) CHURCHILL (Quinta da Gricha), COCKBURN (Quinta dos Canais), Quinta do CRASTO, CROFT (Quinta da Roêda), DOW (Quinta do Bomfim, Quinta Senhora da Ribeira), FONSECA (Guimaraens), GRAHAM (Malvedos), NOVAL (Silval), Quinta do Passadouro, Pintas, Quinta de la ROSA, TAYLOR (Quinta de Terra Feita, Quinta de Vargellas), Quinta do Vale Dona Maria, Quinta do Vale Meão, Quinta do Vallado, Quinta do VESUVIO, WARRE (Quinta da Cavadinha).

Aged tawny Barros, BURMESTER, COCKBURN, DOW, FERREIRA, FONSECA, GRAHAM, Krohn, NIEPOORT, NOVAL, RAMOS PINTO, SANDEMAN, TAYLOR, WARRE.

Colheita Andresen, Barros, BURMESTER, Cálem, Feist, Kopke, Krohn, Messias, NIEPOORT, NOVAL.

Traditional Late Bottled Vintage Andresen, CHURCHILL, Quinta do CRASTO, FONSECA, Quinta do Infantado, NIEPOORT, NOVAL, Poças, RAMOS PINTO, Quinta de la ROSA, SMITH WOODHOUSE, WARRE.

Crusted CHURCHILL, DOW, GRAHAM, FONSECA.

Ruby COCKBURN, FERREIRA, FONSECA, GRAHAM, Quinta de la ROSA, SANDEMAN, SMITH WOODHOUSE, TAYLOR, WARRE.

White CHURCHILL, NIEPOORT.

237

POMMERY *Champagne AC, Champagne, France* High-quality CHAMPAGNE hous
now owned by Vranken, who have maintained the traditional Pommer
style but in recent years have launched 9 – yes 9 – non-vintage cuvées!
can't keep up. Along with Brut Royal and Apanage★, the range nov
includes Summertime blanc de blancs, Wintertime blanc de noirs an
Springtime, a Pinot Noir-dominated rosé. Austere vintage Brut★ i
delicious with maturity, and the prestige cuvée Louise, both white★★
and rosé★★, is the epitome of discreet, perfumed elegance. Best years
(1999) 98 96 **95 92 90 89 88 85 82**.

PONDALOWIE *Bendigo, Victoria, Australia* Dominic and Krystina Morris ar
dynamic producers making a name for their red wines, including som
absolutely ripper Shiraz★, Shiraz-Viognier★ and dramatic, opulen
Tempranillo★★.

CH. PONTET-CANET★★ *Pauillac AC, 5ème Cru Classé, Haut-Médoc, Bordeaux
France* This property's vineyards are located close to those of MOUTON
ROTHSCHILD. Since 1975, when the Tesserons of LAFON-ROCHET bought th
property, there has been a gradual return to the typical PAUILLAC style o
big, chewy, intense claret that develops a beautiful blackcurrant fruit, an
since 2000 the property has been on fine form. It's one of the wines of th
vintage in 2004 and 2005 – and that's saying something. One of the bes
value of the Classed Growths. Best years: 2006 05 04 03 02 **01** 00 **99 98 9**
95 94 90 89 86 85.

PORT See pages 236–7.

NICOLAS POTEL *Burgundy, France* Energetic négociant owned by Cottin
brothers of Labouré-Roi, producing consistently fine wines at attractiv
prices. Particularly strong in their native VOLNAY★★, VOSNE-ROMANEE an
in NUITS-ST-GEORGES★★. Now increasing white wine production. Nicolas i
setting up his own eco-friendly domaine in Beaune from the 200?
vintage. Best years: (2007) 06 05 **04 03 02 99**.

CH. POTENSAC★★ *Médoc AC, Bordeaux, France* Owned and run by th
Delon family, of LEOVILLE-LAS-CASES, Potensac's fabulous success is base
on quality, consistency and value for money. The wine can be drunk a
4–5 years, but fine vintages will improve for at least 10 years. Best years
2006 05 04 **03 02 01 00 99 98 96 95**.

POUILLY-FUISSÉ AC *Mâconnais, Burgundy, France* Chardonnay from 5
villages, including Pouilly and Fuissé. After a period of poor value, ther
are now some committed growers producing buttery, creamy wines tha
can be delicious at 2 years but will often develop beautifully for up to 10
Best producers: D & M Barraud★★, Bret Brothers★★, Cordier★★, Corsin★★
C & T Drouin★, J-A Ferret★★, Ch. Fuissé★★, Guffens-Heynen (VERGET)★★
R Lassarat★★, R Luquet★, O Merlin★★, Robert-Denogent★★, Ch. de
Rontets★★, Saumaize-Michelin★★, Valette★★. Best years: (2007) 06 **05 04 03**
02 00 99.

POUILLY-FUMÉ AC *Loire Valley, France* Fumé means 'smoked' in French
and a good Pouilly-Fumé has a pungent smell often likened to gunflint
The grape is Sauvignon Blanc, and the extra smokiness comes from a
flinty soil called silex. Despite the efforts of a few producers, this is a
disappointingly underperforming and overpriced AC. Best producers:
F Blanchet★, Henri BOURGEOIS★, A Cailbourdin★, J-C Chatelain★, Didier
DAGUENEAU★★, Serge Dagueneau★, André Dezat, A & E Figeat, Ladoucette★
Landrat-Guyollot★, Masson-Blondelet★, M Redde★, Seguin, Sellier, Tinel-
Blondelet★, Ch. de Tracy★. Best years: 2007 **06 05 02 00**.

POUILLY-LOCHÉ AC See POUILLY-VINZELLES AC.

POUILLY-SUR-LOIRE AC *Loire Valley, France* Light appley wines from the Chasselas grape from vineyards around Pouilly-sur-Loire, the town which gave its name to POUILLY-FUMÉ. Drink as young as possible. Best producers: Serge Dagueneau★, Landrat-Guyollot★.

POUILLY-VINZELLES AC *Mâconnais, Burgundy, France* Small AC which, with its neighbour Pouilly-Loché, lies somewhat in the shadow of POUILLY-FUISSÉ. Most wines come through the co-operative, but there are some good domaines. Best producers: Cave des Grands Crus Blancs, la Soufrandière★★, Tripoz★, Valette★. Best years: (2007) 06 05 04 03 02.

CH. POUJEAUX★ *Moulis AC, Haut-Médoc, Bordeaux, France* Frequently Poujeaux is the epitome of MOULIS – beautifully balanced, gentle ripe fruit jostled by stony dryness – but just lacking that something extra to propel it to a higher plane. Attractive at 5–6 years old, good vintages can easily last for 10–20 years. Since 2007 same ownership as Clos Fourtet in ST-EMILION. Best years: 2006 05 04 **03** 02 **01** 00 99 98 96 95 90 86.

PRAGER *Wachau, Niederösterreich, Austria* Toni Bodenstein is one of the pioneers of the WACHAU, producing top dry Rieslings from the Achleiten and Klaus vineyards★★★ and excellent Grüner Veltliners from Achleiten★★. Best years: (Riesling/Grüner Veltliner Smaragd) (2007) 06 05 04 03 02 01 00 99 98 97 96.

PREMIÈRES CÔTES DE BLAYE AC *Bordeaux, France* A much improved AC on the right bank of the Gironde. The fresh, Merlot-based reds are ready in 2–3 years but will age for more. Top red wines can be labelled under the new, quality-driven Blaye AC from 2000. Part of new Côtes de Bordeaux AC from 2007. Best producers: (reds) Bel-Air la Royère★, Confiance★, Gigault (Cuvée Viva★), les Grands Maréchaux, Haut-Bertinerie★, Haut-Colombier★, Haut-Grelot, Haut-Sociando, les Jonqueyres★, Mondésir-Gazin★, Montfollet★, Roland la Garde★, Segonzac★, Tourtes★; (whites) Haut-Bertinerie★, Charron (Acacia★), Cave des Hauts de Gironde, Tourtes (Prestige★). Best years: 2005 04 03 01 00 98 96 95.

PREMIÈRES CÔTES DE BORDEAUX AC *Bordeaux, France* Hilly region overlooking GRAVES and SAUTERNES across the Garonne. For a long time the AC was best known for its Sauternes-style sweet wines, particularly from the communes of CADILLAC, LOUPIAC and STE-CROIX-DU-MONT, but the juicy reds and rosés have now forged ahead. These are usually delicious at 2–3 years old but should last for 5–6 years. Part of new Côtes de Bordeaux AC from 2007. Best producers: (reds) Bauduc★, Carignan★, Chelivette★, Clos Ste-Anne, Grand-Mouëys★, Lamothe-de-Haux, Lezongars★, Mont-Pérat★, Plaisance★, Puy-Bardens★, REYNON★, Ste-Marie (Alios★), Suau★. Best years: (reds) 2005 04 00 98 96 95.

CH. PRIEURÉ-LICHINE★ *Margaux AC, 4ème Cru Classé, Haut-Médoc, Bordeaux, France* Underachieving property that saw several false dawns before being sold in 1999. Right Bank specialist Stéphane Derenoncourt of PAVIE-MACQUIN★★ and CANON-LA-GAFFELIERE★★ fame is now the consultant winemaker, and the wines have more fruit, finesse and perfume, especially the 2004. Best years: 2006 05 04 03 02 01 00 99 98 96 95 90 89.

PRIEURÉ DE ST-JEAN DE BÉBIAN *Coteaux du Languedoc AC, Languedoc, France* One of the pioneering estates in the Midi, producing an intense, spicy, generous red★★, second wine La Chapelle de Bébian and a barrel-fermented white. Best years: (reds) 2006 05 02 01 00 99.

PRIMITIVO DI MANDURIA DOC *Puglia, Italy* The most important appellation for PUGLIA's Primitivo grape, which has been enjoying a renaissance of interest since it was found to be almost identical to

California's Zinfandel. The best wines combine outstanding ripeness an
concentration with a knockout alcohol level. Good Primitivo is also sol
as IGT Primitivo del Tarantino and as Gioia del Colle DOC. Be
producers: Felline★★, Pervini★★, Giovanni Soloperto. Best years: (2007) (06
05 04 03 01 00.

PRIMO ESTATE *McLaren Vale, South Australia* Joe Grilli continues to be one o
Australia's most thoughtful and innovative winemakers. For hi
premium label, Joseph, Grilli adapts the Italian AMARONE method fo
Moda Cabernet-Merlot★★ (★★★ with 10 years' age!) and makes
dense, eye-popping, complex Joseph Red fizz★★. He also does
sensuous Botrytis Riesling La Magia★★, fabulous honeyed fortifie
Fronti★★★, surprising dry white La Biondina Colombard★, cherry-rip
Il Briccone★ (Shiraz-Sangiovese), bright, velvety Merlesco (Merlot
fine, powerful Nebbiolo★ – and superb olive oils★★★. Best years: (Mod
Cabernet-Merlot) (2007) 06 05 04 **02 01 00** 99 98 97 96 95 94 93 91 90.

PRIMO PALATUM *Languedoc and South-West France* One of the new breed o
négociants working between many appellations. Xavier Copel selects th
best wines from CAHORS★, MADIRAN★, JURANCON★, MINERVOIS★, COTES D
ROUSSILLON and other appellations in South-West France an
Languedoc-Roussillon, as well as from BORDEAUX. Cahors cuvée
Classica★ and Mythologia★ are dark and concentrated.

PRIORAT DOCa *Cataluña, Spain* A hilly, isolated
district with very low-yielding vineyards
planted on precipitous slopes of deep slate
soil. Old-style fortified *rancio* wines used to
attract little attention. Then in the 1980s a
group of young winemakers revolutionized
the area, bringing in state-of-the-art winemaking methods and grape varieties such as
Cabernet Sauvignon to back up the native
Garnacha and Cariñena. Their rare,

expensive wines have taken the world by storm. Ready at 5 years old, th
best will last much, much longer. The region was elevated to DOC
status in 2001. Best producers: Bodegas B G (Gueta-Lupía★), Burgos Porta
Capafons-Ossó★, Cims de Porrera★★, CLOS ERASMUS★★★, CLO
MOGADOR★★★, Combier-Fischer-Gérin★★ (Trio Infernal 2/3★★★), L
Conreria d'Scala Dei★, Costers del Siurana (Clos de l'Obac★), J M Fuente
(Gran Clos★★), Ithaca★, Mas La Alta★★, MAS DOIX★★★, Mas d'en Gil (Clo
Fontà★), Mas Martinet (Clos Martinet★), Merum, Alvaro PALACIOS★★★
Pasanau Germans (Finca la Planeta★), Rotllan Torra★, Scala Dei★, Terroir a
Limit/SADIE FAMILY (Dits del Terra★★), VALL-LLACH★★. Best years: (reds) 200
04 03 01 00 99 98 96 95 94 93.

PROSECCO DI CONEGLIANO-VALDOBBIADENE DOC *Veneto, Ital*
The Prosecco grape gives soft, scented wine made sparkling by a secon
fermentation in tank, though Prosecco can also be still, or *tranquillo*
Generally, however, it is a spumante or frizzante for drinking young. Th
Cartizze sub-zone near Valdobbiadene supposedly produces the mos
refined, certainly the most expensive, wines. Best producers: Adami★
Bernardi★, Bisol★, Carpenè Malvolti★, Le Colture, Col Vetoraz★, Nin
Franco★, La Riva dei Frati★, Ruggeri★, Tanorè★, Zardetto★.

PROVENCE *France* Provence is home to France's oldest vineyards but the
region has been better known for its beaches and arts festivals than for it

wines. However, it seems even Provence is caught up in the revolution sweeping through the vineyards of southern France. The area has 5 small ACs (BANDOL, les BAUX-DE-PROVENCE, BELLET, CASSIS and PALETTE), but most of the wine comes from the much larger areas of the COTES DE PROVENCE, COTEAUX VAROIS, Coteaux de Pierrevert and COTEAUX D'AIX-EN-PROVENCE. Vin de Pays des BOUCHES-DU-RHONE is also becoming increasingly important. Reds can be good but are often too lean, rosés are getting fresher, though not less expensive. Whites have a way to go.

J J PRÜM *Bernkastel, Mosel, Germany* Estate making some of Germany's best Riesling in sites like the Sonnenuhr★★★ in WEHLEN, Himmelreich★★ in GRAACH and Lay★★ and Badstube★★ in BERNKASTEL. All have great aging potential. Best years: (2007) 06 05 04 03 02 **01 99 98 97 96 95 94 93 90 88 85**.

S A PRÜM *Wehlen, Mosel, Germany* There are a confusing number of Prüms in the MOSEL – the best known is J J PRUM, but S A Prüm comes a decent second. The estate's most interesting wines are Riesling from WEHLENER Sonnenuhr, especially Auslese★★, but it also makes good wine from sites in BERNKASTEL★ and GRAACH★. Best years: (2007) 06 05 04 **03 02 01 99 97 95**.

PRUNOTTO *Barolo DOCG, Piedmont, Italy* One of the great BAROLO producers, now ably run by Albiera, Piero ANTINORI's eldest daughter. Highlights include Barolo Bussia★★★ and Cannubi★★, BARBERA D'ALBA Pian Romualdo★★, BARBERA D'ASTI Costamiòle★★, BARBARESCO Bric Turot★★ and NEBBIOLO D'ALBA Occhetti★. Also good MOSCATO D'ASTI★, Barbera d'Asti Fiulot★ and ROERO Arneis★. Best years: (Barolo) (2007) (06) 04 **03** 01 **00 99 98 97 95 90 89 88 85**.

PUGLIA *Italy* This southern region is a prolific source of blending wines, but exciting progress has been made with native varieties: red Uva di Troia in CASTEL DEL MONTE; white Greco for characterful Gravina, revived by Botromagno; and Verdeca and Bianco d'Alessano for Locorotondo. The red Primitivo, led by examples from producers under the ACCADEMIA DEI RACEMI umbrella, make a big impact (whether under the PRIMITIVO DI MANDURIA DOC or more general IGTs). But it is the Negroamaro grape grown on traditional bush-trained or *alberello* vines in the Salento peninsula that provides the best wines, whether red or rosé. Outstanding examples include Vallone's Graticciaia★★, Candido's Duca d'Aragona★★, Masseria Monaci's le Braci★★ and Taurino's Patriglione★★. Brindisi and SALICE SALENTINO are two good-value, reliable DOCs.

PUISSEGUIN-ST-ÉMILION AC *Bordeaux, France* Small ST-EMILION satellite. The wines are generally fairly solid but with an attractive chunky fruit and usually make good drinking at 3–5 years. Best producers: Bel-Air, Branda, Durand-Laplagne★, Fongaban, Guibeau-la-Fourvieille, Laurets, la Mauriane★, Producteurs Réunis, Soleil★. Best years: **2005 03 01 00 98 96 95**.

PULIGNY-MONTRACHET AC *Côte de Beaune, Burgundy, France* Puligny is one of the finest white wine villages in the world and adds the name of its greatest Grand Cru, le MONTRACHET, to its own. There are 3 other Grands Crus (BATARD-MONTRACHET, Bienvenues-BATARD-MONTRACHET and Chevalier-MONTRACHET) and 11 Premiers Crus. The flatter vineyards use the Puligny-Montrachet AC. Good vintages really need 5 years' aging, while Premiers Crus and Grands Crus may need 10 years and can last for 20 or more. A few barrels of red wine are made. Best producers: J-M Boillot★★, CARILLON★★★, Chavy★, Deux MONTILLE★, DROUHIN★★,

A Ente★★, B Ente★, JADOT★★, Larue★★, LATOUR★, Dom. LEFLAIVE★★★ O LEFLAIVE★, P Pernot★★, Ch. de Puligny-Montrachet★★, RAMONET★★ SAUZET★★. Best years: (2007) 06 05 **04 02 01 00 99**.

PYRENEES See GRAMPIANS AND PYRENEES.

QUARTS DE CHAUME AC *Loire Valley, France* The Chenin Blanc grape finds one of its most rewarding mesoclimates here. Quarts de Chaume is a 40ha (100-acre) AC within the larger COTEAUX DU LAYON AC overlooking the Loire; steep, sheltered, schistous slopes favour optimal ripening and noble rot. The result is intense, sweet wines with a mineral backbone, which can last for longer than almost any in the world – although many can be drunk after 5 years. **Best producers:** BAUMARD★★★, Bellerive★★ Laffourcade★, Pierre-Bise★★, Jo PITHON★★, Plaisance★, Joseph Renou★★ Suronde★★, la Varière★. Best years: (2007) 06 05 **03** 02 **01 99** 97 96 95 90 89

QUEBRADA DE MACUL *Maipo, Chile* East of Santiago, at the foot of the Andes, this garage winery was created by winemaker Ignacio Recabarren to produce superbly idiosyncratic Cabernet Sauvignon-based Domus Aurea★★, a red packed with MAIPO character. Recabarren left in 2002 and Bordelais Jean-Pascal Lacaze is now in charge. Best years: (Domus Aurea) (2006) 04 03 02 **01 99** 97.

QUEENSLAND *Australia* The Queensland wine industry is expanding fast and now produces more than TASMANIA. Wine is closely linked to tourism. About 60 wineries perch on rocky hills in the main region, the Granite Belt, near the NEW SOUTH WALES border. New areas South Burnett (north-west of Brisbane), Darling Downs (around the town of Toowoomba) and Mount Tamborine in the Gold Coast hinterland are showing promise. **Best producers:** Albert River, Barambah Ridge, BOIREANN★, Robert Channon★, Clovely Estate, Heritage, Jimbour Station, Preston Peak★, Robinsons Family, Sirromet, Summit Estate.

QUERCIABELLA *Chianti Classico DOCG, Tuscany, Italy* This model of a modern Chianti producer serves up a gorgeously scented, rich-fruited CHIANTI CLASSICO★★. But it has made an even greater splash with its 3 SUPER-TUSCAN: Burgundy-like white Batàr★★ from Pinot Bianco and Chardonnay; tobaccoey, spicy Sangiovese-Cabernet blend Camartina★★★; and Palafreno★, a blend of Sangiovese and Merlot. Best years: (Camartina) (2007) (06) 04 **03** 01 99 97 95 90 88.

QUILCEDA CREEK *Washington State, USA* One of America's top Cabernet Sauvignons★★★, a wine with intense concentration and exceptional character. It benefits from cellaring for 7–10 years. Supple, rich Merlot★★★ is produced in small quantities. A less expensive Columbia Valley Red★★ offers a tantalizing glimpse of the winemaking style. Best years: (2006) 05 04 03 **02 01 99** 97.

QUINCY AC *Loire Valley, France* Appealingly aggressive gooseberry-flavoured, dry white wine from Sauvignon Blanc vineyards west of Bourges. Can age for a year or two. **Best producers:** Ballandors★, H BOURGEOIS★, Mardon★, J Rouzé, Silices de Quincy★, Tremblay, Trotereau★.

QUINTARELLI *Valpolicella DOC, Veneto, Italy* Giuseppe Quintarelli is the great traditional winemaker of VALPOLICELLA. His philosophy is one of growing the very best grapes and letting nature do the rest. His Classico Superiore★★ is left in cask for about 4 years and his famed AMARONE★★★ and RECIOTO★★ for up to 7 years before release. Alzero★★ is a spectacular Amarone-style wine made from Cabernets Franc and Sauvignon. Best years: (Amarone) (2007) (06) (04) (03) **01 99 97** 95 93 90 88 85 83.

QUPÉ *Santa Maria Valley AVA, California, USA* Owner/winemaker Bob Lindquist makes a savoury, tasty Bien Nacido Syrah★. His Reserve Chardonnay★★ and Bien Nacido Cuvée★★ (a Chardonnay-Viognier blend) have sublime appley fruit and perfume. A leading exponent of red and white RHONE-style wines, including Viognier★ and Marsanne★. Best years: (Syrah) (2005) 04 03 **02 01 00 99 98 97 96 95 94 91 90**.

CH. DE LA RAGOTIÈRE *Muscadet Sèvre-et-Maine, Loire Valley, France* The inventive Couillaud brothers claim to have salvaged the reputation of Muscadet in US restaurants with M★★, an old-vines wine matured *sur lie* for almost 3 years. The standard Muscadet★ is elegant and built to last, too; lighter ones come from the Couillauds' other property, Ch. la Morinière. Vin de pays Chardonnay is a speciality (Auguste Couillaud★) and a host of experimental varieties appear under the Collection Privée label, including an accomplished Sauvignon Gris★, Viognier and late-harvest Petit Manseng. Best years: (M) **2001 99 97**.

RAÏMAT *Costers del Segre DO, Cataluña, Spain* Owned by CODORNIU, this large, irrigated estate makes pleasant and refreshingly balanced wines from Tempranillo, Cabernet Sauvignon (Mas Castell vineyard★) and Chardonnay. Lively 100% Chardonnay CAVA and upscale red blend 4 Varietales. Best years: (reds) **2005 04 03 01 00 99 98**.

RAMONET *Chassagne-Montrachet, Côte de Beaune, Burgundy, France* The Ramonets (Noël and Claude) produce some of the most complex of all white Burgundies from 3 Grands Crus (BATARD-MONTRACHET★★★, Bienvenues-BATARD-MONTRACHET★★★ and le MONTRACHET★★★) and Premiers Crus including Ruchottes★★★, Caillerets★★★, Boudriotte★★, Vergers★★, Morgeot★★ and Chaumées★★★. If you want to spare your wallet try the ST-AUBIN★★ or the CHASSAGNE-MONTRACHET white★★ or red★★. Best years: (whites) (2007) 06 05 04 02 **01 00 99 97 92 90 89**.

JOÃO PORTUGAL RAMOS *Alentejo, Portugal* João Portugal Ramos is one of Portugal's foremost winemakers. Smoky, peppery Trincadeira★★, spicy Aragonês (Tempranillo)★, powerful Syrah★ and intensely dark-fruited red blend Vila Santa★★ are all superb. Marquês de Borba★ is the label for everyday reds and whites, and a brilliant red Reserva★★ is also made. New World-style Tagus Creek is setting new standards in juicy, affordable styles. Best years: 2005 **04 01 00 99 97**.

RAMOS PINTO *Douro DOC and Port DOC, Douro, Portugal* Innovative PORT company owned by ROEDERER, making complex, full-bodied Late Bottled Vintage★ and aged tawnies (10-year-old Quinta da Ervamoira★★ and 20-year-old Quinta do Bom Retiro★★★). Vintage ports★★ are rich and early maturing. DOURO reds Duas Quintas (Reserva★, Reserva Especial★★) and Bons Ares★ are reliable. Best years: (Vintage) 2004 **03 00 97 95 94 83**.

CASTELLO DEI RAMPOLLA *Chianti Classico DOCG, Tuscany, Italy* Outstanding if French-influenced CHIANTI CLASSICO★★. SUPER-TUSCAN Sammarco, sometimes ★★★, is mostly Cabernet with some Sangiovese; Vigna d'Alceo★★★ adds Petit Verdot to Cabernet Sauvignon. Best years: (Sammarco) (2007) (06) 04 03 **01 00 99 98 97 95**; (Vigna d'Alceo) (2007) (06) 04 03 01 **00 99 98 97**.

RANDERSACKER *Franken, Germany* Important wine village just outside the city of Würzburg in FRANKEN, producing excellent dry Rieslings, dry Silvaners, spicy Traminer and piercingly intense Rieslaner. Best producers: Bürgerspital, JULIUSSPITAL★, Schmitt's Kinder★, Störrlein★. Best years: (2007) 06 05 **04 03 02 01 00 99**.

RAPEL, VALLE DEL *Valle Central, Chile*   One of Chile's most exciting red wine regions, the cradle of Chilean Carmenère, Rapel covers both the Valle del Cachapoal in the north and the Valle de COLCHAGUA in the south. Best producers: Altaïr★/SAN PEDRO, Anakena, CASA LAPOSTOLLE★★ CONCHA Y TORO★★, CONO SUR★, EMILIANA★★, Gracia★, LA ROSA★, MONTES★★ MontGras, Torreón de Paredes, Viu Manent★.

KENT RASMUSSEN *Carneros AVA, California, USA*   Burgundian-style Chardonnay★★ capable of considerable aging and a fascinating juicy Pinot Noir★★ are made by ultra-traditional methods. Also occasional delightful oddities like Alicante and Dolcetto under the Ramsay label. Best years: (Pinot Noir) (2005) **02 01 00 99 98 95 94 91 90**.

RASTEAU *Rhône Valley, France*   The single-village AC is for fortified Grenache red or white wine and a reviving *rancio* version which is left in barrel for 2 or more years. However, much of the best wine from Rasteau is robust dry red, which comes under the COTES DU RHONE-VILLAGES AC. Best producers: E Balme, Beaurenard★, Cave des Vignerons, Mourt de Gautens★★ Perrin★, Rabasse-Charavin, Santa Duc, la Soumade★, du Trapadis★.

RENATO RATTI *Barolo DOCG, Piedmont, Italy*   The late Renato Ratti led the revolution in winemaking in the Alba area with BAROLO and BARBARESCO of better balance, colour and richness and softer in tannins than the traditional models. Today his son Pietro and nephew Massimo Martinelli produce sound Barolo Marcenasco★ and crus Conca★★ and Rocche★★ from the Marcenasco vineyards at La Morra, as well as good BARBERA D'ALBA Torriglione★, Dolcetto d'Alba Colombè★, NEBBIOLO D'ALBA Ochetti★ and Monferrato DOC Villa Pattono★, a blend of Barbera with Cabernet and Merlot.

RAUENTHAL *Rheingau, Germany*   Sadly, only a few producers live up to the reputation earned by this RHEINGAU village's great Baiken and Gehrn sites for intense, spicy Rieslings. Best producers: Georg BREUER★★, Langwerth von Simmern★, Staatsweingut. Best years: (2007) 06 05 04 **03 02 01 99 98**.

CH. RAUZAN-SÉGLA★★ *Margaux AC, 2ème Cru Classé, Haut-Médoc, Bordeaux, France*   A dynamic change in winemaking in 1982 and the purchase of the property by Chanel in 1994 propelled Rauzan-Ségla up the quality ladder. Now the wines have a rich blackcurrant fruit, round, mellow texture, powerful woody spice and good concentration. Second wine Ségla. Best years: 2006 05 04 03 02 **01 00 99 98 96 95 94 90 89 88 86 85**.

JEAN-MARIE RAVENEAU *Chablis, Burgundy, France*   Beautifully nuanced CHABLIS from 3 Grands Crus (Blanchot★★★, les Clos★★★, Valmur★★★) and 4 Premiers Crus (Montée de Tonnerre★★★, Vaillons★★, Butteaux★★★, Chapelot★★), using a combination of old oak and stainless-steel fermentation. The wines can age for a decade or more. Best years: (top crus) (2007) 06 05 04 02 **00 99 97 95 92 90**.

RAVENSWOOD *Sonoma Valley AVA, California, USA*   Zinfandel expert Joel Peterson established Ravenswood in 1976. During the lean years, when most Zin was pink and sweet, he added an intense Chardonnay, a sometimes very good Cabernet Sauvignon★ and several tasty Merlots (Sangiacomo★★). But Zinfandel remains the trump card. Early 21st-century offerings were disappointing – especially large-volume Vintners Blend – but this has now picked up, and Amador★ and Lodi★ wines are tasty and characterful, and sometimes outperform the Sonoma versions (single-vineyard wines can be ★★). New super-premium blend Icon★★ is Syrah-based. Constellation bought the winery in 2001, but Peterson remains in charge. Best years: (Zins) **2002 01 00 99 97 96 95 94 91 90**.

CH. RAYAS *Châteauneuf-du-Pape, Rhône Valley, France* Emmanuel Reynaud, nephew of the eccentric Jacques Reynaud, runs this estate in his uncle's inimitable rule-breaking style, producing usually exotically fragrant rich reds★★★ and whites★★ which also age well. Prices are not cheap and the wines are not consistent, but at its best Rayas is thrilling. The red is made entirely from low-yielding Grenache vines, while the white is a blend of Clairette, Grenache Blanc and (so rumour has it) Chardonnay. Second-label Pignan can also be impressive. COTES DU RHONE Ch. de Fonsalette★★ is usually wonderful. Best years: (Châteauneuf-du-Pape) 2006 05 04 03 **01 99 98 96 95 94 91 90 89 88 86**; (whites) 2006 05 04 **03 01 00 99 98 97 96 95 94 91 90 89**.

REBHOLZ *Siebeldingen, Pfalz, Germany* This estate in the southern PFALZ produces crystalline Riesling★★, Weissburgunder★★ (Pinot Blanc) and Grauburgunder★ (Pinot Gris), with vibrant fruit aromas. Top of the range are intensely mineral dry Riesling★★★ from the Kastanienbusch and Sonnenschein vineyards, powerful dry Gewürztraminer★★ and extravagantly aromatic dry Muskateller★★. The sparkling wine★★, from barrel-fermented Pinot varieties, is among Germany's most elegant. Also Germany's finest Chardonnay★★ and serious Spätburgunder★★ (Pinot Noir) reds. Best years: (whites) (2007) 06 05 04 **03 02 01 00 99**; (reds) (2007) 05 04 03 **02 01 00 99**.

RECIOTO DELLA VALPOLICELLA DOC *Veneto, Italy* The great sweet wine of VALPOLICELLA, made from grapes picked earlier than usual and left to dry on straw mats until February or even March. The wines are deep in colour, with a rich, bitter-sweet cherryish fruit. Top wines age well for 10 years, but most are best drunk young. As with Valpolicella, the Classico tag is important, if not essential. Best producers: Accordini★, ALLEGRINI★★, Bolla (Spumante★★), Brigaldara★, BUSSOLA★★★, Michele Castellani★★, DAL FORNO★★★, MASI★, QUINTARELLI★★, Le Ragose★, Le Salette★, Serègo Alighieri★★, Speri★, Tedeschi★, Tommasi★, Villa Monteleone★★, VIVIANI★★. Best years: (2006) 05 **04 03 01 00 98 97**.

RECIOTO DI SOAVE DOCG *Veneto, Italy* Sweet white wine made in the SOAVE zone from dried grapes, like RECIOTO DELLA VALPOLICELLA. Garganega grapes give wonderfully delicate yet intense wines that age well for up to a decade. One of the best, ANSELMI's I Capitelli, is now sold as IGT Veneto. Best producers: ANSELMI★★, La Cappuccina★★, Cà Rugate★, Coffele★★, Gini★★, PIEROPAN★★, Bruno Sartori★, Tamellini★★. Best years: (2006) 04 **03 01 00 98 97**.

RÉGNIÉ AC *Beaujolais, Burgundy, France* In good years this BEAUJOLAIS Cru is light, aromatic and enjoyable along the style of CHIROUBLES, but can be thin in lesser years. Best producers: DUBOEUF (des Buyats★), Rampon, Gilles Roux/de la Plaigne★, Tracot/ Dubost★. Best years: **2007** 06.

DOM. LA RÉMÉJEANNE *Côtes du Rhône AC, Rhône Valley, France* First-class property making a range of strikingly individual, sometimes heady wines. COTES DU RHONE-VILLAGES les Genèvriers★★ has the weight and texture of good CHATEAUNEUF-DU-PAPE, while COTES DU RHONE Syrah les Eglantiers★★ is superb. Both need at least 3–5 years' aging. Also good Côtes du Rhône les Chèvrefeuilles★ and les Arbousiers (red and white). Best years: (les Eglantiers) 2007 **06 05 04 03 01 00**.

REMELLURI *Rioja DOCa, País Vasco, Spain* Organic RIOJA estate producing red wines with far more fruit than usual and good concentration for aging – the best are ★★. There is also a delicate, barrel-fermented white blend★★. Best years: (Reserva) 2004 03 **02 01 99 98 96 95 94 91 89**.

RETSINA *Greece* Resinated white (and rosé) wine common all over Greece although both production and sales are falling. Poor Retsina is diabolical but the best are deliciously oily and piny. Drink young – and cold.

REUILLY AC *Loire Valley, France* Extremely dry but attractive Sauvigno from west of SANCERRE. Some pale Pinot Noir red and Pinot Gris rosé Best producers: H Beurdin★, G Bigonneau, D Jamain, A Mabillot, J-M Sorbe

CH. REYNON *Premières Côtes de Bordeaux AC, Bordeaux, France* Property of enology professor Denis Dubourdieu. The dry whites, particularly th fruity, minerally Sauvignon Blanc★, are delightful and the red★ ha come on tremendously since 1997. In the same stable is the lovely GRAVE Clos Floridène★★, which is vinified at Reynon. Best years: (reds) 2006 0! **04 03 01 00**; (whites) **2006 05 04 02 01 00 99**.

RHEINGAU *Germany* 3106ha (7675-acre) wine region on a south-facing stretch of the Rhine flanking the city of Wiesbaden, planted mostly with Riesling and some Spätburgunder (Pinot Noir). At their best, the Rieslings are racy and slow-maturing. But famous names are no longer a guarantee of top quality, as a new generation of winemakers is producing many of the best wines. See also ELTVILLE, ERBACH, GEISENHEIM, HATTENHEIM, HOCHHEIM, JOHANNISBERG, KIEDRICH, RAUENTHAL, RUDESHEIM, WINKEL. Best years: (2007) 06 05 04 **03** 02 01 99 98 97.

WEINGUT
FRANZ KÜNSTLER

RHEINGAU
2001
Hochheimer Hölle
Riesling Spätlese
trocken
WEINGUT FRANZ KÜNSTLER D-65239 HOCHHEIM
Qualitätswein mit Prädikat
A.P. Nr. 40-080-013-02
Produce of Germany
750 ml e

RHEINHESSEN *Germany* 26,280ha (65,000-acre) wine region with a number of famous top-quality estates, especially at Bodenheim, Nackenheim NIERSTEIN and Oppenheim. BINGEN, to the north-west, also has a fine vineyard area along the left bank of the Rhine. Further away from the river a handfu of growers, such as KELLER and WITTMANN, have made a name for themselves Riesling accounts for 12% of the vineyard area; Weissburgunder (Pinot Blanc is the rising star. Best years: (2007) 06 05 **04 03 02 01 00 99**.

RHÔNE VALLEY *France* The Rhône starts out as a river in Switzerland ambling through Lake Geneva before hurtling southwards into France. In th area south of Lyon, between Vienne and Avignon, the valley becomes one of France's great wine regions. In the northern part vertigo-inducing slope overhang the river and the small amount of wine produced is of remarkable individuality. The Syrah grape reigns here in COTE-ROTIE and on the great hil of HERMITAGE. ST-JOSEPH, CROZES-HERMITAGE and CORNAS also make excellent reds while the white Viognier grape yields perfumed, musky wine at CONDRIEU an the tiny CHATEAU-GRILLET. In the southern part the steep slopes give way to hot wide plains, with hills both in the west and east. Most of these vineyards are either COTES DU RHONE or COTES DU RHONE-VILLAGES, reds, whites and rosés, bu there are also specific ACs, the best known being CHATEAUNEUF-DU-PAPE GIGONDAS and the luscious, golden dessert wine, MUSCAT DE BEAUMES-DE-VENISE See also BEAUMES-DE-VENISE, CAIRANNE, CLAIRETTE DE DIE, COSTIERES DE NIMES COTEAUX DE L'ARDECHE, COTEAUX DU TRICASTIN, COTES DU LUBERON, COTES DU VENTOUX, LIRAC, RASTEAU, ST-PERAY, TAVEL, VACQUEYRAS, VINSOBRES.

RÍAS BAIXAS DO *Galicia, Spain* The best of GALICIA's DOs, Rías Baixas i making some of Spain's best whites. The magic ingredient is the Albariño grape, making dry, fruity whites with a glorious fragrance and citrus tang. Drink young or with short aging. Best producers: Agro de Bazán★★, Castro Martín, Martín Códax★, Condes de Albarei★, Quinta de Couselo, Fillaboa★★, Adegas Galegas★, Lagar de Besada★, Lagar de Fornelos★, Lusco do Miño★★, Gerardo Méndez (Do Ferreiro Cepas Vellas★★), Viña Nora★, Pablo Padín, Palacio de Fefiñanes★★, Pazo de Barrantes★, Pazo de Señorans★★, Santiago Ruiz★, Terras Gauda★★, La Val★, Valmiñor★.

RIBATEJO *Portugal* Portugal's second-largest wine region straddles the river Tagus (Tejo). Hotter and drier than ESTREMADURA to the west, vineyards in the fertile flood plain are being uprooted in favour of less vigorous soils away from the river, though D F J VINHOS still believes in the quality of the original alluvial sites. The Ribatejo DOC includes 6 sub-regions. Vinho Regional wines are labelled Ribatejano. Best producers: (reds) Quinta da Alorna, Quinta do Alqueve, Casa Cadaval★, Quinta do Casal Branco (Falcoaria★), D F J VINHOS★, Caves Dom Teodosio, Quinta do Falcão, Falua (Reserva★), Fiúza-BRIGHT, Quinta da Lagoalva da Cima★, Companhia das Lezírias, Quinta da Ribeirinha (Vale de Lobos).

RIBERA DEL DUERO DO *Castilla y León, Spain* The dark, mouthfilling reds in this DO, from Tinto Fino (Tempranillo), sometimes with Cabernet Sauvignon and Merlot, are nowadays generally more exciting than those of RIOJA. But excessive expansion of vineyards, increase in yields and excessive use of oak may threaten its supremacy. Best producers: AALTO★★, Alión★★, Arroyo, Arzuaga★, Astrales★, Dominio de Atauta★★, Balbás★, Hijos de Antonio Barceló, Briego, Felix Callejo, Cillar de Silos★, Convento San Francisco★, Hermanos Cuadrado García, O FOURNIER★, Hacienda Monasterio★★, Matarromera★, Montecastro★★, Emilio Moro★★, Pago de los Capellanes★★, Pago de Carraovejas★★, Parxet, Pedrosa, Hermanos Pérez Pascuas, PESQUERA★★, PINGUS★★★, Protos★, Rodero★, Telmo RODRIGUEZ★, Hermanos Sastre★★, Tarsus★, Valdubón, Valduero★, Valtravieso, VEGA SICILIA★★★, Alonso del Yerro★★. Best years: 2005 **04 03 01 00** 99 96 95 94 91 90 89 86 85.

BARONE RICASOLI *Chianti Classico DOCG, Tuscany, Italy* The estate where modern CHIANTI was perfected by Baron Bettino Ricasoli in the mid-19th century. The flagship wine is Castello di Brolio Chianti Classico★★; wine labelled Brolio is effectively a second selection. Riserva Guicciarda★ is good value. SUPER-TUSCAN Casalferro★★ is a Sangiovese-Merlot blend. Best years: (Casalferro) (2007) (06) 04 **03 01 00** 99 97.

DOM. RICHEAUME *Côtes de Provence AC, Provence, France* German-owned property, run on organic principles and producing impressively deep-coloured reds★; Les Terrasses★★ is from Syrah aged in new wood. Best years: (Terrasses) 2005 04 03.

RICHEBOURG AC *Grand Cru, Côte de Nuits, Burgundy, France* Rich, fleshy wine from the northern end of VOSNE-ROMANRE. Most domaine-bottlings are exceptional. Best producers: GRIVOT★★★, Anne GROS★★★, A-F GROS★★★, Hudelot-Noëllat★★, Dom. LEROY★★★, T LIGER-BELAIR★★, MEO-CAMUZET★★★, Dom. de la ROMANEE-CONTI★★★. Best years: (2007) 06 05 04 03 02 **01 00** 99 **98 97** 96 95 93 91 90.

DOM. RICHOU *Loire Valley, France* One of the most consistent and good-value domaines in the LOIRE. Best are the ANJOU-VILLAGES Brissac Vieilles Vignes★★ and sweet COTEAUX DE L'AUBANCE les Trois Demoiselles★★. Les Rogeries★ is a good example of modern dry ANJOU BLANC. Best years: (les Trois Demoiselles) 2006 05 **04 03** 02 01 99 97 96 95 90 89.

MAX FERD RICHTER *Mülheim, Mosel, Germany* Racy Rieslings from some of the best sites in the MOSEL, including WEHLENER Sonnenuhr★★ BRAUNEBERGer Juffer★★ and GRAACHER Domprobst★. Richter's Mülheimer Helenenkloster vineyard produces a magical Eiswein★★★ virtually every year. Best years: (2007) 06 05 **04 03 02 01 99 98 97 96 95**.

RIDGE VINEYARDS *Santa Cruz Mountains AVA, California, USA* Paul Draper's Zinfandels★★★, made with grapes from various sources, have great intensity and long life. Other reds, led by Cabernet-based Monte Bello★★★, show impressive personality. Geyserville★★ is a fascinating blend of Zinfandel with old-vine Carignan, Syrah and Petite Sirah. There's fine Chardonnay★★, too. Best years: (Monte Bello) 2005 03 02 0 **00 99 98 97 95 94 93 92 91 90 87 85 84**.

RIDGEVIEW *West Sussex, England* Specialist sparkling wine producer using classic CHAMPAGNE varieties to make an excellent – and improving – range of wines. Cavendish★★ and Bloomsbury★★ are traditional 3-variety blends; Knightsbridge★ is a blanc de noirs; Fitzrovia★ is a Chardonnay-Pinot Noir rosé. Best years: 2004 03 **02**.

RIECINE *Chianti Classico DOCG, Tuscany, Italy* Small estate in Gaiole making exquisite wines. Yields are low, so there is a great intensity of fruit and a superb definition of spiced cherry flavours. English winemaker Sean O'Callaghan continues to fashion ever better CHIANTI CLASSICO★★, Riserva★★★ and barrique-aged La Gioia★★★. Best years: (La Gioia) (2007) (06) 04 03 **01 99 98 97 95 90**.

RIESLANER One of the few German grape crossings of real merit, Rieslaner resembles Riesling, but with greater breadth and even higher acidity. This makes it an ideal sweet wine grape, as MULLER-CATOIR (Pfalz), KELLER (Rheinhessen) and some Franken growers have demonstrated, with wines frequently ★★.

RIESLING See pages 250–1.

RIESLING ITALICO See WELSCHRIESLING.

CH. RIEUSSEC★★★ *Sauternes AC, 1er Cru Classé, Bordeaux, France* Apart from the peerless Ch. d'YQUEM, Rieussec is often the richest, most succulent wine of SAUTERNES. Cellar for at least 10 years. Dry white 'R' is nothing special. Second wine: Carmes de Rieussec. Owned by LAFITE-ROTHSCHILD. Best years: 2006 05 04 03 **02 01 99 98 97 96 95 90 89 88**.

RIOJA DOCa *Rioja, Navarra, País Vasco and Castilla y León, Spain* Rioja, in northern Spain, is not all oaky, creamy white wines and elegant, barrel-aged reds, combining oak flavours with wild strawberry and prune fruit. Over half Rioja's red wine is sold young, never having seen the inside of a barrel, and most of the white is fairly anonymous. Wine quality, as could be expected from such a large region with more than 300 producers, is inconsistent but a bevy of ambitious new producers is taking quality seriously. Best producers: (reds) ALLENDE★★, Altanza, Altos de Lanzaga★/Telmo RODRIGUEZ, ARTADI★★★, Baron de Ley★, BERBERANA, Bodegas Bilbaínas, CAMPILLO★, CAMPO VIEJO, CONTINO★★, El Coto, CVNE, DOMECQ, FAUSTINO, Viña Ijalba, Lan (Culmen★), LOPEZ DE HEREDIA★, MARQUES DE CACERES★, MARQUES DE MURRIETA★★, MARQUES DE RISCAL★, Marqués de Vargas★★, MARTINEZ BUJANDA, Abel Mendoza★★, Montecillo★, MUGA★, Ostatu, Viñedos de Páganos★★, Palacios Remondo★, REMELLURI★★, Fernando Remírez de Ganuza★★, La RIOJA ALTA★, RIOJANAS★, Roda★★, Benjamin ROMEO★★★, Sierra Cantabria★★, Señorío de San Vicente★★, Tobía, Valdemar★, Ysios;

(whites) ALLENDE★, CAMPO VIEJO, LOPEZ DE HEREDIA★★, MARQUES DE CACERES★, MARQUES DE MURRIETA, REMELLURI★, La RIOJA ALTA★, RIOJANAS★, Valdemar★. Best years: (reds) 2005 **04 01 00 96 95 94 91 89 87 85**.

LA RIOJA ALTA *Rioja DOCa, Rioja, Spain* One of the best of the older RIOJA producers, making mainly Reservas and Gran Reservas. Its only Crianza, Viña Alberdi, fulfils the minimum age requirements for a Reserva anyway. Good, lemony-oaky Viña Ardanza Reserva★ white. Red Reservas, Viña Arana★ and Viña Ardanza★★, age splendidly, and Gran Reservas, Reserva 904★★ and Reserva 890★★ (made only in exceptional years), are among the very best of Rioja wines. Best years: (Gran Reserva 890) **1989 87 85 82 81 78**.

BODEGAS RIOJANAS *Rioja DOCa, Rioja, Spain* Quality winery producing Reservas and Gran Reservas in 2 styles – elegant Viña Albina★ and richer Monte Real★ – plus refined Gran Albina★ and now a more modern Monte Real Crianza. White Monte Real Blanco Crianza★ is one of RIOJA's best. The whites and Reservas can be kept for 5 years after release, Gran Reservas for 10 or more. Best years: (Monte Real Gran Reserva) **1998 96 95 94 91 89 87 85**.

RION *Nuits-St-Georges, Côte de Nuits, Burgundy, France* Patrice Rion was wine-maker at Dom. Daniel Rion from 1979 to 2000, making consistently fine but often austere reds such as VOSNE-ROMANEE les Beauxmonts★★ and les Chaumes★★, ECHEZEAUX and CLOS DE VOUGEOT. His own label brings rich, concentrated BOURGOGNE Rouge★★, CHAMBOLLE-MUSIGNY les Cras★★ and NUITS-ST-GEORGES Clos des Argillières★★ from his own vines plus a small négociant range. Best years: (top reds) (2007) 06 05 04 03 **02 01 00** 99.

RIPOSTE *Adelaide Hills, South Australia* Since leaving KNAPPSTEIN to move to the cool ADELAIDE HILLS, Tim Knappstein has run Lenswood Vineyard and TK Wines. In 2003, the Knappsteins sold the Lenswood Vineyard, although Tim is still able to access its fruit. He now acts as consultant winemaker at new Adelaide Hills winery Wicks Estate and has started his own brand, Riposte. His current focus is on Pinot Noir, Sauvignon Blanc★ and Gewürztraminer★.

RIVERA *Puglia, Italy* The CASTEL DEL MONTE Riserva Il Falcone★ is a good, full-blooded southern red. Also a series of varietals under the Terre al Monte label, best of which are Aglianico★, Pinot Bianco and Sauvignon Blanc.

RIVERINA *New South Wales, Australia* Centred on the town of Griffith and irrigated by the waters of the Murrumbidgee River, the Riverina is an important source of reliable cheap quaffing wines. Many of Australia's best-known brands, though not mentioning the Riverina on the label, are based on wines from here. The potential for quality is definitely there, and locally based companies such as DE BORTOLI (with Sacred Hill, Deen and Montage), MCWILLIAM'S (Hanwood, Inheritance), Nugan Estate★ (Cookoothama, Talinga Park), WESTEND★ (Richland) and Casella (YELLOWTAIL, Yendah) have lifted quality at budget prices. Remarkable sweet wines, led by Noble One Botrytis Semillon★★★ from De Bortoli.

RIVERLAND *Australia* This important irrigated region, responsible for about 12% of the national grape crush, lies along the Murray River in SOUTH AUSTRALIA near the border with VICTORIA. A great deal goes to cask wine and cheap quaffers but an increased awareness of quality has seen inferior varieties replaced and yields lowered. Here and there, wines of real character are emerging, including some remarkable reds from the Petit Verdot grape. Best producers: Angove's, HARDY (Banrock Station, Renmano), Kingston Estate, YALUMBA (Oxford Landing).

RIESLING

If you have tasted wines with names like Laski Riesling, Olasz Riesling, Welschriesling, Gray Riesling, Riesling Italico, Cape Riesling and the like and found them bland or unappetizing – do not blame the Riesling grape. These wines have filched Riesling's name, but have nothing whatsoever to do with the great grape itself.

Riesling is Germany's finest contribution to the world of wine – and herein lies the second problem. German wines fell to such a low level of general esteem through the proliferation of wines like Liebfraumilch during the 1980s that Riesling, even true German Riesling, has been dragged down with it.

So what is true Riesling? It is a very ancient German grape, probably the descendant of wild vines growing in the Rhine Valley. It certainly performs best in the cool vineyard regions of Germany's Rhine, Nahe and Mosel Valleys, and in Alsace and Austria. It also does well in Canada, New Zealand and both warm and cool parts of Australia. It is widely planted in California, less so in northern Italy, and there's a tiny amount in South Africa where new, suitable sites are eagerly being sought by the growing number of Riesling fanatics, and in Chile.

Young Rieslings often show a delightful floral perfume, sometimes blended with the crispness of green apples, often lime, peach, nectarine or apricot, sometimes even raisin, honey or spice depending upon the ripeness of the grapes. As the wines age, the lime often intensifies, and a flavour perhaps of slate, perhaps of petrol/kerosene intrudes. In general Rieslings may be drunk young, but top dry wines can improve for many years, and the truly sweet German styles can age for generations.

WINE STYLES

Germany These wines have a marvellous perfume and an ability to hold on to a piercing acidity, even at high ripeness levels, so long as the ripening period has been warm and gradual rather than broiling and rushed. German Rieslings can be bone dry, through to medium and even lusciously sweet. Styles range from crisp elegant Mosels to riper, fuller wines from the Rheingau and Nahe, with rounder, fatter examples from the Pfalz and Baden regions in the south. The very sweet Trockenbeerenauslese (TBA) Rieslings are made from grapes affected by noble rot; for Eiswein (icewine), also intensely sweet, the grapes are picked and pressed while frozen.

Other regions In the valleys of the Danube in Austria, Riesling gives stunning dry wines that combine richness with elegance, but the most fragrant wines, apart from German examples, come from France's Alsace. The mountain vineyards of northern Italy and the cool vineyards of the Czech Republic, Slovakia and Switzerland can show a floral sharp style. Australia is the southern hemisphere's world-class producer, with cool areas of South Australia, Victoria and Western Australia all offering superb – and different – examples typified by a citrus, mineral scent, and often challenging austerity. New Zealand's style is floral, fresh and frequently attractively off-dry, but with enough acidity to age. South Africa's best examples are sweet, but some dry versions are appearing. Chile is growing some light, fragrant examples. The USA has fragrant dry Rieslings from New York, mostly off-dry from the Pacific Northwest and sweet styles from California, and Canada has its icewines.

BEST PRODUCERS

Germany
Dry BASSERMANN-JORDAN, Georg BREUER, BURKLIN-WOLF, Christmann, HEYMANN-LOWENSTEIN, KELLER, KOEHLER-RUPRECHT, KUNSTLER, J LEITZ, REBHOLZ, SAUER, WITTMANN.

Non-dry DIEL, DONNHOFF, GUNDERLOCH, HAAG, HAART, HEYMANN-LOWENSTEIN, KARTHAUSERHOF, von KESSELSTATT, KUHN, KUNSTLER, Carl Loewen, Dr LOOSEN, MAXIMIN GRUNHAUS, MOLITOR, MULLER-CATOIR, Egon MULLER-SCHARZHOF, J J PRUM, St Urbans-Hof, Willi SCHAEFER, SELBACH-OSTER, WEIL, ZILLIKEN.

Austria
Dry Alzinger, BRUNDLMAYER, Hiedler, HIRTZBERGER, J Högl, KNOLL, Loimer, NIGL, NIKOLAIHOF, F X PICHLER, Rudi Pichler, PRAGER, Schloss Gobelsburg, Schmelz.

France
(Alsace) Dry J-B ADAM, P BLANCK, A Boxler, DEISS, Dirler-Cadé, HUGEL, Josmeyer, Kientzler, Kreydenweiss, A MANN, MURE, Ostertag, SCHOFFIT, TRIMBACH, WEINBACH, ZIND-HUMBRECHT.

Non-dry Léon Beyer, DEISS, HUGEL, Ostertag, TRIMBACH, WEINBACH, ZIND-HUMBRECHT.

Australia
Tim ADAMS, BAY OF FIRES, Leo Buring (Leonay), FERNGROVE, Freycinet, GROSSET, HENSCHKE, HOUGHTON, HOWARD PARK, JACOB'S CREEK (Steingarten), KNAPPSTEIN, Peter LEHMANN (Reserve), Mesh, MOUNT HORROCKS, O'Leary Walker, PETALUMA (Hanlin Hill), Pewsey Vale (Contours), Pipers Brook, SKILLOGALEE.

New Zealand
CLOUDY BAY, DRY RIVER, FELTON ROAD, Foxes Island, FROMM, MILLTON, Mt Difficulty, Mount Edward, PALLISER, PEGASUS BAY, VILLA MARIA.

South Africa
Sweet CLUVER, Neethlingshof.

USA
(Washington) CHATEAU STE MICHELLE (Eroica), LONG SHADOWS (Poet's Leap); *(New York)* Dr Konstantin FRANK.

251

RIVESALTES AC *Roussillon, France*   *Vin doux naturel* from a large area around the town of Rivesaltes. These fortified wines are some of southern France's best and can be made from an assortment of grapes, mainly white Muscat (when it is called MUSCAT DE RIVESALTES) and Grenache Noir, Gris and Blanc. A *rancio* style ages well. Best producers: Baixas co-op, la CASENOVE★, CAZES★★, Chênes★, Fontanel★, Força Réal★, GAUBY★, Joliette★, Laporte, Nouvelles★, Rivesaltes co-op, Sarda-Malet★.

ROBERTSON WO *South Africa*   Hot, dry inland area with lime-rich soils, uncommon in the Cape, that are ideal for vines. Chenin Blanc and Colombard remain the major white varieties, though just over a quarter of all South Africa's Chardonnay also grows here, for both still and sparkling styles. Sauvignon can also be good. Muscadel (Muscat Blanc à Petits Grains) yields a benchmark fortified wine, usually unoaked and released young. A red revolution is under way: Shiraz, Merlot and Cabernet have made an excellent start. Best producers: Graham BECK★, Bon Courage, De Wetshof, Quando, Robertson Winery, SPRINGFIELD ESTATE★, Van Loveren, Weltevrede, Zandvliet.

CH. ROC DE CAMBES★★ *Côtes de Bourg AC, Bordeaux, France*   François Mitjavile of TERTRE-ROTEBOEUF has applied diligence and genius to this property since he acquired it in 1988. Full and succulent, with ripe dark fruit, this wine takes the COTES DE BOURG appellation to new heights. Best years: 2006 05 04 **03 02 01 00 99 98 97 96 95**.

DOM. DES ROCHES NEUVES *Saumur-Champigny AC, Loire Valley, France*   A shift to biodynamic methods and more hands-off winemaking (including less extraction and new oak) has elevated very good wines to a higher level. Fresh, pure and mineral, top cuvées Insolite SAUMUR★★ (Chenin Blanc) and Marginale SAUMUR-CHAMPIGNY★★ (Cabernet Franc) are excellent expressions of fruit and *terroir*; generic Saumur-Champigny and Terres Chaudes★ are good value. Best years: (reds) (2007) 06 05 **04 03 02 01 00 99 97**.

ROCHIOLI *Russian River Valley AVA, California, USA*   Well-known grape growers, the Rochioli family are equally good at winemaking, offering silky, black cherry Pinot Noir★★ and a richer, dramatic West Block Reserve Pinot★★. Also a fine Sauvignon Blanc and a range of cult Chardonnays★★. Best years: (Pinot Noir) (2005) 04 **03 02 01 00 99 98 97**.

ROCKFORD *Barossa Valley, South Australia*   Wonderfully nostalgic wines from Robert O'Callaghan, a great respecter of the old vines so plentiful in the BAROSSA, who delights in using antique machinery to create wines of irresistible drinkability. Masterful Basket Press Shiraz★★, Riesling★★, Moppa Springs★ (Grenache-Shiraz-Mourvèdre), Rifle Range Cabernet★★ and Australia's best sparkling Black Shiraz★★★. Best years: (Basket Press Shiraz) 2006 05 04 03 02 **01 99 98 96 95 92 91 90 88 87**.

ANTONIN RODET *Mercurey, Côte Chalonnaise, Burgundy, France*   Merchant specializing in COTE CHALONNAISE, but with an excellent range throughout Burgundy. Rodet owns or co-owns 5 domaines – Ch. de Rully★, Ch. de Chamirey★, Ch. de Mercey★, Dom. des Perdrix★ and Jacques Prieur★★ – which are the source of the best wines. BOURGOGNE Vieilles Vignes★ is one of the best inexpensive Chardonnays available. Best years: (reds) (2007) 06 05 **03 02 99**; (whites) (2007) 06 05 **04 02 00 99**.

TELMO RODRÍGUEZ *Spain*   The former winemaker for REMELLURI has formed a 'wine company' that is active throughout Spain. With a team of enologists and viticulturists, it forms joint ventures with local growers and manages the winemaking process. The results are often spectacular. Top wines: Molino Real★ (Sierras de MALAGA), Alto Matallana★ (RIBERA DEL

DUERO), Altos de Lanzaga★ (RIOJA), Dehesa Gago Pago La Jara★★ (TORO), Viña 105 (Cigales), Basa★ (RUEDA).

LOUIS ROEDERER *Champagne AC, Champagne, France* Renowned firm making some of the best, full-flavoured CHAMPAGNE around. As well as the excellent non-vintage★★ and pale vintage rosé★★, it also makes a big, exciting vintage★★, delicious vintage Blanc de Blancs★★ and the famous Roederer Cristal★★★ and Cristal Rosé★★★, de luxe cuvées which are nearly always magnificent. Both the vintage and Cristal can usually be aged for 10 years or more; the non-vintage benefits from a bit of aging, too. Best years: (2003) 02 00 **99 97** 96 **95 90 89 88 85**.

ROEDERER ESTATE *Anderson Valley AVA, California, USA* Offshoot of Louis ROEDERER. The Brut★★ (sold in the UK as Quartet) is austere but impressive, a step back from the upfront fruit of many California sparklers, but it will age beautifully. Lovely rosé★★, and the top bottling, L'Ermitage★★★, is stunning. Best years: (L'Ermitage) 1999 97 96 **94 92** 91.

ROERO DOCG *Piedmont, Italy* The Roero hills lie across the Tanaro river from the LANGHE hills, home of BAROLO and BARBARESCO. Long noted as a source of supple, fruity Nebbiolo-based red wines to drink in 2–5 years, Roero has recently been turning out Nebbiolos of Barolo-like intensity from producers such as Correggia and Malvirà. Roero is also the home of the white Arneis grape. Best producers: (reds) G Almondo★, Ca' Rossa★, Cascina Chicco★, Correggia★★, Deltetto★★, Funtanin★, F Gallino★, Malvirà★★, Monchiero Carbone★, Angelo Negro★, Porello★. Best years: (reds) (2007) (06) **04 03 01 00 99**. See also ARNEIS.

ROMAGNA *Emilia-Romagna, Italy* Romagna's wine production is centred on 4 DOCs and 1 DOCG. The whites are from Trebbiano (ineffably dull), Pagadebit (showing promise as both dry and sweet wine) and Albana (Albana di Romagna DOCG can be dry or sweet). The best of the Sangiovese-based reds can rival good CHIANTI CLASSICO. Best producers: (Sangiovese) La Berta★, Castelluccio★★, L Conti★, Drei Donà-La Palazza★★, G Madonia★, San Patrignano co-op/Terre del Cedro★ (Avi★★), Tre Monti★, Zerbina★★.

LA ROMANÉE AC *Grand Cru, Côte de Nuits, Burgundy, France* Tiny Grand Cru★★★ of the very highest quality, owned and now made by Vicomte LIGER-BELAIR; up to 2002 it was distributed by BOUCHARD PÈRE ET FILS. Best years: (2007) 06 05 03 02 99 **98 97** 96.

LA ROMANÉE-CONTI AC *Grand Cru, Côte de Nuits, Burgundy, France* For many extremely wealthy wine lovers this is the pinnacle of red Burgundy★★★. It is an incredibly complex wine with great structure and pure, clearly defined fruit flavour, but you've got to age it 15 years to see what all the fuss is about. The vineyard, wholly owned by Dom. de la ROMANÉE-CONTI, covers only 1.8ha (4½ acres). Best years: (2007) 06 05 04 03 02 01 00 99 98 97 96 95 93 **90 89 88 85 78**.

DOM. DE LA ROMANÉE-CONTI *Vosne-Romanée, Côte de Nuits, Burgundy, France* This famous red wine domaine owns a string of Grands Crus in VOSNE-ROMANÉE (la TÂCHE★★★, RICHEBOURG★★★, ROMANÉE-CONTI★★★, ROMANÉE-ST-VIVANT★★★, ECHÉZEAUX★★★ and Grands-Échezeaux★★★) as well as a small parcel of le MONTRACHET★★★. The wines are ludicrously expensive but can be sublime – full of fruit when young, but capable of aging for 15 years or more to an astonishing marriage made in the heaven and hell of richness and decay. Best years: (reds) (2007) 06 05 04 03 02 01 00 99 98 97 96 95 93 **90 89 85 78**.

ROMANÉE-ST-VIVANT AC *Grand Cru, Côte de Nuits, Burgundy, France* The largest of VOSNE-ROMANEE's 6 Grands Crus. At 10–15 years old the wines should reveal the keenly balanced brilliance of which the vineyard is capable, but a surly, rough edge sometimes gets in the way. Best producers: l'Arlot★★, R Arnoux★★★, S CATHIARD★★, J-J Confuron★★★, DROUHIN★★★, Hudelot-Noëllat★★★, JADOT★★★, Dom. LEROY★★★, Dom. de la ROMANEE-CONTI★★★. Best years: (2007) 06 05 04 03 02 01 **00 99 98 97 96 95 93 90**.

CH. ROMANIN *Les Baux de Provence AC, Provence, France* Jean-Louis Charmolüe, former owner of Ch. MONTROSE in Bordeaux, is now installed at this biodynamically run vineyard. Top wine is Le Coeur du Château Romanin★ from a 4ha (10-acre) parcel of Syrah, Mourvèdre, Cabernet Sauvignon and Grenache. Second wine is La Chapelle de Romanin, while Jean le Troubadour is for everyday drinking. Best years: (Le Coeur) 2005 04 03 01 **00**.

BENJAMIN ROMEO *Rioja DOCa, La Rioja, Spain* ARTADI's former winemaker launched his own estate with a collection of tiny old vineyards, and immediately caused a sensation with his velvety, Burgundian and yet powerful wines, Contador★★★, La Viña de Andrés Romeo★★ and La Cueva del Contador★★. Best years: (2005) 04 03 **02 01 00**.

QUINTA DOS ROQUES *Dão DOC, Beira Alta, Portugal* One of DAO's finest producers, the wines of 2 estates with quite different characters are made here. Quinta dos Roques red★ is ripe and supple, while Quinta das Maias★ is a smoky, peppery red. The top wines are the Roques Reserva★★, made from old vines and aged in 100% new oak, and Touriga Nacional★★. Both estates also have a decent dry white, especially Roques Encruzado★. Best years: 2005 **04 03 01 00 97 96**.

QUINTA DE LA ROSA *Douro DOC and Port DOC, Douro, Portugal* The Bergqvist family have transformed this property into a small but serious producer of both PORT and unfortified DOURO★ (Reserva★★) wines. The Vintage Port★★ is excellent, as is unfiltered LBV★★; Finest Reserve and 10-year-old tawny★ are also good. A special selection vintage port, Vale do Inferno★, was made in 1999 and shows a lovely old vine intensity. Best years: (Vintage) 2004 **03 00 97 96 95 94 92 91**.

ROSÉ DE LOIRE AC *Loire Valley, France* Dry rosé from ANJOU, SAUMUR and TOURAINE. It can be a lovely drink, full of red berry fruits, but drink as young as possible, chilled. It's far superior to Rosé d'Anjou AC, which is usually sweetish without much flavour – though Rosé d'Un Jour is very good rosé from 8 rebellious growers led by Mark Angeli. Best producers: M Angeli/Sansonnière, Hautes Ouches, Passavant, St-Arnoud, Trottières.

ROSÉ DES RICEYS AC *Champagne, France* Still, dark pink wine made from Pinot Noir grapes in the southern part of the CHAMPAGNE region. Best producers: Alexandre Bonnet★, Devaux★, Guy de Forez, Morel.

ROSEMOUNT ESTATE *Hunter Valley, New South Wales, Australia* Winery buying and growing grapes in several regions to produce some of Australia's most popular wines, but many seem sweeter and flatter than before and any sense of 'estate' has virtually disappeared. The flagship Roxburgh Chardonnay★ is undergoing a dramatic and not entirely successful style change. Best of the other whites is Orange Vineyard Chardonnay★. Top-level Show Reserve reds are a bit stodgy, as is dense

Balmoral Syrah, but GSM★ (Grenache-Syrah-Mourvèdre) can be good. After an inspiring start in MUDGEE, the Hill of Gold range has dipped, though Mountain Blue Shiraz-Cabernet★ can be excellent. Best years: (Balmoral Syrah) (2005) 04 02 01 **00 98 97 96 94 92 91 90**.

ROSSO CÒNERO DOC *Marche, Italy* The best wines in this zone, on the Adriatic coast, are made solely from Montepulciano, and have a wonderfully spicy richness. Best producers: Fazi Battaglia★, Garofoli★ (Grosso Agontano★★), Lanari★ (Fibbio★★), Leopardi Dittajuti★, Malacari★, Mecella (Rubelliano★), Monte Schiavo (Adeodato★★), Moroder★ (Dorico★★), Le Terrazze★ (Sassi Neri★★, Visions of J★★), Umani Ronchi★ (Cúmaro★★). Best years: (2007) (06) 04 **03 01 00**.

ROSSO DI MONTALCINO DOC *Tuscany, Italy* The little brother of BRUNELLO DI MONTALCINO spends less time aging in wood, enabling the wines to retain a wonderful exuberance of flavour. In lesser years the best Brunello grapes may cascade here, so off-years (like 2002) can be surprisingly good. Best producers: Agostina Pieri★★, Altesino★, Argiano★, Brunelli★, Camigliano★, Caparzo★, Casanova di Neri★★, Ciacci Piccolomini d'Aragona★★, Col d'Orcia★, Collemattoni★, COSTANTI★★, Fuligni★, Gorelli-Due Portine★, M Lambardi★★, Lisini★, Siro Pacenti★★, Poggio Antico★, Poggio Salvi★, il POGGIONE★, Salicutti★★, San Filippo-Fanti★, Talenti★, Valdicava★. Best years: (2007) 06 05 04 **03 02 01 00**.

ROSSO DI MONTEPULCIANO DOC *Tuscany, Italy* Some VINO NOBILE producers use this DOC in order to improve selection for the main wine; the best deliver delightfully plummy, chocolaty flavours. Best producers: La Braccesca★/ANTINORI, La Ciarliana★, Contucci★, Dei★, Del Cerro★, Il Faggeto★, Fassati★, Nottola★, POLIZIANO★, Salcheto★★, Valdipiatta★, Villa Sant'Anna★. Best years: (2007) 06 **04 03 01**.

ROSSO PICENO DOC *Marche, Italy* Often considered a poor relative of ROSSO CONERO, but it can be rich and seductive when the full complement (70%) of Montepulciano is used, and also when it comes from the more restricted Superiore zone. Best producers: Boccadigabbia★ (Villamagna★★), Le Caniette★, Laurentina★, Monte Schiavo★, Saladini Pilastri★, Velenosi★. Best years: (2007) (06) **04 03 01 00**.

RENÉ ROSTAING *Côte-Rôtie AC, Rhône Valley, France* Modern, oaked, rich wines with deep colour and softly elegant fruit flavours, from some of the best sites in CÔTE-RÔTIE: classic Côte-Rôtie★, Côte Blonde★★ and la Landonne★★. There's a very good CONDRIEU★★ too. Best years: (top crus) 2007 06 05 04 **03 01 00 99 98 95 94 91 90 88**.

DOM. ROTIER *Gaillac AC, South-West France* This GAILLAC estate makes wines using blends of local and more classic grapes. Red Renaissance★, with flavours of wild thyme, brings together Duras, Braucol, Syrah and Cabernet Sauvignon. There are both dry and sweet versions of white Renaissance, based on local grape Len de l'Elh. Best years: (Renaissance red) 2005 04 **03 00**.

GEORGES ROUMIER *Chambolle-Musigny, Côte de Nuits, Burgundy, France* Christophe Roumier is one of Burgundy's top winemakers, devoting as much attention to his vineyards as to cellar technique, believing in severe pruning, low yields and stringent grape selection. Roumier rarely uses more than one-third new oak. His best wine is often BONNES-MARES★★★; other Grands Crus include MUSIGNY★★★, Ruchottes-Chambertin★★ and CORTON-CHARLEMAGNE★★. Best value are usually the village CHAMBOLLE★★ and an exclusively owned Premier Cru in MOREY-ST-DENIS, Clos de la Bussière★★. Best years: (reds) (2007) 06 05 04 03 02 **01 00 99 98 97 96 95 90**.

R ROUSSANNE

ROUSSANNE The RHONE VALLEY's best white grape, frequently blended with Marsanne. Roussanne is the more aromatic and elegant of the two, less prone to oxidation and with better acidity, but growers usually prefer Marsanne due to its higher yields. Now being planted in the Midi. There are some examples in Savoie and Australia. While much of the Roussanne planted in California has been identified as Viognier, there are a few true plantings that produce fascinating complex wines.

ARMAND ROUSSEAU *Gevrey-Chambertin, Côte de Nuits, Burgundy, France* One of the most highly respected CHAMBERTIN estates, with vineyards in Chambertin★★★, Clos-de-Bèze★★★, Mazis-Chambertin★★ and Charmes-Chambertin★★ as well as GEVREY-CHAMBERTIN Clos St-Jacques★★★ and CLOS DE LA ROCHE★★★ in MOREY-ST-DENIS. The long-lived traditional wines are outstandingly harmonious, elegant, yet rich Charles Rousseau has been making these great wines since 1959, and his son Eric has rediscovered consistency of late. Best years: (2007) 06 05 04 03 02 99 96 **93 91 90 89 88 85**.

ROUSSILLON *France* The snow-covered peaks of the Pyrenees form a spectacular backdrop to the ancient region of Roussillon, now the Pyrénées-Orientales *département*. The vineyards produce a wide range of fairly priced wines, mainly red, ranging from the ripe, raisin-rich *vins doux naturels* to light, fruity-fresh vins de pays, and there are now some really exciting table wines, both white and red, being made in Roussillon, especially by individual estates. See also BANYULS, COLLIOURE, COTES DU ROUSSILLON, COTES DU ROUSSILLON-VILLAGES, MAURY, MUSCAT DE RIVESALTES, RIVESALTES.

RUCHOTTES-CHAMBERTIN AC See CHAMBERTIN AC.

RÜDESHEIM *Rheingau, Germany* Village producing silky, aromatic wines from some steep terraced vineyards high above the Rhine (Berg Schlossberg, Berg Rottland, Berg Roseneck and Bischofsberg). Best producers: Georg BREUER★★, Johannishof★, Kesseler★★, Josef LEITZ★★, Ress Schloss Schönborn★. Best years: (2007) 06 05 **04 03** 02 01 99 98 97.

RUEDA DO *Castilla y León, Spain* The RIOJA firm of MARQUES DE RISCAL launched the reputation of this white wine region in the 1970s, first by rescuing the almost extinct Verdejo grape, then by introducing Sauvignon Blanc. Fresh young whites have been joined by barrel-fermented wines aiming for a longer life, particularly at Castilla La Vieja, Ossian and Belondrade y Lurton. Best producers: Alvarez y Diez★, Antaño (Viña Mocén★) Belondrade y Lurton★, Castelo de Medina★, Bodegas de Crianza Castilla La Vieja★, Cerrosol (Doña Beatriz), Dos Victorias (José Pariente★), Hermanos Lurton, MARQUES DE RISCAL★, Viñedos de Nieva★, Ossian★, Palacio de Bornos★, José Pariente★, Javier Sanz★, Vinos Sanz, Viña Sila★ (Naia, Naiades) Sitios de Bodega★, Angel Rodríguez Vidal (Martinsancho★).

RUFFINO *Tuscany, Italy* Huge operation now partly owned by American giant Constellation Brands; production is still controlled by brothers Marco and Paolo Folonari, and is increasingly orientated towards quality. SUPER-TUSCANS include La Solatia★ (Chardonnay); Modus★ (Sangiovese-Cabernet-Merlot); Nero del Tondo★ (Pinot Noir); and the unique blend of Colorino and Merlot, Romitorio di Santedame★★. Ruffino also owns VINO NOBILE estate Lodola Nuova, BRUNELLO I Greppone Mazzi and Borgo Conventi in COLLIO. See also FOLONARI.

RUINART *Champagne AC, Champagne, France* Ruinart has a surprisingly low profile given the quality of its wines. Non-vintage★ is very good, as is Blanc de Blancs★★, but the top wines here are the supremely classy Dom Ruinart Blanc de Blancs★★★ and the Dom Ruinart Rosé★★★. Best years: 2000 98 96 **95** 90 88 85 83 82.

RULLY AC *Côte Chalonnaise, Burgundy, France* Best known for white wines, often oak-aged. Reds are light, with a fleeting strawberry and cherry perfume. Most wines are reasonably priced. Best producers: (whites) d'Allaines★, J-C Brelière★, M Briday★, DROUHIN★, Dureuil-Janthial★, Duvernay, FAIVELEY★, V GIRARDIN★, Hasard★, H & P Jacqueson★★, JADOT★, O LEFLAIVE★, RODET★, Villaine★; (reds) Dureuil-Janthial★, la Folie, H & P Jacqueson★. Best years: (whites) **2007** 06 05; (reds) (2007) **05**.

RUSSIAN RIVER VALLEY AVA *Sonoma County, California, USA* Beginning south of Healdsburg this valley cools as it meanders towards the Pacific. Green Valley, a sub-AVA, is home to IRON HORSE, Dutton-Goldfield and Marimar TORRES. It has now superseded CARNEROS as the top spot in North Coast California for Pinot Noir and Chardonnay. Best producers: Davis Bynum★, DEHLINGER★★, De Loach★, Dutton-Goldfield★★, Merry Edwards★★, Gary Farrell★★, IRON HORSE★★, Kosta-Browne★, Moshin★, Papapietro Perry★, Ramey★★, ROCHIOLI★★, SONOMA-CUTRER★, Rodney Strong★, Joseph SWAN★, Marimar TORRES★★, WILLIAMS SELYEM★★. Best years: (Pinot Noir) (2005) 04 **03 02 01 00 99 97 95**.

RUST EN VREDE *Stellenbosch WO, South Africa* Jean Engelbrecht, son of original owner/winemaker Jannie Engelbrecht, has carried out a thorough springclean and created an upmarket restaurant in the old barrel cellar since returning to run this red-only property. A return to form for this farm's excellent reds is promised under new winemaker Coenie Snyman. Rust en Vrede★, a Cabernet-Shiraz-Merlot blend, reflects the farm's terroir; Shiraz★, Merlot and Cabernet all benefit from young, virus-free vines, showing fine, soft tannins and fresh fruit. Best years: (Rust en Vrede estate wine) **2004** 03 02 01 00 99 98.

RUSTENBERG *Stellenbosch, South Africa* Top-notch wines led by single-vineyard Peter Barlow★★, a big but classically structured Cabernet, and bold Five Soldiers★★ (Chardonnay). There's also a complex, layered BORDEAUX-style blend John X Merriman★★ and lean but scented Roussanne, a first in South Africa. Occasionally produced The Last Straw★★ is a heavenly 'sticky'. A delightful, heady Viognier★★ and increasingly complex

savoury Shiraz★ are the pick of the value Brampton range. Best years: (Peter Barlow) (2005) **04 03 01 99 98**; (Five Soldiers) **2006 05 04 03 02 01 00 99**.

RUTHERFORD AVA *Napa Valley, California, USA* This viticultural area in mid-NAPA VALLEY has inspired hours of argument over whether it has a distinct identity. The heart of the area, the Rutherford Bench, does seem to be a prime Cabernet Sauvignon zone, and many traditional Napa Cabernets come from here and exhibit the 'Rutherford dust' flavour. Best producers: BEAULIEU (Private Reserve★★), Cakebread, CAYMUS★★, FLORA SPRINGS★★, Freemark Abbey★ (Bosché★★), Frog's Leap★★, Hall★, PINE RIDGE★, Quintessa★, Rubicon/COPPOLA★★, Sequoia Grove★, Staglin★★. Best years: (Cabernet) (2005) 04 03 **02 01 00** 99 96 95 94 93 91 90 86.

RUTHERGLEN *Victoria, Australia* This region in north-east VICTORIA is the home of heroic reds from Shiraz, Cabernet and Durif (Petite Sirah), and luscious, world-beating fortifieds from Muscat and Tokay (Muscadelle). Good sherry- and PORT-style wines. **Best producers: (fortifieds) All Saints★, Buller★★, Campbells★★, CHAMBERS★★, MORRIS★★, Stanton & Killeen★★.**

SAALE-UNSTRUT *Germany* Located in the former East Germany, Saale-Unstrut's 658ha (1625 acres) of vineyards can struggle to ripen fully, but quality is steadily improving. Weissburgunder (Pinot Blanc) is the most important quality grape. **Best producers: Gussek, Lützkendorf★, Pawis.**

SACHSEN *Germany* Until recently one of Europe's forgotten wine regions (411ha/1015 acres) on the river Elbe in former East Germany. Now beginning to produce some good wines, the best being dry Riesling, Gewürztraminer, Weissburgunder (Pinot Blanc) and Grauburgunder (Pinot Gris) with snappy acidity and surprisingly high alcohol. **Best producers: Schloss Proschwitz★, Schloss Wackerbarth, Klaus Zimmerling★.**

THE SADIE FAMILY *Swartland WO, South Africa* Eben Sadie takes a non-interventionist approach in his vineyards, with biodynamics playing an increasing role. He crafts a red and a white wine: both benefit from aging. Columella★★, Syrah with a little Mourvèdre, combines richness and power and is clearly influenced by Eben's project in Spain, a PRIORAT called Dits del Terra. Palladius★★, a Viognier-based blend, is a generously textured dry white wine whose flavours evolve endlessly in the glass. A second Swartland venture, Sequillo, produces a bright, mineral-fresh Syrah-based red★★ and elegant barrel-fermented Chenin-based white★★. **Best years: (Columella) 2005 04 03 02 01 00.**

ST-AMOUR AC *Beaujolais, Burgundy, France* The most northerly BEAUJOLAIS cru, much in demand through the romantic connotation of its name. The granitic vineyards produce wines with great intensity of colour that may be initially harsh, needing a few months to soften. **Best producers: des Billards/Loron★, DUBOEUF★ (des Sablons★), des Duc★. Best years: 2007 06 05.**

ST-AUBIN AC *Côte de Beaune, Burgundy, France* Some of Burgundy's best-value wines. Good reds, especially from Premiers Crus like les Frionnes and les Murgers des Dents de Chien. Also reasonably priced, oak-aged whites. **Best producers: d'Allaines★, J-C Bachelet★, F & D Clair★★, M Colin★, Deux MONTILLE★, DROUHIN★, JADOT★, H Lamy★★, Lamy-Pillot★, Larue★★, O LEFLAIVE★, B Morey★, RAMONET★★. Best years: (reds) (2007) 06 05 03 02; (whites) (2007) 06 05 04 02.**

ST-BRIS AC *Burgundy, France* Recently promoted appellation for Sauvignon Blanc; paradoxically, producing less interesting wines than a decade ago. Drink young. **Best producer: J-H Goisot.**

ST-CHINIAN AC *Languedoc, France* Large AC of hill villages set back from the coast, covering strong, spicy red wines with more personality and fruit than run-of-the-mill HERAULT. **Best producers: Berloup co-op, BORIE LA VITARELE★, CANET-VALETTE★, Cazal-Viel★, CLOS BAGATELLE★, HECHT & BANNIER★, Jougla★, Mas Champart★, Maurel Fonsalade★, Moulin de Ciffre, Moulinier, Rimbert★, Roquebrun co-op, Tabatau (Lo Tabataire★). Best years: 2005 04 03 01 00.**

SAINT CLAIR *Marlborough, South Island, New Zealand* A top performer thanks to some great vineyard sites. Whites are led by the intensely fruity Wairau Reserve Sauvignon Blanc★★ and a variety of single-vineyard wines under the Pioneer Block★★ label made when vintage conditions allow. Excellent Reserve Chardonnay★★, tasty Riesling★ and Gewürztraminer★. Vicar's Choice is impressive entry-level label. Various Pinot Noirs★ (Doctor's Creek★★) and serious, chocolaty Rapaura Reserve Merlot★★ lead the reds. Best years: (Sauvignon Blanc) **2007 06 04**.

ST-DÉSIRAT, CAVE DE *St-Joseph AC, Rhône Valley, France* One of the best co-ops in the RHONE VALLEY. The intense, smoky red ST-JOSEPH★ is a bargain, as are local vins de pays. In 2005 it took over the nearby co-op of Sarras, and now accounts for over 50% of all St-Joseph.

ST-ÉMILION AC *Bordeaux, France* The scenic Roman hill town of St-Émilion is the centre of Bordeaux's most historic wine region. The finest vineyards are on the plateau and *côtes*, or steep slopes, around the town, although an area to the west, called the *graves*, contains 2 famous properties, CHEVAL BLANC and FIGEAC. It is a region of smallholdings, with over 1000 properties, and consequently the co-operative plays an important part. The dominant early-ripening Merlot grape gives wines with a 'come hither' softness and sweetness rare in red BORDEAUX. St-Émilion AC is the basic generic AC, with 4 'satellites' (LUSSAC, MONTAGNE, PUISSEGUIN, ST-GEORGES) allowed to annex their name to it. The best producers, including the Classed Growths, are found in the more tightly controlled ST-EMILION GRAND CRU AC category but there are anomalies, e.g. La Mondotte★★. Best years: **2005 03 01 00 98 96 95 90**.

ST-ÉMILION GRAND CRU AC *Bordeaux, France* ST-EMILION's top-quality AC, which includes the estates classified as Grand Cru Classé and Premier Grand Cru Classé (below). The 2006 Classification lists 46 Grands Crus Classés. This AC also includes many of the new wave of limited edition *vins de garage*. Best producers: (Grands Crus Classés) l'ARROSEE★, Balestard-la-Tonnelle★, CANON-LA-GAFFELIERE★★, Clos de l'Oratoire★, la Dominique★, Fleur Cardinale★, Grand Mayne★★, Grand Pontet★, Larcis Ducasse★, Larmande★, MONBOUSQUET★, Pavie-Decesse★, la Tour Figeac★; (others) Bellevue★, Faugères★, Fombrauge★, la Gomerie★, Gracia★, Moulin St-Georges★, Quinault l'Enclos★, Rol Valentin★, TERTRE-ROTEBOEUF★★, Teyssier, VALANDRAUD★★. Best years: **2005 03 01 00 98 96 95 90 89 88**.

ST-ÉMILION PREMIER GRAND CRU CLASSÉ *Bordeaux, France* The St-Émilion élite level, divided into 2 categories – 'A' and 'B' – with only the much more expensive CHEVAL BLANC and AUSONE in category 'A'. There are 13 'B' châteaux, with PAVIE-MACQUIN and TROPLONG MONDOT added in the 2006 Classification. Best producers: ANGELUS★★★, AUSONE★★★, BEAU-SEJOUR BECOT★★, Beauséjour★, BELAIR★, CANON★, CHEVAL BLANC★★★, Clos Fourtet★, FIGEAC★★, la Gaffelière★, MAGDELAINE★, PAVIE★★, PAVIE-MACQUIN★★, TROPLONG MONDOT★★, Trottevieille★. Best years: **2006 05 04 03 02 01 00 99 98 96 95 90 89 88**.

ST-ESTÈPHE AC *Haut-Médoc, Bordeaux, France* Large AC north of PAUILLAC with 5 Classed Growths. St-Estèphe wines have high tannin levels, but given time (10–20 years) those sought-after flavours of blackcurrant and cedarwood do peek out. More Merlot has been planted to soften the wines and make them more accessible at an earlier age. As summers get drier and hotter, these wines are coming into their own. Best producers: CALON-SEGUR★★, COS D'ESTOURNEL★★★, Cos Labory, HAUT-MARBUZET★★, LAFON-ROCHET★, Lilian-Ladouys★, Marbuzet★, MEYNEY★, MONTROSE★★, les Ormes-de-Pez★, PEZ★, Phélan Ségur★. Best years: **2006 05 04 03 02 01 00 96 95 94 90 89 88 86**.

DOM. ST-GAYAN *Gigondas AC, Rhône Valley, France* The Meffre family's holdings include some very old vines, which lend power to the chunky GIGONDAS★ (★★ in top years). Other reds, such as Rasteau, are very good value. Best years: (Gigondas) 2007 06 05 **04 03 01 00 99 98 97 95 90**.

ST-GEORGES-ST-ÉMILION AC *Bordeaux, France* The smallest satellite of ST-EMILION, with lovely, soft wines that can nevertheless age for 6–10 years. Best producers: Calon, Macquin St-Georges★, St-André Corbin★, Ch. St-Georges★, Tour-du-Pas-St-Georges★, Vieux-Montaiguillon. Best years: **2005** 03 01 00 98 96 95 90.

ST HALLETT *Barossa Valley, South Australia* Following a merger with MCLAREN VALE's Tatachilla, then a joint takeover of ADELAIDE HILLS' Hillstowe, all 3 wineries were snapped up by brewer Lion Nathan. So far, the bargain Gamekeeper's Reserve★ red, Poacher's Blend★ white, EDEN VALLEY Riesling★ and The Reward Cabernet★★ all seem to be performing pretty well, as are venerable Old Block Shiraz★ and its Shiraz Siblings Blackwell★ and Faith★, but production of all the labels is now centred on St Hallett, which may strain resources. Best years: (Old Block) (2006) (04) 03 **02 98 96 94 93 91 90**.

ST-JOSEPH AC *Rhône Valley, France* Large, mainly red AC, along the opposite bank of the Rhône to HERMITAGE. Made from Syrah, the reds have mouthfilling fruit with irresistible blackcurrant richness. Brilliant at 1–2 years, they can last for up to 10. The white wines are usually pleasant and flowery to drink young, although an increasing number can age. Best producers: (reds) CHAPOUTIER★, J-L CHAVE★★, Chêne★, L Chèze★, COLOMBO★, Courbis★, COURSODON★★, CUILLERON★★, DELAS★★, E & J Durand★★, P Faury★, Ferme des Sept Lunes★, Florentin★, P Gaillard★★, Gonon★★, GRAILLOT★★, B Gripa★★, GUIGAL★★, JABOULET★, Monier★, Monteillet★★, Paret★, A PERRET★★, C Pichon★, ST-DESIRAT co-op★, TAIN co-op★, Tardieu-Laurent★★, Vallet★, G Vernay★, F Villard★★; (whites) CHAPOUTIER (Granits★★), Chêne★★, L Chèze★, Courbis★ (Royes★★), CUILLERON★★, DELAS★, Ferraton★, P Finon, G Flacher, Florentin★, P Gaillard★★, Gonon★★, B Gripa★, GUIGAL, Monteillet★, A PERRET★, Villard★★. Best years: (reds) 2007 **06 05 03 01 00 99 98 95**; (whites) 2007 **06 05 04 03 00 98**.

ST-JULIEN AC *Haut-Médoc, Bordeaux, France* For many, St-Julien produces perfect claret, with an ideal balance between opulence and austerity and between the brashness of youth and the genius of maturity. It is the smallest of the HAUT-MEDOC ACs but almost all is first-rate vineyard land and quality is high. Best producers: BEYCHEVELLE★, BRANAIRE-DUCRU★★, DUCRU-BEAUCAILLOU★★★, GLORIA★, GRUAUD-LAROSE★★, LAGRANGE★★, LANGOA-BARTON★★, LEOVILLE-BARTON★★★, LEOVILLE-LAS-CASES★★★, LEOVILLE-POYFERRE★★, ST-PIERRE★★, TALBOT★. Best years: 2006 05 04 03 02 **01 00 99 98 96 95 94 90 89 88 86**.

CHÂTEAU BEYCHEVELLE
GRAND VIN 2003
— SAINT-JULIEN —

ST-NICOLAS-DE-BOURGUEIL AC *Loire Valley, France* An enclave within the larger BOURGUEIL AC, and similarly producing light wines from vineyards towards the river, sturdier bottles from up the hill. Almost all the wine is red and with the same piercing red fruit flavours of Bourgueil, and much better after 7–10 years, especially in warm vintages. Best producers: Y Amirault★★, Clos des Quarterons★, Dom. de la Cotelleraie/ Vallée★, L & M Cognard-Taluau★, Vignoble de la Jarnoterie, F Mabileau★★,

J-C Mabileau★, Dom. Pavillon du Grand Clos★, J Taluau★. Best years: (2006) 05 **04 03 02 01** 97 96 95.

ST-PÉRAY AC *Rhône Valley, France* Rather hefty CHAMPAGNE-method fizz from Marsanne and Roussanne grapes. Still white is usually dry, fragrant and mineral on the finish. Best producers: S Chaboud★, CHAPOUTIER, CLAPE★, COLOMBO★, DELAS, Fauterie★, B Gripa★★, J Lemenicier★, TAIN co-op★, Tardieu-Laurent★, J-L Thiers★, Tunnel★, Vins de Vienne, A Voge★ (Fleur de Crussol★★). Best years: **2007 06 05 04 03 01 00 99**.

CH. ST-PIERRE★★ *St-Julien AC, 4ème Cru Classé, Haut-Médoc, Bordeaux, France* Small ST-JULIEN property making wines that have become a byword for ripe, lush fruit wrapped round with the spice of new oak. Drinkable early, but top vintages can improve for 20 years. Best years: 2006 05 04 03 02 **01** 00 **99** 98 96 95 94 90 89 85.

ST-ROMAIN AC *Côte de Beaune, Burgundy, France* Red wines with a firm, bitter-sweet cherrystone fruit and flinty-dry whites. Both are usually good value by Burgundian standards, but take a few years to open out. Best producers: (whites) Bazenet★, H & G Buisson, Chassorney★★, A Gras★★, O LEFLAIVE★, VERGET★★; (reds) A Gras★. Best years: (whites) (2007) **06** 05 04 02; (reds) (2007) **06** 05 03 02.

ST-VÉRAN AC *Mâconnais, Burgundy, France* Often thought of as a POUILLY-FUISSÉ understudy, this is gentle, fairly fruity, normally unoaked Mâconnais Chardonnay. Overall quality is good. Drink young. Best producers: D & M Barraud★, Cordier★, Corsin★★, Deux Roches★, DUBOEUF★, Gerbeaux★, R Lassarat★, O Merlin★, Saumaize-Michelin★, J C Thévenet★★, VERGET★, J-J Vincent★. Best years: (2007) **06**.

STE-CROIX-DU-MONT AC *Bordeaux, France* Best of the 3 sweet wine ACs that gaze jealously at SAUTERNES and BARSAC across the Garonne river (the others are CADILLAC and LOUPIAC). The wine is mildly sweet rather than splendidly rich. Top wines can age for at least a decade. Best producers: Crabitan-Bellevue★, Loubens★, Lousteau-Vieil, Mailles, Mont, Pavillon★, la Rame★. Best years: 2005 **03 02 01** 99 98 97 96 95.

SAINTSBURY *Carneros AVA, California, USA* Deeply committed CARNEROS winery. Its Pinot Noirs★★ are brilliant examples of the perfume and fruit quality of Carneros; the new line of vineyard-designated Pinots, led by the exquisite Brown Ranch★★★, are deeper and oakier, while Garnet★ is a delicious lighter style. The Chardonnays★★ are also impressive, best after 2–3 years. Best years: (Pinot Noir) 2005 04 **03 02 01** 00 99 98 97 96 95.

CASTELLO DELLA SALA *Orvieto DOC, Umbria, Italy* Belongs to the ANTINORI family, making good ORVIETO★ and outstanding oak-aged Cervaro★★★ (Chardonnay and a little Grechetto). Also Pinot Nero★ and sweet Muffato della Sala★★.

DUCA DI SALAPARUTA *Sicily, Italy* Corvo is the brand name for Sicilian wines made by this firm. Red and white Corvo are pretty basic, but there are superior whites, Colomba Platino★ and Bianca di Valguarnera★, and 2 fine reds, Terre d'Agala★ and Duca Enrico★★.

SALICE SALENTINO DOC *Puglia, Italy* One of the better DOCs in the Salento peninsula, using Negroamaro tempered with a dash of perfumed Malvasia Nera for ripe, chocolaty wines that acquire hints of roast chestnuts and prunes with age. Drink after 3–4 years, although they may last as long again. The DOCs of Alezio, Brindisi, Copertino, Leverano and Squinzano, plus various IGTs, are similar. Best producers: Candido★, Casale Bevagna★, Leone De Castris★, Due Palme★, Taurino★, Vallone★★, Conti Zecca. Best years: (reds) (2006) **04 03 01** 00.

SALTA *Argentina* The vineyards of Salta province, 700km (435 miles) north
of MENDOZA, are concentrated along the Calchaquí Valley. The most
important location is Cafayate, at about 1750m (5750 ft), where all the
traditional producers are located, but Colomé (2200m/7200 ft) is also
showing tremendous potential and there are new vineyards going as high
as 3100m (over 10,000 ft) – truly the highest in the world. High altitude,
sandy soils and almost no rain produce wines of intense colour and high
alcohol content, with scented white Torrontés and lush red Malbec. Best
producers: (Cafayate) Etchart, Finca Las Nubes, San Pedro de Yacochuya;
(Colomé) Colomé (Torrontés★).

SAMOS *Greece* The island of Samos has a centuries-old reputation for rich,
sweet, Muscat-based wines. The Samos co-op's wines include deep gold,
honeyed Samos Nectar★★, made from sun-dried grapes; apricotty
Palaio★, aged for up to 20 years; and seductively complex Samos
Anthemis★, fortified and cask-aged for up to 5 years.

SAN ANTONIO VALLEY *Chile* This region is really in two parts: the more
northerly, actually called San Antonio, and the more southerly Leyda.
Closeness to the Pacific Ocean and the icy Humboldt Current decides
whether you are best at snappy Sauvignon Blanc and fragrant Pinot Noir
(Leyda), or scented, juice-laden Syrah (San Antonio). There are half a
dozen estates, but big companies like CONCHA Y TORO, SANTA RITA and
MONTES are also making exciting wine from the region's fruit. Water
shortage is a problem, but expect Leyda in particular to become a new
mini-CASABLANCA. Best producers: CASA MARIN★★, Garcés Silva/Amayna★,
Viña Leyda★★, MATETIC★.

SAN LEONARDO *Trentino, Italy* Marchese Carlo Guerrieri Gonzaga, a
former winemaker at SASSICAIA, has established his Cabernet-Merlot
blend San Leonardo★★★ as the northern equivalent of the famous
Tuscan. Recently launched is an almost equally impressive Merlot called
Villa Gresti★★. Best years: (2007) (06) 04 **03 01 00** 99 97 96 **95**.

SAN LUIS OBISPO COUNTY *California, USA* CENTRAL COAST county best
known for Chardonnay, Pinot Noir, a bit of old-vine Zinfandel, Syrah
and Cabernet Sauvignon. There are 5 AVAs – Edna Valley, PASO ROBLES,
SANTA MARIA VALLEY (shared with SANTA BARBARA COUNTY), Arroyo Grande
Valley and York Mountain. Best producers: Alban★★, Claiborne &
Churchill★, Eberle★, Edna Valley★★, Justin★, Laetitia, J Lohr (Hilltop Cabernet
Sauvignon★), Meridian★, Norman★, Saucelito Canyon★, Savannah-
Chanelle★, Talley★★, Wild Horse★. Best years: (reds) 2005 04 **03** 02 01 00
99 98 97 95 94.

SAN PEDRO *Curicó, Chile* This giant operation produced little of note before
Jacques Lurton arrived as a consultant in 1994. Now, Marco Puyó is the
winemaker and American Paul Hobbs is consultant. San Pedro's
35 South range is pretty good, Castillo de Molina Reservas★ are ripe and
full-bodied, and 1865 Malbec★★ and Cabernet★★ are excellent,
powerful, dark-fruited reds. The Tabalí winery, in LIMARI VALLEY, is
producing memorable Chardonnay★★ and Syrah★★, while Altaïr in
Cachapoal Valley (RAPEL) delivers exuberant, occasionally excessive,
Cabernet-based reds. San Pedro recently added to its portfolio Viña
Leyda, in SAN ANTONIO VALLEY.

SANCERRE AC *Loire Valley, France* White Sancerre can provide the perfect
expression of the bright green tang of the Sauvignon grape, and from a
good grower can be deliciously refreshing – as can the rare Pinot Noir
rosé – but the very best also age well. Some growers produce a richer style

using new oak. Pinot Noir reds from top producers are now a serious proposition. The wines are more consistent than those of neighbouring POUILLY. Prices reflect the appellation's popularity. **Best producers: F & J Bailly★, Balland-Chapuis★, H BOURGEOIS★★, H Brochard★, R Champault★, F Cotat★★, F Crochet★, L Crochet★, Delaporte★, Gitton★, P Jolivet★, Serge Laloue★, Dom. Martin★, A MELLOT★, J Mellot★, P Millérioux★, Mollet-Maudry★, H Natter★, A & F Neveu★, R Neveu★, V Pinard★★, J Reverdy★, P & N Reverdy★, J-M Roger★, VACHERON★★, André Vatan★. Best years: 2007 06 05 02.**

SANDALFORD *Swan Valley, Western Australia* One of WESTERN AUSTRALIA'S original wineries (founded in 1840) and a pioneer of the MARGARET RIVER, where Sandalford planted a large vineyard in 1972. However, it generally underperformed until the arrival of winemaker Paul Boulden in 2001. With the premium wines, Boulden has focused on the Margaret River, and quality has leaped ahead. Whites – Sauvignon Blanc-Semillon, Verdelho★ and Chardonnay★ – are impressive, while the reds are perhaps even better: dark and classically ripe, fleshy Shiraz★★ and Cabernet Sauvignon★★★. Lush Cabernet Prendiville Reserve★★★ raises the bar even further. Budget ranges – Element and Protégé – offer quality at fair prices. **Best years: (Cabernet Sauvignon) (2007) 05 04 03 02 01 00 99.**

SANDEMAN *Port DOC, Douro, Portugal and Jerez y Manzanilla DO, Spain* The PORT operation is now owned by SOGRAPE, but run by George Sandeman (7th-generation descendant of the founder). Excellent aged tawnies: 20-year-old★ and 30-year-old★★. Vintage ports are more patchy. Vau Vintage is the second label, for early drinking. In 2004 Sogrape sold its Jerez assets to Nueva Rumasa (Garvey), which now makes the Sandeman brands as a sub-contractor. **Best years: (Vintage) 2003 00 97 94 66 63 55.**

LUCIANO SANDRONE *Barolo DOCG, Piedmont, Italy* Luciano Sandrone has become one of PIEDMONT'S leading wine stylists, renowned for his BAROLO Cannubi Boschis★★★ and Le Vigne★★★, as well as BARBERA D'ALBA★★ and Dolcetto d'Alba★★, which rank with the best.

SANFORD *Santa Rita Hills AVA, California, USA* Richard Sanford planted the great Benedict vineyard in the Santa Ynez Valley in 1971, thus establishing SANTA BARBARA as a potentially top-quality vineyard region. An estate vineyard planted west of Highway 101 is in the SANTA RITA HILLS, an area that subsequently burst on to the Pinot Noir scene with some spectacular wines. Sanford now makes sharply focused, dark-fruited Pinot Noir★★, Chardonnay★★ and Sauvignon Blanc★. Richard Sanford left the project in 2005 to found high-quality Alma Rosa label. **Best years: (Pinot Noir) 2005 04 03 02 01 00 99 98 97 96 95.**

DOM. LE SANG DES CAILLOUX *Vacqueyras AC, Rhône Valley, France* Top VACQUEYRAS estate with big, authentic red wines led by the old-vines Grenache-Syrah Cuvée de Lopy★★ that bursts with fruit and vigour over 10 or more years. Doucineline★ and Azalaïs★ reds are more restrained. **Best years: 2007 06 05 04 03 01 00 99 98.**

SANGIOVESE Sangiovese, the most widely planted grape variety in Italy, reaches its greatest heights in central TUSCANY, especially in Montalcino, whose BRUNELLO must be 100% varietal. This grape has produced a wide range of sub-varieties, plus a growing number of 'improved' clones, which makes generalization difficult. Much care is being taken in the current wave of replanting, whether in CHIANTI CLASSICO, Brunello di

Montalcino, VINO NOBILE DI MONTEPULCIANO or elsewhere. Styles range from pale, lively and cherryish through vivacious, mid-range Chiantis to excellent top Riservas and SUPER-TUSCANS. Some fine examples are also produced in ROMAGNA. California producers including ATLAS PEAK, SHAFER, Robert Pepi and SEGHESIO are having a go at taming the grape, without much success. Australia has good examples from King Valley in VICTORIA (Gary Crittenden, Pizzini) and MCLAREN VALE (Coriole), but poor-quality clones have thus far hampered progress. Also grown in Argentina and Chile, and both South Africa and NEW YORK are trying it.

SANTA BARBARA COUNTY *California, USA* CENTRAL COAST county, northwest of Los Angeles, known for Chardonnay, Riesling, Pinot Noir and Syrah. The main AVAs are SANTA RITA HILLS, Santa Ynez Valley and most of SANTA MARIA VALLEY (the remainder is in SAN LUIS OBISPO COUNTY), all top areas for Pinot Noir. Best producers: AU BON CLIMAT★★, Babcock, Beckmen★★, Brander★, Brewer-Clifton★★, Byron★★, Cambria, Foxen★★, Hitching Post★★, Lane Tanner★★, Longoria★★, Melville★, Andrew MURRAY★★, Ojai★★, Fess Parker★, QUPE★★, SANFORD★★, Zaca Mesa★. Best years: (Pinot Noir) 2005 04 **03 02 01 00 99** 98 97 95 94.

SANTA CRUZ MOUNTAINS AVA *California, USA* A sub-region of the CENTRAL COAST AVA. Notable for long-lived Chardonnays and Cabernet Sauvignons, including the stunning Monte Bello from RIDGE. Also small amounts of robust Pinot Noir. Best producers: BONNY DOON★★, David Bruce★★, Clos La Chance★, Thomas Fogarty★, Kathryn Kennedy★★, Mount Eden Vineyards★★, RIDGE★★★, Santa Cruz Mountain Vineyard★.

SANTA MARIA VALLEY AVA *Santa Barbara County and San Luis Obispo County, California, USA* Cool Santa Maria Valley is coming on strong as a producer of Chardonnay, Pinot Noir and Syrah. Look for wines made from grapes grown in Bien Nacido and Sierra Madre vineyards by several small wineries. Best producers: AU BON CLIMAT★★, Byron★★, Cambria, Foxen★★, Lane Tanner (Pinot Noir★★), Longoria★, QUPE★★.

SANTA RITA *Maipo, Chile* Long-established MAIPO giant. Red blends such as superb Triple C★★ (Cabernet Franc, Cabernet Sauvignon, Carmenère) and Syrah-Cabernet Sauvignon-Carmenère★ show real flair. Floresta whites (Leyda Sauvignon Blanc★★) and reds (Apalta Cabernet Sauvignon★★) are tremendous. Casa Real★ is expensive and old fashioned, but some people love it.

SANTA RITA HILLS AVA *Santa Barbara County, California, USA* Established in 2002, this small AVA lies at the western edge of the Santa Ynez Hills in SANTA BARBARA COUNTY. Fog and wind from the Pacific keep temperatures cool. Pinot Noir is the primary grape (along with small amounts of Syrah and Chardonnay) and the wines have deeper colour, greater varietal intensity and higher acidity than others in the region. Best producers: Babcock, Brewer-Clifton★★, Clos Pepe★★, Fiddlehead★★, Foley★★, Lafond★, Melville★, SANFORD★★, Sea Smoke★★.

SANTENAY AC *Côte de Beaune, Burgundy, France* Red Santenay wines often promise good ripe flavour, though they don't always deliver it, but are worth aging for 4–6 years in the hope that the wine will open out. Many of the best wines, both red and white, come from les Gravières Premier Cru on the border with CHASSAGNE-MONTRACHET. Best producers: (reds) R Belland★★, F & D Clair★, M Colin★, J Girardin★, V GIRARDIN★★, Monnot★, B Morey★★, L Muzard★★, N POTEL★, Prieur-Brunet; (whites) V GIRARDIN★, Jaffelin, René Lequin-Colin★. Best years: (reds) (2007) 06 05 **03 02** 99.

CASA SANTOS LIMA *Alenquer DOC, Estremadura, Portugal* A beautiful estate with a wide range. Light, fruity and tasty Espiga reds and whites, spicy red★ and creamy, perfumed white Palha Canas, and red and white Quinta das Setencostas★. Also Touriz★ (from DOURO varieties), varietal Touriga Nacional★, Touriga Franca★, Trincadeira★ and Tinta Roriz★ and peachy, herby Chardonnay★.

CAVES SÃO JOÃO *Beira Litoral, Portugal* A pioneer of cool-fermented, white BAIRRADA, and makes rich, oaky Cabernet Sauvignon from its own vines. Rich, complex traditional reds and whites include outstanding Reserva★★ and Frei João★ from Bairrada and Porta dos Cavaleiros★★ from DAO – they demand at least 10 years' age to show their quality.

SARDINIA *Italy* Grapes of Spanish origin, like the white Vermentino and Torbato and the red Monica, Cannonau and Carignano, dominate production on this huge, hilly Mediterranean island, but they vie with a Malvasia of Greek origin and natives like Nuragus and Vernaccia. The cooler northern part (Gallura) favours whites, especially Vermentino, while the southern and eastern parts are best suited to reds from Cannonau and Monica, with Carignano dominating in the south-west. The wines used to be powerful, alcoholic monsters, but the current trend is for a lighter, modern, more international style. Foremost among those in pursuit of quality are ARGIOLAS, SELLA & MOSCA and the Santadi co-op. See also CARIGNANO DEL SULCIS.

SASSICAIA DOC★★★ *Tuscany, Italy* Legendary Cabernet Sauvignon-Cabernet Franc blend. Vines were planted in 1944 to satisfy the Marchese Incisa della Rocchetta's thirst for fine red Bordeaux, which was in short supply during the war. The wine remained purely for family consumption until nephew Piero ANTINORI and winemaker Giacomo Tachis persuaded the Marchese to refine production practices and to release several thousand bottles from the 1968 vintage. Since then, Sassicaia's fame has increased as it proved itself to be one of the world's great Cabernets, combining a blackcurrant power of blistering intensity with a heavenly scent of cigars. It has its

own DOC, within the BOLGHERI appellation, from the 1995 vintage. Best years: (2007) (06) 04 **03 01 99 98 97 95 90 88 85 68**.

HORST SAUER *Escherndof, Franken, Germany* Horst Sauer shot to stardom in the late 1990s. His dry Rieslings★★ and Silvaners★ are unusually juicy and fresh for a region renowned for blunt, earthy wines. His late-harvest wines are unchallenged in the region and frequently ★★★; they will easily live a decade, sometimes much more. Best years: (dry Riesling, Silvaner) (2007) 06 05 **04 03 02 01 00**.

SAUMUR AC *Loire Valley, France* Dry white wines, mainly from Chenin Blanc, with up to 20% Chardonnay; the best combine bright fruit with a mineral seam. The reds are lighter than those of SAUMUR-CHAMPIGNY and Saumur Puy-Notre-Dame, which was recently awarded its own appellation. Also dry to off-dry Cabernet rosé, and sweet Coteaux de Saumur in good years. Best producers: Château-Gaillard★, Clos Rougeard★★, Collier★, Filliatreau★, Fosse-Seche, HUREAU★★, Langlois-Château★, R-N Legrand★, la Paleine★, ROCHES NEUVES★★, St-Just★, Saumur co-op, Tour Grise, VILLENEUVE★★, Yvonne★★. Best years: (whites) 2007 **06 05 04 03 02**.

SAUMUR-CHAMPIGNY AC *Loire Valley, France* Saumur's best red wine.
Cabernet Franc is the main grape, and in hot years the wine can be
superb, with a piercing scent of blackcurrants and raspberries easily
overpowering the earthy finish. Delicious young, it can age for 6–10
years. Best producers: Clos Rougeard★★, de la Cune, Filliatreau★, HUREAU★★,
Lavigne, R-N Legrand★, Nerleux★, la Perruche★, Retiveau-Rétif★, ROCHES
NEUVES★★, St-Vincent★, Patrick Vadé★, Varinelles★, VILLENEUVE★★, Yvonne★.
Best years: (2007) **06 05 04 03 02 01 96**.

SAUMUR MOUSSEUX AC *Loire Valley, France* Reasonable CHAMPAGNE-
method sparkling wines, mainly from Chenin Blanc. Adding
Chardonnay and Cabernet Franc makes the wine softer and more
interesting. Usually non-vintage. Small quantities of rosé are also made.
Best producers: BOUVET-LADUBAY★, Gratien & Meyer★, Grenelle★, la Paleine★,
la Perruche★, St-Cyr-en-Bourg co-op★, Veuve Amiot.

SAUTERNES AC *Bordeaux, France* The name Sauternes is synonymous with
the best sweet wines in the world. Sauternes and BARSAC both lie on the
banks of the little river Ciron and are 2 of the very few areas in France
where noble rot occurs naturally. Production of these intense, sweet,
luscious wines from botrytized grapes is a risk-laden and extremely
expensive affair, and the wines are never going to be cheap. From good
producers the wines are worth their high price – as well as 14% alcohol
they have a richness full of flavours of pineapples, peaches, syrup and
spice. Good vintages should be aged for 5–10 years and often last twice
as long. Best producers: Bastor-Lamontagne★, Clos Haut-Peyraguey★★, Cru
Barréjats★, DOISY-DAENE★★, DOISY-VEDRINES★★, FARGUES★★, GILETTE★★,
GUIRAUD★★, Haut-Bergeron★, les Justices★, LAFAURIE-PEYRAGUEY★★, Lamothe-
Guignard★, Malle★, Rabaud-Promis★, Raymond-Lafon★, Rayne-Vigneau★,
RIEUSSEC★★★, Sigalas Rabaud★★, SUDUIRAUT★★, la TOUR BLANCHE★★,
YQUEM★★★. Best years: 2007 05 03 **02 01 99 98 97 96 95 90 89 88 86 83**.

SAUVIGNON BLANC See pages 268–9.

SAUZET *Puligny-Montrachet, Côte de Beaune, Burgundy, France* A producer with a
reputation for classic, rich, full-flavoured white Burgundies, made in an
opulent, fat style, but recently showing more classical restraint. Sauzet
owns prime sites in PULIGNY-MONTRACHET★ and CHASSAGNE-MONTRACHET★
(Premiers Crus usually ★★), as well as small parcels of BATARD-
MONTRACHET★★★ and Bienvenues-BATARD-MONTRACHET★★★. Best years:
(2007) **06 05 04 03 02**.

SAVENNIÈRES AC *Loire Valley, France* Wines from Chenin Blanc, produced
on steep vineyards south of Anjou. Usually steely and dry, although some
richer wines are being produced by a new generation using new oak and
malolactic fermentation. The top wines usually need at least 8 years to
mature, and can age for longer. There are 2 extremely good vineyards
with their own ACs: la Coulée-de-Serrant and la Roche-aux-Moines.
Best producers: BAUMARD★★, Bergerie, Chamboureau★, Clos de Coulaine★,
CLOS DE LA COULÉE-DE-SERRANT★★, Closel★★, Épiré★★, Damien Laureau★, aux
Moines★, Eric Morgat★, Pierre-Bise★★, Jo PITHON, P-Y Tijou★★. Best years:
(2007) 06 05 **04 03** 02 **01 99 97 96 95 90**.

SAVIGNY-LÈS-BEAUNE AC *Côte de Beaune, Burgundy, France* Large village
with reds dominating; usually dry and lean, they need 4–6 years to open
out. The top Premiers Crus, such as Lavières, Peuillets and La
Dominode, are more substantial. The white wines show a bit of dry,
nutty class after 2–3 years. The wines are generally reasonably priced.
Best producers: S Bize★, Camus-Bruchon★★, Champy★, CHANDON DE

BRIAILLES★, B CLAIR★★, M Écard★★, J J Girard★, V GIRARDIN★, L Jacob★★, Dom. LEROY★★, C Maréchal★, J-M Pavelot★★, TOLLOT-BEAUT★★. Best years: (reds) (2007) 06 05 **03 02 99 96**.

SAVOIE *France* Savoie's high Alpine vineyards produce fresh, snappy white wines with loads of flavour, when made from the Altesse (or Roussette) grape. Drink them young. There are some attractive light reds and rosés, too, and, in hot years, some positively Rhône-like reds from the Mondeuse grape. Most of the better wines use the Vin de Savoie AC and should be drunk young or with 3–4 years' age. The 15 best villages, including Apremont, near Aix-les-Bains, and Abymes, Chignin and Montmélian, near Chambéry, can add their own name to the label. Between Lyon and Savoie are the vineyards of the Vin du Bugey VDQS, with light, easy-drinking reds and whites. **Best producers:** Bouvet★, Dupasquier★, Jacquin★, Magnin★, C Marandon★, Monin, Neyroud, Perret★, A & M Quénard★, J-P & J-F Quénard★, R Quénard★, Ripaille★, Rocailles★, Saint-Germain, C Trosset★; (Bugey) Charlin. See also SEYSSEL.

SAXENBURG *Stellenbosch WO, South Africa* In-demand red wines, led by dense, burly Private Collection Shiraz★★ and an even richer, bigger Shiraz Select★★, plus excellent Cabernet★★ and Merlot★. Private Collection Sauvignon Blanc★★ and Chardonnay★★ head the white range. Drink whites young; reds will improve for 5–8 years. **Best years:** (premium reds) 2005 **04 03 02 01 00 99 98**.

WILLI SCHAEFER *Graach, Mosel, Germany* Classic MOSEL wines: Riesling Spätlese and Auslese from the GRAACHer Domprobst vineyard have a balance of piercing acidity and lavish fruit that is every bit as dramatic as Domprobst's precipitous slope. Extremely long-lived, they're frequently ★★★, as is the sensational Beerenauslese Schaefer produces in good vintages. Even his QbA wines are ★. **Best years:** (Riesling Spätlese, Auslese) (2007) 06 05 04 **03 02 01 99 98 97 96 95 94**.

SCHÄFER-FRÖHLICH *Bockenau, Nahe, Germany* From vineyards in SCHLOSSBOCKELHEIM and the more obscure Bockenau, Tim Fröhlich has since 2003 been producing racy dry Rieslings★★ and sumptuous nobly sweet wines★★★. **Best years:** (2007) 06 05 **04 03 02 01**.

SCHARFFENBERGER CELLARS *Anderson Valley AVA, California, USA* Owned by ROEDERER. Non-vintage Brut★★, with lovely toasty depth, exuberant Rosé★★, and vintage Blanc de Blancs★★ are all excellent.

SCHEUREBE Silvaner x Riesling crossing found in Germany's PFALZ and RHEINHESSEN. In Austria it is sometimes labelled Sämling 88. At its best in Trockenbeerenauslese and Eiswein. When ripe, it has a marvellous flavour of honey, exotic fruits and the pinkest of pink grapefruit.

SCHILCHER Rosé and sparkling wine from the Blauer Wildbacher grape, a speciality of the West STEIERMARK in Austria. Its very high acidity means you either love it or detest it. For me, it's a mood thing. **Best producer:** Strohmeier.

SCHIOPETTO *Friuli-Venezia Giulia, Italy* The late Mario Schiopetto pioneered the development of scented varietals and high-quality, intensely concentrated white wines from COLLIO. Outstanding are (Tocai) Friulano★★, Pinot Bianco★★ and Sauvignon★★, which open out with age to display fascinating flavours. New COLLI ORIENTALI vineyards Poderi dei Blumeri can only add further prestige.

SAUVIGNON BLANC

Of all the world's grapes, the Sauvignon Blanc is leader of the 'love it or loathe it' pack. It veers from being wildly fashionable to totally out of favour depending upon where it is grown and which country's wine writers are talking, but you, the consumers, love it – and so do I. Sauvignon is always at its best when full rein is allowed to its very particular talents, because this grape does give intense, sometimes shocking flavours, and doesn't take kindly to being put into a straitjacket. Periodically, producers lose confidence in its fantastic, brash, tangy personality and try to calm it down. Don't do it. Let it run free – it's that lip-smacking, in-yer-face nettles and lime zest and passionfruit attack that drinkers love. There's no more thirst-quenching wine than a snappy, crunchy young Sauvignon Blanc. Let's celebrate it.

WINE STYLES

Sancerre-style Sauvignon Although it had long been used as a blending grape in Bordeaux, where its characteristic green tang injected a bit of life into the blander, waxier Sémillon, Sauvignon first became trendy as the grape used for Sancerre, a bone-dry Loire white whose green gooseberry fruit and slightly smoky perfume inspired the winemakers of other countries to try to emulate, then often surpass, the original model.

The range of styles Sauvignon produces is as wide as, if less subtly nuanced than, those of Chardonnay. It is highly successful when picked not too ripe, fermented cool in stainless steel, and bottled early. This is the Sancerre model followed by growers elsewhere. New Zealand is now regarded as the top Sauvignon country, and many new producers in places like Australia, South Africa, southern France, Hungary, Spain and Chile are emulating this powerful mix of passionfruit, gooseberry and lime. South African and Chilean examples, from the coolest coastal regions, with tangy fruit and mineral depth, are beginning to challenge New Zealand for quality.

Using oak Sauvignon also lends itself to fermentation in barrel and aging in new oak, though less happily than does Chardonnay. This is the model of the Graves region of Bordeaux, although generally here Sémillon would be blended in with Sauvignon to good effect.

New Zealand again excels at this style, and there are good examples from California, Australia and northern Italy. The mix, usually led by Sémillon, is becoming a classy speciality of South Africa's coastal regions. In Austria, producers in southern Styria (Steiermark) make powerful, aromatic versions, sometimes with a touch of oak. In all these regions, the acidity that is Sauvignon's great strength should remain, with a nectarine fruit and a spicy, biscuity softness from the oak. These oaky styles are best drunk either within about a year, or after aging for 5 years or so, and can produce remarkable, strongly individual flavours that you'll either love or loathe.

Sweet wines Sauvignon is also a crucial ingredient in the great sweet wines of Sauternes and Barsac from Bordeaux, though it is less susceptible than its partner Sémillon to the sweetness-enhancing 'noble rot' fungus, botrytis.

Sweet wines from the USA, South Africa, Australia and, inevitably, New Zealand range from the interesting to the outstanding – but the characteristic green tang of the Sauvignon should stay in the wine even at ultra-sweet levels.

BEST PRODUCERS

France
Pouilly-Fumé J-C Chatelain, Didier DAGUENEAU, Ladoucette, Masson-Blondelet, de Tracy; *Sancerre* H BOURGEOIS, F Cotat, L Crochet, A MELLOT, V Pinard, J-M Roger, VACHERON; *Pessac-Léognan* Dom. de CHEVALIER, Couhins-Lurton, FIEUZAL, HAUT-BRION, LAVILLE-HAUT-BRION, SMITH-HAUT-LAFITTE.

Other European Sauvignons
Austria Gross, Lackner-Tinnacher, POLZ, E Sabathi, TEMENT.

Italy Colterenzio co-op, Peter Dipoli, GRAVNER, Edi Kante, LAGEDER, SCHIOPETTO, Vie di Romans, Villa Russiz.

Spain (*Rueda*) Alvarez y Diez (Mantel Blanco), Castelo de Medina, MARQUES DE RISCAL, Palacio de Bornos, Javier Sanz, Sitios de Bodega; (*Penedès*) TORRES (Fransola).

New Zealand
Astrolabe, Cape Campbell, Clifford Bay, CLOUDY BAY, Crossings, Forrest Estate, JACKSON ESTATE, Lawson's Dry Hills, NEUDORF, PALLISER, SAINT CLAIR, SERESIN, VAVASOUR, VILLA MARIA, WITHER HILLS.

Australia
Bird in Hand, Bridgewater Mill, Brookland Valley, Edwards, HANGING ROCK, HOUGHTON (PEMBERTON), KATNOOK ESTATE, Lenton Brae, Nepenthe, SHAW & SMITH, Stella Bella, Tamar Ridge, Geoff WEAVER.

USA
California Abreu, ARAUJO, Brander, DRY CREEK (DCV3), FLORA SPRINGS (Soliloquy), KENWOOD, KUNDE, Mason, MATANZAS CREEK, Murphy-Goode, Navarro, Quivira, Saracina, SPOTTSWOODE, St. Supery, Voss.

Chile
CASA MARIN (Cipreses), CASAS DEL BOSQUE, CONCHA Y TORO (Terrunyo), Viña Leyda, MONTES (Leyda), SANTA RITA (Floresta).

South Africa
CAPE POINT VINEYARDS, Neil ELLIS, Flagstone, Fryer's Cove, MULDERBOSCH, Oak Valley, SPRINGFIELD ESTATE, STEENBERG, THELEMA, VERGELEGEN.

269

SCHLOSS LIESER *Lieser, Mosel, Germany* Since Thomas Haag (son of
Wilhelm, of the Fritz HAAG estate) took over the winemaking in 1992
(and then bought the property in 97), this small estate has shot to the
top. MOSEL Rieslings★★ marry richness with great elegance. Best years:
(2007) 06 05 **04 03 02 01 99 98**.

SCHLOSS REINHARTSHAUSEN *Erbach, Rheingau, Germany* Estate formerly
owned by the Hohenzollern family, rulers of Prussia. Top sites include
the great ERBACHer Marcobrunn. Much improved under new
management since 2003. Good Rieslings (Auslese, Beerenauslese, TBA
★★) and Sekt★. Best years: (2007) 06 05 **04 03 02 01 99 98 97 96**.

SCHLOSS SAARSTEIN *Serrig, Mosel-Saar-Ruwer, Germany* Fine Saar estate
with somewhat austere Riesling Trocken; Riesling Kabinett★, Spätlese★
and Auslese★★ are better balanced, keeping the startling acidity but
coating it with fruit, often with the aromas of slightly unripe white
peaches. Saarstein makes the occasional spectacular Eiswein★★★. Best
years: (2007) 06 05 04 **03 02 01 99 97 95**.

SCHLOSS VOLLRADS *Oestrich-Winkel, Rheingau, Germany* Quality at this
historic estate has improved greatly this century, with some brilliant
Eiswein★★ and TBA★★. Best years: (2007) 06 05 **04 03 02 01**.

SCHLOSSBÖCKELHEIM *Nahe, Germany* This village's top sites are the
Felsenberg and Kupfergrube, but good wines also come from Mühlberg
and Königsfels. Best producers: Dr Crusius★, DONNHOFF★★★,
Gutsverwaltung Niederhausen-Schlossböckelheim★, SCHAFER-FROHLICH★★.
Best years: (2007) 06 05 **04 03 02 01 00 99**.

DOM. SCHOFFIT *Alsace AC, Alsace, France* One of the two main owners of
the outstanding Rangen Grand Cru vineyard, also making a range of
deliciously fruity non-cru wines. Top-of-the-tree Clos St-Théobald
wines from Rangen are often ★★★ and will improve for at least 5–6 years
after release, Rieslings for even longer. The Cuvée Alexandre range is
essentially declassified ALSACE Vendange Tardive. Best years: (Clos St-
Théobald Riesling) (2007) 05 **04 02 01 00 99 98 97 96 95**.

SCHRAMSBERG *Napa Valley AVA, California, USA* The first CALIFORNIA winery
to make really excellent CHAMPAGNE-style sparklers from the classic
grapes. Though all releases do not achieve the same heights, these wines
can be among California's best, and as good as most Champagne. The
Crémant★ is an attractive slightly sweetish sparkler, the Blanc de
Noirs★★ and the Blanc de Blancs★ are more classic. Bold, powerful
J Schram★★ is rich and flavoursome and increasingly good. Top of the
line is the Reserve Brut★★. Vintage-dated wines can be drunk with up to
10 years' age. 2005 saw the debut of the winery's first red, a 2002 J Davies
Cabernet Sauvignon★★ from Diamond Mountain, in honour of the late
founder, Jack Davies.

SCREAMING EAGLE *Oakville AVA, California, USA* Real estate agent Jean
Phillips first produced a Cabernet Sauvignon from her OAKVILLE valley
floor vineyard in 1992. Made in very limited quantities, Screaming
Eagle★★★ is one of California's most sought-after Cabernets each
vintage, a huge, brooding wine that displays all the lush fruit of Oakville.
Sold in March 2006; the new owners propose to change as little as
possible – except the price. That's gone up to $500 a bottle!

SEGHESIO *Sonoma County, California, USA* Having grown grapes in SONOMA
COUNTY for a century, the Seghesio family is today known for its own
Zinfandel. All bottlings, from Sonoma County★★ to the single-vineyard
San Lorenzo★★ and Cortina★★, display textbook black fruit and

peppery spice. Sangiovese from 1910 vines, known as Chianti Station★, is one of the best in the state. Also look for fascinating Aglianico★ and crisp Italian whites such as Pinot Grigio★ and Arneis★.

SEIFRIED *Nelson, South Island, New Zealand* Estate founded in 1974 by Austrian Hermann Seifried and his New Zealand wife Agnes. The best wines include Sauvignon Blanc★, Gewürztraminer★ and botrytized Riesling★★. Best years: (whites) 2007 06 05 04 03 02 01.

SELBACH-OSTER *Zeltingen, Mosel, Germany* Johannes Selbach is one of the MOSEL's new generation of star winemakers, producing very pure, elegant Riesling★★ from the Zeltinger Sonnenuhr site. Also fine wine from WEHLEN, GRAACH and BERNKASTEL. Best years: (2007) 06 05 **04** 03 02 01 00 99 98 97 96 95.

SELLA & MOSCA *Sardinia, Italy* As well as the rich, port-like Anghelu Ruju★ made from semi-dried Cannonau grapes, this much-modernized old firm, today part of the Campari group, produces good dry whites, Terre Bianche★ (Torbato) and La Cala★ (Vermentino), and oak-aged reds, Marchese di Villamarina★ (Cabernet) and Tanca Farrà★ (Cannonau-Cabernet). Best years: (Marchese di Villamarina) (2007) (06) (05) 04 01 00 97 95.

SELVAPIANA *Chianti DOCG, Tuscany, Italy* This estate has always produced excellent CHIANTI RUFINA. But since 1990 it has vaulted into the top rank of Tuscan estates, particularly with the single-vineyard crus Fornace★★ and Vigneto Bucerchiale Riserva★★★. VIN SANTO★★ is very good. Best years: (Bucerchiale) (2007) (06) 04 01 99 98 95 93 91 90 88 85.

SÉMILLON Found mainly in South-West France, especially in the sweet wines of SAUTERNES and BARSAC, because it is prone to noble rot (*Botrytis cinerea*). Also blended for its waxy texture with Sauvignon Blanc to make dry wine – almost all the great GRAVES Classed Growths are based on this blend. Performs well in Australia (aged Semillon from the HUNTER, BAROSSA and CLARE VALLEY can be wonderful) on its own or as a blender with Chardonnay (the accent over the é is dropped on New World labels). Sémillon is also blended with Sauvignon in Australia, New Zealand, California (including St Supery's Virtu★ white Meritage) and WASHINGTON STATE. In cooler regions of South Africa it is producing some outstanding results, often barrel-fermented, and, increasingly, in flagship blends with Sauvignon.

SEÑA★ *Aconcagua, Chile* Seña is one of those trailblazing wines – initially a joint venture with MONDAVI – that was supposed to change the face of Chilean wine, but didn't, because it was too Californian. Now 100% Chilean-owned (by the Chadwick family of ERRAZURIZ), this ripe, dense Cabernet-based super-blend may indeed blaze a trail because quality has leapt since Errázuriz took total control in 2005.

SEPPELT *Grampians, Victoria, Australia* In one of the year's most controversial moves, Foster's has sold Seppeltsfield (the BAROSSA base of Seppelt and its entire fortified resources) to a group centring on the CLARE VALLEY producer, Kilikanoon. From its GRAMPIANS base, Seppelt continues to excel with its flagship St Peters Shiraz★★, the definitive Show Sparkling Shiraz★★★ and the Original Sparkling Shiraz★. The sparkling whites appear to be suffering from a lack of focus. Drumborg Riesling★ from the super-cool Henty region of southern VICTORIA stands out, and there are some excellent budget-priced table wines in the Victorian range.

SERESIN *Marlborough, South Island, New Zealand*
Film producer Michael Seresin's winery has
made a big impact on the MARLBOROUGH scene
with its range of stylish organic wines. Intense
Sauvignon Blanc★ is best within a year or two
of the vintage, but creamy Chardonnay★★,
succulent Pinot Gris★ and rich, oaky Pinot
Noir★ will age for up to 3 years. **Best years:** (Sauvignon Blanc) **2007 06**.

SETÚBAL DOC *Portugal* Fortified wine from the Setúbal Peninsula south of
Lisbon, which is called 'Moscatel de Setúbal' when made from at least
85% Moscatel, and 'Setúbal' when it's not. **Best producers:** BACALHOA
VINHOS DE PORTUGAL★★, José Maria da FONSECA★★.

SEYSSEL AC *Savoie, France* Known for its feather-light, sparkling wine,
Seyssel Mousseux. With the lovely sharp, peppery bite of the Molette
and Altesse grapes smoothed out with a creamy yeast, it is an ideal
summer gulper. The still white is light and floral, and made from Altesse
and Chasselas. **Best producers:** Mollex★, Varichon & Clerc.

SEYVAL BLANC Hybrid grape whose disease resistance and ability to
continue ripening in a damp autumn make it a useful variety in England,
Canada, NEW YORK STATE and other areas in the eastern US. Gives clean,
sappy, grapefruit-edged wines that are sometimes a very passable
imitation of bone-dry CHABLIS.

SHAFER *Stags Leap District AVA, California, USA* One of the best NAPA wineries,
making unusually fruity One Point Five Cabernet★★ and Reserve-style
Hillside Select★★★. Merlot★★ is also exciting. Relentless★ is made
from estate-grown Syrah. Red Shoulder Ranch Chardonnay★★★ is
classic CARNEROS style. **Best years:** (Hillside Select) (2005) (04) 03 **02 01 00 99
98 97 96 95 94 93 91 90 84**.

SHARPHAM *Devon, England* Beautiful vineyard with consistent winemaking
and a stylish range of still and sparkling wines, including white Bacchus★
and Madeleine Angevine-based Estate Selection, and red Beenleigh
(Cabernet Sauvignon-Merlot).

SHAW & SMITH *Adelaide Hills, South Australia* Tangy Sauvignon Blanc★★
was a runaway success from the first vintage in 1989. The range now
includes Unwooded Chardonnay★, an increasingly brilliant single-
vineyard M3 Chardonnay★★★ and impressive, fleshy, cool-climate
Shiraz★. **Best years:** (M3 Chardonnay) (2007) 06 05 04 **03 02**.

SHERRY See JEREZ Y MANZANILLA DO, pages 174–5.

SHIRAZ See SYRAH, pages 284–5.

SICILY *Italy* Sicily is emerging with a renewed spirit and attitude to wine
production. Those who led the way, such as PLANETA, Duca di SALAPARUTA
and TASCA D'ALMERITA, have been joined by others, including Donnafugata,
the revitalized Spadafora and transformed Settesoli (headed by Diego
Planeta; Inycon is its tasty budget label). Other exciting estates include
Abbazia Santa Anastasia, especially noted for its Cabernet Sauvignon-Nero
d'Avola blend, Litra★★; Cottanera, for excellent varietal Merlot
(Grammonte★★), Mondeuse (L'Ardenza★★) and Syrah (Sole di Sesta★★);
Cusumano, for 100% Nero d'Avola (Sàgana★) and a Nero d'Avola-
Cabernet-Merlot blend (Noà★); Morgante, for a pure Nero d'Avola (Don
Antonio★★); Palari, for its Nerello Mascalese-Cappuccio blend (Faro

Palari★★); and Ceuso, for a Nero d'Avola-Merlot-Cabernet blend (Ceuso Custera★). Firriato, aided by consultant Kym Milne, also makes excellent reds★ and whites★. Latest vineyard destination of choice is high on the slopes of Etna, with grapes like Nerello Mascalese and Carricante. See also MARSALA, MOSCATO PASSITO DI PANTELLERIA.

SIEUR D'ARQUES, LES VIGNERONS DU *Limoux AC, Languedoc, France* This modern co-op makes around 80% of the still and sparkling wines of LIMOUX. The BLANQUETTE DE LIMOUX★ and CREMANT DE LIMOUX★ are reliable, but the real excitement comes with the Toques et Clochers Chardonnays★ (occasionally ★★). The co-op also makes a range of vins de pays and has a joint venture with Philippine de Rothschild (MOUTON-CADET), Baron'arques, and with GALLO in California (Red Bicyclette).

SILENI *Hawkes Bay, North Island, New Zealand* Established by millionaire Graeme Avery, with a view to making nothing but the best, this modern winery brings a touch of the NAPA VALLEY to HAWKES BAY. Refreshing unoaked Chardonnay★, tangy MARLBOROUGH Sauvignon★ and ripe, mouthfilling Semillon★ are all tasty. Pinot Noir★ is good (from Hawkes Bay and Marlborough), as is Merlot (The Triangle★), and Syrah★★ is delicate and scented. Best years: (reds) (2007) **06 04 02 00 98.**

SILVER OAK CELLARS *Napa Valley, California, USA* Only Cabernet Sauvignon is made here, with bottlings from ALEXANDER VALLEY★★ and NAPA VALLEY★★ grapes. Forward, generous, fruity wines, impossible not to enjoy young, yet with great staying power. Best years: (Napa Valley) (2005) (04) 03 **02 01 00 99 97 96 95 94 93 92 91 90 86 85 84.**

SILVERADO VINEYARDS *Stags Leap District AVA, California, USA* The regular Cabernet Sauvignon★ has intense fruit and is drinkable fairly young; Solo★★ and Limited Reserve★★ have more depth and are capable of aging; a STAGS LEAP DISTRICT Cabernet Sauvignon★★ displays the cherry fruit and supple tannins of this AVA. Also a fruity Merlot★, refreshing Sauvignon Blanc★ and Chardonnay★ with soft, inviting fruit and a silky finish. Best years: (Limited Reserve) (2005) (04) (03) 02 **01 99 95 94 91 90.**

SIMI *Alexander Valley AVA, California, USA* Historic winery purchased by Constellation in 1999. Currently the ALEXANDER VALLEY Cabernet Sauvignon★, Chardonnay★ (Reserve★★) and Sauvignon Blanc★ attain fair standards. Best years: (reds) 2005 **01 99 97 95 94 91 90.**

SIMONSIG *Stellenbosch WO, South Africa* Family-run property with broad range of styles. Most consistent are the reds: regular Shiraz and lavishly oaked Merindol Syrah; a delicious unwooded Pinotage★★ and well-oaked old-vine Redhill Pinotage★★; the svelte BORDEAUX-blend Tiara★; and dense, powerful Frans Malan Reserve★, a Cape blend of Pinotage, Cabernet Sauvignon and Merlot. Whites are sound, if less exciting. Cap Classique sparklers, Kaapse Vonkel and occasional Cuvée Royale, are biscuity and creamy. Best years: (premium reds) (2006) **05 04 03 02 01 00 99 98.**

CH. SIRAN★ *Margaux AC, Haut-Médoc, Bordeaux, France* Owned by the same family since 1848, this estate produces consistently good claret – increasingly characterful, approachable young, but with enough structure to last for as long as 20 years. Second wine: S de Siran. Best years: 2006 05 04 03 02 01 00 **99 98 96 95 90 89 86.**

SKALLI-FORTANT DE FRANCE *Languedoc-Roussillon, France* Robert Skalli was a pioneer of varietal wines in the Midi. Modern winemaking and the planting of international grape varieties were the keys to success. After a dip in quality, now one of the most influential producers in the south of France. The Fortant de France brand includes a range of single-variety Vins de Pays d'oc. Grenache and Chardonnay are among the best, along with Reserve F Merlot and Cabernet Sauvignon.

SKILLOGALEE *Clare Valley, South Australia* Very good range from the cool CLARE VALLEY: a stony Riesling★ typical of the region and an attractive lemony Gewürztraminer★. Reds include lovely full, fresh Shiraz★★ and minty Cabernet Sauvignon★★. Also a rich, raisiny Liqueur Muscat★★.

CH. SMITH-HAUT-LAFITTE *Pessac-Léognan AC, Cru Classé de Graves, Bordeaux, France* This property was floundering until a change of ownership in 1990 heralded a decade of hard graft, resulting in massively improved quality. The reds, traditionally lean, now have much more fruit and perfume and can approach ★★. The Sauvignon-dominated white is a shining example of modern white Bordeaux and at best is ★★★. Second wine (red and white): Les Hauts de Smith. Best years: (reds) 2006 05 04 03 02 **01** 00 **99 98 96 95**; (whites) 2006 **05 04 03 02 01 00 99 98 96 95**.

SMITH WOODHOUSE *Port DOC, Portugal* Underrated but consistently satisfying PORT from this shipper in the Symington group. The Vintage★★ is always worth looking out for, as is single-quinta Madalena (made since 1995), and its Late Bottled Vintage★★ is the rich and characterful, figgy, unfiltered type. Best years: (Vintage) **2003 00 97 94 92 91 85 83 80 77 70 63**; (Madalena) **2001 99 98 95**.

SOAVE DOC *Veneto, Italy* In the hilly Soave Classico zone near Verona, the Garganega and Trebbiano di Soave grapes can produce ripe, nutty, scented wines. Since 1992, the blend may include 30% Chardonnay, and good examples are definitely on the increase. Soave Superiore has been DOCG for some years, but the top private producers continue to ignore it in protest at the anomalous rules governing the denomination. Best producers: Bertani★, Ca' Rugate★, La Cappuccina★, Coffele★★, Gini★★, Inama★, MASI★, Pasqua/Cecilia Beretta★, PIEROPAN★★, Portinari★, Prà★★, Suavia★★, Tamellini★. See also ANSELMI, RECIOTO DI SOAVE DOCG.

CH. SOCIANDO-MALLET★★ *Haut-Médoc AC, Haut-Médoc, Bordeaux, France* It wasn't classified in 1855, but every single vintage nowadays outshines many properties that were. The wines massively repay 10–20 years' aging, but exhibit classic Bordeaux flavours from as early as 5 years old. Best years: 2006 05 04 03 02 **01** 00 **99 98 96 95 94 90 89 88 86 85**.

SOGRAPE *Portugal* This Portuguese giant revolutionized quality in some of Portugal's most reactionary wine regions. Mateus Rosé is still the company's golden egg, but Sogrape makes good to very good wines, including VINHO VERDE (Quinta de Azevedo★★), DOURO (Reserva Tinto★), DAO and ALENTEJO (Vinha do Monte and Herdade do Peso★★). A high-tech winery in Dão produces Duque de Viseu★ and premium Quinta dos Carvalhais; varietal Encruzado★ (white) and Touriga Nacional (red) are promising; (red) Reserva★★ is a further step up. Callabriga★ reds from Douro, Alentejo and Dão are based on Aragonês (Tempranillo), blended with local varieties. Subsidiaries FERREIRA, SANDEMAN and Offley provide top-flight ports. Also owns Finca Flichman in Argentina.

SOLAIA★★★ *Tuscany, Italy* One of ANTINORI'S SUPER-TUSCANS, sourced, like TIGNANELLO, from the Santa Cristina vineyard. Solaia is a blend of Cabernet Sauvignon, Sangiovese and Cabernet Franc. Intense, with rich fruit and a classic structure, it is not produced in every vintage. Best years: (2007) (06) 04 03 **01 99 98 97 95 94 93 91 90 88 86 85**.

SOMONTANO DO *Aragón, Spain* This region in the foothills of the
Pyrenees is encountering some difficulties due to uneven quality, too
many indifferent wines and, perhaps, too much success too soon. Reds
and rosés from the local grapes (Moristel and Tempranillo) can be light,
fresh and flavourful, and international varieties such as Chardonnay and
Gewürztraminer can yield promising wines. An interesting development
is the rediscovery of the powerful native red grape, Parraleta, and of old-
vines Grenache. Best producers: Otto Bestué, Blecua★★, ENATE★★, Fábregas,
Irius★, Lalanne★, Laus★, Pirineos★, VINAS DEL VERO★. Best years: (reds) 2005
04 03 01 99 98 97 96.

SONOMA COAST AVA *California, USA* A huge appellation, defined on its
western boundary by the Pacific Ocean, that attempts to bring together
the coolest regions of SONOMA COUNTY. It encompasses the Sonoma part
of CARNEROS and overlaps parts of SONOMA VALLEY and RUSSIAN RIVER. The
heart of the appellation are vineyards on the high coastal ridge only a few
miles from the Pacific. Intense Chardonnays and Pinot Noirs are the
focus. Best producers: FLOWERS★★, HARTFORD FAMILY★★, KISTLER★★, Littorai
(Hirsch Pinot Noir★★★), MARCASSIN★★, W H Smith★★, Sonoma Coast
Vineyards★★ (Balistreri Vineyard★★★), Wild Hog★.

SONOMA COUNTY *California, USA* Sonoma's vine-growing area is big and
sprawling – some 25,500ha (63,000 acres), with dozens of soil types and
mesoclimates, from the fairly warm SONOMA VALLEY and ALEXANDER VALLEY
regions to the cool Green Valley and lower RUSSIAN RIVER VALLEY. The best
wines are from Chardonnay, Sauvignon Blanc, Cabernet Sauvignon,
Pinot Noir and Zinfandel. Often the equal of rival NAPA in quality and
originality of flavours. See also CARNEROS, DRY CREEK VALLEY, SONOMA COAST.

SONOMA-CUTRER *Russian River Valley AVA, Sonoma County, California, USA*
Rich, oaky, popular, but often overhyped Chardonnays. Single-vineyard
Les Pierres★★ is the most complex and richest; Cutrer★★ can also have
a complexity worth waiting for; Founders Reserve★★ is made in very
limited quantities (screwcapped!). Russian River Ranches★ is much
improved in recent releases. Best years: (2005) 04 03 **02 01 00 99** 98 97 95.

SONOMA VALLEY AVA *California, USA* The oldest wine region north of
San Francisco, Sonoma Valley is situated on the western side of the
Mayacamas Mountains, which separate it from NAPA VALLEY. Best varieties
are Chardonnay and Zinfandel, with Cabernet and Merlot from hillside
sites also good. Best producers: ARROWOOD★★, CHATEAU ST JEAN★, B R Cohn,
Fisher★, GUNDLACH-BUNDSCHU★★, KENWOOD★, KUNDE★★, LANDMARK★★,
LAUREL GLEN★★, MATANZAS CREEK★★, MOON MOUNTAIN★★, RAVENSWOOD★, St
Francis★, Sebastiani★. Best years: (Zinfandel) 2003 **01 00 99** 98 97 96 95 94.

DOM. SORIN *Bandol AC, Provence, France* Luc Sorin, from CHABLIS, arrived in
Provence in 1995. As well as red and rosé BANDOL★, he makes various
COTES DE PROVENCE cuvées: white Cuvée Tradition is a mouthwatering oak-
aged blend of Rolle and Sémillon; Terra Amata is crisp pink grapefruit
and cranberry juice-flavoured rosé. Best years: (red Bandol) 2005 **03 01**.

SOUTH AUSTRALIA Australia's biggest grape-growing state, with some
70,000ha (173,000 acres) of vineyards and almost half the country's total
production. Covers many climates and most wine styles, from bulk wines to
the very best. Established regions are ADELAIDE HILLS, Adelaide Plains, CLARE,
BAROSSA and Eden Valleys, MCLAREN VALE, Langhorne Creek, COONAWARRA,
PADTHAWAY and RIVERLAND. Newer regions creating excitement include Mount
Benson and Wrattonbully, both in the LIMESTONE COAST zone.

SPARKLING WINES OF THE WORLD

Made by the Traditional (Champagne) Method

Although Champagne is still the benchmark for top-class sparkling wines all over the world, the Champagne houses themselves have taken the message to California, Australia and New Zealand via wineries they've established in these regions. However, Champagne-method fizz doesn't necessarily have to feature the traditional Champagne grape varieties (Chardonnay, Pinot Noir and Pinot Meunier), and this allows a host of other places to join the party. Describing a wine as Champagne method is strictly speaking no longer allowed (only original Champagne from France is officially sanctioned to do this), but the use of a phrase like Traditional Method should not distract from the fact that these wines are still painstakingly produced using the complex system of secondary fermentation in the bottle itself.

STYLES OF SPARKLING WINE

France French fizz ranges from the sublime to the near-ridiculous. The best examples have great finesse and include appley Crémant d'Alsace produced from Pinot Blanc and Pinot Gris, sometimes with a little Chardonnay too; often inexpensive yet eminently drinkable Crémant de Bourgogne, based mainly on Chardonnay; and some stylish examples from the Loire Valley, notably in Saumur and Vouvray. Clairette de Die and Crémant de Limoux in the south confuse the issue by sometimes following their own idiosyncratic method of production, but the result is delicious.

Rest of Europe Franciacorta DOCG is a success story for Italy. Most *metodo classico* sparkling wine is confined to the north, where ripening conditions are closer to those of Champagne, but a few good examples do pop up in unexpected places – Sicily, for instance. Asti, Lambrusco and Prosecco are not Champagne-method wines. In Spain, the Cava wines of Cataluña offer an affordable style for everyday drinking. German Sekt comes in two basic styles: one made from Riesling grapes, the other using Champagne varieties. England is proving naturally suited to growing grapes for sparkling wine.

Australia and New Zealand Australia has a wide range of styles, though there is little overt varietal definition. Blends are still being produced using fruit from many areas, but regional characters are starting to emerge. Cool Tasmania is the star performer, making some top fizz from local grapes. Red sparklers, notably those made from Shiraz, are an irresistible Australian curiosity with an alcoholic kick. Cool-climate New Zealand is now producing some world-class examples difficult to tell from good Champagne; as in Australia, some have Champagne connections.

USA In California, some magnificent examples are produced – the best ones using grapes from Carneros or the Anderson Valley. Quality has been transformed by the efforts of French Champagne houses. Oregon is also a contender in the sparkling stakes.

South Africa Cap Classique is the local name for the Champagne method. The best are very good and those from the limy soils of Robertson are starting to show particularly well, but too many brands seem to lack the desire to excel. Consistency is a problem; also, high demand means many are released too young.

BEST PRODUCERS

Australia *white* BAY OF FIRES (Arras), BROWN BROTHERS, Cope-Williams, DOMAINE CHANDON (Green Point), Freycinet (Radenti), HANGING ROCK, Stefano LUBIANA, PETALUMA (Croser), Pipers Brook (Kreglinger), Taltarni (Clover Hill), Tamar Ridge, YALUMBA (Jansz), Yarrabank, Yellowglen (Perle); *red* Peter LEHMANN (Black Queen), Charles MELTON, PRIMO ESTATE, ROCKFORD, SEPPELT.

Austria BRUNDLMAYER, Schlumberger.

France *Alsace* Ostertag; *Burgundy* Bailly co-op, Lugny co-op; *Die* J-C Raspail; *Limoux* SIEUR D'ARQUES; *St-Péray* Chaboud, J-L Thiers; *Saumur* BOUVET-LADUBAY, Gratien & Meyer; *Vouvray* CLOS NAUDIN, HUET.

Germany *Pfalz* Bergdolt, REBHOLZ; *Rheingau* BREUER, WEGELER; *Rheinhessen* Raumland.

Italy *Franciacorta* BELLAVISTA, CA' DEL BOSCO; *Trento* FERRARI; *Sicily* TASCA D'ALMERITA.

New Zealand CLOUDY BAY (Pelorus), DEUTZ, HUNTER'S, LE BRUN, Nautilus, No 1 Family Estate, PALLISER.

Portugal Caves ALIANCA, Quinta dos Loridos/BACALHOA, Vértice (Super Reserva).

South Africa Graham BECK, High Constantia, STEENBERG, Twee Jonge Gezellen, VILLIERA.

Spain *Cava* Can Ràfols dels Caus, CODORNIU, Colet, FREIXENET, Parxet, Signat, Agustí Torelló, Dominio de la Vega.

UK BREAKY BOTTOM, CAMEL VALLEY, CHAPEL DOWN, DENBIES, NYETIMBER, RIDGEVIEW.

USA *California* DOMAINE CARNEROS, DOMAINE CHANDON, Gloria Ferrer, HANDLEY, IRON HORSE, J Wine, Laetitia, MUMM NAPA, ROEDERER ESTATE, SCHARFFENBERGER CELLARS, SCHRAMSBERG; *Oregon* ARGYLE.

277

SOUTH-WEST FRANCE As well as the world-famous wines of BORDEAUX, South-West France has many lesser-known, less expensive ACs, VDQS and Vins de Pays, over 10 *départements* from the Atlantic coast to LANGUEDOC-ROUSSILLON. Bordeaux grapes (Cabernet Sauvignon, Merlot and Cabernet Franc for reds; Sauvignon Blanc, Sémillon and Muscadelle for whites) are common, but there are lots of interesting local varieties as well, such as Tannat (in MADIRAN), Petit Manseng (in JURANCON) and Mauzac (in GAILLAC). See also BERGERAC, BUZET, CAHORS, COTES DE DURAS, COTES DU FRONTONNAIS, IROULEGUY, MONBAZILLAC, MONTRAVEL, PACHERENC DU VIC-BILH, PECHARMANT.

SPÄTBURGUNDER See PINOT NOIR.

SPICE ROUTE WINE COMPANY *Swartland WO, South Africa* Owned by Charles Back of FAIRVIEW. Ripe, well-oaked Flagship Syrah★★ and polished Malabar★★ – Shiraz-based and featuring any or all of Mourvèdre, Merlot, Grenache, Viognier and Pinotage, reflecting its Malmesbury *terroir* – now head the pack. Whites showing promise include rich, barrel-fermented Chenin Blanc★ and elegant Viognier. **Best years: (premium reds) 2005 04 03 02 01 00 99.**

SPOTTSWOODE *Napa Valley AVA, California, USA* Replanted in the mid-1990s, this beautifully situated 16ha (40-acre) vineyard west of St Helena has not missed a beat since the winery opened in 1982. Deep, blackberry- and cherry-fruited Cabernet Sauvignon★★★ is wonderful to drink early, but is best at 5–10 years. Sauvignon Blanc★★ (blended with a little Semillon and barrel fermented) is a sophisticated treat. **Best years: (Cabernet) (2005) 04 03 02 01 00 99 98 97 96 95 94 93.**

SPRINGFIELD ESTATE *Robertson WO, South Africa* Abrie Bruwer's approach is strictly hands-off in his efforts to capture his vineyard's terroir. Méthode Ancienne Chardonnay★ is barrel fermented with vineyard yeasts and bottled without any fining or filtration. Not every vintage makes it! Cabernet Sauvignon is also made as Méthode Ancienne★. The unwooded Wild Yeast Chardonnay★ and flinty, lively Life from Stone Sauvignon Blanc★★ are also notably expressive. The Cabernet Franc-Merlot-based Work of Time★ is the farm's first blend. **Best years: (Sauvignon Blanc) 2007 06 05 04.**

STAGS LEAP DISTRICT AVA *Napa County, California, USA* One of California's best-defined appellations. Located in south-eastern NAPA VALLEY, it is cooler than OAKVILLE or RUTHERFORD to the north, and the red wines have a recognisably mellow, balanced character. A little Sauvignon Blanc and Chardonnay are grown, but the true stars are Cabernet Sauvignon and Merlot. **Best producers:** CHIMNEY ROCK★★, Cliff Lede★, CLOS DU VAL★★, HARTWELL★★, PINE RIDGE★★, SHAFER★★★, SILVERADO★★, Robert Sinskey★★, STAG'S LEAP WINE CELLARS★★, Stags' Leap Winery★★.

STAG'S LEAP WINE CELLARS *Stags Leap District AVA, California, USA* The winery rose to fame when its Cabernet Sauvignon came first at the famous Paris tasting of 1976. Cabernet Sauvignon★★ can be stunning, particularly the SLV★★★ from estate vineyards and the Fay★★; the Cask 23 Cabernet Sauvignon★★ can be very good, but is overhyped. After a dip in quality, recent vintages are back on form. A lot of work has gone into the Chardonnay★ (Arcadia Vineyard★★) and the style is one of NAPA's more successful. Sauvignon Blanc★ (Rancho Chimiles★★) is intensely flavoured, with brisk acidity. Founder Warren Winiarski sold the property in 2007 to CHATEAU STE MICHELLE and ANTINORI of Italy. **Best years: (Cabernet) 2004 (03) 02 01 00 99 98 97 96 95 94 91 90 86.**

STANLAKE PARK *Berkshire, England*   Formerly known as Valley Vineyards, this 10ha (25-acre) vineyard has, over the past 20 years, produced many stunning wines. The range includes toasty oaky Fumé and fragrant Regatta and Hinton Grove★ whites; Ruscombe red and occasional barrel-aged Pinot Noir; sparkling Heritage Brut (from Seyval Blanc and other grapes) and Stanlake Park★ (Pinot Noir and Chardonnay).

STEELE *Lake County, California, USA*   Owner/winemaker Jed Steele is a master blender. He sources grapes from all over California and Washington and shapes them into exciting wines, usually featuring vivid fruit with supple mouthfeel. He also offers single-vineyard wines and has, in current release, 4–6 Chardonnays, most ★★. His Zinfandels★★ and Pinot Noirs★★ (CARNEROS, SANTA MARIA VALLEY) are usually very good. Shooting Star label provides remarkable value in a ready-to-drink style.

STEENBERG *Constantia WO, South Africa*   The oldest farm in the CONSTANTIA Valley produces some of South Africa's best and most consistent Sauvignon Blanc: Reserve★★ is smoky and flinty with underlying fruit richness; straight Sauvignon★★ is pure upfront fruit. Barrel-fermented Semillon★★ (occasionally pushing ★★★) matches them in quality. Reds include an irresistible minty Merlot★★, gaining more nuance each year; Catharina★★, a blend featuring Cabernet and Merlot, with Shiraz and a dab of Nebbiolo; and exciting, smoky Shiraz★★. Fast-improving Steenberg 1682 Brut★ Cap Classique fizz is elegant and biscuity. Best years: (whites) 2007 06 05 04 03 02 01 00.

STEIERMARK *Austria*   This 3700ha (9140-acre) region (Styria in English) in south-east Austria is divided into 3 areas: Süd-Oststeiermark, Südsteiermark and Weststeiermark. Technically it is the warmest of the Austrian wine regions, but the best vineyards are in cool, high-altitude sites. The tastiest wines are Morillon (unoaked Chardonnay, though oak is catching on), Sauvignon Blanc and Gelber Muskateller (Muscat). Best producers: Gross★★, Lackner-Tinnacher★, POLZ★★, E Sabathi★, Sattlerhof★, Walter Skoff, TEMENT★★, Winkler-Hermaden★, Wohlmuth★.

STELLENBOSCH WO *South Africa*   This district boasts the greatest concentration of wineries in the Cape, though is only third in vineyard area; the vineyards straddle valley floors and stretch up the many mountain slopes. Climates and soils are as diverse as wine styles; smaller units of origin – wards – are now being demarcated to more accurately reflect this diversity. The renowned reds are matched by some excellent Sauvignon Blanc and Chardonnay, as well as modern Chenin Blanc and Semillon. Best producers: BEYERSKLOOF★, Cordoba★, De Toren★, DE TRAFFORD★★, DeWaal★, Dornier★, Neil ELLIS★★, Ernie ELS★★, Ken Forrester★, The Foundry★★, GRANGEHURST★★, HARTENBERG★, JORDAN★★, KANONKOP★★, Laibach★, L'AVENIR★, Le Riche★, MEERLUST★, Meinert★, MORGENHOF★, Morgenster★, MULDERBOSCH★★, Neethlingshof★, Overgaauw★, Quoin Rock★, RUST EN VREDE★, RUSTENBERG★★, SAXENBURG★★, SIMONSIG★, Stellenzicht★, Sterhuis★, THELEMA★★, Tokara★, VERGELEGEN★★, VILLIERA★, WARWICK★, Waterford★★, Waterkloof (Circumstance★).

STERLING VINEYARDS *Napa Valley AVA, California, USA*   Merlot is the focus here, led by Three Palms★★ and Reserve★★, both packed with ripe, dense fruit. Reserve Cabernet is now ★★. The Winery Lake Chardonnay★ delivers elegant honey and apple fruit. Also Winery Lake Pinot Noir★. Best years: (Merlot) 2002 01 00 99 97 96 94.

SUPER-TUSCANS

Tuscany, Italy

The term 'Super-Tuscans', first used by English and American writers, has now been adopted by Italians themselves to describe the new-style red wines of Tuscany. The 1970s and 80s were a time when enormous strides were being made in Bordeaux, Australia and California, yet these changes threatened to bypass Italy completely because of its restrictive wine laws. A group of winemakers, led by Piero Antinori – who created the inspirational Tignanello and Solaia from vineyards within the Chianti Classico DOCG – abandoned tradition to put their best efforts and best grapes into creative wines styled for modern tastes.

Old large oak casks were replaced with French barriques, while Cabernet Sauvignon and other trendy varieties, such as Cabernet Franc, Merlot and Syrah, were planted alongside Sangiovese in vineyards that emerged with sudden grandeur as crus. Since the DOC specifically forbade such innovations, producers were forced to label their wines as plain Vino da Tavola. The 'Super-Tuscan' Vino da Tavolas, as they were quickly dubbed, were a phenomenal success: brilliant in flavour with an approachable, upfront style. Some found it hard to believe that table wines with no official credentials could outrank DOCG Chianti. A single mouthful was usually enough to convince them.

However, after 9/11 the market for most of the less established Super-Tuscans collapsed, and apart from a few big names it has hardly recovered to date. There seems to be much more interest in international markets in established DOC(G)s such as Brunello di Montalcino and Chianti Classico Riserva.

WINE STYLES

Sangiovese, the Cabernets and Merlot are the basis for most Super-Tuscans, usually in a blend. All also appear varietally, with Sangiovese forming the largest group of top-quality varietal Super-Tuscans. To some Sangiovese-based wines, a small percentage of other native varieties such as Colorino, Canaiolo or Malvasia Nera is added. Syrah is of growing importance, mostly varietally, but also in innovative new blends such as Argiano's Solengo, where it features along with Cabernet and Merlot. Super-Tuscan wines also show considerable differences in vinification and aging. Top wines are invariably based on ripe, concentrated grapes from a site with special attributes.

CLASSIFICATIONS

A law passed in 1992 has finally brought the Super-Tuscans into line with official classifications. Sassicaia now has its own DOC under Bolgheri. Chianti Classico's now independent DOCG could cover many a Sangiovese-based Super-Tuscan, but the majority are currently sold under the region-wide IGT Toscana alongside wines made from international varieties. There are also 3 sub-regional IGTs, but only a few producers use these.

See also BOLGHERI, CHIANTI CLASSICO, SASSICAIA, SOLAIA, TIGNANELLO; and individual producers.

BEST PRODUCERS

Sangiovese and other Tuscan varieties Badia a Coltibuono (Sangioveto), BOSCARELLI, CASTELLARE (I Sodi di San Niccolò), FELSINA (Fontalloro), FONTODI (Flaccianello della Pieve), ISOLE E OLENA (Cepparello), Lilliano (Anagallis), MONTEVERTINE (Le Pergole Torte), Paneretta (Quattrocentenario, Terrine), Poggio Scalette (Il Carbonaione), Poggiopiano (Rosso di Sera), Querceto (La Corte), RIECINE (La Gioia), San Giusto a Rentennano (Percarlo), VOLPAIA (Coltassala).

Sangiovese-Cabernet and Sangiovese-Merlot blends BANFI (Summus), Colombaio di Cencio (Il Futuro), FONTERUTOLI (Siepi), Gagliole, Montepeloso (Nardo), QUERCIABELLA (Camartina), Castello dei RAMPOLLA (Sammarco), RICASOLI (Casalferro), Sette Ponti (Oreno), TIGNANELLO.

Cabernet Col d'Orcia (Olmaia), Fossi (Sassoforte), ISOLE E OLENA (Collezione), Le MACCHIOLE (Paléo Rosso), Nozzole (Il Pareto), Castello dei RAMPOLLA (Vigna d'Alceo), SOLAIA.

Merlot Castello di AMA (L'Apparita), Le MACCHIOLE (Messorio), ORNELLAIA (Masseto), Petrolo (Galatrona), TUA RITA (Redigaffi).

Cabernet-Merlot blends ANTINORI (Guado al Tasso), Argiano (Solengo), BANFI (Excelsus), Capezzana (Ghiaie della Furba), ORNELLAIA (Ornellaia), Poggio al Sole (Seraselva), POLIZIANO (Le Stanze), Le Pupille (Saffredi), Trinoro, TUA RITA (Giusto di Notri).

STONIER *Mornington Peninsula, Victoria, Australia* The peninsula's biggest winery and one of its best, though Lion Nathan, via PETALUMA, now has a controlling interest. KBS Vineyard★★ and Reserve Chardonnay★★ and Windmill Vineyard★★ and Reserve Pinot Noir★★ are usually outstanding, and there are fine standard bottlings in warm vintages.

STONYRIDGE *Waiheke Island, Auckland, North Island, New Zealand* The leading winery on WAIHEKE ISLAND, Stonyridge specializes in reds made from Cabernet Sauvignon, Merlot, Petit Verdot, Malbec and Cabernet Franc. The top label, Larose★★★, is a remarkably BORDEAUX-like red of real intensity. Best years: (Larose) (2007) 05 **04 02 00 99 98**.

CH. SUDUIRAUT★★ *Sauternes AC, 1er Cru Classé, Bordeaux, France* Together with RIEUSSEC, Suduiraut is regarded as a close runner-up to d'YQUEM. Although the wines are delicious at only a few years old, the richness and excitement increase enormously after a decade or so. Seemed to be under-performing in the 1980s and mid-90s but now owned by AXA (see PICHON-LONGUEVILLE) and back on irresistible song. Best years: 2006 05 04 03 **02 01 99 98 97 96 95 90 89 86 82**.

SUMAC RIDGE *Okanagan Valley VQA, British Columbia, Canada* Excellent Sauvignon Blanc★ and Gewürztraminer Reserve★, fine Pinot Blanc and one of Canada's best CHAMPAGNE-method fizzes, Steller's Jay Brut★. Top reds include Cabernet Sauvignon, Cabernet Franc, Merlot, Pinot Noir and Meritage★.

SUNTORY *Japan* Red Tomi and sweet white Noble d'Or (made from botrytized grapes) are top brands for wine made exclusively from grapes grown in Japan. Classic varieties – Cabernets Sauvignon and Franc, Chardonnay, Sémillon and Sauvignon – are also having success.

SUPER-TUSCANS See pages 280–1.

SWAN DISTRICT *Western Australia* The original WESTERN AUSTRALIA wine region and the hottest stretch of vineyards in Australia, spread along the fertile silty flats of Perth's Swan River. It used to specialize in fortified wines, but SOUTH AUSTRALIA and north-east VICTORIA do them better. New-wave whites and reds are fresh and generous. Best producers: Paul Conti, Faber★, HOUGHTON★★, John Kosovich, Lamont★, Oakover, SANDALFORD★★, Sittella, Upper Reach.

JOSEPH SWAN VINEYARDS *Russian River Valley AVA, California, USA* The late Joseph Swan made legendary Zinfandel in the 1970s and was one of the first to age Zinfandel★★ in French oak. In the 80s he turned to Pinot Noir★★★ which is now probably the winery's best offering. Best years: (Zinfandel) 2005 **02 01 99 98 97 96 95**.

SYRAH See pages 284–5.

LA TÂCHE AC★★★ *Grand Cru, Côte de Nuits, Burgundy, France* Along with la ROMANÉE and la ROMANÉE-CONTI, the greatest of the great VOSNE-ROMANÉE Grands Crus, owned by Dom. de la ROMANÉE-CONTI. The wine provides layer on layer of flavours; keep it for 10 years or you'll only experience a fraction of the pleasure you paid big money for. Best years: (2007) 06 05 04 03 02 01 00 99 98 **97** 96 95 93 **90 89 88 85 78**.

TAHBILK *Goulburn Valley, Central Victoria, Australia* Wonderfully old-fashioned family company making traditionally big, gumleafy/minty reds, matured largely in old wood. 1860 Vines Shiraz★ and the Reserve reds – now Eric Stevens Purbrick Shiraz and Eric Stevens Purbrick Cabernet – are full of character, even if they need years of cellaring. White Marsanne★★ is perfumed and attractive, as is a floral-scented Viognier★. Best years: (Eric Stevens Purbrick Shiraz) (2007) (06) (05) (04) 03 02 01 **00 99 98 97 96 94**.

CAVE DE TAIN *Hermitage, Rhône Valley, France* Progressive co-op offering good-value wines from the northern Rhône. Reasonably high quality, despite annual production of 500,000 cases and rather dull basic 'supermarket' cuvées. Impressive CROZES-HERMITAGE les Hauts du Fief★, fine CORNAS★ and both red and white ST-JOSEPH★ and HERMITAGE★. Topping the range are an old-vine red Hermitage Gambert de Loche★★ and a rich Vin de Paille★★. Also still and sparkling ST-PERAY★. Best years: (top reds) 2007 06 05 **04 03 01 00 99 98 97 95**.

TAITTINGER *Champagne AC, Champagne, France* The top wine, Comtes de Champagne Blanc de Blancs★★★, can be memorable for its creamy, foaming pleasures; the Comtes de Champagne rosé★★ is elegant and oozing class. Prélude is an attractive, fuller-bodied non-vintage style made from 4 Grands Crus and aged for 4 years before release. Non-vintage Les Folies de la Marquetterie is from a steeply sloping single vineyard. Best years: 2002 00 **99 98 96 95 90 89 88 85 82**.

CH. TALBOT★ *St-Julien AC, 4ème Cru Classé, Haut-Médoc, Bordeaux, France* Chunky, soft-centred but sturdy, capable of aging well for 10–20 years and increasingly good this century. Also a tasty white wine, Caillou Blanc de Talbot★. Second wine: Connétable de Talbot. Best years: 2006 05 04 03 02 01 00 **99 98 96 95 90 89 88 86 85**.

TALBOTT *Monterey County, California, USA* This estate is known for its Chardonnays from vineyards in the Santa Lucia Highlands in MONTEREY COUNTY. Sleepy Hollow Vineyard★★, Cuvée Cynthia★★ and Diamond T Estate★★ are all packed with ripe tropical fruit and ample oak. Kali Hart Chardonnay★ gives a taste of the style on a budget. Also Chardonnay and Pinot Noir under the Logan label.

TAPANAPPA *Adelaide Hills, South Australia* The partnership of the families of Brian Croser (formerly of PETALUMA), Arnould d'Hautefeuille (BOLLINGER) and Jean-Michel Cazes (LYNCH-BAGES) explores the notion of terroir by following Croser's belief in the importance of 'distinguished sites'. Sublime, complex and mouthwatering Chardonnay from the Croser family's Tiers Vineyard★★ in the ADELAIDE HILLS; one of the country's most elegant Cabernet-Shiraz blends from the mature Whalebone Vineyard★★ at Wrattonbully; and Pinot Noir from the Foggy Hill Vineyard★ on the maritime Southern Fleurieu Peninsula.

DOM. DU TARIQUET *Vin de Pays des Côtes de Gascogne, South-West France* On his huge 853-ha (2,100-acre) property, Yves Grassa, innovative COTES DE GASCOGNE producer, transformed Gascony's thin raw whites into some of the snappiest, fruitiest, almost-dry wines in France. Also makes oak-aged★ and late-harvest★ styles, and Domaine la Hitaire whites.

TARRAWARRA *Yarra Valley, Victoria, Australia* Founder Marc Besen wanted to make a MONTRACHET, and hang the expense. It's a long haul, but the winemakers are doing well: Chardonnay★★ is deep and multi-faceted. Pinot Noir★★ has almost COTE DE NUITS flavour and concentration. Tin Cows is a less pricey brand for both these grapes, plus Shiraz and Merlot. Best years: (Pinot Noir) (2006) 05 04 03 **02 01 99 98 97 96 94 92**.

TASCA D'ALMERITA *Sicily, Italy* This estate in the highlands of central SICILY makes some of southern Italy's best wines. Native grape varieties give excellent Rosso del Conte★★ (based on Nero d'Avola) and white Nozze d'Oro★ (based on Inzolia), but there are also Chardonnay★★ and Cabernet Sauvignon★★ of extraordinary intensity and elegance. Almerita Brut★ (Chardonnay) is a fine CHAMPAGNE-method sparkler. Relatively simple Regaleali Bianco and Rosato are good value.

SYRAH/SHIRAZ

Syrah's popularity is rising fast and it now produces world-class wines in France, in Australia – where as Shiraz it produces some of the New World's most remarkable reds – and in California and possibly South Africa and Chile, too. And wherever it appears it trumpets a proud and wilful personality based on loads of flavour and unmistakable originality.

When the late-ripening Syrah grape is grown in the coolest, most marginal areas for full ripening, such as Côte-Rôtie, it is capable of producing very classy, elegant wines. However, producers must ensure low yields if they are to produce high-quality wines. Syrah's heartland – Hermitage and Côte-Rôtie in the Rhône Valley – comprises a mere 365ha (900 acres) of steeply terraced vineyards, producing hardly enough wine to make more than a very rarefied reputation for themselves. This may be one reason for its relatively slow uptake by growers in other countries, who simply had no idea as to what kind of flavour the Syrah grape produced, so didn't copy it. But the situation is rapidly changing and Syrah's popularity in both the warm and the reasonably cool wine regions of the world becomes more evident with every vintage.

WINE STYLES

French Syrah The flavours of Syrah are most individual, but with modern vineyard practices and winemaking techniques they are far less daunting than they used to be. Traditional Syrah had a savage, almost coarse, throaty roar of a flavour. And from the very low-yielding Hermitage vineyards, the small grapes often showed a bitter tannic quality. But better selections of clones in the vineyard and improved winemaking have revealed Syrah with a majestic depth of fruit – all blackberry and damson, loganberry and plum – some quite strong tannin, occasionally bacon smoke, but also a warm creamy aftertaste, and a promise of chocolate and occasionally a scent of violets. It is these characteristics that have made Syrah popular throughout the south of France as an 'improving' variety for its rather traditional red wines.

Australian Shiraz Australia's most widely planted red variety has become, in many respects, its premium varietal. Shiraz gives spectacularly good results when taken seriously – especially in the Barossa, Clare, Eden Valley and McLaren Vale regions of South Australia. An increasingly diverse range of high-quality examples is also coming from Victoria's high country vineyards, more traditional examples from New South Wales' Hunter Valley and Mudgee, and exciting, more restrained styles from the Great Southern, Grampians, Pyrenees and Adelaide Hills regions, as well as patches of Canberra and Queensland. Just about everywhere, really. Flavours are rich, intense, thick sweet fruit coated with chocolate, and seasoned with leather, herbs and spice, or fragrant, floral and flowing with damson and blackberry fruit.

Other regions In California and Washington State producers are turning out superb Rhône-style blends as well as varietal Syrahs modelled closely on Côte-Rôtie or Hermitage. In South Africa Syrah is the most-planted red variety and, as in Chile, more exciting varietal wines and blends appear every vintage. New Zealand's offerings are thrillingly different. Italy (especially Tuscany and Sicily, often in a blend with Nero d'Avola), Spain, Portugal and Argentina are beginning to shine, and even Switzerland and North Africa are having a go.

BEST PRODUCERS

France
Rhône ALLEMAND, F Balthazar,
G Barge, A Belle, CHAPOUTIER, CHAVE,
Y Chave, Chêne, CLAPE, Clusel-Roch,
COLOMBO, Combier, Courbis,
COURSODON, CUILLERON, DELAS, E & J
Durand, B Faurie, L Fayolle, Gaillard,
J-M Gérin, Gonon, GRAILLOT, Gripa,
GUIGAL, JAMET, Jasmin, V Paris,
ROSTAING, S Ogier, M Sorrel,
Tardieu-Laurent, F Villard; *Languedoc*
ALQUIER, GAUBY, Mas Champart, PEYRE
ROSE, PRIEURE DE ST-JEAN DE BEBIAN.

Other European Syrah
Italy (*Piedmont*) Bertelli; (*Tuscany*)
D'ALESSANDRO, FONTODI, Fossi, ISOLE E
OLENA, Le MACCHIOLE, Poggio al Sole;
(*Sicily*) Cottanera, PLANETA.

Spain Albet i Noya, Castaño,
Casa Castillo, Finca Sandoval,
MARQUES DE GRINON, Enrique
Mendoza, Pago del Ama.

New World Syrah/Shiraz
Australia Tim ADAMS, BAROSSA VALLEY
ESTATE, Jim BARRY, BEST'S, Rolf BINDER,
BROKENWOOD, CLARENDON HILLS,
CLONAKILLA, Craiglee, Dalwhinnie,
D'ARENBERG, Dutschke, FOX CREEK,
GLAETZER, HARDY (Eileen Hardy),
Henry's Drive, HENSCHKE, Hewitson,
HOUGHTON (Gladstones), HOWARD
PARK (Scotsdale), Jasper Hill,
Peter LEHMANN, Charles MELTON,
MOUNT LANGI GHIRAN, PENFOLDS,
PLANTAGENET, PONDALOWIE,
ROCKFORD, SEPPELT (St Peters), SHAW
& SMITH, TORBRECK, TURKEY FLAT,
TYRRELL'S, WENDOUREE, The Willows,
WIRRA WIRRA (RWS), YALUMBA, Yering
Station (Reserve), Zema.

New Zealand Bilancia, CRAGGY
RANGE, DRY RIVER, Esk Valley, FROMM,
Murdoch James, Passage Rock,
Stonecroft, Te Awa, TE MATA,
TRINITY HILL, Vidal, VILLA MARIA.

South Africa BOEKENHOUTSKLOOF,
DE TRAFFORD, FAIRVIEW, The Foundry,
HARTENBERG, SADIE FAMILY, SAXENBURG,
SPICE ROUTE, STEENBERG, Stellenzicht.

USA (*California*) ALBAN, ARAUJO,
Cline, DEHLINGER, Dutton-Goldfield,
Edmunds St John, Havens, Jade
Mountain, Lewis, Andrew MURRAY,
Pax, QUPE, Swanson, Sean Thackrey,
Truchard.

Chile Falernia, MATETIC, MONTES,
Tabalí/SAN PEDRO.

TASMANIA *Australia* Tasmania may be a minor state viticulturally, with only 1200ha (2965 acres) of vines, but the island has a diverse range of mesoclimates and sub-regions. The generally cool climate has always attracted seekers of greatness in Pinot Noir and Chardonnay, and good results are becoming more consistent. Riesling, Gewürztraminer and Pinot Gris perform well, but the real star is fabulous premium fizz. Best producers: Apsley Gorge, BAY OF FIRES★★, Freycinet★★, Stefano LUBIANA★, Moorilla★, Pipers Brook★, Providence, Tamar Ridge★, Wellington★. Best years: (Pinot Noir) 2007 06 05 **03 02 01 00 99 98 97 95 94 93 92 91**.

TAURASI DOCG *Campania, Italy* MASTROBERARDINO created Taurasi's reputation; now the great potential of the Aglianico grape is being exploited by others, both within this DOCG and elsewhere in CAMPANIA. Drink at 5–10 years. Best producers: A Caggiano★★, Feudi di San Gregorio★★, MASTROBERARDINO★★, S Molettieri★, Struzziero, Terredora di Paolo★. Best years: (2007) (06) 04 **03 01 00 98 97 96 94 93 92 90**.

TAVEL AC *Rhône Valley, France* Chunky, alcoholic rosé from north-west of Avignon. Grenache and Cinsaut are the main grapes. Drink at one year old if you want it cheerful, heady, yet refreshing, with food. Best producers: Aquéria★, la Forcadière★, Genestière★, GUIGAL, Lafond Roc-Épine★, Montézargues★★, la Mordorée★★, Vignerons de Tavel, Trinquevedel★.

TAYLOR *Port DOC, Douro, Portugal* The aristocrat of the PORT industry, over 300 years old and still going strong. Now part of the Fladgate Partnership, along with FONSECA and CROFT. Its Vintage★★★ (sold as Taylor Fladgate in the USA) is superb; Quinta de Vargellas★★ is an elegant, cedary, single-quinta vintage port made in the best of the 'off-vintages'. Quinta de Terra Feita★★, the other main component of Taylor's Vintage, is also often released as a single-quinta. Taylor's 20-year-old★★ is a very fine aged tawny. First Estate is a successful premium ruby. Best years: (Vintage) **2003** 00 97 94 92 85 83 80 77 75 70 66 63 60 55 48 45 27; (Vargellas) **2001** 99 98 96 95 91 88 87 86 82 78 67 64 61.

TE MATA *Hawkes Bay, North Island, New Zealand* HAWKES BAY's glamour winery, best known for its reds, Coleraine★★ and Awatea★★, both based on Cabernet Sauvignon with varying proportions of Merlot and Cabernet Franc. Also delicious toasty Elston Chardonnay★. Exceptional vintages of all 3 wines might be aged for 5–10 years. Also scented, peppery, elegant Bullnose Syrah★★ and trailblazing Woodthorpe Viognier★. Best years: (Coleraine) (2006) 05 **04 02 00 98 96**.

TEMENT *Südsteiermark, Austria* Austria's best Sauvignon Blanc★★ (single-site Zieregg★★★) and Morillon (Chardonnay)★★. Both varieties are fermented and aged in oak, giving power, depth and subtle oak character. The Gelber Muskatellers are unusually racy – perfect aperitif wines. Red Arachon★★ is a joint venture with PICHLER and Szemes in BURGENLAND. Best years: (Morillon, Zieregg) (2007) 06 05 **04 03 02 01**.

TEMPRANILLO Spain's best native red grape can make wonderful wine with wild strawberry and spicy, tobaccoey flavours. It is important in RIOJA, PENEDES (as Ull de Llebre), RIBERA DEL DUERO (as Tinto Fino or Tinta del País), La MANCHA and VALDEPENAS (as Cencibel), TORO (as Tinta de Toro), NAVARRA, SOMONTANO and UTIEL-REQUENA. In Portugal it is found in the ALENTEJO (as Aragonez) in the DOURO, DAO and ESTREMADURA (as Tinta Roriz). Wines can be deliciously fruity for drinking young, but Tempranillo also matures well, and its flavours blend happily with oak. It is now being taken more seriously in Argentina, and new plantings have been made in California, Oregon, Washington (CAYUSE), Australia, New Zealand and South Africa.

TEROLDEGO ROTALIANO DOC *Trentino-Alto Adige, Italy* Teroldego is a TRENTINO grape variety, producing mainly deep-coloured, leafy, blackberry-flavoured wine from gravel soils of the Rotaliano plain. Best producers: Barone de Cles★, M Donati★, Dorigati★, Endrizzi★, FORADORI★★, Conti Martini★, Mezzacorona (Riserva★), Cantina Rotaliana★, A & R Zeni★. Best years: (2007) (06) **04 03 01 00 99 97 96 95 93**.

TERRAS DO SADO *Setúbal Peninsula, Portugal* Warm, maritime area south of Lisbon. SETUBAL produces sweet fortified wine. The better reds (based on Castelão) come from the Palmela DOC. A few good whites. Best producers: (reds) Caves ALIANCA (Palmela Particular★), BACALHOA VINHOS DE PORTUGAL★★, D F J VINHOS★, Ermelinda Freitas★, José Maria da FONSECA★★, Hero do Castanheiro, Pegões co-op★, Pegos Claros★. Best years: 2005 04 03 **01 00 99 97 96 95**.

TERRAZAS DE LOS ANDES *Mendoza, Argentina* Offshoot of the Chandon empire, and a terrific source of reds from high-altitude vineyards around LUJAN DE CUYO. Top reds used to be known as Gran Malbec★★ and Gran Cabernet Sauvignon★★, but are now labelled Afincado and heading for ★★★. A joint venture with CHEVAL BLANC of ST-EMILION has yielded Cheval des Andes★★★, a stunning Cabernet Sauvignon-Malbec blend.

CASTELLO DEL TERRICCIO *Tuscany, Italy* Estate in the Pisan hills south of Livorno. Changes in philosophy seem to have deprived top red Lupicaia★★ (Cabernet-Merlot) and less pricey Tassinaia★ (Sangiovese-Cabernet-Merlot) of much of their exciting, potentially ★★★ personality. Rondinaia (Chardonnay)★★ and Con Vento (Sauvignon Blanc)★ are the most interesting whites. Capannino is an inexpensive red. Best years: (Lupicaia) (2006) (04) 03 01 **00 98 97 96 95 94 93**.

CH. TERTRE-RÔTEBOEUF★★ *St-Émilion Grand Cru AC, Bordeaux, France* ST-EMILION's most exceptional unclassified estate. The richly seductive, Merlot-based wines sell at the same price as the Premiers Grands Crus Classés – and so they should. Same ownership as the outstanding ROC DE CAMBES. Best years: 2006 05 04 **03 02 01** 00 **99 98 96 95 94 90 89 88**.

TEXAS *USA* Texas has enjoyed the tremendous wine industry growth that has hit the USA this decade, with the number of wineries soaring to 155, thanks to new investment and government support. The state has 8 AVAs, with the Texas High Plains the most significant. Plantings are tending away from BORDEAUX varieties in favour of Mediterranean and native grapes such as Syrah, Sangiovese and Norton. Thunderstorms are capable of destroying entire crops in minutes. Best producers: Becker, Fall Creek, Flat Creek, Llano Estacado, McPherson, Messina Hof.

THELEMA *Stellenbosch WO, South Africa* This mountainside farm has been among the top Cape wineries for 20 years: Gyles Webb's meticulous attention to detail results in a consistently good range. Leafy wet blackcurranty Cabernet Sauvignon★★, ripe fleshy Merlot★ (Reserve★★), spicy, accessible Shiraz★, barrel-fermented Chardonnay★★, vibrant Sauvignon Blanc★★ and citrus Riesling★ are among the leaders. New ELGIN venture is already showing exciting Sauvignon★ and

Shiraz★. Best years: (Cabernet Sauvignon) (2006) 05 04 03 **01 00 99 98 97 96 95**; (Chardonnay) 2007 **06 05 04 03 02 01 00 99**.

THERMENREGION *Niederösterreich, Austria* Warm, 2330ha (5760-acre) region, south of Vienna, taking its name from the spa towns of Baden and Bad Vöslau. The village of Gumpoldskirchen, near Vienna, has rich and sometimes sweet white wines. The red wine area around Baden produces large amounts of Blauer Portugieser and improving Pinot Noir and Cabernet. Best producers: Alphart, Biegler, Fischer★, Johanneshof★, Schellmann, Stadlmann★. Best years: (sweet whites) (2007) 06 05 **04 03 02 01**.

THIRTY BENCH *Niagara Peninsula VQA, Ontario, Canada* A collaboration of 3 winemakers, Thirty Bench is known for its excellent Rieslings, including Late Harvest and Icewine★, very good BORDEAUX-style red Reserve Blend★ and a fine barrel-fermented Chardonnay★.

THOMAS *Hunter Valley, New South Wales, Australia* Andrew Thomas has been producing exemplary Semillon and Shiraz under his family label since 1999. Braemore Vineyard Semillon★★ is a traditional, ageworthy HUNTER white while the OC Semillon★ is a delicious early-drinking style. Kiss Vineyard Shiraz★★, from old vines, is ripe, powerful, complex and velvety.

THREE CHOIRS *Gloucestershire, England* Martin Fowke makes a large range of wines from 30ha (74 acres) of vines, plus bought-in grapes. New Release is a fresh, fruity white, released in November of vintage year (as with BEAUJOLAIS NOUVEAU). Other successful wines are Bacchus and Sieggerebe varietals, plus occasional Late Harvest dessert wine.

TICINO *Switzerland* Italian-speaking Swiss canton. Eighty percent of production here is Merlot, usually soft and gluggable, but sometimes more serious with some oak barrel-aging. Best producers: Brivio, La Capellaccia★, Delea★, Gialdi, Huber★, Werner Stucky★, Tamborini, Terreni alla Maggia★, Christian Zündel★. Best years: (2007) 06 05 **04 03 02 01 00**.

TIEFENBRUNNER *Alto Adige DOC, Trentino-Alto Adige, Italy* Herbert Tiefenbrunner began his career at this castle (Schloss Turmhof) as a teenager in 1943. In his 80s, he still helps son Christof in the winery, producing 20-plus wine styles, mostly under the ALTO ADIGE DOC. The focus is on purity of fruit and varietal character, mainly among whites, the star being Müller-Thurgau 'Feldmarschall'★★ which, at 1,000m (3280 ft), is too high to qualify as DOC under Italy's relentlessly silly laws. Best years: (Feldmarschall) (2007) 06 **04 03 01 00 99 98 97**.

TIGNANELLO★★ *Tuscany, Italy* In the early 1970s, Piero ANTINORI employed the previously unheard-of practice of aging in small French oak barrels and used Cabernet Sauvignon (20%) in the blend with Sangiovese. The quality was superb, and Tignanello's success sparked off the SUPER-TUSCAN movement. Top vintages are truly great; lesser years are of decent CHIANTI CLASSICO quality. Best years: (2007) (06) 04 **03 01 00 99 98 97 95 93 90 88 85**.

TINTA RORIZ See TEMPRANILLO.

TOCAI FRIULANO Tocai Friulano is a north-east Italian grape producing dry, nutty, oily whites of great character in COLLIO and COLLI ORIENTALI. Friuli producers are awaiting a final ruling on the name, but it looks like they, under pressure from the Hungarians, will have to change it. Perhaps to just plain Friulano? Best producers: Borgo del Tiglio★, Livio FELLUGA★, JERMANN★, Edi Keber★★, Miani★★, Princic★, Ronco del Gelso★★, Russiz Superiore★★, SCHIOPETTO★★, Le Vigne di Zamò★★, Villa Russiz★.

TOKAJI *Hungary* Hungary's classic, liquorous wine of historic reputation, with its unique, sweet-and-sour, sherry-like tang, comes from 28 villages on the Hungarian-Slovak border. Mists from the Bodrog river ensure that noble rot on the Furmint, Hárslevelü and Muscotaly (Muscat Ottonel) grapes is a fairly common occurrence. Degrees of sweetness are measured in *puttonyos*. Discussions continue about traditional oxidized styles versus fresher modern versions. Best producers: Disznókö★★, Château Megyer★★, Oremus★, Château Pajzos★★, Royal Tokaji Wine Co★★, Istvan Szepsy (6 Puttonyos 95★★★, Essencia★★★), Tokaji Kereskedöház★. Best years: **2000 99 97 93**.

TOLLOT-BEAUT *Chorey-lès-Beaune, Burgundy, France* Good reds with lots of fruit and a pronounced new oak character. The village-level CHOREY-LES-BEAUNE★★, ALOXE-CORTON★★ and SAVIGNY-LES-BEAUNE★★ are all excellent, as is the top BEAUNE Premier Cru Clos du Roi★★. Whites are more variable, but at best delicious. Best years: (reds) (2007) 06 05 03 02 01 99.

TORBRECK *Barossa Valley, South Australia* Dave Powell specializes in opulent, well-structured reds from 60–120-year-old Shiraz, Grenache and Mataro (Mourvèdre) vines. Made in minute quantities, the flagship RunRig★★★, single-vineyard Descendant★★ and Factor★★ are all richly concentrated, powerful, complex Shiraz. The Steading★ and Juveniles★ are Grenache-Mataro-Shiraz blends (the latter unoaked), while the Woodcutters White (Semillon) and Red (Shiraz) are lightly oaked, mouth-filling quaffers.

TORGIANO DOC & DOCG *Umbria, Italy* A zone near Perugia dominated by one producer, LUNGAROTTI. Lungarotti's basic Rubesco Torgiano★ is ripely fruity; the Torgiano Riserva DOCG Vigna Monticchio★★ is a fine black cherry-flavoured wine, aged for up to 8 years before release.

TORO DO *Castilla y León, Spain* Mainly red wines, which are robust, full of colour and tannin, and pretty high in alcohol. The main grape, Tinta de Toro, is a variant of Tempranillo, and there is some Garnacha. In the late 1990s, the arrival of some of the top wineries in Spain gave the sleepy area a major boost. Best producers: Viña Bajoz, Fariña★, Frutos Villar (Muruve★), Garanza, Matarredonda, Maurodos★★, Monte La Reina, Numanthia-Termes (Numanthia★★, Termanthia★★★), Pintia★★/VEGA SICILIA, Quinta de la Quietud★, Sobreño, Telmo RODRIGUEZ★★, Toresanas/Bodegas de Crianza Castilla la Vieja★, Vega Saúco, Villaester.

TORRES *Penedès DO, Cataluña, Spain* Large family winery led by visionary Miguel Torres, making good to excellent wines with local grapes, (Parellada, Tempranillo) and international varieties. Viña Sol★ is a good, citrony quaffer, Viña Esmeralda★ (Muscat Blanc à Petits Grains and Gewürztraminer) is grapy and spicy, Fransola★★ (Sauvignon Blanc with some Parellada) is oaky yet refreshingly leafy, and Milmanda★ is a delicate, expressive Chardonnay. Successful reds are soft, oaky and blackcurranty Gran Coronas★ (Tempranillo and Cabernet), fine, relatively rich though increasingly international Mas La Plana★★ (Cabernet Sauvignon), floral, perfumed Mas Borràs (Pinot Noir) and raisiny Atrium★ (Merlot). The top reds – Grans Muralles★★, a blend of Catalan grapes, and Reserva Real★★, a BORDEAUX-style red blend – are fascinating but expensive and improve with every vintage. Best years: (Mas La Plana) **2003 01 00 99 98 97 96 95 94 91 90 88**.

MARIMAR TORRES ESTATE *Sonoma County, California, USA* The sister of Spanish winemaker Miguel TORRES has established her own winery in the cool Green Valley region of SONOMA COUNTY, only a few miles from the Pacific Ocean. She specializes in Chardonnay and Pinot Noir, the best of which are from the Don Miguel Vineyard. The Chardonnay★★ is big and intense, initially quite oaky, but able to age gracefully to fascinating maturity at 10 years old. Recent vintages of full-flavoured Pinot Noir★★ are the best yet. Best years: 2005 03 **02 01 00** 99 98 97 95 94.

MIGUEL TORRES *Curicó, Chile* TORRES' Chilean operation is now producing its best ever wines: snappy Sauvignon Blanc★, grassy, fruity Santa Digna rosé★, weighty, blackcurranty Manso de Velasco Cabernet★★, exciting, sonorous old-Carignan-based Cordillera★★ and Conde de Superunda★★, a tremendous, dense blend based on Cabernet and Tempranillo. Best years: (Manso de Velasco) (2006) 05 04 03 02 **01 00** 99.

CH. LA TOUR BLANCHE★★ *Sauternes AC, 1er Cru Classé, Bordeaux, France* This estate regained top form in the 1980s with the introduction of new oak barrels for fermentation, lower yields and greater selection. Full-bodied, rich and aromatic, it now ranks with the best of the Classed Growths. Second wine: Les Charmilles de la Tour Blanche. Best years: 2006 05 04 03 **02 01** 99 98 97 96 95 90 89 88 86.

CH. TOUR BOISÉE *Minervois AC, Languedoc, France* Top wines here are the red Jardin Secret★, Cuvée Marie-Claude★, aged for 12 months in barrel, the fruity Cuvée Marielle et Frédérique, and the white Cuvée Marie-Claude★, with a hint of Muscat Blanc à Petits Grains for added aroma. Best years: (red) 2004 **03 01 00**.

CH. TOUR DES GENDRES *Bergerac AC, South-West France* Luc de Conti's BERGERACS are made with as much sophistication as the better Crus Classés of BORDEAUX. Generously fruity Moulin des Dames★ and the more serious la Gloire de Mon Père★★ reds are mostly Cabernet Sauvignon. Full, fruity and elegant Moulin des Dames★★ white is a Bordeaux blend of Sémillon, Sauvignon Blanc and Muscadelle. Best years: (la Gloire de Mon Père) 2005 03 **01 00** 99 98.

TOURAINE AC *Loire Valley, France* General AC in the central LOIRE; largely everyday wines to drink young, though its tradition for wines that could do with some aging is being restored by an ambitious minority, many of whose wines are confusingly labelled Vin de Table. Most reds are from Gamay and, in hot years, can be juicy, rustic-fruited wines. There is a fair amount of red from Cabernets Sauvignon and Franc too, and some good Côt (Malbec). Best whites are Sauvignon Blanc, which can be a good substitute for SANCERRE at half the price, and the rare Romorantin; decent Chenin and Chardonnay. White and rosé sparkling wines are made by the traditional method but rarely have the distinction of the best VOUVRAY and CREMANT DE LOIRE. Best producers: Acacias★, Brulée★, Clos de la Briderie★, F Chidaine★, Corbillières★, J Delaunay★, Robert Denis★, David Levin★, Marcadet★, H Marionnet/la Charmoise★, J-C Mandard★, J-F Merieau★, Michaud★, Octavie★, Pavy★, Pré Baron★, J Preys★, Ricard★, Roche Blanc★, Sauvète. Best years: (reds) 2006 **05 04 03 02**.

TOURIGA NACIONAL High-quality red Portuguese grape, rich in aroma and fruit. It contributes deep colour and tannin to PORT, and is rapidly increasing in importance for table wines throughout the country. Small but important plantings in South Africa enhance some of the impressive port styles emerging across the country.

TOWER ESTATE *Hunter Valley, New South Wales, Australia* This syndicate, founded by the late, great Len Evans, focuses on sourcing top-notch grapes from their ideal regions. So, there is powerful, stylish COONAWARRA Cabernet★★, top-flight BAROSSA Shiraz★★, fine floral CLARE Riesling★★, fruity ADELAIDE HILLS Sauvignon Blanc★ and classic Semillon★★, Shiraz★ and Chardonnay★ from the HUNTER VALLEY.

TRAPICHE *Mendoza, Argentina* The fine wine arm of Peñaflor, Argentina's biggest wine producer, where chief winemaker Daniel Pi has triumphantly turned quality around since taking over in 2002. Medalla Cabernet Sauvignon★★ is dense and satisfying, Iscay★ solid and rich, while single-vineyard Malbecs★★ are sumptuous and individual.

TRÁS-OS-MONTES *Portugal* Impoverished north-eastern province, producing pretty rustic stuff. The Vinho Regional is Transmontano. **Best producers: Quinta do Sobreiró de Cima, Casa de Valle Pradinhos.**

TREBBIANO The most widely planted white Italian grape variety. As Trebbiano Toscano, it is the base for EST! EST!! EST!!! and any number of other neutral, dry whites, as well as much VIN SANTO. But there are other grapes masquerading under the Trebbiano name that aren't anything like as neutral. The most notable are the Trebbianos from SOAVE, LUGANA and ABRUZZO – grapes capable of full-bodied, fragrant wines. Called Ugni Blanc in France, where it is primarily used for distilling, as it should be.

TRENTINO *Italy* Wines from this northern Italian region rarely have the verve or perfume of ALTO ADIGE examples, but can make up for this with riper, softer flavours, where vineyard yields have been kept in check. The Trentino DOC covers 20 different styles of wine, including whites Pinot Bianco and Grigio, Chardonnay, Moscato Giallo, Müller-Thurgau and Nosiola, and reds Lagrein, Marzemino and Cabernet. Trento Classico is a DOC for CHAMPAGNE-method fizz. **Best producers: N Balter★, N Bolognani★, La Cadalora★, Castel Noarna★, Cavit co-op, Cesconi★★, De Tarczal★, Dorigati, FERRARI★★, Graziano Fontana★, FORADORI★★, Letrari★, Longariva★, Conti Martini★, Maso Cantanghel★★, Maso Furli★, Maso Roveri★, Mezzacorona, Pojer & Sandri★, Pravis★, SAN LEONARDO★★★, Simoncelli★, E Spagnolli★, Vallarom★, La Vis co-op.** See also TEROLDEGO ROTALIANO.

DOM. DE TRÉVALLON *Provence, France* Iconoclastic Eloi Dürrbach makes brilliant reds★★ (at best ★★★) – a tradition-busting blend of Cabernet Sauvignon and Syrah, mixing herbal wildness with a sweetness of blackberry, blackcurrant and black, black plums – and a tiny quantity of white★★★. Both are labelled Vin de Pays des BOUCHES-DU-RHONE. The reds age well, but are intriguingly drinkable in their youth. **Best years: (reds) (2005) 04 03 01 00 99 98 97.**

TRIMBACH *Alsace AC, Alsace, France* An excellent grower/merchant whose trademark is beautifully structured, emphatically dry, subtly perfumed elegance. Top wines are Gewurztraminer Cuvée des Seigneurs de Ribeaupierre★★, Riesling Cuvée Frédéric Émile★★ and Riesling Clos Ste-Hune★★★. Also very good Vendange Tardive★★ and Sélection de Grains Nobles★★. Trimbach basics are a bit pricey, but enjoyable in their austere manner. **Best years: (Clos Ste-Hune) (2007) (05) 04 03 02 01 00 99 98 97 96 95 93 92 90.**

TRINITY HILL *Hawkes Bay, North Island, New Zealand* Talented owner/ winemaker John Hancock enthusiastically produces many top wines from the Gimblett Gravels area, including flagship Homage Syrah★★★ that's co-fermented with a small amount of Viognier, a fine peppery Syrah★★, an impressively proportioned Merlot★★, gutsy long-lived Cabernet Sauvignon★ and equally heroic Cabernet Sauvignon-Merlot★ plus a big and complex Chardonnay★. Trinity also makes a good job of less mainstream styles such as Tempranillo★, Arneis and Viognier★★. Best years: (reds) (2007) 06 **04 02 00**.

TRITTENHEIM *Mosel, Germany* Important village with some excellent vineyard sites, notably the Apotheke (pharmacy) and Leiterchen (little ladder). The wines are sleek, with crisp acidity and plenty of fruit. Best producers: Ernst Clüsserath★, Clüsserath-Weiler★, GRANS-FASSIAN★★, Milz-Laurentiushof★. Best years: (2007) 06 05 **04 03 02 01 99 98**.

CH. TROPLONG-MONDOT★★ *St-Émilion Grand Cru AC, 1er Grand Cru Classé, Bordeaux, France* Owner Christine Valette has been producing quality wines at this property since the mid-1980s. Her reward – elevation to Premier Grand Cru Classé in 2006. The wines are powerfully structured and mouthfillingly textured for long aging. Best years: 2006 05 **04 03** 02 01 00 **99 98 96 95 94 90 89**.

CH. TROTANOY★★ *Pomerol AC, Bordeaux, France* Another POMEROL estate (like PETRUS and LATOUR-A-POMEROL) which has benefited from the brilliant touch of the MOUEIX family. Back on form after a dip in the mid-80s. Best years: 2006 05 04 03 **02 01** 00 **99 98 96 95 94 90 89 88**.

TUA RITA *Tuscany, Italy* Since the early 1990s, this estate in the MAREMMA has established itself at the top of the Italian Merlot tree with Redigaffi★★★; Cabernet-Merlot blend Giusto di Notri★★ is almost as renowned. Best years: (2006) (05) 04 03 **01 00 99 98 97 96 95**.

CAVE VINICOLE DE TURCKHEIM *Alsace AC, Alsace, France* Important co-op with good basics in all varieties. The Reserve tier of all wines merits ★, while Brand★, Hengst★★ and Ollwiller★ bottlings are rich and concentrated. Reds, rosés and CREMANT D'ALSACE★ are consistent. Best years: (Grand Cru Gewurztraminer) (2007) 05 **04 02 01 00 99 98 97 95**.

TURKEY FLAT *Barossa, South Australia* The Schultz family, BAROSSA growers with substantial holdings of old-vine Shiraz (planted 1847) and Grenache, turned to winemaking in 1990. Deeply flavoured, lush Shiraz★★, delicious Grenache★ and one of Australia's top Rosés★.

TURLEY *Napa Valley AVA, California, USA* Larry Turley's ultra-ripe Zinfandels★★, from a number of old vineyards, are either praised for their profound power and depth or damned for their tannic, high-alcohol, PORT-like nature. Petite Sirah★★ is similarly built. Best years: (Zins) (2005) 04 **03 02 01 00 99 98 97 96 95**.

TURSAN VDQS *South-West France* These wines are made on the edge of les Landes, the sandy coastal area south of Bordeaux. The white is the most interesting: made from the Baroque grape, it is clean, crisp and refreshing. Best producers: Baron de Bachen, Dulucq, Tursan co-op.

TUSCANY *Italy* Tuscany's rolling hills, clad with vines, olive trees and cypresses, have produced wine since at least Etruscan times. Today, its many DOC/DOCGs are based on the red Sangiovese grape and are led by CHIANTI CLASSICO, BRUNELLO DI MONTALCINO and VINO NOBILE DI MONTEPULCIANO, as well as famous SUPER-TUSCANS like ORNELLAIA and TIGNANELLO. White wines, despite sweet VIN SANTO, and the occasional excellent Chardonnay and Sauvignon, do not figure highly. See also BOLGHERI, CARMIGNANO, MAREMMA, MONTECARLO, MORELLINO DI SCANSANO, ROSSO DI MONTALCINO, ROSSO DI MONTEPULCIANO, SASSICAIA, SOLAIA, VERNACCIA DI SAN GIMIGNANO.

TYRRELL'S *Hunter Valley, New South Wales, Australia* Top-notch family-owned company with prime HUNTER vineyards, now expanding into COONAWARRA, MCLAREN VALE and HEATHCOTE, with impressive results. Comprehensive range, from good-value quaffers (Old Winery★, Lost Block★) to excellent Vat 47 Chardonnay★★★ and Vat 9 Shiraz★. Semillon is the speciality, with 4 single-vineyard wines (all ★★) – Lost Block, Stevens, Belford and the rare HVD – and, best of all, the superb Vat 1★★★. Best years: (Vat 1 Semillon) (2003) (02) 01 00 99 **98 97 96 95 94 93 92 91 90 89 87 86 77 76 75**; (Vat 47 Chardonnay) 2003 02 01 **00 99 98 97 96 95 94 91 89**.

UCO VALLEY *Mendoza, Argentina* This valley, in the foothills of the Andes, is an old secret of Argentine viticulture, newly rediscovered. Most vineyards are new but there are precious old plantings too. With vineyards at 1000–1500m (3200–4900 ft) above sea level, it's Argentina's best spot for Chardonnays, especially from the Tupungato area. Reds are also showing fascinating flavours – especially Merlot, Malbec, Syrah and Tempranillo. Best producers: ACHAVAL-FERRER★★, CATENA★★, Clos de los Siete★★, O FOURNIER★★, Salentein★, TERRAZAS DE LOS ANDES★★.

UGNI BLANC See TREBBIANO.

UMATHUM *Frauenkirchen, Neusiedlersee, Burgenland, Austria* Resisting the trend in Austria towards heavily oaked blockbuster reds, Josef Umathum emphasizes finesse and sheer drinkability. The single-vineyard Ried Hallebühl★★ is usually his top wine, but the St Laurent Vom Stein★ and the Zweigelt-dominated Haideboden★ sometimes match it in quality. Best years: (reds) (2007) (06) **04 03 01 00 99**.

UMBRIA *Italy* Wine production in this Italian region is dominated by ORVIETO, accounting for almost 70% of DOC wines. However, some of the most characterful wines are reds from TORGIANO and MONTEFALCO. Latest interest centres on international-style reds made by the ubiquitous Riccardo Cotarella at estates such as Pieve del Vescovo (Lucciaio★★), La Carraia (Fobiano★★), Lamborghini (Campoleone★★) and La Palazzola (Rubino★★).

ÜRZIG *Mosel, Germany* Middle MOSEL village with the famous red slate Würzgarten (spice garden) vineyard tumbling spectacularly down to the river and producing marvellously spicy Riesling. Drink young or with at least 5 years' age. Best producers: J J Christoffel★★, Dr LOOSEN★★★, Mönchhof★★, Peter Nicolay★, Dr Weins-Prüm★. Best years: (2007) 06 05 04 **03 02 01 99 98 97**.

UTIEL-REQUENA DO *Valencia, Spain* Renowned for its rosés, mostly from the Bobal grape. Reds, with Tempranillo often complementing Bobal, are on the up. The groundbreaking Mustiguillo★★ winery now has its own appellation, Vinos de la Tierra Terrerazo. Best producers: Coviñas, Gandía, Palmera (L'Angelet★), Schenk, Torre Oria, Dominio de la Vega.

DOM. VACHERON *Sancerre AC, Loire Valley, France* Unusually for a SANCERRE domaine, Vacheron, now biodynamic, is more reputed for its Pinot Noir reds than for its whites, but the whole range is currently on top form. Intense and expensive Belle Dame★★ red and Les Romains★★ red and white lead the way. The basic Sancerres – a cherryish red★ and a grapefruity white★ – have reserves of complexity that set them above the crowd. Best years: (Belle Dame) 2007 **06 05 04 03 02 01 00 99**.

VACQUEYRAS AC *Rhône Valley, France* Red wines, mainly Grenache, account for 95% of production; they have a warm, spicy bouquet and a rich deep flavour that seems infused with the herbs and pine dust of the south. Lovely to drink at 2–3 years, though good wines will age for 10 years. Best producers: Amouriers★, la Charbonnière★, Clos des Cazaux★★, Couroulu★, DELAS★, Font de Papier★, la Fourmone★, la Garrigue★, JABOULET★, Alain Jaume, Monardière★★, Montirius★★, Montmirail★, Montvac★, SANG DES CAILLOUX★★, Tardieu-Laurent★★, la Tourade★, Ch. des Tours★, Vacqueyras co-op, Verquière★. Best years: 2007 **06 05 04 03 01 00 99 98**.

VAL DE LOIRE, VIN DE PAYS DU *Loire Valley, France* Replaces Vin de Pays du Jardin de la France with effect from the 2007 vintage. It covers all 14 designated wine-producing regions of the LOIRE VALLEY – over 7,300ha (18,000 acres), accounting for around 500,000hl of wine. Key whites are Sauvignon Blanc, Chardonnay and Chenin Blanc, with some Grolleau Gris, Melon de Bourgogne, Folle Blanche and Pinot Blanc. The focus for reds is Gamay, Cabernets Franc and Sauvignon, with some Pinot Noir. It is increasingly a refuge for ambitious producers whose wines punch well above the weight of their appellation, especially in TOURAINE. Best producers: Ampelidae, BOUVET-LADUBAY★, Brulée★, l'ECU★, L Herbel, Henry Marionnet★, Alphonse MELLOT★, J-F Merieau★, RAGOTIERE★★, Ricard.

VAL D'ORBIEU, LES VIGNERONS DU *Languedoc-Roussillon, France* This growers' association is one of France's largest wine-exporting companies, selling in excess of 20 million cases a year. Membership includes several top co-ops (Cucugnan, Cuxac, Montredon, Ribauté) and individual producers (Dom. de Fontsainte, Ch. la VOULTE-GASPARETS). It also owns Cordier in BORDEAUX. Its upmarket blended wines (Cuvée Chouette★, Chorus★, Elysices★, Réserve St-Martin, la Cuvée Mythique★) are a mix of traditional Mediterranean varieties with Cabernet or Merlot.

VALAIS *Switzerland* Swiss canton flanking the Rhône. Between Martigny and Sierre the valley turns north-east, creating an Alpine suntrap, and this short stretch of terraced vineyard land provides many of Switzerland's most individual wines from Fendant, Johannisberger (Silvaner), Pinot Noir and Gamay, and several stunning examples from Syrah, Chardonnay, Ermitage (Marsanne) and Petite Arvine. Best producers: Bonvin★, Cina★, M Clavien★, Cottagnoud★, Dorsaz★, Jean-René Germanier★, Adrian Mathier★, Mercier, Dom. du Mont d'Or★, Provins, Rouvinez★, M Zufferey★.

CH. VALANDRAUD★★ *St-Émilion Grand Cru AC, Bordeaux, France* The precursor of the 'garage wine' sensation in ST-EMILION, a big, rich, extracted wine from low yields, from grapes mainly grown in different parcels around St-Émilion. Recently the core of the wine has been a top-quality limestone-based property and we can now see a real, impressive, consistent Valandraud style developing. Best years: 2006 05 04 03 02 01 00 99 98 96 95.

VALDEPEÑAS DO *Castilla-La Mancha, Spain* Valdepeñas offers some of Spain's best inexpensive oak-aged reds, but there is an increasing number of unoaked, fruit-forward reds as well. In fact, there are more whites than reds, at least some of them modern, fresh and fruity. Best producers: Miguel Calatayud, Los Llanos, Luís Megía, Real, Félix Solís, Casa de la Viña.

VALDESPINO *Jerez y Manzanilla DO, Andalucía, Spain* New owner Grupo Estévez (Marqués del Real Tesoro, Tio Mateo) is probably the quality leader in Jerez today and the pristine quality of Valdespino's sherries has not been affected. Fino Inocente★★, Palo Cortado Cardenal★★★, Pedro Ximénez Niños★★★ and dry Amontillado Coliseo★★★ are stunning examples of sherry's different styles.

VALDIVIESO *Curicó, Chile* Important winery, struggling to get back on track after a few lean years. Varietals are attractive and direct, Reserves from cooler regions a definite step up, and some of the Single Vineyards are quite impressive (Chardonnay★, Malbec★). Multi-varietal, multi-vintage blend Caballo Loco★★ (mad horse) is always fascinating and unpredictable, and Eclat★★, based on old Carignan, is chewy and rich.

VALENCIA *Spain* The best wines from Valencia DO are the inexpensive, sweet, grapy Moscatels. Simple, fruity whites, reds and rosés are also good. Alicante DO to the south produces a little-known treasure, the Fondillón dry or semi-dry fortified wine, as well as a cluster of wines made by a few quality-conscious modern wineries. Monastrell (Mourvèdre) is the main red grape variety. Best producers: (Valencia) Gandía, Los Pinos★, Celler del Roure★, Schenk, Cherubino Valsangiacomo (Marqués de Caro); (Alicante) Bocopa★, Gutiérrez de la Vega (Casta Diva Muscat★★), Enrique Mendoza★★, Salvador Poveda★, Primitivo Quiles★. See also UTIEL-REQUENA.

VALL-LLACH *Priorat DOCa, Spain* This tiny winery, owned by Catalan folk singer Lluís Llach, has joined the ranks of the best PRIORAT producers with its powerful reds★★ dominated by old-vine Cariñena. Best years: (2005) 04 03 **01 00 99 98**.

VALLE D'AOSTA *Italy* Tiny Alpine valley sandwiched between PIEDMONT and the French Alps in northern Italy. The regional DOC covers 17 wine styles, referring either to a specific grape variety (like Gamay or Pinot Nero) or to a delimited region like Donnaz, a northern extension of Piedmont's Carema, producing a light red from the Nebbiolo grape. Perhaps the finest wine from these steep slopes is the sweet Chambave Moscato. Best producers: R Anselmet★, C Charrère/Les Crêtes★, La Crotta di Vegneron★, Grosjean, Institut Agricole Regional★, Onze Communes co-op, Ezio Voyat★.

VALPOLICELLA DOC *Veneto, Italy* Styles range from a light, cherryish red to rich, PORT-like RECIOTO and AMARONE. Most of the better examples are Valpolicella Classico Superiore from the hills north-west of Verona and are made predominantly from Corvina and Corvinone grapes. The most concentrated, ageworthy examples are made either from a particular vineyard, or by refermenting the wine on the skins and lees of the Amarone, a style called *ripasso*, or by using a portion of dried grapes. Best producers: Accordini★, ALLEGRINI★★★, Bertani★, Brigaldara★, Brunelli★, BUSSOLA★★★, Michele Castellani★, Valentina Cubi★, DAL FORNO★★★, Guerrieri-Rizzardi★, MASI★, Mazzi★, Pasqua/Cecilia Beretta★, QUINTARELLI★★★, Le Ragose★, Le Salette★, Serègo Alighieri★, Speri★, Tedeschi★, Villa Monteleone★, VIVIANI★★, Zenato★, Zeni★. Best years: (Valpolicella Superiore): 2006 **04 03 01 00 97 95 93 90**.

VALTELLINA SUPERIORE DOCG *Lombardy, Italy* Red wine produced on the precipitous slopes of northern LOMBARDY. There is a basic light Valtellina DOC red, made from at least 70% Nebbiolo (here called

Chiavennasca), but the best wines are made under the Valtellina Superiore DOCG as Grumello, Inferno, Sassella and Valgella. From top vintages the wines are attractively perfumed and approachable. Sfursat or Sforzato is a dense, high-alcohol red (up to 14.5%) made from semi-dried grapes. Best producers: La Castellina★, Enologica Valtellinese★, Fay★, Nino Negri★, Nera★, Rainoldi★, Conti Sertoli Salis★, Triacca★. Best years: (2007) (06) 04 03 01 99 98 97 95 93 90 88 85.

VAN VOLXEM *Wiltingen, Mosel-Saar-Ruwer, Germany* Roman Niewodniczanski bought this estate, with its great old vineyards in Scharzhofberg and Wiltinger Gottesfuss, in 2000. His style, off-dry and opulent, is atypical and controversial, but often ★★. Best years: (2007) 06 05 04 03 01.

CH. VANNIÈRES *Bandol AC, Provence, France* Leading BANDOL estate, owned by the Boisseaux family since the 1950s. Under a new winemaker, it has leapt into the top ranks. Wood has replaced cement tanks, wines are bottled unfiltered, and the percentage of Mourvèdre has gone from 50 to 95. Besides red Bandol★★, Vannières produces COTES DE PROVENCE and Vin de Pays. Best years: 2005 03 01 00 98 97.

VASSE FELIX *Margaret River, Western Australia* MARGARET RIVER's first vineyard and winery turned 40 by becoming more focused on the region under a new winemaking team. The flagship Heytesbury Chardonnay★★ is tighter, leaner and finer than before, while the powerful Heytesbury Cabernet★ shows greater elegance. There's a decadently rich, profound Cabernet Sauvignon★ and oak-led Shiraz★, and the Chardonnay★ is pleasurable drinking for a modest price. Best years: (Heytesbury Cabernet Sauvignon) (2007) 05 04 01 99 97 96 95.

VAUD *Switzerland* The Vaud's main vineyards border Lake Geneva (Lac Léman), with 5 sub-regions: la Côte, Lavaux, CHABLAIS, Côtes de l'Orbe-Bonvillars, Vully. Fresh light white wines are made from Chasselas; at DEZALEY it gains depth. Reds from Gamay and Pinot Noir. Best producers: Henri Badoux, Louis Bovard★, Dubois, Massy, Obrist, J & P Testuz★.

VAVASOUR *Marlborough, South Island, New Zealand* First winery in MARLBOROUGH's Awatere Valley, now enjoying spectacular success. One of New Zealand's best Chardonnays★★, a fine, lush Pinot Noir★★ and palate-tingling, oak-tinged Sauvignon Blanc★★. Second-label Dashwood is also top stuff, particularly the tangy Sauvignon Blanc★★. In 2006 Vavasour merged with high-flying Waiheke winery GOLDWATER. Best years: (Sauvignon Blanc) 2007 06 04 03.

VEENWOUDEN *Paarl WO, South Africa* The focus here is on reds based on BORDEAUX varieties: sumptuous, well-oaked Merlot★★; firm and silky-fruited Veenwouden Classic★★; and Vivat Bacchus★, with a distinctive Malbec component. A tiny quantity of fine Chardonnay★ is made. Best years: (Merlot, Classic) 2004 03 02 00 99 98.

VEGA SICILIA *Ribera del Duero DO, Castilla y León, Spain* Among Spain's most expensive wines, rich, fragrant, complex and very slow to mature, and by no means always easy to appreciate. This estate was the first in Spain to introduce French varieties, and almost a quarter of the vines are now Cabernet Sauvignon, two-thirds are Tempranillo and the rest Malbec and Merlot. Vega Sicilia Unico★★★ – the top wine – was traditionally given about 10 years' wood aging, but since 1982 this has been reduced to 5 or 6. Second wine: Valbuena★★. A subsidiary winery produces the more modern Alión★★, and the new Pintia★★ winery makes some of the most distinctive wines in TORO. Best years: (Unico) 1996 95 94 91 90 89 87 86 85 83 82 81 80 79 76 75 74 70 68.

VELICH *Neuseidlersee, Burgenland, Austria* Roland and Heinz Velich make
♀ Austria's most mineral and sophisticated Chardonnay★★ from old vines
in the Tiglat vineyard. Also spectacular dessert wines of ★★ and ★★★
quality. Best years: (Tiglat Chardonnay) (2007) 06 **05 04 03 02 01**; (sweet
whites) (2007) 06 05 04 **02 01 99 98 96**.

VENETO *Italy* This region takes in the wine zones of SOAVE, VALPOLICELLA,
BARDOLINO and Piave in north-east Italy. It is the source of a great deal of
inexpensive wine, but the Soave and Valpolicella hills are also capable of
producing high-quality wine. Other hilly areas like Colli Berici and Colli
Euganei produce large quantities of dull varietal wines, but can offer the odd
flash of brilliance. The great dry red of this zone is AMARONE. See also BIANCO
DI CUSTOZA, PROSECCO, RECIOTO DELLA VALPOLICELLA, RECIOTO DI SOAVE.

VERDICCHIO DEI CASTELLI DI JESI DOC *Marche, Italy* Verdicchio,
♀ grown in the hills near the Adriatic around Jesi and in the Apennine
foothills enclave of Matelica, has blossomed into
central Italy's most promising white variety. When
fresh and fruity it is the ideal wine with fish, but
some Verdicchio can age into a white of surprising
depth of flavours. A few producers, notably Garofoli
with Serra Fiorese★★, age it in oak, but even without
wood it can develop an almost Burgundy-like
complexity. A little is made sparkling. Best producers:
(Jesi) Brunori★, Bucci★★, Colonnara★, Coroncino★★, Fazi
Battaglia★, Garofoli★★, Mancinelli★, Monte Schiavo★★,
Santa Barbara★, Sartarelli★★, Tavignano★, Terre Cortesi
Moncaro★, Umani Ronchi★, Fratelli Zaccagnini★; (Matelica)
Belisario★, Bisci★, Mecella★, La Monacesca★★.

VERGELEGEN *Stellenbosch WO, South Africa* This historic farm's Sauvignon
♬ Blancs are considered benchmarks: the regular bottling★★ is aggressive
and racy, streaked with sleek tropical fruit: the single-vineyard
Reserve★★ is flinty, dry and fascinating. Topping both is barrel-
fermented white Vergelegen★★, a Semillon-Sauvignon blend that ages
superbly for 3–6 years. There is also a ripe-textured, stylish Chardonnay
Reserve★★. Reds are even more attention-grabbing: Vergelegen★★★, a
BORDEAUX blend, shows classic mineral intensity, Merlot★★ and
Cabernet Sauvignon★★ are often among South Africa's best. Single-
vineyard Cabernet Sauvignon-based 'V'★★ (sometimes ★★★) is
brilliantly individual. Best years: (premium reds) 2005 **04 03 02 01 00** 99 98.

VERGET *Mâconnais, Burgundy, France* Négociant house run by Jean-Marie
♀ Guffens-Heynen, with outstanding Premiers Crus and Grands Crus
from the COTE D'OR, notably CHASSAGNE-MONTRACHET★★ and BATARD-
MONTRACHET★★★. Guffens-Heynen also has his own domaine, with
excellent MACON-VILLAGES★★ and POUILLY-FUISSE★★. But beware, the wines
are made in a very individualistic style. Best years: (2007) 06 05 **04 02 01 00** 99.

VERITAS See Rolf BINDER.

VERMENTINO The best dry white wines of SARDINIA generally come from
the Vermentino grape. Light, dry, perfumed and nutty, the best
examples tend to be from the north-east of the island, where the
Vermentino di Gallura zone is located. Occasionally it is made sweet or
sparkling. Vermentino is also grown in LIGURIA and TUSCANY, though its

character is quite different. It is believed to be the same as Rolle, found in many blends in PROVENCE. Best producers: (Sardinia) ARGIOLAS★, Capichera★★, Cherchi★, Gallura co-op★, Piero Mancini★, Pedra Majore★, Santadi co-op★, SELLA & MOSCA★, Vermentino co-op★.

VERNACCIA DI SAN GIMIGNANO DOCG *Tuscany, Italy* Dry white wines – generally light quaffers – made from the Vernaccia grape grown in the hills around San Gimignano. It is debatable whether the allowance of up to 10% Chardonnay in the blend is a forward step. There is a San Gimignano DOC for the zone's reds, though the best SUPER-TUSCANS are sold as IGT wines. Best producers: Cà del Vispo★, Le Calcinaie★, Casale-Falchini★, V Cesani★, La Lastra (Riserva★), Melini (Le Grillaie★), Montenidoli★, G Panizzi★, Il Paradiso★, Pietrafitta★, La Rampa di Fugnano★, Guicciardini Strozzi★, Teruzzi & Puthod (Terre di Tufi★★), Casa alle Vacche★, Vagnoni★.

QUINTA DO VESÚVIO★★ *Port DOC, Douro, Portugal* A consistently top vintage PORT from the Symington stable that appears only when the high quality can be maintained. Best with at least 10 years' age. **Best years:** 2004 **03 01 00 99 97 96 95 94 92 91 90.**

VEUVE CLICQUOT *Champagne AC, Champagne, France* Produced by the LVMH luxury goods group, these CHAMPAGNEs can still live up to the high standards set by the original Widow Clicquot at the beginning of the 19th century, although many are released too young. The non-vintage is full, toasty and satisfyingly weighty, or lean and raw, depending on your luck; the vintage★ used to be reliably impressive, but recent releases have shown none of the traditional Clicquot class. The de luxe Grande Dame★★★, however, is both powerful and elegant. Grande Dame Rosé★★★ is exquisite. **Best years:** 2002 00 **99 98** 96 **95 90** 89 88 85 82.

VICTORIA *Australia* Despite its relatively small area, Victoria has arguably more land suited to quality grape-growing than any other state in Australia, with climates ranging from hot Murray Darling and Swan Hill on the Murray River to cool MORNINGTON PENINSULA and GIPPSLAND in the south. The range of flavours is similarly wide and exciting. With more than 500 wineries, Victoria leads the boutique winery boom, particularly in Mornington Peninsula. See also BEECHWORTH, BENDIGO, CENTRAL VICTORIA, GEELONG, GRAMPIANS AND PYRENEES, HEATHCOTE, RUTHERGLEN, YARRA VALLEY.

VIEUX-CHÂTEAU-CERTAN★★ *Pomerol AC, Bordeaux, France* Slow-developing, tannic red with up to 30% Cabernet Franc and 10% Cabernet Sauvignon in the blend, which after 15–20 years finally resembles more a fragrant, refined MEDOC than a hedonistic POMEROL. **Best years:** 2006 05 04 02 01 00 **99 98 96 95 90 89 88 86 85.**

DOM. DU VIEUX TÉLÉGRAPHE *Châteauneuf-du-Pape AC, Rhône Valley, France* The vines are some of the oldest in CHATEAUNEUF and the Grenache-based red★★★ is among the best modern-style wines of the RHONE VALLEY. There is a small amount of white★★, which is rich and heavenly when very young. Good second wine, Vieux Mas des Papes. Also owns improving la Roquette★ in Châteauneuf and les Pallières★★ in GIGONDAS. **Best years:** (reds) 2007 06 05 04 **03 01 00 99 98 97 96 95 90 89 88.**

VILLA MARIA *Auckland and Marlborough, New Zealand* Founder George Fistonich also owns Esk Valley and Vidal (both in HAWKES BAY). Villa Maria Reserve Merlot-Cabernet★★★, Reserve Merlot★★, Esk Valley The Terraces★★★ and Vidal Merlot-Cabernet★★ are superb. Syrahs are among New Zealand's best: Esk Valley and Villa Maria Reserve both ★★★, Vidal★★. Reserve Chardonnay from Vidal★★ and Villa Maria★★ are power-packed wines. The Villa Maria range includes various MARLBOROUGH Sauvignon Blancs, with Clifford Bay★★, Ballochdale★★ and Richmond Brook★★ estates outstanding. Also from Marlborough, impressive Pinot Noir★★, Pinot Gris★, Riesling★ and stunning botrytized Noble Riesling★★★. Best years: (Hawkes Bay reds) (2007) 06 **04** 02 00 98.

CH. DE VILLENEUVE *Saumur-Champigny AC, Loire Valley, France* The secret of this property's success lies in low yields, picked when properly ripe. First-class SAUMUR-CHAMPIGNY★, with concentrated, mineral Vieilles Vignes★★ and le Grand Clos★★. Also good white stainless-steel-fermented SAUMUR★ and barrel-fermented Saumur Les Cormiers★★. Best years: (2007) 06 05 **04** 03 02 01 97 96.

VILLIERA *Stellenbosch WO, South Africa* The speciality is Cap Classique sparklers; stand-outs are Monro Brut★ and the additive-free Brut Natural Chardonnay★. Still whites include Sauvignon Blanc (Bush Vine★), a consistent Riesling and 2 delicious Chenin Blancs★ with different degrees of oaking. Monro, a structured Merlot-led BORDEAUX blend, is best among the reds. Fired Earth★ is a tasty Late Bottled PORT style. Also 'mentor' to neighbouring M'hudi project (Pinotage★).

VIN SANTO *Tuscany, Italy* The 'holy wine' of TUSCANY can be one of the world's great sweet wines – but the term has been wantonly abused (happily the *liquoroso* version, made by adding alcohol to partially fermented must, is no longer recognized as a legitimate style). Made from grapes either hung from rafters or laid on mats to dry, the wines, fermented and aged in small barrels for up to 7–8 years, should be nutty, oxidized, full of the flavours of dried apricots and crystallized orange peel, concentrated and long. Also made in UMBRIA, and in TRENTINO as Vino Santo using the Nosiola grape. Best producers: Castello di AMA★, AVIGNONESI★★★, Fattoria di Basciano★★, Bindella★★, Cacchiano★, Capezzana★★, Fattoria del Cerro★★, Corzano & Paterno★★, FONTODI★★, ISOLE E OLENA★★★, Romeo★★, San Felice★★, San Gervasio★, San Giusto a Rentennano★★★, SELVAPIANA★★, Villa Sant'Anna★★, Villa di Vetrice★, VOLPAIA★★.

VIÑAS DEL VERO *Somontano DO, Aragón, Spain* Minerally unoaked Chardonnay and its toasty barrel-fermented counterpart★ are joined by more original whites such as Clarión★, a blend of Chardonnay, Gewürztraminer and Macabeo. Top reds are Secastilla★★ (old-vines Garnacha with some Syrah), Gran Vos★ (Merlot-Cabernet-Pinot Noir) and the red blend made by its subsidiary Blecua★★.

VINHO VERDE DOC *Minho and Douro Litoral, Portugal* 'Vinho Verde' can be red or white – 'green' only in the sense of being young. The whites are the most widely seen outside Portugal and range from sulphured and acidic to aromatic, flowery and fruity. One or two that fall outside the DOC regulations are sold as Vinho Regional Minho (Quinta da Covela★). Best producers: Quinta de Alderiz, Quinta do Ameal★, Quinta da Aveleda, Quinta da Baguinha★, Encostas dos Castelos, Quinta da Franqueira★, Moncão co-op (Deu la Deu Alvarinho★, Muralhas de Moncão), Muros de Melgaço★, Quintas de Melgaço, Palácio de Brejoeira, Casa de Sezim★, Quinta de Simães, Quinta de Soalheiro★, SOGRAPE (Quinta de Azevedo★★), Quinta do Tamariz★.

VINO NOBILE DI MONTEPULCIANO DOCG *Tuscany, Italy* The 'noble wine' from the hills around the town of Montepulciano is made from the Sangiovese grape, known locally as Prugnolo, with the help of a little Canaiolo and Mammolo (and increasingly, today, Merlot and Cabernet).

At its best, it combines the power and structure of BRUNELLO DI MONTALCINO with the finesse and complexity found in top CHIANTI. Unfortunately, the best was a rare beast until relatively recently; improvement in the 1990s has been impressive. The introduction of what is essentially a second wine, ROSSO DI MONTEPULCIANO, has certainly helped. Best producers: AVIGNONESI★★, Bindella★, BOSCARELLI★★, La Braccesca★★/ANTINORI, Le Casalte★, La Ciarliana★, Contucci★, Dei★★, Del Cerro★★, Fassati★★, Gracciano★, Il Macchione★, Nottola★★, Palazzo Vecchio★, POLIZIANO★★, Redi★, Romeo★, Salcheto★★, Trerose★ (Simposio★★), Valdipiatta★. Best years: (2007) (06) 04 **03 01 00 99 97 95**.

VINSOBRES AC *Rhône Valley, France* Southern RHONE village, AC for red since 2005. A good area for Syrah, which goes into the blend with Grenache. Best producers: Chaume-Arnaud★, Constant-Duquesnoy, Coriançon★, Deurre★, Gramenon, Jaume★, Moulin★, Perrin★, la Vinsobraise co-op.

VIOGNIER Traditionally grown only in the northern RHONE, and a poor yielder, prone to disease and difficult to vinify. The wine can be delicious: pear-fleshy, apricotty with a soft, almost waxy texture, usually a fragrance of spring flowers and sometimes a taste like crème fraîche. New, higher-yielding clones are now found in LANGUEDOC-ROUSSILLON, Ardèche and the southern Rhône as well as in Spain, Switzerland, Italy, Austria, the USA, Argentina, Chile, Australia, New Zealand and South Africa.

VIRÉ-CLESSÉ AC *Mâconnais, Burgundy, France* Appellation created in 1998 out of 2 of the best MACON-VILLAGES. Controversially, the rules outlaw wines with residual sugar, thus excluding Jean Thévenet's extraordinary cuvées. Best producers: A Bonhomme★★, Bret Brothers★, O Merlin★, R Michel★★, Rijckaert★, Cave de Viré★, Ch. de Viré★. Best years: (2007) **06 05 04 02**.

VIRGINIA *USA* Thomas Jefferson's modern-day successors have created a rapidly growing and improving wine industry. Virginia now has more than 120 wineries and 6 AVAs. Aromatic Viognier and earthy Cabernet Franc show most promise, while growers tinker with other varieties such as Petit Manseng and Tannat. Best producers: Barboursville★, Chrysalis, HORTON★, Kluge, Linden★, Rockbridge, Valhalla★, Veritas, White Hall★.

VIVIANI *Valpolicella DOC, Veneto, Italy* Claudio Viviani's 9ha (22-acre) site is turning out some beautifully balanced VALPOLICELLA. The top AMARONE, Casa dei Bepi★★★, is a model of enlightened modernity, and the Valpolicella Classico Superiore Campo Morar★★ and RECIOTO★★ are of a similar quality. Best years: (2006) 04 **03 01 00 97**.

ROBERTO VOERZIO *Barolo DOCG, Piedmont, Italy* One of the best of the new wave of BAROLO producers. Dolcetto (Priavino★) is successful, as is Vignaserra★★ – barrique-aged Nebbiolo with a little Cabernet – and the outstanding BARBERA D'ALBA Riserva Vigneto Pozzo dell'Annunziata★★★. Barriques are also used for fashioning his Barolo, but such is the quality and concentration of fruit that the oak does not overwhelm. Single-vineyard examples made in the best years include Brunate★★, Cerequio★★★, La Serra★★ and Riserva Capalot★★★. Best years: (Barolo) (2007) (06) (04) **03 01 00 99 98 97 96 95 93 91 90 89 88 85**.

COMTE GEORGES DE VOGÜÉ *Chambolle-Musigny AC, Côte de Nuits, Burgundy, France* De Vogüé owns substantial holdings in 2 Grands Crus, BONNES-MARES★★★ and MUSIGNY★★★, as well as in Chambolle's top Premier Cru, les Amoureuses★★★. Since 1990 the domaine has delivered more concentrated wines than before. It is the sole producer of minute quantities of Musigny Blanc★★, but because of recent replanting the wine is currently being sold as (very expensive) BOURGOGNE Blanc. Best years: (Musigny) (2007) 06 05 04 03 00 99 **98 97 96 93 92 91 90**.

VOLNAY AC *Côte de Beaune, Burgundy, France* Some of the most elegant red wines of the COTE DE BEAUNE; attractive when young, good examples can age well. The top Premiers Crus are Caillerets, Champans, Clos des Chênes, Santenots and Taillepieds. Best producers: R Ampeau★★, d'ANGERVILLE★★, H Boillot★, J-M Boillot★★, J-M Bouley★, COCHE-DURY★★, V GIRARDIN★★, LAFARGE★★★, LAFON★★★, Matrot★★, MONTILLE★★, N POTEL★★, J Prieur★★, Roblet-Monnot★, N Rossignol★, J Voillot★★. Best years: (2007) 05 03 **02 99 98 97 96 95 93 91 90**.

CASTELLO DI VOLPAIA *Chianti Classico DOCG, Tuscany, Italy* Light, perfumed but refined CHIANTI CLASSICO★ (Riserva★★). Two stylish SUPER-TUSCANS, Balifico★★ and Coltassala★★, are both predominantly Sangiovese. Sometimes good but not great VIN SANTO★. Riccardo Cotarella (FALESCO) is consultant enologist.

VOSNE-ROMANÉE AC *Côte de Nuits, Burgundy, France* The greatest village in the COTE DE NUITS, with 6 Grands Crus and 13 Premiers Crus (notably les Malconsorts, aux Brûlées and les Suchots) which are often as good as other villages' Grands Crus. The quality of Vosne's village wine is also high. In good years the wines need at least 6 years' aging, but 10–15 would be better. Best producers: R Arnoux★★★, Cacheux Sirugue★★, S CATHIARD★★★, B CLAIR★★, B Clavelier★★, R Engel★★, GRIVOT★★★, Anne GROS★★★, A-F GROS★★, M GROS★★★, F Lamarche★★, Dom. LEROY★★★, Vicomte LIGER-BELAIR★★★, MEO-CAMUZET★★★, Mugneret-Gibourg★★, RION★★, Dom. de la ROMANEE-CONTI★★★, E Rouget★★★. Best years: (2007) 06 05 03 02 01 **00 99 98 97 96 95 93 91 90**.

VOUGEOT AC *Côte de Nuits, Burgundy, France* Outside the walls of CLOS DE VOUGEOT there are 11ha (27 acres) of Premier Cru and 5ha (12 acres) of other vines. Look out for Premier Cru Les Cras (red) and the Clos Blanc de Vougeot, first planted with white grapes in 1110. Best producers: Bertagna★, Chopin★★, C Clerget★, VOUGERAIE★★. Best years: (reds) (2007) 06 05 03 02 01 **00 99 98 97 96**.

DOM. DE LA VOUGERAIE *Côte de Nuits, Burgundy, France* An estate created by Jean-Claude BOISSET in 1999 out of the numerous vineyards – often excellent but under-achieving – that came with Burgundy merchant houses acquired during his rise to prominence since 1964. Wines have been generally outstanding, notably Clos Blanc de VOUGEOT★★★, GEVREY-CHAMBERTIN les Évocelles★★, le MUSIGNY★★★ and Vougeot les Cras★★ reds. Best years: (reds) (2007) 06 05 04 03 02 **01 00 99**.

CH. LA VOULTE-GASPARETS *Corbières AC, Languedoc, France* CORBIERES with flavours of thyme and baked earth from old hillside vines. Good basic Voulte-Gasparets and more expensive Cuvée Réservée★ and Romain Pauc★★. Can be drunk young, but ages well. Best years: (Romain Pauc) 2005 04 03 **01 00 99 98**.

VOUVRAY AC *Loire Valley, France* Dry, medium-dry, sweet and sparkling wines from Chenin grapes east of Tours. The dry wines acquire beautifully rounded flavours after 6–8 years. Medium-dry wines, when well made from a single domaine, are worth aging for 20 years or more. Spectacular noble-rot-affected sweet wines can be produced when conditions are right. The fizz is some of the LOIRE's best. Best producers:

Aubuisières★★, Bourillon-Dorléans★★, Champalou★, F Chidaine, CLOS NAUDIN★★, la Fontainerie★★, Gaudrelle★, Gautier★★, Haute Borne★, HUET★★★, Pichot★★, F Pinon★★, Taille aux Loups★★/BLOT, Vigneau Chevreau★. Best years: 2007 06 05 **04 03 02 01 99 97 96 95 93 90 89**.

VOYAGER ESTATE *Margaret River, Western Australia* Originally planted in 1978 and owned since 92 by mining magnate and teetotaller Michael Wright, who has built one of the most impressive cellar-door complexes in MARGARET RIVER. Stellar Chardonnay★★★, vibrant Sauvignon Blanc-Semillon and grassy Sauvignon Blanc. The Cabernet Sauvignon★ and Shiraz have leapt up a notch in recent vintages.

WACHAU *Niederösterreich, Austria* This stunning 1390ha (3400-acre) stretch of the Danube is Austria's top region for dry whites, from Riesling and Grüner Veltliner. Best producers: Alzinger★★, F HIRTZBERGER★★★, Högl★★, Jamek★, KNOLL★★★, NIKOLAIHOF★★, F X PICHLER★★★, Rudi Pichler★★, PRAGER★★★, Schmelz★★, Freie Weingärtner Wachau★. Best years: (2007) 06 05 04 **03 02 01 00 99 98 97 95 94 90**.

WACHENHEIM *Pfalz, Germany* Wine village made famous by the BURKLIN-WOLF estate, its best vineyards can produce rich yet beautifully balanced Rieslings. Best producers: Josef BIFFAR★, BURKLIN-WOLF★★, Karl Schaefer★, J L WOLF★★. Best years: (2007) 06 05 **04 03 02 01 99 98 97**.

WAGRAM *Niederösterreich, Austria* 2800ha (6920-acre) wine region on both banks of the Danube, stretching from just north of Vienna west to St Pölten. Previously known as Donauland – the name changed in 2007 – Wagram is the source of fine Grüner Veltliners. Best producers: J Bauer★, K Fritsch★, Leth★, Bernhard Ott★★, Wimmer-Czerny★.

WAIHEKE ISLAND *North Island, New Zealand* GOLDWATER pioneered wine-making on this island in Auckland harbour in the early 1980s, and this tiny region is now home to over 30 wineries. Hot, dry ripening conditions have made high-quality Cabernet-based reds that sell for high prices. Chardonnay is now appearing, together with experimental plots of Syrah and Viognier. Best producers: Fenton★, GOLDWATER★★, Obsidian, Passage Rock★, STONYRIDGE★★★, Te Whau★. Best years: (reds) (2007) 05 **04 02 00 99**.

WALKER BAY WO *South Africa* This maritime district on the south coast is home to a mix of grape varieties, but the holy grail of the majority is Pinot Noir, with the hub of activity in the Hemel en Aarde (heaven and earth) Valley. Also steely Sauvignon Blanc, minerally Chardonnay and refined Pinotage. Best producers: Ashbourne★, BOUCHARD FINLAYSON★★, HAMILTON RUSSELL★★, Hermanuspietersfontein, Newton Johnson★. Best years: (Pinot Noir) 2007 **06 05 04 03 02 01 00 99**.

WALLA WALLA VALLEY *AVA Washington State, USA* Walla Walla has over 100 of WASHINGTON's wineries, but 55 have only been producing wine since 1999. Similarly, vineyard acreage, although only 4% of the state total, has trebled since 99 – and is still growing. If you think there's a gold-rush feel about this clearly exciting area you wouldn't be far wrong. Best producers: CAYUSE VINEYARDS★★, DUNHAM CELLARS★, K Vintners★, L'ECOLE NO 41★★, LEONETTI CELLAR★★★, LONG SHADOWS VINTNERS★★, Northstar★, Pepper Bridge★, Reininger★, WOODWARD CANYON★★.

WARRE *Port DOC, Douro, Portugal* Part of the Symington group, with top-quality Vintage PORT★★★ and a good 'off-vintage' port from Quinta da Cavadinha★★. LBV★★ is in the traditional, unfiltered style. Warrior★ is a reliable ruby and Otima a solid 10-year-old tawny; Otima★ 20-year-old is much better. Best years: (Vintage) **2003 00 97 94 91 85 83 80 77 70 66 63**; (Cavadinha) **2001 99 98 96 95 92 90 88 87 86 82 78**.

WARWICK *Stellenbosch WO, South Africa* Warwick produces the complex Trilogy★ BORDEAUX-style blend and a refined, fragrant Cabernet Franc★. The Three Cape Ladies★ red blend includes Pinotage along with Cabernet Sauvignon and Merlot. Whites are represented by an unwooded Sauvignon Blanc and full-bodied, lightly oaked Chardonnay★. Best years: (Trilogy) **2006 05 04 03 02 01 00 99**.

WASHINGTON STATE *USA* Second-largest premium wine-producing state in the US, with more than 500 wineries. The chief growing areas are in irrigated high desert, east of the Cascade Mountains, where the COLUMBIA VALLEY AVA encompasses the smaller AVAs of YAKIMA VALLEY, WALLA WALLA VALLEY, Wahluke Slope, Horse Heaven Hills, Columbia Gorge, Rattlesnake Hills and Red Mountain. Although the heat is not as intense as in California, long summer days with extra hours of sunshine due to the northern latitude seem to increase the intensity of fruit flavours and result in both red and white wines of great depth. Cabernet, Merlot, Syrah, Chardonnay and Semillon can produce very good wines here.

GEOFF WEAVER *Adelaide Hills, South Australia* Low-yielding vines at Geoff Weaver's Lenswood vineyard produce top-quality fruit, from which he crafts limy Riesling★★, crisply gooseberryish Sauvignon★★ and stylish cool-climate Chardonnay★★. Pinot Noir is promising.

WEGELER *Bernkastel, Mosel; Oestrich-Winkel, Rheingau; Deidesheim, Pfalz, Germany* The Wegeler family's 3 estates are dedicated primarily to Riesling, and dry wines make up the bulk of production. Whether dry or naturally sweet Auslese, the best merit ★★ and will develop well with 5 or more years of aging. Consistently good 'Geheimrat J' Sekt★★, too. Best years: (Mosel) (2007) **06 05 04 03 02 01 99 98 97 96**.

WEHLEN *Mosel, Germany* Village whose steep Sonnenuhr vineyard produces some of the most intense Rieslings in Germany. Best producers: Kerpen, Dr LOOSEN★★★, MOLITOR★★, J J PRUM★★★, S A PRUM★, Max Ferd RICHTER★★, SELBACH-OSTER★★, WEGELER★, Dr Weins-Prüm★. Best years: (2007) **06 05 04 03 02 01 99 98 97 95 94**.

ROBERT WEIL *Kiedrich, Rheingau, Germany* Huge investment from Japanese drinks giant SUNTORY, coupled with Wilhelm Weil's devotion to quality, has clearly paid off. Majestic sweet Auslese, Beerenauslese and Trockenbeerenauslese Rieslings★★★ and dry Rieslings★ are crisp and elegant, although the regular wines have been a little disappointing in recent vintages. Best years: (2007) **06 05 04 03 02 01 99 98 96 95**.

WEINBACH *Alsace AC, Alsace, France* This Kaysersberg estate is run by Colette Faller and her two daughters, Laurence (the winemaker) and Catherine. The range is quite complicated. The lightest wines are named in honour of Mme Faller's late husband Théo★★. Ste-Cathérine★★ bottlings come from the Schlossberg and are late picked, though not technically Vendange Tardive; Laurence wines are from the non-cru Altenbourg. Superior bottlings include the vineyard name, and the top dry wine is the special selection Ste-Cathérine Riesling Grand Cru

Schlossberg L'Inédit★★★. Quintessence★★★ – a super-concentrated Sélection de Grains Nobles from Pinot Gris or Gewurztraminer – is not produced every year. All the wines are exceptionally balanced and, while delightful on release, can age for many years. Best years: (Grand Cru Riesling) (2007) 05 **04 02 01 00 99 98 97 96 95 94 93 92 90**.

WEINERT *Mendoza, Argentina* Buying grapes from some of the oldest vineyards in LUJAN DE CUYO, Weinert has built a reputation for Malbec. Its oxidative approach to winemaking creates complex, long-lived reds such as mocha and black cherry Gran Vino★★. Estrella (Star) Malbec★★ is an eccentric red released decades after the vintage.

WEISSBURGUNDER See PINOT BLANC.

WELSCHRIESLING Unrelated to the great Riesling of the Rhine, this grape makes some of the best sweet wines in Austria, but tends to be rather dull as a dry wine. It is highly esteemed in Hungary as Olasz Rizling. As Riesling Italico it is decreasingly planted in northern Italy, where it can produce decent dry whites.

WENDOUREE *Clare Valley, South Australia* Small winery using old-fashioned methods to make enormous, ageworthy reds★★★ from paltry yields off their own very old Shiraz, Cabernet, Malbec and Mataro (Mourvèdre) vines, plus tiny amounts of sweet Muscat★. Reds can, and do, age beautifully for 30 years or more. Best years: (reds) (2006) (05) (04) 03 02 01 **99 98 96 95 94 92 91 90 86 83 82 81 80 78 76 75**.

WESTEND *Riverina, New South Wales, Australia* The Calabria family winery was established in 1945 but has dramatically increased production and improved quality under Bill Calabria in recent years. The 3 Bridges range includes a powerful, robust Durif★ and the lush, honeyed Golden Mist Botrytis Semillon★. Richland is one of Australia's best budget-priced ranges: standout varieties are Pinot Grigio and consistent Sauvignon Blanc. The even cheaper Outback label sometimes hits the mark.

WESTERN AUSTRALIA Only the south-west corner of this state is suited to vines, the SWAN DISTRICT and Perth environs being the oldest and hottest area, with present attention (and more than 230 producers) focused on GREAT SOUTHERN, MARGARET RIVER, Geographe and PEMBERTON. The state produces just over 4% of Australia's grape crush but about 20% of its premium wines.

WIEN *Austria* Region within the city limits of Wien (Vienna). The best wines come from south-facing sites in Grinzing, Nussdorf and Weiden, and the Bisamberg hill east of the Danube. Best producers: Christ, Edlmoser, Mayer, Schilling, WIENINGER★★, Zahel. Best years: (2007) 06 **05 04 03 01**.

WIENINGER *Stammersdorf, Wien, Austria* Fritz Wieninger has risen above the parochial standards of many Viennese growers to offer a range of elegant, well-crafted wines from Chardonnay and Pinot Noir. The best range is often the Select★★, the pricier Grand Select★ being often over-oaked. Recent additions are brilliant white wines from the renowned Nussberg★★ vineyard. Best years: (2007) 06 05 **04 03 01**.

WILLAMETTE VALLEY AVA *Oregon, USA* Wet winters, generally dry summers, and a so-so chance of long, cool autumn days provide sound growing conditions for cool-climate varieties such as Pinot Noir, Pinot Gris and Chardonnay. Dundee Hills, with its volcanic hillsides, is considered the best sub-region. Best producers: ADELSHEIM★, ARGYLE★,

BEAUX FRERES★★, BERGSTROM★★, CRISTOM★, DOMAINE DROUHIN★★, DOMAINE SERENE★★, ELK COVE★, Evesham Wood★, Sineann★, WillaKenzie★, Ken WRIGHT★. Best years: (reds) (2006) **04 03 02 00**.

WILLIAMS SELYEM *Russian River Valley AVA, California, USA* The cult following for the Pinot Noirs, especially the J Rochioli Vineyard★★, has diminished somewhat in recent years, but Williams Selyem continues to make exemplary Pinot Noirs from various regions, including SONOMA COAST★ and ANDERSON VALLEY★. Zins are good too. Best years: (Pinot Noir) 2005 04 **03** 02 01 00 99 98 97 96 95 94.

WINKEL *Rheingau, Germany* RHEINGAU village whose best vineyard is the large Hasensprung but the most famous one is Schloss Vollrads – an ancient estate that does not use the village name on its label. Best producers: Hamm, Prinz von Hessen, Johannishof★★, SCHLOSS VOLLRADS★ (since 1999), WEGELER★. Best years: (2007) 06 05 04 03 **02 01** 99 98.

WINNINGEN *Mosel, Germany* A small group of growers has shown that the steep slopes of this little-known village, particularly the Ühlen and Röttgen sites, can produce excellent Rieslings, especially in a rich dry style. Best producers: HEYMANN-LOWENSTEIN★★, Reinhard Knebel★★, Richard Richter★. Best years: (2007) 06 05 **04 03 02 01** 99.

WIRRA WIRRA *McLaren Vale, South Australia* Outstanding producer with fine ADELAIDE HILLS whites – well-balanced and tangy Sauvignon Blanc★ and tight, fine yet creamy Chardonnay★★ – and soft MCLAREN VALE reds led by delicious The Angelus (Dead Ringer outside Australia) Cabernet★★, chocolaty RSW Shiraz★★ and stylish, concentrated Woodhenge Shiraz★. Recently purchased outstanding Rayner vineyard in the McLaren Vale. Best years: (RSW Shiraz) 2006 05 04 03 **02 01** 98 96 94 91 90.

WITHER HILLS *Marlborough, South Island, New Zealand* Quality-focused winery, bought in 2002 by New Zealand brewing group Lion Nathan; talented founder/winemaker Brent Marris resigned as manager after the 2007 vintage to focus on his label 'The Ned'. A trio of stylish MARLBOROUGH wines – concentrated, pungent Sauvignon Blanc★, fruit-focused Chardonnay★★ and vibrant Pinot Noir★★ – get the best out of the region's grapes. Will the style change post-Marris? We'll have to wait and see. Best years: (Sauvignon Blanc) **2007 06 04**.

WITTMANN *Westhofen, Rheinhessen, Germany* Philipp Wittmann has worked wonders at his family's organic estate, succeeding equally with bold dry Rieslings★★, Chardonnay★★ and voluptuous Trockenbeerenauslese ★★★. Best years: (2007) 06 05 **04 03 02 01**.

J L WOLF *Wachenheim, Pfalz, Germany* Ernst Loosen, of Dr LOOSEN, took over this underperforming estate in 1996. A string of concentrated, mostly dry Rieslings★★ have won it a place among the region's top producers. Best years: (2007) 06 05 **04 03 02 01 99**.

WOODWARD CANYON *Walla Walla Valley AVA, Washington State, USA* Big, barrel-fermented Chardonnays (Celilo Vineyard★) were the trademark wines for many years, but today the focus is on reds, led by Artist Series★★ Cabernet Sauvignon and Old Vines★★ Cabernet Sauvignon. Merlot★★ is rich, velvety and deeply perfumed. Red BORDEAUX-style blend is labelled Charbonneau★, the name of the vineyard where the fruit is grown. Best years: (top Cabernet Sauvignon) (2006) 05 **04 03 02 99**.

KEN WRIGHT CELLARS *Willamette Valley AVA, Oregon, USA* Ken Wright produces more than a dozen succulent, single-vineyard Pinot Noirs. Bold and rich with new oak flavour, they range from good to ethereal, led by the Carter★★, Savoya★★, Guadalupe★★, McCrone★★ and Shea★★.

Fine WASHINGTON Chardonnay from the Celilo Vineyard★★ and a crisp Freedom Hill Vineyard Pinot Blanc★ are made in very small quantities. Best years: (Pinot Noir) 2006 05 **04 03 02 01**.

WÜRTTEMBERG *Germany* 11,500ha (28,415-acre) region centred on the river Neckar. Two-thirds of the wine made is red, and the best comes from Lemberger (Blaufränkisch) or Spätburgunder (Pinot Noir) grapes. Massive yields are often responsible for pallid wines, especially from the locally popular Trollinger grape. A few of the top steep sites are now producing perfumed reds and racy Riesling. Best years: (reds) (2007) (06) 05 04 **03 02 01 99**.

WÜRZBURG *Franken, Germany* The centre of FRANKEN wines. Some Rieslings can be great, but the real star is Silvaner. Best producers: Bürgerspital, JULIUSSPITAL★★, Staatlicher Hofkeller, Weingut am Stein★. Best years: (2007) 06 05 04 **03 02 01 00 99 88 86**.

WYNNS *Coonawarra, South Australia* Wynns' name is synonymous with COONAWARRA. It is now part of the giant Foster's Wine Group, but its personality seems to have suffered less than most of the group's other brands and, except at the top end, prices remain fair. Investment in vineyard rejuvenation is paying off. Wynns is best known for reds, such as good Shiraz★, Cabernet Sauvignon★ and Johnson's Block Shiraz-Cabernet★. Top-end John Riddoch Cabernet Sauvignon★★ and Michael Shiraz★★ were deep, ripe, oaky styles, but latest releases show more restraint and elegance. Also attractive Chardonnay★ and delightful Riesling★. Best years: (John Riddoch) 2005 04 03 **99 96 94 91 90 88 86**.

YAKIMA VALLEY AVA *Washington State, USA* This important valley lies within the much larger COLUMBIA VALLEY AVA. Yakima is planted mostly to Chardonnay, Merlot and Cabernet Sauvignon and has more than 65 wineries. Best producers: Chinook★, DELILLE CELLARS★★, Hogue Cellars, Wineglass Cellars★.

YALUMBA *Barossa Valley, South Australia* Distinguished old firm, owned by the Hill-Smith family, making a wide range of wines under its own name, as well as Heggies Vineyard (restrained Riesling★, plump Merlot★★, opulent Viognier★ and botrytis Riesling★★), Hill-Smith Estate (Sauvignon Blanc★) and Pewsey Vale (fine Riesling★★ and Cabernet Sauvignon★). Flagship reds are The Signature Cabernet-Shiraz★★, Octavius Shiraz★★ and The Menzies Cabernet★★, and all cellar well. New premiums include Old Vine Grenache★★, Contour Riesling★★, Virgilius Viognier★★ and Shiraz-Viognier★. High-quality quaffers like Y Series varietals★ (sometimes ★★) and Oxford Landing Chardonnay, Sauvignon★ and Cabernet-Shiraz are consistently impressive. Angas Brut is big-volume enjoyable fizz, while TASMANIA's Jansz★ (Vintage★★) has added a class act to the flight. Museum Release fortifieds (Muscat★★) are excellent, but rare. Best years: (The Signature red) (2007) (06) 05 **04 03 02 01 00 99 98 97 96 95 93 92 91 90 88**.

YARRA VALLEY *Victoria, Australia* With its cool climate, the Yarra is asking to be judged as Australia's best Pinot Noir region. Exciting also for Chardonnay and Cabernet-Merlot blends and as a supplier of base wine for fizz. Best producers: Arthur's Creek★, COLDSTREAM HILLS★★, CARLEI★★, DE BORTOLI★★, Diamond Valley★★, DOMAINE CHANDON/Green Point★, Métier, MOUNT MARY★★, St Huberts, TARRAWARRA★★, Yarra Burn★, Yarra Yering★★, Yeringberg★, Yering Station★★.

YELLOWTAIL *Riverina, New South Wales, Australia* Yellowtail, Australia's fastest-growing export brand ever, has made the RIVERINA family winery, Casella, a major world player. Artfully crafted but overly sweet wines.

CH. D'YQUEM★★★ *Sauternes AC, 1er Cru Supérieur, Bordeaux, France* Often rated the most sublime sweet wine in the world, Yquem's total commitment to quality is unquestionable. Despite a large vineyard (100ha/250 acres), production is tiny. Only fully noble-rotted grapes are picked, often berry by berry, and low yield means each vine produces only a glass of wine! This precious liquid is then fermented in new oak barrels and left to mature for 3–4 years before bottling. It is one of the world's most expensive wines, in constant demand because of its richness and exotic flavours. The wines took a step forward in quality during the 1990s and seem to have gone even further during the 2000s. A dry white, Ygrec, is made in some years. In 1999 LVMH won a takeover battle with the Lur-Saluces family, owners for 406 years. Best years: 2006 05 04 03 **02 01 00 99 98 97 96 95 94 93 90 89 88 86 83 81 80 79 76 75 71 70 67 62**.

ZILLIKEN *Saarburg, Mosel-Saar-Ruwer, Germany* Estate specializing in Rieslings★★ (Auslese, Eiswein often ★★★) from the Saarburger Rausch vineyard. Best years: (2007) 06 05 04 **03** 02 **01 99 97 95 94**.

ZIND-HUMBRECHT *Alsace AC, Alsace, France* Olivier Humbrecht is one of France's outstanding winemakers, with an approach that emphasizes the individuality of each site and each vintage. Wines from 4 Grand Cru sites – Rangen, Goldert, Hengst and Brand – are superlative (Riesling★★★, Gewurztraminer★★★, Pinot Gris★★★ and Muscat★★), the Rangen in particular producing wines unlike any others in Alsace. Wines from specific non-Grand Cru vineyards such as Clos Windsbuhl and Clos Jebsal are also exceptional. Vendange Tardive and Sélection de Grains Nobles wines are almost invariably of ★★★ quality. Even basic Sylvaners★ and Pinot Blancs★★ are fine. Wines often have some residual sugar, but it's all natural. Best years: (Grand Cru Riesling) (2007) 05 04 **03** 02 01 00 99 98 97 96 95.

ZINFANDEL CALIFORNIA's versatile red grape can make big, juicy, fruit-packed wine – or insipid, sweetish 'blush' or even late-harvest dessert wine. Some Zinfandel is now made in other countries, with notable examples in Australia and South Africa. Best producers: (California) Brown★★, Cline Cellars★★, Dashe★★, DRY CREEK VINEYARD★★, Dutton-Goldfield★★, Gary Farrell★★, FETZER★, HARTFORD★, MARIAH★, Martinelli★★, Nalle★★, Preston★, Rafanelli★★, RAVENSWOOD★, RIDGE★★★, Rosenblum★★, Saddleback★★, St Francis★★, SEGHESIO★★, Trinitas★★, TURLEY★★; (Australia) CAPE MENTELLE★★, Kangarilla Road, Nepenthe★★. See also PRIMITIVO DI MANDURIA.

FAMILIA ZUCCARDI *Mendoza, Argentina* One of Argentina's great success stories. Dynamic owner José Zuccardi has created a range of utterly enjoyable easy-drinking wines, from basic Santa Julia reds★ upwards. Santa Julia Reservas and Zuccardi 'Q'★ (Tempranillo★★) wines have improved dramatically with the introduction of up-to-date equipment. Top-of-the-line Zeta★★, a blend of Tempranillo and Malbec, is a serious yet sensual red. Zuccardi also experiments with more grape varieties than anyone else in Argentina; future triumphs will include such varieties as Marselan, Caladoc, Tannat and Touriga Nacional. Son Sebastian is a whizz-kid with sparklers (red Bonarda★ is ace) and sweeties. He's even made a sweet botrytized Cabernet! My kind of guy.

GLOSSARY OF WINE TERMS

AC/AOC (APPELLATION D'ORIGINE CONTRÔLÉE)
The top category of French wines, defined by regulations covering vineyard yields, grape varieties, geographical boundaries, alcohol content and production method. Guarantees origin and style of a wine, but not its quality.

ACID/ACIDITY
Naturally present in grapes and essential to wine, providing balance and stability and giving the refreshing tang in white wines and the appetizing grip in reds.

ADEGA
Portuguese for winery.

AGING
An alternative term for maturation.

ALCOHOLIC CONTENT
The alcoholic strength of wine, expressed as a percentage of the total volume of the wine. Typically in the range of 7–15%.

ALCOHOLIC FERMENTATION
The process whereby yeasts, natural or added, convert the grape sugars into alcohol (Ethyl alcohol, or Ethanol) and carbon dioxide.

AMONTILLADO
Traditionally dry style of sherry. See Jerez y Manzanilla in main A–Z.

ANBAUGEBIET
German for growing region; these names will appear on labels of all QbA and QmP wines. There are 13 Anbaugebiete: Ahr, Baden, Franken, Hessische Bergstrasse, Mittelrhein, Mosel-Saar-Ruwer, Nahe, Pfalz, Rheingau, Rheinhessen, Saale-Unstrut, Sachsen and Württemberg.

AUSBRUCH
Austrian Prädikat category used for sweet wines from the town of Rust.

AUSLESE
German and Austrian Prädikat category meaning that the grapes were 'selected' for their higher ripeness.

AVA (AMERICAN VITICULTURAL AREA)
System of appellations of origin for US wines.

AZIENDA AGRICOLA
Italian for estate or farm. It also indicates wine made from grapes grown by the proprietor.

BARREL AGING
Time spent maturing in wood, usually oak, during which wine takes on flavours from the wood.

BARREL FERMENTATION
Oak barrels may be used for fermentation instead of stainless steel to give a rich, oaky flavour to the wine.

BARRIQUE
The *barrique bordelaise* is the traditional Bordeaux oak barrel of 225 litres (50 gallons) capacity.

BAUMÉ
A scale measuring must weight (the amount of sugar in grape juice) to estimate potential alcohol content.

BEERENAUSLESE
German and Austrian Prädikat category applied to wines made from 'individually selected' berries (i.e. grapes) affected by noble rot (*Edelfäule* in German). The wines are rich and sweet. Beerenauslese wines are only produced in the best years in Germany, but in Austria they are a regular occurrence.

BEREICH
German for region or district within a wine region or *Anbaugebiet*. Bereichs tend to be large, and the use of a Bereich name, such as Bereich Bingen, without qualification is seldom an indication of quality – in most cases, quite the reverse.

BIODYNAMIC VITICULTURE
This approach works with the movement of the planets and cosmic forces to achieve health and balance in the soil and in the vine. Vines are treated with infusions of mineral, animal and plant materials, applied in homeopathic quantities. An increasing number of growers are turning to biodynamism, with some

BOTTLE SIZES

CHAMPAGNE

Magnum	1.5 litres	2 bottles
Jeroboam	3 litres	4 bottles
Rehoboam	4.5 litres	6 bottles
Methuselah	6 litres	8 bottles
Salmanazar	9 litres	12 bottles
Balthazar	12 litres	16 bottles
Nebuchadnezzar	15 litres	20 bottles

BORDEAUX

Magnum	1.5 litres	2 bottles
Marie-Jeanne	2.25 litres	3 bottles
Double-magnum	3 litres	4 bottles
Jeroboam	4.5 litres	6 bottles
Imperial	6 litres	8 bottles

astonishing results, but it is labour-intensive and generally confined to smaller estates.

BLANC DE BLANCS
White wine made from one or more white grape varieties. Used especially for sparkling wines; in Champagne, denotes wine made entirely from the Chardonnay grape.

BLANC DE NOIRS
White wine made from black grapes only – the juice is separated from the skins to avoid extracting any colour. Most often seen in Champagne, where it describes wine made from Pinot Noir and/or Pinot Meunier grapes.

BLENDING
The art of mixing together wines of different origin, style or age, often to balance out acidity, weight etc. Winemakers often use the term *assemblage*.

BODEGA
Spanish for winery.

BOTRYTIS
See noble rot.

BRUT
French term for dry sparkling wines, especially Champagne.

CARBONIC MACERATION
Winemaking method used to produce fresh fruity reds for drinking young. Whole (uncrushed) bunches of grapes are fermented in closed containers – a process that extracts lots of fruit and colour, but little tannin.

CHAMPAGNE METHOD
Traditional method used for all of the world's finest sparkling wines. A second fermentation takes place in the bottle, producing carbon dioxide which, kept in solution under pressure, gives the wine its fizz.

CHAPTALIZATION
Legal addition of sugar during fermentation to raise a wine's alcoholic strength. More necessary in cool climates where lack of sun produces insufficient natural sugar in the grape.

CHARMAT
See cuve close.

CHÂTEAU
French for castle: widely used in France to describe any wine estate, large or small.

CHIARETTO
Italian for a rosé wine of very light pink colour from around Lake Garda.

CLARET
English for red Bordeaux wines, from the French *clairet*, which was traditionally used to describe a lighter style of red Bordeaux.

CLARIFICATION
Term covering any wine-making process (such as filtering or fining) that involves the removal of solid matter either from the must or the wine.

CLONE
Strain of grape species. The term is usually taken to mean laboratory-produced, virus-free clones, selected to produce higher or lower quantity, or selected for resistance to frost or disease.

CLOS
French for a walled vineyard – as in Burgundy's Clos de Vougeot – also commonly incorporated into the names of estates (e.g. Clos des Papes), whether they are walled or not.

COLD FERMENTATION
Long, slow fermentation at low temperature to extract maximum freshness from the grapes. Crucial for whites in hot climates.

COLHEITA
Aged tawny port from a single vintage. *See* Port in main A–Z.

COMMUNE
A French village and its surrounding area or parish.

CO-OPERATIVE
In a co-operative cellar, growers who are members bring their grapes for vinification and bottling under a collective label. In terms of quantity, the French wine industry is dominated by co-ops. They often use less workaday titles, such as Caves des Vignerons, Producteurs Réunis, Union des Producteurs or Cellier des Vignerons.

CORKED/CORKY
Wine fault derived from a cork which has become contaminated, usually with Trichloroanisole or TCA. The mouldy, stale smell is unmistakable. Nothing to do with pieces of cork in the wine.

COSECHA
Spanish for vintage.

CÔTE
French word for a slope or hillside, which is where many, but not all, of the country's best vineyards are found.

CRÉMANT
French term for traditional-method sparkling wine from Alsace, Bordeaux, Burgundy, Die, Jura, Limoux, Loire and Luxembourg.

CRIANZA
Spanish term for the youngest official category of oak-matured wine. A red Crianza wine must have had at least 2 years' aging (1 in oak, 1 in bottle) before sale; a white or rosé, 1 year.

CRU
French for growth, meaning a specific plot of

land or particular estate. In Burgundy, growths are divided into Grands (great) and Premiers (first) Crus, and apply solely to the actual land. In Champagne the same terms are used for whole villages. In Bordeaux there are various hierarchical levels of Cru referring to estates rather than their vineyards. In Italy the term is used frequently, in an unofficial way, to indicate a single-vineyard or special-selection wine.

CRU BOURGEOIS
French term for wines from the Médoc that are ranked immediately below the Crus Classés (last revised in 2003). Many are excellent value for money.

CRU CLASSÉ
The Classed Growths are the aristocracy of Bordeaux, ennobled by the Classifications of 1855 (for the Médoc, Barsac and Sauternes), 1955, 1969, 1986, 1996 and 2006 (for St-Émilion) and 1953 and 1959 (for Graves). Curiously, Pomerol has never been classified. The modern classifications are more reliable than the 1855 version, which was based solely on the price of the wines at the time of the Great Exhibition in Paris, but in terms of prestige the 1855 Classification remains the most important. With the exception of a single alteration in 1973, when Ch. Mouton-Rothschild was elevated to First Growth status, the list has not changed since 1855. It certainly needs revising.

CUVE CLOSE
A bulk process used to produce inexpensive sparkling wines. The second fermentation, which produces the bubbles, takes place in tank rather than in the bottle (as in the superior Traditional Method). Also called Charmat.

310

CUVÉE
French for the contents of a single vat or tank, but usually indicates a wine blended from either different grape varieties or the best barrels of wine.

DÉGORGEMENT
Stage in the production of Champagne-method wines when the sediment, collected in the neck of the bottle during *remuage*, is removed.

DEMI-SEC
French for medium-dry.

DO
(DENOMINACIÓN DE ORIGEN)
Spain's equivalent of the French AC quality category, regulating origin and production methods.

DOC
(DENOMINAÇÃO DE ORIGEM CONTROLADA)
Portugal's top regional classification for wines.

DOCA
(DENOMINACIÓN DE ORIGEN CALIFICADA)
Spanish quality wine category, intended to be one step up from DO. So far only Rioja and Priorat qualify.

DOC
(DENOMINAZIONE DI ORIGINE CONTROLLATA)
Italian quality wine category, regulating origin, grape varieties, yield and production methods.

DOCG
(DENOMINAZIONE DI ORIGINE CONTROLLATA E GARANTITA)
The top tier of the Italian classification system.

DOMAINE
French term for wine estate.

DOSAGE
A sugar and wine mixture added to sparkling wine

after *dégorgement* which affects how sweet or dry it will be.

EDELZWICKER
Blended wine from Alsace, usually bland.

EINZELLAGE
German for an individual vineyard site which is generally farmed by several growers. The name is preceded on the label by that of the village; for example, the Wehlener Sonnenuhr is the Sonnenuhr vineyard in Wehlen. The mention of a particular site should signify a superior wine. Sadly, this is not necessarily so.

EISWEIN
Rare, chiefly German and Austrian, late-harvested wine made by picking the grapes and pressing them while frozen. This concentrates the sweetness of the grape as most of the liquid is removed as ice. *See also* Icewine.

ESCOLHA
Portuguese for selection.

FEINHERB
Disliking the unsatisfactory term Halbtrocken, some producers prefer the term Feinherb. It lacks legal definition but usually applies to wines with 9–25g per litre of residual sugar.

FILTERING
Removal of yeasts, solids and any impurities from a wine before bottling.

FINING
Method of clarifying wine by adding a coagulant (e.g. egg whites, isinglass, bentonite) to remove soluble particles such as proteins and excessive tannins.

FINO
The lightest, freshest style of sherry. *See* Jerez y Manzanilla in main A–Z.

FLOR
A film of yeast which forms on the surface of fino sherries (and some other wines) in the barrel, preventing oxidation and imparting a tangy, dry flavour.

FLYING WINEMAKER
Term coined in the late 1980s to describe enologists, many Australian-trained, brought in to improve the quality of wines in many underperforming wine regions.

FORTIFIED WINE
Wine which has high-alcohol grape spirit added, usually before the initial fermentation is completed, thereby preserving sweetness.

FRIZZANTE
Italian for semi-sparkling wine, usually made dry, but sometimes sweet.

GARAGE WINE
See vin de garage.

GARRAFEIRA
Portuguese term for wine from an outstanding vintage, with 0.5% more alcohol than the minimum required, and 2 years' aging in vat or barrel followed by 1 year in bottle for reds, and 6 months of each for whites. Also used by merchants for their best blended and aged wines. Use of the term is in decline as producers opt for the more readily recognized Reserva as an alternative on the label.

GRAN RESERVA
Top category of Spanish wines from a top vintage, with at least 5 years' aging (2 of them in cask) for reds and 4 for whites.

GRAND CRU
French for great growth. Supposedly the best vineyard sites in Alsace, Burgundy, Champagne and parts of Bordeaux –

and should produce the most exciting wines.

GROSSLAGE
German term for a grouping of vineyards. Some are not too big, and have the advantage of allowing small amounts of higher QmP wines to be made from the grapes from several vineyards. But sometimes the use of vast Grosslage names (e.g. Niersteiner Gutes Domtal) deceives consumers into believing they are buying something special. Top estates have agreed not to use Gross-lage names on their labels.

HALBTROCKEN
German for medium dry. In Germany and Austria medium-dry wine has 9–18g per litre of residual sugar, though sparkling wine is allowed up to 50g per litre. See Feinherb.

ICEWINE
A speciality of Canada, produced from juice squeezed from ripe grapes that have frozen on the vine. See also Eiswein.

IGT (INDICAZIONE GEOGRAFICA TIPICA)
The Italian equivalent of the French vin de pays. As in the Midi, both premium and everyday wines may share the same appellation. Many of the Super-Tuscan vini da tavola are now sold under a regional IGT.

IPR (INDICAÇÃO DE PROVENIÊNCIA REGULAMENTADA)
The second tier in the Portuguese wine classifications, for regions awaiting approval for DOC. See page 37.

KABINETT
Term used for the lowest level of QmP wines in Germany.

LANDWEIN
German or Austrian 'country' wine; the

equivalent of French vin de pays. The wine must have a territorial definition and may be chaptalized to give it more alcohol.

LATE HARVEST
See Vendange Tardive.

LAYING DOWN
The storing of wine which will improve with age.

LEES
Sediment – dead yeast cells, grape pips (seeds), pulp and tartrates – thrown by wine during fermentation and left behind after racking. Some wines are left on the fine lees for as long as possible to take on extra flavour.

MACERATION
Important winemaking process for red wines whereby colour, flavour and/or tannin are extracted from grape skins before, during or after fermentation. The period lasts from a few days to several weeks.

MALOLACTIC FERMENTATION
Secondary fermentation whereby harsh malic acid is converted into mild lactic acid and carbon dioxide. Normal in red wines but often prevented in whites to preserve a fresh, fruity taste.

MANZANILLA
The tangiest style of sherry, similar to fino. See Jerez y Manzanilla in main A–Z.

MATURATION
Term for the beneficial aging of wine.

MERITAGE
American term for red or white wines made from a blend of Bordeaux grape varieties.

MESOCLIMATE
The climate of a specific geographical area, be it a vineyard or simply a hillside or valley.

MIDI
A loose geographical term, virtually synonymous with Languedoc-Roussillon, covering the vast, sunbaked area of southern France between the Pyrenees and the Rhône Valley.

MOELLEUX
French for soft or mellow, used to describe sweet or medium-sweet wines, particularly in the Loire.

MOUSSEUX
French for sparkling wine.

MUST
The mixture of grape juice, skins, pips and pulp produced after crushing (but prior to completion of fermentation), which will eventually become wine.

MUST WEIGHT
An indicator of the sugar content of juice – and therefore the ripeness of grapes.

NÉGOCIANT
French term for a merchant who buys and sells wine. A négociant-éléveur is a merchant who buys, makes, ages and sells wine.

NEW WORLD
When used as a geographical term, New World includes the Americas, South Africa, Australia and New Zealand. By extension, it is also a term used to describe the clean, fruity, upfront style now in evidence all over the world, but pioneered in the USA and Australia.

NOBLE ROT
(*Botrytis cinerea*) Fungus which, when it attacks ripe white grapes, shrivels the fruit and intensifies their sugar while adding a distinctive flavour. A vital factor in creating many of the world's finest sweet wines, such as Sauternes and Trockenbeerenauslese.

OAK
The wood used almost exclusively to make barrels for fermenting and aging fine wines. It adds flavours such as vanilla, and tannins; the newer the wood, the greater the impact.

OECHSLE
German scale measuring must weight (sugar content).

OLOROSO
The darkest, most heavily fortified style of sherry. *See* Jerez y Manzanilla in main A–Z.

OXIDATION
Over-exposure of wine to air, causing loss of fruit and flavour. Slight oxidation, such as occurs through the wood of a barrel or during racking, is part of the aging process and, in wines of sufficient structure, enhances flavour and complexity.

PASSITO
Italian term for wine made from dried grapes. The result is usually a sweet wine with a raisiny intensity of fruit. The drying process is called *appassimento*. *See also* Moscato Passito di Pantelleria, Recioto della Valpolicella, Recioto di Soave and Vin Santo in main A–Z.

PERLWEIN
German for a lightly sparkling wine.

PÉTILLANT
French for a lightly sparkling wine.

PHYLLOXERA
The vine aphid *Phylloxera vastatrix* attacks vine roots. It devastated European and consequently other vineyards around the world in the late 1800s soon after it arrived from America. Since then, the vulnerable *Vitis vinifera* has generally been grafted on to vinously inferior, but phylloxera-resistant, American rootstocks.

PRÄDIKAT
Grades defining quality wines in Germany and Austria. These are (in ascending order) Kabinett (not considered as Prädikat in Austria), Spätlese, Auslese, Beerenauslese, the Austrian-only category Ausbruch, and Trockenbeerenauslese. Strohwein and Eiswein are also Prädikat wines. Some Spätleses and even a few Ausleses are now made as dry wines.

PRÄDIKATSWEIN
The new term for QmP.

PREMIER CRU
First Growth; the top quality classification in parts of Bordeaux, but second to Grand Cru in Burgundy. Used in Champagne to designate vineyards just below Grand Cru.

PRIMEUR
French term for a young wine, often released for sale within a few weeks of the harvest. Beaujolais Nouveau is the best-known example.

QBA (QUALITÄTSWEIN BESTIMMTER ANBAUGEBIETE)
German for quality wine from designated regions. Sugar can be added to increase the alcohol content. Usually pretty ordinary, but from top estates this category offers excellent value. In Austria *Qualitätswein* is equivalent to German QbA.

QMP (QUALITÄTSWEIN MIT PRÄDIKAT)
German for quality wine with distinction. A higher category than QbA, with controlled yields and no sugar addition. QmP covers 6 levels based on the ripeness of the grapes: *see* Prädikat. The term will

be replaced by Prädikats-
wein from August 2007.

QUINTA
Portuguese for farm or
estate.

RACKING
Gradual clarification of
wine; the wine is
transferred from one barrel
or container to another,
leaving the lees behind.

RANCIO
Fortified wine deliberately
exposed to the effects of
oxidation, found mainly in
Languedoc-Roussillon
and parts of Spain.

REMUAGE
Process in Champagne-
making whereby the
bottles, stored on their
sides and at a progressively
steeper angle in *pupitres*,
are twisted, or riddled,
each day so that the
sediment moves down the
sides and collects in the
neck of the bottle on the
cap, ready for *dégorgement*.

RESERVA
Spanish wines that have
fulfilled certain aging
requirements: reds must
have at least 3 years' aging
before sale, of which one
must be in oak barrels;
whites and rosés must
have at least 2 years' age,
of which 6 months must
be in oak.

RÉSERVE
French for what is, in
theory at least, a
winemaker's finest wine.
The word has no legal
definition in France.

RIPASSO
A method used in
Valpolicella to make wines
with extra depth. Wine is
passed over the lees of
Recioto or Amarone della
Valpolicella, adding extra
alcohol and flavour,
though also extra tannin
and a risk of higher acidity
and oxidation.

RISERVA
An Italian term,
recognized in many

DOCs and DOCGs, for a
special selection of wine
that has been aged longer
before release. It is only a
promise of a more
pleasurable drink if the
wine had enough fruit and
structure in the first place.

SEC
French for dry. When
applied to Champagne, it
means medium-dry.

'SECOND' WINES
A second selection from a
designated vineyard,
usually lighter and
quicker-maturing than the
main wine.

SEDIMENT
Usually refers to residue
thrown by a wine,
particularly red, as it ages
in bottle.

SEKT
German for sparkling
wine. The wine will be
entirely German only if it
is called Deutscher Sekt or
Sekt bA. The best wines
are traditional-method
and made from
100% Riesling or from
100% Weissburgunder
(Pinot Blanc).

**SÉLECTION DE
GRAINS NOBLES**
A superripe category for
sweet Alsace wines, now
also being used by some
producers of Coteaux du
Layon in the Loire Valley
for the most concentrated
wines. *See also* Vendange
Tardive.

SMARAGD
The top of the three
categories of wine from
the Wachau in Austria,
the lower two being
Federspiel and Steinfeder.
Made from very ripe and
usually late-harvested
grapes, the wines have a
minimum of 12% alcohol,
often 13–14%.

SOLERA
Traditional Spanish
system of blending
fortified wines, especially
sherry and Montilla-
Moriles.

SPÄTLESE
German for late-picked
(riper) grapes. Often
moderately sweet, though
there are dry versions.

SPUMANTE
Italian for sparkling.
Bottle-fermented wines
are often referred to as
metodo classico or *metodo
tradizionale*.

SUPÉRIEUR
French for a wine with a
slightly higher alcohol
content than the basic AC.

SUPERIORE
Italian DOC wines with
higher alcohol or more
aging potential.

SUR LIE
French for on the lees,
meaning wine bottled
direct from the cask/
fermentation vat to gain
extra flavour from the lees.
Common with
quality Muscadet, white
Burgundy, similar
barrel-aged whites and,
increasingly, commercial
bulk whites.

TAFELWEIN
German for table wine.

TANNIN
Harsh, bitter, mouth-
puckering element in red
wine, derived from grape
skins and stems, and from
oak barrels. Tannins
soften with age and are
essential for long-term
development in red wines.

TERROIR
A French term used to
denote the combination of
soil, climate and exposure
to the sun – that is, the
natural physical
environment of the vine.

**TRADITIONAL
METHOD**
See Champagne method.

TROCKEN
German for dry. In most
parts of Germany and
Austria Trocken matches
the EU definition of
dryness – less than 9g per
litre residual sugar.

313

TROCKENBEEREN-AUSLESE (TBA)
German for 'dry berry selected', denoting grapes affected by noble rot (*Edelfäule* in German) – the wines will be lusciously sweet although low in alcohol.

VARIETAL
Wine made from, and named after, a single or dominant grape variety.

VDP
German organization recognizable on the label by a Prussian eagle bearing grapes. The quality of estates included is usually – but not always – high.

VDQS (VIN DÉLIMITÉ DE QUALITÉ SUPÉRIEURE)
The second-highest classification for French wines, behind AC.

VELHO
Portuguese for old. Legally applied only to wines with at least 3 years' aging for reds and 2 years for whites.

VENDANGE TARDIVE
French for late harvest. Grapes are left on the vines beyond the normal harvest time to concentrate flavours and sugars. The term is traditional in Alsace. The Italian term is *vendemmia tardiva*.

VIEILLES VIGNES
French term for a wine made from vines at least 20 years old. Should have greater concentration than wine from younger vines.

VIÑA
Spanish for vineyard.

VIN DE GARAGE
Wines made on so small a scale they could be made in one's garage. Such wines may be made from vineyards of a couple of hectares or less, and are often of extreme concentration.

VIN DE PAILLE
Sweet wine found mainly in the Jura region of France. Traditionally, the grapes are left for 2–3 months on straw (*paille*) mats before fermentation to dehydrate, thus concentrating the sugars. The wines are sweet but slightly nutty.

VIN DE PAYS
The term gives a regional identity to wine from the country districts of France. It is a particularly useful category for adventurous winemakers who want to use good-quality grapes not allowed under the frequently restrictive AC regulations. Many are labelled with the grape variety.

VIN DE TABLE
French for table wine, the lowest quality level.

VIN DOUX NATUREL (VDN)
French for a fortified wine, where fermentation has been stopped by the addition of alcohol, leaving the wine 'naturally' sweet, although you could argue that stopping fermentation with a slug of powerful spirit is distinctly unnatural.

VIN JAUNE
A speciality of the Jura region in France, made from the Savagnin grape. In Château-Chalon it is the only permitted style. Made in a similar way to fino sherry but not fortified. Unlike fino, *vin jaune* usually ages well.

VINIFICATION
The process of turning grapes into wine.

VINO DA TAVOLA
The Italian term for table wine, officially Italy's lowest level of production, is a catch-all that until recently applied to more than 80% of the nation's wine, with virtually no regulations controlling quality. Yet this category also provided the arena in the 1970s for the biggest revolution in quality that Italy has ever seen, with the creation of innovative, DOC-busting Super-Tuscans. *See* Super-Tuscans in main A–Z.

VINTAGE
The year's grape harvest, also used to describe wines of a single year. 'Off-vintage' is a year not generally declared as vintage. *See* Port in main A–Z.

VITICULTURE
Vine-growing and vineyard management.

VITIS VINIFERA
Vine species, native to Europe and Central Asia, from which almost all the world's quality wine is made.

VQA (VINTNERS QUALITY ALLIANCE)
Canadian equivalent of France's AC system, defining quality standards and designated viticultural areas.

WEISSHERBST
German rosé wine, a speciality of Baden.

WO (WINE OF ORIGIN)
South African system of appellations which certifies area of origin, grape variety and vintage.

YIELD
The amount of fruit, and ultimately wine, produced from a vineyard. Measured in hectolitres per hectare (hl/ha) in most of Europe and in the New World as tons per acre or tonnes per hectare. Yield may vary from year to year, and depends on grape variety, age and density of the vines, and viticultural practices.

WHO OWNS WHAT

The world's major drinks companies are getting bigger and, frankly, I'm worried. As these vast wine conglomerates stride across continents, it seems highly likely that local traditions will – for purely business reasons – be pared away, along with individuality of flavour. It's not all bad news: in some cases wineries have benefited from the huge resources that come with corporate ownership, but I can't help feeling nervous knowing that the fate of a winery rests in the hands of distant institutional investors. Below I have listed some of the names that crop up again and again – and will no doubt continue to do so, as they aggressively pursue their grasp of market share.

Other wine companies – which bottle wines under their own names and feature in the main A–Z – are spreading their nets. GALLO has agreements with SIEUR D'ARQUES in southern France, Leonardo Da Vinci winery in Tuscany, MCWILLIAM'S of Australia and Whitehaven of New Zealand. The HESS COLLECTION in California owns Peter LEHMANN in Australia, GLEN CARLOU in South Africa and Colomé in Argentina. As well as Ch. MOUTON-ROTHSCHILD, the Rothschild family have other interests in France, co-own OPUS ONE and, in partnership with CONCHA Y TORO, produce ALMAVIVA in Chile.

The never-ending whirl of joint ventures, mergers and takeovers shows no signs of slowing down: the following can only be a snapshot at the time of going to press.

AXA-MILLESIMES

The French insurance giant AXA's subsidiary owns Bordeaux châteaux PETIT-VILLAGE, PICHON-LONGUEVILLE, Pibran and SUDUIRAUT, plus Dom. de l'Arlot in Burgundy, Ch. Belles Eaux in the Languedoc, TOKAJI producer Disznókö and PORT producer Quinta DO NOVAL.

CONSTELLATION BRANDS

The world's largest wine company got even bigger in December 2007 when it acquired Beam Wine Estates (part of Fortune Brands), with a portfolio that included California's ATLAS PEAK, CLOS DU BOIS, GEYSER PEAK, Buena Vista, Gary Farrell and Wild Horse. US-based wine, beer and spirits group Constellation Brands merged with Australia's BRL Hardy in 2003. BRL Hardy had already looked outside Australia to New Zealand's NOBILO (Selaks, White Cloud) – and in 2003 launched Shamwari ('Friendship') wines in South Africa; Australian brands include Banrock Station, BAROSSA VALLEY ESTATE, BAY OF FIRES, Brookland Valley, HARDYS, HOUGHTON, LEASINGHAM, Moondah Brook, Stonehaven and Yarra Burn. In late 2004 Constellation bought the prestigious Robert MONDAVI Winery and all its entities, including OPUS ONE (although it later surrendered Italian premium wines Luce della Vite and ORNELLAIA to FRESCOBALDI). Robert Mondavi Winery is now part of Constellation's Icon Estates division, along with FRANCISCAN Oakville Estate, Estancia, Mount Veeder Winery and SIMI in California and Columbia Winery in Washington. Other US brands include Blackstone and RAVENSWOOD in California and Covey Run in Washington's Columbia Valley. Constellation also owns Chile's Veramonte, and acquired Canada's Vincor in 2006; the deal included Kim Crawford in New Zealand, Kumala in South Africa, Australia's Amberley Estate and Goundrey, Toasted Head in California, Hogue Cellars in Washington State, as well as INNISKILLIN, Jackson-Triggs and other producers in Canada. One of the UK's top-selling brands, Stowells, is part of Constellation, which also has a 40% stake in Italy's RUFFINO.

FOSTER'S GROUP

The wine division of Foster's, the Australian brewing giant, was founded on the twin pillars of Australia's Wolf BLASS and BERINGER in California. In May 2005 Foster's won control of Southcorp, Australia's biggest wine conglomerate. It currently controls around 60 different brands and producers. In California it owns, among others, Carmenet, CHATEAU ST JEAN, Chateau Souverain, Etude, Meridian, St Clement and Stags' Leap Winery. Australian brands include Annie's Lane, Baileys of Glenrowan, Leo Buring, COLDSTREAM HILLS, Devil's Lair, Jamiesons Run, LINDEMANS, Metala, Mildara, Greg Norman, PENFOLDS, ROSEMOUNT ESTATE, Rothbury Estate, Rouge Homme, Saltram (Mamre Brook), Seaview, SEPPELT, T'Gallant, Tollana, WYNNS, Yarra Ridge and Yellowglen. Foster's also owns MATUA VALLEY and Secret Stone in New Zealand.

FREIXENET

The CAVA producer owns a number of other Spanish wineries (including Castellblanch, Conde de Caralt, Segura Viudas, René Barbier, and Valdubón in RIBERA DEL DUERO) and companies in California, Mexico, Chile and Argentina. It also owns the Champagne house of Henri Abelé, Bordeaux négociant/producer Yvon Mau and Australia's Wingara Wine Group (Deakin Estate, KATNOOK ESTATE).

JACKSON FAMILY

Jess Jackson, founder of California's KENDALL-JACKSON, has a growing portfolio of brands in California, including ARROWOOD, Atalon, Byron, Cambria, Cardinale, Edmeades, Freemark Abbey, HARTFORD, La Crema, La Jota. Lokoya, MATANZAS CREEK, Murphy-Goode, Pepi, Stonestreet and Vérité. Jackson also owns Calina (Chile), Yangarra Estate (Australia), Château Lassègue (ST-EMILION) and Villa Arceno (Tuscany).

LVMH

French luxury goods group Louis Vuitton-Moët Hennessy owns Champagne houses MOET & CHANDON (including Dom Pérignon), KRUG, Mercier, RUINART and VEUVE CLICQUOT, and has established DOMAINE CHANDON sparkling wine companies in California, Australia and Argentina. It also owns Ch. d'YQUEM, CAPE MENTELLE in Australia, CLOUDY BAY in New Zealand, NEWTON in California, and TERRAZAS DE LOS ANDES in Argentina. In early 2008 LVMH acquired the prestigious Bodega Numanthia-Termes in TORO, Spain.

PERNOD RICARD

The French spirits giant owns Australia's all-conquering JACOB'S CREEK brand, along with Wyndham Estate and the Orlando, Gramp's, Poet's Corner and Richmond Grove labels. Pernod Ricard's empire also encompasses New Zealand's mighty MONTANA (CHURCH ROAD, Corbans, Lindauer, Stoneleigh), Champagne producers MUMM and PERRIER-JOUET, Californian fizz MUMM NAPA, Long Mountain in South Africa and a number of Argentinian producers, including Balbi, Etchart and Graffigna. In Spain Pernod Ricard controls CAMPO VIEJO, Palacio de la Vega, Marqués de Arienzo, Siglo and Tarsus, among others, and in Georgia it has a 75% stake in Georgian Wines & Spirits.

INDEX OF PRODUCERS

Numbers in **bold** refer to main entries.

317

318

321

323

339

FRANCE

Alsace (vendanges tardives)	97	96	95	90	89	88	86	85	83	82
	8◆	8◆	9◆	10◆	9◆	8◆	8◆	9◆	7◇	10◆
Champagne (vintage)	97	96	95	90	89	88	86	85	83	82
	6◆	9◇	8◆	9◆	8◆	9◆	7◆	8◆	7◇	9◆

Bordeaux	97	96	95	94	90	89	88	86	85	83
Margaux	6◇	8◆	8◆	6◇	10◆	8◆	7◆	8◆	8◆	9◇
St.-Jul., Pauillac, St-Est.	6◇	9◆	8◆	7◇	10◆	9◆	8◆	9◆	8◆	7◇
Graves/Pessac-L. (red)	6◇	8◆	8◆	6◇	8◆	8◆	8◆	6◇	8◆	8◇
St-Émilion, Pomerol	6◇	7◆	9◆	6◇	10◆	9◆	8◆	7◆	9◆	7◇

Bordeaux (cont.)	82	81	75	70	66	61	59	55	53	49
Margaux (cont.)	8◇	7◇	6◇	8◇	7◇	10◇	8◇	6◇	8◇	9◇
St.-Jul. etc. (cont.)	10◆	7◇	8◇	8◇	8◇	10◇	9◇	8◇	9◇	10◇
Graves etc. (R) (cont.)	9◇	7◇	6◇	8◇	8◇	10◇	9◇	8◇	8◇	10◇
St-Émilion etc. (cont.)	9◇	7◇	8◇	8◇	6◇	10◇	7◇	7◇	8◇	9◇

Sauternes	97	96	95	90	89	88	86	83	80	76
	9◆	9◆	7◆	10◆	9◆	9◆	9◆	9◆	7◇	8◇
Sauternes (cont.)	75	71	67	62	59	55	53	49	47	45
	8◇	8◇	9◇	8◇	9◇	8◇	8◇	10◇	10◇	9◇

Burgundy

Chablis	97	96	95	92	90	89	88			
	7◇	9◆	8◆	7◇	10◇	8◇	8◇			
Côte de Beaune (wh.)	97	96	95	93	92	90	89	88	86	85
	8◇	6◇	9◇	7◇	8◇	7◇	9◇	6◇	8◇	8◇
Côte de Nuits (red)	97	96	95	93	90	89	88	85	83	78
	8◆	9◆	7◆	8◆	9◆	7◇	8◇	9◇	6◇	10◆